THE EVIDENTIAL FOUNDATIONS
OF PROBABILISTIC REASONING

THE EVIDENTIAL FOUNDATIONS OF PROBABILISTIC REASONING

DAVID A. SCHUM

Northwestern University Press
Evanston, Illinois

Northwestern University Press
Evanston, Illinois 60208-4210

Originally published in hardcover in 1994 by John Wiley & Sons,
Inc., New York. Copyright © 1994 by John Wiley & Sons, Inc.
Northwestern University Press paperback published 2001 by
arrangement with John Wiley & Sons, Inc. All rights reserved.

Printed in the United States of America

10 9 8 7 6 5 4 3 2 1

ISBN 0-8101-1821-1

Library of Congress Cataloging-in-Publication Data
Schum, David A.
    The evidential foundations of probabilistic reasoning / David A.
Schum.
       p. cm.
    Originally published: New York : Wiley, c1994, in series: Wiley
series in systems engineering.
    Includes bibliographical references and index.
    ISBN 0-8101-1821-1 (pbk. : alk. paper)
    1. Evidence. 2. Inference. 3. Probabilities. I. Title.
BC171.S38 2001
121'.65—dc21   00-045260

The paper used in this publication meets the minimum
requirements of the American National Standard for Information
Sciences—Permanence of Paper for Printed Library Materials,
ANSI Z39.48-1984.

For Brian and Edward
filii carissimi

Preface

Here is a book about the evidence we gather and use as a basis for drawing conclusions about matters of interest in our work and in other parts of our daily lives. Certain attributes of evidence are commonly recognized. In any inference task our evidence is always incomplete, rarely conclusive, and often imprecise or vague; it comes from sources having any gradation of credibility. As a result conclusions reached from evidence having these attributes can only be probabilistic in nature. Probabilistic reasoning requires many difficult judgments in the process of establishing the credentials of evidence in terms of its relevance, credibility, and inferential force. No evidence comes to us with these credentials already established.

This book provides a detailed examination of the various properties and uses of evidence and the judgmental tasks they entail. Many interesting and important evidential subtleties lie just below the surface of probabilistic reasoning. If they are recognized, these subtleties can be exploited during the process of drawing a conclusion. But evidence bearing on possible conclusions is rarely provided for us. Also examined in this book are various processes by which evidence may be generated or discovered. In many instances conclusions are based upon large masses of evidence. The manner in which we marshal, organize, or juxtapose our evidence has a bearing not only upon the discovery of new evidence and new possible conclusions but also upon the final conclusions that we reach. Probabilistic reasoning and discovery involve a rich array of intellectual tasks. This book presents an analysis of the requirements of these tasks, but it does not provide an assessment of the extent to which people perform them wisely. I believe that we need to be better informed about the nature of these tasks before we attempt to pass any firm judgments about the wisdom of the people who perform them.

One trouble is that insights about the properties and uses of evidence are not to be found in any single discipline. We might say that the house of evidence has many mansions. No person I know lives in all of them. But we can certainly visit these different mansions and meet the people in them who have unique and valuable things to tell us about evidence, its properties and uses, and its discovery. Over the years I have visited a number of the mansions of evidence; this book records observations I have made on these visits. The mansions of evidence I have visited include those occupied by scholars and practitioners in the fields of law, philosophy and logic, probability, semiotics, artificial intelligence, psychology, and history. It will be apparent that my visits have been of greater duration in some mansions than they have been in others. I believe it very useful to bring together, in a single work, insights about evidence that come from these disciplines. I have been encouraged in this venture by the comments of many graduate students (mostly engineers) who have attended seminars that I offer concerning the discovery and use of evidence in probabilistic reasoning. There are other treatises on evidence, but most of them are written to satisfy the needs of persons in a particular discipline.

Visiting the different mansions of evidence seems quite prudent for several reasons. Many currently important areas of research are multidisciplinary in nature. The research interests of my graduate students over the past several years certainly reflect this characteristic. Persons in one discipline often draw upon evidence gathered by persons in another. In some cases we may fail to apprehend the significance of evidence from another discipline; in other cases we may expect more of such evidence than it can deliver. It is also true that persons in one discipline may be quite unaware of important insights about evidence acquired by persons in another discipline. To cite an important example, scholars of evidence in jurisprudence have provided us with a very rich legacy of scholarship and experience on a wide variety of important evidential and inferential matters. The existence of this legacy and its application in a variety of other disciplines should be more widely advertised (a task I undertake in this work).

Another reason for visiting the different mansions of evidence concerns the tutoring that we typically receive regarding the inferential use of evidence. A substantial number of the topics in this book are not covered in courses in logic, probability, and statistics. Courses in logic rarely dwell upon the task of drawing conclusions from masses of evidence whose items take different discernible forms. Courses in statistics only concern evidence arising from repetitive or replicable processes; they do not consider evidence about the singular or unique events of interest in so many disciplines. In addition, courses in logic or statistics do not typically inform us about problems we encounter when we must construct, often lengthy, reasoning chains in defense of the relevance and credibility of evidence. Probabilists and researchers in artificial intelligence, along with others, have taken an interest in complex inference problems (now termed *inference networks*). Research in this area has focused mainly upon the development of efficient algorithms for combining the many probability judgments required in these problems. However, what is commonly overlooked in such study is the richness of the evidential foundations for these complex inferences.

The audience that I have in mind for this book consists of students, researchers, and practitioners in every discipline in which there is concern about evidence and its inferential use. The only major requisite for mastering the contents of this book is a willingness to consider scholarship from many different disciplines. Purely structural issues occupy us in Chapters 3 and 4 as we consider the construction of arguments made in defense of the relevance and credibility of individual items and of masses of evidence. Probabilistic and structural matters are encountered in Chapters 5 through 8 as we consider the task of assessing the inferential force of evidence. The mathematics involved in discussing these matters is quite elementary. In Chapters 7 and 8 I have provided over one hundred numerical examples to illustrate the workings of various probabilistic expressions for the inferential force of evidence and the subtleties they reveal. The essential topic in Chapter 9 is the imaginative reasoning processes that provide a basis for the discovery or generation of new evidence and new hypotheses. In discussing these topics, we will encounter the activities of some very interesting characters (both real and fictional) who have emerged during the history of concern about the discovery and use of evidence. I have given examples from real life or from works of fiction to illustrate many of the evidential issues that I discuss.

I now invite you to consider the possibility that there can be a science of evidence. Others have extended this same invitation, as you will see in the first chapter.

DAVID A. SCHUM

Fairfax, Virginia
January 1994

Acknowledgments

In preparing this book and in performing the research on which portions of it are based, I have been blessed with splendid colleagues and financial assistance; who could ask for more? I particularly thank Andy Sage, Ward Edwards, and Austin Kibler for their encouragement of my past and current efforts to bring together a variety of scholarship bearing on the study of evidence. Ward must accept either the credit or the blame for having first stimulated my interest in probability and evidence many years ago. In my studies I have been very grateful for the support of the National Science Foundation, which came in the form of Grants SOC77-28471 and SOC80-24203 to Rice University and Grants SES87-04377 and SES90-07693 to George Mason University. The research that I performed would simply not have been possible without this support.

On my visits to the mansions of evidence which I mentioned in the Preface, I encountered the works of many persons who have contributed so much to our present understanding of evidence. For the sake of being inclusive, I now thank all of you whose names appear in my reference list. Alas, many of these persons will not now hear my earthly thanks. But there are persons, now very much alive, whom I have met in these mansions and for whom I have such admiration and affection. In the field of evidence law Professors Terry Anderson, Lash LaRue, Richard Lempert, Peter Tillers, and William Twining have been especially helpful and very patient in answering questions I asked while a tourist in this field. For the past eight years I have thoroughly enjoyed my active collaboration with Peter Tillers in research on a variety of evidential matters. In philosophy I have found the works of L. Jonathan Cohen to be particularly inspiring, and I thank him for his helpful advice on matters that arose during the preparation of this book. In addition Douglas

Stalker and Walter Wehrle have been so helpful during my visits to the mansion of philosophy. I thank Ryzsard Michalski for his guidance on issues in artificial intelligence; I also thank him for inviting me to be more than just a tourist in this mansion. In the mansion of probability theory I owe so much to Paul Pfeiffer, a colleague and friend of long-standing, whose wisdom and patience so strongly encouraged my studies of probability and evidence.

Other colleagues have helped me during the preparation of this book. Tony Zawilski and Ray Curts (both hardened and shameless engineers) read the entire manuscript and also made substantive contributions that are acknowledged in the text. Richard Evans and Scott Hornung made very helpful comments about portions of this work. I also wish to express my gratitude to Dana Andrus, who edited the manuscript, and Rosalyn Farkas of John Wiley & Sons. No author has ever had better editorial assistance.

Now comes the customary and, in this case, necessary disclaimer. Be assured that all of the persons mentioned above provided me with good advice and sound arguments. I may not, however, have acquired a similarly sound understanding, and in truth, I did not follow all of the advice I received. Any imperfections in this work are the result either of my own obstinacy or lack of understanding.

D.A.S.

THE EVIDENTIAL FOUNDATIONS
OF PROBABILISTIC REASONING

Chapter 1

A Discourse on Evidence

Perhaps I should begin this discourse with a careful definition of the word *evidence*. However, this task is not quite so easy as it may appear. So I will beg your indulgence and ask you to accept, for the moment, the following rather casual interpretation of this word: We commonly use the term evidence with reference to observable phenomena upon which we base inferences about matters of interest and importance to us. We often make additional reference to the context in which some body of evidence arises; thus we speak of scientific evidence, medical evidence, legal evidence, and so on. One question concerns the extent to which evidence may share common properties regardless of the phenomena it reveals. Stated another way, we might inquire about the extent to which evidence can be studied abstractly without reference to any particular situation in which the evidence arises. It may seem obvious that the engineer, physician, auditor, and sociologist use different evidence in order to draw conclusions of importance to them. But some items of evidence seem to differ more in substance than they do in form or structure. In addition different disciplines encounter different mixtures of structurally discernible forms and combinations of evidence. My belief, which I will attempt to justify in these pages, is that there are many things to be said about evidence that are independent of its content or substance. This book contains a collection of thoughts about evidence that I hope you will find interesting and useful regardless of your disciplinary background and interests. I begin by attempting to find some common ground for a discourse about evidence that is not dependent upon the setting in which evidence is first discovered and then used for the purpose of drawing conclusions.

1.1 FINDING COMMON GROUND

One attribute of human inference common across different situations is that *conclusive* evidence is either in very short supply or is quite impossible to arship in others. As we will observe, some disciplines are in possession of valuable information about the structure of evidence, while other disciplines have more to tell us about the process of assessing the inferential force or strength of evidence.

1.2 IS A GENERAL DISCOURSE ON EVIDENCE NECESSARY?

Even if you accept the fact that substantively different evidence can have various common properties and that inferences in different contexts may involve different mixtures of recurrent forms and combinations of evidence, should you care? If the topic of evidence is so important in various disciplines, where are books with such titles as "Evidence for the Engineer," "Evidence for the Psychologist", and "Evidence for the Auditor"? These are several possible answers to this question which I will mention at this point; other answers will emerge as we proceed.

One reason for dwelling upon general properties of evidence is that so many of our inferential activities are now interdisciplinary in nature. Inferences that we make often require at least some understanding of evidence on a variety of matters. Consider an engineer in the act of designing a certain system and attempting to draw a conclusion about how successful will be the actual implementation of this system among persons for whom it is intended. Evidence is necessary regarding the physical properties of the system itself and of the environment in which it will function. But evidence is also necessary about the behavior of the people who are to be users of this system or who are to be affected in some way by its employment. Thus physical evidence about the behavior of devices mingles with behavioral evidence regarding various human skills and other characteristics. Having some understanding of general properties of evidence assists us in judging how various forms of evidence stand in relation to the conclusions that we must draw. Such judgments are not always easy when we consider evidence obtained from disciplines other than our own. In some cases we may fail to comprehend the significance of evidence from other disciplines, while in other cases we may expect more of such evidence than it can deliver. It is often helpful to consider the process of inference in different disciplines. One person who noted this fact was the historian Marc Bloch. As he said (1953, 18–19): "Each science, taken by itself, represents but a fragment of the universal march toward knowledge. . . . in order to understand and appreciate one's own methods of investigation, however specialized, it is indispensible to see their connections with all simultaneous tendencies in other fields."

Another reason for the study of general properties of evidence concerns a methodological gap that is now observable in so many contexts and is growing larger while we are now discussing it. Our current methods for gathering, storing, retrieving, and transmitting information far exceed, in number and effectiveness, our methods for putting this information to inferential use in the drawing of conclusions from it. Persons in many different disciplines including engineering, artificial intelligence, probability, philosophy, and psychology are now actively engaged in the development of computer-based methods for assisting people whose inferences involve complex arguments based upon masses of evidence. I believe that the success of such ventures rests, at least in part, upon a better understanding of the various forms, combinations, properties, and uses of evidence.

One topic of current interest, among persons devoted to reducing the size of this methodological gap, involves development of methods for the analysis of *inference networks* as representations for often complex arguments based upon a mass of evidence (e.g., Pearl 1988; Shafer and Pearl 1990; Neapolitan 1990). Most of the inference network research has been focused upon various computational algorithms for propagating or aggregating probabilities associated with elements of these networks. However, much less attention has been paid to a variety of issues concerning the different forms and combinations of evidence that serve to "activate" an inference network. As I mentioned earlier, inferences can usually be decomposed to different levels of granularity, and we are often faced with a choice about the level of detail at which an analysis will be made. Careful study of the evidential foundations of an inference network identifies many important subtleties that may be easily overlooked and also makes clear the various roles of evidence in the analysis of an inference network. An inference network can be viewed as a *mental model* of an inference task constructed by one or more persons with requisite knowledge in the problem domain of interest. An interesting question, later discussed, concerns whether such construction must always be considered an art form.

It might easily be argued that there already are many books on evidence for engineers, psychologists, auditors, and others, but they simply do not have titles such as those suggested above. For example, a student or practitioner of medicine can consult a number of textual and other reference sources on hematology and from them obtain an account of accumulated wisdom regarding the signs and symptoms of various blood disorders. An acoustical engineer has similar access to an abundant collection of physical and psychophysical data relevant to the design and use of audio systems. A sociologist has access to a variety of data concerning the dimensions of intergroup conflict. Some of these works offer various models for combining data in multivariate analyses. Some of these models are deterministic, while others are stochastic or probabilistic in nature. So it can be argued that the coverage of evidence relevant in various disciplines is substantial, and there is little need to engage in any general discourse about evidence.

Trouble arises, however, when we compare examples and cases mentioned in texts, classrooms, and many research reports with the situations we encounter in our everyday lives. There is often an obvious misfit in terms of substance and/or complexity between text or class examples and the *unique* situations we face in our work. We discover that the inferences our work requires rest upon varieties of evidence that seem to bear in many ways upon possible conclusions. We also discover that the training we might have had in logic, probability, and statistics does not seem to have captured the true complexity of the inference tasks we now face. Having access to a mass of evidence is one thing; constructing defensible arguments on the basis of this evidence is quite another. This is particularly true in situations in which we have a variety of evidence whose exact bearing upon hypotheses that we entertain is not always obvious. Some disciplines have recognized problems associated with lack of specific tutoring in the properties, uses, and discovery of evidence; here are two examples.

It might be thought that of all disciplines imaginable, training related to the inferential use of evidence would be the most thorough in the field of law. After all, the use of evidence seems to be the stock-in-trade of practicing attorneys. However, a renowned legal scholar and educator, William Twining, has recently argued that the training typically received by attorneys is mainly rule centered, involving the admissibility of evidence at trial, and ignores issues concerning the use of evidence in inferences about matters in contention (Twining 1984). A similar view is taken by David Binder and Paul Bergman, who argue that courses and texts in law schools never systematically consider processes by which litigators gather, analyze, and use evidence to prove matters at issue (1984, xvii). Nonlawyers may interpret these statements somewhat frivolously to mean that advocates' training consists mainly of studies of what they can get by with at trial. However, in Chapter 2 we will return to legal scholarship on evidence, at which point I will argue that this work forms the major source of inspiration for anyone interested in a study of the general properties and uses of evidence.

The inferential use of evidence also appears to be the stock-in-trade of the practicing physician. However, a view similar to that of legal educators has been stated regarding the kind of training routinely provided in medical diagnosis and treatment (Wulff 1981, 1). Wulff tells us that medical students spend their days and nights reading thousands of pages on anatomy, physiology, pathology, surgery, and many other subjects. Training on how to utilize all of this knowledge in making correct diagnostic and therapeutic decisions then occurs at the bedside in (supervised) contact with patients. Preparation and training of this kind is necessary, but Wulff argues that attention should also be given to the many evidential, inferential, and decisional matters he discusses in his book. In many contexts inference or diagnosis might be considered more an art than a science; this raises an interesting question.

1.3   CAN THERE BE A SCIENCE OF EVIDENCE?

I suspect that the answer to this question depends upon how we choose to employ the word *science*. The *Oxford English Dictionary* (OED) lists several common uses of this term, including one that is general and one that is quite restricted. In a general sense the word science simply refers to a particular branch of knowledge or a recognized department of learning. In a more restricted sense this term refers to a connected body of demonstrated truths or observed facts classified under general laws, with the added requirement that it includes trustworthy methods for the discovery of new truths. As long as we confine ourselves to the general usage just noted, I do not believe it does any harm to talk about a *science of evidence*.

One person who I believe would agree with what I have just said is a man whose works I will mention with great frequency throughout this book. John Henry Wigmore (1863–1943) is certainly the most prolific and arguably the most profound scholar of evidence in modern times. Wigmore was a professor of law and for many years Dean of the Law School at Northwestern University. It would be very difficult to overestimate Wigmore's influence on our judicial system. It is virtually impossible to find a treatise on evidence in legal affairs that does not refer to Wigmore's work. Wigmore wrote on matters concerning the admissibility of evidence at trial, but he was equally concerned about inferential issues in the evaluation of evidence. One of his works is entitled *The Science of Judicial Proof: As Given by Logic, Psychology, and General Experience, and Illustrated in Judicial Trials*. In this book, first published in 1913, Wigmore took on the task of offering guidance to attorneys preparing for trial and confronted with the task of constructing defensible arguments based upon masses of evidence having a variety of logically distinguishable properties. This work was never popular among the practicing attorneys for whom it was intended; there is a recent analysis of reasons why this has been so (Twining 1985, 164–166). One thing clear, however, is that Wigmore was far ahead of his time. As early as 1913 he recognized the methodological gap I mentioned above, and he also anticipated current interest in *inference networks* and *fuzzy probabilities*, two topics of interest to us later on (Tillers and Schum 1988).

That Wigmore believed a science of evidence is possible is perhaps best indicated by the following quotation given in the frontispiece of his *Science Of Judicial Proof* (1937, 3d ed.). This quotation comes from *The Big Bow Mystery* written by Israel Zangwill:

" Have you ever given any attention to the Science of Evidence?" said Mr. Grodman.

"How do you mean?" asked the Home Secretary, rather puzzled, but with a melancholy smile. "I should hardly speak of it as a science; I look at it as a question of common sense".

"Pardon me sir. It is the most difficult of all the sciences. It is indeed rather the science of the sciences. What is the whole of inductive logic, as laid down (say) by Bacon and Mill, but an attempt to appraise the value of evidence, the said evidence being the trails left by the Creator, so to speak? The Creator has (I say it in all reverence) drawn a myriad of red herrings across the track. But research on the subject. In this chapter I will argue that discovery-related processes that are both imaginative and efficient depend, at least to some extent, upon the manner in which we have marshaled or organized our existing thoughts and evidence. In the final chapter I will attempt to synthesize various evidential matters presented in this discourse and to show their relevance in a variety of disciplines and inferential contexts.

I began this chapter by postponing an attempt to define the word *evidence*. All I said was that this is no easy task; I will now begin to tell you why this is so.

Chapter 2

The Study of Evidence

Careful study of evidence requires examination of recorded experience and scholarship in many different areas. No single discipline can lay claim to all advancements that have been made in our understanding of evidence, its properties, and its uses. In this chapter we will encounter the thoughts of logicians, philosophers, probabilists, jurists, and others whose scholarship defines the essential evidential and inferential issues that we will examine throughout this discourse. Study of the properties and uses of evidence involves matters about which there will be continuing dialogue and, perhaps, no final answers. As we proceed, we will encounter many interesting characters, some of whom may have had very little idea of the role they would play in shaping our concepts of evidence and its use in probabilistic reasoning.

2.1 EVIDENCE, OBSERVATIONS, AND ABSTRACTIONS

For a start, we might believe that the term *evidence* is easily defined, since its use is so common. But many other terms used in connection with human intellectual processes, such as *intelligence*, *learning*, and *rationality*, are also in very common use but are known to be resistant to easy definitions. In my opening remarks in Chapter 1, I used the term evidence rather casually with reference to observable phenomena upon which we base inferences. The truth is that many persons have, without complete success, sought a definition of evidence that will satisfy the requirements of every situation in which the term is used. One trouble is that we often use the term evidence interchangeably with other terms such as data, information, facts, and knowledge. There are distinctions among these terms that deserve careful attention. Here is another attempt to answer the following question.

a myriad of red herrings across our tracks, and so the physical evidence we obtain is rarely conclusive on matters of interest to us. Speaking of the *signs of nature,* we will in Chapter 9 encounter the thoughts of persons in the field of *semiotics,* that discipline whose major interest concerns the identification, meaning, and affect of the signs of nature.

Suppose we take as a point of departure a view of evidence that includes the testimonial assertions or authoritative records that come from people and physical objects or things. Presumably, if I am to make use of any of these phenomena in an inference of concern, I must be able to observe them in some way. I must hear the testimony and observe the authoritative records and physical objects. In some contexts it is taken as obvious that evidence always concerns observables. For example, in discussing inductive inference in science, Wesley Salmon tells us: "We observe that human beings utilize what may be roughly characterized as inductive or scientific methods of extending knowledge from the observed to the unobserved" (1979, 6). On an empiricist view, our knowledge of the world is limited to what we can observe with our senses and then infer from these observations. A natural question raised by my very restrictive definition of evidence is, Does evidence always involve that which we can observe in some way? Here is an example of entirely legitimate evidence about events that no one might have observed directly.

Consider what Hacking calls *authority* as a species of evidence that we obtain from people. In our daily inferences we probably do not routinely make reference to the recorded teachings of ancient authorities such as Aristotle, St. Augustine, Galen, or Hippocrates. But we do often make use of records obtained from what we regard as authoritative sources. On some occasions we consult a variety of tables and other documents for evidence we cannot obtain by our own personal observations. For example, suppose that knowing the time of high tide, the time of sunset, or the lunar phase that existed in Miami, Florida, on March 1, 1992, would be important evidence in some current inference of importance to you. Unless you were in Miami on this date and could have recorded these phenomena, you have no choice but to consult appropriate tide tables and almanacs. You observe the tide tables or the almanacs but not the tides, the sun, or the moon themselves. Almost certainly no one else made observations of these tabled values either; they were calculated on the basis of other knowledge regarding the behavior of celestial bodies. So you might regard tabled information of this sort as a surrogate for direct observations that you cannot or did not make. Abraham Lincoln once made use of entries in an almanac as evidence impeaching the credibility of a witness who asserted that he had seen, at 11:00 PM by the light of a full moon, a defendant named Cal Armstrong kill a man. The almanac showed that on the night in question there was a new moon, and thus no moonlight at all (Wigmore 1937, 435).

But there is another important case to be considered regarding evidence and observation. Suppose that in some situation you *expect* to observe something and are unable to do so. Perhaps this something is not there (your expectation is wrong) or perhaps you were looking in the wrong place. But it may also seem possible that someone is concealing the thing you expected to observe. If so, you might regard your present failure to find what you expect as evidence of concealment, which in turn may have an inferential bearing upon hypotheses you are considering. In another situation you might ask a person for information or might request some physical item; this person refuses to answer your question or refuses to provide you with this item. All of these situations involve *missing evidence*, evidence expected but not observed. Suppose a person or an organization refuses to produce evidence for your inspection or refuses to produce testimony about a certain matter. For over two hundred years our legal system has, in many situations, sanctioned the drawing of an adverse inference from a person's failure to produce evidence. The grounds for this adverse inference reside in a presumption that the evidence is unfavorable to the person refusing to produce it, otherwise it would have been forthcoming. So missing, and therefore unobserved, evidence can itself be evidence in certain cases, as we will discuss in Sections 3.4 and 7.6. However, the empiricist might be entitled to claim that you did in fact "sense" something; you sensed the fact that you are unable to obtain the evidence you expected or you observed that some person refused to answer your query or to produce what you requested.

Achinstein provides several interpretations of evidence including one he favors (1982, 322–336). He says that e is *potential* evidence on hypothesis H if and only if (1) e is true, (2) e does not make H necessary, (3) the probability of H on evidence e is substantial, and (4) the probability of an explanatory connection between H and e is substantial. Achinstein's characterization is valuable because it summarizes several points about evidence that we must examine quite carefully. First, we will often have uncertainty about whether or not evidence e "is true," and we have to be able to represent the nature of this uncertainty. In part this will involve specifying exactly what evidence we believe we have. Second, if evidence e does not entail (or make necessary) hypothesis H, this simply means that e is inconclusive; this is essentially what I (and Hacking) have stipulated so far. But assumptions 3 and 4 raise issues concerning the *relevance* and the *force* of e on H and the nature of the argument or chain of reasoning that links e and H. These important matters will be of concern to us throughout this discourse.

At this point you might believe that I face the unenviable task of attempting to complete the rest of this book about a concept that resists a ready or even a noncircular definition. However, I take great comfort in the fact that there are thousands of books and papers written, and eagerly read, on intelligence, learning, rationality, and other concepts that offer obstinate resistance to definition. Attempts to provide an exact definition of the word evidence bring to mind what psychologists often call an *absolute* or *exact judgment*, as opposed to a *relative judgment*. In many situations absolute or exact judgments are difficult or impossible to make. I show you a light and ask you how bright it is; this calls for an absolute or exact judgment on your part. You say this makes no sense at all, since you seem to have no internal scale similar to watts or lumens to which you might refer in making any exact judgment about the brightness of a light. Now I show you two lights and ask you to tell me if one seems brighter than the other. This task now makes sense to you, and so you tell me that one light is brighter than the other or that they both seem equally bright. There is now an abundance of research on our natural ability to make *relative* judgments of many different sorts (e.g., Warren and Warren 1968; Marks 1974; Stevens 1975; Baird and Noma 1978).

If we have difficulty defining evidence absolutely or exactly, perhaps we can obtain some *relative* sense of what *evidence* means by comparing this word with others that either seem related to it or are used synonymously. The word *evidence* is often associated with the words *fact, data, information,* and *knowledge.* There are distinctions among these four terms that bear careful examination when they are related to the concept of evidence. As we proceed, I hope to dispel any thoughts you might have that we are just splitting hairs and quibbling about words. The matters we are now discussing are most important in any careful analysis of the properties of evidence and its various roles in probabilistic inference.

2.1.2   Evidence, "Facts," and Abstractions

As we have observed, the *OED* equates *evidence* and *fact;* so do many people in discussing the grounds for conclusions they have reached. We often hear someone saying that an inference or a decision was based "on the facts." Presumably this person means that the decision or conclusion was based upon evidence of some kind and not just upon idle guess or speculation. In our legal system use of the word fact is widespread; jurors are called *fact finders,* pretrial discovery-related processes are said to involve *fact investigation,* advocates construct *factual theories,* and what happens at trial is described as *fact determination.* On occasion the word fact is intensified, and we hear of "hard facts." As we also observed, the *OED* tells us that a fact is "that which has actually happened or is the case." Not a bad idea then to give some attention to what constitutes a "fact" and to consider the extent to which we can ever "know the facts." In giving attention to the relationship between evidence and facts, we will be able to obtain some understanding about where evidence stands in relation to possible conclusions that we might reach. Since the semantics or meaning of evidence and fact is at issue, perhaps we ought to consult a semanticist.

One person who has written extensively about "facts" is the semanticist Wendell Johnson (1946, ch. 5). Johnson tells us that problems we encounter in assessing the state of our knowledge and understanding of the world center on our use of words to reflect reality or what "actually happens"; the words we attach to things are not the same as the things themselves. He also tells us that "knowing the facts" is a deceptively simple statement that leaves much to chance and takes much for granted. In particular, the statement "knowing the facts" or knowing "what actually happened" assumes that a fact is observable and that we would all instantly recognize one when we observe it. Johnson argues that there are at least four important points about "facts" which we ought to consider.

The first is that "knowing the facts" is quite impossible if what we mean is that we have *all the facts*. We often hear someone say: "I am waiting to decide until I have all the facts"; Johnson says this person will simply never be able to make a decision. Hemple says this person would have to wait till the end of the world (1966, 11–12). Part of the reason is that we obtain only as many of the facts as our senses or sensing devices allow. Our observations of any kind produce only an *abstraction* or *representation* of an object, event, or situation and not these things themselves. Thus your visual observation of an object or an event is not the same as the object or the event itself. No radar image or photograph of an object is the same as the object itself; a television tape recording of an event is not the same as the event itself. Each one of our senses provides only certain kinds of information. Our sensory modalities are also not infallible; the same is true for any electronic or mechanical sensing device.

Second, we may reasonably disagree among ourselves about "what the facts are" in any situation. This is one reason why there are court trials; people disagree, often violently, about what the facts are in some situations. The observation of any object, event, or situation is a personal affair and people are known to differ widely in their sensory capacity, objectivity, attentiveness, and other observational characteristics. As we proceed, I will frequently mention the importance of a person's *standpoint* in the discovery and evaluation of evidence. In the process I will draw upon the work of William Twining and Terry Anderson, both of whom have much to tell us about the importance and influence of a person's standpoint on what evidence will be discovered, what possibilities will be entertained, what arguments will be constructed from the evidence to these possibilities, and what inferential force will be assessed for these arguments (Twining and Miers 1982; Twining 1990; Anderson and Twining 1991). In short, persons having different standpoints may see "the facts" quite differently.

A third characteristic of facts is that many of them do not seem to be stationary; what is taken to be fact today may not be perceived so a month or a year from now. Suppose that some time ago you heard about an event from a person whose credibility you had every reason to endorse. You accepted what this person told you as fact, and acting upon it, you drew a certain conclusion that influenced some choice you made. You now have reason to repent the conclusion you drew and the choice you made, and in the process you discover some new information that bears adversely upon the credibility of the person whose word you trusted. This information now makes you question the wisdom of your readiness to accept as fact what this person told you. What we often term "hard facts" may be difficult to obtain. In some cases we may discover that what is taken to be a "hard fact" actually rests upon a theory or conjecture. The philosopher Lakatos gives us an example of a researcher who took his observation of pure chlorine to be a hard fact when, in truth, this "hard" fact rested upon a theory then prevalent about how "pure" chlorine could be obtained (1970, 44).

Finally, Wendell Johnson tells us that what is taken as fact depends upon the extent to which observations made by different persons are corroborative. The more persons who, on independent observation, take some event to be fact, the more certain we can be that we do have a fact on our hands. The trouble of course is that many observations cannot be easily verified or corroborated; this is often true of events that have happened in the past. It is true in other situations such as in my earlier example of a patient with a headache; by what means does a doctor verify this claim so that it can be accepted as fact? Three centuries before Wendell Johnson, Thomas Hobbes (1651) advised that we will never have absolute but only conditional knowledge of facts (1988 ed., 30–31).

Taking all of these matters into consideration, it appears that we would be quite prudent to separate the terms *evidence* and *fact*. We may have various kinds of evidence about some event, but if this evidence is to any degree inconclusive, we are not entitled to say that this evidence entails the factual occurrence or the truth of this event. Stated another way, *evidence about some event and the actual occurrence of this event are not the same*, and we may be misled if we take them to be. Figure 2.1 illustrates a distinction that I will make throughout this discourse on evidence. In this figure E* represents evidence that event E happened or is true. As you see E* and E are not the same; from evidence E* I must *infer* whether or not E actually happened or is true (E^c, read E-complement, means E did not occur). Under a stipulation that all evidence is inconclusive to some degree, this inference can only be expressed in probabilistic terms.

The exact nature of the inferential step from E* to E depends, as we will see, upon what kind of evidence is E* and how it was obtained. For example, evidence E* might represent a person's testimony that event E occurred. In this case we may wish to decompose the inference from E* to a conclusion about whether or not E happened in fact. As we will later observe in Section 3.2.3, a certain decomposition reveals various attributes of the credibility of the person who testifies E*. Other stages of reasoning (indicated by the dashed

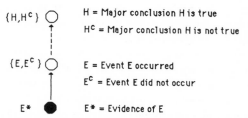

FIGURE 2.1   An event distinguished from evidence of its occurrence.

arrow in Figure 2.1) may indicate the inferential bearing of events E and E^c on possible conclusions or major hypotheses {H, H^c}. As we will see, these stages of reasoning concern the relevance of evidence E^* on these hypotheses. Figure 2.1 makes clear the distinction I wish to make between evidence and and the actual or factual occurrence of the event(s) reported in evidence. I am not alone in making this distinction; it has also been thought necessary by jurists (e.g., Wigmore 1937, 45, 318–320) and by some probabilists (e.g., Keynes 1921, 181).

It might be argued, however, that the analysis illustrated in Figure 2.1 is somewhat misleading, or in any case incomplete. You might say that what is a "fact" is that I received evidence E^*; whether this evidence favors E or E^c is another matter. I take evidence E^* as some fact from which I draw an inference about whether or not what E^* reveals is factually true. So it may be that there are two "facts" to be considered here: (1) the fact of my receiving the evidence, and (2) what the evidence reports as alleged fact. My analysis so far only involves a distinction between evidence about some event and the factual occurrence of this event. In discussing Achinstein's analysis of evidence, I mentioned that we have to consider very carefully what exactly is the evidence we have. Suppose, for example, that I use E^* to represent, as evidence, a testimonial assertion I receive from somebody that event E occurred. But you could inquire about whether or not E^* is actually a "fact"; perhaps I was hallucinating and this person said nothing at all. I might also have been mistaken about what some source actually asserted. On this analysis the only things "factual" are the sensory, perceptual, or other mental events that lead me to believe that I have just heard evidence E^*. Perhaps this is what Wendell Johnson had in mind when he said that "facts" are personal matters.

2.1.3 Evidence, Data, and Information

We often use the Latin word *datum* or its plural form *data* in place of the word evidence. The *OED* defines *datum* as "a thing given or granted; something known or assumed as fact, and made the basis of reasoning or calculation; an assumption or premise from which inferences are drawn." Evidence forms the basis for reasoning, and we speak of drawing a conclusion from "given" evidence; so equating the words data and evidence seems, on the surface, to invite no difficulties. However, the trouble is that there are untold billions of data lurking in libraries, file cabinets, and computer memories; are all of these billions of data evidence? In its current data base the Internal Revenue Service has on record the datum that I underpaid my income tax for the year 1990 (I did of course later pay the amount that the IRS said I owed). In drawing a conclusion about the present state of your health a physician would almost certainly never think of using this IRS datum about me as evidence in a medical diagnosis about the condition of your health even if she knew of it and had access to it. We would all agree that my past tax underpayment in 1990 seems to have no *relevance* on any conclusion regarding the present state of your health. So we might simply state: A *datum becomes evidence in a particular inference when its relevance to this inference has been established.* Unfortunately, no datum comes to us with already-established relevance "credentials." The relevance of any datum has to be established by cogent *argument.* In Chapter 3 we will examine the process of establishing the relevance of evidence by arguments or chains of reasoning.

We might all agree that evidence should provide at least some *information,* or we could never draw any conclusion from it. A coded message we cannot decipher or a message written in some obscure dialect we cannot translate are both uninformative and would ordinarily be useless as evidence, or so it seems. However, in some circumstances we might be inclined to take as evidence just the receipt of a message from a particular source on a particular occasion. That someone tried to communicate with us may be evidence in certain situations, even if we cannot understand the message being sent. Perhaps this will happen if or when we receive a message from some extra-terrestrial civilization.

At least one person suggests that we distinguish between the terms evidence and information. In a work summarizing many of his thoughts about prob-abilistic reasoning, I. J. Good argues that evidence is always taken to be either for or against some hypothesis or is mentioned with explicit reference to some hypothesis and its negation. But he argues that information does not neces-sarily make explicit reference to the process of discriminating among hy-potheses we entertain (1983, 186). Though we suppose that evidence is in-formative in our inferences, we do not have to suppose that all items of information or data are now or will be evidence in any particular inference.

2.1.4 Evidence and Knowledge

I have another reason for summoning the courage to continue this book even though the term evidence is so very difficult to define in a completely satis-factory way. Today many persons, without any discernible embarrassment, seem willing to refer to themselves as "knowledge engineers" when in fact the term *knowledge* has resisted definition as obstinately as any term we will encounter. Philosophers continue to argue about what it means to say that "*X knows* that E is true." Most evidential issues have roots in epistemology. We may easily be able to say we have evidence in some inferential situation, but we will not so easily be able to say what knowledge we have on the basis of this evidence. Here is just one illustration; others will appear as we proceed.

In a probabilistic inference about whether or not hypothesis H is true, we both agree that event E, if it occurred, would strongly favor H being true. The trouble is that neither you nor I were privy to the situation in which E might or might not have occurred; so we have to determine how we will obtain such "knowledge." I say: "Let us ask person P, she will *know* whether or not E happened." Suppose that upon inquiry P says: "Yes, event E did happen."

We now have two questions: Does P know that event E happened? Do we ourselves now know that E happened as a result of what P just told us? Person P is the source of our present evidence about event E. As we will later discuss in Section 3.2, the foundation of all argument made on the basis of any kind of evidence is the credibility of the source(s) from which our evidence comes (including our own direct observations). Study of the credibility-related foundations of probabilistic argument involves epistemological issues we cannot ignore if our aim is to improve our understanding of the properties and uses of evidence. There are of course epistemological issues that accompany other elements of the process of drawing conclusions from evidence. Even if we are willing to say that our evidence provides knowledge, we might not be entitled to say that we then have knowledge regarding a particular conclusion on which this evidence seems relevant.

When all is said and done we may not be able to define the word evidence so that everything acceptable in all recognized disciplines is included and everything else is excluded. Different disciplines set their own experience-based standards and expectations as far as evidence is concerned. Here are examples of such standards and expectations that have come from the fields of history, medicine, and law. The historian Winks asserts (1968, xv):

> Evidence means different things to different people, of course. The historian tends to think mainly in terms of documents. A lawyer will mean something different by the word, as will a sociologist, or a physicist, or a geologist, or a police officer at the moment of making an arrest. For certain problems evidence must be "hard," while for others it may be "soft." Even if no acceptable or agreed-upon definitions of evidence may be given, most of us recognize intuitively what we mean when we use the word.

We should not infer from Winks' account that historians employ only documentary evidence. As Bloch tells us (1953, 66): "The variety of historical evidence is nearly infinite. Everything a man says or writes, everything that he makes, everything he touches can and ought to teach us about him." Lichtman and French list eighteen substantive classes of evidence routinely evaluated by historians (1978, 19).

To physicians the word evidence may mean any or all of the following: (1) demographic data, (2) subjective symptoms observed by the patient (e.g., dizziness, depression, headaches), (3) objective symptoms also observed by the patient (e.g., swollen ankles, jaundice, blood in urine), (4) physical signs observed by the doctor (e.g., heart murmer, enlarged liver), (5) paraclinical findings (e.g., X rays, blood chemistry, urinalysis), and (6) other information about the patient's past history such as smoking or drinking habits and life style (Wulff 1981, 8–9). In the field of law, evidence is commonly described as a means of proof of matters at issue in a dispute and mainly involves testimony, things ("real" or tangible evidence), and documents (Twining 1990, 179; Wigmore on Evidence, vol 1, 1983, 6–12).

2.2 RHETORIC, LOGIC, AND PHILOSOPHY

Having considered what evidence *is*, we must now give attention to what evidence *does* in inferences that cannot be demonstrative or deductive. The incomplete and inconclusive evidence we receive from sources having any gradation of credibility or reliability allows us to draw conclusions that have to be hedged probabilistically. Keynes tells us that the theory of probability is concerned with knowledge we obtain by *argument,* in particular, by those arguments that justify only some degree of certainty about possible conclusions (1921, 3). A natural question then is, What role does evidence play in argument? As we proceed, I will mention how some evidence can open up a line of argument or a chain of reasoning to a possible conclusion while other evidence bears upon our judgments about the strength or weakness of the links in these reasoning chains. Development of ideas concerning the inferential uses of evidence has taken place over many centuries.

2.2.1 Persuasive Arguments and Valid Arguments

The exact origins of interest in the evidential foundations of argument are buried somewhere in antiquity. However, it has been suggested that interest in the study of evidence may have coincided with the intertwined development of *rhetoric,* the study of *persuasive* argument, and *logic,* the study of *valid* argument (Twining 1990, 4–5). As we know, people are often persuaded by arguments that are not valid; on other occasions valid arguments fail to be persuasive. One place to begin a search for the origins of interest in evidence is in Greece in the fifth-century BC. It was during this period that tyrannies began to give way to democratic institutions; many historians associate interest in rhetoric with the emergence of democracy. Citizens of this period became increasingly inclined to seek redress of grievances in courts or in other hearings and for this purpose they often employed *rhetors* (speakers) whose task was to persuade courts or tribunals of the merits of their clients' cases. From such beginnings a general interest in persuasive discourse eventually emerged. As the historian Will Durant put it: "Oratory, stimulated by democracy and litigation, became one of the passions of Greece" (1939, 430).

One Greek who lived during this period was Corax of Syracuse (in Sicily) who, around 466 BC, wrote a treatise entitled *Techne Logon* (The Art of Words). None of Corax's work survives, and we know of it only through the writings of others. Corax discussed arguments "from probabilities" and offered various prescriptions for the construction and delivery of effective oral arguments, particularly in forensic or legal matters. Corax also had students who seem to have exported his teachings on rhetoric to other parts of Greece. In Athens those who studied and taught rhetoric were called "Sophists." Apparently some Sophists taught that any means could be employed in order to persuade an audience. Originally the term Sophist referred simply to one who taught for a fee; the most influential Sophist being Protagoras (Russell

1960, 73). It was only later that the term "sophistry" came to indicate specious, deceptive, or threadbare arguments. It is quite common today to associate the term "rhetoric" with florid discourse (frequently on political matters) that is exciting to the passions instead of appealing to the intellect. Starting in the Middle Ages, emphasis began to be placed by teachers of rhetoric on theatrics and the ornamentation of argument. In addition to learning about such legitimate matters as elocution or the style of effective speech, students were also carefully tutored in the use of gestures and postures that might be most appealing to an audience. The study of rhetoric, along with grammer and logic, remained part of a *trivium* of "core courses" taught in many universities until quite modern times.

Among the persons not persuaded by all of the rhetorical teachings of the Sophists were Plato and Aristotle. In fact, in a work entitled *Sophistical Refutations* Aristotle replied to the Sophists by compiling a list of fallacies to which many of their apparently persuasive arguments were prone. This same list is included in most modern texts on logic and critical thinking (e.g., Copi 1982, 97–137; Engel 1986; Fogelin 1987, 69–101). The list includes *petitio principii* (begging the question), *ad hominem* (arguing against a person rather than to an issue), *post hoc ergo propter hoc* (after which therefore on account of which), and *ad misericordiam* (an appeal to pity). Logic is concerned with prescriptions for valid inference, the systematic study of which originated in the work of Aristotle. There are, however, traces of earlier study of rules for valid inference (Kneale and Kneale 1984, 1–22).

It is certainly true that long before Aristotle people were capable of recognizing and constructing valid arguments. But Aristotle seems to have been the first to note the distinction between the form and the content of an inference. He recognized that certain formal rules for inference would apply regardless of the content or substance of the inference. In his work *Prior Analytics* Aristotle formulated rules for inference involving class membership, where a *class* refers to some totality or universe of discourse. Inferences concerning class membership are called *syllogisms*, a form of argument in which there are premises and a conclusion. Today we say that an inference is deductively valid if the truth of its premises makes necessary the truth of its conclusion. Thus, if it is true that all A's belong to class B, and if it is true that this particular X is an A, we conclude necessarily that X is a member of class B. But, as Reichenbach noted, the price paid by deductive inference for the necessity of its conclusions is their emptiness (1968, 81). In deductive inference a conclusion reveals only that which is already evident in its premises.

What we require in our daily lives are inferences whose conclusions go beyond evidential premises. Consider an engineer who has conducted a series of bench tests of a new device in which this device performed perfectly on each test. To what extent does the evidence supplied by these tests entitle this engineer to conclude that this device will later perform perfectly "in the field" and under conditions that might not have been included in the earlier tests? Here is an auditor who has examined a sample of a client's business transactions and finds no irregularities in them. To what extent does this evidence allow the auditor to conclude that *none* of this client's transactions involve irregularites? Here is an antibiotic known in many past instances to cure a certain bacterial infection. To what extent can a physician now conclude on the basis of this past experience that this antibiotic will provide a cure for the next *new* patient who has this bacterial infection? In each of these examples the engineer, auditor, and physician entertain conclusions that go beyond evidential premises. But these inferences have another characteristic; they all involve evidential premises that provide *some* but not conclusive grounds for belief in any of the possible conclusions being entertained. Today we use the term *induction* to refer to reasoning that provides only some but not complete grounds for a conclusion. Inductive inferences that go beyond evidential premises or that have content not present in these premises, such as in the three examples above, are said to be *ampliative* in nature because such reasoning amplifies our knowledge (Cohen 1989a, 1–2).

The term *induction* arose in efforts to translate a word (epagoge) used by Aristotle in describing reasoning from particular cases to universal truths (Kneale 1952, 24–25). Assessing Aristotle's contribution to our present understanding of induction is not an easy matter since there are differing views about what Aristotle actually said and meant in his discussions of what we now term *inductive reasoning*. In fact on this matter Bertrand Russell claims that Aristotle is a "battleground" (1960, 195). It does appear that Aristotle had no conception of induction specifically connected to probability (Kneale 1952, 24). This does not mean, however, that Aristotle had no conception of probability. Indeed in his *Rhetoric* Aristotle tells us that probability refers to what happens "for the most part" (1357a 35–36, Barnes ed., 1991, 2157), or what "usually" happens (1402a 23, Barnes ed., 1991, 2236).

Aristotle also used the concept of probability in connection with *generalizations* commonly asserted as a basis for reasoning. As we will note in Section 3.3.1, our legal system supposes that we all have a stock of commonsense generalizations that we can apply in inferences from evidence given at trial. Here are two such generalizations that Aristotle asserted in his *Rhetoric* (1392b 25–26; 1393a 7, Barnes ed., 1991, 2219): (1) ". . . if a man was going to do something, he has done it, for it is *likely* that the intention was carried out"; (2) " . . . if it is clouding over, it is *likely* to rain" (italics mine). So Aristotle gives us a foretaste of what we now call *fuzzy* probabilities, those asserted using words such as *likely* (more on fuzzy probability in Section 5.6).

For Aristotle, induction refers to the passage from particulars to universals, and he discusses two different cases. In his work *Prior Analytics* Aristotle describes what is now termed *summative* or *complete* induction, a form of reasoning that is in fact deductive in nature; here is an example. Suppose a flight attendant knows that there are fifty passengers who have made reservations for a certain flight and that they are all now in the waiting area. As the passengers file through the gate, the attendant collects a ticket from each passenger and observes that, when the last one has gone through, fifty tickets have been collected. The attendant then concludes necessarily that *every* passenger on the plane is ticketed. Here we have the passage to a general conclusion from a complete enumeration of particulars. Such a conclusion, however, is hardly ampliative or goes beyond the particulars upon which it is based. Nor is such a conclusion justified if we have not examined all possible particulars.

In his *Posterior Analytics* Aristotle used the term induction in another sense that Kneale refers to as "intuitive" induction (1952, 24–37). Aristotle's basic interest was in the demonstrative establishment of universal truths from primary premises in the form of particulars. The trouble, which he recognized, concerns how we obtain knowledge of these particulars. If they have also to be established demonstratively from other particulars, then we have an infinite regress on our hands. Aristotle argued that it must be "intellectual intuition" that grasps the particulars from which we establish universals. Kneale notes that this is a form of induction in which the universal is exhibited as implicit in known particulars, something that requires experience and observations. In describing Aristotle's second form of induction, Keynes simply notes that it is a process by which observation of particulars, in which some abstract notion is exemplified, enables us to realize and comprehend the abstraction itself (1921, 274). Some writers have claimed that Aristotle's "intutitve" induction is actually not even an inference. The reason is that it is not a type of argument involving premises and a conclusion but simply the process of guessing based upon the perception of relations (Cohen, M., and Nagle 1934, 275).

2.2.2   Evidence and Enumerative Induction

Having examined Aristotle's summative or complete induction in which a universal is established by enumerating all possible particulars, we might inquire about inference in situations in which not all particulars can be enumerated. Suppose, again, that there are fifty people in the airline's waiting area. This time, however, the flight is behind schedule, and in order to save time, the flight attendant considers collecting tickets from just the first twenty-five passengers in line. Could the attendant, on evidence that the first twenty-five passengers had tickets, conclude with certainty that all fifty passengers have tickets and allow the remaining twenty-five to pass through the gate without the further hinderance of collecting their tickets? For a variety of reasons no airline would sanction such an inference or such a procedure. It seems clear from the examples he provided that Aristotle never meant to suggest a form of inductive reasoning that generally proceeds by a simple enumeration of individual cases (Kneale and Kneale 1984, 36). But inferences based upon the enumeration of instances have been made for centuries. The tabulation of outcome *frequencies* is an enumerative process upon which all statistical inferences are based.

Induction based upon the enumeration of individual cases cannot establish conclusively the truth of any hypothesis or generalization even if all evidential cases examined to date have been favorable to this generalization (the uninteresting exception involves summative or complete induction). The future, in the form of the next case we observe, may not resemble the past in the form of previous favorable cases we have examined. Absent clairvoyance, we cannot know in advance that the next case will be favorable as have been all previous cases. Regardless of how many favorable cases we have observed in the past, all it takes is one unfavorable case to undermine some generalization that we are considering. There are many examples of such calamity; here is one that comes from the mathematician Leonard Euler (Sominskii 1961). Suppose we conjecture that the quadratic expression $x^2 + x + 41$ generates only prime numbers for integer values of $x \geq 0$. For $x = 0$ the result is 41, for $x = 1$ the result is 43, and for $x = 2$ the result is 47, all of which are primes. Each new trial thereafter inspires confidence in our conjecture, and so we persist in this empirical process. Even at the 40th observation this quadratic expression continues to generate prime numbers, since $x = 39$ produces 1601, which is prime. Now comes calamity for the conjecture since on the 41st observation, when $x = 40$, the expression generates the number $1681 = (41)^2$, which is not a prime number. Proof by a purely empirical process does not work in mathematics as Euler's example shows. We encounter difficulties with empirical means of proof in other situations as well.

It would certainly be comforting to know that there are uniformities in nature so that things that have worked in the past will continue to work in future. In lieu of absolute certainty about uniformities in nature, most of us seem willing to settle for an expression of the likeliness that something will work in future, given evidence about the number of times it has worked in the past. I have flown on commercial airliners on many past occasions and have survived each time. I now contemplate another flight next week and ponder the extent of the uniformity of nature as far as it concerns airplanes on which I am a passenger. If I were certain that this plane would crash, I would not get aboard. On the other hand, if I were certain that this plane would not crash and that I would arrive safely, I would not buy flight insurance. I will fly next week and also purchase flight insurance; this demonstrates some but not complete faith in this particular uniformity. Bertrand Russell mentioned some of the dangers in placing faith in the uniformity of nature. As he said (Russell 1921, 63): "Domestic animals expect food when they see the person who usually feeds them. We know that all these rather crude expectations of uniformity are liable to be misleading. The man who has fed the chicken every day throughout its life at last wrings its neck instead, showing that more refined views as to the uniformity of nature would have been useful to the chicken."

2.2.3   Evidence and Eliminative Induction

Nineteen centuries separate Aristotle and Francis Bacon (1561–1626), whose major work *Novum Organum* (A New Instrument), written in 1620, is taken to be the first attempt at an inductive logic (Reichenbach 1968, 82–83), or at least the first attempt to justify the procedures of natural scientists (Kneale 1952, 48–49). Earlier in Section 2.1.1 we noted Hacking's idea that progress in developing schemes for inductive reasoning was retarded by a conception of evidence that was incomplete. It appears that the use of evidence of "things that could point to other things" began to emerge only in the 1600s and in what Hacking terms the "low" sciences. Perhaps we should be a bit careful here lest the impression is conveyed that there was nothing useful happening in the natural sciences until the 1600s and only in Western cultures.

As one example, considerable progress was made long before the 1600s in a field today called *physiological optics;* a survey of this progress appears in the work of Yves Le Grand (1975, 4–7). As early as the second century AD, the Greek naturalist Galen had correctly identified various parts of the eye such as the conjunctiva, cornea, iris, aqueous humor, crystalline lens, vitreous humor, retina, choroid layer, and sclera. This early Greek knowledge would have been destroyed had it not been for the efforts of later Islamic scholars who added their own discoveries to this growing body of knowledge. In the ninth century AD, Hunain Ibn Ishaq produced the first detailed diagram of the eye. In the tenth century AD, Ibn al Haitham (also known to us as Alhazen) correctly inferred elements of the geometry of vision. In the twelfth century AD a prominent Islamic scholar, Averroes, located the retina as the site of photoreception. Many other examples might be given of similar advances made in natural science before the 1600s.

Francis Bacon may have had reverence for Aristotle generally, but he had no particular reverence for Aristotle's logic and its influence upon reasoning in science. Aristotle's works—*The Categories, On Interpretation, Prior Analytics, Posterior Analytics, Topics,* and *Sophistical Refutations*—have been collectively called the *Organum,* or instrument for acquiring scientific knowledge. In the *Novum Organum* Bacon hoped to supply natural scientists with some new tools. In *The Great Instauration* (Renovation), a preamble to his *Novum Organum,* Bacon says (Burtt collection, 1939, 15–16):

> For in the ordinary logic almost all work is spent about the syllogism. Of induction the logicians seem hardly to have taken any serious thought, but they pass by it with a slight notice, and hasten on to the formulae of disputation. I on the contrary, reject disputation by syllogism, as acting too confusedly, and letting nature slip out of its hands.

He then adds:

> But the greatest change I introduce is in the form of induction and the judgment made thereby. For the induction of which the logicians speak, which proceeds by simple enumeration, is a puerile thing; concludes at hazard; is always liable to be upset by contradictory instance; takes into account only what is known and ordinary; and leads to no result.

Not every subsequent natural scientist heeded Bacon's advice about the hazards of induction by enumeration. We are told that the chemist Antoine

Lavoisier did claim (erroneously) in 1789, on the basis of a strictly enumerative process, that all acids contain oxygen (Gjertsen 1989, 90). As a remedy to the deficiencies of enumerative induction, Bacon advocated an eliminative process in which evidence is to be used not in accumulating support for hypotheses but in an effort to eliminate them. If some hypothesis or generalization can be overthrown by a single negative instance, then perhaps we should structure our observational procedures and evidence gathering with elimination in mind. He believed that, of affirmative and negative instances regarding some hypothesis or claim, negative instances are the more forceful. Major sections of the *Novum Organum* contain lists of what Bacon termed aphorisms. One such list contains Bacon's observations on *The Interpretation of Nature and The Kingdom of Man*. In *Aphorism xlvi* on this list Bacon gives us an anecdote regarding the power of a negative instance. He tells of an ancient who was shown pictures of persons who had paid their vows to the gods and as a result had escaped shipwreck. This ancient was then asked whether or not he did acknowledge the power of the gods. Bacon tells us that the ancient replied: "Aye, but where are they painted that were drowned after their vows" (Burtt collection, 1939, 36).

Bacon's new instrument for the advancement of science consisted of an observational process in which we "interrogate Nature in order to be able to tabulate both the various circumstances in which instances of the phenomenon (the 'nature') under investigation have been found to be present and also the circumstances under which they have found to be absent" (Cohen, L. J., 1989a, 5). Of course it is true that the wider the array of circumstances we examine, the more confidence we can have in any explanation of the phenomenon of concern. Thus eliminative induction is also *variative* in nature. We do not gather support for a generalization by accumulating favorable instances of it. What we should do according to Bacon is to examine a variety of circumstances in an attempt to eliminate alternative explanations. In the *Novum Organum* Bacon tells us how this process allowed him to isolate motion as the cause of heat. In assessing the significance of Bacon's work, we encounter the same difficulty we did in the case of Aristotle's "intuitive" induction; different persons have interpreted Bacon in different ways.

One issue concerns whether or not Bacon believed we could use his new tools to establish with certainty the truth of some hypothesis or generalization. Jonathan Cohen argues that Baconian induction has been seriously misrepresented by his modern interpreters (1989a, 5). In particular, Cohen mentions the work of R. L. Ellis (1859) as propagating the idea that a distinguishing characteristic of Baconian induction is "absolute certainty." Ellis had a direct influence upon Keynes, since he also argued that Bacon believed one element of the preference for eliminative over enumerative induction concerned the possible attainment of inductive certainty using his eliminative methods (1921, 267). But Cohen argues that Bacon had a "gradualist" conception of induction and that at any stage of inquiry we may be less than certain about the truth of some hypothesis or generalization (1989a, 4–13). In the *Preface* to his

Novum Organum, Bacon asserts (Burtt collection, 1939, 24): "Now my method, though hard to practice, is easy to explain; and it is this. I propose to establish progressive stages of certainty."

Part of the difficulty I believe is that many of us come to accept the idea that *certainty* is fixed and that what can only be graded is *uncertainty.* This, at any rate, is the view one obtains from conventional probability. All probabilities greater than zero but less than one are said to grade the extent of our uncertainty about some hypothesis. A probability of 1.0 means some hypothesis is certain to be true, and a probability of zero means this hypothesis is certain not to be true. In fairness, however, it seems that there is no particular reason why we cannot speak of gradations of certainty that occur at various stages of inquiry, as Bacon did in describing his new tool for science.

Though we honor Bacon for setting thoughts about inductive reasoning on a more productive course, the method he advocated is not rich enough by itself to provide us with all of the tools we need in gathering new understanding about the parts of nature of interest to us. One person who built upon Bacon's insights about induction was John Stuart Mill (1806–1873). Mill believed that a more mature conception of inductive reasoning should include methods for identifying *causes.* This seems natural and desirable since many of the inferences required of us involve judgments about causal connections. In business affairs we seek probable causes of a bank failure; engineers seek probable causes of failure of a device or system; in criminal law magistrates make probable cause rulings affecting the possible further incarceration of a person arrested. In a work entitled *System of Logic* (1843) Mill discussed five experimental methods for isolating causes. Although they are called "Mill's methods," they have a earlier origins (Gjertsen 1989, 93). Very informative discussions of Mill's methods are given by Skyrms (1986, 75–128) and Cohen (1989a, 29–39). Cohen notes that these methods are Baconian in spirit because they are variative and basically eliminative in nature.

Thoughts about eliminative and variative induction coming from Bacon and Mill had an influence upon others. The jurist Wigmore claimed that inferences at trial are inductive in nature and, in at least some instances, require the use of methods such as Mill's (1937, 18–48). Then we have Sir Arthur Conan-Doyle, whose character Sherlock Holmes seems definitely to have been Baconian. In the mystery *The Sign of the Four* Holmes tells Watson (Baring-Gould 1967, vol. 1, 638): "How often have I said to you that when you have eliminated the impossible, whatever remains, *however improbable, must be the truth.*" Some persons accept the necessity of eliminative induction in various circumstances but also believe Holmes' view of this process to be rather naive (e.g., Earman 1992, 163–185). Suppose, for example, that a criminal investigator considers ten possible suspects. As the investigation proceeds, the evidence serves to eliminate nine of them. It does not necessarily follow that the remaining suspect is the one who committed the crime. The trouble is that this investigator may not even have entertained as a possible suspect the person who actually committed the crime. The process of *dis-*

covering or *generating* hypotheses or possibilities seems to involve reasoning that is not necessarily inductive in nature as we will consider in Section 2.6 and in Chapter 9. Bacon seems not to have distinguished between the processes of discovery and inductive proof, but Mill did claim that his methods, if not instruments for discovery, were at least instruments of proof (Cohen 1970, 128–129; 1989, 11).

The influence of Bacon and Mill extends to the present day and is particularly noticeable in courses we may take in experimental design. For example, the idea of a *control group* is traceable to Mill's methods. Students of experimental design learn something about the difficulties of identifying appropriate controls in order to isolate causal factors. We will return to Mill's methods when we encounter *causality,* yet another term that resists definition (Section 4.3). The distinction between enumerative and eliminative induction does not involve arcane matters devoid of practical importance. Indeed, as we will discuss in Chapter 5, there is considerable controversy about what is meant by the concept of *weight of evidence.* An important part of this controversy involves the distinction between enumerative and eliminative induction. Perhaps we should not expect to find that the force or weight of evidence is graded in the same way in these two different forms of inductive reasoning.

2.2.4   Arguments about Induction

Some scholars have assigned to evidence a primary place in logic and philosophy. For example, the adequacy or probative (inferential) value of evidence is said to be a major concern in logic (Cohen, M., and Nagle 1934, 5). Ayer tells us that the study of evidence best captures the stage to which philosophy has progressed (1984, 18). Evidence has been described as the central factor in producing belief (Nozick 1981, 257). If the use of evidence is so compelling in allowing us to draw conclusions, how is it that we cannot defend *ampliative inference* based upon evidence as being ideal or "rational"? Recall that an ampliative inference is one whose conclusion goes beyond and thus amplifies the content of evidential premises. Suppose that as a researcher or practitioner in some area, you have reached a conclusion based upon evidence that you would not hesitate to present to your colleagues and severest critics. What philosophers tell you, however, is that the evidence-based inferential process that you have employed cannot be defended as the most rational or wisest process you could have used. Your natural reply might be: "What other process do you recommend?" Even your harshest critic might hesitate to recommend that you employ a clairvoyant, resort to the recorded wisdom of ancient thinkers, seek a solution by means of divine revelation, or deduce a conclusion "from self-evident first principles in one glorious exercise of logical or mathematical skill, as once suggested by Descartes" (Cohen, L. J., 1989, 7).

It has been said that induction is "the queen of science and the scandal of philosophy." The person initially skeptical about the credentials of ampliative induction was the Scots philosopher David Hume. In his *Treatise of Human Nature* (1739, bk. I, pt. III) Hume argued that we could never completely justify reasoning from the observed to the unobserved. Given a modern interpretation, Hume's argument was that ampliative inference could not be established by nonampliative (deductive) means, for this would show that ampliative inference is not ampliative after all. On the other hand, to justify ampliative inference by an ampliative method involves an obviously circular argument (Salmon 1975, 5–11). Such an argument would essentially say that, in the future, the future will resemble the past because, in the past, the future has resembled the past. Since Hume's time philosophers have made many attempts to justify the inductive process whose use is so common in so many situations (e.g., Swinburne 1974; Cohen, L. J., and Hesse 1980).

Earlier I pondered the wisdom of trying to complete a book on the topic of evidence because it resists definition. I now face an additional burden since it appears that the use of evidence as a basis for inference cannot be rationally justified. Since you now have this book in your hands, you can infer that I did not worry excessively about this problem. I believe that I am in good company in moderating the extent to which I am troubled over the problem Hume posed for all of us. In his Inaugural Lecture entitled *The Warrant of Induction*, given at Cambridge University in January 1988, D. H. Mellor begins as follows: "This lecture will last less than twenty-four hours. I know that, and so do you. And you knew it before I said so. How? Because you knew that lectures don't last twenty-four hours." Mellor goes on to say that this particular induction by members of his audience is warranted by their own evidence about the length of lectures they have heard in the past. The major source Mellor draws upon in his lecture is a paper entitled *Truth and Probability* by F. P. Ramsey (1926). In this paper Ramsey said: "We are all convinced by inductive arguments, and our conviction is reasonable because the world is so constituted that inductive arguments lead on the whole to true opinions. We are not, therefore, able to help trusting induction, nor if we could help it do we see any reason why we should, because we believe it to be a reliable process" (Mellor collection, 1990, 93). Mellor concludes his lecture by discussing the typical terseness of lectures of the sort he has given. As his closing remark he states: "And so you do know already that its terse— that it will last less than twenty four hours—because, as you will see at the end of this sentence, that belief of yours is not only warranted, it's true." Whereupon Mellor's lecture ended well shy of twenty-four hours.

Apart from the issue of whether or not ampliative inference can be justified, philosophers have found other things to argue about; one concerns the relative importance of enumerative and eliminative or variative induction. In statistics courses we learn about inferential methods based upon the enumerative process of accumulating frequencies. We also learn that the confidence we can have in some relative frequency depends upon the size of the sample upon which it is based. The establishment of relative frequencies assumes the existence of a process that can be replicated or observed repeatedly. We also learn to distinguish between statistical and scientific hypotheses, though the linkage between the two is rarely made clear (Edwards, W., 1965, 400–402). By the process of eliminative induction we employ a series of *different* evidential tests, each one designed to eliminate certain possibilities we might entertain. In one exchange Burks argued that induction involves a hierarchy of rules and methods and that the methods found at one level incorporate those found at lower levels. In science Burks claims that eliminative and variative methods are found quite high in this hierarchy but that enumerative methods are basic and operate from the lowest level on up (1980, 172–189). In reply, L. J. Cohen argued that both forms of induction have a place but that the relative positions of enumerative and variative induction depend upon the situation (1980, 190). As we will observe, inductive inference is necessary in situations in which no enumeration is possible.

I mentioned that the lack of conclusive evidence means that inductive conclusions we reach must be hedged probabilistically in some way. The trouble is that there are different ideas about how we ought to grade the uncertainty or the degree of certainty with which we state inductively reached conclusions. Some of these ideas concern the enumerative-eliminative distinction we have been discussing. There is at least one view that states that we should not even try to hedge conclusions probabilistically by any means. The philosopher Karl Popper (1968, 1972) has argued that in science, at least, there is no room for probabilities. Popper agrees that theories can never be proved but only disproved, so his methods resemble induction by elimination to the extent that they allow us to falsify theories on the basis of different evidential tests. If a theory cannot be proved, it can at least be *corroborated* to the extent that it passes the evidential tests we devise. Popper claims that science should take no interest in theories that have high probabilities. His claim is that we need theories that are rich and powerful in the sense that they allow us to generate entirely new facts; such theories, he says, are always *improbable* in the nature of things.

Popper gives us a valuable lesson which we will have occasion to recall in our later discussion of alternative views about what the *weight* of evidence means. He tells us that in responding to an opposing view, we should always attempt to put this view in its best possible light or else our criticism of it will not be worth very much (1968, 260, n. 5). There is considerable controversy about probabilistic reasoning in general and about the weight of evidence in particular. In not all of the published research on this matter have opposing views been put to their best advantage.

I mentioned that induction has been termed the "scandal" of philosophy. But inductive reasoning seems to be related to other intellectual activities such as learning (e.g., see De Finetti 1972, 147; Michalski 1991). Learning is sometimes characterized as a change in behavior as a result of experience. In inductive inference we revise our beliefs about the truth of hypotheses on the basis of evidence we obtain. Psychologists, among others, have been actively engaged in research on human learning for decades. Researchers in artificial intelligence have attempted to design various "knowledge-based" systems to assist people in the performance of various inferential or diagnostic tasks. It has recently been remarked that induction, as the scandal of philosophy, has now become the scandal of psychology and artificial intelligence as well, since neither of these areas have been particularly able to describe and to facilitate the processes of induction and learning (Holland et al. 1989, 1).

2.2.5 Evidence and Chains of Reasoning

To set the stage for discussion of an important inferential issue, we return briefly to the topic of missing evidence. As you may recall from an earlier example, one form of missing evidence is that which you expect but are unable to find. There seem to be three possibilities: (1) The evidence does not exist, (2) you looked in the wrong place, or (3) someone is concealing it. When I first began to study evidence in the 1960s, I came to the conclusion that single-stage inductive reasoning is very rare except in contrived abstract examples. Upon close examination, reasoning from evidence to possible conclusions always seems to involve more than one stage. In Chapters 7 and 8 I will present analyses of a wide assortment of common properties and subtleties in evidence, every one of which involves consideration of a chain of reasoning in which there are often many links. Recognizing that human inductive reasoning usually has many stages, I began in the 1960s to take an interest in what is now called *multistage, hierarchical,* or *cascaded* inference. Seeking inspiration for the study of cascaded inference, I consulted a variety of sources in logic and philosophy and could find only scant reference to problems associated with chains of reasoning. Since I did not believe logicians and philosophers were concealing this information from me, I concluded that they were either unconcerned about the topic, occupied by other matters, or that I was simply looking in the wrong places. Here are two examples of what I was then able to find regarding chains of reasoning.

In his *Treatise of Human Nature* Hume records (Selby-Bigge ed., 1975, 144):

> 'Tis certain, that when an inference is drawn immediately from an object, without any intermediate cause or effect, the conviction is much stronger, and the persuasion more lively, than when the imagination is carry'd thro' a long chain of connected arguments, however infallible the connexion of each link may be esteem'd. 'Tis from the original impression, that the vivacity of all the ideas is deriv'd, by means of the customary transition of the imagination; and 'tis evident this vivacity must decay in proportion to the distance, and must lose somewhat in each transition.

As I will later discuss, I must take issue with Hume's belief that the "vivacity" of an inference always decays in proportion to the number of links in a chain of reasoning. As we will see, this depends upon how a chain of reasoning from evidence to conclusions is constructed and how adequate is other evidence that bears upon the strength or weakness of each link in this chain.

As I have noted, even the "simplest" of inferences can be decomposed, and the level of decomposition one employs is quite arbitrary. One source from whom I received this inspiration is the logician John Venn. In his *Principles of Inductive Logic,* Venn states (1907, 506):

> When a "sequence" is shown to us, that is, when there are two groups respectively, of antecedents and consequents, with any appreciable interval between them, however minute this interval may be, we know well enough that if we choose to examine more closely we can subdivide this by the interposition of other so-called links, and so on indefinitely. Nature is continuous, and it depends entirely upon the degree of minuteness to which we decide to work, and upon the existence of appropriate names for the intermediate events, whether or not we impose any of these links.

Philosophers and logicians have certainly recognized the existence of chains of reasoning and, at least in Venn's case, have recognized the arbitrariness in forming them. But for inspiration regarding the ubiquity and importance of cascaded inference, we must turn to our colleagues in jurisprudence. It was in legal evidence scholarship that I found my "missing evidence" about cascaded inference.

2.3 EVIDENCE, PROBABILITY, AND STATISTICS

Let me now add the word *probability* to the growing list of terms that withstand our best efforts to define them. I know of one work that begins with an attempt to define this word, continues with various interpretations of it, and ends 252 pages later with a tentative definition that is guaranteed not to please everyone (Weatherford 1982). My experience with the word *evidence* allows me to have great sympathy for Weatherford. For some people the word probability is immediately associated with numbers between zero and one that are used to grade the extent of our *uncertainty* about events, statements, or possible conclusions. Others, who have not had the benefit of conventional tutoring in probability, may simply associate this word either with numerical terms such as percentages and odds or with other words such as *likeliness* that are often used as synonyms. In common with other subjects such as psychology, probability may be said to have a very long past but a very short history. I will try to explain this curious situation in just a moment. It is very common to associate the beginnings of probability theory with early calculations involving games of chance. However, the history of the origin and development of probability theory is a far richer intellectual enterprise and involves the fields of law, religion, politics, history, and business. We are blessed with some splendid historical accounts of the development of the concept of probability. The ones I have relied upon are the works of Todhunter (1865), David (1962), Epstein (1967), Hacking (1975), Shapiro (1982), Stigler (1986), Daston (1988), and Gigerenzer et al. (1991).

2.3.1 Interpretations of Probability

The concept of probability has now been interpreted in so many different ways that it is difficult even to decide how these various interpretations might best be categorized. My major concern in this chapter is to establish connections between the concepts of evidence, induction, and probability in order to facilitate our later discussion of the properties of and subtleties in various forms and combinations of evidence. The categorization I will make of important conceptions of probabilistic reasoning requires a brief survey of how the concept of probability seems to have emerged during its long past but short history.

The long past of probability extends back at least to paleolithic times when early peoples seem to have regularly employed devices similar to what we now call dice. Among present-day gamblers dice are frequently called "bones." It happens that the heel bone of certain running animals is called an *astragalus* or *talus*. Smoothed and marked bones of this sort are found among the artifacts left behind by cave dwellers (David 1962). Hacking claims that these bones are the earliest known randomization devices (1975, 1). Early peoples may have used these devices for gambling or as a means of forecasting the future. Whatever their original purpose, these devices appear regularly in later cultures up to the present day. Epstein (1967) provides us with an interesting history of the development and use of various devices for gambling or for divining the future. All of these devices have a common characteristic: They are constructed so as to produce outcomes by *chance,* at random, or without design. But the "short history" of probability dates back not much over 400 years when various persons first began to become interested in calculating chances associated with various gambling devices. Sometime between 1524 and 1550 Gerolamo Cardano wrote a treatise entitled *Liber De Ludo Alea* (Book on Games of Chance) that was in fact a manual for gamblers. Cardano died in 1576, and his work was not published until 1663 (Todhunter 1865, 1). Some of the works of Kepler and Galileo also reveal their interests in calculating chances.

In spite of these earlier works it is common to associate the beginnings of the short history of probability calculation with the mathematician Blaise Pascal (1623–1662). In fact in some historical accounts the precise date of July 29, 1654, is taken to mark the beginning of mathematical probability (Todhunter 1865, 7–21). It was on this date that Pascal began to communicate with another mathematician Pierre de Fermat (1608–1665) about a problem that had been posed to Pascal by a reputed gamester named Chevalier de Mere. This problem, called the "problem of points," involved a game in which a player had to gain a certain number of points in order to win. The problem posed by de Mere was how to divide the stakes between two players if one of the players had to leave before the game was played out. It was supposed by Pascal and Fermat that on any trial of this game each player had an equal chance of winning a point. From such a beginning a widespread interest developed among mathematicians in the calculation of *aleatory* probabilities, those associated with games of chance (the Latin word *alea* is variously translated as a single die, dice game, chance, risk, or venture).

The calculation of aleatory probabilities is an exercise in counting or enumeration under two assumptions. First, suppose a game in which there is some *finite* number $n(S)$ of possible outcomes on any of the well-defined trials of this game; S represents the entire collection of these possible outcomes. Second, suppose that each of these outcomes have an *equal probability* of occurring on any given trial. If we define E to be a subset of the outcomes in S that have some common property, the probability of E, $P(E)$, equals $n(E)/n(S)$, where $n(E)$ refers to the number of outcomes having the property that defines E. Thus, for example, we determine the probability of rolling a seven using two ordinary and fair six-sided dice to be 6/36, since on exactly six of the thirty-six possible outcomes the upturned numbers on the two dice sum to seven. Anyone familiar with the subject of combinatorial analysis knows that the counting exercises involved in determining aleatory probabilities can be quite difficult for certain kinds of games. Here is an example that illustrates just one of the many historical oddities associated with games of chance.

In the game of poker, played using a well-shuffled ordinary deck of fifty-two cards, two of the possible five-card hands are a *flush* and a *straight*. A *flush* is a hand containing five cards all of the same suit (clubs, spades, hearts, or diamonds), provided these five cards are not also consecutively ranked (if the five cards were also in consecutive ranks, then the hand would be called *straight flush*). A *straight* is a five card hand in which the cards can be placed in consecutive ranks, provided that the five cards are not also of the same suit (here again we would have a *straight flush*). If we adopt the usual convention that an ace can be played "high or low" (either ranked above a king or ranked below a two) there are $n(F) = 5108$ possible five-card hands that are flushes and $n(G) = 10,200$ possible five-card hands that are straights. Now there are $n(S) = 2,598,960$ possible five-card hands. If we assume that these hands have equal probability of occurring, the probability of a flush $P(F) = 5108/2,598,960 = 0.0020$ and the probability of a straight $P(G) = 10,200/2,598,960 = 0.0039$. As you can see, a flush is just slightly less probable than a straight. Yet, long before anyone could determine these probabilities, it was common to value a flush more than a straight (Hacking 1975, 53). We can only speculate about the reason why human intuition became so well-informed in this matter. Perhaps someone before Pascal's time knew about the combinatorics involved in determining card-hand probabilities. We might even suppose that there was some heroic person with an abundance of leisure time who actually tabulated the 5108 different flushes and the 10,200 different straights.

The aleatory probability calculations of Pascal and other later mathematicians provided a basis for belief about the chances of winning in games such as dice, cards, and roulette wheels. But, as in other periods of human history, people in the 1600s were also interested in the formation of beliefs concerning other matters about which there was uncertainty. In particular, court officials and jurors formed beliefs about the guilt or innocence of a defendant; shepards of the church as well as members of their flocks formed beliefs about events having religious significance, including of course events of a miraculous nature; merchants formed beliefs about whether or not the goods they shipped overseas would arrive in good order; and historians formed beliefs regarding the probable occurrence of interesting past events. All of the beliefs just mentioned seem to have a common characteristic: They are probabilistic in nature, but they involve evidential processes in which the aleatory assumptions of a finite number of equally likely outcomes make no sense. Despite the nonaleatory nature of the situations in which such beliefs were formed, attempts were made to apply the rigor and precision of mathematics to belief formation in these matters.

Thus Hacking argues that the emergence of probability in the 1600s had a certain duality (1975, 11–17). On the one hand, probability involved aleatory processes that produce stable *relative frequencies*. Most aleatory devices involve a certain *visible symmetry* designed to reinforce the idea that we should be *indifferent* about which outcome will be generated on any given trial. For example, a die that on close inspection appears to be fair should show the number five on roughly 1/6 of the occasions on which it is thrown. On the other hand, probability took on an *epistemic* face and concerned the *reasonable belief* a person might have in situations, such as those described above, that cannot be construed in terms of replicable games of chance. Courts, clerics, merchants, historians, and others in the 1600s began to be concerned about probabilistic beliefs and about how the strength of these beliefs, on various forms of evidence, might reasonably be graded. Some mathematicians of the period took these problems as their own and began to be concerned about probabilities associated with legal evidence, religious miracles, business ventures, and historical events. Of particular interest was the application of mathematical probability to inferential problems in jurisprudence, to which I will return in Section 2.4. I must add that there is some debate about whether Hacking's duality covers all of the shades of probability that appear to have emerged around the time of Pascal; probability in the 1600s may have had other faces as well (Daston 1988, 11–12; Shapiro 1982).

Another important event that took place in the 1600s was the founding of *statistics*. The person whose name is usually associated with this event is John Graunt (1620–1674), a London merchant who began to take an interest in what we would today call *vital statistics*, those associated with birth, mortality, and the causes of mortality. His work concerned the tabulation of relative frequencies for processes that, although repetitive in nature, could involve no aleatory assumptions. A relative frequency is, like an aleatory probability, a ratio determined by enumeration. In some series of N trials or observations the ratio $n(E)/N$ is the number of times an outcome favorable to event E was observed in the N observations that were taken. Of course this relative frequency cannot be taken to be equivalent to the probability of E, since we might have taken any number of other observations of this process. In short, the relative frequency $n(E)/N$ is simply an *estimate* of the probability of E, $P(E)$. We might expect, however, that this estimate would get better as N increases. In the late 1600s James Bernoulli discovered the first of what have been termed the "laws of large numbers." Bernoulli proved that if we consider a sufficiently long series N of observations, the probability can be made as close to 1.0 as we please that $n(E)/N$ will lie as close to $P(E)$ as we please. Notice, however, that we cannot define the limiting value of a relative frequency to be a probability by Bernoulli's result since this would involve a circular argument; the convergence process Bernoulli discussed is itself probabilistic in nature.

In 1632 Graunt began to publish what he termed *Bills of Mortality* containing statistical summaries of records kept by parish clerks in the city of London. Here are two examples from Graunt's Bills of Mortality for the years 1632 (Newman 1956, vol. 3, 1425) and 1665 (David 1962). In 1662, of 9584 christenings, 4994 (52.1%) were males and 4590 (47.8%) were females. Also in 1662, of 9535 persons buried, 4932 (51.7%) were males and 4603 (48.3%) were females. Notice here the roughly equal number of christenings and burials. How things changed in 1665! In this year there were 9967 christenings (51.3% male and 48.7% female), but there were 97,306 burials, more than ten times the number in 1632. The explanation is that 1665 was a plague year; of the 97,306 burials, 68,596 (70.5%) of these persons were recorded as having died of the plague. Mortality tables involving relative frequencies such as those compiled by Graunt began to provide a basis for the emergence of interest in annuities and insurance of various forms.

An even shorter part of the history of probability concerns the first attempt to put this concept on an axiomatic footing. This happened in 1933 in a treatise entitled *Foundations of the Theory of Probability*, written by the Russian mathematician A. N. Kolmogorov. In this work Kolmogorov introduced probability as a mathematical *measure* assigned to *events*, as subsets of outcomes in a complete and nonempty collection S. We commonly refer to S as a *sample space* or as a *basic space* of outcomes. As a measure-theoretic concept, probability thus has a life of its own and can be studied in the abstract without reference to any particular context in which it may be applied. Kolmogorov's probability measure has various properties specified by or derivable from the axioms he asserts. We have to consider the extent to which these axioms provide a suitable basis for a concept of probability that covers all situations in which we use evidence as a basis for conclusions that can only be probabilistic in nature. In different views of probability there are different conceptions of the weight or force of evidence. In some of these views, probability-related metrics will not conform to properties of probability grounded upon the following axioms of Kolmogorov.

Kolmogorov first considers a *probability system* whose basic ingredients consist of (1) a nonempty basic space S of elementary outcomes, (2) a "suitable" class **C** of events, and (3) a *probability measure P* defined for each event E in class **C**. What is meant by a "suitable" class **C** requires some explanation. Kolmogorov wished to have a concept of probability that would be rich and flexible enough to allow assignment of probability in a consistent way to *Boolean combinations* of events. We form such combinations by the operations of union, intersection, and complementation. Suppose that S is finite such that $n(S) = t$. In this case there are 2^t possible subsets (events) in S. These possible events include S itself, which we call the *sure event*, and $\emptyset$, which we call the *impossible event*. If we let **C** be the class consisting of all these 2^t possible events, then we are assured that any Boolean combination of events in **C**, formed by a countable (finite or countably infinite) number of the operations of union, intersection, and complementation, will also be an event in **C**. Thus, for example, if events E and F are members of **C**, then so are the events E^c (not-E), $E \cup F$, and $E \cap F$. In the case of finite S, the class **C** of all 2^t possible subsets of S is a "suitable" class.

Trouble arises, however, when S is infinite; in this case we cannot simply take **C** to be the set of all subsets of S. There are certain pathologies that can arise. If we suppose that **C** has the following three properties, we can be assured that **C** will be "suitable" in the sense mentioned above: (1) $\emptyset$ and S are events; (2) if E is an event in **C**, then so is E^c; and (3) if we have a countable sequence of events, the union of events in this sequence is an event in **C** and the intersection of the events in this sequence is also an event in **C**. A class **C** of subsets (events) of S having these three properties is alternatively called a *Borel field*, a *sigma field*, or a *sigma algebra* of subsets (events).

Kolmogorov's probability measure, defined on subsets of "suitable" class **C**, has three basic properties: (1) $P(E) \geq 0$ for any event E in class **C**, (2) $P(S) = 1.0$, and (3) $P(E \cup F) = P(E) + P(F)$ if E and F are any two mutually exclusive or disjoint events in **C**. Thus Kolmogorov's probabilities are numbers between zero and one that are *additive* across mutually exclusive events. From these three basic axioms regarding Kolmogorov's probability measure, many other properties can be derived. For example, $P(E^c) = 1 - P(E)$; $P(\emptyset) = 0$; if E is a subset of F, then $P(E) \leq P(F)$; and, in general, $P(E \cup F) = P(E) + P(F) - P(E \cap F)$.

It is not an accident that aleatory probabilities $n(E)/n(S)$ and relative frequencies $n(E)/N$ conform to Kolmogorov's probability measure. Both aleatory probabilities and relative frequencies are enumerative in nature and occur in repeatable or replicable situations. In fact, in applications of his probability system and measure, Kolmogorov assumes a repetitive process (1933, 3). He also asserts (1964, vol. 2, 231):

Since it cannot be doubted that statistical laws are of great importance, we turn to the question of methods of studying them. First of all, one thinks of the possibility of proceeding in a purely empirical way. Since a law of probability exhibits itself only in mass processes, it is natural to imagine that in order to discover the law we must conduct a mass experiment. Such an idea, however, is only partly right. As soon as we have established certain laws of probability by experiment, we may proceed to deduce from them new laws of probability by logical means or by computation, under certain assumptions.

Quite obviously, the quantities Kolmogorov had in mind when he formulated his axioms were either aleatory probabilities or relative frequencies, both associated with *enumerative* induction. But in our historical excursion we have also encountered induction that is *eliminative* in nature, and we have encountered *epistemic* probabilities or degrees of *reasonable belief* as asserted by people in many nonenumerative situations. Can we expect that probabilities conforming to those in Kolmogorov's axiom-based system will necessarily capture all aspects of our credal or belief states and will also be congenial to induction that is eliminative in nature? Answers to this question provide a basis for categorizing contemporary views of probability.

For our present purposes I shall adopt a distinction made by Jonathan Cohen (1977, 1989a). We can sort most interpretations of probability into two categories bearing the names *Pascalian* or *non-Pascalian*. This distinction simply acknowledges the lineage of interest in probability calculation traceable to the work of Blaise Pascal. Pascalian interpretations of probability have a common feature: They all employ a metric of probability that conforms to Kolmogorov's three probability measure axioms just mentioned. But probabilities having these metric properties have been interpreted in various ways depending upon the situation in which they are encountered. The number of different interpretations of Pascalian probabilities you will find depends upon where you look. Fine (1973) lists nine specific interpretations, Cohen (1989a) lists six specific interpretations, and Weatherford (1982) lists four entire *classes* of interpretations. As Cohen remarks, we seem to have an embarrassment of riches as far as alternative interpretations of Pascalian probabilities are concerned (1989a, 81). Not all of these interpretations are crucial in our present discourse on evidence, its properties, and its subtleties. However, one Pascalian interpretation that we will encounter repeatedly is the *subjectivist* or *personalist* view of probability. On this interpretation we are entitled to grade epistemic degrees of belief using probabilities that conform to Kolmogorov's axioms. In fact, as we will later discuss in Section 2.3.5, many people hold the view that any "rational" numerical expression of our probabilistic beliefs must conform to the properties of Kolmogorov's probability measure.

In Chapter 5 we will encounter three non-Pascalian views of probabilistic reasoning whose essential probability-related metrics do not conform to the Kolmogorov axioms. Quite recently Jonathan Cohen (1977) has given us a system of probabilities that is expressly congenial to eliminative and variative induction. He refers to this system of probabilities as *Baconian*, acknowl-

edging the lineage of interest in eliminative induction traceable to Francis
Bacon. As we will observe in Section 5.5, Baconian probabilities do not in
the least resemble Pascalian probabilities. Baconian probabilities are only
ordinal in nature and grade the extent to which hypotheses are successful in
resisting our best attempts to eliminate them on the basis of a variety of
different relevant evidential tests. A major property of Pascalian probabilities
is their *additivity* across mutually exclusive events; if these events are also
exhaustive, then the probability assigned to them must sum to one. As we
will see in discussing Glenn Shafer's work in Section 5.4, it has been recognized
since the 1600s that additive expressions of probability are not always adequate
in capturing certain credal or belief states that all of us naturally experience.
In his major work Shafer (1976) offers an epistemic system of *belief functions*
whose properties are not necessarily Pascalian in nature. Finally, I have noted
that both Aristotle and Wigmore had conceptions of probability that we would
today describe as *fuzzy* in nature. In many of our daily inferences, ampliative
or otherwise, the ingredients of inference (evidence, hypotheses, and generalizations that link them) are *imprecise*. Since this is so, it seems natural
that we should only be able to state probabilistic conclusions with imprecision.
Lotfi Zadeh and his many colleagues have provided us with methods of fuzzy
or approximate reasoning (see Yager et al. 1987 for a collection of Zadeh's
most important works). The fuzzy probabilities Zadeh discusses and that we
will consider in Section 5.6 are not Pascalian.

The process of drawing probabilistic conclusions from evidence in any
context imaginable is of course a *behavioral* task. I have already stated my
belief that probabilistic reasoning is an enormously rich intellectual activity.
The more I observe such activities in many different contexts, the richer they
appear to me. I simply do not believe it possible to capture all of this behavioral richness within the confines of any single formal system of probabilities that now exists or that any of us is likely to invent. Thus, as you will
see, I take a very tolerant view of both Pascalian and non-Pascalian systems,
all of which capture certain elements of the behavioral richness of inductive
reasoning based upon evidence. I may be wishy-washy in other matters, but
I believe my present tolerance for diversity in thinking about human reasoning
is not an example. However convenient it would be, philosophically or otherwise, I do not believe we will be able to tie all of human probabilistic
reasoning into one neat bundle.

2.3.2 Probability and Evidence

We have considered ampliative induction as the process of forming probabilistically hedged conclusions on the basis of evidence. So it seems obvious
that the probabilities we assign to our conclusions depend upon the evidence
we have. If we gather new evidence, we may have to *revise* our probabilities.
One characteristic of inductive conclusions is that they are *tentative* in nature
and are subject to change in light of new evidence we obtain. Stated another

way, as we *learn* new things, our probabilistic beliefs may change. All of this now seems quite obvious, and it is therefore quite surprising to discover that the idea of probability being relative to evidence is quite recent on the historical time scale of probability. This relation appears to have been first made explicit by a person named Kahle who, in 1735, published a now-unobtainable work entitled *Elementa Logicae Probabilium*. This, at any rate, is the conclusion of Keynes (1921, 90–91) and Kneale (1952, 9–13) who attempted to trace studies of the linkage between probability and evidence. However, it might be noted that persons earlier than Kahle seem to have understood this linkage. For example, in his *Essay Concerning Human Understanding* (1690), Locke said that there were two grounds for probability: "Conformity with our own experience, or the testimony of other's experience" (Nidditch ed., 1991, 405). Testimony is evidence, and so are our own observations.

We will have to exercise some care in discussing the relationship between evidence and probability. The reason is that the evidence we have may play different roles in allowing us to estimate, judge, or calculate probabilities. What we will have in many situations is evidence and *evidence about the inferential strength of this evidence;* here are two examples. As we recall, John Graunt gave us statistical evidence that, in the year 1665, 70.5% of deaths recorded that year by parish clerks in London were caused by the plague. Suppose we wish to use this evidence in drawing a conclusion about the true proportion of people who died of the plague in London in the year 1665. In doing so, we would be well-advised to consider other evidence bearing upon the confidence we can place in Graunt's statistical evidence. This additional evidence might concern such matters as (1) the number of citizens in London whose names would never have appeared in parish registers, (2) the accuracy and care with which the cause of death was diagnosed in those days, and (3) the accuracy and completeness with which parish clerks maintained their records.

Earlier I promised that we would meet some interesting characters during our discourse on evidence. In their journey to the western islands of Scotland in 1773, Samuel Johnson and his biographer James Boswell visited the Island of Iona where are buried many ancient kings of Scotland, Ireland, and Norway. Many of their gravestones were not readable in 1773. Noting this, Johnson remarked that some of these graves undoubtedly contained men who did not expect to be so soon forgotten. In our studies of evidence in different contexts we will encounter persons who perhaps did not know they would be so long remembered. Two such persons may have been Lewis Pelser and Dominic Constantino, both of whom, on April 15, 1920, were laborers at the Rice & Hutchins shoe factory in South Braintree, Massachusetts. Their names will live as long as the murder trial of Nicola Sacco and Bartolomeo Vanzetti is an object of study. This promises to be a very long time since there has been no more celebrated trial in American legal history. Sacco was charged with first-degree murder and Vanzetti charged as an accomplice in the slaying of a payroll guard named Alessandro Berardelli during a robbery that took place In South Braintree on the above date. Pelser, a witness for the prosecution, identified Sacco as being at the scene of the crime. Pelser said that, hearing shots, he looked out the window and observed a person who looked like Sacco (at trial Pelser identified Sacco as one of the persons he had seen). Constantino, a witness for the defense, asserted that, when the shooting started, he observed Pelser to be under a workbench (Sacco-Vanzetti case, trial transcript, 1969, 1167–1168). In this instance Pelser gave identification evidence bearing upon whether or not Sacco was guilty as charged; Constantino gave evidence about the credibility of Pelser's evidence.

Any formal or logical system of probability needs to incorporate some mechanism for *revising* probabilities in light of new evidence we obtain. Stated another way, we need to have a concept of probability that allows for the combination of new evidence with old in the process of revising the strength of our beliefs, regardless of the nature of the evidence we have. On a Pascalian interpretation the mechanism for probabilistic belief revision is provided by a process called *conditioning* that allows us to determine probabilities that have been revised or conditioned. The essential property of a conditional probability is given in Pascalian terms *by definition* and is not asserted in the form of an axiom. As we learn in elementary probability courses, the probability of E, *given* F, is *defined* as $P(E|F) = P(E \cap F)/P(F)$ provided that $P(F) \neq 0$. Kolmogorov took this to be a definition except he used a different notation (1933, 6). For the probability of E, given evidence F, he used the notation $P_F(E) = P(E \cap F)/P(F)$ provided that $P(F) \neq 0$. So, $P(E|F) = P_F(E)$. In essence P_F is a new probability measure we apply to E when we are given F. I am going to preserve both notations for a conditional probability since mixing the two notational schemes conveys important information about the process of conditioning (Pfeiffer and Schum 1973, 86, 102–104). Also, in keeping with notational conventions, I will hereafter suppress the intersection symbol ($\cap$); thus, for example, $E \cap F = EF$.

We ought to investigate the grounds for defining the probability of E, given or conditional upon evidence about F, as the ratio of $P(EF)$ to $P(F)$. Let us appeal to the situation depicted in Figure 2.2. I am going to interpret this

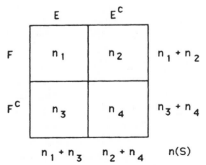

FIGURE 2.2 Partitioning outcomes in a game of chance.

situation in terms of a game of chance under aleatory assumptions; it could just as easily represent a replicable or frequentistic situation in which aleatory assumptions would not make any sense. Earlier in Figure 2.1, I made a distinction between evidence of an event and the event itself. For the sake of simplicity in explaining the situation in Figure 2.2, let us suppose we can take evidence F^* as equivalent to F; this means we do not question the credibility of our source of information about event F.

Suppose a game of chance in which there is a finite number $n(S)$ of equally likely outcomes. In Figure 2.2 we have partitioned the $n(S)$ outcomes in S in two ways: in terms of events $\{E, E^c\}$ and in terms of events $\{F, F^c\}$. First, we can determine the aleatory probability of E to be $P(E) = (n_1 + n_3)/n(S)$, where $(n_1 + n_3)$ is the number of outcomes favorable to event E. Notice that this probability is relative to our entire sample space S which contains all $n(S)$ possible outcomes. Now suppose we learn that event F has occurred; that is, one of the outcomes favorable to event F has occurred. We observe that the number of outcomes favorable to event F is $n(F) = (n_1 + n_2)$. Having been told that event F did happen our task is to determine the probability of E in light of this revelation; our interest must therefore concern the *ratio* of the number of outcomes that favor *both* E and F to the number of outcomes that favor F. This proportion is $n_1/(n_1 + n_2)$, which we notationally represent by $P(E|F)$ or, in Kolmogorov's terms, by $P_F(E)$.

Two things have happened in this process. First, in determining the (un-conditional) probability of E, we considered E by itself. But when we learned that F occurred, we were forced to become interested in the *joint* occurrence of E and F. Second, in the process, we changed our sample space from S to F; once we learned that an outcome favorable to F had occurred, we could forget about the $(n_3 + n_4)$ outcomes that correspond to the nonoccurrence of F. Thus we reduced our sample space from $n(S)$, when we determined $P(E)$, to $n(F) = (n_1 + n_2)$, when we determined $P(E|F)$. Using Kolmogorov's notation, we began with a probability measure $P(\ )$, which we applied to event E, and then adopted a revised measure $P_F(\ )$, which we applied in determining the probability of E given F. The question of course is: Does our new conditional probability measure $P_F(\ )$ have the same properties as specified by the Kolmogorov axioms? The answer is yes, and this is precisely the reason why the definition $P(E|F) = P_F(E) = P(EF)/P(F)$, for $P(F) \neq 0$, has been taken seriously in Pascalian interpretations. It is an easy matter to show that (1) $P(E|F) \geq 0$, (2) $P(S|F) = 1.0$, and (3) $P(E \cup F|G) = P(E|G) + P(F|G)$ if events E and F are mutually exclusive.

I wish to carry this conditioning process one stage further in order to capture several important features of Pascalian conditioning. The process of conditioning may be carried out repeatedly since we learn about new things all the time. We began with $P(E)$, found evidence about F, and determined the conditional probability $P(E|F) = P_F(E)$. Now suppose we discover additional evidence about event G and inquire about how this further influences the probability of E. In one set of terms, we have passed from $P(E)$ to $P(E|F)$

and now to $P(E|FG)$. By our definition, $P(E|FG) = P(EFG)/P(FG)$, for $P(FG) \neq 0$. Here we see that we have made a further revision in our sample space from F to FG. So, in Pascalian terms, the process of *repeated conditioning* involves successive redefinition of a sample space during which we focus our attention on smaller collections of outcomes. We might say that probability revision in Pascalian terms involves making finer distinctions. Mixing together the two notational schemes we have used, we can observe other important facts about Pascalian probability conditioning.

First, it can be argued that *all* Pascalian probability measures are conditional. Our determination of $P(E)$ is conditional upon a particular well-defined sample space S, together with assumptions about the likeliness of outcomes in S. In some Pascalian interpretations S plays the role of "background knowledge" we may have. Some of this background knowledge might consist of "ground rules" for probability determination such as the aleatory assumptions in our present example. In Section 5.4 we will consider whether or not we always have such well-defined background knowledge in nonenumerative inferences.

So we might well have begun with $P(E|S) = P_S(E) = P(ES)/P(S) = P(E)$; this is true since $ES = E$ and $P(S) = 1$ by axiom. But now we have discovered evidence about two events F and G and wish to know what the Pascalian conditioning mechanism says about the successive revision of the probability of event E in light of this evidence. Let us first begin with $P(E|S) = P_S(E) = P(E)$. When we discovered evidence of F, we now have $P(E|SF)$ which, in Kolmogorov's notation, is $P_{SF}(E)$. Now $P_{SF}(E) = P(ESF)/P(SF) = P(EF)/P(F) = P(E|F)$ for $P(F) \neq 0$. This is true since $ESF = EF$ and $SF = F$. But, if all of our probabilities are taken to be initially conditional upon S, so are the probabilities of EF and of F. So $P(E|SF) = P_{SF}(E) = P_S(EF)/P_S(F) = P_S(E|F)$. This last expression is important because we now see that both $P(E)$ and our revised probability $P(E|F)$ are conditional upon S. In probability revision we do not forget about background knowledge when we obtain new evidence.

When we then discovered evidence of event G, we have $P(E|SFG) = P_{SFG}(E)$. Since $SFG = FG$, we have $P(E|FG) = P_{FG}(E)$ which can also be written as $P_G(EF)/P_G(F) = P_G(E|F)$. Now we can see the benefit of this hybrid notational exercise. We commonly speak of events such as F and G as "conditioning events" in the sense that they may condition our belief about some other event E. The fact that $P(E|FG) = P_G(E|F)$ makes clear that what we are conditioning or revising, when we obtain additional evidence G, is the probability of E conditional upon F. The probability of E, given old evidence F and new evidence G, results from a revision of the probability of E, given old evidence F. But we appear to have lost "background knowledge" S in the above process. However, it can easily be restored since $P(E|SFG) = P_{SFG}(E) = P_{SG}(EF)/P_{SG}(F) = P_{SG}(E|F)$. For the sake of simplicity in manipulating complicated Pascalian probability expressions, we often suppress a term signifying "background information." But, by definition, this term is always lurking in the background and can be brought forth when necessary. In our work involving the capturing of attributes of the credibility of sources of evidence (in Section 7.3) we will draw upon the fact that $P(E|FG) = P_G(E|F) = P(E|SFG) = P_{SG}(E|F)$.

Historians of probability have given us no definite time at which the Pascalian interpretation of a conditional probability as a ratio of other probabilities first emerged. It does appear, however, that the essential idea of conditioning in aleatory and frequentistic situations (as illustrated in Figure 2.2) has been around for quite some time. But there was some occasional confusion between a *joint* probability and a *conditional* probability; for example, Laplace employed joint probability expressions instead of the conditional probability expressions required in certain calculations he made (Stigler 1986, 115–116). It is often easy to confuse a joint probability like $P(EF)$ with a conditional probability $P(E|F)$; minor changes in wording make all the difference. In just two situations are these two probabilities the same for events with nonzero probability: (1) when E and F are mutually exclusive, or (2) when $P(F) = 1.0$ (i.e., when F = S). One interpretation of Pascalian conditional probabilities is that they are *normalized* joint probabilities. The word *normalized* in this context means making probabilities sum to one. In the definition $P(E|F) = P(EF)/P(F)$, the term $P(F)$ is a normalizer (provided it is not zero). The role $P(F)$ plays is to ensure that $P(E|F) + P(E^c|F) = 1.0$, as they must for coherence with the Kolmogorov axioms.

A careful examination of the basic Pascalian mechanism for probability revision is necessary. The examples of Pascalian probability revision I have given involve either aleatory probabilities or relative frequencies. The essential Pascalian conditioning mechanism can be generalized in various ways as we will observe as we proceed. But, it is both fair and important to enquire about the extent to which we can expect the Pascalian interpretation of conditioning to represent probabilistic belief revision in all of ampliative inference. We must ask whether or not this interpretation will capture all of the richness of probabilistic reasoning in all epistemic situations and in conditions under which inferences are based upon the eliminative use of a variety of evidence.

2.3.3 Frequentistic and Singular Evidence

We encounter many instances of the truth of the following assertion: *Though all statistical reasoning is probabilistic, not all probabilistic reasoning is statistical.* There is a very unfortunate confusion of terms that occurs in a wide assortment of literatures. Many persons often use the term "statistical reasoning" with reference to probabilistic reasoning that is based on evidence patently nonstatistical in nature. Inferences at trial provide many examples. Nicola Sacco either did or did not kill Alessandro Berardelli on one occasion, April, 15, 1920. Lewis Pelser either saw Sacco at the crime scene on this particular date or he didn't. Dominic Constantino either saw Pelser under the workbench when the shooting started or he didn't didn't see him there on this single occasion. We cannot replay the world over again N times to gather any relative frequency estimates of probabilities we might require in an inference about whether or not Sacco murdered Berardelli. The events of concern in this instance are singular, unique, or one of a kind. In so many situations in which we form probabilistic beliefs, we have no relevant statistics to go on because they are unobtainable. In many instances it may even be quite difficult to determine what is a relevant statistic (Lindley 1985, 16).

The distinguishing characteristic of frequentistic or statistical evidence is that it is always *numerical* in nature. A *statistic* is a numerical index or measure of some characteristic of a *sample* of observations of phenomena of various sorts. Common forms of statistical evidence are measures of central tendency (mean, median, mode, etc), variability (range, variance, standard deviation, etc.), and association (covariance, correlation, etc.); there are many others as well. Such evidence is gathered and regularly used in virtually every context imaginable and can concern any phenomenon that can be repeatedly observed. From statistical evidence we often attempt to draw conclusions about various characteristics of some population from which we believe the sample of observations has been selected. On other occasions, however, statistical evidence is used in inferences regarding individuals. In medicine, for example, we might use accumulated statistical evidence regarding certain indicators of risk in cardiac surgery in order to draw a conclusion about whether or not a particular new patient, whose risk indicators we have observed, will survive cardiac surgery. In these inferences we have to be concerned about the extent to which this statistical evidence will apply to a specific new patient who certainly has unique characteristics. Conclusions reached on the basis of statistical evidence are necessarily probabilistic since statistical evidence, like any other form of evidence we are considering, is incomplete, inconclusive, and unreliable to some degree.

In Section 2.2.5 I noted that some evidence allows us to form chains of reasoning leading to possible conclusions being entertained. As we will observe in Section 3.3, each link in a reasoning chain has to be defended by a generalization that licenses reasoning from one stage to another. In some cases we are able to test these generalizations with statistical evidence. In other cases we must employ nonstatistical evidence. In still other cases we may have no evidence and must, in order to draw any conclusion at all, be willing to give a generalization the benefit of our doubt. In many instances the chains of reasoning we construct will outrun the evidence we have to support or weaken the linkage between one reasoning stage and another.

2.3.4 Probabilistic Rules for Induction

As noted earlier, Francis Bacon is usually credited with making the first attempt to formulate a logic of inductive reasoning. Who shall we credit for being the first to formulate a rule for probability calculations in reasoning tasks that are inductive? The name commonly given in answer to this question is the Reverend Thomas Bayes, F.R.S. (1702–1761), a nonconformist minister of Tunbridge Wells, England. Biographical details on Bayes are rather sparse (e.g., Barnard 1958, 293–295; Lindley 1990, 10–11) but are sufficient to indicate that, in addition to being a man of the cloth, he knew enough mathematics to justify his election as a Fellow of the Royal Society in the year 1742. Though his published mathematical works are small in number they are now judged to be very high in quality. Bayes wrote on the topics of asymptotic series and on the topic of *fluxions* (what we now call *derivatives* in differential calculus). But Bayes's claim on our attentions concerns a certain result he described in a paper entitled *An Essay toward Solving a Problem in the Doctrine of Chances,* which appeared in *The Philosophical Transactions of the Royal Society* (vol. 53, for the year 1763, 370–418). Bayes did not himself attempt to publish this work. It was found among his effects after he died in 1761 by Richard Price, the executor of Bayes's will, who recommended its publication in the *Transactions of the Royal Society.*

The mathematical result Bayes describes in this paper is now known as *Bayes's rule* or *Bayes's theorem.* The problem Bayes addressed in his paper can be described in modern terms as follows: Consider a binary or Bernoulli process that generates either a success (s) or a failure (f) on any trial or performance of this process. Suppose that the probability of a success on any trial, $P(s) = p$, is unknown to us except that we suppose $0 < p \leq 1.0$. We perform a series of n such trials under the assumption that p stays the same from trial to trial. Suppose we observe some number r of successes in these n trials. The problem addressed by Bayes was: How shall we determine the probability that p lies between any two values a and b, given that we have observed r successes in n such trials? In modern symbols the required probability is a conditional having the form $P(a \leq p \leq b|r$ successes in n Bernoulli trials). Our inference here concerns p, so the interval $[a, b]$ represents one hypothesis about possible values p could take on. The evidence we have on the hypothesis that p lies in this interval is the r successes we have just observed in the n trials we have performed. So the above probability has the form $P(\text{hypothesis}|\text{evidence})$.

To Richard Price belongs credit for observing that the problem Bayes posed and the result he described have generality far beyond the Bernoulli process of concern to Bayes. In a letter to John Canton of the Royal Society, printed as a preface to Bayes's paper, Price observes (1763, 370–375):

> Every judicious person will be sensible that the problem now mentioned is by no means merely a curious speculation in the doctrine of chances, but necessary to be solved in order to secure a sure foundation for all our reasonings concerning past facts, and what is likely to be hereafter. Common sense is indeed sufficient to shew us that, from the observation of what has in former instances been the consequence of a certain cause or action, one may make a judgment what is likely to be the consequence of it another time, and that the larger number of

experiments we have to support a conclusion, so much the more reason we have to take it for granted. But it is certain that we cannot determine, at least not to any nicety, in what degree repeated experiments confirm a conclusion, without the particular discussion of the beforementioned problem; which, therefore is necessary to be considered by any one who would give a clear account of the strength of *analogical* or *inductive* reasoning; . . . .

Bayes's paper is as widely cited as it is unread. The exact manner in which Bayes determined $P(a \leq p \leq b|r$ successes in n trials) can be observed either in Bayes's paper itself (see Pearson and Kendall 1970, 131–153 for a reprinted version) or in comments upon his solution (e.g., Fisher 1959, 10–15; Daston 1988, 257–267). I will first present Bayes's rule in its simplest possible form as it is given in most texts on probability. This form will allow me to illustrate its most controversial element. Then we will consider what we must do in order to make Bayes's rule capture some important evidential distinctions we have already made.

Suppose we have an interest in whether or not hypothesis H is true, and we believe that event E, if it occurred, would be a relevant though inconclusive premise upon which to base a probabilistic inference about the truth of H. Hypothesis H might represent some past or future situation that is the subject of our inferential interest. In most discussions of Bayes's rule no distinction is made between E*, as evidence about event E, and event E itself. Suppose, for the moment, we take E* to be the same as E. In other words, let us assume that we have *perfectly* credible evidence about the occurrence of event E. As illustrated by Bayes's solution to the Bernoulli problem mentioned above, we have $P(H|E)$ or (in Kolmogorov's notation) $P_H(E)$ which, on the Pascalian definition of a conditional probability, can be expressed as $P(HE)/P(E)$, for $P(E) > 0$. Now, applying what is known as the *general product rule* (or *chain rule*) for conditional probabilities, we can express $P(HE)$ as $P(H)P(E|H)$; this rule simply follows from the definition of a conditional probability as defined. So we have $P(H|E) = P(H)P(E|H)/P(E)$, for $P(E) > 0$, as the simplest possible case of Bayes's rule. The term $P(E)$ is the "normalizer" we discussed that ensures that $P(H|E) + P(H^c|E) = 1.0$. We can determine $P(E)$ by means of another property of conditional probabilites called the *law of total probability*. Starting with $P(E) = P(EH) + P(EH^c)$, and using the general product rule, we have $P(E) = P(H)P(E|H) + P(H^c)P(E|H^c)$.

Clearly there is nothing remarkable about Bayes's rule; it is a simple consequence of the properties of Pascalian probability and the way in which a conditional probability is defined within this system. If you accept these properties and this definition, then you must also accept Bayes's rule as a logical consequence. So far, so good. But it is only when we examine the ingredients of Bayes's rule and consider how they might be obtained in practice that controversy arises. What we wish to calculate, $P(H|E)$, is called the *posterior probability* of H; the probability of H *after* we found out about E. The term

$P(E|H)$ is called a *likelihood*, and as I will later explain in detail (Section 5.3), it is the term in Bayes's rule that concerns the inferential force or strength of our evidence. The remaining term $P(H)$ is called the *prior probability* of H; the probability of H *before* we found out about E. This prior probability term has been the major source of controversy about the use of this rule.

Suppose that E is the very first item of evidence we have considered in our inference about H. If this is so, where does $P(H)$ come from? Stated in other words, how do we get the process of probabilistic inference started? There are quite different interpretations of what Bayes himself said in answer to these questions in the particular problem he posed. On one interpretation (e.g., Fisher 1959, 11–12; Hacking 1965, 199–200) Bayes supposedly advocated a *flat* or a *uniform* prior probability distribution across $0 < p \leq 1.0$. Such a distribution corresponds with what is described as the *principle of insufficient reason* (e.g., Stigler 1986, 127); it has also been described as *Bayes's postulate* (e.g., Fisher 1959, 11). This postulate, applied in our modern interpretation of Bayes's rule, would mean that we begin a probabilistic inference about hypothesis H by supposing that $P(H) = P(H^c) = 1/2$. If this is so, then the posterior probability $P(H|E) = P(E|H)/[P(E|H) + P(E|H^c)]$ since the prior terms would cancel out. But there are arguments that Bayes did not really take the principle of insufficient reason to form the starting place for probabilistic inference (Stigler 1986, 127–131).

This principle of insufficient reason was, however, taken by the mathematician Pierre Simon Laplace (1749–1827) as the starting point for inference in a situation in which we seek to determine the probability that the future will resemble the past. Again consider a Bernoulli process that generates successes (s) and failures (f) in a situation in which $P(s)$ is unknown to us. Suppose we have observed a sequence of n successes in a row and contemplate the probability that the next observation we take will also be a success. If we let F = the event that the next observation will be an s and let E = the event that the preceding n observations have also resulted in an s, then we have the conditional probability $P(F|E)$. In determining $P(F|E)$ Laplace assumed that all values of $P(s) > 0$ were equally probable [for an account of Laplace's derivation of $P(F|E)$, see Parzen 1960, 121–124]. His result, called the *Laplace rule of succession*, is that $P(F|E) = (n+1)/(n+2)$. On first inspection this rule seems sensible; the longer the past sequence of successes we have observed, the more likely it is that another success will occur. But this rule leads to some absurdities and self-contradictions (Kneale 1952, 203–205). It suggests, among other things, that a person now age eighty has a better chance of living another year than does a person now age ten. In addition, if $n = 0$ (we have made no previous observations), the rule of succession tells us that the probability of the first success should be $1/2$; this contradicts the principle of insufficient reason upon which this rule is based.

My first encounter with Bayes's rule was in 1960 in a graduate course in statistics. One of the texts assigned was *The Design of Experiments* by Sir R. A. Fisher (1960). In the second chapter of this work Fisher gives a summary of the various reasons why statisticians have rejected Bayes's rule in enumerative or frequentistic inference. Fisher observes that advocates of Bayes's rule "seem forced to regard mathematical probability, not as an objective quantity measured by observable frequencies, but as measuring merely psychological tendencies, theorems respecting which are useless for scientific purposes" (1960, 6–7). If probabilities are viewed only in terms of relative frequencies, then it might seem impossible to determine any prior probabilities unless we make some sort of estimate about their value. Such an estimate might be based upon whatever background knowledge (S) we have. In this case our prior on some H is the conditional probability $P_S(H) = P(H|S)$. It is interesting to note that, in this edition of *The Design of Experiments*, Fisher did not acknowledge the existing work of F. P Ramsey, L. J. Savage, and B. de Finetti (and others) who had advocated a subjectivist or personalist interpretation of probability. On this interpretation Bayes's rule is accessible to anyone (statistician or otherwise) willing to encode prior beliefs or expectancies in probabilistic form (for a collection of papers on subjective probability, see Kyburg and Smokler 1964). Statisticians to this day argue among themselves about whether or not the use of Bayes's rule is justified in statistical inference. Their arguments play almost no role in this present discourse on evidence.

In its commonly expressed form, Bayes's rule says *very* little about probabilistic reasoning. All it says is that we revise a prior probability to a posterior probability in response to evidence that has some specified probabilistic force graded in terms of likelihoods. But Bayes' rule can be made to say very much more about probabilistic inference and about the force of evidence. The first step in doing so is to distinguish between evidence E^* and event E itself. Thus, in the simple case we are considering and acknowledging the distinction just made, $P(H|E^*) = P(H)P(E^*|H)/P(E^*)$. The term $P(E^*|H)$ forces us to consider the nature of the probabilistic linkage between evidence E^* and hypothesis H. For a start, the linkage between E^* and event E may involve other events, as I mentioned in Section 2.1.2. In addition E itself may be only indirectly linked to H through other events interposed between E and H. In short, we have to make Bayes's rule respond to the cascaded, hierarchical, or multistage inferences mentioned in Section 2.2.5. The second thing we need to incorporate is the fact that we will have *many* items of evidence to consider, so we will have to employ the *repeated conditioning* mentioned above in Section 2.3.2. For example, we may have evidence items E^*, F^*, and G^* and consequently must consider $P(H|E^*F^*G^*)$. Each of these three items of evidence may have different patterns of linkage with H. They may also be linked to one another in various ways. It is under such conditions that we begin to form the idea of our inference problem as resembling a *network* of arguments that may be related in interesting and difficult ways.

Asking the question Who invented Bayes's rule? is like asking Who is buried in Grant's tomb? Recently Stephen Stigler asked the first of these questions in an informative and interesting paper (1983, 290–296). Upon careful examination of the available evidence on this question, Stigler gives (subjective) odds of three to one that the person who first saw the essentials of Bayes's rule was not Thomas Bayes but the Cambridge University mathematician Nicholas Saunderson (1682–1739). Incidently Stigler's odds rest upon uniform prior probabilities. Whoever first saw the essentials of the rule we now credit to Thomas Bayes, we have to accept the fact that there are other rules for ampliative inference that have to be considered. Jonathan Cohen tells us that John Stuart Mill tried, without complete success, to fit a Pascalian interpretation of probability to his conceptions of eliminative induction (1989a, 29–39). In Section 5.5 we will consider Cohen's arguments about why there must be non-Pascalian rules for combining evidence in ampliative inference that proceeds by elimination. When we discuss Glenn Shafer's system of belief functions in Section 5.4, we will encounter another expression called *Dempster's rule* for combining subjective gradings of the *support* we believe our evidence provides for hypotheses in epistemic situations. Shafer (1986b, 155–179) mentions how the essentials of Dempster's rule were foreseen in the late 1600s in the work of the Bishop of Bath and Wells, George Hooper (1640–1727), and in the work of the Alsatian mathematician Johann Heinrich Lambert (1728–1777).

2.3.5 Probability and "Rational" Inference

Words such as *rational, optimal,* and *ideal* repeatedly occur in discussions of human inference and choice. Each one of us hopes to draw conclusions from evidence and to make choices that can be defended or perceived as being wise. What constitutes "rational" probabilistic inference and choice is a very difficult question. Rescher (1988) gives us a very good account of how many difficulties there are. Experience teaches that we often draw conclusions from evidence that later turn out not to be correct. In many situations, of course, we have no way of knowing whether or not our conclusions and choices were correct. Seventy years have now gone by since Sacco and Vanzetti were convicted of first degree murder; there is still argument about whether or not the verdict reached by the jury was justified by the evidence given at trial (e.g., Kadane and Schum 1991). The very nature of the evidence we are considering precludes our being correct all of the time in our inferential behavior. The fact that evidence in our daily inferences is incomplete, inconclusive, and comes from sources having imperfect credibility means that we can expect to draw incorrect conclusions on occasion. For several reasons many modern scholars of inference and choice recommend that we grade inference and decision behavior in terms of the processes that were employed in reaching a conclusion or making a choice and not in terms of the outcomes that resulted (e.g., von Winterfeldt and Edwards 1988, 3).

Confining attention to ampliative inference based upon evidence, it would certainly help to have standards for rationality, optimality, or wisdom in such tasks. We might choose to call such standards *normative* in the sense that they tell us how such tasks *ought to be* performed. One issue that now divides Pascalians and non-Pascalians is whether or not norms for all of ampliative inference are to be found within the Pascalian interpretation of probability. In her account of the early history of probability, Lorraine Daston shows us that concern about rational inference and the development of mathematical probability were bound together. She begins (1988, xi):

> What does it mean to be rational? This book is about a two-hundred-year attempt to answer this question, the classical theory of probability. . . . Mathematical probability theory was to be the codification of a new brand of rationality that emerged at approximately the same time as the theory itself, or rather of a more modest reasonableness that solved everyday dilemmas on the basis of incomplete knowledge, in contrast to the traditional rationality of demonstrative certainty. As the probabilists never tired of repeating, their theory was intended to reduce this prosaic good sense to a calculus.

These early probabilists began to lay the groundwork for what, on some accounts, is a system of probability that does in fact capture rationality or at least reasonableness in probabilistic reasoning. There are today many learned individuals who believe that rationality in probabilistic reasoning involves behavior that is *coherent* or *consistent* with the Kolmogorov axioms asserted in Section 2.3.1 and with Bayes's rule as a consequence of these axioms and the definition of a conditional probability as given in Section 2.3.2 (e.g., Horwich 1982; Skyrms 1986; Lindley 1985). One argument frequently given in support of such standards of inferential rationality is that coherence with these standards grants us immunity from exploitation on the part of unscrupulous individuals who know something about *Dutch books*. A Dutch book is a combination of wagers that assures that you will lose money regardless of what happens; here is an example given by Winkler (1972, 23–25).

A *reference contract* is a prize for which you have to bid in order to obtain it. For example, I allow you to bid on a reference contract that says I will pay you $3 if it rains tomorrow. In thinking about how much you would pay me for this contract, you would naturally consider the probability of rain tomorrow. If you were *certain* that it will *not rain* tomorrow, you would of course not even consider this contract. If you were certain that it will rain tomorrow, you would try to get me to sell this contract to you for less than $3. But if you were uncertain about whether or not it will rain tomorrow the amount you would pay depends upon how probable you believe is rain tomorrow and how probable you believe is no rain tomorrow. I ask you for these probabilities, and you reply: $P(\text{rain}) = 2/3$ and $P(\text{no rain}) = 2/3$ in clear violation of Kolmogorov's axioms, one derived property of which is that $P(E) + P(E^c) = 1.0$. Noticing this, I now offer to let you bid on two reference contracts: (1) one that pays $3 if it rains and (2) one that pays $3 if it does not rain. Your probabilities imply that you would be willing to pay $2 for each of these contracts since your stated probabilities in each case correspond to betting odds of 2:1. If I can get you to purchase each of these reference contracts, you will win $3 on one of them since it will either rain or not rain tomorrow. But you will have paid me a total of $4 and will end up with a net loss of $1 no matter what happens. A person who can be exploited in this and other similar ways is often called a *money pump*.

In aleatory and frequentistic situations we have no trouble about such exploitation since probabilities and estimates of probabilities in these situations are automatically coherent with the Kolmogorov axioms and the definition of a conditional probability. What is at issue as far as exploitation is concerned are the epistemic probabilities we assert as indications of the strength of our beliefs based upon inconclusive evidence. It can be shown that epistemic coherence with these axioms and the definition of conditional probability makes you immune to being exploited as a money pump (e.g., Skyrms 1986, 185–197). On this view, "rationality" or "coherence" in inference refers to the manner in which you express your beliefs in probabilistic terms. But we have to consider whether all that matters for rationality in probabilistic reasoning is consistency in expressing credal or belief states. As Jonathan Cohen remarked: "The coherence of your credence function will not save you from bankruptcy if you persistently bet with people who are better informed than yourself" (1980, 196). In Section 5.5 we will observe how Cohen's system of Baconian probabilities for eliminative induction rests upon consideration of *how much* evidence we have considered and how completely it covers matters judged to be relevant in our inference. In addition we will consider, in Section 5.4, Shafer's account of various belief states that are not to be captured in Pascalian terms. Finally, in Section 5.6 we will consider Zadeh's interest in the role of imprecision in commonsense reasoning and the non-Pascalian rules that are required.

2.4 EVIDENCE IN JURISPRUDENCE: "BEATING AND BOULTING THE TRUTH"

We come at last to the discipline that provides us with the richest legacy of scholarship and recorded experience concerning evidence, its properties, and its uses. I believe there are several reasons why this legacy has accumulated within the field of jurisprudence and why knowledge of the existence of this legacy is so important for persons in many other disciplines. Our Anglo-American system for settling disputes involves procedures that have been hammered out over many centuries. By examining scholarship on evidence in jurisprudence we gain an appreciation for the astonishing variety of subtleties in evidence and argument; these same subtleties can be observed in the inference tasks we face in other contexts. Thus evidence scholarship in jurisprudence should not go unnoticed by scientists, engineers, physicians, auditors, historians and others concerned about the properties and uses of evidence.

2.4.1   Juries and the Adversarial Process

A basic characteristic of the Anglo-American system for settling disputes is
its *adversarial* nature. In such a system it is to be expected that one side of
a matter in dispute will meticulously examine the evidence and arguments
presented by the other. In a famous passage Sir Matthew Hale argued that
questioning by the parties in contention, their advocates, judges, and juries
is a better process for "beating and boulting the truth" than other systems
lacking this adversarial characteristic (1739, 164). Some persons have suggested that we view the process of argument in any context as being adversarial in nature. For example, the philosopher Stephen Toulmin observed
(1964, 7):

> Logic is concerned with the soundness of the claims we make—with the solidity
> of the grounds we produce to support them, the firmness of the backing we can
> provide for them—or, to change the metaphor, with the sort of *case* we can
> present in defence of our claims. The legal analogy implied in this last way of
> putting the point can be of real help. . . . Logic (we may say) is generalised
> jurisprudence.

Interest in the properties and uses of evidence seems to have coincided
with developments of the jury system as we now know it. The history of the
development of our jury system makes very interesting reading (e.g., Holdsworth 1903, vol. 1, 135–169; Wells 1911, 347–361; Plucknett 1956, 106–138;
Pollock and Maitland 1968; Van Caenegem 1988, 62–84). Many of the attributes of the jury system that we now take for granted were a long time in
coming. Our modern jury system has its roots, frail though they were, in
Britain in the tenth through thirteenth centuries. Since this is so, we might
expect there to have been both Scandinavian and Norman influences. In the
year 977 the Saxon King Aethelred II, in what is termed the *Wantage Code*,
empowered his reeves (officers) in each local community to go out with twelve
of the king's thegns (retainers) and "swear on relics that they would neither
accuse any innocent person or protect any guilty one" (Stenton 1962, 502–
503). These bodies of twelve individuals were later called *presentment juries*
and performed an accusatorial function; they *presented* charges against a
person. These presentment juries were the forerunner of our modern *grand
juries*. It is from these presentment juries that *petty juries* (ordinary trial juries)
were eventually formed. When the Normans came in 1066 they brought with
them an inquisitorial system of justice which still exists in some countries.
Courts in an inquisitorial system have officials who play the joint role of
prosecutor and judge. In the century following the Norman conquest there
came to be two bodies of jurors: presentment juries for criminal matters and
assize juries for civil matters.

A person presented with a charge in a crown or criminal case in the eleventh
and twelfth centuries bore the burden of *proving his innocence*. Trials of the

period had an interesting sequence of events: judgment, trial, and sentence. At the judgment stage a defendant chose one of three ways of proving his innocence at trial. He could, along with others if he could find them, *swear on oath* to his innocence. It was then believed that God would immediately strike dead any person who swore a false oath. A second option involved various *ordeals* such as carrying a hot iron for a certain length of time. The burn of an accused who carried a hot iron was examined after an interval of time and, if there was no putrifaction in the wound, the person was judged innocent. A special ordeal called the "cursed morsel" was reserved for defendants who were members of the clergy (Plucknett 1956, 114–115). The accused swallowed items of food in which were concealed various objects. If the accused did not choke on this object, he was judged innocent. The third option was *trial by battle* in which it was believed that God would side with the accused only if he were innocent. There is a noticeable lack of evidence in these early trials; in all cases the verdict was left to *judicium Dei* (the judgment of God).

Proof by oath eventually became suspect and was not allowed in criminal cases after the twelfth century (as Shakespeare was later to write in act III, scene 2, of *A Midsummer Night's Dream*: "Weigh oath with oath and you will nothing weigh"). At the Fourth Lateran Council in 1215 Pope Innocent III finally ordered members of the clergy not to bless any of the ordeals, so they declined as a method of "proof." Holdsworth mentions another reason for this decline: Such ordeals rarely delivered convictions expected by the crown (1903, vol. 1, 143). Trial by battle as a "proof" method also declined but was not in fact abolished by statute in England until the year 1819 (Plucknett 1956, 118). Another event of some importance occurred in the year 1215 when, at Runnymede on Monday, June 15, King John signed the document called *Magna Carta*. Clause 39 of this document asserts that the king will not proceed with force against any man, or send others to do so, except by the lawful judgment of his peers (*judicium parium*) or by the law of the land. Some have interpreted *judicium parium* to mean trial by jury, but this seems not to have been the original intent. The historian Poole notes that the significance of Magna Carta belonged to the future (1955, 476–477). It seems that this document became important not for what it actually said but for what people thought it said.

A gap was created with the decline of proof by oath, ordeal, or combat. To fill this gap presentment juries were transformed, by degrees, into trial juries that began (barely) to resemble our juries of today. There were no set procedures for these early juries to follow, and they were allowed to obtain any kind of evidence by any means. Of greatest importance was that these early trial juries consisted of accusers, witnesses, and others with a vested interest in the case. It was not until the 1700s that jurors lost the characteristic of also being witnesses (Holdsworth 1903, vol. 1, 157). Thus it comes as no surprise to learn that early trials by jury were stoutly resisted by persons accused of a crime. In an account of early opposition to trial by jury, Wells relates (1914, 97–110):

> Men, confronted by a jury trial, stood mute in antagonistic silence, refusing, in dogged obstinacy, even to speak when confronted with this means of proving their innocence, which was too often a method of heaping up against them the slanders, the malicious gossip, the misconception and the ill-will of the envious, and the condemnation of self-righteous neighbors.

Persons refusing to submit to trial by jury were forced to experience *peine forte et dure* (hard and long punishment). Wells gives us an interesting account of just how hard and long this punishment actually was. He also tells us that as late as 1728 persons accused were mistreated in various ways if they refused to plead guilty or innocent (1914, 104). It was not until 1827 that courts would automatically enter a plea of not guilty on behalf of a defendant who refused to plead (Holdsworth 1903, Vol. 1, 155).

By a statute of Edward III in 1352, a person accused could challenge the suitability of any juror who had joined in his indictment (Wells 1911, 360). This important statute marked the beginning of development of the jury as an impartial body of persons who were informed about the matter at issue by evidence provided by external witnesses. As reliance upon external witnesses increased so did interest in the kinds of evidence they provided as well interest in witness credibility and competence. But another trouble arose when juries began to deliberate upon evidence supplied by persons who were not themselves jurors. The crown and the courts did not always get the verdicts they expected or wanted. In these early times jury service was not always pleasant; jurors could be attainted (accused of giving a false verdict) and could be severely punished for two reasons. They could be legitimately attainted for malfeasance such as taking bribes or misrepresenting their interests in the case; they could also be attainted for drawing conclusions from evidence that differed from those congenial to the interests or expectations of the courts or the crown. This second ground for attainting jurors amounted to state control over trial verdicts and was as grossly unfair to defendants as it was unpleasant to jurors.

Such control did not disappear until 1670, thanks to the efforts of Chief Justice John Vaughn in the celebrated trial of Edward Bushell. William Penn (the Quaker founder of the State of Pennsylvania) and another Quaker named William Mead had been tried for causing a riot but were acquitted by a jury of which Bushell was a member. Bushell and other jurors were, in turn, charged with reaching a verdict counter to what the court regarded as full and manifest evidence against Penn and Mead. Chief Justice Vaughn made a ruling in this landmark case that established the independence of juries. He argued that jurors could not answer questions of law, and that courts could not answer questions of fact. In our courts today jurors, not the courts, rule on the weight of evidence and on the credibility of witnesses from whom the evidence comes.

Other important evidential developments came slowly, one of which concerns the right to cross examine adverse witnesses. This right was not fully developed until the 1700s at which point Hale could justly claim that the adversarial process was suited to "beating and boulting the truth." It has been claimed that the right of cross examination is what makes the entire jury process efficacious (Wigmore on Evidence, vol. 5, 1974, 32–36). By these and other slow and painful steps, an adversarial legal process emerged in which evidence is evaluated by individuals who claim to have no vested interest in the cases being tried. At various steps in this developmental process came increasing concern about the characteristics of evidence and rules concerning its admissibility. As we proceed, I will return to the history of interest in the various forms and combinations of evidence that developed during the emergence of our system of justice.

2.4.2 Our Courts as Evidential Clearinghouses

I believe there is another reason why the level of concern about the properties and uses of evidence is so strong in the field of law. The disciplines of law and, perhaps, history are the only ones known to me in which evidence of *every* substantive variety imaginable must be evaluated. This suggests the metaphor of our courts as evidential *clearinghouses*. In financial terms a clearinghouse is a place where checks are exchanged and accounts settled. In our courts evidence and arguments are exchanged by the parties in contention and accounts, of various sorts, are settled. In both civil and criminal litigation any substantive variety of evidence is likely to be encountered. Here are some examples having a contemporary flavor since they each involve particular *expert witnesses* who may be called upon to explain the significance of the evidence being considered. First, suppose civil litigation involving a suit for damages following an airline accident. In such cases courts are likely to hear testimony from aeronautical, electronic, and mechanical engineers, meteorologists, flight crews, and air traffic controllers. In a case of embezzlement courts may hear evidence from auditors, accountants, bankers, and other financial experts. In a murder trial courts may hear testimony from weapons experts, physicians, fingerprint and DNA analysts, and chemists. If the defendant raises a plea of insanity courts may hear testimony from psychiatrists, psychologists, and other behavioral scientists.

For courts and juries to make sense out of masses of substantively different varieties of evidence, scholars in law have had to give attention to two major evidential questions: (1) How does the evidence stand in relation to the persons who will draw conclusions from it? (2) How does the evidence stand in relation to the matters at issue in some dispute? The first question essentially involves the means by which the user of evidence can assess its credibility, reliability, or authenticity. The second question involves various ways in which the evidence may be relevant to matters at issue. As we will see in Section 3.4, these two questions provide the fundamental basis for a useful categorization of evidence regardless of its substance.

2.4.3 Bentham and Wigmore

After the 1600s, when the reliance of courts and juries upon external sources of evidence was firmly established, there began to be developed a system of rules concerning what would be acceptable evidence in various forms of litigation. Thus began the emergence of the *law of evidence*. The reader interested in a survey of this branch of law can do no better than to read Chapter 6 in William Twining's recent book (1990, 178–218). Twining tells us that the law of evidence has often resembled Gruyère (Swiss) cheese in the sense that there are more holes than cheese. He says these laws also resemble the Cheshire cat in *Alice in Wonderland* that kept appearing and disappearing (1990, 197). For our present purposes there are two names that stand out in the developing field of evidence law: in England, Jeremy Bentham (1748–1832) and in the United States, John Henry Wigmore (1863–1943). The reason for interest in Bentham and Wigmore is that they both proposed what we may regard as the first *theories of evidence*. They were both concerned about the properties and uses of evidence that are now of interest to us. In another work Twining (1985) gives a masterful account of the essentials of the theories of evidence of Bentham and Wigmore.

Bentham and Wigmore are the two leading figures in what may be termed the *rationalist-empiricist* tradition of evidence scholarship (Twining 1985, ix, 16f). In essence this view first supposes that the settlement of disputes should proceed on the basis of a "rational" consideration of evidence instead of the "irrational" methods such as trial by oaths, ordeals, or battle that characterized the early history of the Anglo-American judicial system. Second, this view supposes that "rational" inferences at trial are grounded in the English empiricist teachings of Francis Bacon, John Locke, and John Stuart Mill. In this rationalist-empiricist view the matters at issue in a dispute are to be ". . . proved to specified standards of probability on the basis of the careful and rational weighing of evidence which is both relevant and reliable . . ." (Twining, 1985, 15–16).

Bentham's major work on evidence is a five-volume treatise entitled *Rationale of Judicial Evidence* (1839). Bentham's view was that no evidence should be excluded from consideration at trial. In this respect his views of evidence correspond to those in Scandinavian countries whose legal systems permit "free proof" (any evidence is admitted) (Ekelof 1983, 9). Bentham discussed a variety of evidential matters, including the means by which evidence arises, circumstantial evidence, chains of reasoning from evidence, the subjective nature of evidence evaluation, hearsay, the authentication of evidence, and the means by which the probative (inferential) force of evidence might be assessed. Bentham's work suffers on just one account: It is wretchedly difficult to read. Even the legal historian Plucknett noted this fact (1956, 74).

In several other works I have described how I first encountered Wigmore's works and how significant they have been as a source of inspiration in my own formal and empirical studies of the process of weighing evidence (Schum 1980, 187–188; 1990, 79–80). In addition to his treatise *The Science of Judicial Proof*, mentioned in Section 1.3, I have given careful attention to his multiple-volume work entitled *A Treatise on the Anglo-American System of Evidence in Trials at Common Law* (cited throughout this discourse as *Wigmore on Evidence*). I know of no other studies of evidence that are as comprehensive as Wigmore's. We have discussed Aristotle's *Organum* and Francis Bacon's *Novum Organum* for science. Wigmore's objective was to provide a *Novum Organum* for the study of judicial evidence (Wigmore 1913). Anyone whose aspirations include constructing a theory of evidence, studying human inference behavior, or constructing computer-based systems that exhibit "intelligent" inference behavior should not be innocent of Wigmore's works. Following are the major reasons why I have taken Wigmore's work so seriously.

In his multiple-volume *Treatise* Wigmore gives us an encyclopedic account of the rich array of evidential and inferential subtleties any theory of evidence must be prepared to capture. This account also provides historical information about when these subtleties first began to be recognized by our courts. In the *Science of Judicial Proof* Wigmore first gives us an account of certain logically discernible forms of evidence and their inferential uses at trial. His account of the inferential uses of evidence is remarkably similar to the one Toulmin later gave in his theory of argument construction (Toulmin 1964; Toulmin, Reike, and Janik 1984). Wigmore also convinces us that most inferences at trial are "catenated" (cascaded or hierarchical) and involve chains of reasoning. Of greatest contemporary interest are Wigmore's *analytic* and *synthetic* methods for inference on the basis of masses of evidence belonging to different identifiable species. In Section 4.4.2 I will discuss this part of Wigmore's work in some detail because I believe it has great relevance for current research on *inference networks*. Wigmore was the first person to be concerned about how we might make sense out of masses of evidence.

2.4.4   The "New Evidence Scholarship": History Repeats Itself

The very earliest probabilists in the 1600s sought inspiration from, and possible applications of their work in, a variety of human affairs including jurisprudence. Daston refers to these attempts as the *moralization* of mathematics (1988, ch. 6). There is much more to this story, some of which is relevant at this point; other parts of this story are relevant when we consider specific credibility-testimony issues in Section 7.3. In the 1600s not every person believed there was an easy fit between mathematical probability and inference based upon evidence given at trial; one such person was Pierre de Montmort

(1678–1719). Montmort seems to have been convinced that laws governing the physical universe did not apply to the ordinary affairs of people and that our limited intellects are incapable of comprehending the complexity of relationships involved in our daily affairs (Daston 1988, 317). In any case Montmort was pessimistic about applying the emerging calculus of probability in many human affairs including trials at law. Both Daston (1988, 370–386) and Zabell (1988) tell us about the decline of interest that subsequently took place in attempts to apply probability to inferential problems in legal and other human affairs. In the case of credibility-testimony problems, however, Zabell notes that interest among probabilists did not expire until 1901 (1988, 350). Zabell attributes this decline, in part, to an increasing emphasis on an empirical or frequentistic basis for probabilities. As I will note in Section 3.3, there are rarely any relative frequencies available to support assessments of attributes of the credibility and competence of witnesses.

It is possible that the decline of interest in "moralizing" mathematics had very little impact upon jurists who were already accustomed to working things out for themselves. What is clear is that no probabilist had ever given attention to the task of weighing *entire masses* of evidence given at trial. As Wigmore noted (1937, 8): "The logicians have furnished us in plenty with canons of reasoning for specific single inferences; but for a total mass of contentious evidence in judicial trials, they have offered no system." Wigmore devised an analytic and synthetic method for drawing conclusions from a mass of evidence, as we will consider in Section 4.4.

But history has a way of repeating itself; quite recently there have been several conferences at which jurists, philosophers, probabilists, and others have discussed a variety of evidential issues. Two of these conferences, held at Oxford University in 1984 and 1988, were hosted by Adrian Zuckerman of the Oxford Law Faculty. A third conference was held at the Boston University Law School in 1986, and a fourth was held at Cardozo Law School in New York in 1991. Collections of papers given at the 1986 and 1991 conferences are available (Tillers and Green 1986, 1988; Tillers 1991). My colleague Peter Tillers, in addition to hosting the 1986 and 1991 conferences, now hosts the monthly *International Seminar on Evidence in Litigation* at Cardozo Law School to which scholars from *many* disciplines are invited to discuss their work on evidence and inference.

The disciplines of law and probability have changed considerably during the past three hundred years. But many important evidential issues are still with us, and so are persons from the past. At all of the conferences mentioned above Francis Bacon has been ably represented in the work of Jonathan Cohen; at the 1986 conference Hooper and Lambert were represented in the work of Glenn Shafer; and Thomas Bayes has been represented by Ward Edwards, Stephen Feinberg, and others. One issue, much debated in all of these conferences, concerns which of several alternative views of probabilistic reasoning has the most to say about evidential matters in trials at law. Montmort has also been ably represented at all of these conferences by the many contemporary jurists who are quite sceptical about the extent to which *any* formal system of probabilistic reasoning can capture matters vital in assessments of evidence in legal contexts (e.g., see Nesson 1986, 521–539; Zuckerman 1986, 487–508; Allen 1991, 373–422; Anderson 1991, 783–791; Bergman and Moore 1991, 589–619; Thompson 1991, 725–781).

It is always difficult to identify the exact stimulus for any behavioral response. Thus it is difficult to say precisely what caused the resurgence of collaboration among jurists, probabilists, and others in the study of evidence. Some suggestions are given in a work by Richard Lempert (University of Michigan Law School) who applied the description *new evidence scholarship* to refer to an increased level of interest among jurists in the process of proof and its relation to probabilistic and other related matters. As he stated (Lempert 1986, 439–440):

> Today I think we are seeing the fruits of this burgeoning interest and the talent it has attracted. Evidence is being transformed from a field concerned with the articulation of rules to a field concerned with the process of proof. Wigmore's other great work [*Science of Judicial Proof*] is being discovered, and disciplines outside the law, like mathematics, psychology, and philosophy, are being plumbed for the guidance they can give.

But the guidance Lempert discusses has been bidirectional. I am able to comment on many of the topics in this book largely because of the inspiration and guidance I have received from Wigmore and from many contemporary scholars of evidence in jurisprudence. In every contact I have had with evidence scholars in jurisprudence I have received so much more than I have been able to give.

2.5 THEORIES OF EVIDENCE: ARGUMENT STRUCTURE AND EVIDENTIAL FORCE

Acknowledging how difficult it is to give an uncontroversial definition of the word *evidence,* we might consider what seems to constitute a reasonable *theory of evidence.* Our present survey of thoughts about evidence and related matters at least allows us to show what difficulties await anyone who proposes a theory of evidence together with the claim that it is comprehensive. For a start, it seems there are two major elements necessary in any comprehensive theory of evidence; they may not be sufficient, as I will later explain. The first element is *structural* in nature and concerns the manner in which evidence items are to be linked to hypotheses or possible conclusions as well as to each other. What is being structured are *arguments*, often having many stages or steps, that show the *relevance* of evidence on conclusions we entertain as well as its credibility. One difficulty, noted by Wigmore, is that we encounter *masses* of evidence and are faced with the task of structuring what often turn out to be stunningly complex arguments linking this evidence to possible conclusions. As noted earlier, we also have to face the fact that arguments we construct can never be defended as being uniquely "correct."

The second element involves the fact that we are rarely able to draw any conclusion just by staring at the argument structures we have created. What we need in addition are ways of grading the *strength, force,* or *weight* of elements of our arguments and ways of *combining* these gradings in defensible ways. The strength, force, or weight of evidence and argument seems to be an *intensive* dimension and so we can suppose that there are various ways in which these characteristics can be graded numerically. We know that these gradings must be probabilistic in nature, given that the evidence we have is incomplete, inconclusive, and lacks credibility to some degree. Having graded the strength, force, or weight associated with elements of our arguments, we must also have some means for combining these gradings in order to determine which, if any, conclusion seems most favored by our evidence and the arguments we have structured from it.

Bentham, Wigmore, and others have provided us with a place to start as far as the structural elements of a theory of evidence are concerned. Indeed it is these structural considerations that allow us to identify various characteristics of evidence that apply regardless of its substance. It would have been far too much to ask of these persons that, in addition to their other accomplishments, they should also have been probabilists. As we will discuss in Section 4.4, one of the reasons why Wigmore's analytic and synthetic methods for complex argument construction never gained acceptance was that they incorporated no specific rules for aggregating evidential force assessments within and across arguments. As we will see in Chapter 5, probabilists have given us various systems for grading and combining the force, strength, or weight of evidence. In at least one instance a theory of evidential weight has been taken to be a theory of evidence. In his very influential work, *A Mathematical Theory of Evidence,* Glenn Shafer begins (1976, 3):

> The mathematical theory presented in this essay is at once a theory of evidence and a theory of probable reasoning. It is a theory of evidence because it deals with weights of evidence and with numerical degrees of support based on evidence. It is a theory of probable reasoning because it focuses on the fundamental operation of probable reasoning: the combination of evidence.

I yield to no one in my admiration for Shafer's work; this will certainly be apparent by the number of times I will draw upon his insights. But I believe there is more to a theory of evidence than consideration of the support it provides. There are many structural matters involving the forms, combinations, and uses of evidence that cannot be overlooked in any comprehensive theory of evidence. Work on these structural matters has been going on for very long time, particularly in jurisprudence. I note that in several later works, Shafer demonstrated his concern about the structure of probabilistic arguments (e.g., 1986a, 1988). Of particular interest to us will be his thoughts on how we might proceed when the level of detail in our arguments outruns the evidence we have to support such detailed analysis. Until quite recently probabilists of a Pascalian persuasion have not given much attention to structural matters. In my own work I have applied Pascalian and other methods in studying matters related to the force of evidence of every structrual form and combination of evidence I could discover; the results of this study form the subject matter of Chapters 7 and 8. In addition the current work on inference networks has obvious structural attributes, as I will later discuss.

The combination of structural and force-related elements just discussed often proves difficult when applied to real-life inferences. As I noted in Chapter 1, most inferences in our daily lives involve mixtures of reasoning forms. I believe that "pure" inductive reasoning tasks are hard to find outside the classroom. Cognitive models or networks we construct to represent our arguments will exhibit both causal and noncausal linkage patterns of the sort we will discuss in Section 4.3. Both the structural and force-related elements we have to consider are subject to revision in light of new evidence and insight. In other words, the cognitive structure of an inference problem "grows," or at least "mutates," over time and in response to newly discovered evidence and hypotheses. As a result our beliefs about the inferential force or weight of our evidence may change throughout the life of an inference problem. As I will discuss in Chapter 9, there are many different strategies that might be employed for marshaling or organizing our thoughts and our evidence during an inference task. Each strategy we employ emphasizes different distinctions in our evidence, and so we expect that the manner in which we marshal thought and evidence has a bearing upon the perceived structure of arguments we make and upon our beliefs about the inferential force of our evidence.

Taken together, structural considerations and *different* formal systems for probabilistic reasoning contribute to our understanding of the evidential foundations of the complex inferences that are the subject matter of this book. Each of the different formal probability systems we will encounter, in its own special way, is informative in our efforts to understand complex inference. They may also be informative about yet another possible element of a comprehensive theory of evidence.

2.6 DISCOVERING EVIDENCE

It might be argued that a theory of the properties and uses of evidence ought to be kept separate from any theory about how evidence is discovered or generated. There are of course other things to be discovered in inference tasks besides evidence. In particular, we have to discover or generate hypotheses or possible conclusions as well as evidential tests of them. The generation of new ideas in the form of hypotheses, as well as the generation of evidential tests of these hypotheses, is an exercise in imaginative reasoning. In fact there is considerable room for imaginative thinking in the process of constructing defensible and persuasive argument from masses of evidence. We might suppose that formal systems of probability only concern matters of inductive proof and not matters of discovery. But, as I will argue in Chapter 9, each one of the systems of probabilistic reasoning we consider does have distinct *heuristic* value in suggesting questions that might be asked of and about our evidence. One of the most appealing features of Shafer's work is his emphasis upon the creative attributes of probabilistic reasoning (1976, 279–286).

One trouble is that imaginative and creative thought processes are not well-understood (some persons prefer a distinction between imagination and creativity). The American philosopher Charles Sanders Peirce coined the term *abduction* with reference to the process of generating new ideas, in the form of hypotheses, together with evidential tests of them (Buchler collection, [1901] 1955, 150–156). There is some argument, discussed in Chapter 9, about the extent to which abduction differs from what we have termed *ampliative induction*. There now exists an array of interesting scholarship on the process of discovery, investigation, or inquiry. As we will see, this is an enterprise shared by many persons including philosophers, semioticians, mathematicians, psychologists, and the writers of fiction.

Finally, the reader should *not* infer, from my preceding comments, that I am now preparing to launch, in subsequent chapters, what I regard as a comprehensive theory of evidence. The fact that we cannot easily define the concept of evidence does not, by itself, prevent me from doing so. I have a better reason for not making so bold a claim. I have adhered quite obstinately to a research agenda I established nearly thirty years ago when I began to study evidence and its role in inference. The major item on my agenda has always been to discover what lies below the surface of the task of drawing conclusions from evidence having different properties and uses. There are many important but inconspicuous details of inference that have largely gone unnoticed except by scholars of evidence in jurisprudence. Years ago, on a trip to the Yosemite Valley, I was chided for spending so much of my time turning over rocks to see what I could find. There are many such rocks in probabilistic reasoning, and I have turned over quite a few of them. The balance of this book describes what I and others have found beneath them. The major factor preventing me from saying that I am now prepared to offer a comprehensive theory of evidence is that there are still so many evidential rocks left unturned.

Chapter **3**

Structural Issues I: Studying the Properties of Evidence

Our examination of evidence and its relation to argument structuring comes in two parts. In the present chapter we will attend to various structural matters that assist us in obtaining a better understanding of important properties of recurrent forms and combinations of evidence. Then in Chapter 4 we will discuss a variety of structural issues associated with the construction of complex and interrelated arguments based upon a mass of evidence whose items have properties we now begin to identify. As I claimed in Chapter 1, evidence can be classified in various ways that assist in its study and analysis. Drawing upon recorded experience and scholarship regarding evidence in legal contexts, I mentioned in Section 2.4.2 that there seem to be two basic dimensions for classifying evidence. One dimension concerns how an item of evidence stands in relation to matters at issue in an inference problem. As we will see, this dimension concerns the *relevance* of evidence. The other dimension concerns how the user of an item of evidence stands in relation to this item. This dimension concerns the *credibility* of evidence and how it may be either supported or undermined. Taken together the relevance and credibility dimensions suggest informative analyses of the inferential force, strength, or weight of identifiable forms and combinations of evidence. Such analyses form the subject matter of Chapters 5 through 8.

On the surface, at least, items of evidence often have similar properties, even though they reveal different content or substance. We employ a variety of images such as those obtained by photography, X-ray, radar, infrared, and other sensing devices. We might, for example, identify a class of photographic evidence because of the physical similarity of photographs. Reliance is often placed on the testimonial assertions of people, so we might designate a class of evidence as being testimonial in nature. Other evidence exists in the form of documents of various sorts, so we might specify a class of evidence as being documentary in nature. This kind of one-dimensional and superficial evidence categorization can be misleading. For example, all photographs do not have the same inferential status in the same or in different inference tasks any more than do all testimonial assertions from people or all documents. Physically similar items of evidence may have quite different bearings upon possible conclusions as the following example illustrates:

Suppose we have two photographs A and B. Photo A, allegedly taken on a certain date at Loch Ness in Scotland, shows what appears to be a large creature with a very long neck emerging from the surface of the loch (you may have seen such a photograph in various news accounts of the "Loch Ness Monster"). This photo is being offered as evidence in an inference about whether or not such creatures now exist in this loch. Photo B shows a well-known public official X shaking hands with Y, an equally well-known (at least to the FBI) member of a crime syndicate. This photo, taken three years ago, is now being introduced as evidence in X's trial for allegedly accepting a large bribe from Y last January. Suppose, for the moment, that both photos are entirely authentic; they have not been retouched or altered in any way and they are known to have been taken on the dates and in the places alleged. The bearing of Photo A upon whether or not there are uncommon creatures in Loch Ness seems more direct than does the bearing of photo B upon whether or not X took a bribe from Y. All Photo B shows is that X and Y shook hands three years ago; it does not show X taking money from Y. So any classification of evidence based only upon superficial similarities will not be useful. In our efforts to say general things about evidence we are advised to consider both the relevance and credibility dimensions. The credibility dimension concerns how seriously we should consider evidence that is offered or discovered; the relevance dimension concerns how we believe the evidence bears upon possible conclusions we entertain.

3.1 RELEVANCE AND ARGUMENT

Unfortunately, evidence rarely comes to us with already-established credentials regarding its relevance, credibility, and force. Such credentials have to be established by argument and in most cases by the use of other evidence whose credentials must, in turn, be established. Yes, there is often the possibility of an infinite regress. We may have evidence A, evidence B about evidence A, evidence C about evidence B about evidence A, . . . , ad infinitum. As an example, suppose W tells us that he observed an event whose occurrence or nonoccurrence seems relevant in an inference problem we face. A short time later, X gives us some information that seems very damaging to W's credibility. Then Y gives us information very damaging to X's credibility. Finally, Z reports information damaging to Y's credibility. Such situations do arise in various contexts and have been given the name: *a wilderness of mirrors* (Martin 1980). In Section 2.1.2 we considered the plight of a person who wishes to have "all the facts" before a conclusion is drawn or a decision is made. Having "all the facts" in some inference problem may place us on the infinite regress just mentioned. In most situations we will naturally have only limited amounts of time and inclination to deliberate upon the credentials of evidence we employ in an inference problem. We must often believe some things and not others, even though we may agree that there is other information "out there" that might alter our beliefs. There are situations in which we are forced to suspend or withhold belief. In some extreme cases, such as those involving a "wilderness of mirrors," we may even experience inferential paralysis and be quite unwilling or unable to draw any conclusion.

One thing apparent is that we may reasonably disagree about the credibility, relevance, and force of any item of evidence. For a variety of reasons you and I might disagree about the authenticity of the photograph alleging the existence of a Loch Ness monster. We might also disagree about the relevance of the photo of public official X shaking hands with crime boss Y as it bears on the issue of whether or not X accepted a bribe from Y. We have different backgrounds, experiences, skills, motives, and other individual characteristics. In short, the same evidence can be viewed from different perspectives or standpoints. We begin with a close examination of the concept of evidential relevance.

3.1.1 Defining Relevance

The term *relevance* is very broadly applied; it is common to speak of relevant hypotheses, relevant assumptions, relevant arguments, relevant variables, and so on. Common synonyms for the term *relevant* are pertinent, appropriate, related, connected, and apposite. Many texts in logic dwell upon the relevance of arguments. The reason is that the most frequently made criticism of an argument is that it is "beside the point" or "irrelevant" (Walton 1989, 60–61). Some of the fallacies in deductive argument, recognized since the time of Aristotle, are said to be *fallacies of relevance,* since they all concern instances in which premises are logically irrelevant to and are therefore incapable of establishing the truth of conclusions (Copi 1982, 98–99). The term *non sequitur* (it does not follow) is used with reference to a faulty argument. It has been argued that the concept of relevance is fundamental to our understanding of the processes of human cognition and communication and that the efficiency of such processes demands a focus upon information that is relevant (Sperber and Wilson 1986). In science there is a continuing search for variables that are relevant or that play a role in explanations of phenomena of interest.

In directing our attention to the relevance of evidence, we can at least initially expect that evidence is relevant if it is somehow pertinent or that it makes a difference in some way. But this account is not satisfactory of course, since we have not yet asked a relevant or pertinent question as far as relevance is concerned; the question is, Relevance to what? In Section 2.1.3, in trying to find a definition for the word evidence, I noted the connection between the words evidence and data, at which point I argued that a datum becomes evidence when its relevance in some inference has been established. Charles Darwin once asserted that any observation (datum) must be for or against some view if it is to be of any service at all (as quoted in Copi 1982, 477). Thus, in discussing the relevance of evidence, we have to be specific regarding the matter about which an item of evidence might be for or against. Fortunately we can draw upon the experience and wisdom of our colleagues in jurisprudence who, not unexpectedly, have been concerned about what *relevant evidence* means. In our *Federal Rules of Evidence,* Rule FRE-401 makes the following definition (Mueller and Kirkpatrick 1988, 33):

> "Relevant evidence" means evidence having any tendency to make the existence of any fact that is of consequence to the determination of the action more probable or less probable than it would be without the evidence.

In other words, FRE-401 tells us that evidence is relevant in an inference task if it causes you to change your probabilistic belief (one way or another) about some matter that is important in this task. On this interpretation we can easily apply FRE-401 to scientific and other contexts. For example, in the study of visual thresholds, the state of dark adaptation of a person's retina is relevant in an inference about this person's absolute visual sensitivity (the least amount of quantal energy that this person can detect). In an inference about the absolute level of sensitivity of someone's eye, you would revise your opinion upon evidence that this person had been in the dark for the last thirty minutes. The belief you revised refers to the state of your opinion before you received this evidence. Experiments such as those performed by Hecht, Schlaer, and Pirenne (1942) provide you with some grounds for this revision in your belief. Their research shows the nature of the dependence of absolute visual threshold upon states or levels of several variables they identified in addition to retinal dark adaptation.

The concept of relevance can be interpreted in relation to another concept, that of the *inferential force* of evidence. In Chapter 5 we will consider this concept in some detail and from different points of view. For the moment, however, let us just say that the inferential force of an item or body of evidence concerns *how much* and *in what direction* (i.e., toward which hypothesis) we revise our probabilistic beliefs on the basis of evidence. We might say that evidence is relevant if it has *some force* in allowing us to change our beliefs in a particular inference task. All FRE-401 requires is that evidence make some material or important proposition "more or less probable" than it was before this evidence was obtained. But it does not say anything about how much more or less probable this proposition must be. The qualifiers "more or less probable" and "some inferential force" are of course imprecise or fuzzy, as we will note in Section 5.6. In many contexts, law being an example, we have to adopt imprecise standards for a variety of reasons. Here are two reasons why attempting to increase the precision of a definition of relevance in terms of inferential force presents problems. First, as I noted several times, opinions differ considerably about how we might grade the inferential force of evidence. Second, even if agreement could be reached about a metric for evidential force, we would still be faced with the task of determining a *relevance threshold* on this metric, a point above which evidence would be deemed relevant and below which evidence would be deemed irrelevant. An Advisory Committee of the United States House of Repesentatives Judiciary Committee, commenting upon FRE-401, noted that attempts to make any more stringent or precise requirements for evidential relevance in legal contexts would be "unworkable and unrealistic" (Mueller and Kirkpatrick 1988, 34).

Thresholds aside, we have to ask whether it even makes any sense to attempt to grade the degree of relevance of evidence. Given the relation between relevance and inferential force, we might suppose that the more inferential force on some matter an item of evidence appears to have, the more relevant it is on this matter. There are several difficulties with this supposition. First, we have to ask whether or not it is even meaningful to say that one item of evidence is more (or less) relevant than another. On one view of probability we will examine in Chapter 4, the concept of relevance is related to the concept of probabilistic dependence (e.g., Pearl 1988, 13); there are gradations of such dependence. On another view, the relevance of evidence in eliminative or variative inference is linked in to its ability to eliminate or falsify hypotheses being considered (Cohen, L. J., 1977, 1989a). Keynes equates relevance with the increase in the *weight* of an argument (1921, 72). He uses the term *weight* in a way similar to its use in Jonathan Cohen's Baconian system of probabilities to be discussed in Section 5.5. In Chapter 5 I will discuss a variety of metrics for grading the inferential force and weight of evidence, but I will not say that these metrics also grade the relevance of evidence. There are very good reasons why I am hestitant to do so.

In grading evidential relevance in terms of inferential force, we have to be precise about what is relevant. Suppose that event E, if it occurred, would allow us to make a strong revision in our belief about the likeliness of hypothesis H. We might say that knowledge of E would certainly be relevant in our inference about H. But we have no direct information about E and must rely upon person W, who reports E* that event E did occur. The trouble is that we come to know various things about W, including the fact that he has very poor observational capacity and was in fact intoxicated at the time he says he made his observation of event E. In short, we believe that W could not have discriminated between the occurrence and the nonoccurrence of E at the time of his observation. As a result W's report has not removed any of our uncertainty about whether or not event E occurred. As we will see in Chapter 7, under such conditions W's evidence E* has no inferential force on H, even though the event he reports is indeed relevant in our inference about H. Here we have another reason why it is prudent to separate evidence E* and the event E described by this evidence; failure to do so masks many important distinctions we are obliged to consider. In the present example, although event E is relevant in our inference, evidence E* about this event has no inferential force. Under a strict interpretation of FRE-401, we would have to regard W's evidence E* as irrelevant in our inference about H, even though we strongly believe that the event he reports is relevant in this inference.

Though we cannot give any precise numerical standard for the relevance of evidence, I believe it is quite important to note that there are different ways in which evidence can be perceived as relevant in some inference task. I might say, in other words, that there are different reasons why evidence seems relevant. In some cases evidence seems relevant because we can construct a direct chain of reasoning from the evidence to some major, ultimate, or final hypothesis of concern. In other cases, however, we may have evidence from which we can form no such chains of reasoning, but the evidence seems relevant all the same because it bears upon the strength or weakness of links in the chains of reasoning we have already established from other evidence. In short, we may have *ancillary* evidence about other evidence and about links in the chains of reasoning established from other evidence. Ancillary evidence seems to acquire relevance because of its assocation with other evidence whose relevance on major hypotheses can be certified by a specific argument. I will mention in Section 3.3.3 how relevance acquired by ancillary evidence also rests upon specific arguments.

Finally, there is an additional trouble with the concept of relevance we have considered thus far. It is true that evidence can allow us to revise our beliefs about hypotheses or possibilities already noticed or discerned. But evidence can also allow us to *revise existing hypotheses themselves*. As I will note later in Section 4.5.5, evidence we take seriously can often become incorporated in existing hypotheses as we refine these hypotheses or make them more specific. Evidence can also allow us to *generate* entirely new hypotheses. It seems too restrictive to associate a concept of the relevance of evidence just with some existing collection of hypotheses or possibilities. We need a concept of evidential relevance that is broad enough to apply to the very important discovery-related matters we will dwell upon in Chapter 9 and to the fact that our entire conception or structure of an inference problem may change as we gather new evidence. In anticipation of these matters we might, at this stage, say that evidence is relevant if it allows us to revise our beliefs about the likeliness of any existing hypotheses or if it allows us to revise one or more existing hypotheses or to generate entirely new ones.

3.1.2 Relevance and Standpoint

Two or more persons asked to offer an explanation of some phenomenon, draw a conclusion about some matter, or make a prediction will very likely disagree to some extent. We might easily explain such variance in terms of individual differences or human perversity and let it go at that. This is not helpful, however, since collections of individuals are often called upon to share their differences in an attempt to arrive at a conclusion that can, if possible, be endorsed by all. In many situations one person or group, holding a certain belief, may attempt to persuade other individuals or groups to hold this same belief. Disappointment and often anger follow when such persuasive efforts fail. Person A notes with disdain how obtuse B is in failing to see the merit of A's arguments from a certain body of evidence. In the study of evidence and its various roles in probabilistic inference, we are not at liberty to dismiss human diversity simply as a fact of life. Indeed in analyses we make of evidence we often wish to exploit our differences in an effort to obtain increased insight about difficult inference problems we face. Inquiring about specific reasons why B fails to accept what seems obvious, A may obtain additional insight and perhaps become willing to alter his own beliefs. When we disagree about the relevance, credibility, or force of evidence, we may save time and adrenaline by attempting to identify the locus of our disagreement so that it may perhaps be resolved . In part this involves attending to the structural matters we are now considering. It also involves willingness to observe an inference problem from more than one *standpoint* or perspective.

Although our immediate concern is with the relevance of evidence, matters involving the idea of standpoint or perspective arise throughout the *entire* process of inference, including problem identification and structuring as well as the generation and assessment of all problem ingredients. Two persons who have made the idea of clarifying standpoint central in their analyses of evidence are Terence Anderson and William Twining (e.g., see Anderson and Twining 1991; Twining and Miers 1982; Twining 1990). Though their ideas on the role of standpoint in evidential analyses are stated within the context of law, I believe they are equally important in other contexts. Let us suppose that, as a researcher or practitioner in your chosen area, you face the task of publicly defending a conclusion you have reached. You might also face the task of defending the methods you are now using or contemplate using in an effort to reach a conclusion. Anderson and Twining tell us that there are three things you should be prepared to declare for your own benefit as well as for the benefit of members of your audience who are trying to determine whether or not your conclusions and/or methods of analysis can be taken seriously. I will illustrate these three declarations now with reference to the relevance of evidence, but I will return to them in connection with other matters.

The first declaration involves an answer to the question: *Who am I?* This might seem a foolish question, since you already know who you are and so do members of your audience. But the question is not idle, since its answer requires more than just stating your name. As we all know, the same person may "wear several different hats" or play different roles. For example, a physician may wear the hat of researcher as well as practitioner; an academician may wear the hats of researcher and of teacher (although many will justifiably argue that these two hats are not so different after all). A legal scholar attempting an analysis of an already-decided case often wears the hat of an historian, since the evidence in this case as well as its outcome are now part of the past. So the answer to this question involves specifiying what hat you are now wearing with reference to the inferential matter of present concern. It may seem obvious that the role a person is playing in some inferential task determines, in part, what evidence this person will judge to be relevant. However, unless this person's role in this situation is made clear, others may wonder why this person judged some data to be relevant evidence and others not.

One reason why persons wearing different hats make different relevance assessments is that the questions they ask and the hypotheses or possibilities they entertain are different. Imagine that a police officer, an attorney, and a news reporter arrive at the following scene: A man is lying unconscious on the floor of a parking garage and is bleeding from head injuries. The police officer might reasonably make certain observations and ask certain questions bearing upon whether or not the man's injuries are the result of a criminal act. The attorney might be inclined to make certain observations and ask certain questions bearing upon whether or not there are grounds for a civil damage suit. The news reporter's inquiries might well concern whether or not this event is newsworthy. To change the metaphor, we could also say that instead of people wearing different hats, they make observations through different lenses. The view of a scene through the police officer's lens may not be identical to the view of this same scene through the lenses of the attorney or the news reporter. People who entertain different possibilities may naturally discern different evidence as being relevant.

The second standpoint element involves answers to the question, *At what stage in what process am I in?* Human inference tasks unfold over time and involve different reasoning processes at different stages in the "life cycle" of these tasks. I asserted in Section 1.1 that inferences in real life seem to involve *mixtures* of different forms of reasoning that have been identified. In another work I discussed how inference problems in legal contexts resemble stage plays in which various acts, scenes, and collections of actors can be discerned (Schum 1986). I believe the same is true regarding inference problems in many other contexts, although the ordering of inferential acts and scenes will differ from one context to another. Anderson and Twining recommend that we identify the inferential "play" in which we are now appearing as well as the act/scene in which our present evidential analysis appears. Such identification has a bearing upon evidential relevance in several ways.

An item of evidence taken as relevant at one stage (act/scene) of an inference task may be dismissed as irrelevant at another; there are many possibilities. We may, at some point in an inference task, eliminate a certain hypothesis or possibility. Some of the evidence relevant on this hypothesis may seem quite irrelevant on other hypotheses we retain. For example, in an investigation into the slaying of victim V, it is learned that suspect A threatened on several occasions to kill V. This certainly seems relevant on whether or not A is the culprit. Some time later, however, we learn that A has an airtight alibi, so we eliminate A from consideration. Evidence of this threat by A would seem to have little bearing upon whether or not suspect B is the guilty party if no conceivable connection could be established between A and B. We would, for example, have to be able to rule out the possibility that B had knowledge of A's threats. It can also happen of course that evidence judged irrelevant at one stage can be perceived as relevant at a later stage when we finally discern some hypothesis upon which this evidence seems to bear.

The perceived nature of evidential relevance can change as the development of an inference problem unfolds. An item of evidence taken to be only ancillary in nature at one stage can, at a later stage, have a more direct inferential bearing upon some new hypothesis. For example, an historian may at one stage discover an item of evidence that seems to bear only upon the authenticity of a certain document, upon which a chain of reasoning has been formed to some major hypothesis of historical interest. Suppose that this evidence item concerns some aspect of the behavior of the person who allegedly drafted this document. We would, in light of earlier comments, label this behavioral information as ancillary evidence, since it may either strengthen or weaken a link in the chain of reasoning from the document to the major hypotheses at issue. At a later stage, however, this same evidence about this person's behavior may be judged to have a more direct bearing upon another major hypothesis that was not earlier discerned.

The third standpoint declaration recommended by Anderson and Twining involves an answer to the question, *What am I trying to do?* People have different objectives and perform various evidential analyses that serve different purposes. Clarifying your own objectives and the purposes for some analysis of evidence can assist your audience and can often diffuse criticism. The police officer, attorney, and news reporter perhaps had quite different objectives at the time they viewed the man bleeding on the floor of the garage parking lot. We might expect that these persons make relevance judgments within the context of their own objectives. The basic research objectives of an academician may not be so honored by a practitioner in some area in which the academician believes her research to have strong applicability. Factors deemed highly relevant to the academician may not be so perceived by the practitioner, and vice versa. The pursuit of some objectives involves inferences concerning events in the past; other objectives involve predictive inferences about future events. In some situations, science for example, we can construct a model or representation of a situation in which inferences are required and then await the verdict of evidence we collect about whether or not nature behaves in accordance with our model. In other cases, models or representations of an inference problem are constructed and then revised on the basis of evidence as it is gathered or discovered. As we will note again in Chapter 4, some inference tasks are recurrent, while others are unique. A person's standpoint plays a role in any structural process in inference, regardless of the manner in which this structuring takes place.

3.1.3 Establishing the Relevance of Evidence: An Example

To illustrate the process of establishing the relevance of an item of evidence, I have chosen an example I do not regard as trivial. This example comes from an actual inference problem, and it is at least as difficult as any I could have contrived. As I mentioned at the outset of this discourse, we perform inferences every day that are truly complex when examined carefully. I will ask you to consider the following evidence actually presented in the celebrated murder trial of Sacco and Vanzetti which I mentioned briefly in Section 2.3.2. Although it involves inference in a court trial, I believe this example illustrates relevance considerations that occur in other contexts as well.

The murder with which Sacco and Vanzetti were charged took place in South Braintree, Massachusetts, on April 15, 1920. Several weeks later, on May 5, 1920, the two were arrested on a streetcar outside of Campello, Massachusetts; they were charged at the time with being "suspicious persons." Both Sacco and Vanzetti were carrying concealed revolvers at the time of their arrest, a fact neither one of them contested. The following evidence was admitted, without defense objection, by Judge Webster Thayer as relevant on the issue of whether or not Sacco, with the assistance of Vanzetti, took the life of Alessandro Berardelli during a robbery of a payroll Berardelli was carrying at the time. Police Officer Michael J. Connolly testified that following the arrest: *Sacco attempted on several occasions to put his hand under his overcoat in spite of being warned* (by Connolly) *not to do so"* (Sacco-Vanzetti case: trial transcript, vol. 1, 1969 ed., pp 751–763). There was testimony that Vanzetti made similar gestures which, allegedly, the police took to be threatening. For our present purposes we will confine attention just to Connolly's testimony about Sacco. What we have to consider are possible grounds for accepting that this testimony has relevance in allowing someone to revise a belief about whether or not Sacco killed the payroll guard Berardelli on April 15, 1920, in South Braintree.

In our daily activities we all leave behind signs, markers, indications, or traces of these activities. Thus it is not unusual that our legal system recognizes that, when a crime has been committed, certain *traces* are left behind by the person(s) committing the crime. Wigmore refers to such traces as a form of *retrospectant* evidence regarding events that happen *after* the performance of some action. He also tells us about forms of *prospectant* and *concomitant* evidence, those which refer to events occurring *before* and *during* the performance of some action (1937, 136–160). Some of the traces left behind following a crime are physical in nature such as footprints, fingerprints, and objects of various kinds. Other traces left behind are mental in nature and concern the effects upon a person's mental state of having committed a crime.

One kind of mental trace evidence is said to be *consciousness of guilt*. If Sacco had robbed and shot Berardelli, as alleged, we suppose that he would be conscious or witting of this fact and that such consciousness would presumably have affected his subsequent behavior in various ways. If we could prove that a person is conscious of having committed a crime, this would certainly provide a basis for belief revision about whether or not he actually committed the crime. The trouble of course is, How do we ever prove that a person was, on some past occasion, conscious of any particular activity? A person, such as Sacco, who denies having performed an act will also deny having been conscious of performing it. But, as noted above, we can suppose that a person's consciousness of having performed some act will affect his/her subsequent behavior in observable ways. So our present task is to try to connect what Connolly testified about Sacco's hand movements following his arrest on May 5, 1920, with Sacco's being then conscious of the fact that he committed the crime on April 15, 1920.

Figure 3.1 shows the general nature of the task we face in an attempt to justify the relevance of Officer Connolly's testimony on the issue whether nor not Sacco shot and killed Berardelli on April 15, 1920. Based upon our discussion of trace evidence, courts would allow an inference from Sacco's consciousness of having robbed and shot Berardelli to the ultimate hypothesis that Sacco did in fact rob and shoot Berardelli (this inference is shown by the solid arrow in Figure 3.1). Consciousness of guilt is taken to be relevant on guilt itself. However, courts also recognize that consciousness of guilt,

FIGURE 3.1 An example of the defense of evidential relevance.

though relevant, would not be conclusive. It is well-known that people frequently confess to crimes they did not commit. In some cases it may be true that people, in various states of delusion, may consciously imagine that they have committed certain acts in which they have had no part. The relevance issue we face in this exercise is to determine whether or not the police officers' testimony about actions by Sacco following his arrest is relevant on the issue of Sacco's being conscious of his having robbed and shot Berardelli.

It seems apparent that we need to set up some *line of reasoning* or *argument* that seems to justify why the police officers' testimony about Sacco's alleged hand movements should cause us to change our beliefs about whether or not Sacco was, at the time of his arrest, conscious of his guilt in the Berardelli slaying. This line of reasoning, yet to be constructed, is shown by the dashed line in Figure 3.1. One way to approach the problem of setting up such a line of reasoning or argument is to try to imagine what uncertainties exist between Sacco's alleged actions on May 5, 1920, and Sacco's consciousness at this time of having committed a *particular crime* earlier on April 15, 1920. All sorts of things come to mind. Sacco may not have attempted to put his hand under his coat. There is evidence that Connolly and other officers fabricated this story. Sacco may have attempted to put his hand inside his coat but not for the purpose of drawing the weapon he was carrying. He may have had an itch he wished to scratch. He might have reached for the weapon he was carrying for the purpose of handing it over to the officers. Sacco may have been conscious of having been involved earlier in suspicious activities, but ones that had nothing whatever to do with the crime in South Braintree on April 15, 1920. The message here is that the act of forming a line of reasoning or argument from evidence is also the act of laying bare various sources of uncertainty you can imagine that exist between your evidence and what you are trying to infer from it. In every inferential context there are often many sources of uncertainty that can be revealed in a careful analysis of an argument, from an item of evidence to some major or ultimate hypothesis.

To make any reasonable assessment of the relevance of Officer Connolly's testimony, we ought to consider carefully what is involved in such an assessment. There is some disagreement about how we might best describe the process of establishing the relevance of evidence by argument. In Section 3.1.6 we will return to Sacco's alleged actions following his arrest and what might be argued about their relevance in his trial.

3.1.4 Argument Ingredients, Methods, and Metaphors

Suppose we have an item of evidence E^* and contemplate its relevance on hypothesis or possibility H. Suppose you and I believe that E^* allows a revision of belief about the likeliness of H, but how are we to persuade others that such revision is justified? Our persuasive efforts seem to rest upon the cogency of the argument we construct that links E^* and H. Let us first suppose that evidence E^* does not entail the truth of H and that we intend to make no statement to this effect. In short, and in keeping with what we discussed earlier, we regard E* as *inconclusive* evidence of H. So we begin to construct a *chain of reasoning* or an *argument* from E* to H. The reasoning chain we construct is shown in Figure 3.2a. We both agree that evidence E* bears inconclusively upon E; just because we have evidence E* does not entail that E in fact occurred. You then say: If E did happen, then F *might have* occurred. Thinking further, you say: And if F occurred, then H *might have* occurred (or might occur). By such means we have linked E* and H by a series of inferential steps we both regard as plausible. Constructing such reasoning chains often requires considerable intellectual effort not always rewarded by its persuasive effect on others. Be assured that you will have at least some grounds for questioning links in the chain of reasoning I will construct re-

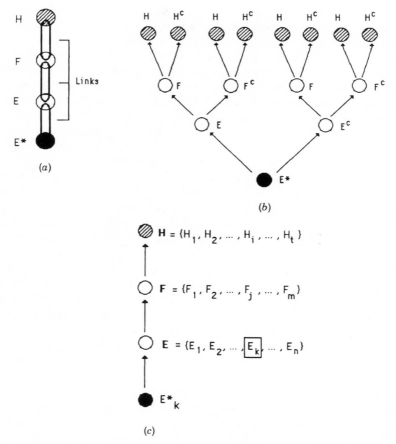

FIGURE 3.2 Chains of reasoning. (a) Links in the chain. (b) Reasoning routes. (c) Possibilities at each stage of reasoning.

garding the relevance of the police officer's testimony regarding Sacco's actions following his arrest.

Metaphors are useful, and we can hardly do without them. At the same time, they can often be misleading or incomplete in various ways. The "chain" of reasoning shown in Figure 3.2*a* is at least incomplete because it fails to describe all the linkages that we have to acknowledge. Notice in the paragraph above, that we have hedged our conclusions at each reasoning stage using the words *might have* regarding the occurrence of E, F, and H. So from evidence E* we have to consider at least two possibilities: E either occurred or it did not (E^c). At the next stage, either F occurred or it did not (F^c), and at the final stage, either H is true or it is not (H^c). I could have used the future tense here if F or H concern matters that have not yet happened. In a medical context, for example, H might represent the possibility that patient P will die if surgery is performed and E* some diagnostic evidence taken as relevant on this possibility. Shown in Figure 3.2*b* are the eight possible chains of reasoning or *reasoning routes* (another metaphor) that we must consider, given our present uncertainties about E, F, and H.

Our present belief about the relevance of E* on H might be stated in terms of any one of these routes. We might have stated the preceding relevance argument in other terms. For example, evidence E* favors the occurrence of E, E favors the occurrence of F, and F favors the truth of H. Such a statement would mean that we are taking the route shown as E*–E–F–H in Figure 3.2*b*. But we need not take this route in order to show the relevance of evidence E*. For example, E* would also be relevant if, following one of these reasoning routes, we were led to the nonoccurrence of H (H^c). For example, we might argue that E* favors E, E favors F^c, and F^c favors H^c. So it seems necessary for us to identify situations in which evidence is either *favorably relevant* or *unfavorably relevant* on some hypothesis. Thus E* may be either favorably or unfavorably relevant on H. Our relevance argument might involve any of these eight possible chains of reasoning or reasoning routes in Figure 3.2*b*. Later, in Sections 7.1 and 7.2, we will examine some very interesting issues involving the *transitivity* of inferential reasoning. For example, we might say that E* favors E, E favors F, and F favors H only to discover situations in which we cannot also say, transitively, that E* favors H. Different formal systems of probability identify different conditions under which inferential transitivity is conferred.

Figure 3.2*b* illustrates a binary situation in which we only consider the occurrence/nonoccurrence or the truth/falsity of matters at each link in our reasoning chains. In many situations our inferences require that we make finer than binary distinctions. Shown in Figure 3.2*c* is a situation in which we let the boldface letters **E, F,** and **H** stand in for *variables* having any number of states, levels, or possibilities. The binary situation depicted in diagram *b* is clearly a special case of the one shown in diagram *c*. We might even regard **E, F,** and **H** as *random variables,* in the sense that there is uncertainty about what state any of these variables is in as far as our present inference is concerned As shown, **E** has **n** possible states, **F** has **m** possible states, and **H** has **t** possible states. Our evidence in this case, E_k^*, is that variable **E** is in state k. The number of possible reasoning routes of course increases as we make finer distinctions at each stage of reasoning. In the example in Figure 3.2c there are **n** × **m** × **t** possible reasoning routes from E_k^* to some state of **H.** Taking one of these routes, we might seek to defend the relevance of E_k^* on **H** by asserting that E_k^* changes our assessment of the likeliness of H_i and, possibly, the likeliness of other states of **H** as well. The reason why I say "possibly" here is that we will consider evidence that seems to bear upon one hypothesis but says nothing about other hypotheses.

Before we discuss other possible linkages not shown in any of the diagrams in Figure 3.2, we need to consider what terms we might apply to various stages of reasoning we identify and to discuss what means we have for defending our assertions of relevance in terms of the chains of reasoning or arguments we construct. We have already discussed how difficult it is to define the term *evidence.* This acknowledged, E^* at the bottom of a reasoning chain represents what we are taking as the basis for revising our belief about H. Various labels have been applied to the possibilities that exist at subsequent stages of reasoning from E^*. To illustrate, we consider the binary situation in which we have {E, E^c} at the first stage, {F, F^c}, at the second stage, and {H, H^c} at the final stage in Figure 3.2b. We might first say that {E, E^c} , {F, F^c} , and {H, H^c} are pairs of *hypotheses* or *possibilities* that exist at each of the stages of reasoning we have identified. We might even distinguish among these pairs by saying that {E, E^c} and {F, F^c} are pairs of *interim hypotheses* and that {H, H^c} represents a pair of *ultimate, major,* or *final hypothesis* in the sense that, as far as our present inference is concerned, whether or not H is true is the major inferential issue we are now considering.

Wigmore certainly enjoyed inventing new terms, some of which we now consider. From evidence such as E^* we try to prove various things (at least in a probabilistic sense). Using the Latin *probandum,* meaning *that which is to be proved,* Wigmore (1937, 9) would say that E and E^c represent *interim* probanda, F and F^c represent *penultimate* probanda, and H and H^c represent *ultimate* or final probanda. Toulmin uses the term *claim* with reference to that which we seek to prove (1964, 97). So we might label these pairs at each stage of reasoning as a *claim* and a *counterclaim.* It probably makes no difference which of these alternative labels we employ. However, when we begin to attach probabilities to links or stages of chains of reasoning, we will encounter some resistance to the use of certain terms. For example, I might say that any of the above pairs are binary *event classes* such as {H, H^c}. Further I might say that my inference involves whether or not *event* H occurred or is true. Keynes, for one, would object to my using the term *event* with reference to any of the pairs in our reasoning chain if I then applied a probability distribution to these pairs. He argues that probability is appropriately applied to *propositions* and not to events (1921, 5). But Kolmogorov would not so object, since, as we noted in Section 2.3.1, a basic element of his probability system concerns a probability measure P applied to events (subsets) in a "suitable class" **C**.

The term *event* has a very specific definition within the conventional system of probabilities grounded on the Kolmogorov axioms we considered. Within this system an event E is defined as a subset of outcomes in some well-defined sample space S, all of which are consistent with a proposition that defines E. Using one particular notational scheme, if we let Π_E be read as *the proposition that defines E*, and if we let s be an outcome in S, then $E = \{s: \Pi_E(s) \text{ is true}\}$. In words, E is the set of all outcomes s for which Π_E is true when it is applied to any of the outcomes in this set (Pfeiffer and Schum 1973, 43). If you look back at what we have covered so far, you will see that I have used the term event several times in making a distinction between event E and evidence E^* that event E occurred. I think it is quite natural, for example, to discuss the occurrence or nonoccurrence of *events* that Officer Connolly described in his testimony. It is also necessary to note that his testimony does not entail the occurrence of the events he reported. In such cases I have used the term event in a very general sense to indicate something that may or may not happen; I will continue to do so. In fact my subsequent use of the term event will be nonrestrictive. We will wish to consider instances which make necessary the specific definition $E = \{s: \Pi_E(s) \text{ is true}\}$ because of the subject matter of an inference. In Chapter 5, we will note some additional distinctions that seem necessary when we discuss the inferential force of evidence and argument.

We can hardly persuade anyone of the relevance of E^* on hypothesis H simply by drawing a diagram such as the ones in Figure 3.2. People whose opinions we are trying to influence will wish to know why we believe we are entitled to reason from one stage to another such as from E^* to E to F to H in our example. Here we encounter another necessary ingredient of argument that has been given various names. For each reasoning stage or step identified we have to make an assertion about what we believe provides the ground for or gives us license to take each one of these steps. Among some logicians and legal scholars such assertions are called *generalizations* (e.g., Cohen, L. J., 1977, 1989a; Binder and Bergman 1984; Anderson and Twining 1991). Other writers refer to such assertions as *warrants* (e.g., Toulmin 1964; Toulmin, Reike and Janik, 1984). Whether we call them generalizations or warrants, the intent is the same; they are assertions we make about why we believe we are entitled to reason from one stage to another.

In reasoning from E^* to E at the first step, I might assert the following: If we have evidence that an event occurred, this event *usually* (*often, sometimes, frequently*, etc.) did occur. Thus I believe we have some degree of license to reason from evidence E^* to E, the event(s) reported in the evidence. But notice that I have hedged this generalization or warrant; I did not say: When we have evidence that an event occurred, this event necessarily occurred. If it is inconclusive, evidence about some event does not allow me to say that the occurrence of this event is certain. Which hedge I choose depends upon the strength of my own belief based upon the experiences I have had in evaluating this kind of evidence. At the next stage I might say: If something like E happens, then something like F *usually* (*often, sometimes, frequently*) happens. Again, my experience does not allow me to say that E makes F necessary, and so I hedge this connection in some manner consistent with my own experience. At the final stage I assert: If something like F happens, then something like H *usually* (*often, sometimes, frequently*) happens. These three generalizations or warrants have something in common: They are assertions about what happens *in general* (the very reason why they are called *generalizations*). What is at issue is whether the generalizations we assert hold in the particular situation that forms the subject matter of an inference. This requires us to put our generalizations to various tests, as the following example illustrates:

Suppose we let E* represent the following testimony from Officer Connolly: "*Sacco attempted on several occasions to put his hand under his overcoat in spite of being warned* (by Connolly) *not to do so.*" Then let E represent the event: *Sacco did attempt on several occasions to put his hand under his overcoat in spite of being warned* (by Connolly) *not to do so.*" Suppose you agree with the following generalization: If a person says that an event happened, then this event often did happen. This would provide at least some license for an inference from Connolly's testimony E* to E, as defined above. The trouble is that this generalization says nothing whatever about Officer Connolly, Sacco, or any other aspect of this particular assertion by Connolly and the circumstances under which he made it. In short, without much difficulty we can begin to imagine specific reasons why this generalization could be undermined in its present application to Connolly's testimony. So the issue is: How do we determine whether this generalization holds in this particular instance? The answer is: We put this generalization to the test by gathering and using ancillary evidence regarding Connolly's credibility as a source of information about Sacco's behavior following his arrest.

To return to the abstract example illustrated in Figure 3.2*a*, we would need at least plausible generalizations and, if possible, ancillary evidence in an effort to persuade someone of the relevance of E* on hypothesis H. Figure 3.3 shows two metaphors we might employ to illustrate how generalizations and ancillary evidence are used to defend the relevance of evidence. While we can say that generalizations and ancillary evidence help us to defend the strength of links in chains of reasoning we construct, we can also say that generalizations and ancillary evidence represent the "glue" that holds our arguments together. Naturally there will be argument about whether we have used either the correct or strong enough "glue" to hold our arguments together. The role of generalizations and their backing by ancillary evidence is sufficiently important that we will return to this topic in Section 3.3. As we will observe, these two ingredients are also necessary in our attempts to grade the inferential force of evidence.

I have mentioned that inferences can always be decomposed and that no particular inference decomposition can be regarded as uniquely "correct" or

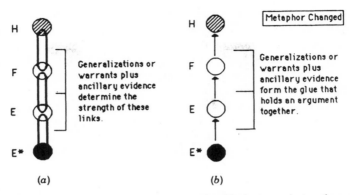

FIGURE 3.3 Metaphors to illustrate the strength of links in a chain of reasoning. (a) Factors affecting link strength. (b) The "glue" that holds arguments together.

"final." The construction of an argument in defense of the relevance of evidence in any context is a subjective or behavioral experience. Though we rely upon our own experience as well as the experience of others in making relevance assessments, there are no normative or prescriptive standards we can apply in the construction of arguments in any particular context. In our effort to convince someone of the relevance of E^* on hypothesis H, using the reasoning chain E^*–E–F–H, this person might argue that we have left out step G between F and H and that the chain should read: E^*–E–F–G–H. Another person might argue that we have misidentified one or more of the steps. In Section 3.2 I will show how certain forms of evidence require us to make a further decomposition of the step between evidence E^* and the event E reported in this evidence. Someone else might argue that the generalization we assert at some step is faulty or that the ancillary evidence we employ to test a generalization has little or no force on this generalization.

3.1.5 Masses of Evidence and Multiple Arguments

The inferences required in our work and in other parts of our lives rarely involve single and simple chains of reasoning such as the one depicted in various forms in Figures 3.2 and 3.3. We usually have some body of evidence whose individual items bear in different ways upon hypotheses of interest. But there is an additional difficulty: Evidence items may *bear upon each other* in interesting and often complex ways. Examined carefully, inferences in real life involve many arguments or lines of reasoning from many evidence items. It is also true that the arguments we construct can be related in various ways. Careful analysis of multiple arguments based upon a mass of evidence reveals some remarkably subtle evidential characteristics which, if recognized, can be exploited in the task of drawing conclusions. As we consider masses of evidence and more complex relevance arguments other metaphors will come to mind.

Figure 3.4*a* illustrates a virtue of careful argument construction that may be overlooked. Suppose, as in our earlier abstract illustration, we have formed an argument in defense of the relevance of evidence E* on major hypotheses/claims/probanda **H** = {H, H^c}. Our argument involves *interim* classes of events **E** = {E, E^c} and **F** = {F, F^c}. Suppose that this chain of reasoning is viewed as plausible by even our severest critic. One thing we can note is that if E* is relevant on **H**, then so would be evidence regarding **F**, since **F** represents a stage in our defense of the relevance of E*. In fact evidence about **F** would seem to be more directly relevant on **H**, since, according to our argument, **F** is logically less remote from **H** than is **E**, regarding which we have evidence E*. The act of laying out *plausible* stages of argument has distinct heuristic value since the stages we identify also serve to identify additional evidence having relevance. Thus, as 3.4*a* shows, we may subsequently obtain evidence about **F**. Suppose we obtain evidence F* that event F occurred or that proposition F is true. Figure 3.4*a* also shows how it is possible in some situations to obtain direct evidence H* about an ultimate or major hypotheses H. Suppose that hypothesis H represents some past event. We might be able to find someone to tell us directly whether this event did

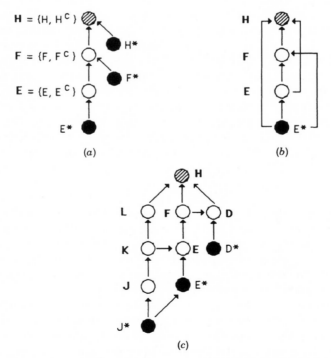

FIGURE 3.4 Linkage patterns. (a) Assistance in generating new evidence. (b) Possible linkage patterns in single chain. (c) More complex linkage patterns.

occur. In the diagram H* represents evidence that H occurred or is true. However, if H represents some future event, we would hardly have access to direct evidence about this event unless we could obtain the services of a true clairvoyant.

Figure 3.4*b* is the first in a series of illustrations I will provide concerning the fact that evidence such as E* may bear in more than one way upon hypotheses H. In our abstract example so far we have evidence E* linked to H via E and F. But, in addition to being linked to H via E and F, E* might have another direct linkage to one or the other of the states of H. There are even other possibilities we have to consider. Evidence E* might have a more direct bearing upon F in addition to its bearing via E, and E might have a more direct bearing upon H in addition to its bearing via F. These additional linkages involving the elements of argument are extremely important in our attempts to capture a wide array of important and interesting subtleties in evidence. We will consider these linkages in detail in Chapters 5 through 8. In the conventional view of probability, they all involve the concept of *conditional nonindependence* which, as we will discuss, is a simple idea that has quite profound inferential consequences.

Illustrated in Figure 3.4*c* is a situation in which we have three evidence items, each of which suggests a line of argument to major or ultimate hypotheses H. As shown, evidence J*, E*, and D* all have their own bearings upon H; arguments establishing their relevance have various numbers of stages or steps. But Figure 3.4*c* also illustrates another important matter, which is that arguments we construct can themselves be linked or related in various ways. First, notice the linkage between K, in the argument from J*, and E, in the argument from E*. Suppose that knowing what state K is in (e.g., knowing whether K or K^c occurred) would have a bearing upon how inferentially important is one of the states of E (i.e., E or E^c). The same may be said about the linkage shown between F and D. Figure 3.4*c* shows yet another form of linkage, the one shown between evidence items J* and E*. We have to allow for the possibility that whatever our items of evidence are, they are themselves linked in various ways. For example, suppose that J* is a report made by John and E* is a report made by Ellen. It is often very prudent to inquire whether what Ellen reported was influenced by John and what he reported. Perhaps John coerced Ellen into telling us that event E occurred, or Ellen coerced John into telling us that event J occurred. Of course we need no such coersion for these reports to be linked. Perhaps Ellen found out that John would tell us about J, and on this basis Ellen decided to tell us that event E happened.

What we must routinely manage in many different disciplines and contexts are inferences that, when subjected to careful analysis, involve various patterns or mixtures of the all the situations depicted in the three diagrams in Figure 3.4. If, using the structural matters we have discussed so far, we attempted to construct arguments in defense of the relevance of some mass of evidence we have, we might easily describe what we have just constructed as a complex *inference network*. There is even more structural complexity to come when we consider (in Section 3.3) the generalizations and ancillary evidence that support or weaken the links in chains of reasoning we have constructed. We might perform the task of structuring an inference network in different ways depending upon the specific task we face, the stage of work we are in, and what our objectives seem to be. In short, the standpoint issues discussed earlier are very important in determining how a person might proceed with such structuring. In Sections 4.4 and 4.5 we will examine some alternative ways in which complex inference networks can be constructed.

Finally, we often hear a person's argument being described as "threadbare" to indicate that it is weak in some way. This suggests yet another metaphor by means of which we consider the *fabric* of our arguments from evidence. I believe this metaphor to be fitting since, as the diagrams in Figure 3.4 illustrate, we can readily discern both *warp* (vertical) and *weft* (lateral) threads in a complex argument. The more vertical threads we chart, the more lines of argument we can bring to bear on major hypotheses of interest. The weft threads are interesting since, as later discussed, they involve various subtleties we have recognized regarding relations between elements of our arguments and among the items of evidence upon which they rest. We add even more weft threads when we can back up the stages of our arguments by appropriate generalizations and ancillary evidential tests of them.

3.1.6 Defending the Relevance of Evidence: An Exercise

As an exercise in establishing the relevance of evidence, we now consider how Officer Connolly's testimony about Sacco's actions following his arrest on May 5, 1920, may be defended as relevant on the issue of whether or not Sacco was, at the time of his arrest, conscious or witting of his guilt in the South Braintree murder that took place on April 15, 1920. What we will try to do is to fill in a specific argument that I indicated by the dashed line in Figure 3.1. Here is some additional backgound information that bears upon the standpoint we might adopt in our attempt to defend the relevance of this item of evidence. First, the prosecution was never obliged at trial to construct an argument in defense of the relevance of Connolly's testimony. Had they known what they were in for if they were asked to perform such a task, the prosecution might have had second thoughts about introducing Connolly's testimony. As we will see, there appear to be many sources of uncertainty between Connolly's testimony and the major issue in this case. The relevance of Connolly's testimony seems to have been assumed by both the prosecution and the defense. The defense certainly took considerable pains to counter Connolly's testimony. However, it seems that the defense recognized only some but not all of the uncertainties associated with this testimony.

We are now considering matters that have been over (but certainly not done with) since 1927 when Sacco and Vanzetti were executed following the failure of numerous appeals on their behalf. They were convicted of first-degree murder in July 1921; the sentence of death they received was not carried out until six years later. So our standpoint is that of historians, since we are attempting to analyze past events regarding a matter that has already been decided. However, in trying to defend the relevance of Connolly's testimony regarding Sacco's actions following his arrest, we have also to play the role of prosecutor seeking to convince judge, defense counsel, and jurors of the relevance of this testimony. Should we fail in our attempt to defend the relevance of this testimony, we may conclude that an error was made as far as the relevance of this evidence is concerned. As our objective we might assert that we are here illustrating the difficulties that we may face in many real-life inference tasks when and if we are asked to defend the relevance of evidence we employ in order to change our own minds as well as the minds of others.

Figure 3.5 shows one possible argument that we could construct in defense of the relevance of Connolly's testimony. At the bottom of this chain of reasoning is Connolly's testimony E_1^*; at the top of the chain H represents the *ultimate* prodandum, hypothesis, claim, or fact-in-issue in this case (as far as just Sacco is concerned). All other propositions or statements in this figure are listed as E_1 through E_7 and are *interim* probanda or hypotheses that form our present attempt to link Connolly's evidence to the ultimate probandum or hypothesis. We must first consider what generalizations or warrants we might assert to license each of the eight numbered links in this chain of reasoning. The direction of the arrows shows the direction of our reasoning in this exercise. To proceed, we will make one stipulation, namely that Sacco was carrying a concealed revolver. Recall that this was not contested by the defense and was known before the trial by both sides.

Step 1 (from E_1^* to E_1). As a first step we need to link Connolly's testimony E_1^* to the event he reports E_1. To license this reasoning step, we might assert: *The events reported by police officers testifying under oath usually have occurred.* Different persons might use different hedges here instead of *usually*. Some will want to make it stronger and others weaker.

Step 2 (from E_1 to E_2). Supposing for the moment that E_1 is true, we might also suppose that it is possible that Sacco's intention, in his attempts to reach inside his coat, was to draw the revolver stuck in his belt. To license this reasoning step, we might assert: *Persons who are arrested while carrying concealed weapons often attempt to grasp these weapons.* Again, you may wish to use a different hedge here instead of *often*.

Step 3 (from E_2 to E_3). Supposing for the moment that Sacco did intend to draw his revolver, we seem entitled to suppose E_3, that he might also have intended to use this revolver or threaten to use it on the arresting officers. As a generalization we might assert: *Arrested persons who attempt to draw*

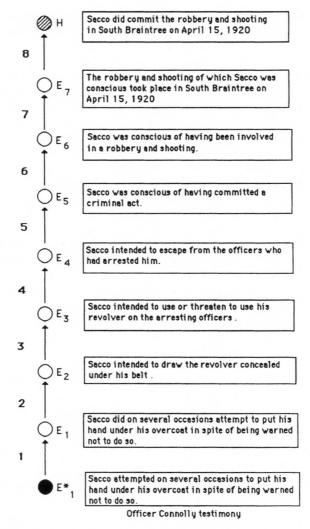

FIGURE 3.5 An exercise in defending the relevance of evidence.

concealed weapons will very often intend to use these weapons to threaten or harm arresting officers.

Step 4 (from E₃ to E₄). Supposing that Sacco did intend to use or threaten to use his revolver on the arresting officers, we might also be entitled to suppose E_4, that his further intention was to escape from custody. We certainly do not believe that if he did make use of his revolver or threaten to do so, he would then linger in the vicinity to see what would happen. To license step 4, we might assert: *Persons who intend to use or threaten to use weapons on arresting officers will most often do so because of their intention to escape from custody.*

Step 5 (from E_4 to E_5). Suppose that Sacco did intend to escape from police custody; one possibility is E_5, that he was conscious of having committed actions for which he might be arrested. As a generalization we might assert: *Persons who intend to escape from arresting officers are usually conscious of having committed a criminal act.*

Step 6 (from E_5 to E_6). Suppose E_5, that Sacco was conscious of having committed a criminal act. He might of course have committed acts of varying seriousness. We know, for example, that he was illegally carrying a concealed weapon and that he was involved in other activities that aroused the attention of the police. In particular, both he and Vanzetti were involved in the distribution of anarchistic literature which, although not a criminal offense, did attract the attention of the police. But we seem entitled to suppose that if Sacco was conscious of having committed acts for which he could be arrested or detained, then he would very likely be conscious of having been involved in a serious criminal act such as robbery and shooting. To license our reasoning at step 6, we might assert: *Persons who are conscious of having committed a criminal act will very likely be conscious of having committed acts of a serious nature, such as robbery and shooting.*

Step 7 (from E_6 to E_7). So far, at E_6, we have Sacco being possibly conscious of having been involved in a robbery and shooting. It is possible, of course, that he could have been involved in other robberies and shootings instead of the one that took place in South Braintree on April 15, 1920. The prosecution never suggested or had any evidence that Sacco was involved in other crimes of this sort. Regardless of whether Sacco had been involved in similar crimes, we might be entitled to suppose that he would be able to recall or be conscious of particular instances of crimes such as the one described in E_7. The generalization we might assert linking E_6 and E_7 is: *If a person is conscious of having performed some serious criminal action on one or more past occasions, then this person is usually conscious of particular instances in which this action has been performed.*

Step 8 (from E_7 to E_8). This final step involves a generalization that seems to form the basis for our legal system's acceptance of the relevance of evidence of *consciousness of guilt*. This generalization might be read as follows: *A person conscious of having committed a specific criminal act very likely committed it.* Notice that this generalization, like all the others, is hedged; it does not say that persons conscious of having committed a criminal act are certain to have committed it. We have to allow for the possibility of a person's self-delusion, as I noted above.

In attempting to establish the relevance of Connolly's testimony, we are led to construct a chain of reasoning having, in this example, a large number of links. I believe this particular example to be well chosen if you *disagree* with it in some way. An example in which the relevance of evidence seems obvious to everyone is also not very instructive; it would also not tend to resemble many situations in real life in which establishing the relevance of evidence may be quite difficult. I could never claim that the chain of reasoning I have constructed is uniquely suitable. You may note one or more inter-mediate links you believe that I should have inserted. In fact I know of at least two links that I have purposely omitted but will identify in Section 3.3.1; these two additional links concern Officer Connolly's credibility. You might also disagree about the manner in which I have labeled or described the interim hypotheses or probanda at each stage.

Disagreement is possible about any of the generalizations I asserted at each reasoning step, as well as about the manner in which I hedged them. Your present standpoint might be quite different from the one I adopted as I constructed this chain. Suppose you agree at least about the number of links in this chain of reasoning. As you can see, I have identified seven sources of uncertainty interposed between evidence E_1^* and H, one at each reasoning step. For every E noted in this chain there is an E^c. For example, for E_2 we will also have E_2^c, that Sacco had no intention of drawing his revolver; at E_6 we also have E_6^c, that Sacco was not at all conscious of having been involved in a robbery and shooting. So Connolly's testimony E_1^* seems logically quite remote from H. We might say that in our defense of the relevance of this testimony we are out on an inferential limb of considerable length. How strong this limb will seem depends upon the adequacy of the generalizations asserted and upon what ancillary evidence we have to support these gener-alizations. All I have done so far is to propose what I regard as a plausible linkage between E_1^* and H in this case. However, we might later conclude that Connolly's testimony has no inferential force, and is therefore irrelevant, despite this linkage. We should also note that if we have eight binary stages in the inference depicted in Figure 3.5, there are $(2)^8 = 256$ possible reasoning routes from Connolly's testimony E_1^* to H or to H^c.

Constructing a specific relevance argument such as the one in Figure 3.5 seems like a very compulsive exercise. It is an exercise that is only rarely undertaken even when human lives are at stake, as in the case of Sacco and Vanzetti. It is easy to argue that important inferences ought to be based upon careful analysis of this sort. Such a case is difficult to make when an inference is based upon a mass of evidence and when a conclusion is required in a short time. Suppose you believe that the relevance of Connolly's testimony could be established using a much shorter chain of reasoning. In particular, suppose you try to eliminate the steps shown as E_1 through E_6 in Figure 3.5. To do this, you would have to be able to assert a single generalization that links E_1^* to E_7. We might try to assert one, but I fear it would not be very persuasive. For example, we might assert: *If a police officer, under oath, testifies that a* *person arrested and carrying a concealed weapon tried on several occasions to put his hand under his coat, then this person arrested* (hedge required here) *is conscious of having been involved in a robbery and shooting that took place on some occasion in the past.* We would have a job on our hands trying to make this generalization convincing regardless of the hedge we employed.

All of the generalizations I asserted regarding the reasoning stages or links shown in Figure 3.5 are examples of what might be termed *commonsense* generalizations. To assert them, I required no special knowledge or expertise. They are indeed exactly the sort of commonsense generalizations our legal system supposes any juror-eligible person already has "stocked" as a result of his/her life experiences. This is one reason why I will frequently employ evidential examples from law in this discourse; most of us have no difficulty in relating to such examples. But now consider the establishment of the relevance of an item of evidence in other contexts such as science, engineering, history, auditing, or any other specific area you choose. It seems almost certain that generalizations asserted in such areas are not simply matters of common sense but require specific background knowledge of the situation in which an inference is required. This is one reason why there are so many "expert witnesses" who testify at trial. In a suit for damages following an aircraft accident, aeronautical engineers and others will have to explain the relevance, on the possible causes of an accident, of evidence of a very thin coating of ice on the leading edges of the aircraft's wings.

Finally, there is one more matter to discuss concerning the chain of reasoning in Figure 3.5. Suppose you agree that I have established a plausible chain of reasoning between Connolly's testimony and H, that Sacco did commit the murder in question. As I mentioned above, FRE-401 requires that relevant evidence must allow us to believe that H is more probable or less probable than it was before we obtained this evidence. We have not yet discussed how much force Connolly's testimony has on H; to do so requires attention to a variety of other matters. For the moment, however, I will ask you simply to note that the truth of a statement or proposition shown at any stage of the reasoning in Figure 3.5 would represent just inconclusive evidence regarding the truth of the statement at the next higher stage. For example, suppose that E_1 is true; Sacco did attempt to put his hand under his coat on several occasions in spite of being warned not to do so. This would be inconclusive evidence that he intended to draw his concealed revolver. Any of us could think of reasons why he might have wished to put his hand under his coat for other purposes. As another example, assume the truth of E_5, that Sacco was conscious of having committed a criminal act. This would be inconclusive evidence that Sacco was conscious or witting of having been involved in a robbery and shooting. The reasoning chain from E_1^* to H is a good example of what has been termed *cascaded, hierarchical,* or *multistage* inference. In law such inferences are said to be catenated (Wigmore 1937, 13–15) or to involve *inference upon inference* (Wigmore on Evidence, Vol. 1A, Tillers rev., 1983, 1107–1142). In our daily activities I believe we encounter very few inferences that are not cascaded, hierarchical, or catenated. The next topic we will discuss alerts us to the fact that there are often additional links in chains of reasoning that are associated with the source(s) of evidence.

3.2 THE FOUNDATIONS OF ARGUMENT

As we have just seen by example, we need plausible arguments in order to certify the relevance of evidence on possible conclusions. I mentioned earlier that the act of constructing an argument in defense of the relevance of some item of evidence is also the act of identifying what you believe to be potential sources of uncertainty that may lurk between your evidence and the possible conclusions you might draw from it. Of all the uncertainties that exist in reasoning from evidence none, I believe, are more interesting than those associated with the evidence itself and the sources from which we receive it. Stated another way, the foundation of all argument based on evidence concerns the nature of the evidence itself and credibility of the sources from which it comes.

I have at several points emphasized the distinction between evidence about some event and the event itself. The sad truth is that evidence is not always what it appears to be. Evidence E* may appear to reveal the occurrence of event E when, in truth, E did not happen. Documents may be forged, blood test results inaccurate, X-ray or radar images misinterpreted, and testimony untruthful. This much is obvious; what is not so obvious is that what we believe we know about the evidence itself and the source(s) from which it comes can often be at least as valuable inferentially as what the evidence itself seems to reveal. We will be able to capture these additional sources of inferential value by means of the linkage patterns illustrated above in Figure 3.4*b*.

As I have noted, one dimension for categorizing evidence concerns how a person performing some inference task stands in relation to the various items of evidence being considered. In examining this dimension, we must attend to the physical properties of evidence, to the manner in which it came into existence, and to the source(s) from which it was received. In some cases the person evaluating an item of evidence is, by direct observation and through the medium of her own senses, able to judge what events the evidence reveals. Thus, from my wife's observation of a lunch sack on the table this morning after I have left the house, she might infer that I forgot to bring my lunch with me when I went to work. In other words, she has tangible evidence of a lunch sack on the table and might infer from it that I forgot to bring my lunch with me. But tangible evidence is often not what it appears to be. The sack she sees might not contain my lunch; it might contain the assorted trash I collected from my car last night. Even if the sack contained a lunch, she might not be entitled to conclude that I forgot to bring a lunch today. I may foolishly have packed another lunch this morning in complete forgetfulness that I packed one last night, which my wife kindly put on the table this morning so that I would not forget it. In other situations, revelation of events comes through the medium of another person's senses, for example, as when we listen to a person tell us about his observations of the occurrence of some event. As we will see, there are several possible bases for such testimonial evidence.

In short, on some occasions we have a primary interface with something of inferential interest that is provided by our own senses. In other instances this interface is provided by the senses of some other person(s). Recalling our discussion in Section 2.1.1 about the use of authoritative records and missing evidence, we may encounter situations in which certain revelations having inferential significance are not the result of anyone's direct sensory interface with the things revealed. What we are obliged to do in assessing both the relevance and the force of evidence is to ask a variety of questions about our evidence and about the manner in which we obtained it.

3.2.1 Questions about Evidence and Its Sources

Suppose that there is an item of evidence whose relevance you have estab-lished in an important inference task. A major question you might ask is, *How do I stand in relation to this evidence?* This is an important question. It involves whether or not you can examine the evidence to determine *for yourself* what it reveals. First, suppose that the evidence you have is *tangible,* in the sense that you can in some way examine it to determine what it reveals. In some cases you can make such a determination on your own. My wife could examine the lunch sack she observed to determine whether or not it contained my lunch. In other cases, however, we might need assistance in determining what some item of tangible evidence reveals. I have on several occasions examined samples of rocks that were brought back from the *Apollo* voyages to the moon. I can see the rocks well enough, but since I am no geologist, I cannot determine much about what they reveal. There are of course many different kinds of things we can examine for ourselves, including objects, documents, sensor images, measuring devices, and a variety of rep-resentations such as maps, charts, and diagrams. Our colleagues in law give particular labels to some of these tangibles (e.g., Graham 1989, 3). Objects or things we can examine are called *real evidence*. In addition to *documentary evidence*, there is a category of evidence labeled *demonstrative;* this includes maps, charts, diagrams, models, or other demonstrations. All of these kinds of tangible evidence are open to our direct examination. What they actually reveal in particular instances is not always obvious.

From tangible evidence E^* you (possibly with the assistance of someone else) can determine whether this evidence reveals the occurrence of some event E. We might say that with tangible evidence you have a direct interface with the objects, documents, images, measuring devices, and other things that reveal information of various sorts. Of course you may be wrong in your judgment about what some tangible evidence item does reveal. Objects can be contrived, documents forged, measuring devices inaccurate, and images, charts, and so on, can be constructed in various ways in an effort to mislead you. In addition your own observational and interpretational capabilities may be imperfect for various reasons. But now suppose that the evidence you have received comes from another person in the form of an assertion by this person that some event of interest occurred or is true. In law, at least, it is customary to call such evidence *testimonial*. Although the person providing you with testimony is certainly tangible in the sense that you can directly hear what he says, the event(s) he reports to you may not be open to your direct examination. For example, Officer Connolly testified to the occurrence of certain actions by defendant Sacco that allegedly happened in the past. Connolly alleges that he had interface with these happenings, while persons charged with evaluating this evidence could never themselves have had such direct sensory interface. If they did have, they would never have been jurors in this case.

So with testimonial evidence you stand to varying degrees more remote from the occurrence or nonoccurrence of events than you do when you have tangible evidence of these events. However, we have to be a bit careful here. Suppose you have tangible evidence in the form of a document that you can examine to your heart's content. However, what is of interest to you in this document is an account of an event F that, according to the document, took place two years ago. What is tangible to you is of course the document and not whatever event F refers to; so you are certainly remote from event F. However, you would in this case be less remote from F than you would be if, instead of examining the document yourself, person P reported to you that she had examined this document and its account of event F. There is of course the possibility that P misread this document or is not being truthful about its contents. So in this instance P's observational and reporting behavior provide additional sources of uncertainty.

When a person testifies about some event, we are entitled to inquire about how this person obtained her information about this event. Questions raised in such inquiry are as varied as they are interesting. There seem to be three possibilities. First, she could have made a *direct observation* in some situation in which this event could either have happened or not. Stated in other words, she could have had some direct sensory interface herself with these possible events. Testimony on the basis of direct observation can of course only concern past events or events that happen in the rapidly fleeting "present."

Another very interesting possibility is that a person could have obtained information about certain events from another source. We might refer to such evidence as being that which we obtain at *secondhand*. We did not hear about these events from some primary source who made a direct observation but from an intermediary. It is common to call a primary source "the horse's mouth." For example, person P tells us that person Q said that event E happened. We are also entitled to inquire how Q obtained the information that P reports to us. By such inquiry we might discover that the information, reported by the person with whom we have a direct interface, came rather from a chain of sources, some of which may not be other persons. For example, we might encounter a situation in which P tells us that Q said he saw a document containing an assertion that R said that S said she observed event E. If you think such situations are rarely encountered, listen very carefully to what you hear news commentators report. Another name commonly given to secondhand evidence is *hearsay*. In Section 7.4 we will return to an analysis of this very interesting form of evidence obtained through chains of human or other sources. The number of occasions on which we have to make use of secondhand or nth-hand information is truly astonishing. In some situations we hear testimony in which no primary source (a person making a direct observation) can be identified. We have a name for such testimony; it is called *rumor* or *gossip*.

In addition to obtaining information about events by direct observation or at secondhand, the person who reports to us may have obtained information in a third way, *by inference*. Person X tells us that event E occurred, and we inquire how he obtained this information. He may tell us: "I observed events C and D, and so I inferred or guessed that event E also occurred." In legal contexts such evidence is called *opinion evidence*. In this case X neither made a direct observation regarding E nor did he hear about E from someone else; he inferred that E happened because of other things he observed or was told. He could of course have drawn such an inference from evidence other than from his own direct observations. For example, X might have said: "I heard about event C from John and heard about event D from Dick, and so I concluded that event E must also have happened." Since we do not have access to true clairvoyants when we need them the most, it is clear that testimonial evidence regarding future events can only be what we have termed opinion evidence. Thus a physician who asserts that patient A will die if some surgery is not performed is drawing an inference based upon evidence concerning past or current events.

So testimonial evidence from a particular person can itself have different groundings. But such evidence has other characteristics we have to recognize. In some situations a person P will give *unequivocal* testimony that a certain event E did occur; person P asserts: "Event E did occur." Still we might have uncertainty about whether E did occur, even though P's testimony is not equivocal or is not hedged in any way. In Section 3.2.3 we will examine some of the specific sources of uncertainty we face as far as P's credibility is concerned. In other situations a person may give testimony that is equivocal in nature. There are at least two ways in which such equivocation may be expressed. In one case we may ask P whether event E occurred, and P responds by saying such things as "I couldn't tell," "I don't remember," or "I don't know." Such extreme equivocation may indicate an act of honest self-impeachment on P's part; he actually does not know or remember whether E occurred. However, P's extreme equivocation is also consistent with the possibility that P does know or can remember whether E happened but, for various reasons, refuses to tell us. The name commonly given this form of behavior is *stonewalling*. In other situations, however, P may hedge or equivocate in less extreme ways. He may state, for example: "I believe it *very probable* that E did occur." His assertion here is an example of what we will, in Section 5.6, call *fuzzy probabilities*. In some situations he may attach specific numbers to grade the strength of his belief regarding E; he might assert: "I am 70% sure that E did occur."

Another question of inferential importance in evaluating testimonial evidence involves whether the testimony was solicited or given voluntarily. This matter is important regardless of whether the testimony is stated equivocally or unequivocally. If we ask person P whether event E happened, we presumably already appreciate the possible relevance of evidence about E in the inference task we face. But this might not necessarily be the case if P voluntarily tells us that event E happened. It may be true that P volunteered this testimony in the hope that we will perceive this evidence as relevant in a certain inference task P supposes us to face. In many contexts it is prudent to inquire about the reasons why a person volunteers testimony. Suppose we believe this person to be untruthful in his report that event E occurred. We ought to inquire, for example, about possible reasons why this person chose this particular lie in preference to others he might have told. The reasons we uncover may have inferential significance on their own. In some situations tangible evidence may be provided voluntarily rather than being solicited. Motivational issues, having interesting implications, are bound to arise when a document embarrassing to one public official is allegedly "leaked" to the press by another public official.

Both tangible and testimonial evidence have a property that needs to be recognized. Such evidence can reveal the occurrence or nonoccurrence of some event(s). Evidence revealing the occurrence of some event is said to be *positive evidence;* that which reveals the nonoccurrence of events is said to be *negative evidence*. There are some interesting issues here that bear upon the discovery or generation of evidence as well as upon assessments of the relevance, credibility, and force of evidence. It is often common to focus on evidence regarding the occurrence of events and easy to overlook evidence regarding the nonoccurrence of events. In any inferential context it is just as important to inquire about what did not happen as it is to inquire about what did happen. Celebrated examples of the inferential relevance and force of negative evidence are provided in several of the Sherlock Holmes mysteries we will examine in Section 7.7. There is no order of precedence between positive and negative evidence as far as either relevance or force are concerned. Tangible or testimonial evidence about the nonoccurrence of an event can be just as relevant and inferentially forceful as evidence about the occurrence of events.

Either tangible or testimonial evidence rests, at some stage, upon someone's observations, your own or those of another person. Again, if no person can be identified who made a relevant observation of an object, event, or situation, our hearing about the occurrence or nonoccurrence of an event may be classed as rumor or gossip. But we briefly discussed situations in which evidence expected is either not found or is not produced on request, and we began to inquire why this is so. Evidence we regard as *missing* may be either tangible or testimonial in nature. You take your car in for service and are astounded by the amount you are charged. One expensive item involved replacement of your fuel pump. You ask to see your original pump that was replaced, and the mechanic tells you that he discarded it and cannot show it to you. You might easily regard his failure to produce this tangible evidence with some suspicion. A person tells an insurance investigator, "It's none of your business" when the investigator asks whether or not her front door was locked on the day several expensive items were allegedly stolen from her home. Our failure to find evidence where we expect to find it or the failure of persons to produce things or provide testimony can in many cases be regarded as a form of evidence. It is quite important to note that having no evidence about event E is not the same as having evidence that E did not occur. The distinction between negative evidence and missing evidence is not always made.

I also mentioned briefly that there are other kinds of information we often use as evidence that do not rest upon someone's direct observation. We make frequent use of records we regard as authoritative, and we also take certain things for granted without further evidence. One form of authoritative record is an air or nautical almanac that provides the declination and hour angle of celestial bodies at various times and locations. Other examples include tables of chemical compounds, physical constants, mathematical formulas, and tidal occurrances. If you used such information in an inference task, you would ordinarily not be obliged to prove that the information is trustworthy or that someone actually observed it in some way. You would of course be obliged to prove that you extracted the correct information from any such authoritative records. Other information often used in an inference is normally accepted without further proof. For example, you would not be obliged to provide further proof about such statements as: heroin is a narcotic substance, gasoline is a flammable substance, or that the population of New York City exceeds that of Omaha. As we will later see, these are examples of *accepted facts* that, in a court trial, could be judicially noticed or accepted by the court.

The evidential distinctions we have just made are of great importance as far as the manner in which the *credibility* or *believability* of evidence is established. Before we proceed, we must dwell for a moment on the term *credibility*. This term is used in a variety of ways; for example, it is common to speak of credible evidence, credible sources of evidence, and credible stories, narratives, or explanations. I believe this term is quite appropriate for use in inference from evidence, since the very foundation of argument from evidence E* concerns the degree to which we feel entitled *to believe* that event E did occur, based upon evidence E* that it did. In establishing the credibility of this evidence, we must look to the credibility of the source from which it came.

Other terms are frequently used in place of the term credibility. For example, it is quite common to describe either evidence or sources of evidence as being *reliable*. One jurist insists that we speak of reliable rather than credible witnesses (Stone 1984, 100–107) The trouble here is that the term reliability has quite specific meaning in different contexts. For example, in the field of engineering the reliability of a device is defined as the probability that this device is still functioning at a specific time t (Leon-Garcia 1989, 163–164). In the field of testing in the behavioral sciences the reliability of a test concerns the extent to which a test gives repeatable results (Nunnally 1967, 191). In this sense reliability means the extent to which a test is self-consistent. My colleague Tony Zawilski suggests that a "reliable" witness might be one who is always available to give testimony, whether or not we can believe what he says. There is much more to the believability of evidence than the term reliability conveys.

A major problem we face in establishing the evidential foundations of our arguments is that the manner in which we establish the credibility of evidence depends upon what kind of evidence we have. Credibility, like other characteristics, has many attributes; this is certainly true when this term is applied to human sources of evidence. Attributes of the credibility of tangible evidence are not the same as attributes of the credibility of testimonial evidence. One additional term often used in place of credibility is the term *accuracy;* we may often speak of accurate evidence or accurate sources. As we will observe, accuracy is just one attribute of credibility.

3.2.2   The Credibility of Tangible Evidence: Its Authenticity and Accuracy

People may have a natural preference for tangible evidence on the ground that such evidence appears to "speak for itself." What this means is that tangible evidence is open to direct inspection by persons who intend to use it in drawing a conclusion. We may all have a tendency to trust our own senses over the senses of others who provide testimonial evidence about what they observed. The trouble is that tangible evidence can be misleading in many different ways, so we have to give special attention to attributes of the credibility of tangible evidence, the first of which is its *authenticity*. An object or a thing, we say, is authentic when it is exactly what it appears or is claimed to be. Many people have purchased what they believed to be an original work by a famous artist only to be told later that they paid a huge sum of money for a very competent forgery. Other persons have, until they were apprehended, made substantial fortunes distributing currency whose counterfeit nature required an expert to discover. In some instances establishing the authenticity of tangible evidence is a matter of life or death.

The weapon found on Sacco when he was arrested by Officer Connolly was a 32-caliber Colt revolver. During the autopsy he performed, Dr. George B. Mcgrath extracted four 32-caliber bullets from the body of Alessandro Berardelli, the payroll guard Sacco had allegedly slain in South Braintree. Mcgrath identified each of these bullets by a roman numeral he had etched on the base of each bullet with a surgical instrument. He testified that the bullet he labeled "III" was the one that caused the death of Berardelli. A 32-caliber bullet with a "III" etched on its base was shown at the trial, and ballistics experts testified that this bullet had indeed been fired through Sacco's Colt. To this day there is considerable disagreement about whether bullet III shown at the trial as having been fired through Sacco's Colt was the same bullet III that Dr. Mcgrath extracted from the body of Berardelli (e.g., see Young and Kaiser 1985; Starrs 1986). Bullets were test-fired through Sacco's Colt before the trial, and there is certainly the possibility that one of these test-fired bullets was substituted for the one extracted by Dr. Mcgrath from Berardelli's body. Sacco and Vanzetti may have been executed on the basis of tangible evidence that was not authentic.

If you discover tangible evidence yourself, you know how it came into existence. If tangible evidence is given to you by someone else, you have to be concerned about who discovered it, when was it discovered, how was it maintained, and who had access to it before before you observed it. What we are discussing here is called the *chain of custody* of tangible evidence. All sides still debating the case of Sacco and Vanzetti agree that the chain of custody of the tangible evidence introduced at their trial was, charitably, very weak (e.g., Starrs 1986b, 1051–1056). The authentication of tangible evidence is necessary whether the evidence is an object, a document, an image, a record, a measurement, or a demonstration. The historian may be concerned about the authenticity of an ancient document, and an auditor may be concerned about the authenticity of a client's sales transactions. You might be very concerned about the chain of custody of a blood, urine, or tissue sample collected from you by your physician for analysis in a laboratory. Misidentificiation of such samples is not unheard of. Authentication often requires the very close attention of experts whose background and training allows them to comment on whether some item of tangible evidence is what it appears to be. As expected, in jurisprudence matters concerning the authenticity of tangible evidence have been carefully studied (e.g., Lempert and Saltzburg 1977, 1045–1053). I will later mention some of the work by semioticians on authenticity matters.

Our sensory capabilities are limited in various ways, so devices have been designed to extend the range of things we can observe. These devices produce images or records of various kinds that we can examine with our own senses. For this reason we may class these images and records as tangible evidence. Thus we can examine photographs, X-ray images, radar images, and so on.

No sensing device, human, mechanical, or electronic, is infallible. We have natural questions concerning the inherent *accuracy* of sensing devices, but we also recognize that these devices can be influenced and tampered with in various ways. For example, radars can be jammed, and they are affected by changes in atmospheric and other conditions. So, when we examine sensor images, we face with some uncertainty what they reveal.

But sensing devices can be exercised over and over again, so we may obtain some assessment of the degree to which they are able to make discriminations of importance to us. In the process we may be able to express this discrimination capability in probabilistic terms. Suppose that a sensor is designed to tell whether event E ocurred; the sensor either reports E^*, that the event occurred, or E^{c*}, that the event did not occur. On the basis of many trials on which this sensor is employed, we may obtain statistical estimates of the conditional probabilities: (1) $P(E^*|E)$, the sensor's *hit rate* or *true-positive* rate, (2) $P(E^*|E^c)$, a *false-positive* rate, (3) $P(E^{c*}|E^c)$, a *correct rejection* or *true negative* rate, and (4) $P(E^{c*}|E)$, a *miss* or *false-negative rate*. In the study of the credibility of evidence, whether tangible or testimonial, some very useful ideas have come from the *theory of signal detection and recognition* (e.g., Swets 1964; Green and Swets 1966; Egan 1975). Though this theory was originally developed in connection with the design of better physical sensing devices it has considerable applicability to human detection and recognition capability, as we will see.

Physical measuring devices also have limits on their accuracy. The strain gauge or voltmeter used by an engineer, as well as the anemometer used by a meteorologist, have error tolerances and require periodic recalibration. In many situations experience allows the user of some measuring device to form error estimates using well-known probability distributions. We must also interpret various forms of demonstrative evidence with some care. Suppose that an inference rests upon statistical data someone has presented in graphic form which you can directly observe. Anyone who has taken a course in statistics learns how easy it is to mislead someone by means of descriptive statistics. The graph you are now examining was prepared by a public official and shows a precipitous decline in the rate of unemployment over the past two years. However, as a result of your statistical training you are astute enough to note that the axes of this graph have been scaled to magnify what is really an almost trivial decline in this rate. Now you have an inference regarding whether this official was just poorly trained or is attempting to mislead you.

3.2.3 Testimony and Attributes of the Credibility of Human Sources

I have claimed that there are no simple inferences except perhaps those provided in classroom examples. Apparently direct inferences can be decomposed to reveal many additional sources of uncertainty. We often simplify inferences by suppressing or overlooking sources of uncertainty. The trouble is that it is rarely easy to determine conditions under which we may safely suppress uncertainties we do recognize. A careful examination of evidence and its sources reveals a variety of uncertainties related to the evidence and how it was obtained. In examining attributes of the credibility of tangible and testimonial evidence, we encounter very difficult matters about which some divergence of opinion is to be expected. There are interesting and difficult epistemological issues that we cannot easily dismiss. These issues arise when we carefully consider the question, How do I stand in relation to the evidence I have? We now consider how we might identify attributes of the credibility of human sources or witnesses who give testimony. Most human characteristics have many attributes; credibility is no exception.

It is important to note first that, as users of evidence, we make observations whether the evidence is tangible or testimonial. As tangible evidence I consider a photograph in which I observe Ron coming out of Joe's house. I might be mistaken; it might have been Don and not Ron coming out of Joe's house. Instead, as testimonial evidence I hear you assert that you saw Ron coming out of Joe's house. You might have been mistaken in your observation, since it could have been Don instead of Ron. Another possibility in this testimonial case is that I misheard what you testified. Rather, you said it was Don coming out of Joe's house; I thought you said it was Ron. In the case of tangible evidence my own credibility as an observer is at issue. In the case of testimony, however, my own credibility as well as yours is at issue. Unless you have a disability you recognize, in a crucial inference task you would normally prefer to trust your own senses over the senses of someone else. In some cases trust in our own senses might be misplaced. My own quite uneducated olfactory and gustatory capabilities do not allow me to make the same discriminations in judging the quality of wine as those possible for a professional wine taster. In addition my eyesight and hearing are not as acute as they used to be.

To begin an analysis of attributes of the credibility of human observers, let us first appeal to common experience. Suppose that a person makes an observation of some kind and then tells someone else about what she observed. Here are three generalizations about human observational and reporting behavior I believe to be relatively uncontroversial.

1. People do not always report the events they believe to have occurred. We might restate this generalization to read: *When a person reports having observed the occurrence of an event, this person (usually, often, frequently, etc) believes this event to have happened.* Some hedge is required, since we do not suppose that people always testify in accordance with their beliefs.

2. The beliefs people have as a result of an observation do not always correspond to the sensory evidence they received during this observation. We might assert: *If, on observation, a person believes that an event has occurred, then this person (usually, often, frequently, etc.) has re-*

ceived sensory evidence of this event. This generalization allows for the possibility that a person's beliefs are not consistent with the sensory evidence this person obtained.

3. The evidence of our senses is not infallible. We might assert: *If a person's senses provide evidence of an event, then this event (usually, often, frequently, etc.) has occurred.* This allows for the possibility that a person's senses might have been inaccurate or were misled in some way.

No one knows exactly what chain of neurophysiological and other events takes place between the time a person's sensory end organs are stimulated and the time this person tells someone about what information this simulus provided. But the generalizations just noted allow us to identify three important attributes of the credibility of human observers. In fact there is a happy coincidence among these three commonsense generalizations, with some thoughts from epistemology, some results from experimental psychology, and several centuries of recorded experience in jurisprudence.

In Figure 3.6a person W reports E* that event E occurred. We wish to make an inference about whether or not event E did happen as W reports. Appealing to the first generalization above, we ask: Does W believe that event E occurred? This question involves W's *veracity* or truthfulness, since we would not say that W is truthful in this report unless she believed what she told us. As I will discuss later in Section 7.3.2, there has been an unfortunate tendency among probabilists to say that a witness is truthful only if the event she reports actually occurred. The trouble is that a person can be entirely truthful in reporting an event when this event did not in fact occur. Quite simply, a person could very easily be truthful but inaccurate or unobjective as an observer. A certain person believes that the traffic light is on red and tells us so when in fact it is on green. She just happens to be red-green color-blind and is not untruthful. As Figure 3.6a shows, the first stage in our inference about whether E happened concerns whether W believes what she reported.

Suppose we believe that W believes that event E happened. For the moment let us suppose that she is truthful in reporting to us what she believes. The second generalization asserted above holds out the possibility that W might believe that E happened despite the sensory evidence she obtained. Perhaps she so strongly expected or wished event E to occur that she would believe it did regardless of what her senses told her. I believe the credibility attribute of concern here is one we can justifiably call *objectivity.* An objective observer would be one who attends to the evidence of her senses and who does not let her motivations or expectancies determine what she will believe. As one philosopher put it, our beliefs are supple or elastic and are subject to a variety of influences (Nozick 1981, ch. 3). Information-carrying signals, as inputs to our sensory-perceptual systems, are not written upon a blank mental tablet. Other things are already written there in the form of our past experience, motivations, expectancies, and even instructions given by other

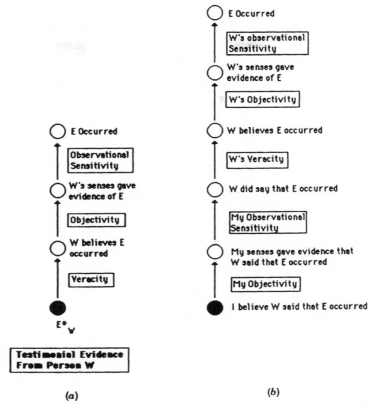

FIGURE 3.6 The foundation for testimonial evidence. (a) Attributes of the credibility of a human source. (b) An expanded foundation for testimonial evidence.

persons. So the second stage of our inference from E* to event E concerns whether W obtained sensory evidence of event E. Essentially we ask, Is W's belief about E consistent with the evidence she obtained from her senses?

The third generalization above asserts that evidence from our senses is not perfect. Stated in other words, sensory evidence is inconclusive to some degree. Suppose we believe that W did obtain sensory evidence about event E. The question is, How good was this evidence? This question involves W's *observational sensitivity* or *accuracy* and various factors upon which it might depend such as the conditions of observation and her physical condition at the time of observation. In discussing tangible evidence, I mentioned how sensing devices can be deceived in various ways. Our own senses are also subject to deception. Given the conditions of observation and the acuteness of her senses, we have to inquire about whether W could have discriminated between the occurrence and nonoccurrence of event E. If we suppose that

W did make an observation concerning event E, her senses provide the essential interface with this event. The final stage of the inference shown in Figure 3.6a concerns the quality of this interface and whether we can conclude that E did happen.

So we have decomposed our inference from E^* to E or E^c into three steps, each one corresponding to an identifiable attribute of the credibility of witness W. Later in Chapter 7 we will make finer distinctions involving these attributes than we have made so far. For example, we have to allow for the possibility that W made no observation and has made up her story about the occurrence of event E. We also have to allow for the possibility that attributes of the credibility of a person may be dependent upon states or levels of other factors we are considering in an inference. As we will see, these additional complexities can be trapped in terms of the linkages depicted in Figure 3.4b.

Before we examine what scholarship in various disciplines has to say about these three human credibility attributes, there are more credibility-related matters we need to examine as far as W's testimonial evidence is concerned. I mentioned above that in evaluating testimonial evidence, we have to be concerned about our own credibility as observers in addition to the credibility of the person providing us with testimony. Figure 3.6b shows some additional sources of uncertainty in my inference from W's testimony E^* as to whether the event she reported did occur. Acknowledging that my receipt of W's report is a sensory event, my inference appears to be grounded upon what I believe I heard W telling me. As the diagram shows, my inference about whether event E happened is grounded on my belief that W said E^*, that event E happened. Was I objective in forming this belief? Perhaps I so strongly wished or expected W to tell me that event E happened that I would believe she did regardless of what my senses recorded. In addition I have also to be concerned about my own observational sensitivity; I may have misheard what W said. Taking my own observational capabilities into account I have exposed two additional sources of uncertainty in my inference from W's testimony to the event she reports.

Figure 3.7 shows a decomposition of an inference from tangible evidence E^* to whether event E occurred or is true. It may be quite common to believe that this inference involves just a single stage as Figure 3.7a shows. However, as shown in Figure 3.7b, I might say that my inference in this case is grounded just upon my *belief* that E^* reveals E. Taking into account my own objectivity and observational sensitivity, this single stage inference can be decomposed into one having two stages. As an example, you hear about an inference that currently troubles me; this inference concerns whether I will be able to pay my bills at the end of the month. You decide to send me some favorably relevant tangible evidence in the form of a check for fifty dollars. I open your letter, see the check, and immediately send you profuse thanks for the check you have sent me for five hundred dollars, the amount I estimated I will need to pay my bills. The extra zero I thought your check contained came either from my wishing this were so or from my own inaccuracy or inattention in

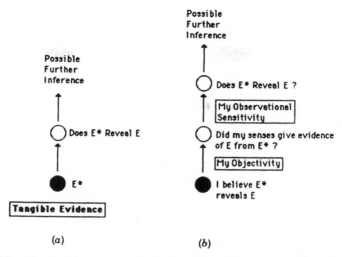

FIGURE 3.7 The foundation for tangible evidence. (a) Basic linkage pattern. (b) An expanded linkage pattern.

observing the amount on your check. Taking into account all of the credibility matters we have discussed so far, a comparison of Figures 3.6b and 3.7b shows one reasons why a person might prefer tangible rather than testimonial evidence of E.

In several other works I have given an account of scholarship from three different disciplines that has led me to believe that we need to consider veracity, objectivity, and observational sensitivity as major attributes of the credibility of human sources of evidence (Schum 1989; 1991; 1992). Here is a brief account of what this scholarship suggests. The first matter concerns the particular decomposition shown in Figure 3.6a. In this diagram I have decomposed an inference about whether event E happened, based upon W's testimony E*, into three stages, each of which identifies an attribute of W's credibility. You might inquire about the ordering of these three stages and, in particular, why veracity occurs at the first stage, then objectivity, and then observational sensitivity. One source of inspiration for this decomposition comes from the work of epistemologists concerned about the requisites for knowledge. Here is a difficult question: What does it mean to say that person W knows that E is true? One answer, the subject of ongoing controversy, is to say that W knows that E happened if (1) E did happen, (2) W believes that E happened, and (3) W is *justified* in believing that E happened. This account is sometimes called the *standard analysis of knowledge,* and it has been the subject of considerable debate among philosophers (O'Connor and Carr 1982; Shope 1983; Roth and Galis 1984; Pollock 1986; Moser 1991). Much of this debate has centered on the justification condition, which is why I placed emphasis on the word *justified.*

This standard account says that knowledge is *justified true belief*. One writer on the topic of knowledge argues that a belief is justified if it rests upon nondefective evidence (Chisholm 1982, 43–49). Look, again, at diagram *a* in Figure 3.6; start at the top with event E and then move *down* the reasoning chain. Suppose that event E occurred, W obtained good or nondefective sensory evidence of E, and then W believed the evidence of her senses. On this ordering of events, we might says that W "knows" that event E occurred. Suppose that W then tells us E*, that event E occurred; are we entitled to say that we also "know" that E occurred? The first problem of course is that W's testimony concerns a past event. Unless we were there to see it happen for ourselves, we have no way of verifying its occurrence. Even if we did ourselves observe E, we have our own objectivity and observational sensitivity to consider. We can only infer what W sensed and believed based upon her testimony (and what we discover about her credibility). In short, all we "know" is that W told us that E occurred. Depending upon how fine a decomposition we prefer to make of this situation, we might instead say that all we have, as Figure 3.6*b* illustrates, is a belief that W told us that E occurred. So, considering only W's testimony, our inference about whether event E happened involves a chain of inferences about what W believes, what W sensed, and then whether event E happened. If we consider our own observational credibility in observing W's testimony, our chain of reasoning is even longer, as Figure 3.6*b* shows.

The standard account of knowledge just mentioned is not the only one that might be given. Still, this account is very useful as a heuristic in our effort to establish attributes of the credibility of human sources of evidence. It has an even greater virtue, namely it is entirely consistent with experience regarding witness credibility accumulated by our legal system at least since the year 1352. As noted in Section 2.4.1, it was in this year that a statute of Edward III marked the beginning of impartial juries who deliberate upon evidence supplied by external witnesses. In our Anglo-American legal system interest in witness credibility issues began around this period. I began to give an account in Section 2.3 of interest among early probabilists in problems associated with the credibility of testimony and how this interest waned over the years because no statistical records can be kept of a person's credibility attributes such as veracity, objectivity, and observational sensitivity. Nevertheless, in the 1700s Nicholas Bernoulli once argued that a person's trustworthiness could be measured by taking a ratio between the number of occasions on which this person gave confirmed true testimony to the number of occasions on which he gave testimony (Daston 1988, 312). For obvious reasons Bernoulli's advice was never taken seriously by courts.

Courts and advocates have, over the centuries, found *nonstatistical* ways of assessing the credibility of witnesses. The essential method is to ask a *variety* of different questions about the credibility-relevant behavior of witnesses and other factors that might influence a person's credibility. Certain answers to these questions form ancillary evidence bearing upon attributes of the credibility of a witness. What has been especially interesting to me is the fact that we can quite conveniently categorize most of this evidence in terms of the three credibility attributes just mentioned. The chain of reasoning suggested by epistemological analyses of knowledge corresponds with centuries of experience in legal affairs. Shown in Figure 3.8 is a categorization of credibility-relevant evidence in terms of witness veracity, objectivity, and observational sensitivity. First, observe that I have categorized credibility-relevant evidence in terms of its specificity on the three attributes we have identified. Most credibility-relevant evidence is very specific to one of the three attributes. Some evidence such as self-contradiction may bear either on a person's veracity or objectivity. And some evidence, such as the existence of contradictory testimony from another person, is quite unspecific. Does this mean that my categorization scheme fails? I believe that the answer is no for the following reason: Like any other form of evidence, ancillary evidence bearing on credibility varies in the specificity with which it points to some matter. For example, evidence that the robber was male, though important, does not point to any particular male. In the same way the mere existence of contradictory evidence does not say which credibility attribute is being

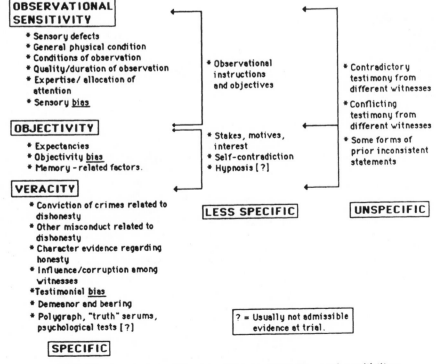

FIGURE 3.8 Categories of evidential tests of testimonial credibility.

challenged. I will return to the various kinds of credibility-related evidence in Figure 3.8 later in Section 7.3.2 when we consider the inferential force of testimonial evidence.

My account of attributes of the credibility of testimony is also consistent with that branch of experimental psychology called *sensory psychophysics*. One of the major topics in this area concerns human ability to detect and recognize information-carrying signals. The trouble in such study is that there is no device we can employ to tell when a person has "sensed" some signal; perhaps there will be in the future. Studies of human sensory capabilities thus rest upon testimonial evidence given by persons about, for example, whether or not they heard or saw some stimulus. Traditionally psychologists have never believed that a person's report of the observation of some stimulus is *direct* evidence that this person actually "sensed" this stimulus. They have been astute enough to recognize, as we noted above, that external stimuli are written on a mental tablet that has many other things already written on it. In particular, psychologists recognize that a person may believe certain events have occurred or not occurred despite the evidence of their senses. A person may report having seen or heard something because he either wished or expected it to occur.

Until about thirty years ago there was never any way of experimentally separating what I have termed *observational sensitivity* from what I have termed *objectivity*. In the early 1960s, however, many psychologists began to view human detection and recognition capabilities in terms of the theory of signal detection (TSD), which they imported from the field of electrical engineering (e.g., Swets 1964; Green and Swets 1966). This theory allows us to study, among other things, the sensitivity of our senses in a way that is not confounded by our motivations, expectancies, and other factors that influence our objectivity. When we consider various ways of grading the inferential force of testimonial evidence in Chapter 7, I will also borrow some very useful terms and concepts from TSD.

Attributes of a person's credibility have other properties that unfortunately are not always recognized. First, a person's veracity, objectivity, and observational sensitivity are always dependent upon the event this person reports. People may be more truthful and objective about some matters than they are about others; they may also have greater powers of sensory discrimination regarding some events than they have about others. These attributes of credibility are also dependent upon time and situation. The fact that a person has always been truthful in past testimony does not entail that he will be truthful on this present occasion. Again, I note that what we believe we know about the credibility of a person who gives us testimony is often at least as inferentially important as what this person tells us.

3.2.4 Credibility and Competence

There is more than one term used with reference to human sources of evidence. It is common, in law and elsewhere, to speak of the *competence* of a witness. Generally a competent witness is a person who could have made some relevant observation and who also understands what she has observed. Thus an engineer having years of experience in matters concerning the construction and maintenance of jet engines would be thought competent in presenting evidence regarding an accident in which engine failure is one possibility being considered. The trouble is that the competence of a person does not entail his credibility, and vice versa. Suppose you have a friend whose general credibility is the envy of your community. But unless this person also is also a trained physician, you would not consider her as a source of information regarding the medical problem you now have. On the other hand, *experts* having made first-hand observations of some events may be untruthful in telling others about these events. I know of no research of any kind on the relationship that exists, if any, between the competence and credibility of people as sources of evidence. It seems a safe strategy to regard these two characteristics as orthogonal or independent. Without fear of controversy we might assert the generalization: *Not all credible persons are competent, and not all competent persons are credible.*

3.3 RELEVANCE, CREDIBILITY, AND ANCILLARY EVIDENCE

We discussed in Section 3.1.4 how arguments from evidence to hypotheses or possibilities rest upon appropriate generalizations and ancillary evidence. As illustrated in Figure 3.3, generalizations and ancillary evidence determine the strength of links in a chain of reasoning or, if you like, they form the "glue" that holds an argument together. Some ancillary evidence may strengthen this glue, and other ancillary evidence may weaken it. Let us return for a moment to Officer Connolly's testimony about Sacco's alleged actions following his arrest. My attempt to defend the relevance of Connolly's testimony required a chain of reasoning having a large number of links, stages, or steps. From what we have just discussed about the credibility of human sources of evidence we might also be inclined to insert additional links in this chain of reasoning that are associated with attributes of Connolly' credibility. Remember that each additional link we insert represents a source of uncertainty we recognize. The additional credibility-related links are inserted as shown in Figure 3.9. We now have a chain of reasoning having ten links, steps, or stages. Notice that I have listed three as being associated with Connolly's credibility and seven as being associated with the relevance of what he asserted on major issue H.

3.3.1 Generalizations about Relevance and Credibility

In an argument from evidence to some major, ultimate, or final conclusion, the generalizations we assert can bear upon the relevance of this evidence or upon the credibility of the source from which it comes. I have already proposed generalizations for the relevance stages shown in Figure 3.9; these generalizations appear in Section 3.1.6. To accommodate the credibility-related steps

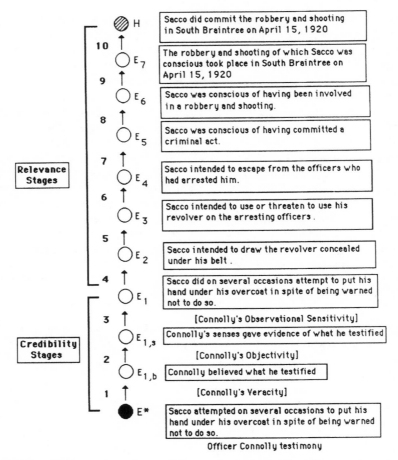

FIGURE 3.9   Establishing the credibility and relevance of evidence: An example.

we have now inserted, I must revise the first generalization I asserted for step 1 in Figure 3.5. The generalization I asserted read: *The events reported by police officers testifying under oath usually have occurred.* Since we are now considering Connolly's veracity, objectivity, and observational sensitivity, we need to decompose the generalization just asserted. Here are some possible generalizations we might assert:

Veracity (Credibility Stage 1). *If a police officer testifying under oath asserts that an event occurred, then this officer (usually, probably, very often, etc.) believes this event to have occurred.*

Objectivity (Credibility Stage 2). *If a police officer believes an event to have occurred, this event was (usually, often, probably, etc.) evidenced by this officer's senses.*

Observational Sensitivity (Credibility Stage 3). *If an officer's senses give evidence of an event, this event (usually, often, probably, etc.) occurred.*

There might be some objection to my categorizing these generalizations into those concerning relevance and those concerning credibility. It can be argued that all generalizations concern relevance; the question is, Relevance to what? The three generalizations I just asserted concern the relevance of Connolly's testimony E* on the event he testifies. These generalizations say that matters associated with his veracity, objectivity, and observational sensitivity provide a plausible basis for an inference from E* to the event he asserted. Then the remaining seven generalizations all bear upon the relevance of the event he asserted to the final issue H. Recognizing this, I believe it does no harm to categorize these generalizations in terms of the credibility and relevance stages of the argument shown in Figure 3.9.

You can choose your own hedges in each of the above credibility-related generalizations, and you are of course entitled to assert entirely different generalizations if you believe these to be unsatisfactory. The trouble is that any collection of the ten generalizations I have now asserted regarding the relevance and credibility of Connolly's testimony may be defective as far as Connolly and his testimony about Sacco are concerned. We need ancillary evidence to test each of these generalizations. Earlier I mentioned that I deliberately chose the testimony given by Officer Connolly to illustrate several matters that are not easy to illustrate using simpler examples. I do not regard this example as either pathological or even unusual because of the number of reasoning stages it reveals. On careful examination, inferences we routinely perform may contain at least as many stages as the ones shown in Figure 3.9.

One important matter concerns just the generalizations we have considered regarding the relevance and credibility of Connolly's testimony. First, suppose that you found the generalizations I asserted to be convincing or at least plausible. Suppose further that we had no ancillary evidence on any of these generalizations. We might still proceed to revise our belief about Sacco's guilt (H) based upon Connolly's evidence (E*) in Figure 3.9 just by giving each of these generalizations the benefit of the doubt or by assuming that they hold in this particular instance involving Connolly and Sacco. If we were to do this, we would be facing an inference upon inference having the ten stages shown in Figure 3.9. In Section 7.1 we will be much concerned about the length of reasoning chains and what chain length by itself says about the force of evidence. If we had no ancillary evidence to support the ten stages of reasoning from Connolly's testimony, we might easily recognize that we would be out on a very long and slender inferential limb.

In such instances in which we seek to draw conclusions from *unsupported generalizations*, we might do well to heed the comments made by a civil appeals judge in trial that took place in 1942. The judge remarked (Maguire et al., 1973, 875):

Inferences alone may, if reasonable, provide a link in a chain of evidence and constitute in that regard substantial evidence. But an inference cannot be piled upon an inference, and then another inference upon that, as such inferences are unreasonable and cannot be considered as substantial evidence. Such a method could be extended indefinitely until there would be no more substance to it than the soup Lincoln talked about that was "made by boiling the shadow of a pigeon that had been starved to death."

Thus, unsupported in any way by ancillary evidence, the inference shown in Figure 3.9 has about as much strength as the soup Abraham Lincoln once described. However, in Chapter 7 we will observe that *supported* chains of reasoning of any length can be very strong indeed, particularly when they involve the extra links shown above in Figure 3.4*b*.

3.3.2 Forms of Ancillary Evidence

Ancillary evidence can be of any variety we discussed in Section 3.2.1; it can be tangible, testimonial, information from authoritative sources, missing evidence, or accepted facts. Here are two examples of ancillary evidence. The first concerns a matter involving the credibility of Officer Connolly's testimony, and the second concerns the relevance of his testimony. There is evidence bearing upon Connolly's veracity, only some of which was available for use by the defense at the trial in 1920. Other evidence only became available after the trial and, though it is useful in postmortem analyses, it was not helpful to the defendants. As Young and Kaiser have discovered, Officer Connolly never made any mention, before the grand jury or during other pretrial hearings, of either Sacco or Vanzetti making suspicious or threatening hand movements. In addition, after the trial, a police associate of Connolly's told defense investigators that several other police associates of Connolly were no longer speaking to him because of the testimony he gave (1985, 68–70, 163). This ancillary evidence casts some doubt upon whether Connolly actually believed the testimony he gave at trial.

Examine Figure 3.9 again, and at stage 7 note that from an inference about Sacco's intention to escape police custody we further infer that he was conscious of having commited a criminal act. Sacco himself testified that he believed he was being arrested because of his political beliefs and not because he had committed any crime. Sacco further testified, as ancillary evidence on this matter, that the first question asked of him and Vanzetti during their initial interrogation by the police was whether they were radicals or socialists. Sacco's contention was that he knew that his distribution of anarchistic literature had attracted the attention of the police.This was certainly not a criminal act and, in any case, had nothing to do with the crime in South Braintree.

3.3.3 On the Indirect Relevance of Ancillary Evidence

At various points I have mentioned how ancillary evidence is used to test, *in particular instances,* the generalizations asserted to license reasoning stages from directly relevant evidence to major hypotheses or possibilities. Some ancillary evidence may favor (or support) a generalization, and some may disfavor it. Consider the reasoning linkages or stages in Figure 3.10 from directly relevant evidence E* to major hypotheses **H** (recall that **H** represents a class of hypotheses such as H and H^c). Suppose we have asserted convincing, or at least plausible, generalizations that license each of these linkages; these generalizations are shown as **G₁** through **G₄** in Figure 3.10. Now we wish to test whether these generalizations apply *in this particular instance* by performing evidential tests of them. We immediately encounter another relevance issue, for obviously we must be able to defend the pertinence of any evidential test on a particular generalization we have asserted; here is an example.

In Section 3.2.3 I asserted the following generalization regarding a person's observational sensitivity: *If a person's senses provide evidence of an event,*

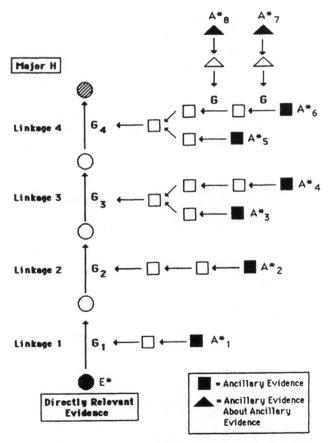

FIGURE 3.10 Generalizations and ancillary evidence as a basis for judging the strength or weakness of links in a reasoning chain.

then this event (usually, often, frequently, etc.) has occurred. Examples of tests of this generalization are given in Figure 3.8. The inferential issue here concerns whether a person can have discriminated between the occurrence and nonoccurrence of the event she reports. Suppose we now wish to test this generalization to see whether it applies to this witness whose testimony we are now considering. In such an inference we would naturally be concerned about our witness' sensory capabilities, physical condition, the conditions of observation, and so on.

The trouble is that the relevance of ancillary evidence may not always be as obvious as it is in the example just given. In some cases we will have to construct quite elaborate arguments to justify the indirect relevance of ancillary evidence. In addition we may often encounter quite massive amounts of ancillary evidence. Consider the ancillary evidence labeled items labeled A^* in Figure 3.10. In some cases, as shown by ancillary evidence A_1^* and A_2^* bearing on $\mathbf{G_1}$ and $\mathbf{G_2}$ at linkages 1 and 2, the defense of indirect relevance may be quite simple. The other cases shown at linkages 3 and 4 involve more complex arguments. Earlier I mentioned the infinite regress possible when we consider evidence, evidence about evidence, evidence about evidence about evidence, and so on. The argument shown at linkage 4 illustrates a simple example. The two evidence items A_7^* and A_8^* represent ancillary evidence about the ancillary evidence shown as A_6^*. As an example, suppose a person (an expert witness perhaps) who provides A_6^* that bears indirectly upon generalization $\mathbf{G_4}$, at linkage 4. Item A_7^* may be evidence supporting or impeaching the credibility of what this person reports.

I will later return to Figure 3.10 in a discussion of possible controversy about the manner in which I have structured the role of ancillary evidence. In Chapter 4 we will begin to consider complex and interrelated arguments based upon masses of evidence. Using one metaphor, we will describe such argument structures as *inference networks*. These networks will be complex enough if we just attended to directly relevant evidence items and the arguments they suggest. When we consider ancillary evidence items, together with arguments they suggest, we may be facing the problem of having inference networks *embedded within* other inference networks. This is what Figure 3.10 illustrates. We have one argument structure linking E^* with $\mathbf{H}$. Other networks embedded in this structure are those involving the ancillary evidence and their associated arguments. As we will see, there is more than one way to structure inference networks. Some may argue that we can always put all of our arguments on one "super" network; however, I do not believe this is always possible or advisable.

3.4 COMMON FORMS OF EVIDENCE

We come at last to a discussion of how we might usefully categorize evidence regardless of its substance or content. The scheme I will describe is based upon discussion of the structural matters in the preceding sections of this chapter. Some persons have grown very old in their attempts to find comprehensive categorizations of various subjects. For example, to my knowledge no one has been successful in finding a comprehensive categorization of human decision tasks. In my present attempt to categorize evidence, I may fare no better (I am certainly growing older). You may be able to see distinctions that I have not made. One distinction I will make is open to question, for reasons I will discuss. Indeed I have changed my mind several times regarding previous categorizations I have attempted (Schum 1987; 1990). My interest in classifying evidence stems from a reading of treatises in law on the subject of evidence. Although my classification scheme is based upon some concepts employed by evidence scholars, it does not resemble any scheme in this area I presently know about. For example, Wigmore (1937) categorized evidence into just three classes, as I will explain in Section 5.1. The scheme I now present in Figure 3.11 has fifteen categories. By itself, the task of taxonomy is not very interesting. But it does often lead us to make distinctions that are useful for various purposes. I have mentioned how our colleagues in jurisprudence have had to be able to recognize certain common properties of evidence in order to cope with the incredible substantive variety of evidence that arises in litigation.

The classification of any item of evidence is, of course, always made relative to the particular inferential situation in which it is used. We may employ an

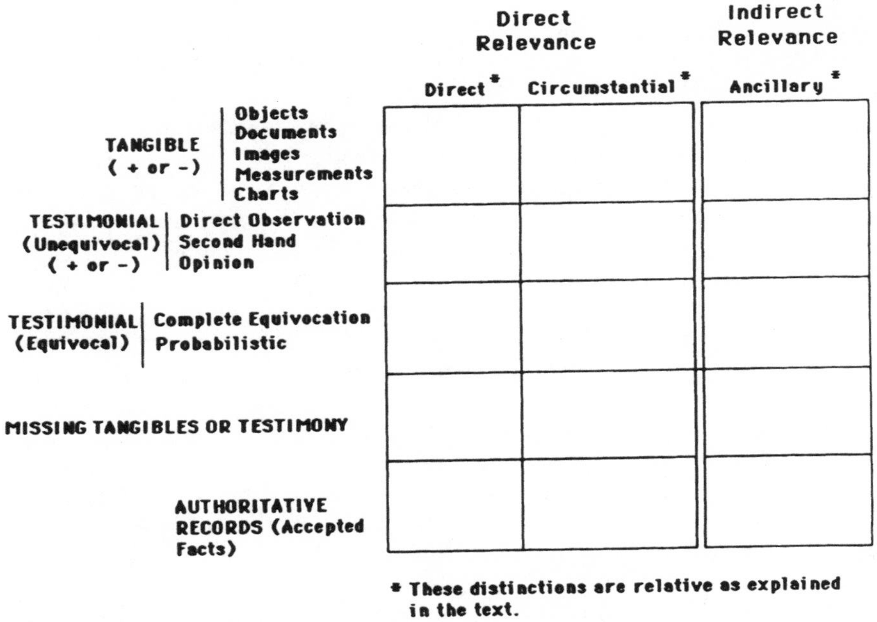

		Direct Relevance		Indirect Relevance
		Direct[*]	Circumstantial[*]	Ancillary[*]
TANGIBLE (+ or –)	Objects Documents Images Measurements Charts			
TESTIMONIAL (Unequivocal) (+ or –)	Direct Observation Second Hand Opinion			
TESTIMONIAL (Equivocal)	Complete Equivocation Probabilistic			
MISSING TANGIBLES OR TESTIMONY				
AUTHORITATIVE RECORDS (Accepted Facts)				

[*] These distinctions are relative as explained in the text.

FIGURE 3.11 Categories of recurrent forms of evidence.

item of evidence in more than one inference problem; its status in one problem may be quite different from its status in another. Evidence classification is relative in other ways, as I will discuss momentarily. The rows in Figure 3.11 correspond to the various types of evidence we identified in response to the question, How do we, as users of an item of evidence, stand in relation to it? The distinctions we made in Section 3.2 allow us to discern five essential categories: (1) various kinds of tangible evidence, (2) unequivocal testimony (from another person) based upon direct observation, obtained at second-hand, or as the expression of an inference or opinion, (3) two species of equivocal testimony (from another person), (4) missing tangible or testimonial evidence, and (5) evidence from authoritative records. The plus and minus signs associated with tangible and unequivocal testimonial evidence refer to the positive and negative evidence we discussed. Again, positive evidence records the occurrence of something, and negative evidence records the non-occurrence of something.

Have I left anything out as far as the rows in Figure 3.11 are concerned? A statistician, for example, might wonder why I have excluded "statistical evidence." No such class is needed, I believe, since various descriptive statistical analyses concern observations of various phenomena, some of which are tangible and some of which are revealed by the testimony of witnesses. In some cases we may even perform statistical analyses of missing data or of items selected from authoritative records. Here are some examples. First, suppose we are performing an exercise, common in industrial situations, called *acceptance sampling*. A large lot of items has been produced, and we wish to draw a conclusion about the proportion of items that are defective in this entire lot. If the proportion of defective items is sufficiently large, we might decide to discard the entire lot. Not being able to examine every item in this lot, we take a random sample of, say, 100 items from this lot. We observe that 8 of these items are defective. Our statistic is the relative frequency 8/100, and upon this datum we must draw a conclusion about the true proportion of items that are defective in the entire lot. The individual items are tangible evidence, and we can examine each item to determine whether it is defective. Suppose instead that our statistical exercise involves an opinion survey. We wish to determine the proportion of people in some community who believe a public offical should be removed from office. We take a sample of testimonial evidence from these persons that indicates their inference or opinion about this matter.

The rows in Figure 3.11 cover the physical kinds of evidence of which I am currently aware. This scheme easily covers Hacking's classification of evidence in terms of people and things that point to other things (see Section 2.1.1). It also covers the kinds of historical, medical, and legal evidence we considered briefly in Section 2.1.4. But, as I will discuss in a moment, we may encounter interesting combinations of these physical kinds of evidence.

The columns in Figure 3.11 arise in response to the question, How does an evidence item stand in relation to the matters at issue in an inference problem? Answers to this question involve the nature of the relevance of evidence, as we discussed in Section 3.1. An item of evidence is directly relevant if we can form a chain of reasoning or an argument from this evidence to a major or final hypothesis. As illustrated in Figure 3.10, evidence that is indirectly relevant bears upon the strength or weakness of links in chains of reasoning set up by directly relevant evidence. Two species of directly relevant evidence can be discerned: direct evidence and circumstantial evidence. I have referred to all indirectly relevant evidence as *ancillary evidence*. Notice that these three evidence categories each carry an asterisk. The status of an evidence item in these categories is relative *within* an inference problem, as I will explain.

Let us begin with the most controversial of the three categories of evidence just identified. I have borrowed the term *direct evidence* from our colleagues in law. Evidence is said to be direct when it goes in one reasoning step to a matter revealed in the evidence. If you believe the evidence to be perfectly credible, that settles the matter. Suppose that I come to your house today, and you observe that I am wearing a cast on my arm. You have direct evidence that I have a cast on my arm. The cast itself is tangible; you can see it for yourself. If you believe the evidence of your senses, you are entitled to conclude that I do have a cast on my arm. As another example, in a trial we have an eyewitness W who asserts: "I saw X (the defendant) shoot Y (the victim)." Here is a direct testimonial assertion about a major matter at issue. If you believe W to be perfectly credible, that (apparently) settles the matter in one reasoning stage as far as your belief is concerned; you believe X did shoot Y. Another way to describe direct evidence is to say that such evidence, if perfectly credible, would be *conclusive* on some issue. You might regard your direct observation as conclusive evidence that I have a cast on my arm. In the testimonial example, W's eyewitness testimony would be conclusive on the matter he asserts only if you believed he was a *perfectly* credible witness.

But there is an interesting difficulty associated with direct evidence that I tried to anticipate in our earlier discussion. I just asserted that direct evidence, if believed, goes in a single step to something revealed by the evidence. But we have discussed at several points how *any* inferential step can be decomposed. This presents us with the following problem: If we say that evidence is direct, we have to specify the event, proposition, or statement upon which it is direct evidence. Let us first consider the tangible evidence you have about the cast on my arm. Look at Figure 3.7a again. Suppose that E* represents your observation of the cast on my arm; let E be the event that I do have a cast on my arm. If you believe the evidence of your senses, that seems to settle it, E did occur or is true. But Figure 3.7b shows another construal of this same situation in which your inference is grounded on your present belief that your senses told you I have a cast on my arm. So, on this construal, your belief about what you saw is direct evidence, not on my having a cast on my arm but only on what your senses recorded. You are entitled to believe your senses recorded my having a cast on my arm only if you believe you are a perfectly *objective* observer. You might have expected or wished to see me with a cast on my arm, and you would believe it so regardless of what your senses recorded.

Now consider the testimonial situation involving eyewitness testimony from witness W. Suppose that E represents the hypothesis that X shot Y, and E* represents W's testimony that X shot Y. Since witness W is a human observer, we have to be concerned about his veracity, objectivity, and observational sensitivity. If we adopt the credibility-related chain of reasoning shown in Figure 3.6a, we see that W's testimony E* cannot be direct evidence of E, since it involves three stages of reasoning about W's veracity, objectivity, and observational sensitivity. On this construal of credibility assessment, W's testimony E* is direct evidence only on what W believes, not on whether or not E is true. If we thought W perfectly truthful, we could take E* as conclusive evidence only that W believes that X shot Y and not that X did in fact shoot Y.

Suppose you hold your own objectivity and observational sensitivity in sufficient esteem so that, as far as you are concerned, you have conclusive evidence that I do presently have a cast on my arm. Unless you have X-ray vision you cannot see what is beneath this cast. One possibility is that I have broken my arm. Let us say that the existence of a cast on my arm is just *circumstantial evidence* that I have broken my arm. All circumstantial evidence has the following characteristic: *Even if this evidence is perfectly credible, it is still inconclusive* about some matter to which it is inferentially related. Figure 3.12 illustrates the distinction between direct and circumstantial evidence. In Figure 3.12a your observation E* is direct evidence of E, that I have a cast on my arm. This assumes your perfect credibility as an observer. In Figure 3.12b your observation E* is just circumstantial evidence that my arm is broken. Such evidence is inconclusive on F even if you regarded yourself to be completely credible as an observer. For any number of reasons I might be wearing this cast to convince you or others that I have injured my arm when in fact I have not. As another example of circumstantial evidence, recall the example in Section 2.1.1 involving your inference about whether your neighbor is keeping a dog in his apartment. The can of dog food you observed in his kitchen, the spots on his carpet, and the scratches on his tables are all items of circumstantial evidence that he is keeping a dog. The reason is that all of these observables have other possible explanations.

Figure 3.12b illustrates how distinctions between direct and circumstantial evidence are always relative within some inference problem. We might regard your observation E* as direct evidence at one stage of reasoning and circumstantial evidence relative to higher stages of reasoning. As a final example of the distinction between direct and circumstantial evidence, consider again Officer Connolly's testimony about Sacco's alleged hand movements after his arrest. We can now give a more precise characterization of this testimonial evidence. Using the chain of reasoning shown in Figure 3.9, we may characterize Connolly's testimony as being direct, but certainly not conclusive, evidence on Connolly's beliefs about what he observed and very weak cir-

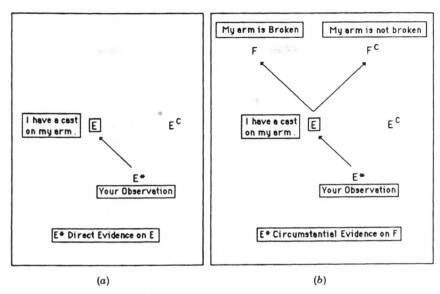

FIGURE 3.12 Comparison of direct and circumstantial evidence.

cumstantial evidence on H, that Sacco committed the crime for which he was charged. The more sources of uncertainty that exist between evidence E^* and hypothesis H, the weaker is the circumstantial connection between E^* and H.

Ancillary evidence always has relative features as I indicated by the asterisks in Figure 3.11. Evidence is always ancillary relative to an inference regarding some major, final, or ultimate hypothesis, possibility, or possible conclusion. As an illustration consider Figure 3.10 again. Suppose that generalization G_1 concerns an attribute of the credibility of the source of evidence E^*. Suppose that the ancillary evidence A_1^* represents evidence bearing upon G_1. This evidence itself might be both direct evidence, at one level, and circumstantial evidence, at another level, as far as G_1 is concerned. But, relative to the argument from E^* to hypotheses **H**, A_1^* is ancillary because it bears upon the strength or weakness of one of the linkages licensed by G_1 between E^* and **H**. In this abstract example we could say that ancillary evidence A_1^* is direct or circumstantial evidence bearing upon the credibility of the source of E^* but only ancillary evidence on major hypotheses **H**.

As Figure 3.11 shows, there are fifteen possible combinations of the rows and columns. Thus, for example, tangible evidence of some form might be direct, circumstantial, or ancillary in nature relative to some problem and within a particular chain of reasoning. The same is true for the other four basic types of evidence in the remaining rows. The risk in presenting any taxonomy is that it immediately invites efforts to find cases that do not seem to fit. One of the easiest ways to defeat a taxonomy is to find items that seem to belong in more than one advertised category. In some cases, as the following example illustrates, we may appear to have various mixtures of the kinds of evidence indicated by the rows in Figure 3.11.

The company at which you are presently employed has invested all of its employees' retirement funds, including your own, with the Acme Assured Annuity Association (AAAA). Last week you heard that your favorite television program "Hindsight" would present an expose of AAAA's financial dealings at 10:00 PM last night. You had to miss this program, but you set your VCR appropriately and you have a television tape of this program. You now run the tape, and during the program a former employee of AAAA, named White, is being interviewed. You hear White assert: "Before I left AAAA I saw a letter from Blue (Chief Executive Officer of AAAA) to Green (Blue's executive assistant) in which Blue wrote: 'We had both better leave the country before the trouble starts; do you want to face 10,000 angry folks who are going to hear they will have nothing to retire on but social security'?" How are we to categorize this chilling evidence regarding the present state of your retirement funds?

Your television tape is *tangible* evidence in the sense that you can examine it over and over again to make sure you heard White correctly. White's evidence, however, is *testimonial* in nature, but the information he relates has been obtained at *secondhand* from his alleged reading of a *document* describing an assertion Blue allegedly made to Green. If you trust your senses, you may regard your tape as direct evidence on White's assertion. However, this evidence appears weakly *circumstantial* in an inference about the present state of your funds. The chain of reasoning from White's testimony to hypotheses representing the present condition of your retirement account might be even longer than the one I constructed for Officer Connolly's testimony in the Sacco and Vanzetti case. Though entirely fictitious, this television tape example seems quite representative of the "evidence" we are frequently provided in many parts of our daily lives. At least some people are inclined to accept as evidence a supermarket tabloid's assertion that a famous movie star recently had a child, out of wedlock mind you, with an extraterrestrial.

I do not regard the types of evidence shown in the rows of Figure 3.11 to be mutually exclusive. We may indeed encounter evidence to which more than one of these row labels might be attached. Deciding how you stand in relation to a certain item of evidence may require careful thought. I believe the categorization scheme in Figure 3.11 assists in this process. I will use this scheme for several purposes in later parts of this discourse. In Section 9.3.3, I will discuss how this scheme is *substance-blind* because it rests only upon inferential considerations and not on any involving content or substance.

3.5 RECURRENT COMBINATIONS OF EVIDENCE

So far we have considered how *individual* evidence items might be classified regardless of their substance or content. Usually in our daily inference tasks we have multiple items of evidence to consider. It is natural to inquire about whether or not there are identifiable ways in which evidence items occur in combination. In fact in an account of any analysis of evidence we have made it is very common to use words that describe relationships that seem to exist between one item of evidence and another. These words are often used rather imprecisely, and we may fail to make distinctions that can be revealed in a careful structural analysis of evidence. Attention to the structural matters we now consider allows us to add considerable precision in any account of how evidence items stand in relation to each other. The structural matters we consider are also quite informative about issues concerning the credibility and the force of evidence items when they are taken in combination.

3.5.1 Dissonant Evidence: Contradiction and Conflict

The different conceptions of evidential force, strength, or weight we consider in Chapter 5 have at least this attribute in common: They all suppose that relevant evidence has vectorlike properties. Evidence points inferentially in one direction or another and with a certain gradation of force. For the moment let us consider just the *inferential direction* of evidence. The direction in which an item of evidence points refers to the hypothesis we believe it favors over other hypotheses being considered. When we have a body of evidence items to consider, we may observe that some evidence favors one hypothesis and other evidence favors another. In such cases we may say that our evidence is *dissonant* to some degree. Regardless of context, we might only rarely encounter evidence that is entirely *harmonious* in the sense that all evidence items favor the same hypothesis. A person who says he always encounters harmonious evidence might well look to his methods of gathering evidence; perhaps he only considers evidence that favors possibilities he expects or wishes to be true.

I believe there to be two essential ways in which evidence can be dissonant, but labeling them presents a problem. All dissonant evidence conflicts, diverges, or is at variance in terms of its inferential implications. One particular species of dissonant evidence is contradictory in nature. The trouble, as I will now attempt to explain, is that not all dissonant or conflicting evidence is necessarily contradictory. I will reserve the term *conflicting* for a particular form of dissonance that does not involve a contradiction.

Figure 3.13 illustrates the distinction I wish to make. Figure 3.13a illustrates *contradictory evidence:* One person or sensor reports E_1^*, that event E occurred, and another person or sensor reports E_2^{c*}, that this *same* event E did *not* occur. The situation shown in 3.13a is of course just a special case of evidential contradiction. Any evidence items reporting *mutually exclusive* events are contradictory. Suppose that **E** represent a class of mutually exclusive events $\{E_1, E_2, \ldots, E_i, \ldots, E_j, \ldots, E_n\}$. By definition, mutually exclusive events cannot happen together, and so these reports are contradictory if one source reports that E_i occurred and another reports that E_j oc-

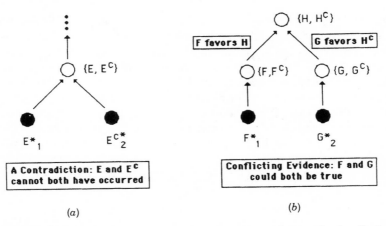

FIGURE 3.13 Dissonant evidence. (a) Contradictory evidence. (b) Conflicting evidence.

curred. Since contradictory evidence involves events that cannot have occurred jointly, we naturally look to the credibility of our sources of this evidence; clearly one of the sources or sensors is wrong. As I noted in discussing Figure 3.8, the existence of contradictory testimony from a human source signals the need for careful credibility assessment, but by itself a contradiction does not tell us what attribute of a person's credibility is being questioned.

We may have contradictory evidence provided by any number of sources. Suppose that some number r of sources report that event E happened and $(n - r)$ of sources report that E did not happen. As we will discuss in Section 8.3.1, it is not a very sensible strategy to attempt to resolve evidential contradictions simply by "counting heads" on each side. Figure 3.13a depicts a contradiction involving directly relevant evidence. The three dots above the arrow pointing from {E, E^c} in this figure simply indicate that the evidence we have about events in this class is relevant on events at higher stages in a chain of reasoning to our major hypotheses. But ancillary evidence can also be contradictory. Suppose that E_1^* in Figure 3.13a is testimony from a person named Henry. In assessing the credibility of Henry's testimony, we hear contradictory evidence regarding his observational sensitivity. Martha says that Henry was not wearing his strongly corrective glasses at the time of his alleged observation; Marvin, on the other hand, says that Henry was wearing his glasses at this time.

What I will term *conflicting evidence* is illustrated in Figure 3.13b. Suppose that a person or sensor reports the occurrence of event F, which we believe to favor hypothesis H. Then another person or sensor reports the occurrence of event G, which we believe to favor H^c. The two items of evidence in this case are conflicting in the sense that they are at variance as far as their directional properties are concerned: One favors one hypothesis, and the other favors another hypothesis. But this is also a property of contradictory evidence, since a report of E may favor one hypothesis and a report of E^c may favor another. What separates conflicting and contradictory evidence is the fact that the events reported in the conflicting case may *both* have happened. As we observed, the events reported in contradictory evidence cannot have occurred jointly.

As an example of evidential conflict, suppose that H in Figure 3.13*b* represents the hypothesis that patient P will survive a particular form of open-heart surgery, and H^c represents the hypothesis that P will not survive this surgery. Two classes of diagnostic events $\mathbf{F} = \{F, F^c\}$ and $\mathbf{G} = \{G, G^c\}$ are considered for this patient. Suppose that F is the event that a patient is less than forty years of age and that G is the event that a patient has had previous heart surgery. The evidence we have is F^*, that patient P is less than forty years old, and G^*, that he has had previous heart surgery. On the basis of past experience suppose that it is known that the occurrence of F points inferentially to H and that the occurrence of G points inferentially toward H^c. Now it is certainly possible for a patient to be less than forty years of age and also to have had previous heart surgery (there is conflict here but no contradiction). As another example, suppose that S is a suspect in an investigation of a robbery of a convenience store. We have discovered evidence that S had the opportunity to commit this crime; he was observed running away from this convenience store just moments after the robbery took place. We suppose that this evidence favors S's guilt. But we also have evidence that S has no record of prior misbehavior of any kind; we suppose that this favors his innocence.

These two examples of evidential conflict allow us to observe another distinction between contradictory and conflicting evidence. In either case we have the task of attempting to resolve the evidential dissonance each reveals. In the case of contradiction the only resolution possible involves the credibility of the sources of our evidence. The reason is that we cannot have E occurring and not occurring at the same time (or, more generally, we cannot have mutually exclusive events happening together). But resolving evidential conflict may be considerably more complicated. It may be possible to resolve conflict with reference to the credibility of our sources. Perhaps patient P lied about his age, or perhaps the witness was inaccurate in her identification of suspect S in the robbery investigation. Other explanations are also possible. In our heart surgery example a more detailed analysis of our evidence may reveal that the conflict we perceived can be explained away on other grounds.

In my example so far I have considered F_1^* and G_2^* *separately* and said that one favored H and the other H^c. A more detailed analysis may show that the *joint occurrence* of these two evidence items may favor one of these states over the other. It may happen, for example, that patient age and prior surgery as diagnostic variables are *not independent* in their effects upon H and H^c. In the robbery example S's running away from the convenience store might easily be explained away by other evidence we have suggesting that S, as well as others, were fleeing the scene to avoid being molested by the person who actually committed the robbery.

In some works the terms *contradiction* and *conflict* are frequently used synonymously with reference to evidential dissonance. For example, in his discussion of the "embarrassment" of evidential dissonance, Shafer (1976, 223) notes, in connection with a discussion of his formal system for grading evidential support:

> . . . one might be tempted to argue that degrees of support based on evidence *ought* to be consonant—that dissonance is always a symptom of some mistake in assessing the evidence, and that such mistakes call for immediate correction. After all, if two items of evidence contradict each other, must not one of them be wrong?

As just mentioned, not all dissonant evidence is contradictory, as Shafer seems to imply. Contradictions require attention to source credibility. Conflicting evidence requires attention to source credibility as well as to our interpretations of the events being reported. What to do about evidential dissonance is a vexing problem for philosophers (e.g., see Levi 1980, 14–15). The trouble is that on certain views of probability we are permitted to assign positive belief to incompatible hypotheses when evidence is contradictory or conflicting. This troubles some persons more than it does others, as we will discuss in Section 8.1

3.5.2 Harmonious Evidence: Corroboration and Convergence

Certain evidence items taken in combination are harmonious in the sense that they are directionally consistent as far as the possibilities they favor. Two important kinds of evidential harmony can be discerned; they are illustrated in Figure 3.14. The first kind, called *corroborative evidence,* has two meanings as illustrated by the two cases in Figure 3.14a. One form of corroborative evidence exists when two or more sources, human or otherwise, report the occurrence of the same event. In case 1 in this figure two sources report E*, that event E occurred. But the word corroborative is used in another sense illustrated in case 2 of Figure 3.14a. In this case one source reports E*, that event E occurred, and another source provides ancillary evidence favorable to the credibility of the source reporting E*.

The fact that evidence is corroborative in either case does not mean we should be any less concerned about source credibility than we are in the case of dissonant evidence. Suppose that E_1^* and E_2^* are testimonial assertions from two persons. It is quite conceivable that either one is lying, unobjective, or observationally insensitive. It is also possible that the two sources have not given independent testimony; perhaps one source influenced the other in some way. Officer Connolly's testimony about Sacco was corroborated by another

Corroboration

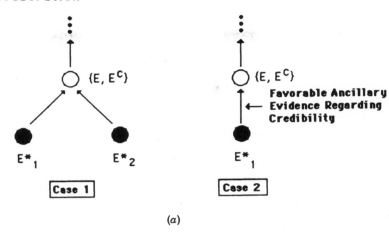

Case 1   Case 2

(a)

Convergence [With Possible Enhancement]

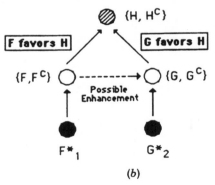

(b)

FIGURE 3.14 Consonant evidence. (a) Two forms of corroborative evidence. (b) Convergent evidence.

police officer named Merle A. Spear who reported the same events as Connolly. There is evidence that Spear gave quite different evidence before the trial but changed his testimony so that it would agree with Connolly's account (Young and Kaiser 1985). In case 2 in Figure 3.14a either the source giving evidence E* or the source of the ancillary evidence may have assorted credibility defects.

Figure 3.14b illustrates another way in which evidence can be harmonious. In this case two or more sources provide evidence of *different* events, all of which favor the same possibility. Such evidence is said to be *convergent*. In the abstract example in this figure, one source reports F*, that event F occurred, and another source reports G*, that event G occurred. Suppose our belief is that both events F and G favor H over H^c. Convergent evidence is quite interesting because, on careful analysis, we have to consider the possibility that two or more items of convergent evidence may mean more to us, when considered jointly, than they do if we considered them separately. One way to illustrate this situation is by means of the dashed line connecting {F, F^c} and {G, G^c}. It may happen, for example, that event F, if it occurred, would *enhance* the inferential force of event G on hypotheses {H, H^c}. If we examined G_2^* by itself, we might assign less force to it than if we recalled having evidence F_1^*, about event F. We might say in such cases that items of evidence can be *synergistic* in their inferential effects on hypotheses being considered. In Section 8.2.2 we will discuss ways of capturing this synergism in terms of the probabilistic concept of *conditional nonindependence*.

Finally, when we examine the task of assessing the inferential force of these recurrent combinations of evidence (Chapter 8), we will observe that corroboration and contradiction are two sides of one "inferential coin"; conflicting and converging evidence are two sides of another. On one view of the force of evidence we will be able to observe quite interesting formal similarities between the two sides of each of these "coins."

3.5.3 Two Species of Evidential Redundancy

In the evidential synergism we have just discussed one item of evidence can act to *enhance* the inferential force of another. We have also to consider situations in which one item of evidence may seem to *diminish* the value of another item. In such cases we might say that the second of these two items of evidence seems *inferentially redundant* to some degree, given the first item. Common synonyms for the word redundant are repetitious, superfluous, extra, and excess. The term *redundance* is used in a variety of situations. In designing a system an engineer may incorporate redundant subsystems that serve as backups; if one subsystem fails another takes over. In the field of communications theory the concept of redundance plays a very important role (e.g., Shannon and Weaver 1963, 13–14; Pierce 1961, 149–150, 164–165). The capacity of a communication system is linked to the redundance of messages sent via this system. Suppose that the same message is repeated over and over again on some communication channel. Each repetition of this message has lower information value and takes up transmission time that could be used for more informative messages. Thus redundancy acts to reduce the effective channel capacity of a transmission system. On the other hand, some message redundancy is necessary to increase the reliability of messages transmitted over "noisy" channels; there are various ways in which redundancy can be used in an effective manner (Singh 1966, 39–58).

We also discover that human languages are quite redundant for several reasons. In the English language, for example, words are constructed from twenty-six characters. There are less than half a million words in the English language; this number is minute relative to the number of words that might be formed using these twenty-six characters, even if we restricted word length to a relatively small number of characters. As an example, if our language contained all possible character orderings then the following three-letter sequences would be words: ZEJ, ZOJ, ZQZ. The fact that all possible character combinations are not used adds redundance and offers protection against communication error. The redundance of our language allows us to correct misspelled words. In reading this text, if you encountered the term "evidenxe" you would correctly infer that this symbol sequence "evidenxe" is the word "evidence" misspelled, since there is no word "evidenxe" in our language. Another source of language redundance involves the fact that there are sequential dependencies that exist among the letters in words and also among the words in sentences. In communication theory the redundance of transmissions can be measured in various ways, none of which is completely satisfactory (Staniland 1961, 21–22). However, in Section 8.4 we will be able to borrow from communication theory a measure of redundance that provides considerable insight into problems we encounter in grading the inferential redundance of evidence.

Redundance seems to be a mixed blessing. Having backup subsystems costs money but increases reliability. Redundance in communications systems reduces channel capacity but guards against errors. Applying the concept of redundance to evidence, we observe the same mixed blessing. As we will now observe, redundant evidence provides verification, but such evidence can be overvalued or "double-counted." There seem to be two basic ways in which two or more items of evidence can be inferentially redundant. Figure 3.15*a* illustrates a situation in which two sources or sensors report the occurrence of the same event. In other words, they provide the corroborative evidence discussed in Section 3.5.2 and illustrated in Figure 3.14*a*, case 1. Corroborative evidence of this sort involves repetition and is therefore potentially redundant. For this reason we label this species of redundance *corroborative*. In the left-hand diagram of Figure 3.15*a* we have two sources reporting the occurrence of the same event E. So the question arises, Does the second report of E have any inferential force, given our receipt of the first report? The answer of course depends upon the credibility of *both* sources. If we believe the first source to be perfectly credible, we would have conclusive evidence that E occurred, in which case the second report would tell us nothing new and would be inferentially valueless. Suppose, however, that we have reason to doubt the credibility of the first source. Then the second source's report of E can have inferential value to the extent that the second source is credible.

The left-hand diagram in Figure 3.15*a* shows a situation in which event E, as reported by two sources, is relevant in an inference regarding hypotheses {H, H^c}. In Section 8.4.3 we will discuss a formal way of showing how there is a "well" of inferential force on {H, H^c} associated with event E. How much of the force in this well we can draw out, as a result of hearing about E from the first source, depends upon this source's credibility. If the first source is perfectly credible, we draw all of the force out of this well, and there is

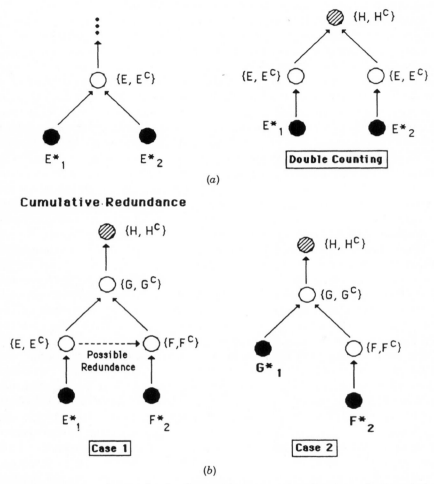

FIGURE 3.15 Two forms of redundant evidence. (a) Corroborative. (b) Cumulative.

nothing remaining to apply to the second report of E. In this situation the second report is completely redundant and has no inferential force. But, to the extent that the first source is not completely credible, there is inferential force remaining in this well, which we could then apply to the second report of event E depending upon the credibility of the second source. In such cases the second report is only partially redundant depending upon the credibility of the both sources. The same idea extends to the general case in which we might have corroborative reports about the same event from some number *n* of sources. There are additional subtleties in corroborative evidence to be discussed in Section 8.4.3 that are associated with the possibility of inferentially interesting behavior on the part of our sources.

When we hear about the same event from two or more sources, there is always a danger that we will assign more inferential force to these reports than they may deserve. In legal contexts such behavior is called *double counting* (Lempert 1977). Shown in the right-hand diagram of Figure 3.15a is an illustration of double counting. In this situation we have two sources reporting the occurrence of the *same* event E. Double counting amounts to a belief that the report from each source involves a different event E, each having its own "well" of inferential force. But this is inappropriate, since there is just one event E and just one "well" of inferential force. As an example of corroborative redundancy, suppose that your child's face looks flushed, her forehead feels warm, and your thermometer shows that her body temperature is 102 degrees Fahrenheit. Here we have three different sensors telling you the same thing, your child has a fever. Having a fever may have a certain well of inferential force on various possible illnesses your child might have. If you double-counted this evidence, as illustrated in Figure 3.15a, you would be supposing that each of these three sensor reports has its own well of inferential force on these possible illnesses.

Evidence can be redundant, or at least partially so, without being repetitious. Figure 3.15b shows two examples of what I have termed *cumulative redundance*. I have borrowed the term *cumulative* from our colleagues in law (e.g., Lempert 1977). Generally this term is used with reference to evidence that does not seem to add anything to evidence already provided. It forms one ground for objecting to the admissibility of evidence. Such objection is based upon the possibility that jurors may overvalue cumulative evidence. As an example, first consider case 1 and suppose the following events in a murder investigation: H = Mary did it, G = Mary was at the scene of the murder, E = Mary's fingerprints are on a table in the room where the murder was committed, and F = Mary's fingerprints are on a chair in the room where the murder was committed. Suppose we receive evidence E* and F* about events E and F. Notice that E and F are *different* events. On an inference about whether Mary was at the scene of the murder {G, G^c}, event F, if true, would not add much to what we would already know if we already believed E to be true. If we found Mary's fingerprints in one part of the room, it seems quite likely that we would find her fingerprints in another part of this room. So, as the dashed line in case 1 of Figure 3.15b indicates, the occurrence of event E acts to diminish the inferential force of event F or, in other words, to make event F inferentially redundant to some degree. It is true that all we have is evidence E* and F*, perhaps obtained from an FBI lab. It is possible that either or both of these fingerprints were wrongly associated with Mary. How redundant is F*, given that we already know about E*, depends in part upon the credibility of both items of evidence.

Case 2 in Figure 3.15b shows another example of cumulative redundance. Again, suppose that H = Mary did it, and G = Mary was at the scene of the murder. But in this case we let F = Mary's car was at the scene of the murder at the time it was committed. Suppose that we have a witness Robert who asserts G^*, that he saw Mary at the scene of the murder. Then comes Harriet who asserts F^*, that she saw Mary's car at the scene of the murder at the time it was committed. Is Harriet's assertion redundant, given Robert's assertion? Unless Mary's car being at the scene had some significance on its own, we would have to say that, if we believed Robert's testimony that Mary was at the scene of the murder, then discovering that Mary's car was at the scene of the murder does not tell us very much in addition to what we already know. In other words, if Mary were at the scene (G), this makes her car being there (F) quite probable whether or not Mary actually committed the crime. How redundant Harriet's assertion F^* is depends in part upon how credible Robert seems. Suppose, for example, we have evidence suggesting that Robert has very poor eyesight; perhaps he did not observe Mary after all. In this case Harriet's assertion may be nonredundant to some degree. In Section 8.4.4 we will be able to give a rather thorough account of the variety of factors that influence the degree of redundance in situations that are illustrated in Figure 3.15b.

We have now attended to various structural matters associated with the task of establishing the relevance and credibility credentials of evidence. We have also considered a variety of purely structural matters of importance in the study of various identifiable forms and combinations of evidence. The trouble is that the complex inference tasks we routinely encounter involve mixtures of the forms and combinations of evidence we have examined. Establishing the relevance and credibility credentials of a mass of evidence is no easy task. We must now turn our attention to additional structural matters that arise when we face the task of trying to make sense out of an existing mass of evidence or the task of determining the structure of an inference problem that we believe will involve many complex and interrelated arguments.

Chapter **4**

Structural Issues II: Inferences Based Upon a Mass of Evidence

The structural matters we considered in Chapter 3 are helpful in identifying recurrent forms and combinations of evidence. But we have only examined these evidential forms and combinations in isolation and have not yet considered situations in which we may encounter *mixtures* of them. To set the stage for the major topics in Chapter 4, we begin by considering inferences in which we may need to construct several or many lines of argument based upon a mass of evidence in which there are mixtures of these recurrent forms and combinations. We will also observe that the structuring of an inference problem need not always proceed from evidence to major or final hypotheses. In some situations we may be able to construct a model of an inference problem before we gather any evidence. In constructing these models, we will often find it necessary to reason from hypotheses to possible evidence. The models we construct may contain many elements whose probability, based upon various patterns of evidence, may be of interest to us. In such cases it is often not even possible to specify what we regard as major, ultimate, or final hypotheses.

In this chapter I will introduce a language appropriate for describing a structured inference as an *inferential network*. In his *Dictionary of the English Language* (1773, 4th ed.) Samuel Johnson defined a *network* as: "Any thing reticulated or decussated, at equal distances, with interstices between the intersections." The networks of interest to us have particular properties. But it seems unlikely that current definitions of a network will become quite so famous as Johnson's description.

4.1 MIXTURES OF EVIDENTIAL FORMS, COMBINATIONS, AND SUBTLETIES

Figure 4.1 illustrates the kinds of situations we may often encounter when we attempt to draw a conclusion from a mass of evidence. This figure shows how some of the evidential forms and combinations we have identified may be embedded in others. It also represents a case in which we may have multiple lines of argument on some collection of major, ultimate, or final hypotheses of interest. There are two kinds of symbols in this figure which we will identify as *nodes* (represented by the circles) and *arcs* (represented by lines with arrows).

There are three varieties of nodes in this figure. Filled circles represent evidence (e.g., B*), open circles represent interim possibilities or hypotheses, and the cross-hatched circle represents major, ultimate, or final hypotheses. Notice that the nodes representing either interim or major hypotheses are labeled with a bold letter. A bold letter represents an exhaustive class of mutually exclusive possibilities or hypotheses. To make matters simple, suppose that each of the bold letters in this figure identifies a binary class of hypothetical events or propositions. For example, $\mathbf{H} = \{H, H^c\}$ represents a major or ultimate hypothesis H and its logical complement H^c. Nodes $\mathbf{A_1} =$

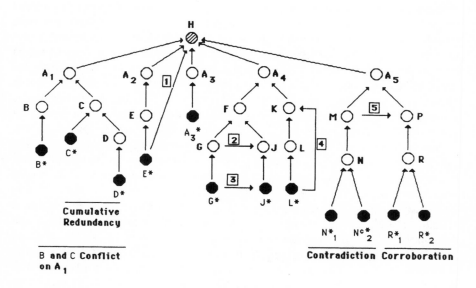

FIGURE 4.1 An example of embedded evidential subtleties in an inference network.

$\{A_1, A_1^c\}$ through $A_5 = \{A_5, A_5^c\}$ represent classes of events or propositions that bear a direct probabilistic relation to hypotheses in **H**. We can also say that these five nodes are *adjacent* to **H**. Class **B** = $\{B, B^c\}$ represents the occurrence or nonoccurrence of B. Evidence nodes allow us to preserve the distinction between evidence of an event and the event itself. Thus, for example, from some source we have received evidence B^* that node **B** is in state B; in simpler terms, B^* is evidence that event B occurred. In Figure 4.1 the arcs or arrows represent a probabilistic linkage and, in this example, also show the direction of our inference. We suppose, for example, that evidence B^* has some probability under either B or B^c; in other words, B^* is inconclusive evidence of event B.

In Figure 4.1 we have a collection of twelve evidence items, subsets of which are linked by argument to one of the **A** event classes. For example, evidence items B^*, C^*, and D^* are linked to A_1. Notice that evidence E^* is linked through **E** to A_2 but is also linked directly to **H**; I will explain the significance of this double linkage momentarily. One way to view the evidential situation in Figure 4.1 is to say that we have five lines of argument, each identified by an **A** event class, that bear upon hypotheses **H**. So, for example, we might say that we have evidence B^*, C^*, and D^* bearing upon line of argument A_1. It is frequently useful to identify an argument in terms of the event class at the node in an argument that is most directly linked or is adjacent to one's major hypotheses. For example, in an inference in a legal matter **H** might represent whether a person is guilty of first-degree murder. Event classes $A_1 = \{A_1, A_1^c\}$ through $A_5 = \{A_5, A_5^c\}$ might indicate points or elements that the prosecution has to prove at trial in order to sustain this charge. Thus $A_1 = \{A_1, A_1^c\}$ might indicate whether or not this person intended to kill the victim; $A_2 = \{A_2, A_2^c\}$ might indicate whether or not this person fashioned this intention beforehand (the killing was premeditated). So we might identify, by means of A_1 and A_2, an intention argument and a premeditation argument.

Suppose, for the moment, we believe that A_1 is in state A_1 and that A_2 is in state A_2; in other words, we believe events A_1 and A_2 have occurred. These two events might not favor the same hypothesis in **H**. For example, A_1 might favor H and A_2 favor H^c. For a start we might have a situation in which events at different nodes adjacent to **H** are themselves conflicting, some of these events favor H and others favor H^c. Next observe that in only one case have we been able to obtain evidence about one of these **A** event classes directly: There is evidence A_3^* that event A_3 occurred or is true. The rest of the evidence concerns events from which one of states of any **A** event class are *indirectly* inferred. For example, whether A_4 is in state A_4 or in state A_4^c is indirectly inferred from evidence G^*, J^*, and L^*. The twelve items of evidence depicted in Figure 4.1 can be of any sort we discussed. For example, they may be various items of *tangible* or *testimonial* evidence. To simplify this figure, I have only shown items of evidence that are *directly relevant* on hypotheses **H**. Each of the twelve items of evidence in this figure is connected by specific argument to **H**. Not shown in this figure is any of the *ancillary evidence* we might also have that either supports or weakens any of the inferential linkages illustrated. How we should best chart ancillary evidence may be controversial, as noted later in Section 4.5.4.

Figure 4.1 also illustrates the manner in which various evidential combinations and subtleties can be embedded in others. First, suppose that events A_1 and A_2 are conflicting in the manner noted above. Now consider node A_1, and notice that we have two lines of reasoning on this event class involving events at nodes **B** and **C**. We have evidence B*, that B occurred, and C*, that C occurred. It may be the case that B and C *conflict* in their inferential implications on A_1. For example, suppose that B favors the occurrence of A_1 and that C favors its nonoccurrence A_1^c. We now have the conflict involving B and C embedded in the conflict involving events A_1 and A_2. But we also notice another subtlety here. We have *direct* evidence C* about event C and also evidence D* that can only be *circumstantial* evidence of C. If we believe the source reporting C*, that C occurred, then the evidence D* would be to some degree *cumulatively redundant* in the manner discussed in Section 3.5.3.

We have circumstantial evidence E* linked to A_2 through node **E**. But E* has another linkage with **H** (in the manner described in Figure 3.4*b*). Another example of an "extra" linkage in Figure 4.1 involves evidence L* being linked to node **K** as well as to node **L**. Such extra linkages are quite important because they allow us to capture the fact that the credibility of a source of evidence may be dependent upon events other than those reported in the evidence. Such *state-dependent* credibility, as we will later describe it, can be an important source of additional inferential force. As noted earlier, information we have about a source of evidence can often be as valuable as the information the source reports.

Some rather complex arguments link evidence G*, J*, and L* to node A_4. Events in nodes **G** and **J** may be either *synergistic* or *cumulatively redundant* in the manner discussed in Sections 3.5.2 and 3.5.3. For example, we might believe that event J has more/less inferential force if we also knew that G was true. In addition we depict a linkage between evidence items G* and J*. By this linkage we simply indicate that these two items of evidence may not have been independently given. Various possible interactions among sources of evidence, if recognized, are also potential origins of additional evidential force. Finally, there are two lines of argument on node A_5, one involving node **M** and another involving node **P**. It may be that these two lines of argument are not independent; perhaps events M and P are either synergistic or redundant. The argument involving **M** is based upon *contradictory* evidence about the state of node **N**. The argument involving **P** is based upon *corroborative* and possibly redundant evidence about events in node **R**.

Figure 4.1 illustrates just some of the evidential situations we encounter as we carefully analyze a mass of evidence in order to determine what we believe is its bearing upon major hypotheses of interest to us. The mass of evidence and the arguments illustrated by this figure now begin to resemble an *inference network*. In Sections 4.4 and 4.5 we will consider scholarship from several different disciplines that concerns both the construction and the application of inference networks. We now examine different ways in which inference problems, requiring various structural approaches, might come into existence.

4.2 STRUCTURING AND STANDPOINT

There are at least two reasons why this is an exciting time to have an interest in probabilistic reasoning. For the first time in the long past (but short history) of probability we have well-articulated *alternative* views about how we should draw conclusions from incomplete and inconclusive evidence. We introduced some of these alternative views in Section 2.3 and will consider them in more detail in Chapter 5. Another cause for excitement is that there are more disciplines involved in research on probabilistic reasoning than ever before. In some cases persons in one discipline may be quite innocent of advancements that have taken place in others. This is to be expected, since the literature on probabilistic reasoning is now so vast. Each discipline brings new perspectives and methods to the study and performance of probabilistic inference. Persons employing new methods and procedures in one discipline may believe the ones employed in others to be uncommonly strange. For example, there may now be some readers wondering why I have drawn all of my inference-related diagrams with the arrows pointing in the "wrong" direction. In some current works I will mention it is customary to structure inference from hypotheses to evidence and not the other way around as I have done.

In discussing the concept of evidential relevance in Section 3.1.2, I mentioned the importance of declaring one's standpoint along lines suggested by Anderson and Twining (1991). The same ideas regarding standpoint are of importance in the structuring of an inference problem and in a choice of methods for drawing a conclusion from available evidence. A defense of any conclusion drawn from some mass of evidence inevitably involves the standpoint questions: (1) Who am I (i.e., what "hat" am I wearing)? (2) At what stage in what process am I? (3) What am I trying to do? My belief is that attention to issues raised by such questions gives us better hope of understanding and integrating scholarship from different disciplines on complex probabilistic inferences we so frequently encounter. Persons in different disciplines have different standpoints and have adopted different approaches to the structuring and performance of probabilistic inference. Following are three matters bearing upon one's standpoint that allow us to obtain a greater appreciation for the different forms of inference structuring now in existence.

4.2.1 Cycles of Discovery, Inference, and Choice

Only in classroom illustrations do inference problems emerge in well-posed form in which hypotheses as well as relevant evidential tests of them are known or given. In natural settings hypotheses, evidence, and the arguments that link them have to be generated or discovered. At some stage a conclusion is required, so we have to marshal our thoughts and our evidence in order to draw a conclusion. In many situations the process of inference is embedded in the further process of choice in which various actions are contemplated. Each possible action has certain consequences whose value we might assess in various ways. One trouble is that persons having different disciplinary interests and objectives will experience different cycles of these three activities: *discovery, inference,* and *choice;* the following are some examples:

In another work I mentioned that our Anglo-American judicial system offers the only instance known to me in which discovery, inference, and choice generally proceed in this particular sequence (Schum 1986). Advocates for either side in a dispute gather evidence on their own and from each other, if they can, *before* a trial or some other form of settlement commences. Although there are exceptions in which new evidence is generated at trial (exaggerated in *Perry Mason* episodes on television), both sides are usually content if discovery is completed before a trial commences, thus reducing the chances of an unpleasant surprise. Members of a fact-finding body are then involved in the inferential activity of assessing the relative merits of the evidence and arguments as presented by each side. There is then an episode in which the fact finders deliberate upon the evidence and arguments and render a decision or verdict. Such decisions can of course be challenged and appeals made to higher courts, but these challenges are usually based upon alleged procedural or other trial irregularities. An advocate cannot challenge a verdict simply because she does not agree with it.

Now consider a medical situation in which you, the patient, consult one or more physicians in the hope of correcting a complaint you now have about your physical condition. You would first assume, and hope, that the physicians' discovery processes do not terminate at some specified point other than the one at which they finally determine the cause of your complaint. Unless your health insurance is adequate, you may of course run out of money before the cause of your complaint is discovered. Ceaseless discovery takes place in contexts such as science, engineering, business, and historical research. In medicine and in other contexts entire sequences of decisions are required, each resting upon new evidence and additional inferences. Your physician may have to try out several different remedies before one is found that removes the cause of your complaint, or at least provides you with some relief from the unpleasant symptoms you may experience. Sequences of inferences and decisions are also required in business and in other contexts.

In some situations the process of probabilistic inference may be an end in itself as far as knowledge acquisition is concerned. Consider the historian engaged in the study of a pattern of past events or the cosmologist studying the makeup and origin of the universe. Evidence-based conclusions in either of these areas have importance on their own even if they are not necessarily embedded in specific choices. No choice now made by an historian can affect the course of events that led to the signing of *Magna Carta* by Prince John in 1215; nor can any choice made by the cosmologist change how the universe will continue to evolve. It can be argued of course that the historian and the cosmologist do have choices that result from their inferential activities such as whether to engage in further investigations in some area, whether to publish results, or whether to seek additional grant support. The point is simply that probabilistic inference is often an end in itself. Analyses now being made of the evidence in the Sacco and Vanzetti case are obviously too late to be of any use to these two persons. But they are of interest in studies of the conduct of trials and the process of drawing conclusions from a mass of evidence.

So it seems natural that persons experiencing different cycles of discovery, inference, and choice may view their inferential activities in different ways and adopt different methods for drawing conclusions from evidence. Such standpoint-related matters also affect how well any new methods for assistance in probabilistic inference will be received. We will return to cycles of discovery, inference, and choice again in Chapter 9 when we consider discovery-related activities in more detail.

4.2.2 Recurrent and Nonrecurrent Inferences

The fact that there are recurrent forms and combinations of evidence may lead us to believe that there are also recurrent inferences having virtually identical structural properties. If this were so, we could invest in the development of structural "templates" that could be used repeatedly in appropriate circumstances. I admit to having some ambivalence regarding the existence of inferences for which such templates might be constructed. On the one hand, I believe that all inference tasks we perform have unique elements. At the same time, I also believe that there are certain classes of recurrent inference tasks having many common elements; some of these tasks will be mentioned in Section 4.5.

The structuring of any inference problem requires time and effort. The willingness of a person or organization to expend resources on a detailed structuring of an inference is related in part to the number of occasions on which this same (or nearly the same) inference will be required. There are recurrent inferential problems in areas such as medicine, business, and weather forecasting in which it makes sense to engage in extensive structrual and related exercises. The payoff for such exercises can be some form of computer assistance in the performance of a recurrent inference task. Some methods of assistance come in the form of *expert* or *knowledge-based* systems. For very complex inference tasks users of these systems bear several burdens, only some of which are structural in nature. Even if a structure for some recurrent inference can be decided, there is still the burden of obtaining many probabilistic assessments from persons having the requisite knowledge and background for such assessments. An additional burden appears in the development of efficient algorithms for the synthesis of these probabilistic assessments necessary in order to draw a conclusion.

In the past few years there has been significant progress in developing the structural and algorithmic requirements for various computer-based systems for assistance in complex inference tasks. Some expert systems have been designed for complex and recurrent inferences. But there are now computer-based systems available for use in situations in which inferences may be unique or nonrecurrent, provided that they are not too complex. Such methods rest upon the important concept of an *influence diagram*, introduced by Howard and Matheson (1984). Systems based upon the use of influence diagrams have the added advantage of offering convenient ways for combining the activities of inference and choice. Persons developing these systems have found it necessary to devise structural mechanisms that are congenial to the needs of users having many different objectives. In Section 4.5 we will discuss various structural elements of current work on expert systems and influence diagrams.

4.2.3 Divide and Conquer: Levels of Inference Decomposition

At several points I have noted that chains of reasoning in an inference task can be decomposed to various levels of "granularity." The level of inference decomposition a person identifies depends upon her knowledge, constraints, and objectives. In other words, a person's present standpoint in an inference task governs, at least to some extent, how minutely this person will examine possible sources of uncertainty that may affect the credibility, relevance, and force of evidence. Existing computer-based methods for assisting people in the performance of inference and choice tasks all rest upon a strategy we may call *divide and conquer*. Difficult inference and choice tasks are decomposed into a number of elements. For example, we decomposed an inference from Officer Connolly's testimony to a major hypothesis in the Sacco and Vanzetti case (Figures 3.5 and 3.9). For some difficult inference based upon a mass of evidence the presumption underlying the divide-and-conquer strategy is that it is less difficult to make probabilistic judgments about the decomposed elements of an inference than it is to make an overall or *holistic* judgment based on the entire mass of evidence. In the decomposition process we identify what we believe to be major sources of uncertainty in an inference task. These uncertainties are assessed separately and then combined according to some algorithm we believe to be appropriate. By such means a person is at least relieved of the burden of combining uncertainty from many sources.

Over two centuries ago Samuel Johnson commented upon this strategy. In his *Rambler* No. 137 of July 9, 1751 (Yale ed., vol. 4, 1969, 361), Johnson noted:

> Divide and conquer is a principle equally just in science as in policy. Complication is a species of confederacy, which, while it continues united, bids defiance

to the most active and vigorous intellect; but of which every member is separately weak, and which may therefore be quickly subdued if it can once be broken.

Apparently Johnson was somewhat uncertain about the general suitability of divide and conquer strategies, since he also noted in his *Rambler* No. 43 for August 14, 1750 (Yale ed., vol. 3, 1969, 236):

There is, indeed, some danger lest he that too scrupulously balances proba bilities, and too perspicaciously foresees obstacles, should always remain in a state of inaction.

When computer-based divide and conquer strategies for inference were first proposed over thirty years ago (Edwards 1962), there was scant realization of the very large number of probabilistic ingredients often revealed in the decomposition of even "simple" inferences. In some cases the assessment of all recognized probabilities would amount to inferential paralysis. One trouble was that none of us involved in this research had yet read Wigmore's work on methods for the analysis and synthesis of complex masses of evidence. Wigmore was certainly aware of the number of ingredients that can be discerned in a decomposition of inference, as we will discuss in Section 4.4. But there are other difficulties in divide and conquer strategies for inference quite apart from the number of probabilistic assessments that are required. Some decomposed probabilistic assessments may be exceedingly difficult, since they require us to consider unfamiliar distinctions involving the evidence we have and how it is linked to other elements revealed in the decomposition of an inference.

In some cases various objectives and constraints may force us to settle for a level of task decomposition that overlooks certain evidential distinctions and suppresses uncertainties we know exist. Such "coarse" decomposition may still be preferable to holistic inference, since we may have no idea how many sources of uncertainty a person may have suppressed in the process of making holistic or global judgments. There is now a significant literature on the uses and limitations of both decomposed and holistic inference (e.g., Twining 1990, 238–242).

4.2.4 A Standpoint for the Study of Evidence

Since the early 1960s I have adhered quite obstinately to a research agenda whose major item involves examining evidence under a conceptual "microscope" consisting of both structural and probabilistic elements. As a student of evidence and its many important but often-inconspicuous properties, I have adopted a certain standpoint that has influenced the manner in which I tend to structure inferences in which various evidential properties and subtleties might be revealed. Since we will shortly consider the work of persons having other agenda and standpoints, I should attempt to clarify my own standpoint as far as it concerns the analyses of evidence I will present in this discourse.

In Section 2.4 I mentioned how much I have been influenced by the work of scholars of evidence in jurisprudence, particularly the work of Wigmore and his contemporary advocates Terry Anderson, Peter Tillers, and William Twining. I have already noted how answers to the following two questions provide a basis for studying various recurrent forms and combinations of evidence: How does the user of an item of evidence stand in relation to it? How does the evidence stand in relation to matters about which conclusions are to be drawn? With a focus upon these two questions it is quite natural to consider inference structures that proceed directionally *from evidence to hypotheses*. All of Wigmore's analyses of evidence, some of which we will consider in Section 4.4, are structured directionally from evidence to major hypotheses. All of the inferential diagrams I have presented so far have this same directional property.

But probabilistic inference can in fact be *bidirectional*. It is just as natural to inquire about the probability of evidence E*, assuming hypothesis H, as it is to inquire about the probability of hypothesis H, in light of evidence E*. Different directional construals of an inference suit different purposes. Chapters 5 through 8 contain a variety of probabilistic analyses of the various forms and combinations of evidence we have considered. All of these analyses rest upon expressions for grading the *inferential force* of evidence. It is by means of such analyses that the true richness of evidence can be observed. All the diagrams I will use to illustrate these analyses will exhibit an inferential direction from evidence to hypotheses. Though such diagrams will violate some current conventions for structuring evidence-hypotheses relations in inference networks, I will carefully describe the purpose of my structural analyses in order to prevent confusion on the part of readers who may be familiar with other current work in this area. Despite of structural differences there are no inconsistencies between the analyses I present and those using other structural procedures.

4.3   RELEVANCE AND CAUSALITY

The evidence and hypotheses in any inference task refer to events that occur at various times. So it is natural for us to examine instances in which we might say that one event somehow brings about or causes the occurrence of another event. Here we encounter another concept that has been the subject of endless controversy, What does it mean to say that event A *causes* event B? There are no simple answers to this question; issues raised in attempts to answer it cannot be dismissed in any account of the role of evidence in probabilistic reasoning. I believe there are at least four related reasons why the topic of causality is important in this discourse on evidence and why discussion of it can best be introduced in terms of the structural matters we are now considering.

I argued in Section 3.1.1 that evidence is relevant if it allows us to revise our beliefs about the likeliness of any existing hypothesis or if it allows us to revise one or more existing hypotheses or to generate entirely new ones. Attempts to justify the relevance of evidence involve constructing chains of reasoning between evidence and hypotheses. Recall that no item of evidence comes to us with already-established relevance "credentials." In many inference tasks the hypotheses under consideration represent possible causes for various patterns of observable effects. In such cases we may be able to trace what we regard as a causal linkage from some ultimate or major hypothesis to events or effects that are observable. If such linkage can be established, evidence of these effects would be relevant in an inference about these hypothesized causes. But there are many instances in which evidence can be justified as relevant on hypotheses of interest when links in a chain of reasoning may indicate no causal connection. A careful examination of the relationship between relevance and causality is an important part of any discourse on evidence.

Describing the connection between causality and probability is a difficult and interesting task. As we will discuss at greater length, it is often necessary to consider causation in probabilistic terms. I might be willing to say that my use of an insecticide has caused the death of the insects I now see prostrate in my flower pot, believing all the while that there is some probability they have expired for other reasons. The insecticide might not work all the time; some insects might have overeaten or died of old age. The connection between causality and *probabilistic dependence* is one that deserves careful attention. Consider Figure 4.2, and note that it is a copy of Figure 4.1 with two changes made: The evidence nodes have been removed, and the arc directions (arrows) have been reversed. This illustrates how we might have structured this inference problem from the top down in advance of obtaining any evidence. Observe that there are nineteen nodes in this hypothetical inference problem. Also observe the important fact that every node is not linked to every other node. Indeed the distinguishing feature of this structured inference problem is that it prescribes a *specific* pattern of probabilistic dependence among these nodes. For example, we are supposing that the state of node **J** depends, probabilistically, just upon the states of nodes **F** and **G** and not upon the

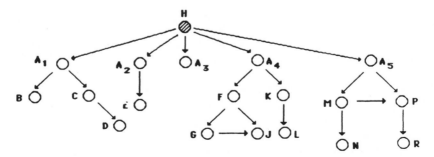

FIGURE 4.2 An inference network illustrating dependency structuring.

states of any other node. In short, we suppose that every node in this inference problem is not connected to every other node. We would experience quite an inferential nightmare if we believed that the state of every node in this figure was influenced by the states of every other node. We will discuss instances in which there is some basis for introducing a causal element in the structuring of an inference problem. We might, for example, be willing to assert that if node A_1 is in state A_1, this would cause node **C** to be in state C which, in turn, would cause node **D** to be in state D. Identifying causal patterns can often simplify complex inferences, but we should not suppose that such identification is a required element of all probabilistic reasoning.

Two other reasons for our present focus on causality concern the very important role of *time* as a factor in assessments of the inferential force of evidence and in the construction of persuasive means for defending conclusions we reach. We expect that there is a definite temporal ordering inherent in any causal relation. If I say that event C caused event E to happen, it would ordinarily be supposed that event C occurred before E. There is, as noted later on, serious discussion about why we should be obliged to suppose that causes always precede their effects. As an illustration of the importance of event ordering, consider the following three events:

A = I left school today preoccupied with thoughts about causality.

B = I ran into the rear end of a car ahead of me in traffic.

C = I had two double scotch whiskeys at a bar.

In any subsequent litigation regarding this matter, I would certainly prefer the event ordering ABC over the ordering ACB. The ordering ABC suggests that my inattention was the probable cause of the accident, about which I later attempted to console myself by means of alcohol. The ordering ACB, however, suggests that my alcohol-impaired performance was the probable cause of the accident, the penalties for which are quite severe. In Section 5.2.1 we will examine the important role of time in assessing the inferential force of evidence.

Finally, suppose we obtain all the evidence shown in Figure 4.1. This figure contains our careful charting of what we believe to be the bearing of this evidence on whether hypothesis H is true. This chart even shows an assortment of evidential subtleties we have recognized. Then, using one of the methods we will discuss in Chapter 5, we assess the inferential force of this evidence on hypotheses $\mathbf{H} = \{H, H^c\}$ and draw the probabilistic conclusion that H is true. We might even supply a specific probabilistic hedge on this conclusion if we perform the necessary calculations. Despite our careful structuring and probabilistic analysis, our efforts may fail to be persuasive for a number of reasons, one of which concerns the fact that graphic structures and probabilistic calculations convey only some of the information one would like to have before accepting the conclusion we have endorsed. In particular, our structural and probabilistic analysis may not, by themselves, *explain why* one should conclude at least tentatively that H is true, based on the evidence we offer. In many contexts it is necessary for us to provide some explanatory account of why the conclusion we endorse should be accepted in preference to others. So we construct stories or scenarios in an effort to explain why the evidence points in one direction rather than in another. There are often distinct temporal and causal elements in such explanations, as we discuss in Section 4.6.

4.3.1 Interpretations of Causality

Here is a sample of ideas drawn from the many extensive and profound works on the topic of causality. Books by J. L. Mackie (1974) and by H. L. A. Hart and T. Honoré (1985) offer particularly valuable and readable assessments of scholarship on causality that extends back at least to the time of Aristotle. The analyses of causality given by Hume in his *Treatise of Human Nature* (1739) and his *Enquiries Concerning Human Understanding* (1777) have been called the most significant and influential single contribution in the study of causation (Mackie 1974, 3). However, Hume gave more than one account of causation, a fact that has vexed scholars interested in this topic. In book I, part III, section XIV of the *Treatise*, Hume first defined a cause to be (1739, Selby-Bigge ed., 1975, 172):

> . . . *an object precedent and contiguous to another, and where all the objects resembling the former are plac'd in a like relation of priority and contiguity to those objects, that resemble the latter; . . . .*

Hume then added that a cause is:

> *An object precedent and contiguous to another, and so united with it in the imagination, that the idea of the one determines the mind to form the idea of the other, and the impression of the one to form a more lively idea of the other; . . . .*

These two definitions have been thought difficult to reconcile, since Hume adds a psychological or behavioral element in the second definition (Mackie 1974, 3). In section VII, part II, of the *Enquiries* Hume gives yet another definition of a cause to be (1777, Nidditch 3d ed., 1989, 76):

> . . . *an object, followed by another, and where all objects similar to the first are followed by objects similar to the second. Or in other words where, if the first had not been, the second had never existed.*

In this third definition we read in a *necessity* requirement, since Hume asserts that an effect will not occur in absence of its cause.

Reduced to essentials Hume's requisites for causality involve the *contiguity* in space and time of cause and effect, the *succession* of effects following causes, and the *necessary connection* between cause and effect. Hume also noted in section IV, part I, of the *Enquiries* that knowledge of cause-effect relations is always the product of experience and that such knowledge can never be obtained by a priori reasoning (1777, Nidditch 3d ed., 1989, 27).

Modern scholars have provided other interpretations of causality and new thoughts about how causal relations may be discerned. Bunge (1979) emphasizes that causes involve relations among events rather than among properties, states, or ideas. Every effect is generated by its cause, causation itself being a form of energy transfer. The causal generation of events is lawful rather than capricious, and although we may say that event C causes event E with a certain probability, strict causality is not stochastic or probabilistic (1979, xix). Interpretations of casuality frequently make reference to conditions of *necessity* and *sufficiency*. At least one person has suggested that it is more useful to talk about necessity and sufficiency than it is to talk about causes and effects (Skyrms 1986, 84–88). The reason is that causality is commonly associated with either, both, or neither of the conditions of necessity and sufficiency. Figure 4.3 illustrates the distinction between these two conditions.

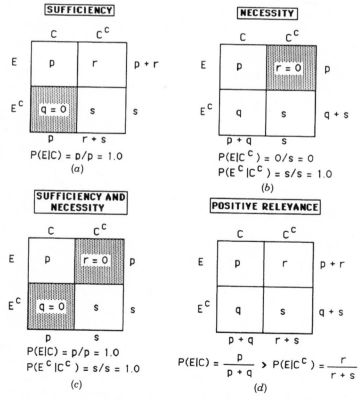

FIGURE 4.3 Causality, relevance, and probabilities.

A probabilistic interpretation of necessity and sufficiency is not only helpful but, on some accounts, necessary. Four probabilities (p, q, r, and s) appear in the four conditions illustrated in Figure 4.3. Let C = cause present and C^c = cause absent; let E = effect present and E^c = effect absent. The probabilities p, q, r, and s refer to the four possible *joint occurrences* of {C, C^c} and {E, E^c}; for example, $p = P(CE)$. Let us suppose that these are conventional probabilities having the requirement that $p + q + r + s = 1.0$. Shown in Figure 4.3*a* is a situation involving what we may term *strict causal sufficiency*. If effect E *must* happen in the presence of cause C, then C is said to be sufficient for causing E. Beyond certain dosage levels the administration of strychnine is sufficient, guaranteed, or certain to cause my death. In a conventional probabilistic sense we can say that a strict condition of causal sufficiency means that the probability of effect E, given cause C, is one; that is $P(E|C) = P(EC)/P(C) = p/p = 1.0$. Conventionally this means that the probability of my not dying, given this requisite doseage of strychnine, $P(E^c|C)$, is zero. As this figure shows, there is nevertheless some probability of my death, given the absence of this requisite doseage of strychnine; this conditional probability is $P(E|C^c) = r/(r + s)$. I may die as a result of any number of other causes.

The condition we may call *strict causal necessity* is illustrated in Figure 4.3*b*. Cause C is said to be a necessary cause of effect E if E cannot happen when C does not happen. Thus oxygen (C) is a necessary cause of combustion (E), since combustion cannot take place in the absence of oxygen; probabilistically $P(E|C^c) = 0/s = 0$. But notice that the presence of oxygen does not guarantee combustion; it is not a sufficient condition, since we may have $P(E^c|C) = q/(p + q) > 0$. Combustion of a substance also requires a sufficiently high temperature. *Strict sufficiency and necessity* together are illustrated in Figure 4.3*c*. In this case the presence of cause C guarantees the occurrence of effect E and the absence of cause C guarantees the nonoccurrence of effect E. Thus, for example, in professional basketball making a one-point free throw or a two-point basket or a three-point basket is both a necessary and sufficient cause of scoring. A team scores if one of these events happens and does not score if one of these events does not happen; probabilistically $P(E|C) = P(E^c|C^c) = 1.0$.

As noted above, Hume emphasized that the discernment of causal connections always rests upon experience; that is, they have to be discovered by empirical means. In his *System of Logic* John Stuart Mill (1853) mentioned five methods for the discovery of causal connections. Thorough and critical analyses of these methods appear in works by Copi (1982, 409–461), Skyrms (1986, 75–114), and L. J. Cohen (1989a, 29–39). As we noted in Section 2.2.3, Mill's methods are basically eliminative in nature; they are designed to allow us to rule out factors we suspect as causes of certain phenomona. His *method of agreement* allows us to rule out candidates for necessary causes of some event. Referring to Figure 4.3*b*, cause C cannot be a (strictly) necessary cause of effect E if this effect appears in the absence of C. For example, a variety of different bacteria may be suspected of causing a certain illness. Consequently we examine a large number of persons with this illness in order to observe one or more bacteria that are always present when this illness occurs. Mill's *method of difference* allows us to rule out candidates for sufficient causes of some event. In Figure 4.3a we observe that C cannot be (strictly) sufficient to cause E if E does not occur when C is present. Fifty people attend a dinner and consume food from a smorgasbord; ten of them become violently ill. Identifying foods eaten by the persons who did and who did not become ill allows us to rule out certain foods as being sufficient causes of the illness that resulted.

Common use of the term *causality* rarely corresponds to the "strict" sufficiency and necessity conditions illustrated in Figures 4.3a, b, or c. In many situations we simply say that causes raise the probability of their effects (Eells 1991). I cannot assert that my insecticide is a strictly sufficient condition for killing insects if I know that this chemical is effective only, say, 90% of the time. So in Figure 4.3a we may have $q > 0$. I use the spray, and it does not kill insects. I would certainly not say that the use of this spray is a necessary cause of the insects' death, since, if I had the inclination to do so, I could kill them in a variety of other ways. Thus in Figure 4.3b we may have $r > 0$. The situation we may regularly encounter is shown in Figure 4.3d in which we suppose that all four probabilities p, q, r, and s are nonzero. Suppose that, on evidence, I have grounds for believing that the death of the insects I find in my flower pot is more likely if I used the insecticide than if I did not; probabilistically $P(E|C) > P(E|C^c)$. In such cases Mill says that cause C has *positive relevance* on effect E. Other persons have said that C in this case is at least a *contributory cause* of effect E (Wulff 1981, 58).

Mill's use of the term *relevance* in connection with the situation in Figure 4.3d is interesting and one that we will discuss further in Chapter 5. The two probabilities $P(E|C)$ and $P(E|C^c)$ are called *likelihoods;* their ratio $P(E|C)/P(E|C^c)$ is appropriately called a *likelihood ratio*. A likelihood ratio is one possible means for grading the inferential force of evidence of effect E on cause C. Evidence of effect E has positive relevance on C if $P(E|C)/P(E|C^c) > 1.0$. I will also note, in Chapter 5, that a likelihood ratio interpretation of relevance seems entirely consistent with the definition of relevance in Federal Rule of Evidence FRE-401, as discussed in Section 3.1.1.

Experience shows that agents we identify as causal either do not work all the time or are not unique in producing some effect. If we try to identify causality with necessity and sufficiency jointly, as in Figure 4.3c, we are implying the existence of a unique cause; every time C happens, E happens, and when C does not happen, neither does E. So we have to consider instances involving the possibility of a *plurality* of causes as when, for example, an airliner crashes on takeoff during a snowstorm. The causes identified may include such matters as inadequate wing de-icing, inappropriate control settings, and pilot inexperience. But there seems to be trouble in saying that an effect can have a plurality of causes. Some have argued that when a situation is described with enough precision, plurality disappears and a single cause can be identified (Copi 1982, 412). However, it is frequently difficult to identify an effect with enough precision in order to isolate a unique cause. Even if an aircraft's flight recorder and the pilots survive, we may not be able to reconstruct the circumstances of the crash in enough detail to isolate a single cause of this calamity.

Someone once said that time is nature's way of preventing everything from happening all at once. We encounter events that follow in succession. In situations in which we imagine a chain of events that seem to be connected, it is common to distinguish between *proximate* and *remote* or *distal* causes. Harold dies at age forty-three, and a county medical examiner, too lazy to perform an autopsy, certifies the cause of Harold's death as "Harold's birth forty-three years ago." Asked to account for his foolishness, the medical examiner defends his certification by saying that Harold's being born is a necessary condition for his having died. Although we cannot dispute this fact, our interests lie in somewhat less remote causes for Harold's death. Many things have happened to Harold since he was born, including his ingestion of a large quantity of cocaine shortly before he expired. So the record is amended by the new medical examiner to read that the proximate cause of Harold's death was an overdose of cocaine.

When we encounter the topic of *correlation* in statistics courses, we are (or should be) informed that a high correlation between two variables does not necessarily indicate any causal relation between them. We might, for example, discover a high statistical correlation, over the last twenty-five years, between the yearly average price of wheat in Armenia and yearly number of high school dropouts in Lufkin, Texas. Our assessment of how one effects the other would require a remarkably vivid imagination. Our best bet would be to say that such an association is accidental. Study of causation on the part of philosophers includes an analysis of ways in which we might distinguish between accidental and lawlike conditions. How do we discriminate between a situation in which C lawfully causes E and one in which the association between C and E is accidental? Skyrms mentions that the difference between law and accident involves the distinction between parts and wholes (1986, 120–128). Laws are truths that are universally applicable. Nonuniversal or local truths may be accidental, as in the instance of a statistical relation between Armenian wheat prices and high school dropout frequency in Lufkin, Texas.

One means of portraying a causal relation involves the idea of a *counterfactual conditional*. On this interpretation event E is said to be causally dependent upon a distinct event C if and only if C and E both occur, *but if C had not occurred then E would not have occurred*. This interpretation brings to mind Hume's third definition of causality (cited above) as ". . . an object followed by another, and where all objects similar to the first are followed by objects similar to the second. Or in other words where, *if the first had not been, the second had never existed*." Modern interpretations of causality in terms of counterfactual conditionals are to be found in the works of J. L. Mackie (1974, 29–58) and D. Lewis (1973, 556–567; 1986). In terms of the strict conditions shown in Figure 4.3, it seems that a counterfactual conditional can only be linked to *necessity* or to *necessity and sufficiency*. Interpreted probabilistically, the counterfactual assertion *if C^c then E^c* means that $P(E^c|C^c) = 1.0$; this also means that $P(E|C^c) = 0$. For $P(C^c) > 0$ to have $P(E|C^c) = 0$, we require $P(EC^c) = r = 0$ as it is only in Figures 4.3*b* and 4.3*c*. Thus there may be some uncertainty about what is precisely meant by a counterfactual assertion.

Not every counterfactual assertion is meant to sustain a cause. I might assert: "If Bill Clinton were under thirty-five years of age, he would not now be president." Such an assertion simply bears upon a requirement of our Constitution and does not suggest that Bill Clinton's being over thirty-five causes him to be president. One reason for interest among philosophers in counterfactual conditionals involves the claim that lawlike connections sustain counterfactual conditionals in ways that accidental connections do not. To illustrate, I will contrast an example of a lawlike connection that I have shamelessly borrowed from Skyrms (1986, 127) with the accidental connection I made up involving affairs in Armenia and Lufkin, Texas. Following Skyrms, I make the assertion that at a pressure of one atmosphere, heating pure water to a temperature of 100 degrees centigrade *causes* it to boil. Here is a glass of pure, cold water at a pressure of one atmosphere. I assert counterfactually: If this water had been heated to a temperature of 100 degrees centigrade, it would have boiled. Such is my faith in a physical uniformity of nature involving the boiling point of water.

Now suppose that, over the past twenty-five years, the (linear) correlation between yearly average wheat prices in Armenia and the yearly high school dropout frequency in Lufkin, Texas, is remarkably high (as close to 1.0 as you please). When yearly average wheat prices rise in Armenia, so rises the yearly dropout frequency in Lufkin; when these average wheat prices fall, so does the yearly dropout frequency. Visting Lufkin this year, we note in the newspapers that the dropout frequency is as high as it has ever been. On the way to Lufkin we read about the high average wheat prices in Armenia this year. In our discussion with the mayor of Lufkin I mention the correlation and assert that the events in Armenia are causing the events in Lufkin. I even assert counterfactually: If the wheat prices in Armenia had been lower this year, then your dropout frequency would have been lower. Asked by the mayor to explain why this would be so, I discover that there is virtually nothing I can draw upon to sustain this counterfactual, particularly since the area in East Texas around Lufkin has never been noted for growing wheat. Knowledge of the yearly wheat prices in Armenia and the correlation might allow me to predict the dropout frequency in Lufkin; but such knowledge would not allow me to explain the connection.

Counterfactual accounts of causality always need to be qualified in various ways summarized by Mackie (1974, 29–58). One important qualification can be illustrated as follows: Again, consider my example in which, distracted by thinking about causality on the way home from work, I run into the rear end of the car ahead of me in traffic. I am cited by a traffic officer for failing to maintain control of my vehicle, so I must appear in court. At the trial the judge asks for my view of what caused the accident and I say, "The fact that there was a car ahead of me." I add the counterfactual assertion, "After all, if there had been no car ahead of me the accident would not have happened." As factually true as this assertion is, it would not be persuasive to the judge or to anyone else. The reason is that the presence of other vehicles is part of the *standing or background conditions* of traffic. Any reasonable cause, such as my inattentive driving, must stand out against this background. I would probably fare no better if I had asserted that the cause of the accident was the car ahead of me slowing down; if this car had not slowed down the accident would not have occurred. Traffic laws require drivers to allow a safe enough distance between their cars and others so that they can respond to changes in the speed of cars ahead of them, which is another standing condition of traffic.

Counterfactual accounts of causality are vulnerable for various reasons, and there is now a substantial literature on this matter (e.g., see van Fraassen, 1980, 112–130; Horwich 1987, 157–176). According to van Fraassen, counterfactual conditional assertions such as "if C had not occurred, then E would not have occurred" involve if-then relations (implications) that are not the same as the implications usually studied in logic, all of which conform to the *law of weakening*. According to this law, the statement "if A, then B" entails the statement "if A and C, then B." For example, consider the rolling of two ordinary dice; let A = the sum of the numbers showing up is seven when both dice are rolled, and B = the sum of the numbers showing up is at most eight when both dice are rolled. In this situation event A obviously implies event B, a condition that would continue to hold even if we added the event C = the person rolling the dice is left-handed. Rolling a seven entails rolling at most an eight regardless of what else we know. The following example is based upon one used by van Fraassen to illustrate what he views as a disconnect between a counterfactual assertion and a statement of causal necessity. The problem concerns a failure of the counterfactual conditional to conform to the law of weakening.

Suppose I assert that a necessary condition for lighting this match is that I strike it on something. At the moment I have not struck this match on anything, and it is not lit. I assert counterfactually: "If I strike this match, it will light." The trouble with this implication is that it does not weaken appropriately, since it does not follow that "if I first soak this match in water and then strike it, it will light." The argument given by van Fraassen is simply that conditionals in natural language do not always conform to the law of weakening and that this is the result of a *ceteris paribus* clause that is always implicit in a counterfactual conditional. Ceteris paribus clauses include such matters as the standing or background conditions mentioned in my traffic example. Such conditions, likely to be viewed differently by different people, make counterfactual conditional assertions context dependent, which van Fraassen argues limits their application in areas such as science.

When the facts of some matter are in dispute, as they are in a court trial, we may often have a clash of counterfactual conditional statements. Here is an example from a court trial in England (*R v. Merrifield*) as noted by Geach (1976, 91–92):

Defense: If the deceased had not been given rat poison, she'd have died just as fast from liver disease.

Prosecution: If the deceased had not had liver disease, she'd have died just as fast from rat poison.

Geach goes on to note that important matters sometimes hang on which counterfactual assertion one adopts, since in this case it was the accused who faced the possibility of execution.

Like Hume, most of us suppose that causes always precede effects. There is, however, serious discussion of "backward causation" (e.g., see Mellor 1985, various entires; Horwich 1987, 91–109). The philosopher A. J. Ayer takes it as necessarily true that causes precede effects but also notes that accounting for this temporal relation is not so easy (Ayer 1986, 170–175). There are various relations that can be established between the conditions of sufficiency and necessity illustrated in Figure 4.3. In particular, if C is a sufficient condition for E, then E is a necessary condition for C. If C is a necessary condition for E, then E is a sufficient condition for C; there are other relations that can be noted (Skyrms 1986, 85–88). Ayer claims that the existence of these relations between sufficiency and necessity seems to confound our attempts to require that causes precede effects, when causality is interpreted in terms of necessity and sufficiency. What we do recognize is that there are common fallacies associated with causation (e.g., Engel 1986, 160–165). Based upon past experiences I assert that washing my car causes it to rain; this is an example of *post hoc, ergo propter hoc*. You point out to me how difficult it might be for me to sustain the counterfactual: "If I do not wash my car, then it will not rain." Occasionally the joint occurrence of two events is taken as evidence of causality when their joint occurrence is simply an accident.

4.3.2 Causality, Probability, and the Relevance of Evidence

The term *causality* is often associated with the term *dependence;* we say that the occurrence of effect E depends upon the occurrence of cause C. In conventional probability theory the related terms *dependence* and *independence* have quite specific meanings that are not always consistent with the meaning of these terms in ordinary discourse. Probabilistically two events A and B are said to be *independent* when $P(A|B) = P(A)$. Thus probabilistic independence represents a *failure of conditioning;* the probability of A does not change when we also find out that B happened. Another way of stating conditions for probabilistic independence follows from the definition of a conditional probability: $P(A|B) = P(AB)/P(B)$. Independence of A and B requires that $P(AB)/P(B) = P(A)$ or, equivalently, that $P(AB) = P(A)P(B)$. This last equation is called the *product rule for independent events.* If we divide both sides of this equation by $P(A)$, we have $P(B|A) = P(B)$. Thus no temporal ordering of the occurrence of A and B is implied by independence, since saying $P(A|B) = P(A)$ is the same as saying that $P(B|A) = P(B)$. The concept of independence in ordinary discourse is not so precisely defined. Part of the difficulty arises because probabilistic independence concerns a probability measure and not the events to which this measure is applied (e.g., Pfeiffer 1990, 76). For example, the terms *mutually exclusive* and *independent* are often used synonymously on the ground that independent events ought to have nothing to do with each other. However, it is easily shown that, for nonzero $P(A)$ and $P(B)$, events A and B cannot be both mutually exclusive and independent.

If $P(A|B) \neq P(A)$ or, equivalently, $P(AB) \neq P(A)P(B)$, events A and B are said to be *nonindependent* or *dependent.* Like probabilistic independence, probabilistic dependence is blind to event ordering, since, if $P(A|B) \neq P(A)$, then $P(B|A) \neq P(B)$. Examine Figures 4.3a, b, and c again for the *strict* conditions of sufficiency, necessity, and sufficiency and necessity. Given one restriction, each of these strict conditions specifies a particular temporally ordered probabilistic dependency relation. The restriction is this: Suppose that we believe that $P(C) > 0$ and $P(E) > 0$. All this means is that we do not regard events C and E either to be *impossible* or to be *null events.* In conventional probability impossible events have zero probability. Null events are events that, though logically possible, have zero probability. In the case of sufficiency we see that the product rule for independent events fails to apply, since $P(CE^c) = 0 \neq P(C)P(E^c) = ps$. The same thing happens in the strict necessity condition in Figure 4.3b, since $P(C^cE) = 0 \neq P(C^c)P(E) = sp$. Independence fails on both counts in strict necessity and sufficiency for similar reasons, since $P(CE^c) = 0 \neq P(C)P(E^c) = ps$, and $P(C^cE) = 0 \neq P(C^c)P(E) = sp$. Thus we see that these three strict conditions are probabilistic dependency relations. The fact that we assume that C must always precede E is quite incidental as far as this probabilistic dependence is concerned.

Let us now examine these same three conditions from an inferential point of view supposing that we observe, as evidence, either of the effects E or E^c and wish to draw a conclusion from such evidence about cause C or its nonoccurrence C^c. To do this, we will again consider the likelihood ratios introduced in the previous section. For effect E we have the likelihood ratio $P(E|C)/P(E|C^c)$, and for the nonoccurrence of this effect E^c we have the likelihood ratio $P(E^c|C)/P(E^c|C^c) = [1 - P(E|C)]/[1 - P(E|C^c)]$. Taking *sufficiency* first, suppose that E = the event that I have just died; E^c = the event that I am now alive, C = the event that I consumed a large dose of strychnine, and C^c = the event that I did not consume this large dose of strcyhnine. I am found dead, and so you have evidence that event E has occurred. This is very *inconclusive* evidence that I consumed the strychnine. Although $P(E|C) = 1.0$, as we noted in discussing sufficiency, $P(E|C^c) = r/(r + s)$ is as close to one as you please, since there are any number of other causes for my death. This means that the likelihood ratio $P(E|C)/P(E|C^c)$ is as close to one as you please. However, finding that I am alive (E^c) is *conclusive* evidence that I have not consumed a large dose of strychnine. In this case we have $P(E^c|C) = 0$, and $P(E^c|C^c) = s/(r + s)$ is as large as you please.

Now consider the necessity condition in Figure 4.3*b* and the following situation: Suppose that there are two boxes B_1 and B_2. Box B_1 has eight red objects and two white objects in it, but B_2 has ten white objects and no red objects in it. These two boxes are hidden behind a screen. Suppose I flip a fair coin to select one of these boxes. From the box I have selected I draw a single object at random and show it to you. You observe the object I have selected but not the box I have selected it from. Let C = I have chosen B_1, and let C^c = I have chosen B_2. A *necessary* cause (C) of my showing you a red object (E) is my having selected B_1, since there are no red objects in B_2. In this case $P(E|C) = p/(p + q) = 8/10$ and $P(E|C^c) = 0$. So, if I show you a red object, this is *conclusive* evidence that I have chosen B_1. In this case the likelihood ratio $P(E|C)/P(E|C^c)$ is undefined, but observe that for fixed $P(E|C)$, this ratio goes to infinity as $P(E|C^c)$ goes to zero. But now suppose that the object I show you is white (E^c); this would be just *inconclusive* evidence, since there are white objects in both boxes. The draw of a white object is also inconclusive evidence in favor of my having selected it from B_2, since $P(E^c|C) = q/(p + q) = 2/10$ and $P(E^c|C^c) = s/s = 10/10 = 1.0$.

To illustrate sufficiency and necessity in Figure 4.3*c*, all we have to do is to change the distribution of the red and white objects in boxes B_1 and B_2. Suppose that B_1 contains ten red objects and no white objects, while B_2 contains no red objects and ten white objects. In this case my having selected B_1 for the drawing of an object is both a necessary and sufficient condition for my showing you a red object. My selecting B_2 is a necessary and sufficient condition for my showing you a white object. In this case my showing you a red object is *conclusive* evidence that I have selected B_1, since $P(E|C) = 1.0$ and $P(E|C^c) = 0$. My showing you a white object is *conclusive* evidence of my having selected B_2; in this case $P(E^c|C) = 0$ and $P(E^c|C^c) = 1.0$.

These three examples have two things in common. First, they all suppose that C precedes E. In the first example, I might have ingested the strychnine (C) and then died (E); it could not have happened the other way around. In the other two cases I select a box first and then show you objects selected from it. The second common feature of these examples is that they involve *strict* or deterministic conditions (of sufficiency, necessity, or sufficiency and necessity). But, as discussed earlier, in our everyday affairs we may have to cope with situations in which the causes we identify may not work all of the time either sufficiently or necessarily. Thus we are led to the situation depicted in Figure 4.3d in which the joint events CE, CE^c, C^cE, and C^cE^c all have nonzero probability. Following Mill, we labeled this situation as one involving probabilistic relevance. It is certainly true that the evidence in the three cases in Figures 4.3a, b, and c is relevant; in fact in every case the evidence is not only relevant but can be conclusive depending upon whether we observe E or E^c. The issue we now have to face concerns the nature of the relationship between relevance and causality. As we have just seen, the evidence in cases of strict necessity/sufficiency conditions is relevant. Can evidence be relevant in situations (1) in which there are not strict conditions of necessity/sufficiency and (2) in which we may not wish to specify any sufficiency or necessity conditions on the events involved in some chain of reasoning constructed in defense of the relevance of evidence?

Answering part (1) of this question seems straightforward. In the case of *sufficiency*, suppose that last night I sprayed the flowers in my pot with insecticide. Today you observe several insects eating away at my flowers and regard this as relevant but only inconclusive evidence that I did not spray these flowers recently. You happen to know that the insecticide I use does not work all the time so that the probability of an insect's not dying (E^c), given its having been sprayed with insecticide (C), is nonzero. In the case of *necessity*, suppose that box B_1 still contains eight red objects and two white objects. However, by mistake I get one red object among all the other white objects that are in box B_2. If you knew this, your observation of a single red object would still of course be relevant but be now just inconclusive evidence that I chose B_1. So, when we depart from conditions of strict sufficiency and necessity, the effects we observe continue to be relevant but are now just inconclusive evidence in inferences about causes. So it appears that we can make the generalization that a nonstrict causal relation between C and E makes evidence about E relevant but always inconclusive in an inference about C. It would always be necessary for us to be able to defend the existence of this causal connection. We have already discussed the necessity for defending the relevance of any evidence.

In answer to part (2) concerning relevance in noncausal situations, consider the chain of reasoning illustrated in Figure 4.4. Joe has been accused of robbing a liquor store and now stands trial. At the trial Mike testifies that he saw Joe's car a short distance from this store just a few minutes before the store was robbed. Mike does not say that he saw Joe. It seems quite easy to defend the relevance of Mike's evidence on the major fact in issue: whether or not Joe committed this robbery. We argue: If Joe's car was at the scene of the robbery shortly before it was committed, then Joe might have been there, and, if Joe was at the scene shortly before the robbery was committed, he might have have been the one who committed it. This chain of reasoning has two credibility-related links I will explain in a moment. Notice in the direct linkage between Mike's evidence (E^*) and hypothesis H, I have not

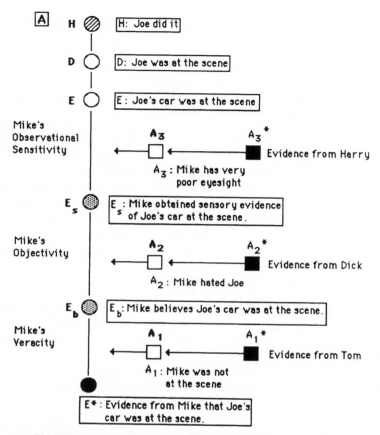

FIGURE 4.4 An illustration of relevance without causality.

put any arrows. The reason is that we might have structured this argument in either direction. There is one condition of *necessity* here which we can assert counterfactually: If Joe had not been at the scene of the robbery, he could not have committed it. Quite possibly Joe might have been involved in planning the robbery but had no hand in carrying it out; however, he is presently accused of being the robber.

But now consider the linkage between event D = Joe was at the scene, and event E = Joe's car was at the scene. We would be hard-pressed to find either a necessary or sufficient condition in the linkage between these two events. It is neither necessary or sufficient for Joe's car to be at the scene in order for Joe to be there himself. It is neither necessary nor sufficient for Joe's being at the scene himself for his car to be there. Joe could have used any number of other means of transportation to the scene, and someone else might have borrowed or stolen Joe's car and drove it to the scene (without Joe). Joe could have been at the scene without his car being there, and Joe's car could have been at the scene without Joe being there. In terms of conventional probability, the inferential force of Mike's testimony depends in part upon how different are the probabilities $P(E|D)$ and $P(E|D^c)$. How different these probabilities are depends upon the strength of the generalization we might assert to link them and on the kind and amount of ancillary evidence we have that backs this generalization (we discussed these matters earlier in Section 3.3).

But Figure 4.4 shows other *ancillary* evidence we may have regarding Mike's credibility as a source of evidence about Joe's car being at the scene. Recall that ancillary evidence acquires relevance if it bears upon the strength or weakness of links in reasoning chains set up by directly relevant evidence such as Mike's testimony. We might have any amount of ancillary evidence bearing upon Mike's veracity, objectivity, and observational sensitivity as a source of information about Joe's car. For example, suppose that Tom tells us that, at the time of the robbery, Mike was with him (Tom) many miles aways from the scene of the robbery; if so, Mike could not have observed Joe's car at the scene of the robbery. This ancillary evidence goes to Mike's veracity and suggests that Mike does not believe what he testified. We might have Dick's testimony that Mike hated Joe and had frequently mentioned how much he would like to see Joe in trouble. Such evidence bears either on Mike's objectivity or veracity. Finally, we might have Harry's testimony that Mike has very poor eyesight. Such ancillary evidence would certainly be certified as relevant, even though we would be very hard-pressed to discern any causal linkage among these ancillary events and other events on this argument structure. For example, we ask what bearing does Joe's car being at the scene have upon the state of Mike's eyesight?

As this example illustrates, we need not suppose any causal connections between events for evidence about these events to have inferential relevance and force. Our colleagues in law have studied causal linkages in detail (e.g., Hart and Honoré, 1985). They have also made rather precise distinctions among direct, immediate, intervening, proximate, remote, and superceding causes (Gifis 1984, 62–63). Jurists have also made very detailed studies of evidential relevance. I am unable to find any reference in the literature on legal evidence that suggests any required connection between the concepts of relevance and causality. Our Federal Rule of Evidence FRE-401 on relevance talks only about the revision of beliefs based on evidence and not about any conditions of necessity and/or sufficiency.

4.3.3 Relevance, Causality, and the Structuring of Complex Inferences

I noted that every inference task we encounter in our daily lives is complex when examined carefully. If we had the time and the inclination, we could decompose what appears to be a very simple inference and in the process discover important sources of uncertainty that we may have overlooked in a superficial analysis. It is certainly true, however, that some inferences involve more evidence and more elaborate arguments than do others. In many situations we may feel quite overwhelmed by the amount of evidence available and wonder how we are to make sense of it all. Masses of evidence we routinely encounter contain mixtures of every recognizable form and combination of evidence we considered in Chapter 3. Some models we construct help us to organize evidence we already have. In other cases, particularly in recurrent inferences, quite elaborate models of an inference task are constructed in advance of the gathering of evidence in any particular application of the model. Models of an inference problem, whether recurrent or not, are frequently revised in light of new insights and evidence; on occasion their major purpose is to guide the discovery of new evidence.

In the remaining sections of this chapter we will consider various methods that have been proposed for assisting persons who encounter inference tasks having any gradation of complexity. Most of these methods incorporate specific rules for combining probabilistic assessments of the inferential force of evidence. Our present interest is in the structural details of these methods; we will later discuss their probabilistic elements. The topics of relevance and causality we have been discussing are quite important in any survey of these methods. All methods we will discuss involve means for charting chains of reasoning that link evidence and various hypothetical elements of an inference model. Some methods focus just on evidential relevance and make no mention of any causal linkages among their elements. Other methods are sometimes advertised as being causal in nature when, as we will observe, they apply equally well in instances in which we are quite unwilling or unable to specify any causal connections among elements of an inference problem.

4.4 INFERENCE NETWORKS I: WIGMORE AND HIS CONTEMPORARY ADVOCATES

As I noted in Section 2.4.3, Wigmore's work *The Science of Judicial Proof* (1937) was intended as a *Novum Organum* for the study of how a conclusion might be reached and defended when it rests upon a mass of what he termed *mixed evidence*. In using the term *mixed,* he was referring to different forms and combinations of evidence such as those we discussed in Chapter 3. However, Wigmore did not recognize all of the forms and combinations we identified. In *The Science of Judicial Proof* Wigmore's standpoint was essentially that of an instructor attempting to tutor advocates preparing for trial and being faced with the task of defending the relevance, credibility, and force of their evidence on issues in contention. As is common in contentious matters, one side can expect that its arguments from evidence will be quite ruthlessly decomposed by the other side. So Wigmore's basic advice was to lay out very carefully arguments to be made from *all of one's evidence,* also taking into account whatever evidence is obtainable from one's opponent. By such means points of inferential weakness and strength in an argument can be identified. My present task is to show how Wigmore's basic structural methods for defending the relevance, credibility, and force of evidence have application in any context in which we seek to draw conclusions based upon masses of mixed evidence.

4.4.1 Basic Inferential Uses of Evidence

I will begin as Wigmore did (1937, 18–37) by identifying certain basic inferential (or probative) uses of evidence. Such identification, illustrated in Figures 4.5 and 4.6, makes use of the evidence forms and combinations we identified in Chapter 3. First, consider Figure 4.5a. Suppose I am trying to convince you to believe that hypothesis H is true. To do so, I initially offer

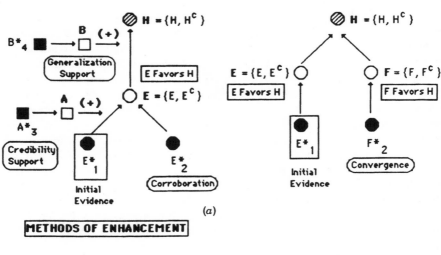

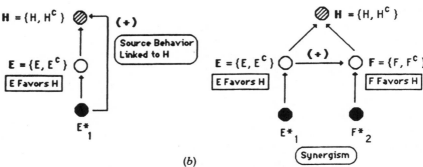

FIGURE 4.5 Methods for supporting or enhancing the value of evidence.

evidence E_1^*, that event E occurred. One basic element of my task is to try to convince you that event E, if it did occur, strongly favors the occurrence of H over its nonoccurrence (H^c). I argue that the known occurrence of E would be strong but *circumstantial* evidence favoring H. I make no claim that E, if true, is conclusive on H. Evidence E_1^* can be any form of evidence we considered in Chapter 3. I have several options for supporting my claim regarding the inferential significance on H of this initial evidence E_1^*. I can first attempt to convince you that event E did happen, as E_1^* alleges, by presenting another item of evidence E_2^* that *corroborates* evidence E_1^*. I might instead or in addition present *ancillary evidence* A_3^* regarding event A that, if true, is favorable to the credibility of evidence E_1^*. In Figure 4.5 the ($+$) sign means that A is favorable evidence strengthening the linkage between E_1^* and E.

From this corroborative evidence as well as the favorable credibility-related evidence, you might agree that event E did occur. But you are also entitled to ask the question, So what? Perhaps you do not agree that E favors H as strongly as I do. Suppose I assert a generalization to the effect that whenever something like E happens, H is also very likely to happen. Another kind of evidence I can introduce is ancillary evidence B_4^*, that event B occurred. Suppose that B, if true, supports or backs the generalization I have asserted as far as this particular inference is concerned. The ($+$) sign on the inference from event B indicates that B is favorable to the generalization that licenses the linkage between E and H. Figure 4.5a shows another option I have in my efforts to convince you of the truth of H. Suppose I introduce evidence F_2^*, that event F occurred. I argue that event F, if true, also favors the occurrence or truth of H. Evidence F_2^* and E_1^* are *convergent* in favoring H.

If I am astute enough, I may have other options in my efforts to convince you about the strong probability of H being true. Figure 4.5b shows two ways in which I may even enhance the value of evidence I have introduced. First, suppose I have ancillary evidence that the behavior of the source of evidence E^* is itself inferentially interesting. I might say that the fact that this particular source reported E^* means that this evidence has more value to us than if we knew for sure that event E happened. Later, in Section 7.2, we will be able to give a very precise probabilistic interpretation of why it is true that in certain circumstances evidence about an event can have more inferential value than the *known occurrence* of this event. There is yet another option illustrated in Figure 4.5b. In addition to introducing evidence F_2^* that converges with E_1^*, I might be able to show how these two items of evidence, taken together, more strongly favor H than they do if we considered them separately. This involves the evidential *synergism* we discussed in Chapter 3.

Exhausting as many of these options as my evidence allows, I rest my case and ask you whether or not you now conclude that H is true. You say that the evidence so far has been given *ex parte* (from one side only) and that you wish to have evidence from someone not quite so committed to the truth of H as I seem to be. So you find a person willing to take an adversarial view regarding the evidence I have introduced and the arguments I have made. The options available to this adversary are illustrated in Figure 4.6. The first evidential option available to my adversary is one of *denial*, as illustrated in the left-hand diagram in Figure 4.6a. My adversary can, in two ways, deny that event E occurred as reported in my initial evidence E_1^*. Perhaps my adversary will be able to produce *contradictory* evidence E_2^{c*}, that event E did not occur. Failing this, my adversary may be able to impeach the credibility of my evidence by introducing ancillary evidence A_3^*, that is unfavorable to the credibility of E_1^*. The $(-)$ sign indicates the unfavorable nature of this

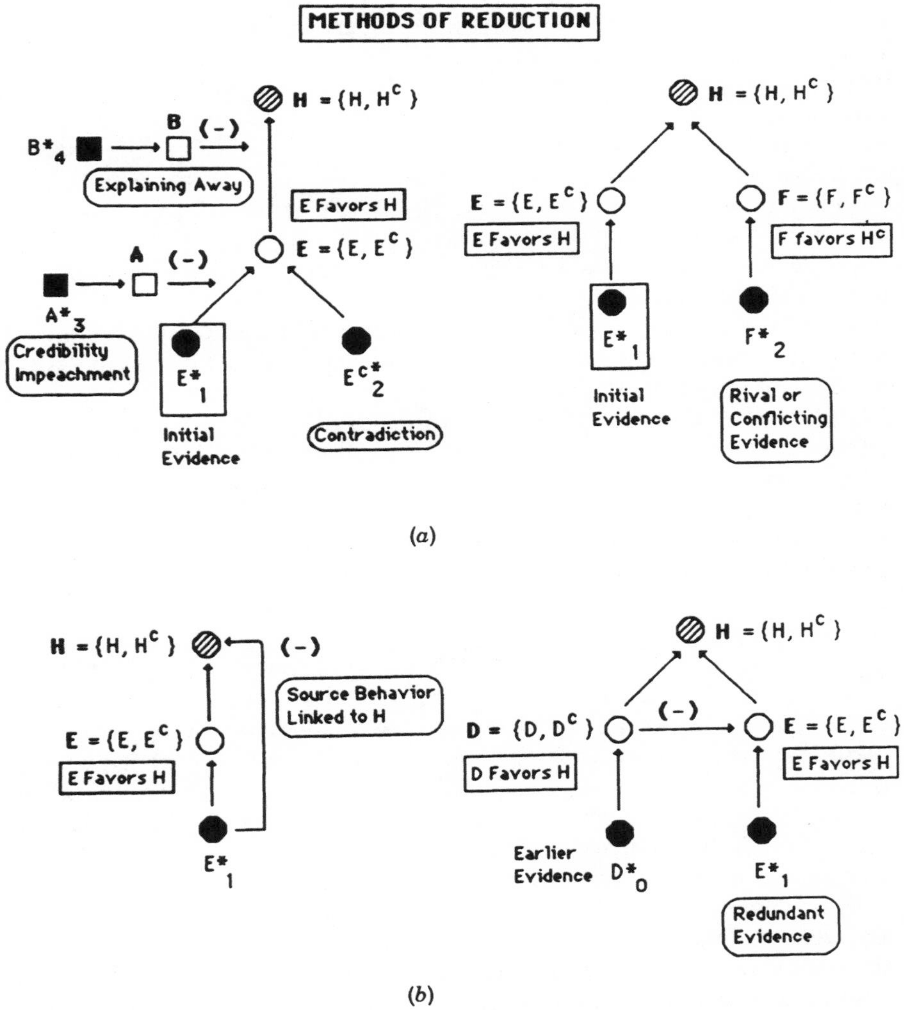

(a)

(b)

FIGURE 4.6 Methods for reducing the value of evidence.

credibility-related evidence; such evidence acts to reduce or sever completely the linkage between E_1^* and E. Instead, or in addition, my adversary can return to the question, So what if event E did occur? The adversary may introduce ancillary evidence B_4^*, that event B occurred, where in this case B is unfavorable to the generalization I asserted that licenses the linkage between E and H. By such means the adversary hopes to show that event E has substantial likeliness given H^c. In other words, what I said about the inferential effect of E on H can be *explained away*. In addition the adversary may be able to introduce rival or *conflicting* evidence such as F_2^* shown in the right hand diagram of Figure 4.6a.

Other options available to my adversary are shown in Figure 4.6b. First, my opponent could introduce ancillary evidence showing that my evidence E_1^* actually has more inferential force on H^c than the known *nonoccurrence* of event E. The argument might read: The evidence from this particular source depends not only on whether or not E occurred but also upon whether or not H occurred. The ancillary evidence might allow us to believe the evidence from this source is more likely if H did not occur. Finally, suppose that my evidence E^* is not the first I have given you; I might have given you earlier evidence D_0^* about event D that also, according to me, favors H. My adversary might be able to argue that evidence E^* says nothing inferentially in addition to what D_0^* said and is thus redundant evidence.

Evidential exchanges such as those in the preceding example take place routinely. Trials at law are certainly adversarial but so are the inferential activities of scientists, engineers, historians, physicians, auditors, and many others who, as Toulmin noted, have to make a case why their conclusions should be favored over others. Wigmore's methods, which we now consider, were developed for the purpose of assisting persons facing the task of constructing and defending conclusions, based upon a mass of mixed evidence, in situations in which not everyone will agree about the relevance, credibility, and force of this evidence.

4.4.2   Analysis and Synthesis: Wigmore's Key Lists and Evidence Charts

Given a mass of evidence whose items seem to bear in different ways upon possible conclusions we entertain, how do we make sense of it all? One approach is to attempt to simplify an inference by ignoring evidence whose relevance, credibility, or force seems doubtful or, in any case, difficult to defend. The trouble is that a skillful adversary or critic may actively undertake such an activity and, in the process, undermine our own analysis. We would of course be quite embarrassed when inquiries are made regarding why we ignored any evidence that appears unfavorable to the conclusion we advocate. So we have to account for all evidence we have that seems to bear in any way on possible conclusions being entertained. We might also attempt to reduce our intellectual labor by relying upon any rhetorical skills we might have in persuading others to accept the conclusion we may view as obvious. This insults the intelligence of others who choose to make a more critical analysis of the available evidence. Arguments made from a mass of available evidence may miscarry unless careful attention is paid to their construction. As we have discussed, evidence comes with no relevance, credibility, and inferential force credentials; these credentials have to be established by careful argument.

Wigmore argued that unsystematic or casual attention to the construction of arguments invites many difficulties. When we have a mass of evidence to evaluate, the intellectual burden of making sense of it all is certainly heavy. One major problem involves the simple fact that we have somehow to keep many things in mind all at once, a task most of us find quite difficult. Some items of evidence are linked in quite complex ways to matters at issue, as we discovered in an analysis of the relevance of Officer Connolly's testimony (Figure 3.9). Some evidence sets up chains of reasoning to major possible conclusions, while other (ancillary) evidence bears upon the strength or weakness of links in these chains. Arguments we make may often be linked in inferentially important ways, and we may note interesting linkages among the items of evidence we have. Wigmore believed it was necessary for us to have some means of assistance in the difficult process of marshaling our thoughts and our evidence as we attempt to construct valid and persuasive arguments on conclusions we advocate. Stated in other words, he believed we need assistance in the task of seeing "the big picture," in the form of an overall conclusion, that can result only through an appropriate juxtaposition of evidential and argumentational details. As Wigmore argued (1937, 858–859):

> Our object then should be by some system of symbols: *To perform the logical (or psychological) process of consciously juxtaposing the detailed related ideas, for the purpose of producing rationally a single final idea.* An ideal method should satisfy this requirement: *To the extent that the mind is unable consciously to juxtapose a larger number of ideas, each coherent group of detailed constituent ideas must be reduced in consciousness to a single idea; until at last the mind can consciously juxtapose them with due attention to each, so as to produce its single final idea.*

So, in an effort to assist us in constructing "the big picture" in a complex inference, Wigmore developed what he termed a *chart method* for constructing arguments from a mass of evidence. This method has both analytic and synthetic elements. As a first illustration of the Wigmore's *analytic* process, consider again the argument I constructed in Figure 3.9 regarding Officer Connolly's testimony. Observe that this argument consists of eleven statements or propositions, ten of which are *probanda* or matters to be proved. One of these statements is the evidence itself (E^*) and one is the major fact-in-issue (H); all other statements are intermediate or interim hypotheses or probanda that link E^* and H. By such analysis I constructed an argument from E* to H. Suppose that this sort of analysis is performed for every argument that is to be made from the evidence we have. Each statement that is made in this stage of argument construction is given an identifying number; the entire collection of statements we have made for every argument we have constructed is called a *key list*. Such a list contains all the statements describing each item of evidence we have and propositions at each stage of reasoning from this evidence to our final or ultimate hypotheses.

Such analyses will often result in a key list containing hundreds or even thousands of statements. What help is this in obtaining "the big picture" as far as a complex inference is concerned? Wigmore argued that to get the "big picture," we do need a picture showing how all of these statements or propositions fit together. Thus the *synthetic* element of Wigmore's method consists of constructing what he called an *evidence chart*. Earlier, in discussing Figure 4.1, I mentioned that an argument from evidence to hypotheses (and vice versa) can be represented by two kinds of elements which I identified as nodes and arcs. Nodes consist of certain statements or propositions, and arcs specify their probabilistic linkages. Wigmore developed a very elaborate syntax of symbols for representing nodes and arcs; his syntax is shown in Figure 4.7. His node symbols refer to various propositions and to identified kinds of evidence. The arc symbols refer to linkages, of various inferential strength, among probanda. We need not consider the definitions Wigmore gave to all of these symbols (for an account of these definitions, see Wigmore 1937, 862–

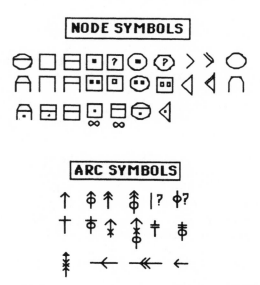

FIGURE 4.7 Wigmore's syntax of node and arc symbols.

868; Tillers and Schum 1988, 929–930; Anderson and Twining 1991, 112–115). A brief example will convey the essentials of Wigmore's original evidence charting method.

Figure 4.8 shows a small extract from an evidence chart Wigmore constructed (1937, 876–881). This figure shows Wigmore's key list and accom-

EVIDENCE CHART: SYNTHESIS

ISSUE: DID Y DIE OF POISON ?

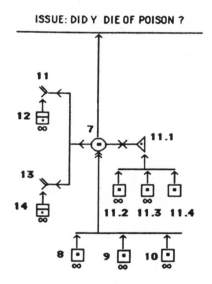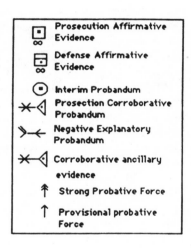

ONE LINE OF ARGUMENT BY THE PROSECUTION

KEY LIST: ANALYSIS

7. Y died, being apparently in health, within three hours after the drink of whiskey.
8-10. Y's wife and the Northingtons witness to 7.
11. Y might have died by colic from which he had often suffered.
11.1 Colic would not have had as symptoms the leg cramps and teeth-clenching; only strychnine could produce these.
11.2 Y's wife and the Northingtons witness to Y's cramps and teeth-clenching.
11.3 Expert witness to significance of symptoms.
11.4 No testimony as to strychnine traces in body by post mortem.
12. Anon witness to his former attacks.
13 Y might have died from the former injury to his side.
14 Anon witness to that injury

FIGURE 4.8   A portion of a Wigmore evidence chart (from Wigmore 1937, 876–881).

panying chart for one of the prosecution's lines of argument on an issue in the murder case *Hatchett v. Commonwealth,* that was tried in Virginia in 1880. Briefly, the prosecution alleged that Oliver Hatchett knowingly gave whiskey containing strychnine to Moses Young who drank some of this whiskey and died a short time later. Hatchett was convicted of murder, but an appeal was filed on his behalf. Wigmore charted the evidence as it appeared in the transcript of the appeals court. Some of the actual trial witnesses were not named in these appellate records; they were identified as "Anon" in Wigmore's charts. There were three elements of the charge against Hatchett, one of which concerned whether or not Young actually died of poison. One line of prosecution argument on this charge rested upon the testimony of three witnesses that Moses Young was in good health until he drank the whiskey (key list items 8–10). The defense countered with evidence that Young suffered from colic and that he had also recently been injured in the side by a cart (items 12 and 14). The prosecution also introduced evidence from three witnesses (item 11.2) who told of Young's behavior after he drank the whiskey. They said he clenched his teeth and said that he had severe cramps. An expert witness (11.3) testified that these symptoms were associated with strychnine poisoning but not with colic. Wigmore noted (item 11.4) that there was no evidence obtained post mortem about strychnine traces in Young's body.

In Figure 4.8 I have explained the meaning of the symbols Wigmore used in charting this collection of evidence. The first six symbols shown are node identifiers. All of Wigmore's symbols for evidence contain an infinity symbol (∞) at the bottom; the two that are shown represent affirmative evidence from prosecution and from defense. The other node identifiers concern probanda or interim hypotheses. The last two symbols are arc labels, and it is here that we must pause to consider Wigmore and probability. Though Wigmore was no probabilist, he did appreciate that the connections or arcs between nodes on his charts indicated probabilistic connections, those showing the probative (inferential) force of one node on another. He graded the strength of these connections in words rather than in numbers, as the two examples show. All of the other arc symbols in Figure 4.7 are verbal probative force indicators. In modern terms these verbal inferential force qualifiers are *fuzzy* in nature, as we will discuss in Chapter 5.

Wigmore was very careful to stress that any evidence chart can only reflect the beliefs of the person(s) who construct it and that no chart could indicate what he called "absolutely correct" beliefs (1937, 860–862). In modern terms, Wigmore made no *normative* claims about this method. He went on to say that although logicians and others have given us methods for assessing the probative force of individual inferences, they have given us nothing useful for grading the net effect of a mass of mixed evidence on a single probandum. He added in a footnote that such methods might someday be discovered. There are grounds for belief that the "someday" Wigmore mentioned has now arrived. Finally, I noted in Section 4.3.2 that the concepts of *relevance* and *causality* are not mixed together in scholarship on evidence in the field of law. At no point in describing his analytic and synthetic methods does Wigmore suggest that the arcs on his networks necessarily indicate causal influences or relations.

4.4.3 A Modern Face on Wigmore's Evidence-Charting Methods

Wigmore's analytic-synthetic method for constructing arguments from a mass of mixed evidence deserves a far better hearing than it ever received from the audience for whom it was intended (trial attorneys). As William Twining notes, Wigmore's methods went over like a "lead balloon" (1985, 164–166). Some of the reasons are quite obvious; many people are naturally averse to any form of symbolic representation. Wigmore was hardly parsimonious in his selection of symbols used to identify the nodes and arcs on his evidence charts. Even if he had employed a much smaller syntax of symbols, the task of charting detailed arguments from a mass of evidence can be a true chore. Twining tells of an evidence chart that measures 37 feet in length (1984, 30–31). It is said that a picture is worth a thousand words. But, if the picture itself becomes sufficiently complex, some of the advantage may be lost. Nevertheless, Wigmore argued that the more complex the inferential task, the more we stand in need of some method for making sense out of the evidence we have.

It might be argued that Wigmore's methods apply only in situations in which we already have all the evidence at hand; that is, the process of discovery has been completed. However, Wigmore extended his charting methods so that they could also be useful during investigative or discovery activities in which new evidence and hypotheses are being generated (1937, 994–1003); we will return to his discovery-related charts in Section 9.4.2. Whether or not we have all available evidence at hand when we begin any charting exercise, we have to suppose that we may need to make frequent revisions in charting our arguments. Some of these changes are necessary because of new evidence, while others become necessary as a result of new or corrected insight. Constructing an evidence chart can be a true chore; making revisions in it is no fun either, since the effects of new evidence or corrected insight may be widespread throughout an evidence chart. Although one might be inclined to use Wigmore's fuzzy evidential force qualifiers, Wigmore gave us no rules by which we could aggregate these qualifiers in reaching a final conclusion.

For these reasons, and others to be noted, it seems easy to dismiss Wigmore's chart method as being of historical interest only among scholars of evidence in jurisprudence. However, the inferential problems his methods address remain in every current discipline and in fact grow more intense in light of our enhanced methods for gathering, transmitting, and storing information. Human inference tasks have certainly not become easier since Wigmore's time. But Wigmore's essential ideas are quite alive and appear to be taken more seriously now, certainly in more disciplines, than they were in his time. Wigmore's *Science of Judicial Proof* has been out of print for many years and can only be found in law libraries. But there is now available a work entitled *Analysis of Evidence: How to Do Things with Facts Based upon Wigmore's Science of Judicial Proof* (Anderson and Twining 1991). This book contains a through and critical assessment of Wigmore's methods for coping with masses of evidence. It also offers a revised version of these methods in which many of the difficulties inherent in Wigmore's original methods have been overcome. But this book is also about the thoughts of Anderson and Twining on evidence and inference. I know of no work in which the astonishingly subtle elements of everyday reasoning are better illustrated than they are in the work *Analysis of Evidence*.

Peter Tillers was asked to revise volume I of Wigmore's treatise on evidence. Because of his awareness of and appreciation for the many advancements in probabilistic reasoning that have taken place since the 1940 edition, this volume is now double its original size (*Wigmore on Evidence*, vols. 1 and 1A, 1983, Tillers rev.). Tillers' discussions of *relevance* (vol. 1A, 944–1095) and *inference-upon-inference,* or *cascaded inference* (vol. 1A, 1106–1138) are masterful accounts of legal interpretations of these most important concepts. For the past five years Tillers and I have studied a variety of evidential issues, some of which involve Wigmore's evidence charting methods. In modern terms, one obvious difficulty with his original methods is that they are not "user-friendly." Wigmore could not have anticipated the advantages now offered by modern computer facilities. With the active collaboration of Anderson and Twining, Tillers and I have recently devised a computer-based system for Wigmorean evidence marshaling and argument structuring (Schum and Tillers 1990). Two of the "user-friendly" elements of this system are illustrated in Figure 4.9. A complex argument can be broken down into sectors, each of which is constructed on a single card (or display). Using a much-simplified set of symbols for nodes and arcs, a chart sector can be very rapidly constructed (and revised) using the graphics capabilities of this system. One vexing problem with Wigmore's original method results from a person's having to go back and forth between chart and key list. In our system a structured argument and its associated key list appear side by side. The example shown in Figure 4.9 is Wigmore's structuring of another element of the *Hatchett v. Commonwealth case.*

Constructing an evidence chart along lines suggested by Wigmore may seem to be a very compulsive exercise. The layout of arguments based upon a mass of evidence requires careful thought. Wigmorean methods are no substitutes for careful thought; they simply provide us with some means for being systematic as we think carefully about the relevance, credibility, and inferential force of all of our evidence. It seems that the more there is at stake in some inference and/or decision task, the more we should be inclined to reason carefully about these matters. As Twining has noted, there are

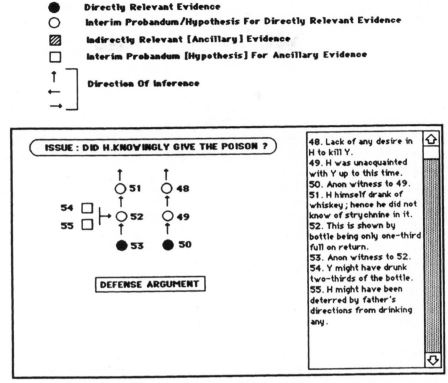

FIGURE 4.9 Computerized Wigmorean argument structuring.

distinct pedagogical reasons for careful evidence charting exercises. As he relates (Twining 1984, 31):

> Doing such exercises should drive home the lesson that analysis of evidence involves careful exploration of *relations between propositions;* it should help to make the student aware of the complexity of such relations and of the many possibilities of logical jumps and of fallacious reasoning when a mass of evidence is involved. Wigmore's method lays a foundation for a systematic approach to analyzing disputed questions of fact; it sets forth a disciplined approach to charting the overall structure of a case, and to digging out unstated, often dubious propositions, and to mapping all the relations between all the relevant evidence.

Such methods have more than pedagogical virtue and are of course applicable in any inferential context. They can also play an important heuristic role in suggesting new possibilities and new evidence. Wigmore's methods can also assist in research that has as its objective the careful analysis of complex inferences. As an example, Jay Kadane (of Carnegie Mellon University) and I are now engaged in a probabilistic analysis of evidence bearing upon the verdict rendered in the Sacco and Vanzetti case (for a preliminary account of this study see Kadane and Schum 1991). The evidence given in this trial runs to 2272 pages. In addition at least as much evidence has been discovered since the trial. To make sense of all of this old and new evidence, we resorted to Wigmore's methods. Careful analysis of this sort is necessary in order for any probabilistic assessment to make sense. Our present charting of the old and new evidence now has twenty sectors, one of which is shown in Figure 4.10. This chart shows identification evidence bearing upon whether Sacco was at the scene of the robbery and shooting when it took place (item 18 on the chart). We have already met two of the characters (Lewis Pelser and Dominic Constantino) in Section 2.3.2. Recall that Pelser said he saw Sacco at the scene, but Constantino said Pelser was under a workbench when the shooting started. The various symbols on this chart identify both directly relevant and ancillary evidence given by both prosecution and defense witnesses and to new evidence discussed in the work of Young and Kaiser (1985). Despite its apparent complexity, this chart (and others like it) does facilitate

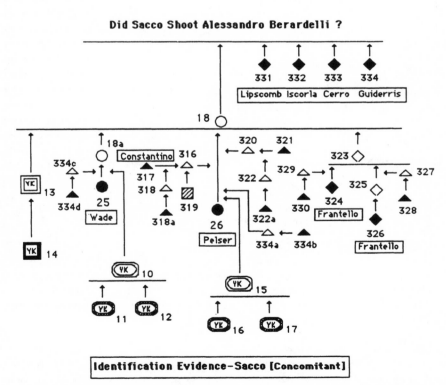

FIGURE 4.10   Wigmorean analysis in the case of Sacco and Vanzetti.

probabilistic assessments. The chart simply shows an analyst's perception of how all of the evidential pieces fit together.

4.5 INFERENCE NETWORKS II: MODERN CONCEPTIONS

The first study of inference networks I know of is described in Wigmore's *Novum Organum* for judicial proof (1913). If Wigmore came back to life today, he would be puzzled, and perhaps amused, upon hearing that his evidence charts are *directed acyclic graphs whose nodes indicate propositions and whose arcs represent fuzzy probabilistic linkages among these nodes*. A network is a particular species within a more general class of formal structures called *graphs*. The study of graph structures is an important area of mathematics having applications in virtually every discipline (e.g., Busacker and Saaty 1965). Within the past dozen years or so there has been an increasing amount of research on applying graph theory to analyses of complex probabilistic inferences.

Persons currently performing analyses of probabilistic inference in terms of graph theory often have different standpoints than the ones typically adopted by Wigmore and others within the context of law. First, the Wigmore inference networks we have considered should not be viewed as paradigmatic for all complex probabilistic reasoning. As we will observe, there are many probabilistic reasoning problems whose basic structure differs from the ones Wigmore addressed within the field of law. In short, Wigmore evidence charts form just one important special case of inference networks. Second, a Wigmore evidence chart may be constructed and found very useful by persons who have absolutely no intention of supplying probabilities for all the linkages that are revealed on such charts. In other contexts, however, an inference network is constructed for the express purpose of identifying specific probabilistic assessments that an inference problem seems to require. One trouble is that the more evidence we have and the more complex are our structured arguments, the more probabilities are involved. Remember that the act of laying out an argument in detail is also the act of identifying uncertainties. At some point we begin to become concerned about the computational burden of aggregating or combining all of these uncertainties in defensible ways in order to draw a final conclusion. A major element of the standpoint in many current studies of inference networks concerns finding *efficient* computational methods for probability aggregation. In some instances we will discover that this computational burden cannot be shouldered by even the most modern computer facilities.

4.5.1 Graphs and Inference Networks

There are just a few concepts from graph theory we will need to consider in order to discuss important structural matters related to the relevance, credibility, and force of different forms and combinations of evidence. Neapolitan gives a more thorough account of the essentials of graph theory applied to inferential networks (1991, ch. 3). In discussing Figures 4.1 and 4.2, I mentioned that the evidential diagrams we consider have two essential ingredients: nodes and arcs. Every *graph* contains nodes and arcs, so all of the evidence-related diagrams I have shown you are graphs. In symbols $G = (N, A)$ means that graph G contains a collection N of nodes and a collection A of arcs or linkages among the nodes in N.

Consider Figure 4.1 again, and suppose that we remove the arrows from all the lines. If we did this, Figure 4.1 would be called an *undirected graph*. In such instances the arcs or lines connecting nodes indicate a linkage whose direction is not specified. When we put the arrows back on the lines or arcs, we have an example of a *directed graph* or, more simply, a *digraph;* all inference-related graphs are digraphs. The direction of the arrows in a digraph used to portray an inference problem can indicate various things such as the direction of inference from one node to another, the inferential influence of one node on another, or the probabilistic dependence among nodes. In some cases we may be willing to say that the directed arcs indicate a causal relation. It is common to identify an arc in terms of the two nodes it links. Thus in Figure 4.1 the arc connecting nodes **D** and **C** is written as the ordered pair **(D, C)**. By convention, the first member of this pair indicates the node at the tail of the arrow or the node at which the arc originates. Two nodes linked by an arc are said to be *adjacent*.

Figure 4.1 illustrates another important property of the digraphs of interest to us. If you start at any node on this graph and follow the arrows, you will never end up back at the node from which you started. A directed graph having such a property is called a *directed acyclic graph* (DAG). Graphs that are directed and acyclic are often called *networks*. All of Wigmore's evidence charts have this acyclic property as well as do all of the inference-related diagrams in our entire discussion of evidence. In a directed acyclic graph we will never find ourselves on an inferential "loop" that leads us back to where we started. Other graph-related concepts are better illustrated using Figure 4.2. The first is the idea of a *chain* involving some number of arcs. Observe, for example, that there is a chain consisting of three arcs that links node **H** with node **D**; the arcs are **(H, A₁)**, **(A₁, C)**, and **(C, D)**. A DAG or network is said to be *singly connected* if for any two nodes we select there is at most one chain between them. Thus we see that the network in Figure 4.2 is *not* singly connected, since there is more than one chain leading to node **J** and more than one chain leading to nodes **P** or **R**. For example, we can follow the chain **A₄, F,** to **J** and also the chain **A₄, F, G,** to **J**. In Chapter 6 we will examine some of the important probabilistic consequences associated with networks that are not singly connected. Many of the evidential subtleties we will investigate in Chapters 7 and 8 involve networks that are not singly connected.

Networks or DAGs suggest familial relations among their nodes involving the familiar terms: parent, child, ancestor, and descendant. The terms parent and child refer to nodes that are adjacent. In Figure 4.2 node **C** is a *parent* of **D**, and correspondingly node **D** is the *child* of node **C**. Observe that some nodes have more than one parent and some parents have more than one child. For example, the parents of node **J** are nodes **F** and **G**; node **A₄** has two children, nodes **F** and **K**. Some nodes such as **F** and **K** have a common parent; other nodes such as **K** and **M** have different parents. Now take any two nodes on this network and call them **X** and **Y**. If there is an inferential chain leading from **X** to **Y**, then **Y** is said to be a *descendant* of **X** and **X** is said to be an *ancestor* of **Y**. Any node can thus have any number of ancestors or descendants. For example, the ancestors of node **L** are the nodes **H**, **A₄**, and **K**; the descendants of node **A₁** are **B**, **C**, and **D**. Observe that in this particular network all of the nodes labeled with open circles have a common ancestor, namely **H**; in turn **H** has as descendants all the rest of the nodes in this network. If a node has no parents, such as **H** in Figure 4.2, it is called a *root node*.

If we let $G = (N, A)$ represent the DAG or network in Figure 4.2, we will observe that it consists of $N = 19$ nodes and $A = 20$ arcs. The number of arcs in this DAG is very small relative to the number of arcs possible if we supposed that every node were adjacent to every other node. In structuring an inference problem, we will commonly not suppose that every node is related to every other node. In fact the particular nodes and arcs we include determine the uniqueness of a given inference problem; different problems will have different numbers of nodes and arcs. It is also true that the same problem structured by different persons may contain different nodes and arcs depending upon how differently these persons perceive this problem. Wigmore was correct; no inference network we construct can be defended as being the normatively "correct" construal of a given problem.

Using the graph-related concepts we have just discussed, we can begin to identify some very general structural differences that may exist among inference problems encountered in various contexts. Some inference problems will have basic structural characteristics resembling those addressed by Wigmore and others who study inference in legal contexts. In other situations the inference problems we encounter may have quite different structural attributes. Two examples illustrating major structural differences are shown in Figure 4.11. Shown in Figure 4.11*a* is a class of inference problems in which there is a *single root node* **U** representing some collection of ultimate, major, or final hypotheses (or *probanda*, as Wigmore called them). In many situations it is customary, and frequently necessary, to specify hypotheses in **U** that are both mutually exclusive and exhaustive. In short, exactly one of the hypotheses in **U** must be true. In many situations, law being an example, we can identify a collection of nodes that represent major lines of argument on hypotheses in **U**, as Figures 4.1 and 4.2 also illustrate. Wigmore referred to

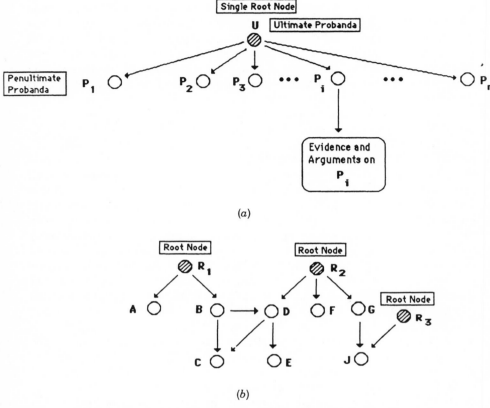

(a)

(b)

FIGURE 4.11 Two examples of inference network generation.

hypotheses identifying these lines of argument as *penultimate probanda*, shown in Figure 4.11a as P_1, P_2, . . . , P_n. We ordinarily suppose that each of the penultimate nodes identifies a class of mutually exclusive and exhaustive hypotheses or possibilities. We might then think of each P_i as being a "hook" upon which we hang, by argument, whatever evidence we have on P_i. The general structural case depicted in Figure 4.11a often applies to inferences in many situations such as medicine, history, and business.

But there are many other inferences routinely performed that do not lend themselves to the situation depicted in Figure 4.11a in which we have a single root node representing ultimate or final hypotheses. In many situations the nature of our inference problem requires us to model or represent some complex process that we believe gives rise to evidence we now have or might have. In some cases, such as the one depicted in Figure 4.11b, it may happen that more than one root node can be identified; then it may be difficult to specify what constitutes our major, ultimate, or final hypotheses. Notice that the network shown in Figure 4.11*b* is in every sense a DAG. The one I have illustrated is not singly connected and represents some fairly complex patterns of probabilistic dependence or influence. It is sometimes argued that an inference network represents what we believe to be causal influences among variables or factors in an inference. There is some controversy concerning use of the term *causal* in describing the patterns of influence among nodes on a network.

4.5.2 Inference Networks, Causality, and Dependence

To continue our discussion of current methods for structuring inference networks, we need just a few probabilistic concepts that arise in the conventional, or Pascalian, view of probability introduced in Section 2.3.1. As I noted earlier, inference networks are often constructed to identify probabilistic elements of an inference problem, each of which has to be assessed by some means. I believe it is fair to say that the Pascalian system of probability predominates in current work on inference networks. Bayes's rule, introduced in Section 2.3.4, forms the mechanism in this system for combining probabilities associated with arcs on an inference network. Consider Figure 4.12 which is intended to illustrate how the structure of the nodes and arcs on an

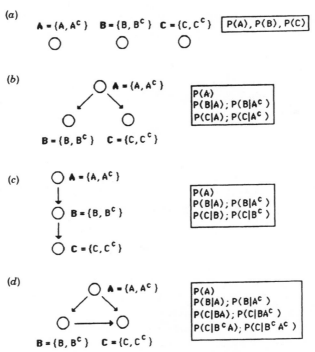

FIGURE 4.12 Inference networks and their probabilistic ingredients.

inference network actually prescribes both the *number* and the *form* of prob-abilistic assessments we need to make. First, suppose, as shown in Figure 4.12*a*, we have three nodes **A, B,** and **C,** each of which represents a binary process (e.g., node **A** can either be in state A or state A^c). Also suppose that, as best we can tell, what state any process is in depends in no way upon what state any other process is in. For example, suppose that A = Tom is intoxicated, B = Dick is intoxicated, and C = Harry is intoxicated. Tom, Dick, and Harry live in different parts of the country and have never had any contact with each other. So it seems plausible to suppose that these events are *completely independent*. What this means is that the *product rule* for independent events we discussed in Section 4.3.2 holds for any way we can form intersections of the events A, B, and C. For the three pairwise inter-sections, $P(AB) = P(A)P(B)$, $P(AC) = P(A)P(C)$, and $P(BC) = P(B)P(C)$. For the intersection of all three events, $P(ABC) = P(A)P(B)P(C)$. It happens that the condition of complete independence also holds if we replace any or all of these events by their complementary events. For example, $P(AB^c) = P(A)P(B^c)$ and $P(A^cBC) = P(A^c)P(B)P(C)$.

Observe in Figure 4.12*a* that we have listed these three nodes but have not connected them by any arcs. This reflects our belief that there is no probabilistic dependence between the three processes represented by these nodes. Given this condition of complete independence, we can determine by means of *just three* probabilities, $P(A)$, $P(B)$, and $P(C)$, the probabilities associated with all possibilities concerning who is and who isn't intoxicated. There are eight possibilities including ones in which all three are intoxicated and none are intoxicated. These eight possibilities are shown in the diagram in Figure 4.13. For binary event classes such diagrams are called *minterm maps* (they have other names in various disciplines). Given binary event classes, a minterm map represents the finest possible partitioning of some sample space or universe of discourse. Any inference about who is and who is not intoxicated would be completely specified if we knew the probabilities

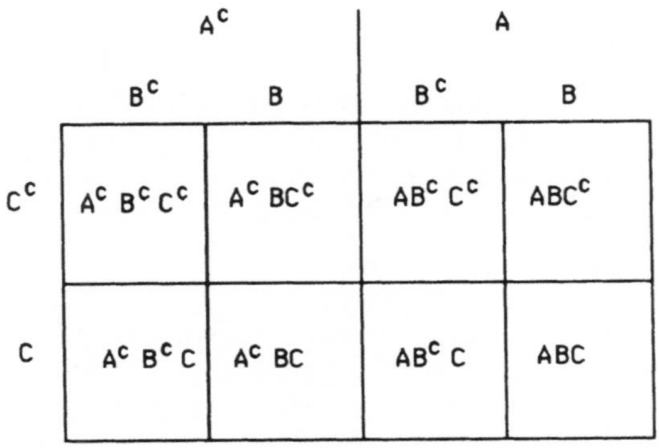

		A^c		A	
		B^c	B	B^c	B
C^c		$A^c B^c C^c$	$A^c BC^c$	$AB^c C^c$	ABC^c
C		$A^c B^c C$	$A^c BC$	$AB^c C$	ABC

FIGURE 4.13 A minterm map illustrating possible joint events.

for each of the minterms or joint events in Figure 4.13. A condition of complete independence would allow us to determine each of these eight probabilities according to the product rule. In the Pascalian system probability *normalizes* (sums to 1.0) across events that are mutually exclusive and exhaustive; for example, $P(A^c) = 1 - P(A)$. Under an assumption of complete independence we can determine, say, the probability that Tom but not Dick or Harry is intoxicated. This probability $P(AB^cC^c) = P(A)[1 - P(B)][1 - P(C)]$. *Moral of story:* The burden of assessing probabilities is minimal when all processes of concern are completely independent.

The trouble is that most inferences involve processes or variables that are *nonindependent* in various ways, with genuinely interesting evidential subtleties. A casual assumption of complete independence among identified processes would in most cases invite inferential calamity. So we have no choice but to do our best at capturing what we believe are avenues of probabilistic *dependence* among processes of concern. To do so, we link nodes representing these processes by various patterns of arcs. I can think of no inference problem, outside of the classroom, whose structure is either provided for us or immediately apparent. Constructing a network representation of an inference problem is a purely subjective judgmental task, one likely to result in a different structural pattern by each person who performs it. In the contemporary literature on inference networks there is now some controversy concerning what people should and do attend to when such tasks are performed. As we will see in just a moment, this controversy concerns whether such structuring always involves the tracking of *causal* relations.

As I will now illustrate by means of Figures 4.12*a*, *b*, and *c*, each probabilistic dependency we introduce increases the number of probabilistic assessments that are required. As background for Figure 4.12*b* suppose you hear me say I have a throbbing headache and you also believe I may be staggering a bit; you entertain the possibility that I am intoxicated. Let A = I am intoxicated, B = I have a headache, and C = I am staggering. Suppose you decide that intoxication causes a person to have a headache and to stagger, so you construct the inference network shown in Figure 4.12*b*. For simplicity let us ignore nodes representing the evidence you received about me and focus on the events your evidence revealed. Since we have three binary event classes, we have the same set of joint events or minterms shown in Figure 4.13. As an example, consider the event ABC that I am intoxicated, I have a headache, and I am staggering. According to the *general product rule* (often called the *chain rule*) for determining the probability of joint events, we can express $P(ABC) = P(A)P(B|A)P(C|BA)$. As it happens, there are five other formally equivalent ways to apply the chain rule in decomposing $P(ABC)$. For example, it is also true that $P(ABC) = P(C)P(B|C)P(A|BC)$. In general, when there are n events in an intersection, there are $n!$ such decompositions.

One basis for choosing the decomposition $P(ABC) = P(A)P(B|A)P(C|BA)$ is that A is a root node (i.e., it has no parents). In this example the events in A are not dependent upon anything except the *back-*

ground information (S) we discussed in Section 2.3.2. Recall that S is, by definition, always lurking in the background, even though we may suppress it on occasion to make equations simpler. You have said that my suspected intoxication may have caused my headache, so you suppose that B is dependent upon A. Your arc from **A** to **B** reflects this dependence and gives rise to the conditional probabilities $P(B|A)$ and $P(B|A^c)$. You need to express how likely is my headache if I am intoxicated and if I am not intoxicated. By your causal argument you suppose that $P(B|A) \neq P(B)$. This indicates your belief that B is not independent of A; perhaps you believe that $P(B|A) > P(B)$. I am more likely to have a headache, given that I am intoxicated, than I am to have a headache if you had not taken my intoxication into account. In the binary case we are considering, to say that $P(B|A) \neq P(B)$ is also to say that $P(B|A) \neq P(B|A^c)$. In short, you are arguing that the probability of my having a headache depends upon whether or not I am intoxicated.

Now consider the term $P(C|BA)$ in our decomposition of $P(ABC)$. The network you have constructed in Figure 4.12*b* reflects your belief that events at node **C** depend upon events at node **A** but not upon events at node **B**. Notice that there is no arc connecting **B** and **C** (we will add one in a later example). Stated another way, **C** has only one parent, that being node **A**. The absence of an arc between **B** and **C** indicates your present belief that whether or not I stagger depends only upon whether or not I am intoxicated and not upon whether or not I have a headache. There are several consequences of this assumption reflected in the inference network in Figure 4.12*b*. The first is that we can shorten $P(C|BA)$ to read $P(C|A)$. The statement $P(C|BA) = P(C|A)$ means that C and B are independent, *conditional upon* A. In words it states that, if you knew or assumed I was intoxicated (A), the probability of my staggering (C) would not be affected by further information (B) that I have a headache. My staggering and my having a headache are independent, conditional upon my being intoxicated. The absence of an arc between **B** and **C** has another consequence, namely it reflects your belief that $P(C|B^cA) = P(C|A)$. If you assumed that I am intoxicated, you would not change your belief about the probability of my staggering if you also knew that I did *not* have a headache. This is our first exposure to the related topics of *conditional independence* and *conditional nonindependence*. These are perhaps the most important probabilistic concepts in any Pascalian or conventional account of inference networks. In Chapters 5 and 6 we will devote considerable attention to these concepts and the role they play in capturing evidential subtleties.

Collecting what we have so far, we can determine $P(ABC)$ in terms of the chain rule as $P(ABC) = P(A)P(B|A)P(C|A)$. As Figure 4.12*b* shows there are just five probabilities required in this case in order to determine probabilities associated with all of the eight possibilities in Figure 4.13. There are in fact ten probabilities we need, but five of these are determined by the normalization property. For example, from $P(A)$ we have $P(A^c) = 1 - P(A)$. As far as event B is concerned, we need to have the probabilities

$P(B|A)$ indicating how likely is my headache, given that I am intoxicated, and $P(B|A^c)$ indicating how likely is my headache, given that I am not intoxicated. By the normalization property of Pascalian probability, $P(B^c|A) = 1 - P(B|A)$, and $P(B^c|A^c) = 1 - P(B|A^c)$. We also need probabilities of my staggering given my being intoxicated, $P(C|A)$, and my not being intoxicated, $P(C|A^c)$. From these, by normalization, we obtain $P(C^c|A)$ and $P(C^c|A^c)$.

Now suppose that someone introduces a temporal factor and argues that what you observed about my behavior is the result of a causal chain involving nodes **A**, **B**, and **C**, as shown in Figure 4.12c. The argument goes: My intoxication (last night) caused me (now) to have a throbbing headache which, in turn, is causing me to stagger about. In short, I have a hangover. On this argument the proximal cause of my staggering is my throbbing headache. Once again, let us consider $P(ABC)$ and decompose it according to the chain rule while noting that **A** is still the root node. We have $P(ABC) = P(A)P(B|A)P(C|BA)$, as in the preceding example. The difference is that node **B** is now the parent of node **C**; in the preceding example **A** was the parent of **C**. Also notice the absence of an arc between **A** and **C**. This encodes a belief that whether or not I am now staggering is independent of whether or not I was intoxicated last night, once you know whether or not I presently have a throbbing headache. Figure 4.12c shows the five probabilities we need to determine the probability of each of the eight possible minterms shown in Figure 4.13. Observe that two of the conditional probabilities are different from those required in the preceding example; we need $P(C|B)$ and $P(C|B^c)$ instead of $P(C|A)$ and $P(C|A^c)$. For example, $P(ABC) = P(A)P(B|A)P(C|B)$. The independence of C and A, given B, allows us to say that $P(C|BA) = P(C|B)$.

Finally, suppose you decide to argue that my present unsteadiness may depend jointly upon my having been intoxicated and my now having a throbbing headache. To represent this situation, you form the network shown in Figure 4.12d which is the same as the one in Figure 4.12b except that you add an arc between nodes **B** and **C**. What you are saying here is that my staggering about may be due jointly to my overindulgence and to my having a throbbing headache. In other words, unsteadiness is not independent of intoxication, whether or not I have a headache. To find the probability of all possibilities in Figure 4.13, we now need to have the seven probability assessments shown in Figure 4.12d. You might, for example, believe that the probability of my staggering about is greater, given that I have a headache and was intoxicated [$P(C|BA)$], than it is given any of the other three possibilities concerning events in nodes **B** and **A**.

Let us pause for a moment to consider the causal elements I introduced in these examples. Suppose you labeled the inference networks in Figures 4.12b, c, and d as *causal networks* to indicate your belief that what allowed you to construct them was your prior experience in perceiving causal associations between phenomena. You argue: Intoxication frequently causes headaches, and intoxication and/or headaches can frequently cause people to stagger about. If you sought to defend your label *causal network* in terms of the *necessity* and *sufficiency* conditions we discussed in Section 4.3.1, you would encounter some difficulties. Would you say, for example, that intoxication is either a necessary or a sufficient condition for a person to have a headache or to stagger about? You would probably not do so, since your accumulated experience would also allow you to believe that intoxicated persons frequently do not have headaches and do not stagger about. You would also say that either headaches or staggering about can occur for reasons other than intoxication. But we might all agree that the presence of a throbbing headache and staggering have some *positive relevance* in an inference about whether a person is or was intoxicated.

Two of the most influential current works on inference networks are those by Pearl (1988) and by Lauritzen and Spiegelhalter (1988). In both of these works, and in others stemming from them, I have noticed what I believe to be an unfortunate linkage between the terms *causality* and *relevance*. My belief is that possible implications drawn from a confusion of these terms may in fact serve to limit the perceived range of applicability of these works. Let us first hear about *relevance* from Judea Pearl; he asserts that relevance is a relation indicating a potential change of belief due to a change in knowledge (1988, 18). Here we agree for reasons I mentioned in Section 3.1. Regarding *causation*, Pearl observes: "Causation is a language with which we can talk efficiently about certain structures of relevance relationships, with the objective of separating the relevant from the superfluous" (1988, 18). Here we partially agree for reasons I tried to make clear in Section 4.3.2. If there is some condition of necessity or sufficiency involving events H and E, then evidence about E would certainly be relevant in an inference about H. But evidence might be judged entirely relevant on H even when we would be very hard-pressed to show how H has caused E or E has caused H.

As I see it, the major trouble caused by the manner in which Pearl links relevance and causality concerns what he says about the major thrust of his own work on inference networks. I have said that the Pascalian system of probability dominates current work on inferential networks and that Bayes's rule forms the principle device according to which probabilistic assessments on the arcs of a network are aggregated in order to reach a conclusion. It is now customary to call such networks *Bayesian networks*. As Pearl tells us: "Bayesian networks are DAGs in which the nodes represent variables, the arcs signify the existence of direct causal influences between the linked variables, and the strengths of these influences are expressed by forward conditional probabilities" (1988, 117). To require that the arcs of an inferential network signify direct causal influences is to hamstring the entire enterprise of applying conventional probability theory in the analyses of inferential networks. If I believed that such causal linkages are necessary, I would not be able to complete the rest of this book. In Chapters 6, 7, and 8 I will apply Bayesian networks in analyses of many different evidential situations. Leaving quite apart what it means to say that A causes B, I would have to exercise more imagination than I could ever muster in order to convince you that causation forms the essential basis for every arc I will identify in my analyses.

I promised earlier that I would give examples of recurrent inferences in which it makes sense to devote the time and energy to a very careful structuring of a complex inference network. As my first example, Lauritzen and Spiegelhalter have incorporated a Bayesian inference network as part of an expert system for assisting the diagnosis of certain kinds of neurological disorders. In an account of this network they began by describing it as a *causal network* (1988, 158). However, in response to several comments from members of their audience, they agreed that other descriptions would be more suitable, one of which is the term influence diagram (1988, 216). I will discuss influence diagrams in the next section. Saying that arcs on an inference network simply represent avenues of probabilistic influence removes any controversy associated with the term causation. Neapolitan, in discussing causal networks, concludes that a more suitable descriptive term might be *independence networks* (1991, 176–190). This term seems quite appropriate since the act of laying out an inference network is also the act of specifying dependencies among nodes. One way of hamstringing an inference is to suppose that every recognized element of an inference somehow depends upon every other element. Constructing an inference network is also the act of localizing probability assessments. The parents of any node show exactly what probabilistic influence, and none other, exists on events at this node. The more independencies we can safely identify, the lighter is our burden of probability assessment.

4.5.3 Emerging Technologies for Complex Inference

Here is a brief account of some of the major structural issues reflected in the work of persons now engaged in research on inference networks. Efforts to provide computer assistance to persons attempting to draw conclusions from masses of evidence date from the work of Ward Edwards (1962). Edwards proposed a system called PIP (Probabilistic Information Processing) in which people provide various probabilistic judgments and computers combine them according to Bayes's rule. The first proposals for PIP were structurally very simple, as illustrated in Figure 4.14. Suppose that an inference concerns hypotheses at a single root node **H**. Users of PIP were first asked to assess a distribution of prior probabilities across hypotheses in **H**. Then, as each item of evidence E_i^* arrived, a user was asked to make a probabilistic assessment of the inferential force of E_i^* on hypotheses in **H**; they did so using the likelihood ratios we discussed earlier in Section 4.3.1. The importance of possible conditional nonindependence of evidence was recognized at the time (e.g., Schum 1966, 1969). Users of PIP were cautioned to give attention to whether or not any new item of evidence seemed nonindependent of any

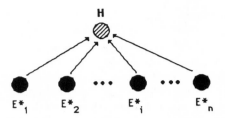

FIGURE 4.14   The inferential structure of Edwards's original PIP system.

previous evidence, conditional upon any of the hypotheses in **H.** In early versions of PIP no attempt was made to structure arguments in defense of the relevance and credibility of any evidence. This caused troubles, since it is often extremely difficult to judge the inferential force of evidence on some hypotheses in the absence of an argument that links evidence and hypotheses. In short, the earliest versions of PIP involved inferences that were not decomposed. Some persons refer, somewhat unkindly, to the inferential structure underlying the first applications of PIP as an "idiot's version" of the application of Bayes's rule.

Various attempts were subsequently made to extend Edwards's PIP idea to situations in which we do wish to decompose an inference task by charting arguments from evidence to major or ultimate hypotheses. An example is Anne Martin's (1980) system called CASPRO (cascaded inference program). This system allows one to determine likelihood ratios associated with items of evidence linked in various ways to major hypotheses at a single root node. Consider the inference network shown in Figure 4.1, and note that there are twelve items of evidence linked by arguments to a single root node **H.** Also observe that the DAG representing this network is not singly connected. Martin's system employs a Bayesian algorithm that allows one to determine, in terms of likelihood ratios, the inferential force on **H** of each of these evidence items. A wide assortment of evidential subtleties such as those revealed in Figure 4.1 can be captured by CASPRO.

In a series of papers and in a recent book, Judea Pearl and his colleagues have made further advances in applying Bayes's rule to complex inferences. (e.g., Pearl, 1982, 1988, 1990; Pearl and Verma, 1987). Consider the inference network in Figure 4.15, which is a copy of Figure 4.11b with one addition. Suppose, as Figure 4.15 illustrates, we have evidence A* that node **A** is in state A. We may wish to determine how this evidence affects our probabilistic belief regarding events at any other node on this network. Notice that the network in these figures has more than one root node. For example, we might wish to determine how evidence A* affects our belief about the state of root node R_2 or any other node in this network such as node **D.** Assuming that we have assessed appropriate probabilities associated with the root nodes and the arcs on this network, Pearl offers a method for determining how receipt of evidence A* causes probabilities to *propagate* through this network and

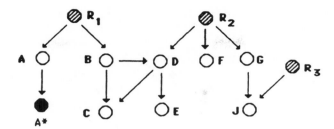

FIGURE 4.15 Evidence on a node in an inference network.

how such propagation affects our beliefs at other nodes. Such probability propagation is *bidirectional* in nature; when a network is "activated" by evidence, any node may receive probabilistic "messages" from its sources of probabilistic influence, namely its parents and its children. Thus, for example, when evidence A* arrives, node **D** may receive probabilistic messages from its parents **B** and R_2 and from its children **C** and **E,** all of whom in turn have received messages from their parents and children.

Pearl, Lauritzen, and Spiegelhalter, among others, have been appropriately concerned about developing efficient algorithms for probability propagation in complex inference networks. Trouble arises when inference networks are not singly connected. This trouble has at least three faces, the first of which involves *computational complexity.* When nodes on an inference network are not singly connected, they may receive messages from many parents and children. When we imagine many nodes receiving messages from many parents and children, we can also imagine that the message-passing process required for equilibrium takes many calculational steps each of which consumes time. It is of interest to know, for example, how many computational steps would be required for the propagation process to reach equilibrium as we seek to determine our beliefs regarding node **D** in Figure 4.15, based upon new evidence A* or on other evidence we may have. As I have mentioned several times, our inferences would often be paralyzed if we supposed that "everything was dependent on everything else" in a network we are constructing. This is one reason why the search for network independencies is so important. It happens that inference may also be paralyzed under certain circumstances even if we had access to the most powerful computer imaginable.

It has recently been shown that there are some classes of inference network problems, involving non-singly connected graphs, that are said to be *NP-Hard* (Cooper 1990). In the field of computer science attention has been given to the problem of determining the difficulty of a problem in terms of its size. We may think of the size of a problem in terms of the number of ingredients or variables it involves. Thus, for example, the inference problem shown in Figure 4.1 is more difficult than any of the ones shown in Figure 4.12. So we suppose that the length of time necessary to solve any problem that can be represented as a graph increases as the number of nodes and arcs increases. The length of time required depends upon the function showing the nature of this increase. The time required to solve some problems increases as a polynomial function of their ingredients, but the time required for others increases exponentially with their ingredients. For small numbers of ingredients the difference between these two functions is small. But as the number of ingredients increases, the difference becomes very large in favor of exponential functions. You might try this out using the two functions $f(n) = n^2$, a polynomial term, and $g(n) = 2^n$, an exponential, where n is the number of problem ingredients. For $n = 4$, $f(4) = 16 = g(4)$. For $n = 10$, $f(10) = 100$, but $g(10) = 1024$. Now try out $n = 50$ in both of these functions.

The letters *NP* mean *nondeterministic polynomial* with reference to the time it takes to solve a problem. The term *nondeterministic* refers to the nature of the computer involved in the solution process; our present interest concerns the term *polymonial*. There is a class of problems called *NP-complete* problems for which no one has yet discovered an algorithm that can solve them in a time proportional to a polynomial function of their ingredients. There may be such a solution one day, but so far no one has found it. The worst case would be a situation in which this solution time increases exponentially with the number of ingredients. Now, *NP-hard* problems are those that appear to be *at least as difficult* as NP-complete problems. Cooper concludes that the search for general algorithms for probability propagation in non-singly connected inference is fruitless and that we may have to settle for what he terms special-case, average-case, and approximation algorithms (1990, 393). Research on computational complexity problems is relevant in many situations. The seminal work in this area seem to be that of Gary and Johnson (1979); tutorials appear in the works of Parker and Rardin (1988, 11–51) and Neapolitan (1990, 300–305), and a very readable layperson's account is given by Poundstone (1990, 160–188).

One problem often overlooked in the current literature on inference networks concerns the burden of assessing probabilities. If an inference is to be analyzed in Bayesian terms, every arc you see on an inference network requires *at least two* probability assessments. The burden of assessment for singly connected networks can be heavy enough; for non-singly connected networks it can be crushing. The basic trouble is that non-singly connected graphs signal conditional nonindependencies such as the one illustrated in Figure 4.12*d;* many evidential subtleties lurk within these nonindependencies. In probabilistic inference what we do not take account of can often hurt us very badly. A major intellectual difficulty concerns how we may best exploit evidential subtleties we recognize, even if we have access to the most modern computer facilities. If enough are recognized, we may discover that there is no computer that could propagate, in a life time, all of the probabilities in the inference network we have constructed.

One of the most promising forms of computer assistance now available rests upon the idea of an *influence diagram* first introduced by Howard and

Matheson (1984; based upon an earlier unpublished work in 1980). As noted in Section 4.2.1, probabilistic inference is often embedded in a decision task. An influence diagram is a DAG having three basic kinds of nodes: those associated with probabilities, decisions, and values. The states of a decision node refer to possible actions or choices; the states of value nodes represent decision consequences together with their assessed values. If an influence diagram has only probability nodes, it does not differ from any of the DAGs we have already considered. For our present purposes we will consider influence diagrams having just probability nodes whose various states represent propositions whose probability is of interest. Persons involved in research on the applications of influence diagrams are unanimous in their view that the arcs on such diagrams do not necessarily indicate any causal linkage (Howard and Matheson 1984; Schacter 1986; Shachter and Heckerman 1987). More recently Howard has argued that even the term *probabilistic dependence* used with reference to an arc may be misleading, since it may often imply a causal linkage (1989, 904). Howard states that the most suitable description of the influence or relation indicated by an arc is conveyed by the term *relevance*. Thus an inference network might also be described as a *relevance diagram*. We have now come full circle to our original discussion of relevance and causality. I believe Howard's account of the meaning of arcs on an inference network to be the most general and most appropriate.

There are now several commercially available software systems for the construction and Bayesian analysis of inference networks; some are based upon influence diagram research and others upon algorithms developed by Pearl and by Lauritzen and Spiegelhalter. Figure 4.16 is an influence or relevance diagram recently presented by Ward Edwards in his discussion of the use of influence diagrams in the analysis of legal cases (1991, 1025–1074). I use this particular example for the purpose of comparing modern inference network analyses and Wigmore's original method for argument construction. Edwards's analysis involves evidence in one of the same cases (*Hatchett v. Commonwealth*) that Wigmore used to illustrate his methods. Earlier, in Section 4.4.2, I described a small portion of Wigmore's analysis of the evidence in this case (see Figure 4.8). Structurally Wigmore's and Edwards's inference networks are quite different, even though they both qualify as DAGs. This difference is to be expected since Wigmore and Edwards had quite different standpoints and, as we will see, quite different constraints.

If we were to examine Wigmore's entire evidence chart for *Hatchett v. Commonwealth,* we would see that it has the same basic form as the one shown in Figure 4.11a (his entire chart is shown in Wigmore, J., 1937, 876–877, and in Anderson and Twining 1991, *Teacher's Manual,* 130–132). A single root node **U** represents the ultimate probandum (matter to be proved) in this case: whether or not Oliver Hatchett murdered Moses Young. There were three penultimate probanda in this case: P_1: Did Moses Young die of poison? P_2: Did Oliver Hatchett give poison to Moses Young? P_3: Did Hatchett knowingly give the poison to Moses Young? All of the evidence and

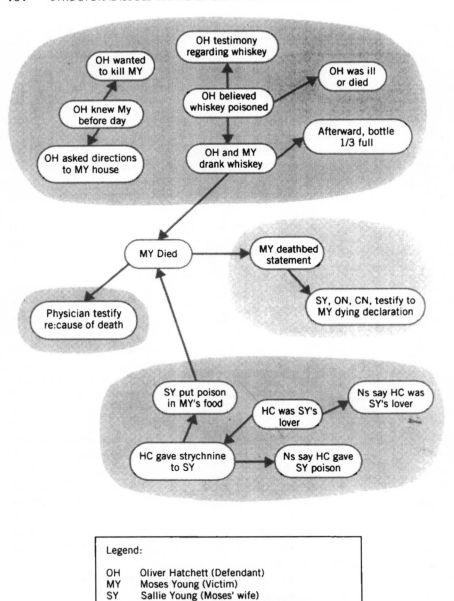

FIGURE 4.16 A Bayes's net for *Hatchett v. Commonwealth* (after Edwards 1991, 1046).

arguments Wigmore presents "hang" on one or the other of these three penultimate issues. In Figure 4.8 is one of three lines of argument Wigmore constructed that bears upon P_1. Wigmore also charted the defense's counterarguments such as the one shown in Figure 4.9. Wigmore essentially saw his evidence charting methods as a device for assembling *all* recognized pieces of an inferential puzzle, subject to the constraint that the assembled puzzle would be structured in terms of the major points or elements at issue in a legal case. But Wigmore was unconstrained by any system of probability. He never mentions Bayes's rule, and he was quite innocent of the concept of conditional independence. Nevertheless, he did recognize that the evidential relevance arguments being constructed have linkages that are probabilistic in nature. He did his best with what he had available to him, verbal expressions of probative or inferential force.

When examined carefully, Edwards's influence diagram analysis of this case more closely resembles the DAG shown in Figure 4.11*b* than it does the one in Figure 4.11*a*. First, Edwards's diagram in Figure 4.16 reveals the existence of three root nodes: R_1: Oliver Hatchett believed that the whiskey was poisoned. R_2: Oliver Hatchett knew Moses Young before the day Young died. R_3: Henry Carroll was Sallie Young's lover. Second, notice that there is no node specifically representing the ultimate probandum concerning whether or not Oliver Hatchett murdered Moses Young. However, the possibility that Hatchett murdered Young appears by virtue of the manner in which Edwards partitioned the states of the node labeled *MY died*. In order to understand Edwards's analysis, you must have more details of this case.

Moses Young, aged 65, was in poor health; he suffered from colic and had been injured in his side after having been struck by a cart. Oliver Hatchett claims that his father (Littleton Hatchett) gave him a jug of whiskey to take to Moses. Oliver gave two different accounts of what his father told him about the whiskey. He first said his father told him that the whiskey would "fix" Moses Young. He later retracted this statement and said that he had no knowledge that the whiskey was poisoned. On the day in question Oliver took the whiskey to Moses who lived about three miles from the Hatchetts. There is evidence that Oliver did not know Moses; he had to make inquiries about where Moses lived. Oliver and Moses first had dinner, and then Oliver asked Moses to go outside and have a drink of the whiskey he had brought. Moses drank from the bottle and returned it to Oliver who then started on his way home. The bottle, later examined, was about 1/3 full. Moses then went inside his house and shortly began to complain of a pain in his side. Moses allegedly told his wife Sallie that Oliver had "tricked him in a drink of whiskey." Moses then fell to the floor, writhed in pain for some time, and expired about three hours later.

There were three persons present with Moses until he died: Sallie and two neighbors Osborne and Charlotte Northington. All three testified that Moses, in a dying declaration, had claimed that Oliver had killed him with the whiskey. Unaccountably there was no postmortem analysis of Moses' body, and no analysis was ever made of the contents of the whiskey bottle. However, at trial two physicians were asked to testify about the cause of Moses death. They both testified that, from the descriptions of Moses behavior before he died they "supposed" he had died from strychnine poisoning. A man named Henry Carroll had also been indicted with Oliver Hatchett; the Northington's testified that Henry was Sallie Young's lover. Three weeks before Moses' death Henry had given Sallie a bottle he said contained strychnine and had instructed Sallie to put some in Moses' coffee. The Northingtons knew about this but did not tell Moses; neither did they tell Moses that Henry was Sallie's lover. No attempt was made by the prosecution to show that Oliver ever knew of Henry's delivery of the strychnine to Sallie.

Now back to the node in Figure 4.16 labeled *MY died*. In partitioning this node Edwards considered four possibilities: Q_1: Moses died of poison in the whiskey only. Q_2: Moses died of poison in his food only. Q_3: Moses died of poison in his food and in the whiskey. Q_4: Moses died of other causes. Oliver Hatchett was guilty of murder only if Q_1 or Q_3 is true. Edwards's influence diagram shows his conception of lines of probabilistic influence among certain major events in this case as revealed in the appeals court transcript. Unlike Wigmore's analysis, Edwards's does not chart all of the evidence revealed in this transcript. Wigmore's inference network for this case contains 68 nodes, many of which represent ancillary evidence and arguments that follow from this evidence; Edwards's influence diagram contains just 17 nodes. I note here that Edwards certainly has no aversion to inference networks containing many nodes. As I write this chapter, Edwards and his colleagues (Bruce Abramson, John Brown, Alan Murphy, and Bob Winkler) are busy constructing an inference network, called HAILFINDER, to improve the forecasting of severe weather in Colorado. This network now has over 70 nodes and requires more than 4500 probability assessments. The number of nodes and probability assessments is sure to grow as their work proceeds.

There was a major constraint on Edwards's analysis of *Hatchett v. Commonwealth* that Wigmore did not experience. Edwards's constraint was Bayes's rule; the computer-based influence diagram system Edwards used in his probabilistic analysis of this case incorporates a Bayesian algorithm for the propagation of probabilities throughout a network. Thus Edwards was first obliged to consider the possibility of conditional nonindependence among his nodes. Observe that there are four clusters of nodes shown in a shaded region of Figure 4.16. Also observe that there are no arcs connecting nodes in one cluster with nodes in another. Possible conditional nonindependencies are localized within a cluster; the clusters themselves are conditionally independent. Edwards assessed his own probabilities associated with the nodes and arcs on his diagram. His influence diagram program then told him that the posterior probability of Q_1, on the charted evidence, is 0.548 and that the probability of Q_3 on this evidence is 0.104. Combined, these probabilities told Edwards that the probability that Oliver Hatchett murdered Moses Young, on the evidence considered, is 0.652. Not believing that this probability corresponds to "beyond reasonable doubt," Edwards concluded that the case against Oliver Hatchett should have been overturned by the appeals court. He was later to discover that this was in fact the opinion rendered by the appeals court. Another constraint on Edwards's analysis involves ancillary evidence and how it should be incorporated in an inference network. There is likely to be controversy about this matter, as we now discuss.

4.5.4 Charting Ancillary Evidence: Networks within Networks?

The reader knowledgeable about the theory of graphs is entitled to believe that I have committed some serious transgressions regarding the manner in which I have constructed network representations of various evidential situations. By definition, an arc connects nodes; this is the reason why an arc is represented by an ordered pair of the nodes it connects, such as the arc **(D, C)** in Figure 4.1. Examine Figures 3.10 and 4.4, in both of which I attempted to illustrate the role of ancillary evidence in determining the strength of an inferential linkage between two nodes. Observe in either figure that I have arcs leading from a node to an arc. For example, Figure 4.4 shows an arc pointing from node A_1 to the arc between nodes E^* and E_b. In graph theory such arc-to-arc connections have no meaning. I will state again what I mean by such arc-to-arc linkages, and then we can argue about whether they make any sense.

In my discussion of Figure 4.4 I left the arcs connecting E^* and H undirected simply to acknowledge the fact that chains of reasoning can be constructed in either direction. For present purposes suppose that this chain of reasoning was constructed from Mike's evidence E^* to hypotheses at node **H**, H is the event that Joe did it. Imagine that arrows inserted on these arcs would point upward. Now consider the first link in this chain of reasoning. Suppose that I ask you to infer that Mike probably believes that Joe's car was at the scene, given that we have his testimony that he saw Joe's car at the scene. You ask me why you should be entitled to make this inference. In reply I assert the following generalization: If a person says an event happened, then this person probably (usually, often, frequently) believes this event did occur. With some choice of hedge here you might easily accept this commonsense generalization. But, because it is a generalization, you begin to be interested in whether or not this generalization holds in this particular instance involving Mike, the testimony he has given, and other elements of the situation in which he gave this testimony. In short, depending upon what we know about Mike, this generalization might or might not be such a good one in the present circumstances. As discussed in connection with Figure 4.4, whether or not Mike believes what he testified concerns his veracity. So we begin to collect whatever evidence we can find that bears upon his truthfulness.

Some of the general kinds of veracity-related evidence we might discover are shown in Figure 3.8. In Figure 4.4 my example of ancillary evidence involves testimony from Tom that Mike was not at the scene and could therefore not have made the observation he says he made. If true, Tom's assertion suggests that Mike made up the story of Joe's car being at the scene, a story he does not actually believe. We might easily discover other ancillary evidence bearing upon Mike's veracity or on any other of the credibility-related attributes illustrated in Figure 4.4. The *mass* of evidence bearing, say, on Mike's veracity, could contain any of the forms of evidence described in Figure 3.11. In addition we might also observe that our arguments rest upon any of the evidence combinations noted in Figures 3.13, 3.14, and 3.15. In short, we might have a variety of evidence and some very complex arguments, all bearing upon Mike's veracity.

Another example of arc-to-arc linkages involves the identification evidence about Sacco and whether or not he was at the scene of the crime (Figure 4.10). Notice the extensive ancillary evidence and arguments bearing on the linkage between nodes 26 and 18. These evidence items and arguments provide the basis for judging the inferential force of Pelser's testimony (node 26) on the events to which he testified (node 18). Recall that he testified seeing Sacco at the scene of the crime.

Modern work on inference networks connects structural and probabilistic elements in ways that Wigmore could never have imagined. The current work in this area I have mentioned so far involves quite sophisticated applications of Bayes's rule. Such networks are usually described as *Bayes nets*; Edwards's influence diagram in Figure 4.16 is a Bayes net. To employ any Bayes net you need conditional probability assessments on arcs, as I illustrated in Figure 4.12. One issue rarely discussed at length in current inference network literature concerns the means of support for these probability assessments. We are told that they can be relative frequencies, if available, but are subjective probability assessments otherwise. Assessments concerning unique or singular events are necessarily subjective. My argument is that conditional probabilities on the arcs of a network must be supported by appropriate generalizations and by at least some evidence and argument bearing upon these generalizations. My arc-to-arc connections simply show the influence of ancillary evidence and argument on the strength of other arcs.

In some cases we may encounter situations like the one depicted in Figure 4.17. Consider the inference network we have constructed; the nodes contain all of the major possibilities of interest to us in this inference problem. This is called our *main network*. Suppose that the probabilities on the arcs on this network require subjective assessments that we must support in some way. Such support is provided by networks *ancillary* to our main network. But these ancillary networks involve arcs that have to be supported, so we gather further evidence and construct ancillary networks in defense of the arcs on our first ancillary network. How far we carry this process of structuring networks-within-networks depends upon how compulsive we are, in addition to whatever temporal and other constraints we face. What we face here is the very issue of granularity of analysis I have mentioned several times. As my

MAIN NETWORK

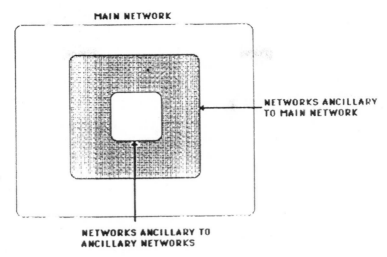

NETWORKS ANCILLARY
TO MAIN NETWORK

NETWORKS ANCILLARY TO
ANCILLARY NETWORKS

FIGURE 4.17   Networks within networks.

colleague Tony Zawilski put it, current work on inference networks supposes that everything ancillary to a main network can somehow be "sucked into" it. Sucking one network into another may involve a considerable suppression of uncertainties and may give rise to later repentance when the importance of these uncertainties is realized.

My analysis of networks within networks, involving what I have termed arc-to-arc connections, will not please everyone. Here are two arguments that might be raised. First, it might be believed that we can always link an ancillary argument to a node on our main inference network. If so, perhaps we can always have just one "super network" that incorporates all of our evidence. I do not believe this can generally be done, and as an example I ask you first to consider nodes E and A_3 in Figure 4.4. Suppose I change the arc from A_3 so that it connects with node E. In a Bayesian analysis this would require me to assess the conditional probabilities $P(A_3|E)$ and $P(A_3|E^c)$. The first probability concerns how likely is Mike to have very poor eyesight if Joe's car was at the scene of the crime. You might agree when I say: I don't see the connection. I would also have great difficulty inserting other nodes between E and A_3 to establish this connection. Instead, I decide to connect nodes E_s and A_3, since this looks more promising. With such a connection I would need to assess the probabilities $P(A_3|E_s)$ and $P(A_3|E_s^c)$. This first says: How likely is Mike to have very poor eyesight, given that he obtained sensory evidence of event E? Unfortunately, this won't work either. The trouble is that the linkage between nodes E_s and E concerns just how good was the sensory evidence Mike might have received as a result of his alleged observation. His having poor eyesight bears upon *how good* this sensory evidence was and not upon whether or not he actually received it. Other, objectivity-related, evidence bears upon whether or not he actually received sensory evidence of event E.

Another argument might say that I can always find a node to insert between nodes **E** and **E$_s$** to which I can link **A$_3$** with an arc. This is easier said than done. Consider the two events: E = Joe's car was at the scene and E$_s$ = Mike obtained sensory evidence of Joe's car at the scene. Even if we could trace the precise chain of physical and neurophysiological events that occur between E and E$_s$, we would not know which one to link to the ancillary node unless we had a precise description of the reasons why Mike has poor visual acuity.

It is interesting to note that Wigmore evidence charts never contain any of the arc-to-arc connections that appear on evidence diagrams I have presented. For example, Figure 4.8 shows several nodes regarding ancillary matters (items 11, 11.1, and 13) linked to a node (item 7) on Wigmore's main network. To this extent Wigmore's charts correspond more closely with the requirements of graph theory than do the inference networks I have constructed so far. Does this show that my arc-to-arc connections make no sense after all? Remember that Wigmore did not have Bayes's rule and conditional probabilities in mind as he constructed his charts. If we attempted to supply probabilistic ingredients associated with the arcs on Wigmore's network, we would experience some difficulties. One probability we would need is P(item 11.1| item 7), which reads: How likely is strychnine and not colic to produce symptoms such as those Moses Young exhibited, given that Moses Young died (apparently in health) within three hours after drinking the whiskey? I cannot see any dependence here. Whether strychnine rather than colic produces symptoms such as those Moses Young exhibited depends in no way upon whether any particular individual, Moses included, died three hours after drinking whiskey.

My belief is that if Wigmore were alive today and inclined to construct Bayes nets, he would have to change the manner in which he charted his ancillary evidence. First consider item 7, that Moses Young died (apparently in health) within three hours after drinking the whiskey. Two probabilities a Bayes net analysis would require are P(item 7| Young died of poison) and P(item 7| Young did not die of poison). These probabilities might be assessed provided we had ancillary evidence to support them. Moses Young's dying, whether or not he was poisoned, is a singular event for which there are no relative frequencies. What we have as evidence bearing upon the strength of these probabilities is item 11 (that he had colic), item 11.1 (that strychnine but not colic could have produced his symptoms), and item 13 (that he had previously suffered an injury to his side). The manner in which a person charts evidence depends on this person's standpoint, one element of which is the person's objectives. One of my own objectives in constructing inference networks is to show how much probability theories together with structural considerations have to tell us about evidence. The probabilities I will discuss in later chapters have to be supported in some way by ancillary evidence in situations in which we will not be able to form direct linkages between this ancillary evidence and nodes on our main inference network. If we could do so, then we would not call such evidence *ancillary*. To say that we can always form a single inference network that incorporates *all* the evidence we have is also to say that there is no such thing as ancillary evidence. I am not prepared to say that this is so.

One person who can come to our assistance regarding the charting of ancillary evidence is Ron Howard, one of the founders of the entire influence diagram enterprise. In a recent paper Howard discusses the role influence diagrams can play as *knowledge maps* (1989). By such means we attempt to capture a person's knowledge about some matter in a way that allows the drawing of conclusions from this knowledge. Some of the knowledge maps Howard discusses have nodes connected to other nodes with arcs that Howard indicates by dashed lines. He tells us that some portions of knowledge maps are *evocative* in the sense that their function is just to "evoke the proper considerations when making the judgments required in the assessed knowledge map" (Howard 1989, 907). I believe that it is accurate to say that ancillary evidence and arguments from it are evocative in the sense that they allow us to assess probabilities associated with nodes on the "main" portion of an inference network or influence diagram.

Figure 4.18 is a revised version of Figure 4.4 and one that is, I believe, congenial to Howard's ideas about evocative portions of an inference network or influence diagram. I have even drawn the arcs from the top down in keeping with custom in constructing influence diagrams. Notice that my arrows from ancillary evidence and arguments are now dashed lines and that they now connect to nodes rather than to arcs (as in Figure 4.4). I have only this hesitation in doing so. If such a scheme is employed, it should be made clear that any evocative arc (dashed line) refers to the *probabilities* required at a node on the main network and not to events at the node itself. For example, in Figure 4.18 the dashed arc connecting nodes A_3 and E_s concerns information that supports the assessment of the conditional probabilities on the arc connecting E_s and E; these probabilities are $P(E_s|E)$ and $P(E_s|E^c)$. There may be no conceivable influence, dependence, or relevance between *nodes* A_3 and E_s, as my examples above were intended to show.

Persons who shudder at the thought of inference networks embedded within other inference networks will not find much comfort from these comments about evocative portions of a network and how they may best be indicated symbolically. Suppose we have a mass of ancillary evidence and some complex arguments, all of which are evocative in allowing us to assess particular probabilities on our "main" inference network. These evocative arguments may themselves require further evocative elements which, in turn, may require others. As I said earlier, these matters all concern the level of granularity at which we are willing and able to decompose a probabilistic inference.

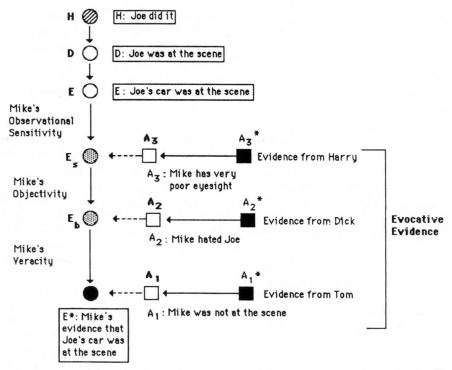

FIGURE 4.18 Ancillary evidence as evocative evidence on an inference network.

4.5.5 On the Mutation of Hypotheses

As I mentioned briefly in Section 2.3.5, Bayes's rule is not the only act in town these days as far as probabilistic reasoning is concerned. Another act, having a sizable audience, involves the system of *belief functions* given us by Glenn Shafer (1976). Inference networks can also incorporate belief functions (e.g., Shenoy and Shafer 1986; Shenoy, Shafer, and Mellouli, 1988). I will presently focus upon some structural ideas from Shafer's work that I believe are important to keep in mind as we attempt to construct an inference network in the face of new evidence and revised insights. To make matters as simple as possible, suppose an emerging inference network having a single root node **H** consisting of a collection of hypotheses about what has happened or will happen in a part of the world of interest to us. As we gather evidence that we believe is relevant on the states of H, we expect that this evidence will allow us to revise our probabilistic beliefs about which of these hypotheses is true or correct. From our discussion in Chapter 3, we would not say our evidence is relevant unless this were so. But other things happen as we obtain new evidence. Our hypotheses themselves may have to be revised or changed in various ways, and some will be eliminated entirely. We may also have to generate new hypotheses in order to account for evidence we discover. In short, the states of node **H** may undergo various mutations in light of our new evidence and new insights. Such mutations can of course occur at any node on our emerging network.

As an example, suppose we are police investigators called upon to draw conclusions about what has caused the death of a victim we shall call Vic. Vic's body was found on the floor of the garage attached to his home. On the way to the scene we decide to be open-minded, so we entertain four initial hypotheses about the cause of Vic's death. These hypotheses are collected at root node H_0 = {H_1: natural causes, H_2: suicide, H_3: accident, and H_4: criminal act}. In Shafer's terms H_0 represents our initial *frame of discernment;* this frame simply indicates our initial assessment of the possibilities. These possibilities are obviously vague or undifferentiated, and we suppose that we must *refine* them in some way or make them more specific. We could not, for example, conclude our investigation with the simple assertion that Vic's death was the result of a criminal act. If a criminal act was performed in this case, we are obliged to discover the person(s) responsible. Clearly a person's frame of discernment depends upon his or her standpoint. Thus the views of Shafer on frames of discernment coincide with those of Anderson and Twining on standpoints. If a news reporter had been called to the scene, she might have entertained the frame: H_0' = {There's a story here, There is no story here}; an attorney arriving at the scene might entertain the frame H_0'' = {There's a damage suit here, There is no damage suit here}.

As police investigators we begin by making observations and asking questions. The massive head injuries Vic suffered are not likely to have been self-inflicted. An autopsy reveals that Vic had been in perfect health. We can find no evidence to indicate that Vic's injuries were the result of accident. Before we eliminate any possibilities, we would be well-advised to consult Jonathan Cohen's thoughts about *eliminative induction*, which I will discuss in more detail in Section 5.5. As a result of questions we ask and evidence we gather, we begin to refine our possibilities; Figure 4.19 shows an example of this refinement process. We find no wallet in Vic's clothes; however, it is found outside his garage. His wallet contains no money or credit cards. At this point we refine H_4 to include the possibilities shown in this figure as $H_{4.1}$, $H_{4.2}$, and $H_{4.3}$. Vic could have been assaulted during a robbery; his assault could have been made to appear to be a concomitant of robbery (we had no trouble finding his wallet). But it is also possible that there was no robbery; Vic might not have been carrying money or credit cards, and he might himself have dropped his wallet outside his garage.

But we do find something else on Vic's person, several ounces of cocaine. So we begin to entertain the possibility that what happened to Vic occurred as a result of a drug deal gone sour. Two possibilities depending upon whether Vic was a pusher or just a user of narcotics are shown as $H_{4.2.1}$ and $H_{4.2.2}$ in

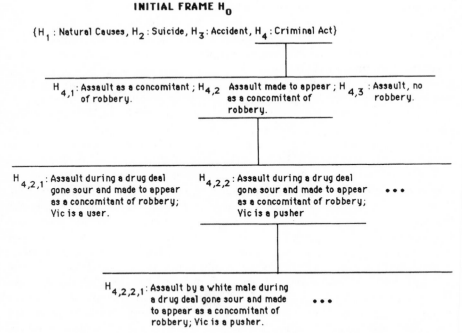

FIGURE 4.19 An illustration of the mutation of hypotheses.

Figure 4.19. The three dots following $H_{4,2,2}$ indicate that there are other possibilities in our refinement of $H_{4,2}$. A neighbor who lives across the street from Vic says she saw a white male running away from Vic's house shortly after the believed time of Vic's assault. So we may now refine $H_{4,2,2}$ to incorporate this new evidence; one possibility is shown in the figure as $H_{4,2,2,1}$. The essential message in Figure 4.19 is that new believable evidence gets incorporated in the hypotheses we entertain; this is what the process of hypothesis refinement is all about. The example shown in Figure 4.19 is very simple; other evidence we have may cause similar refinements of any of the hypotheses being entertained at some stage in the emergence of an inference problem. For example, in light of new revelations we may also be able to refine $H_{4,3}$. The result is that our frame of discernment involving just one node on an inference network may become very complex indeed. The trouble is that new evidence and insights may cause similar mutations of the possibilities at any node.

Shafer's work alerts us to the fact that an inference network is often a "growing thing." Questions we ask and answers we obtain give rise to altered frames of discernment of hypotheses or possibilities. In turn these altered frames cause us to revise our beliefs about the relevance, credibility, and force of evidence we already have as well as new evidence we may discover.

4.6 OTHER STRUCTURES: NARRATIVES, STORIES, AND SCENARIOS

Wigmorean evidence charts, influence diagrams, Bayes nets, or other forms of inference network analyses might not, by themselves, be persuasive in defense of a stated conclusion. Wigmore himself recognized this fact and noted that another structural method was necessary in any attempt to persuade others to accept a conclusion drawn from a mass of evidence. He termed this additional structuring device the *narrative method*, one in which we rearrange ". . . all the evidential data under some scheme of logical sequence, narrating at each point the related evidential facts, and at each fact noting the subordinate evidence on which it depends; concluding with a narrative summary" (1937, 821). Having noted the importance of narratives, Wigmore then proceded to draw an inappropriate conclusion about them. Comparing the narrative method with his evidence charting methods, he states that the narrative method ". . . is the simpler method, more readily used by the beginner, and the more akin to the usual way of describing an evidence problem" (1937, 821–822). As we will see, there is nothing simple about constructing a narrative account of a complex matter, particularly when this narrative is being used for *explanatory* purposes.

The brevity of my present comments on structural matters associated with narratives, stories, and scenarios is not an indication of the strength of my belief in the importance of such activities. I will in fact return to some of these matters in later chapters. People tell stories all the time, and do so for different reasons. In law, for example, advocates tell stories in an effort to convince jurors (Twining 1990, 219–261); jurors in turn appear to tell stories to themselves regarding the evidence they have heard and seen (Pennington 1981; Hastie, Penrod, and Pennington 1983, 22–23; Pennington and Hastie 1991, 1992). Persons in virtually every discipline construct narrative accounts of the results of their findings in order to give reasons why certain conclusions seem to be favored over others. In many cases these accounts have at least a temporal element; often they have a causal element.

Following are two quite different evidence-related reasons why we construct narratives, stories, or scenarios. Before I begin, I should add that some have made distinctions between the terms scenario, story, and narrative (Twining 1990, 219–261). The word *scenario* is sometimes used simply to indicate that a background or scene has been set for the discussion of salient events; in other words, a scenario may be just a description of a situation. Ordinarily we expect that every *story* has a beginning, a middle, and an end; a scenario may have no beginning or end. Twining notes that a story ". . . is a narrative of particular events arranged in a time sequence and forming a meaningful totality." He then adds: ". . . I shall equate narrative with storytelling: one narrates stories, but describes situations" (1990, 223). On Twining's argument the only distinction involves scenarios and stories/narratives.

4.6.1 Scenarios and the Discovery of Evidence

Consider Figure 4.19 again, and note the pattern of refinement that proceeds from H_4 to $H_{4.2.2.1}$. At each stage of refinement, based upon new evidence we gather, we are able to entertain more substantive conjectures about what happened to Vic. Even after we have ruled out natural causes, suicide, and accident, we have only the vaguest of conjectures; it simply reads: "So far, it looks like Vic died of foul play." At the next stage our conjecture might read: "It looks like someone assaulted Vic and tried to make it appear that this assault took place during a robbery of him." At a further stage a possible conjecture is: "Vic dealt in narcotics and was assaulted by a customer who tried to make the assault look like it took place during a robbery of Vic." Finally, we have the conjecture: "Vic dealt in narcotics and was assaulted by a white male customer who tried to make his assault look like it took place during a robbery of Vic." Notice that each of these conjectures gets more substantive, less vague, and begins to resemble a narrative. But these emerging conjectures all have one outstanding characteristic: They do not outrun the evidence we have. There is nothing imaginative about these accounts, they are simply hypotheses embellished by evidence we take seriously. As I will now illustrate, we frequently construct scenarios in which our imaginations do outrun the evidence we have.

The construction of scenarios is a very good device for generating or discovering new evidence (Tillers and Schum 1991). An account of background knowledge we believe we have often suggests new knowledge which we might obtain. Figure 4.20 illustrates some of the matters involved in constructing a scenario for heuristic purposes. Suppose we have five items of evidence (A^*, B^*, C^*, D^*, and E^*) that, at the moment, we believe to be credible and relevant to some hypothesis or possibility of interest. Let us refer to these evidence items as *benchmarks*. Further, suppose that these benchmark evidence items refer to events that have happened at various points in time. So we order the evidence according to what we now believe to be the temporal order in which the events reported in this evidence actually occurred. Of course this is a conjecture; the events, if they did happen, may have occurred in a different order. The ordering shown in Figure 4.20 does *not* refer to the

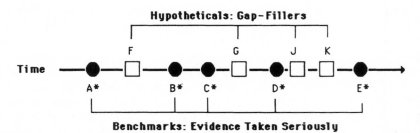

FIGURE 4.20 The ingredients of a scenario.

order in which we received evidence about these events; this is a different matter entirely having possible inferential significance on its own.

If we attempted to construct a scenario about what happened in this situation, just using these five evidence items, we would naturally expect there to be some gaps in it. We might, for example, believe event A to be a possible *distal* cause of event B; what we should like to have is evidence about a more *proximal* or *immediate* cause of B. So we insert an event (F) between A* and B* that refers to this proximal cause. We reason: If A happened, it might have caused F, and if F happened, it might have been a possible cause of B. At the moment we have no evidence about F. This event is *hypothetical,* and its appearance in our scenario simply fills in a gap between events A and B, about which we do presently have evidence. We need not suppose that all hypotheticals or gap-fillers are events in some causal chain. We have evidence that event C occurred prior to event D. Suppose that these events refer to the behavior of some person who first did C and later did D. We suppose that if this person did C and then later D, he must have had some help in doing D. So we insert event G to indicate the involvement of another person. Each hypothetical we insert suggests new evidence we might discover. The heuristic merit of scenario construction is apparent; each hypothetical we imagine suggests questions whose answers come from evidence we obtain. Naturally we may have to revise our scenario when and if evidence about these hypotheticals can be discovered. For example, we may eventually obtain evidence that event F did not occur as we hypothesized.

The construction of scenarios may profitably take place in any context and may involve such matters as aircraft accident investigation, historical research, the audit of a firm, or the diagnosis of mental disorders. The situation depicted in Figure 4.20 is just one among several different ways in which we can marshal existing evidence to facilitate the process of discovering new possibilities and evidence. We will discuss additional methods for achieving this objective in Chapter 9. The essential structural mechanism in a scenario is a conjectural *temporal ordering* of events, some of which are evidenced and others not.

4.6.2 Structuring and Explanations

Using the structural and/or probabilistic methods that you find most congenial to your interests, you have now reached a conclusion in an inference problem. In any report of this conclusion to others you would expect to be asked to *explain how and why* you reached this conclusion. The *how* part of this requirement seems easy enough. In most situations it would ordinarily be expected that you reached your conclusion as a result of reasoning based on evidence and that it was neither revealed to you in a dream nor inspired by consultation with a clairvoyant. You would certainly be prepared to discuss the possibilities you entertained, the arguments you constructed from the evidence you considered, and the probabilistic methods you might have used to reach your conclusion. But the *why* part of this requirement seems more difficult to answer. Other conclusions were possible, and your audience is entitled to learn why you have drawn the particular conclusion you are now prepared to report. In this sense *explaining why* involves a *defense* of the conclusion you have reached. Explaining why something is so involves problems of great concern among philosophers; there is an abundance of work on this topic and no small amount of controversy.

If the context of an inference problem is science or engineering, it might be expected that an explanation would involve causal elements. In an explanation of why an airliner crashed, it might be said that inappropriate control settings, wing icing, pilot inattention, or other conditions contributed to the occurrence of the accident. In such instances it would ordinarily be supposed that a *succession* of events led up to the accident and that conditions such as those mentioned were *antecedents*. Such causal explanations fall heir to all of the problems noted in Section 4.3. But in the physical sciences many explanations can be deduced from lawful relations involving not the succession but the *coexistence* of certain factors. Hempel gives an example involving the behavior of a simple pendulum (1965, 352). The period t (measured in seconds) of a simple pendulum is related to its length l (in centimeters) by a law that reads $t = 2\pi(l/g)^{1/2}$, where g is acceleration in free fall. Hemple notes that the length and period of a pendulum coexist; in other words, we would not say that a pendulum's having a period of two seconds was caused by its having a length of 100 centimeters.

A relation between *explanation* and *prediction* is often expected in scientific contexts. Our being able to explain some phenomenon potentially allows us to predict occurrences of this phenomenon. Unfortunately, in the behavioral sciences, for example, it is often possible to predict the occurrence of some behavioral event without necessarily being able to explain it. For example, there are various psychophysical "laws" showing relationships between physical energy Φ and reported sensations Ψ. In studying the relation $\Psi = f(\Phi)$, various functions f have been proposed; some are logarithmic and others power functions. Such functions account for observed experimental data and can be used for predicting the magnitude of a sensory response to some level of signal energy. But they are not necessarily explanations of how our sensory modalities function in response to various magnitudes of signal energy. They can, however, be suggestive of explanations (e.g., Stevens 1975, 202–226).

Causal explanations are of course desired in the behavioral and social sciences. In such contexts inference problems involving an astonishing number of factors are routinely encountered, and as a result tracing causal chains can be very difficult. It has recently been noted that causal explanations in the behavioral and social sciences frequently fail because they lack *depth* (Miller 1987, 98–104). For example, suppose that cause C_1 helps to bring about effect E. Miller argues that C_1 is a *shallow* cause of effect E if there is another cause C_2 that can undermine C_1 in one of two ways. First, if C_1 had not occurred, E would have happened anyway. In this case C_2 plays the role of a causal substitute for C_1 and brings about E in another way. Second, C_2 might have given rise to C_1 but is so intimately connected with C_1 that it cannot be identified as a remote cause of E. Thus, even if an inference network we have constructed contains defensible causal linkages, it may not always be easy to translate this network into an explanation. Causal explanations are also expected in historical research and are frequently embedded in narratives or stories. As I noted earlier, we expect stories to have a beginning, a middle, and an end. One argument is that in historical research, an explanation is what fills in the middle between the beginning and end; such explanations frequently involve *changes* in events that are often nested within other changes (Danto 1985, 233–256). Thus, for example, a narrative historical account of X's behavior might include an attempted explanation of why X held a certain view at one time and then acted contrary to this view at a later time.

In common discourse, giving an explanation of something to a person means helping this person to understand it. The success of such explanatory efforts depends in part upon the intelligence, background, and other characteristics of the person to whom the explanation is given. Often an explanation is given using terms and concepts whose familiarity is assumed. Such efforts often miscarry because of incorrect assumptions about what background information is necessary for a person to understand an explanation. As an example, many early texts on probability and statistics introduced the idea of independence by means of the product rule and let it go at that. Not all definitions have explanatory value. A common "explanation" of independence was "independence means that $P(AB) = P(A)P(B)$." Even for a person who already understands what a conventional probability means, there is nothing particularly understandable about this explanation unless the concept of a conditional probability has already been introduced. Independence *means* the failure of conditioning where $P(A|B) = P(A)$. Events A and B are independent if knowing or assuming B does not change the probability of A. Hempel argues that reducing an explanation to familiar terms is neither necessary nor sufficient as far as acceptable scientific explanations are concerned (1965, 432).

Explaining why a particular conclusion was drawn from a mass of evidence may be quite difficult. It is certainly true that none of the structural devices we have discussed in this chapter are themselves explanations. Attention to the task of structuring arguments, required in the employment of any of these devices, would certainly be helpful in constructing any explanation of why particular conclusions were reached in preference to others that are possible. In the absence of attention to these structural matters, a person asked for an explanation may suddenly be forced to bring many things to mind. All of the structural matters discussed in this chapter offer ways in which such tasks can be made easier. In instances in which no probabilistic analyses are intended, methods based upon those developed years ago by Wigmore may be very helpful. When complex probabilistic analyses are desirable or necessary, there are now ways in which many such analyses can be made easier by existing computer facilities.

Chapter 5

On the Inferential Force of Evidence

We have now considered at some length a variety of structural matters associated with establishing the relevance and credibility of evidence. None of these structural matters requires a commitment to any particular view of probability. We needed no theory of probability to tell us how we might, as in Chapter 3, categorize recurrent forms and combinations of evidence and determine attributes of the credibility of evidence. Nor did we need any theory of probability in Chapter 4 to inform us about the various uses of evidence and the manner in which complex networks of arguments, based on a mass of evidence, might be constructed. Relevant evidence was defined as that which allows us to change our beliefs about the likeliness of hypotheses or possibilities of interest. In other words, relevant evidence has *some force* in probabilistic belief revision, and we suppose therefore that evidential force is to be graded in probabilistic terms. The issue now to be examined concerns the manner in which we might determine *how much force* evidence has under various circumstances.

On this issue there is substantial controversy. In fact one of the major points of disagreement among current views of probabilistic reasoning concerns exactly what the force of evidence means and how it might be graded. It is very common to use the terms *force, strength,* or *weight* synonymously when discussing how much belief revision evidence seems to justify. But I have avoided interchanging these terms because the term *evidential weight* has a particular meaning in some views of probabilistic inference that it does not have in others. The term *evidential force* is less controversial, so I have employed it in my discussions so far.

Section 2.3.1 contained a very brief introduction to alternative formal systems of probabilistic reasoning now being actively considered. In the process of introducing these alternatives I announced my commitment to a belief that no single view of probabilistic reasoning captures all of the behavioral richness evident in such tasks. Each of the views we will discuss employs a unique way of grading the inferential force of evidence. One result is that we can now view the concept of evidential force from different standpoints or, if you like, through different conceptual lenses. My present objective is to put these alternative views of the task of weighing evidence in their best possible light. From experience I do know that an ecumenical posture in discussing probabilistic reasoning invites criticism. I am more than willing to accept this risk since each one of these views is heuristically valuable in any study of evidence and its properties.

5.1 THE FORCE OF EVIDENCE: HISTORICAL COMMENTS

Dating the emergence of interest in any attribute of evidence cannot be accomplished with any precision. So it is with the concept of the inferential force of evidence. In an attempt to find a suitable definition of the word *evidence* in Section 2.1, I mentioned Ian Hacking's suggestion that progress in inductive reasoning was retarded from the time of Aristotle to the 1600s because the concept of evidence was underdeveloped. Evidence was thought to involve either authoritative sources or testimony, both of which involve *people*. Missing until the 1600s was a concept of evidence that included *things* that could point to other things. Consequently early discussions bearing on the force of evidence tended to focus on people and the value of their testimony. For example, there are several biblical prescriptions for the value of testimony: ". . . for any iniquity . . . at the mouth of two witnesses or at the mouth of three witnesses shall the matter be decided" (*Deuteronomy* 19:15); "If thy brother trespass against thee, then take with thee one or two more, that in the mouth of two or three witnesses every word may be established" (*Matthew* 18:16). Thus the intuition of the ancients suggested that at least *corroboration* is an element in determining the force of testimonial evidence.

In the emergence of our Anglo-American system of laws, progress in understanding what factors contribute to the inferential force of evidence could hardly be made as long as trial verdicts were left to the judgment of God. As noted in Section 2.4.1, the emergence of juries, as bodies of disinterested persons who deliberate upon evidence supplied by external witnesses, did not occur until the thirteenth century. As Wigmore put it, "With the full advent of the jury, in the 1200s, the general surroundings of the modern system were prepared, for then the tribunal was to determine by its own conscious persuasion of the facts, and not merely by supervising external tests" (*Wigmore on Evidence,* vol. 1, Tillers rev., 1983, 607). Progress toward a more complete understanding of attributes of the inferential force of evidence came only by degrees. This was due in part to the strong resistance against trial by jury (see Section 2.4.1). Such resistance was still found three hundred years later during the reign of Elizabeth I. Plucknett provides us with an account of the main disadvantages of being a defendant in an Elizabethan criminal trial (1956, 434). The accused was kept in confinement until the trial, could not prepare for his defense, had no notice of the evidence against him, and had no counsel before or during the trial. At trial the accused had no right to confront witnesses against him or to require originals of documents introduced as evidence against him.

But it was also during the reign of Elizabeth I that a landmark statute was introduced (1563) that compelled the attendance of witnesses at trial and made witness perjury a crime (Plucknett 1956, 436). However, considerable reliance was still placed upon the swearing of oaths by a witness. Wigmore tells us of the Duke of Norfolk's treason trial that took place in 1571. A sworn witness named Richard Candish testified to treasonable words allegedly uttered by Norfolk. In reply, Norfolk attempted to discredit Candish whereupon the judge, Serjeant Barham, interjected: "He is sworn, there needeth no more proving" (*Wigmore on Evidence,* vol. 7, Chadbourn rev., 1940, 247). In this period began controversy regarding the suitability of *numerical systems* for determining the force of evidence. Based upon biblical prescriptions for corroboration such as those noted above, canon or ecclesiastical law had developed an elaborate numerical system for determining the strength of evidence. For example, if you brought charges against a cardinal, you would have been required to bring as many as 44 witnesses to support your case. In the Romanesque law of continental Europe, the value of testimony was even measured in halves and quarters depending on who provided the testimony; this practice did not cease until the 1800s. Only by degrees came the idea of analyzing and valuing the credibility and force of testimony rather than simply counting heads on either side of a matter in dispute (see *Wigmore on Evidence,* vol. 7, 1940, 241–255 for a history of numerical systems).

Let us leave jurisprudence for the moment. John Locke had much to say about the inferential force of evidence in his *Essay Concerning Human Understanding* (1689, Nidditch ed., 1991). Locke's discussion of probability and what he termed *degrees of assent* reflects his concern about the inferential force of many of the forms and combinations of evidence we considered in Chapter 3. At the beginning of his discussion he tells us (Nidditch ed., 1991, 655–656):

> *Probability* then, being to supply the defect of our Knowledge, and to guide us where that fails, is always conversant about Propositions, whereof we have no certainty, but only some inducements to receive them for true. The *grounds of it* are, in short, these two following: *First,* The conformity of any thing with our own Knowledge, Observation, and Experience. *Secondly,* The Testimony of others, vouching their Observation and Experience. In the Testimony of others, is to be considered, 1. The Number. 2. The Integrity. 3. The Skill of the Witnesses. 4. The Design of the Author, where it is out of a Book cited. 5. The Consistency of the Parts, and Circumstances of the Relation. 6. Contrary Testimony.

Thus Locke had the beginnings of an understanding of the credibility-related matters I introduced in Section 3.2 and will again examine in Chapter 7. In addition he distinguished between tangible evidence (open to our own observations) and testimonial evidence (that which comes from observations or experience of others). But he went even farther in noting the existence of what are termed *accepted facts* (see Figure 3.11) whose probability, he said, rises near to certainty. As examples Locke gave: ". . . That Fire warmed a Man, made Lead fluid, and changed the colour or consistency in Wood or Charcoal: that Iron sunk in Water, and swam in Quicksilver . . ." (1689, 662). He also acknowledged what he termed *concurrent* testimony (labeled *corroboration* in Figure 3.14), *contradictory* testimony, and *hearsay,* all of which we considered in Chapter 3. Of hearsay he said (1689, 664):

The Being and Existence of the thing itself, is what I call the original Truth. A credible Man vouching his Knowledge of it, is a good proof: But if another equally credible, do witness it from his Report, the Testimony is weaker; and a third that attests the Hear-say of an Hear-say, is yet less considerable. So that *in traditional truths, each remove weakens the force of the proof.*

In Chapter 7 we will examine formal processes that tell us precisely how much the force of evidence is weakened when it is passed through a chain of sources. This problem is simply a special case of determining the strength of an inference as a function of the number of links in a chain of reasoning that supports the inference.

In the 1600s began, in Daston's words, the *moralization* of mathematics as it concerns the calculation of probabilities (1988, 296–369). Attempts were made to determine probabilities associated with religious, historical, political, business, legal, and other events for which the aleatory assumption of a finite number of equally likely outcomes makes little sense. In line with a lingering emphasis on evidence from people rather than about things, a major focus in these early studies was upon what were termed *credibility-testimony* problems. As Gigerenzer et al. have noted, " Almost every probabilist from Jacob Bernoulli through Poisson tried his hand at the probability of testimony, and Montmort was exceptional in asking whether such matters were really legitimate applications of the mathematical theory" (1991, 28). Even Samuel Johnson commented on the force of testimony, saying that testimony was like an arrow shot from a longbow; its force depends upon the strength of the hand that draws the bow (Boswell 1791, 1098). I believe there are quite definite reasons, to be discussed in Chapter 7, why early and later probabilists were never successful in capturing what is involved in assessing the inferential force of testimonial evidence.

One element of the inferential force of testimony that did not escape the attentions of early probabilists and philosophers concerns the *rareness* or improbability of the event reported in testimony. Issues of event rareness are certain to arise in any discussion of probabilities associated with miracles, a subject of fascination among early probabilists. In his *Enquiries,* Hume noted: "Suppose, for instance, that the fact, which the testimony endeavours to establish, partakes of the extraordinary and the marvelous; in that case, the evidence, resulting from the testimony, admits of a diminution, greater or less, as the fact is more unusual" (1777, 113). Laplace noted that the probability of error or of falsehood is greater when events asserted in testimony are more extraordinary (1796, 114). In Chapter 7 I will provide equations that illustrate rather clearly how event rareness and importance interact with witness credibility in determining the inferential force of testimony.

Returning to legal scholarship, Jeremy Bentham (1839) was certainly interested in the task of assessing the inferential force of testimony. He even proposed a numerical scale for testimonial force assessment that Twining has called a "thermometer of persuasion" (1985, 56). Values on this scale range from plus ten to minus ten with positive values indicating gradations of force favoring H and negative values indicating gradations of force favoring not-H; zero indicates no inferential force. Bentham believed there were four essential questions to be answered in determining the force of an item of testimony: (1) How confident is the witness in the truth of the event asserted? (2) How conformable to general experience (i.e., how rare) is the event asserted? (3) Are there grounds for suspicion of the untrustworthiness of the witness? (4) Is the testimony supported or doubted by other evidence? Bentham also realized that there had to be some methods for aggregating these force assessments across items in some mass of evidence, but he was not so sure that this aggregation process necessarily follows any strict mathematical axioms (Twining 1985, 52–56).

I end this brief history of the concept of evidential force with Wigmore. I have already noted in Section 4.4.2 that Wigmore seems to have been the first to provide a systematic means for establishing the probative or inferential force of a mass of evidence items belonging to various logically distinguishable forms. Figure 4.8 illustrates Wigmore's methods for grading the force of evidence in *fuzzy* terms. This figure also illustrates his recognition of the fact that inferences from evidence involve often complex chains of reasoning to which he applied the term *catenated.* In fact the whole of Wigmore's *Science of Judicial Proof* (1937) might be regarded as a treatise on the task of establishing the force of evidence. This treatise has five major parts. The first one is a discussion of how the nature of judicial proof is mainly inductive in nature. The next three parts concern circumstantial, testimonial, and immediate, direct, or "real" evidence. But Wigmore objected to the term "real" evidence and used instead a quaint term he invented: *autoptic proference.* We might translate this term as "the offering of a self-visible thing" or as *res ipsa loquitur* (the thing declares itself). I will have more to say on Wigmore's evidential distinctions in a moment. The fifth major part of his treatise concerns the analysis of masses of evidence mixed with respect to the three forms of evidence he recognized. In this final part he presents the details of his analytic-synthetic method for charting evidence (as described in Section 4.4).

In contrast, not three but fifteen forms of evidence appear in the taxonomy I provided in Section 3.4 (see Figure 3.11). I have made certain distinctions Wigmore did not make. First, he argued that testimonial and circumstantial evidence are mutually exclusive. But then, by frequent examples, he demonstrated how circumstantial evidence frequently has a base in testimony (e.g. Wigmore 1937, 15). Thus your testimony about seeing the can of dog food in your neighbor's kitchen provides me with circumstantial evidence that your neighbor is keeping a dog in his apartment. Even if I believed you are perfectly credible as a source of evidence, the can of dog food is just inconclusive evidence that your neighbor is keeping a dog. Your direct observation of a cast on my arm provides you with just circumstantial evidence that my arm is broken or otherwise injured. I might be wearing this cast to court undeserved sympathy or for some other purpose rooted in deception. My belief, stated by means of Figure 3.11, is that the terms *tangible* and *testimonial* exist on a different dimension than does the term *circumstantial* and that the first two can intersect with the third in classifying evidence. Thus I do not believe that the first two and the third of these terms represent mutually exclusive cases.

Wigmore's discussions of "real" evidence or "autoptic proference" are interesting and illustrate his view of common legal assumptions about inferences from such evidence. Suppose that a "thing" like a gun or a knife is presented at trial. On Wigmore's argument, such things speak for themselves, and the court is uninterested in inferences about the existence of such things that members of a tribunal might draw as a result of their sensory evidence of these things. As he notes, "A psychologist might say that the Court is to use its sense perception as a basis of inference to a judgment; but this is a distinction which cannot be accepted in judicial proof, because the Court recognizes none such; it takes the results of its senses as immediate and final knowledge" (1937, 11, n. 2). He later explains that courts adopt this view because things presented in court are examined under ideal conditions, are observable simultaneously by all parties, and any unfamiliar details of things can always be explained by expert witnessses (1937, 806). In symbols, Wigmore's argument reads as follows. Suppose that E = the existence of a "thing" and that E* is my sensory evidence of this "thing." On Wigmore's account, courts take my sensory evidence of E* and thing E to be one and the same. I prefer not to take such a leap of faith in this discourse, since there are many situations in which it seems very prudent to keep E* and E separate, even when what is presented to our senses is tangible in nature. As discussed in Section 2.1.2, our senses or any sensing devices provide only abstractions of things and not things themselves. I add, finally, that many modern evidence scholars examine very carefully the inferences made by fact finders as a result of their sensory experience of all sorts of evidence (e.g., Friedman 1987; Tillers and Schum 1992).

5.2 GRADING THE FORCE OF EVIDENCE

How are we to measure the force of evidence items either taken alone or in the aggregate? Suppose that we take as a starting place Hume's assertion: "Thus all probabilistic reasoning is nothing but a species of sensation. . . . When I am convinc'd of any principle, 'tis only an idea, which strikes more strongly upon me. When I give the preference to one set of arguments above another, I do nothing but decide from my feeling concerning the superiority of their influence" (1739, Selby-Bigge ed., 1975, 103). As Daston mentions, Hume's thoughts about the force of evidence, including testimonial evidence about miraculous events, did not go unscathed, particularly at the hands of Richard Price who introduced Bayes's rule to the Royal Society (1988, 325–330). No matter; Hume's assertion gives us a place to start. As we will see, others appear to have taken Hume's probability-sensation analogy seriously. I take it to be common experience that when we are presented with evidence, we have *feelings* about the extent to which this evidence can act to change our beliefs. However, I would also suppose that most of us are not aware of any numbers floating around in our heads as these feeling arise. But, when prompted, we can provide numerical assessments of the strength of our beliefs based upon evidence or even about the force of evidence. In the field of sensory psychophysics numerically expressed human judgments about the strength of our sensations, opinions, and so on, are taken very seriously and with good reason. Numerically expressed human judgments form the basis for useful measures of the brightness of lights, the loudness of sounds, the saturation of colors, and many other sensory events. Progress in the lighting, sound, and color industries has depended in part upon systematic research on human sensory capabilities and limitations; much of this research rests upon numerical judgments.

In psychophysics it is common to distinguish between *prothetic* and *metathetic* judgments (these terms were introduced by S. S. Stevens 1957). Prothetic judgments are *intensive* in nature and involve something added or taken away from something else. Thus, if one light seems brighter than another having the same spectral composition, it is just because the brighter light source applies *more* radiant energy to our senses. Metathetic judgments, on the other hand, are *qualitative* in nature and involve one thing substituted for something else. Thus judgments of hues or colors are qualitative in nature and involve *different* retinal elements being excited by lights having different spectral compositions. I must add that not all psychologists agree with Stevens' prothetic-metathetic distinctions (Warren and Warren 1963, 800–804). On Hume's argument, probabilistic reasoning involves intensive or prothetic judgments. Judgments about the force of argument or of evidence involve an intensive judgmental dimension. This is reflected in the terms *inferential force, strength,* or *weight.* There are different views about how such an evidential attribute should be graded. However, in all views there is agreement that relevant evidence has *vectorlike* properties: It applies *force* in certain *directions*, toward one hypothesis or collection of hypotheses, or toward others. Our first task is to observe what basic ingredients seem to be involved in judgments of the inferential force of evidence.

5.2.1 What Determines the Force of Evidence?

The various structural matters to which we attended in Chapters 3 and 4 provide us with a start in determining the basic ingredients we need to consider in assessing the inferential force of evidence. In constructing arguments bearing upon the credibility and relevance credentials of evidence, we also begin to lay the groundwork for an assessment of its inferential force. Let us consider relevance first and observe that relevant evidence is that which seems *important* because it allows us to change our opinion by some amount and in some direction. A defense of the importance or relevance of evidence rests upon the structural matters discussed in Section 3.1. In some situations evidence seems important because it allows us to change our opinion about the *relative likeliness* of hypotheses. In other situations evidence seems important because we believe it provides a certain level of *support* for some hypothesis or collection of hypotheses. Distinctions between these two interpretations form the subject matter of Sections 5.3 and 5.4. Evidence may also seem important in cases in which we devise evidential tests in an attempt to *eliminate* certain hypotheses or possibilities. The actual elimination of some hypothesis, if justified, would be an extreme revision of opinion. In Section 5.5 we consider the weight of evidence in variative and eliminative inference. We have also considered *ancillary evidence* as that which allows us to support or diminish the credibility and force of other evidence. Recall that the essential role of ancillary evidence is to tell us how adequate are the generalizations we assert to license stages of reasoning we identify based on evidence we believe is directly relevant on major hypotheses.

When we receive an item of information there are two questions that immediately arise: So what? Can we believe it? The first is a relevance question and the second a credibility question. I make no claim that these two questions are always considered in this order. We might, for example, receive some news we believe is credible and only later perceive its relevance in an inference we were not obliged to make when we received this news. If we believed the event(s) reported or observed by some means had no bearing at all in the inference at hand we would not necessarily be concerned about the *credibility* of the source of information about the reported event(s). Having established that a certain item of information has some importance in an inference task we ask: Can we believe it? Answers to such questions involve the credibility-related foundations for argument discussed in Sections 3.2 and 3.3. As noted, there are different credibility-related questions for different forms of evidence. In assessing the credibility of tangible evidence, we require answers

to questions concerning its authenticity and accuracy. Establishing the credibility of testimony requires answers to questions regarding the veracity, objectivity, and observational sensitivity of human witnesses.

In assessing the inferential force of evidence, there are other ingredients
to consider apart from relevance and credibility. In my brief historical account
of matters concerning inferential force I mentioned early recognition of the
importance of the *rareness* or improbability of the event(s) reported in testimony. As we will see in Chapter 7, we have to consider the rareness of
other events besides the one(s) reported in evidence. For example, we may
not consider the event reported in someone's testimony to be at all rare. But
what we do consider to be a rare event is this person's testimony about this
event. Perhaps the event reported in this testimony is quite embarrassing or
unfavorable to the interests of the person providing the testimony. Rareness
issues arise for events at *any* stage in chains of reasoning we construct from
evidence to hypotheses.

Speaking of chains of reasoning, the force of an item of evidence is certainly
related to the *number of links* we can identify in a chain of reasoning from
this evidence to major hypotheses of interest. Recall that each link we identify
represents a source of uncertainty we have recognized. How evidential force
is related to reasoning chain length is the subject of Section 7.1.1. Chains of
reasoning from individual items of evidence can of course be linked together.
So we also suppose that the force of one item of evidence will also depend
upon other directly relevant evidence we have.

It is quite common to apply the terms evidential force, strength, and weight
to individual items of evidence or to entire bodies of evidence. However, not
all views of probabilistic reasoning provide measures of the force of individual
items of evidence. When considering an entire body of evidence and the
extent to which it allows us to change our beliefs, it is also natural for us to
consider the *sufficiency* of the evidence we have. This raises a very important
matter concerning the *completeness* of our evidence and the extent to which
it covers matters we judge to be relevant in our inference. On the Baconian
view of probabilistic reasoning examined in Section 5.5, the *weight* of evidence
is said to depend upon the *amount* of evidence we have considered and the
extent to which it is sufficient in covering matters we believe to be relevant
in an inference.

As I mentioned earlier, the force of one item of evidence may depend
upon other evidence we have. In Figures 3.14*b* and 3.15*b* I gave examples
of situations in which one item of evidence may either enhance or diminish
the value of another. As we proceed, we will examine other situations in
which the inferential force of one item of evidence may depend in very
complex ways upon the *background* provided by other items of evidence we
have. I once proposed an analogy between the tasks of assessing the force of
evidence and perceiving the color or brightness of an object (Schum 1977).
The perceived color or brightness of an object depends in part upon the color
or brightness of the background against which it is presented. Similarly the

perceived inferential force of one item of evidence depends in part upon its relation to other items in a background of existing evidence. But, as Glenn Shafer tells us (Section 5.4), we may not always be able to say exactly what this background contains. There may be other things in this background beside evidence items; it might also contain assumptions that we make about how our evidence came into existence.

Some items of evidence are very complex and may record the occurrence or nonoccurrence of many events. Some of these events may be either directly or indirectly relevant on matters at issue, but some of them may seem entirely *collateral* in nature. That persons X and Y were seen together at a certain time and place may be inferentially interesting. But what either X or Y were wearing at the time may seem inferentially uninteresting. However, collateral details may become important in assessments of the credibility of witnesses. If a witness reports collateral details that seem unusual, or if two or more witnesses disagree about collateral details, then there often are grounds for questioning the credibility of witnesses.

Finally, *time* plays many important roles in any assessment of the inferential force of evidence. In discussing time and causal chains in Section 4.3, I mentioned how the believed temporal ordering of events influences conclusions we might draw from evidence about them. One ordering of events may mean one thing, and another ordering may mean something quite different. The world is also changing all the while we are trying to understand it well enough in order to draw conclusions from evidence we obtain. In many contexts the nonstationarity of the world invites many difficulties. As time passes and work on an inference problem proceeds, we obtain new insights and gather new and different forms of evidence. As a result we may entertain new or revised hypotheses or possibilities; such additions or revisions may give rise to altered impressions of the force of existing evidence. As mentioned several times, generalizations form the "glue" that holds our arguments together. In some contexts these generalizations may become obsolete over time, so our "glue" comes unstuck. We assert a generalization that we believe warrants an inference from E to F. Someone says: "This generalization might have held two months ago, but it doesn't hold today." Part of this difficulty arises because of our discovery of new evidence that may force us to revise or qualify generalizations we have made. In short, any element of arguments that we may construct regarding the relevance and credibility of evidence may have to be revised at any time. Such revisions will certainly affect our impressions of the inferential force of items or bodies of evidence.

5.2.2 Backing Assessments of the Inferential Force of Evidence

Suppose that an inference involves whether or not hypothesis H is true. A body of evidence judged to be relevant in this inference has been assembled, and arguments justifying its relevance have been constructed. In the process the strength of the credibility-related foundations of these arguments has also been considered. The question is now asked: How much force does this assembled evidence have as far as our beliefs about whether or not H is true? Suppose some numerical grading of the force of this evidence is requested. Where do these numerical gradings come from, and how much confidence can we place in them? In other words, what is it that backs or provides a basis for these numerical assessments?

In answering this question, the ideas we discussed in Sections 3.1, 3.2, and 3.3 become important. In these earlier sections we discussed how various *generalizations* form the "glue" that holds stages of our relevance and our credibility-related arguments together. To grade the extent to which these generalizations actually apply in a particular inference, we put them to various tests with reference to this inference. In situations in which our inferences involve replicable processes, we may have statistical or frequentistic backings for these generalizations. In nonreplicable situations involving singular or unique events, we may either support or weaken a generalization on the basis of ancillary evidence resulting from a *variety* of different tests of these generalizations. So in nonfrequentistic situations any subjective judgments of probabilities involving links or arcs on an inference network are based upon ancillary evidence together with accumulated experience with similar or related phenomena. Just how we might use this ancillary evidence and experience in defense of probability judgments is a matter that we must consider very carefully if we expect others to take these probabilities seriously.

5.2.3   Measurement Scale Issues and Assumptions

In discussing various formal or mathematical rules for combining probabilistic ingredients, it is very easy to neglect the apparent or assumed numerical properties of these ingredients. All but one of the numerical methods we will examine for grading the inferential force of evidence rest on specific arithmetic operations for combining or aggregating probabilistic ingredients. In addition we may often wish to make various mathematical transformations of the results of applying these methods, the most common being a logarithmic transformation. The question we now ask is, When does it make sense to add, subtract, multipy, divide, and make various transformations of the probabilistic ingredients these aggregational methods require? A quick but not entirely satisfactory answer is that it depends upon how the probabilistic ingredients were obtained. We suppose that the probabilistic ingredients we employ in grading the force of evidence *measure* something. The different rules we will discuss require different kinds of ingredients or measures that often rest upon human judgment. It is entirely appropriate to inquire about the scale properties of these ingredients.

In the physical sciences concern about the process of measurement is reflected in the classic works of N. R. Campbell (1920, 1928). One topic of interest among measurement theorists is the classification of different scales of measurement. Campbell distinguished between what he termed *funda-mental* and *derived* measures. Fundamental measures rest upon no prior measurements and include, as examples, measures of volume or mass that can be made directly. Others are derived since they rest upon other measures; for example, measures of density require prior measures of mass and of volume. Concern about measurement scales is intensified in the behavioral sciences because so many interesting behavioral attributes are not directly measurable and are observable only through the medium of human judgment. The psychophysicist S. S. Stevens classified scales of measurements in terms of their mathematical properties (e.g., 1946, 1951, 1–49; 1959, 18–61). Most students in the behavioral sciences soon become familiar with Stevens' classification of measurement scales. In recent years so have many students in statistics, since Stevens' measurement scale classification has a bearing upon the appropriateness of various descriptive statistics.

According to Stevens the most primitive level of measurement occurs when we use numbers only to identify or name things. Numbers used in this way are said to have *nominal* properties only. For example, in a statistical survey persons are assigned a number indicating their religious preference. Any numbers will do as long as the they preserve the identity of each religious affiliation; in fact letters would do just as well. Numbers are used on occasion simply to stand things in order and are then said to have *ordinal* scale properties. You might assign the numbers one through five to indicate the order of your preference for five different beverages. In ordinal measurement there is no claim regarding equal scale units. Thus, for example, the difference in preference between the beverages you assigned the numbers one and two might be quite different than the difference in your preference for the ones you assigned the numbers four and five.

Some measurements involve scales that have equal units; they are called *interval* (or sometimes *cardinal*) scales. Examples are the Fahrenheit and centigrade temperature scales. If we do have a defensible unit of measurement, it is meaningful to talk about sums and differences; the difference between 40 and 35 degrees Fahrenheit is taken to be the same, in a physical sense, as the difference between 20 and 15 degrees Fahrenheit. But, taking ratios of these numbers may make no sense, since the zero point on such scales is arbitrary. Stevens also noted the existence of *logarithmic interval* scales such as the familiar *decibel* scale for sound intensity measurement and the *Richter* scale for measuring the intensity of earthquakes. The units on logarithmic interval scales signify equal ratios but not equal differences. For example, a decibel (db) is defined as db $= 10 \log_{10} [E_s/E_t]$, where energy E_t provides a base for the measurement of energy E_s. There is a zero point on such a scale (when $E_s = E_t$), but it is arbitrary, since it depends upon a choice of E_t. A scale of measurement such as a yardstick has equal units signifying equal differences and a nonarbitrary zero point. Scales having these properties are said to be *ratio* scales. Numbers on such scales can be meaningfully added, subtracted, multiplied, or divided.

If we take Stevens seriously, we cannot add and subtract numbers unless they represent measures on an interval or cardinal scale, and we cannot add, subtract, multipy, and divide numbers unless they represent measures on a ratio scale. This has a bearing, for example, on the appropriateness of various statistics. Some statistics that are appropriate when we have equal scale intervals are questionable when we have just ordinal measures (e.g., Stevens 1951, 25). Not everyone is convinced by Stevens classification of numerical scales and its implications for statistics and other areas (e.g., see Ellis 1968; Savage 1970; Hays 1988, 66–72). Our present concern about scales of measurement involves probabilities and related quantities that are either estimated using relative frequencies or assessed subjectively. Relative frequencies result from counting or enumerative processes. Counting processes are usually said to involve ratio scales; on occasion counting is said to involve an even higher-order scale called an *absolute* scale.

To explore the relevance of measurement scales to probabilistic assessments, first consider the Pascalian conditional probability $P(E|F)$, the probability of event E, given another event F. By definition, $P(E|F) = P(EF)/P(F)$. If E and F result from replicable processes, we can determine an estimate of $P(E|F)$. Let $r(E|F)$ be a relative frequency estimate of $P(E|F)$, where $r(E|F) = r(EF)/r(F)$. Now $r(EF) = n(EF)/N$ and $r(F) = n(F)/N$, where $n(EF)$ is the number of times we observed E and F together, $n(F)$ is the number of times we observed F, and N is the total number of our observations. In our estimate $r(E|F) = r(EF)/r(F)$ we are justified in dividing these two numbers, since they were both obtained by counting processes. If we then produced the relative frequency $r(E|F^c)$ by similar means, we would have no trouble justifying taking the ratio $r(E|F)/r(E|F^c)$ an estimate of the likelihood ratio $P(E|F)/P(E|F^c)$. But what happens in instances in which $P(E|F)$ and $P(E|F^c)$ are both subjectively assessed by a person?

Suppose that events E and F are singular or unique so that there are no possible relative frequency estimates of the probability of these events. To judge the values of $P(E|F)$ and $P(E|F^c)$, we suppose that there is a generalization linking E and F, some ancillary evidence on the suitability of this generalization, and the knowledge and experience of the person asked to assess these values. In some works it is customary to identify a *subjective estimate* of a probability with special symbols such as $\Psi(E|F)$ and $\Psi(E|F^c)$. The question is, What scale properties shall we ascribe to the judgments $\Psi(E|F)$ as an assessment of $P(E|F)$ and $\Psi(E|F^c)$ as an assessment of $P(E|F^c)$? Unless we suppose that people have internal probability judgmental scales on which there are equal intervals, we have to rule out both ratio and interval scales in Stevens's classification. The result is a conclusion that such subjective assessments have only ordinal properties. If so, it would make no sense to add or subtract assessments like these or to take ratios of them such as $\Psi(E|F)/\Psi(E|F^c)$. The issue is quite important, since it involves whether or not it makes sense to combine such subjective ingredients according to arithmetic formulas such as Bayes's rule and others to be discussed. The problem becomes more acute in applying these formulas in complex inference networks when it may happen that different required probability assessments are made by different people. The question is, How meaningful is a result obtained by the arithmetic combination of subjective assessments made by different persons?

Perhaps some of these scale-related questions could be settled by empirical means. There is an abundance of research on human judgments of many kinds. Some of this research shows that we are all very good at making relative judgments of various sorts, including judgments of ratios. As we now turn our attention to numerical schemes for grading the inferential force of evidence, let it simply be said that an *assumption* commonly made is that it makes sense to perform probabilistic calculations in which subjective ingredients are combined arithmetically. Whether or not this assumption is justified in any particular instance is a matter I will not pursue further. The reason is simply that I will use these various algebraic methods for grading the force of evidence only to illustrate what various formal rules for probabilistic reasoning have to tell us about the properties of and the subtleties in evidence.

5.3 PASCALIAN GRADATIONS OF THE FORCE OF EVIDENCE

As discussed in Section 2.3.4, Bayes's rule emerges in the conventional or Pascalian system of probability as the canon or prescription for belief revision on the basis of evidence. We suppose that various metrics for grading the inferential force of evidence in the process of belief revision are to be found by examining Bayes's rule. We will indeed make such an examination. But history records another account, that makes no reference to Bayes's rule, about how the force of evidence might be graded in terms of conventional probabilities. This account concerns a combination of thoughts from the philosopher Hume, G. T. Fechner (one of the founders of the discipline of psychophysics), and the American philosopher Charles S. Peirce.

I began Section 5.2 by noting Hume's observation that all probabilistic reasoning is a species of sensation; we favor one argument over another because we *feel* that it is superior. I have always taken Hume's thoughts on this matter quite seriously despite objections raised by Richard Price and others. One reason is that I believe sensory analogies to be very useful in studying various matters concerning the inferential force of evidence. After all, probabilistic reasoning and the evaluation of evidence in any context are behavioral tasks. I have already noted that the force of evidence seems to exist on a prothetic or intensive judgmental continuum and that the contrast mechanisms apparent in sensory judgments also appear in judgments of the force of evidence. We can credit three Germans, all trained in the physical sciences, with being the first persons to perform experimental studies of the relation between physical magnitudes and sensory magnitudes. They are Ernst H. Weber (1795–1878), Gustav T. Fechner (1801–1887), and Wilhelm Wundt (1832–1920). Classic historical accounts of this early research on sensory processes are the ones given by E. G. Boring (1942, 1950).

Some of the major problems addressed by Weber, Fechner, Wundt, and other persons in psychophysics are reminiscent of the *mind-body* problem of interest in philosophy. This issue is: How do mental events correspond to or interact with physical events, if they do so at all? The very name *psychophysics* suggests preoccupation with the mind-body problem. Fechner tells us that lying abed one day (October 22, 1850, to be exact) he perceived the general features of a mathematical rule for relating internal sensory events and external physical events. Drawing upon elements of the earlier work of Weber and others, Fechner proposed that the magnitude of a sensation is proportional to the logarithm of the physical energy that produced it. This relation is now called the "Weber-Fechner law" or simply "Fechner's law." Fechner was a physicist who, it is said, had no desire to be remembered by posterity as a psychologist (Boring 1950, 275). In recent times another psychophysicist, S. S. Stevens, spent a fair amount of his life attempting to prove that sensory and physical events are related according to power functions and are not related logarithmically as Fechner proposed (e.g., Stevens 1962, 1–33; 1975).

The American philosopher Charles Sanders Peirce (1839–1917) knew of Fechner's law and made it central in his studies of the inferential force of evidence and the grading of belief intensity (1878, in Houser and Kloesel 1992, 159). Like Bentham, Peirce thought we needed some kind of "thermometer" for grading the intensity of belief. But, unlike Bentham's "thermometer of persuasion" (see Section 5.1), the scale on Peirce's thermometer was consistent with Pascalian or conventional probabilities. As belief in H increases, belief in not-H decreases. But Peirce noted that his thermometer involves another consideration (1878, 159):

> It is that our belief ought to be proportional to the weight of evidence, in this sense, that two arguments which are entirely independent, neither weakening nor strengthening each other, ought, when they concur, to produce a belief equal to the sum of the intensities of belief which either would produce separately.

Peirce knew about conventional rules for combining probabilities. However, he seems not to have appreciated any distinction between chances (the aleatory conception) and epistemic probability. In particular, Peirce knew of the product rule for independent events. To make belief intensities additive rather than multiplicative, he proposed that the scale on his thermometer correspond to the logarithm of *chance* which, he noted, was in keeping with Fechner's law. As Peirce tells us, "It is entirely in harmony with this law that the feeling of belief should be as the logarithm of the chance; this latter being the expression of the facts which produces the belief" (1878, 159). Peirce went on to say that in the *balancing of reasons* involving arguments pro and con, we should simply subtract the logarithms for con arguments from those for pro arguments to produce a final belief. One trouble with Peirce's idea is that logarithms of Pascalian probabilities are always less than or equal to zero.

5.3.1 Posterior and Prior Probability Measures

Other persons since Peirce have had an interest in grading the intensity of belief and the force of evidence, but unlike Peirce, they have made reference to Bayes's rule. If H is some hypothesis of interest and E^* is some evidence, Bayes's rule says that $P(H|E^*) = P(H)P(E^*|H)/P(E^*)$. At this point I will ask you to recall earlier discussion in Section 2.3.2 of the omnipresence of S, representing our universe of discourse or background information. We can suppress S to make equations simpler, but it is always there and can be recalled when necessary. Arguments about what S may mean in various situations I will defer to Section 5.4. Consider the terms $P(H|E^*)$ and $P(H)$ in Bayes's rule. The term $P(H|E^*)$ is a *posterior probability*, representing the probability of H after you take account of evidence E^*. The probability $P(H)$ is the *prior* probability of H or the probability of H before you considered E^*. One possible measure of the force of evidence E^* is simply the *posterior–prior difference* $d = P(H|E^*) - P(H)$. This difference is one measure of the change in a probabilistic belief about H as a result of evidence E^*. Thus we might interpret **d** as a measure of the inferential force of E^* in an inference about H. The value of **d** may of course be positive or negative, depending upon whether $P(H)$ is greater than or less than $P(H|E^*)$. If **d** = 0, this means that E^* has caused no change in the probability of H. We might be willing to say that E^* is irrelevant in this case, but we have to keep in mind that E^* is evidence that event E occurred. We might believe that event E, if it did occur, would be highly relevant as far as H is concerned.

Posterior–prior differences are discussed as measures of evidential force in a variety of contexts (e.g., Horwich 1982, 51–72; Achinstein 1983, 322–350; Friedman 1987, 673). One such usage brings to mind Peirce's belief intensity thermometer having a logarithmic scale. In the field of statistical communications theory the process of communication in the presence of noise is viewed as an inductive inference task. The probabilities of concern in this theory are taken to be Pascalian, so Bayes's rule is employed in the following situation. Suppose that H is a particular message that might have been transmitted and that E^* is a noisy signal we have received. The posterior $P(H|E^*)$ is the probability of message H being transmitted, given the noisy signal E^*; $P(H)$ is the prior probability of the message being transmitted. Colin Cherry has noted that this inference involves weighing the evidence on H provided by noisy signal E^*. He mentions a measure $I_{E^*} = \log P(H|E^*) - \log P(H)$ which, he says, grades the *information content* of noisy signal E^* (Cherry 1959, 200–201). We should note that I_{E^*} is also equal to $\log[P(H|E^*)/P(H)]$, in which case we consider the ratio $r = P(H|E^*)/P(H)$ and not the difference $d = P(H|E^*) - P(H)$.

Unfortunately, there is trouble associated with grading the force of evidence in terms of either **d** or **r**, as defined above. The trouble is that changes in belief measured on a probability scale can be very misleading. What appears to be an insignificant belief change on a probability scale can in fact be a profound change on another scale directly related to probabilities; this scale involves the familiar term *odds*. First, suppose we have hypothesis H and its complement H^c. The odds of H to H^c, which we will refer to as $\Omega(H:H^c)$, has the following definition: $\Omega(H:H^c) = P(H)/P(H^c) = P(H)/[1 - P(H)]$. So we could determine $\Omega(H:H^c)$ if we knew $P(H)$. But we could also determine $P(H)$ if we knew $\Omega(H:H^c)$, since a little algebra applied to the above definition shows that $P(H) = \Omega(H:H^c)/[1 + \Omega(H:H^c)]$. We might refer to $\Omega(H:H^c)$ as the *prior odds* of H to H^c, since we have not taken evidence E^* into account. Now let us consider the *posterior odds* of H to H^c, given evidence E^*, which we symbolize as $\Omega(H:H^c|E^*)$. The same definition applies, and we have $\Omega(H:H^c|E^*) = P(H|E^*)/P(H^c|E^*) = P(H|E^*)/[1 - P(H|E^*)]$. So, $P(H|E^*) = \Omega(H:H^c|E^*)/[1 + \Omega(H:H^c|E^*)]$. Conventional probabilities have a scale from zero to one, but odds exist on a scale from zero to infinity. Here lies the basic trouble with grading the force of evidence on a probability scale. This scale has an upper bound (1.0); as we get closer to this bound, changes toward it can only be very slight. This problem is illustrated in Figure 5.1*a*.

(*a*) Posterior – Prior Probability Measures

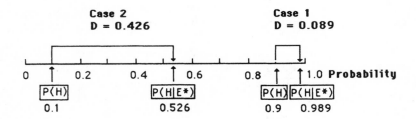

(*b*) Odds Measures

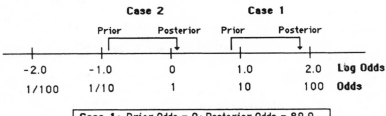

FIGURE 5.1   Examples of two different Pascalian gradings of the inferential force of evidence.

Case 1 (Probabilities). Suppose that $P(H) = 0.9$ and $P(H|E^*) = 0.989$. In this case $d = 0.989 - 0.9 = 0.089$. We might be inclined to say that evidence E^* has not much inferential force since our beliefs were changed by a probability difference of just 0.089. We might also observe that $r = 0.989/0.9 = 1.09$ is also rather small; our posterior probability is just 1.09 times the value of our prior probability.

Case 2 (Probabilities). Suppose, instead, that $P(H) = 0.10$ and $P(H|E^*) = 0.526$. In this case we would have $d = 0.526 - 0.10 = 0.426$ and $r = 0.526/0.10 = 5.26$. Here we might be inclined to say that the inferential force of E^* is quite substantial, since we experienced a probability change of 0.426 and our posterior probability is now 5.26 times the value of our prior.

But what I will now show you is that the belief revisions in these two cases are identical on another scale; they could in fact have been caused by the very same evidence. This new interpretation is illustrated in Figure 5.1*b*.

Case 1 (Odds). Using $P(H) = 0.9$ and $P(H|E^*) = 0.989$ as in case 1 for probabilities, we determine prior odds $\Omega(H:H^c) = 0.9/0.1 = 9$, and posterior odds $\Omega(H:H^c|E^*) = 0.989/0.011 = 89.91$. Let us keep track of the ratio of posterior to prior odds; this ratio is 9.99.

Case 2 (Odds). Using $P(H) = 0.10$ and $P(H|E^*) = 0.526$ as in case 2 for probabilities, we determine prior odds $\Omega(H:H^c) = 0.1/0.9 = 1/9$, and posterior odds $\Omega(H:H^c|E^*) = 0.526/0.474 = 1.11$. The ratio of posterior to prior odds in this case is 9.99, the same as in case 1.

Figure 5.1*b* shows the results of our analysis of the inferential force of evidence E^* when we consider posterior and prior odds rather than probabilities. The odds for each of our two cases are shown on a log scale; this is very convenient for illustrating an interesting property of the force of evidence in terms of log odds. On such a scale the force of evidence is *additive*, and this again brings to mind Peirce's thermometer for grading the intensity of belief. One matter Peirce did not consider was that evidence having any force at all causes a *change* in belief, which we must determine in order to grade the force of evidence in Pascalian terms. This is the essential message in Bayes's rule. Construed in terms of probability changes, cases 1 and 2 appear different. Construed in terms of prior odds, posterior odds, and their ratio, these two cases are identical. The ratio of posterior to prior odds is the same in each case. This belief change in either case could have been due to the same item of evidence. Stated another way, an item of evidence whose force is graded in terms of the ratio of posterior to prior *odds* will have the same measured force in changing a prior belief regardless of the strength of a prior belief. This fact is not apparent when evidential force is graded simply in terms of *posterior–prior probability* differences or ratios. We now consider another very important ingredient of Bayes's rule that is equivalent to a ratio of posterior to prior odds.

5.3.2   Likelihood and Likelihood Ratio Measures

As a measure of the force of evidence, the trouble with the posterior–prior odds ratio we have just considered is that it assumes we already know the posterior odds $\Omega(H:H^c|E^*)$. If we had not already determined $\Omega(H:H^c|E^*)$, we would then have no way of grading the force of evidence E^*. But there are other ingredients in Bayes's rule that directly concern evidence E^* and allow us to determine an evidence-related quantity that is equivalent to the ratio of posterior to prior odds; these ingredients are the *likelihoods* we mentioned earlier in Section 4.3.1. The very simple form of Bayes's rule we have considered shows us that $P(H|E^*) = P(H)P(E^*|H)/P(E^*)$. We made use of $P(H|E^*)$ in determining posterior odds, and we used $P(H)$ in determining prior odds. So, according to Bayes's rule, the change from $P(H)$ to $P(H|E^*)$ somehow involves the likelihood $P(E^*|H)$, but there is another likelihood we need to consider. The probability $P(E^*)$ appears in the denominator of Bayes's rule. Let us assume that E^* is only inconclusive evidence of H. This means that we might have E^* when H is true, but we might also have E^* when H is not true. So we need to consider $P(E^*) = P(E^*H) + P(E^*H^c)$. Using the general product rule for determining the probability of joint events, we have $P(E^*) = P(H)P(E^*|H) + P(H^c)P(E^*|H^c)$. Thus we see that two likelihoods are necessary $P(E^*|H)$ and $P(E^*|H^c)$. These are the same terms we discussed earlier in connection with Mill's ideas about causality and probabilistic relevance. Evidence E^* is positively relevant on H if $P(E^*|H) > P(E^*|H^c)$ and positively relevant on H^c if $P(E^*|H) < P(E^*|H^c)$.

Let us now see how these two likelihoods are related to the ratio of posterior to prior odds. We need to note first that $P(E^*|H)$ and $P(E^*|H^c)$ can be any two probabilities; they need not sum to one since they both involve E^*. There is another form of Bayes's rule, called the *odds–likelihood ratio* form, that shows the direct connection between these likelihoods and the ratio of posterior to prior odds. Consider the posterior probabilities $P(H|E^*) = P(H)P(E^*|H)/P(E^*)$ and $P(H^c|E^*) = P(H^c)P(E^*|H^c)/P(E^*)$. If we divide $P(H|E^*)$ by $P(H^c|E^*)$, $P(E^*)$ drops out, and we are left with $P(H|E^*)/P(H^c|E^*) = [P(H)/P(H^c)][P(E^*|H)/P(E^*|H^c)]$. Here we have three ratios, so we have to suppose that none of the denominators in any of these ratios is zero. Using our definition of prior and posterior odds, we have $\Omega(H:H^c|E^*) = \Omega(H:H^c)[P(E^*|H)/P(E^*|H^c)]$. The ratio of the two likelihoods is of course called a *likelihood ratio,* and for evidence E^* we give it the symbol $L_{E^*} = [P(E^*|H)/P(E^*|H^c)]$. So the odds–likelihood ratio form of Bayes's rule can be expressed as $\Omega(H:H^c|E^*) = \Omega(H:H^c)L_{E^*}$. This means that $L_{E^*} = \Omega(H:H^c|E^*)/\Omega(H:H^c)$; in words, the likelihood ratio is equivalent to the ratio of posterior to prior odds. Expressed in logarithms, $\log L_{E^*} = \log \Omega(H:H^c|E^*) - \log \Omega(H:H^c)$.

We are told by I. J. Good that the British mathematician A. M. Turing was the first to propose $\log L_{E*} = [\log \Omega(H:H^c|E^*) - \log \Omega(H:H^c)]$ as a measure of the *weight of evidence* E^* (1983, 36–38). The measures L_{E*} and $\log L_{E*}$ have *many* interesting properties that I will describe and exploit as we proceed. Since it is a ratio of positive probabilities, L_{E*} is always > 0 if E^* is inconclusive and $P(E^*|H) \neq 0$. We might note at this point that $\log L_{E*} = \log[\Omega(H:H^c|E^*)/\Omega(H:H^c)]$ has all of the properties of the decibel or Richter-scale measures we considered earlier. In S. S. Stevens scale-classification scheme, $\log L_{E*}$ belongs in the class called *logarthmic interval* scales. Such scales have a zero point that is arbitrary. In the case of $\log L_{E*}$ the zero point is scaled with reference to $\Omega(H:H^c)$, which can be any value greater than zero. When $\Omega(H:H^c|E^*) = \Omega(H:H^c)$, $L_{E*} = 1$ and $\log L_{E*} = 0$; in this case E^* has no inferential force. Values of $L_{E*} > 1$ or $\log L_{E*} > 0$ mean that E^* favors H over H^c by an amount indicated by the size of L_{E*}. Values of $L_{E*} < 1$ or $\log L_{E*} < 0$ mean that E^* favors H^c over H by an amount indicated by the size of L_{E*}. In legal contexts it has been noted that L_{E*} captures the basic idea of the relevance of evidence as prescribed by Federal Rule of Evidence FRE-401, which we discussed in Section 3.1.1 (Lempert 1977).

Measured in terms of log likelihood ratio, the force of evidence has the *additivity* first mentioned by Peirce as a desirable property for a measure of the force of evidence. As an illustration, suppose we have two items of evidence E^* and F^*. From Bayes's rule, $P(H|E^*F^*) = P(H)P(E^*|H)$ $P(F^*|E^*H)/P(E^*F^*)$ and $P(H^c|E^*F^*) = P(H^c)P(E^*|H^c)P(F^*|E^*H^c)/P(E^*F^*)$. If we divide these two posterior probabilities, $P(E^*F^*)$ drops out, and we have $\Omega(H:H^c|E^*F^*) = \Omega(H:H^c)L_{E*} [P(F^*|E^*H)/P(F^*|E^*H^c)]$. The term in the brackets here is also a likelihood ratio; to see what it measures, let us draw upon the *hybrid notation* for conditional probabilities mentioned earlier in Section 2.3.2. Using this scheme, we can express $P(F^*|E^*H)$ as $P_{E*}(F^*|H)$ and $P(F^*|E^*H^c)$ as $P_{E*}(F^*|H^c)$. Here we have a *conditional independence* issue. Bayes's rule requires us to determine whether or not E^* and F^* are independent, conditional upon H or H^c. The hybrid terms $P_{E*}(F^*|H)$ and $P_{E*}(F^*|H^c)$ help us to recognize that we are asked to assess the values of $P(F^*|H)$ and $P(F^*|H^c)$ in light of evidence E^*. First, suppose that the force of evidence F^* on H and H^c does depend upon E^*. In this case we say that $P(F^*|E^*H) = P_{E*}(F^*|H) \neq P(F^*|H)$ and $P(F^*|E^*H^c) = P_{E*}(F^*|H^c) \neq P(F^*|H^c)$. In words, these inequalities say that the force of evidence F^* on H and H^c does depend upon E^*. We could express this in ratio form by saying that $L_{F*|E*} = P(F^*|E^*H)/P(F^*|E^*H^c)$ does not equal $L_{F*} = P(F^*|H)/P(F^*|H^c)$. Then we have $\Omega(H:H^c|E^*F^*) = \Omega(H:H^c)(L_{E*})(L_{F*|E*})$. Dividing both sides by prior odds, we have $\Omega(H:H^c|E^*F^*)/\Omega(H:H^c) = (L_{E*})(L_{F*|E*})$. In logs we have $\log[\Omega(H:H^c|E^*F^*)/\Omega(H:H^c)] = \log L_{E*} + \log L_{F*|E*}$. In words, the total force of evidence E^* and F^* is indicated by the sum of their log likelihood ratios.

Next, suppose that E^* and F^* are independent, conditional upon H and upon H^c. If so, $P(F^*|E^*H) = P_{E*}(F^*|H) = P(F^*|H)$ and $P(F^*|E^*H^c) =$

$P_{E*}(F^*|H^c) = P(F^*|H^c)$. In this case we have $L_{F*|E*} = L_{F*} = P(F^*|H)/P(F^*|H^c)$. We can then express $\Omega(H:H^c|E^*F^*) = \Omega(H:H^c)(L_{E*})(L_{F*})$. Dividing both sides by prior odds, we have $\Omega(H:H^c|E^*F^*)/\Omega(H:H^c) = (L_{E*})(L_{F*})$. In logs we have $\log[\Omega(H:H^c|E^*F^*)/\Omega(H:H^c)] = \log L_{E*} + \log L_{F*}$. In log likelihood ratio terms, the force of evidence is always additive whether or not the evidence items are conditionally independent. This additivity property extends to any number of evidence items. We should also note that some items may favor H and others H^c. Those favoring H^c over H will have a negative value of $\log L$. This corresponds to Peirce's argument that in the balancing of reasons, we should subtract the logarithms for con arguments from those for pro arguments.

It is also possible to grade the force of evidence in terms of the difference between likelihoods. On Nozick's account the difference $s = P(E^*|H) - P(E^*|H^c)$ is said to be a measure of the *support* evidence E^* provides to H (1981, 252). The difference s can be negative; then we might say that in such cases it is a measure of the support E^* gives to H^c. There will be argument about whether this likelihood difference is an appropriate measure of evidential support. In Section 5.4 we will consider a different measure of evidential support that makes no use of likelihoods. Nozick's measure s has some useful properties, but for reasons that follow, I will confine my attention to likelihoods and their ratios as Pascalian measures of the force of evidence.

5.3.3   Expanded Forms of Likelihoods and Their Ratios

As a canon for probabilistic reasoning, Bayes's rule certainly looks unpromising in its commonly encountered forms. Take the odds–likelihood ratio form $\Omega(H:H^c|E^*) = \Omega(H:H^c)L_{E*}$. All Bayes's rule says here is that we convert prior odds into posterior odds by multiplying prior odds by the likelihood ratio for evidence E^*. Bayes's rule looks no more promising in the general case in which we have an exhaustive collection n of mutually exclusive hypotheses. Then we would determine the posterior probability of H_i, given evidence E^*, by

$$P(H_i|E^*) = \frac{P(H_i)P(E^*|H_i)}{\sum_{k=1}^{n} P(H_k)P(E^*|H_k)}$$

All Bayes's rule says in this case is that the posterior probability of H_i is the normalized product of the prior probability of H_i and the likelihood of evidence E^*, given H_i. As I mentioned several times earlier, probabilistic reasoning is a very rich intellectual activity. How are we to capture any of this richness by the apparently sterile processes revealed in these equations?

Since the 1960s a major item on my research agenda concerns attempts to make Bayes's rule capture some of the inferential richness I observed while reading legal and other treatises on evidence and inference. Within the Pascalian system of probability, the obvious place to start such a venture is with terms in Bayes's rule that concern the evidence we have; these terms are likelihoods and their ratios. The prior probabilities (or odds), though a subject of controversy regarding how they are to be initially assessed, are hardly interesting as far as the richness of probabilistic reasoning is concerned. In my judgment, we begin to capture the richness of probabilistic inference when we focus on the many interesting forms and combinations of evidence we considered in Chapter 3 and on the more complex structural matters we discussed in Chapter 4. A focus on evidence, likelihoods, and likelihood ratios shows us how we might begin to make Bayes's rule capture some of the richness of probabilistic inference.

First, as mentioned in Chapter 3, a chain of reasoning between E^* and H may involve many links. Stated another way, a defense of the relevance of E^* on H might involve any number of reasoning stages. We can immediately specify one intermediate link involving events $\{E, E^c\}$; recall that E^* is just evidence that event E occurred. If E^* is testimonial evidence about event E, we might further decompose the linkage between E^* and E in the manner discussed in Figure 3.6a. Such decomposition captures elements of the credibility of the source of evidence E^*. In turn, event E might be linked to H by any number of reasoning stages, an extreme example of which is provided in Figure 3.9 for Officer Connolly's testimony in the Sacco and Vanzetti case. In short, our inference from E^* to H will be *cascaded, hierarchical,* or *catenated* (as Wigmore termed it). In Chapters 6 and 7 I will discuss how likelihoods and their ratios can be expanded in order to incorporate cascaded inferences. In their expanded forms likelihoods and likelihood ratios may contain many ingredients, some of which force us to give attention to the conditional independence or nonindependence of events at various stages of reasoning. Many of the important subtleties in the various forms of evidence shown in Figure 3.11 can only be revealed by such expansions.

Few conclusions are drawn on the basis of a single item of evidence. In Chapter 4 we considered inferences based upon entire masses of evidence of different forms. But we also recognized the existence of recurrent combinations of evidence (Figures 3.13, 3.14, and 3.15). Appropriate expansions of likelihoods and their ratios provide a basis for the careful analysis of evidential conflict, contradiction, corroboration, synergism, and redundance. Such analyses, also involving the important concept of conditional nonindependence, form the subject matter of Chapter 8. Expansions of likelihoods and their ratios reveal many interesting things about how the Pascalian approach to inference, via Bayes's rule, can capture evidential subtleties. Among the most interesting subtleties are those associated with the rareness of events. A fundamental fact about expanded likelihoods and their ratios is that *they respond both to ratios and to differences in their ingredients.* Consider the following two pairs of likelihoods: $[P(E|H) = 0.9, P(E|H^c) = 0.1]$ and $[P(E|H) = 0.09, P(E|H^c) = 0.01]$. Though the ratios of the likelihoods in each pair are the same (9), the difference between members of each pair is different; 0.8 for the first pair and 0.08 for the second. In the second pair E is ten times less probable under H and H^c than it is in the first pair. We will see that likelihood ratios respond quite differently to pairs of ingredients such as the two just given. In Section 7.1.3 you will also see why I was "murdered" by a colleague for having discovered this fact about Bayes's rule.

By means of expanded likelihoods and their ratios Bayes's rule can indeed be made to capture much of the richness evident in probabilistic inference. However, applying these Bayesian ideas in actual circumstances requires additional considerations not yet discussed. It may be necessary for us to consider additional structuring exercises in assessing the probabilistic ingredients these likelihood ratios require. We may also come to realize that the arguments upon which these likelihood ratios rest outrun the evidence we have to support the judgments they require. In such cases we may have to be content with simpler arguments and resort to different ways of grading the force of evidence.

5.4 BELIEF FUNCTIONS: GRADING EVIDENTIAL SUPPORT

I have used the term *Pascalian* with reference to any view of probabilitistic reasoning consistent with the Kolmogorov axioms and the particular definition of a conditional probability we have considered. Bayes's rule is a consequence of these axioms and definition. As we have just observed, there are certain measures of the inferential force of evidence that stem from an examination of the likelihood ingredients of Bayes's rule. In my introductory comments about the Pascalian system (Section 2.3), I noted that Kolmogorov had an *enumerative* conception of probability in the back of his mind as he formed his axiomatic system. I also noted that both the aleatory (chance) and relative frequency interpretations of probability rest upon *counting* processes. There has been lingering controversy, often quite heated, about the extent to which we should accept the Pascalian system in general and Bayes's rule in particular as guides to life in probabilistic inference, especially when our evidence and hypotheses refer to singular or unique events whose probability can rest on no overt enumerative process. The history of interest in probability calculation reveals that chance, relative frequency, and epistemic conceptions of probability developed side by side. On the epistemic view a probability simply grades the intensity of a person's belief about the likeliness of some event based upon whatever evidence this person has to justify this belief. The issue is: Should all epistemic gradations of probabilistic belief conform to Pascalian rules?

We now examine a body of work suggesting that epistemic gradations of probabilistic belief can be expected to conform to Pascalian rules on just some occasions. On other occasions we may be quite justified in expressing probabilistic beliefs that conform to other rules. For example, on Pascalian rules probabilistic belief must normalize or sum to one across an exhaustive collection of mutually exclusive hypotheses. Thus, if you hear me say that, on present evidence, the probability of H is 0.6, it might be expected that I would also have to say that on this same evidence the probability of H^c is 0.4. But, on the view we now examine, it may be quite appropriate for me to *withold* some of my belief depending upon various properties of the evidence that I have. I might not always feel justified in allocating all of my present belief to either H or H^c. In the work of Glenn Shafer and his colleagues we find a categorical rejection of the idea that Bayes's rule is *the* normative standard for all probabilistic inference based on evidence.

5.4.1 Partial Beliefs and Their Judgmental Foundations

If I regarded hypothesis H as being conclusively proved by some item or body of evidence, I might say that my belief in H is *complete;* H is certain and that's the end of it! As far as H is concerned I have no uncertainties or doubts; my belief is completely committed to H. If I lacked conclusive evidence for H, I might still believe that H is true, but my committment would be only *partial,* since I do have some uncertainties or doubts about H. In some instances I might even say that I have accepted H, even though I do not completely believe in H. Some persons strongly advise us to distinguish between *belief* and *acceptance* (Cohen, L. J., 1992). A major issue concerns how we ought to grade partial beliefs. The Pascalian system of probability offers an alternative: The posterior probabilities in Bayes's rule grade the extent of our uncertainty about H after we have considered some body of evidence. Thus Bayes's rule can be construed as a theory of partial belief. I might choose to estimate posterior probabilities directly or I might choose to calculate them on the basis of priors and likelihoods, both of which require judgments of various kinds. In either case the resulting posterior probabilities have to obey certain rules if they are to be accepted as Pascalian in nature. In particular, as my posterior belief in H increases, my posterior belief in H^c must decrease. Calculations made using Bayes's rule ensure that this will happen provided that judgments of priors and likelihoods also have Pascalian properties.

The judgmental and subjective nature of probabilistic inference has been a bitter pill for many to swallow. Even those persons whose names have been most directly associated with a subjective or personal interpretation of probability have often skirted issues concerning direct numerical judgments of probability. Chances and relative frequencies often seem comfortably objective since they appear to rest only upon enumeration. However, the many subjective or judgmental ingredients in any statistical analysis are often overlooked (Savage 1961). In statistics the confrontation between frequentists and subjectivists has gone on for many years and still continues. To suggest that probabilities are numbers that have to be judged by people raises a connection between probabilistic inference and psychology that many are loath to accept. In a postscript to his paper *Truth and Probability* (1926), Frank P. Ramsey claimed that a defect in this paper was that it took partial belief as ". . . a psychological phenomenon to be defined and measured by a psychologist" (1929, 95). He went on to say that this would be quite unacceptable in a developed science.

Psychologists themselves are often concerned about the acceptability of human numerical judgments, even though such judgments are routinely employed in many forms of behavioral research. Here is an example from sensory psychophysics. Suppose I show you two lights A and B and I ask you to answer the following question: If we label the brightness of light A as 10, what brightness label would you assign to B? Suppose you believe that light B is twice as bright as A; if so, you would presumably assign the number 20 to light B. If you thought light B to be half as bright as A, you would assign the number 5 to light B. The psychologist S. S. Stevens probably spent more time than anyone else in collecting numerical judgments like these. But he noted that numerical judgments, regardless of their consistency, are rarely persuasive (1962, 32). To eliminate the need for numerical judgments in studying the relations between physical and sensory events, Stevens developed a procedure involving what he termed *cross-modality matches*. In such a procedure a person uses one sensory modality as a basis for judgments about another modality. For example, people were asked to adjust the loudness of a sound so that it would match the brightness of a light; another technique was to indicate the loudness of a tone by means of squeezing a handgrip attached to a dynamometer. In Stevens's experiments the psychophysical relations established by such cross-modality matches generally agreed with those obtained using direct numerical judgments. It might be argued that to avoid numerical judgments, a person could just as easily indicate the intensity of belief in some hypothesis by means of adjusting the apparent brightness of a light or the loudness of a tone.

On some early accounts subjective or personal probabilities were allowed as inferable from a person's choices or from the odds a person might quote in a wager or bet. Savage considers a person who has uncertainty about some event A and who is confronted with a wager involving whether or not A has occurred (or will occur). On Savage's account the probability of A for this person refers to the odds that this person would just barely offer for A over not-A in this wager (1962, 11–12). The person Savage has in mind is somewhat idealized or "coherent," in the sense that this person would never make a combination of wagers in which he is sure to lose. Such wagers involve the "Dutch book" mentioned earlier, in Section 2.3.5. Ramsey discussed conditional probabilities such as P(A|B) that are inferable from a person's bets on A that are valid only if B is true (1926, 76). Modern interpretations of subjective or personal probabilities frequently make no mention of inferring probabilities from wagers. For example, von Winterfeldt and Edwards simply assert that (1) all uncertainties are inherently of the same kind, (2) probabilities are useful numbers with which to measure uncertainties, and (3) probabilities are personal degrees of belief about uncertain events (1986, 91).

In the work of Glenn Shafer we find a specific commitment to a judgmental basis for probabilistic reasoning, even in situations involving chances and relative frequencies. Shafer's major contribution has been to provide a theory about how we might grade the support that evidence provides hypotheses and about how these gradings of support may be combined to indicate the strength of our belief in these hypotheses. Shafer is quite specific in telling us that evidential support is the result of a judgmental process. In what may be regarded as his major work he states: "Whenever I write in this essay of the 'degree of support' that given evidence provides for a proposition or of the 'degree of belief' that an individual accords the proposition, I picture in my mind an act of judgment" (1976, 20). He goes on to say that he does not pretend that there is any objective relation between the evidence and a proposition that determines a precise numerical degree of support. Nor does he claim that there is any precise number that can always reflect a person's judgment of evidential support. He simply supposes that if required, a person can make a numerical judgment that reflects this person's belief about the degree to which evidence supports a proposition. Shafer argues that inferences about a person's probabilities from wagers or bets completely ignore the evidential foundation for these probabilities. For Shafer, Bayes's rule is a useful but not entirely adequate theory of partial belief.

5.4.2 On the Weight and the Support of Evidence

Shafer's work on the grading of evidential support allows us to begin considering elements of the controversy surrounding use of the term *evidential weight*. As noted, Peirce believed that the weight of evidence was proportional to the logarithm of *chance*, in agreement with Fechner's psychophysical law, and that such weights could be added together. Later Turing proposed that we measure the weight of evidence in terms of log likelihood ratio for each evidence item. The aggregate weight of some body of evidence items, conditionally independent or not, is the algebraic sum of the individual log likelihood ratios. Shafer also discusses a logarithmic measure of the weight of evidence that applies under certain circumstances (1976, 77–78). This measure gives us some insight into Shafer's general views about the relation between evidential support and evidential weight. In Shafer's account of the force or weight of evidence, we focus on the *support* that evidence seems to provide for some hypothesis. To grade the support provided by a certain item or body of evidence, Shafer suggests that we can use numbers in the interval $[0, 1]$. However, we are permitted to use these numbers in allocating evidential support to hypotheses or possibilities in ways that are not sanctioned in the Pascalian view of probabilistic reasoning. Shafer tells us that under certain conditions the weight (w) of an item or body of evidence is related to the support (s) it provides according to the expression $w = -\log(1 - s)$. As s approaches zero, so does w; as s approaches 1, w becomes infinite. It will be instructive to compare Shafer's concept of evidential weight or support with the other concepts of evidential weight that we have considered.

On Peirce's account, taken literally, we focus on *chances* associated with evidence, so we might say that $w = \log(c)$, where c is some aleatory probability. In the likelihood ratio account we focus on the *relative likeliness* of evidence under two different hypotheses by considering $w = \log(p/q)$, where p and q are two Pascalian likelihoods such as $P(E^*|H)$ and $P(E^*|H^c)$. These two likelihoods might be chances or relative frequencies, but they might also be subjective or personal probabilities. As I noted earlier, $w = \log(p/q)$ has all the characteristics of a decibel measure. I also mentioned Nozick's measure of evidential support $s = (p - q)$ as the difference between two Pascalian likelihoods. But, in Shafer's stated relation $w = -\log(1 - s)$, what status does evidential support s have? Is it a chance, a relative frequency, a subjective probability, or something else? Recalling Shafer's comments about the judgmental nature of evidential support, the relation $w = -\log(1 - s)$ indicates that evidential weight is simply a transformation or another way of grading a *judgment* made by a person about the support that evidence provides to a proposition. Other probabilists have not been quite so straightforward in acknowledging the role of judgment in determining probabilities or in grading the force of evidence.

As an illustration of how we might use Shafer's concept of evidential support, let us reconsider the inference about whether or not your neighbor is keeping a dog in his apartment in violation of the rules. Earlier I used this situation to illustrate the role of evidence of tangibles or things that can point to other things. Suppose you have no tangible circumstantial evidence such as the table scratches, the carpet spots, or the dog food you observed in your neighbor's apartment. Instead, all you have at present is testimony from person P telling you that your neighbor does have a dog in his apartment. You wonder whether P is credible as a source of information in this case. Suppose H^* represents testimony from P that your neighbor is keeping a dog in his apartment and that H represents the event that your neighbor is in fact keeping a dog in his apartment. One thing you might do is to lay out a chain of reasoning from H^* to H along lines suggested by my analysis of the attributes of the credibility of witnesses as illustrated in Figure 3.6a. On this analysis you identify three stages of reasoning associated with P's credibility attributes: veracity, objectivity, and observational sensitivity. In Chapter 7 we will consider how we might use a decomposed likelihood ratio to assess the inferential force of testimony about some event in an inference about whether this event did happen. But Shafer tells us that we may often form arguments that outrun the evidence we have to support them (e.g., 1986a). Perhaps you have no specific ancillary evidence bearing upon one or more of the three credibility attributes just mentioned. In such cases you may have to resort to a simpler argument such as the one that follows:

As far as person P is concerned, suppose that the best you can do is to give P a single probability as a gradation of his credibility. You say there is a 90% chance that P is credible in this case and a 10% chance that he isn't. What do these judged probabilities mean? Figure 5.2 gives one interpretation of these two ordinary probabilities that will illustrate a simple instance of how Shafer proposes we grade the support that evidence H* provides hypothesis H. You think carefully about P's testimony H* and what it means to say that there is a 90% chance he is credible in this situation. You reason as follows: If P is credible, this means that H is true. In other words, if P is credible, H* entails H; and you believe that there is a 90% chance that this is so. That P's credibility means H is true is indicated by the single line from C: "P is credible" to H in Figure 5.2. To say that there is a 90% chance that H* means H is also to say in Shafer's terms that H*, together with what you believe about P, supports H to degree 0.9.

However, if P is not credible (C^c), this does not necessarily mean that your neighbor is not keeping a dog in his apartment. P might have made up a story that happens to be true (there are other possibilities). In fact, your deciding that P's not being credible could mean either H or H^c, as shown by the two lines from C^c in Figure 5.2. Thus your believing that P's being credible is only *compatible* with H, whereas P's not being credible is *compatible with both* H and H^c. The question now to be answered involves what happens to the 10% chance you assigned to P's not being credible. Since you believe that P's not being credible is compatible with both H and H^c, you have no basis for saying that his evidence provides any direct support for H^c. Thus you cannot commit the remaining 0.1 evidential support to H^c. The best you can do is to leave

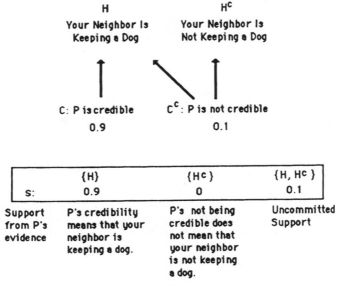

	{H}	{H^c}	{H, H^c}
s:	0.9	0	0.1

| Support from P's evidence | P's credibility means that your neighbor is keeping a dog. | P's not being credible does not mean that your neighbor is not keeping a dog. | Uncommitted Support |

FIGURE 5.2 An example illustrating evidential compatibility and support.

this 0.1 of evidential support *uncommitted* among H and H^c, as shown in Figure 5.2. The evidential support of 0.1 applied to {H, H^c} essentially means that this support might go to H or to H^c, but you have no present basis for saying which way it should go.

A very important element of Shafer's scheme for allocating evidential support to hypotheses concerns the zero support given specifically to {H^c} in the present example. At the moment, based just on P's testimony and what you believe about his credibility, there is no direct support for the possibility that your neighbor is not keeping a dog. In a conventional assignment of Pascalian probabilities, P(H^c) = 0 would mean that H^c is impossible and that no further evidence could cause you to change your mind about the impossibility of H^c. But all you have said by assigning zero support to H^c is simply that P's not being credible is incompatible just with H^c. A statement about the lack of support for H^c is not the same as saying that H^c is impossible. Indeed you allow for the possibility that H^c may be true in your uncommitted assignment of 0.1 support to {H, H^c}. Thus in Shafer's system a lack of support for some hypothesis does not mean that this hypothesis is impossible. There may be new evidence that will offer some support directly to H^c. When we consider rules for combining evidential support across items or bodies of evidence, we will observe how a possibility lacking evidential support at one stage can acquire support at another.

In more abstract terms, what we have in this example are two sets of possible answers to questions we have asked: Is P credible? Is your neighbor keeping a dog? Shafer refers to the sets of possible answers to such questions as *frames of discernment*. The frame concerning person P in our present example is **C** = {C, C^c}, where C = P is credible and C^c = P is not credible. The frame concerning your neighbor is **H** = {H, H^c}, where H = your neighbor is keeping a dog and H^c = he isn't keeping a dog. It is most important in understanding Shafer's view about evidential support to recognize that any discernment of possibilities in a frame depends upon what evidence we already have, what beliefs we presently hold, and what distinctions we wish to make. Our frame of discernment or frame of reference regarding possibilities we entertain may be entirely different depending upon what we believe we know and what distinctions we believe are necessary to make. This brings to mind our earlier discussion (in Sections 3.1 and 4.2) of the thoughts of the legal scholars Anderson and Twining on the role of a person's *standpoint* throughout the entire process of probabilistic reasoning. Our frames of discernment or reference, or our standpoints, depend upon our present state of knowledge, what we are trying to accomplish, and where we presently are in the process of inference about matters of interest. Here is an example of how your present frames of discernment, as shown in Figure 5.2, might have been entirely different.

In our example so far both frames **C** and **H** are very coarse, vague, or undifferentiated. This is a reflection of what you presently know about person P and of what distinctions regarding your neighbor you thought were important. Considering frame **C**, to say simply that P is either credible or not credible is to state only coarse or undifferentiated possibilities. But this is entirely consistent with your present lack of specific evidence about P's credibility. At the moment you might have only vague impressions about his credibility. But suppose you had a variety of specific evidence bearing upon P's veracity, objectivity, and observational sensitivity. Some of this evidence might have strengthened or weakened your beliefs about any of these credibility attributes. In such a case you might have been able to entertain a more refined frame **C'** having the following eight possibilities:

C_1: P is honest, objective, and observationally accurate.

C_2: P is honest, objective, but not observationally accurate.

C_3: P is honest, not objective, but observationally accurate.

C_4: P is honest, not objective, and not observationally accurate.

C_5: P is not honest, but objective, and observationally accurate.

C_6: P is not honest, but objective, and not observationally accurate.

C_7: P is not honest, not objective, but observationally accurate.

C_8: P is not honest, not objective, and not observationally accurate.

The accumulated credibility-relevant evidence you have might allow you to assign chances to each of these eight possibilities that are more specific or refined. If you did have such evidence, you might also entertain using a Bayesian likelihood ratio method for grading the weight of P's evidence on H and H^c as we will later do in Chapter 7. Such a method rests upon the argument shown in Figure 3.6*a*.

In your original frame **H**, you only considered whether or not your neighbor was keeping a dog in his apartment. Perhaps you should consider some more refined possibilities such as those now listed in a refined frame **H'**:

H_1: Your neighbor owns the dog he is keeping in his apartment.

H_2: Your neighbor is keeping a dog, owned by a friend, for an extended period of time.

H_3: Your neighbor is keeping a dog, owned by a friend, for a very short period of time.

H_4: Your neighbor is not keeping any dog in his apartment.

These refined distinctions become necessary when you consider what kind of action you might take if indeed your neighbor presently has a dog in his apartment. You might complain to your landlord if H_1 or H_2 were true, but not necessarily if H_3 were true. As easily discovered, the compatibility judgments between elements of frames **C'** and **H'** are considerably more complicated than were those involving elements of our original frames **C** and **H**. For example, you might agree that C_1, listed above, is compatible with H_1,

H_2, and H_3. You believe that your neighbor is truthful, objective, and observationally accurate in his telling you that your other neighbor is keeping a dog. But his evidence in this case may be compatible with or mean any of these three possibilities. It might not be such an easy task to state which of the four hypotheses in **H'** are compatible with, say, C_3 that P as an honest and accurate but not an objective observer. These refined frames of discernment and more complicated compatibility judgments make the assignment of evidential support a more difficult matter. For example, suppose that the evidence you have suggests that there is a 20% chance that C_3 is true; P is honest and accurate but not necessarily objective. It might be quite difficult to decide how you should allocate $s = 0.20$ to the hypotheses in **H'**. We need to consider carefully the options we have in Shafer's scheme for allocating evidential support.

In Shafer's system we are entitled to allocate evidential support to *combinations* or *subsets* of hypotheses. Suppose we entertain an exhaustive class of n mutually exclusive hypotheses or possibilities. Let this class of hypotheses be called our *frame of discernment*. The number of possible combinations or subsets of these hypotheses is 2^n. For this reason the collection of all 2^n subsets of hypotheses is called a *power set*. For our initial frame **H** = {H, H^c}, the collection of possible subsets (or power set) is {H}, {H^c}, {H, H^c}, and ∅, where ∅ means the empty or vacuous set. For our refined frame **H'**, whose four members are listed above, there are $2^4 = 16$ possible subsets including singletons, pairs, triples, the set of all of them {H_1, H_2, H_3, H_4}, and the set of none of them {∅}. Clearly the difficulty of the judgmental task we face in allocating evidential support depends upon how extensive is our list of hypotheses as well as upon the compatibility relations we are able to discern. To illustrate some options that Shafer's scheme allows us in allocating evidential support to subsets of hypotheses, let us consider a case in which frame **F** is an exhausive collection of just three mutually exclusive hypotheses {H_1, H_2, H_3}. The power set for **F** is shown in Figure 5.3.

Frame F = {H_1, H_2, H_3}

Power Set of Hypotheses in F							
{H_1}	{H_2}	{H_3}	{H_1,H_2}	{H_1,H_3}	{H_2,H_3}	{H_1,H_2,H_3}	∅
Case 1. s{ }: 0	0	0.8	0	0	0	0.2	0
Case 2. s{ }: 0.7	0	0	0	0	0.3	0	0
Case 3. s{ }: 0.5	0.2	0	0	0	0	0.3	0
Case 4. s{ }: 0	0	0	0	0	0	1.0	0
Case 5. s{ }: 0.6	0.3	0.1	0	0	0	0	0

FIGURE 5.3 Examples of Shaferian evidential support assignment.

The five cases in Figure 5.3 each illustrate three major rules imposed in Shafer's scheme for allocating evidential support to possible subsets of hypotheses. At no point in his work does Shafer claim that these rules and their various consequences are normative in the sense that they prescribe rational probabilistic reasoning. He simply argues that they make sense in many situations (1976, 6). First, observe that the numbers representing evidential support (s) assigned in any of these cases are numbers in the interval $0 \leq s \leq 1.0$. Note also that the values of s sum to 1.0 across the *power set* in every case. Finally, notice that the number $s = 0$ is assigned to $\emptyset$ in every case. These three rules are assumed to hold in *every* possible case. To this extent the numbers s resemble ordinary probabilities. However, what can make support assignments non-Pascalian in nature is the fact that we are permitted to allocate evidential support to *subsets of two or more* hypotheses. Such assignment indicates varying degrees of lack of commitment on our part. As illustrated in my example involving P's testimony about the dog in your neighbor's apartment, there are instances in which we cannot always focus evidential support with precision and are therefore obliged to be noncommital in various ways.

Consider case 1 in which we have $s\{H_3\} = 0.8$ and $s\{H_1, H_2, H_3\} = 0.2$. Here is a case in which we say that some evidential possibilities we are considering seem compatible with (or mean) H_3 to degree 0.8. However, there are other evidential possibilities that could mean any of the three hypotheses, so we have no choice but to be noncommital in assigning support of 0.2 to the set $\{H_1, H_2, H_3\}$. The evidence we have seems to support H_3 quite strongly, but it could also mean any of the three hypotheses with a degree of precision we are presently unable to discern. In case 2 we are slightly more commital than in case 1, since we believe that the evidence in this case specifically means H_1 to a certain degree though it might mean either H_2 or H_3 which to a specific degree we cannot now decide.

Case 3 shows an instance in which our evidence, and what we believe we know about it, offers a specific degree of support to each of the incompatible hypotheses H_1 and H_2. It was stipulated that H_1 and H_2 are mutually exclusive or incompatible. In this case we are saying that possible evidential states seem compatible with specific incompatible hypotheses. We also say that 0.3 of our available evidential support cannot be committed to any particular hypothesis. Case 4 is an instance in which we are completely noncommital in assigning evidential support; in this case we simply say that the evidence could mean H_1, H_2, or H_3 but not in any settled proportion among these possibilities. This is a very important case; as we will later discuss, cases like this one concern the important concept of *ignorance as lack of belief*. Finally, case 5 shows an instance in which our evidential support assignment is entirely consistent with Pascalian rules for ordinary probabilities, since we have allocated all of our support in specific amounts to each one of the exhaustive and mutually exclusive hypotheses H_1, H_2, and H_3. Notice in this case that we have not been in any way noncommital in assigning evidential support. We might say that the evidence in this case allows us to focus evidential support in a precise way to each of the hypotheses we are considering. We will return to this case in Section 5.4.4 when we discuss a relationship that exists between Shafer's system and a particular result that follows from Bayes's rule.

5.4.3   Justifying Probabilistic Judgments

When a person makes a numerical probabilistic judgment of some kind, how are we to tell whether this number has been picked out of thin air or is the result of a careful judgmental process? Stated another way, if we are forced to rely upon this person's probabilistic judgment, how much confidence can we have in it? Shafer has considerable interest in such matters. In Chapters 3 and 4 I went to some lengths to illustrate how the credibility and relevance of evidence have to be justified by arguments. What we now consider are various ways in which judgments about the inferential force of evidence must also be justified by arguments. I noted earlier that all the arguments we make about the relevance and credibility of evidence are specific to the person constructing them. An argument constructed by A may not be persuasive to B. In any case there seem to be no arguments from or about evidence that are uniquely "correct." Different persons may entertain different possibilities and make different distinctions.

In a recent work Shafer and Tversky offer a constructive approach in which the process of weighing evidence and making probabilistic judgments can be likened to a thought experiment whose design influences the adequacy of results. The thought experiments in this process are *arguments* that are always open to criticism and counterargument (1985, 40). They note further that any theory of probabilistic judgment requires three elements: (1) a judgmental vocabulary whose elements are numbers on a scale, (2) semantics that show how judgments made in terms of this vocabulary are to be interpreted, and (3) a calculus for combining judgments made on a chosen scale. Thus, for example, we might employ a "Bayesian design" for a judgmental thought experiment that employs (1) a Pascalian probability scale, (2) an interpretation of these probabilities in terms of such things as chances, frequencies, or betting odds, and (3) Bayes's rule as a device for combining judgments made on a Pascalian scale. A Bayesian design may on occasion be quite useful provided that we have some means of justifying our choice of numbers on a Pascalian probability scale that are being used to indicate the force of evidence. In some cases we may experience considerable difficulty in justifying the numbers we have chosen. Here is an example that illustrates some of Shafer's concerns.

In discussing the relevance and credibility of evidence in Chapter 3, I presented what I believe to be a nontrivial example of how these credentials of evidence have to be established by argument. For this purpose I chose Officer Connolly's testimony in the Sacco and Vanzetti case. The basic argument I constructed, involving the relevance and credibility of Connolly's testimony, is shown in Figure 3.9, which I will ask you to consider again.

Suppose you ask me how strong I believe that Connolly's evidence is in an inference about whether Sacco committed the murder with which he was charged. The argument shown in Figure 3.9 may be regarded as the beginning of a thought experiment. This detailed argument identifies what I presently believe to be the major sources of uncertainty lurking between Connolly's testimony and the hypothesis H, concerning Sacco's alleged guilt. Suppose I elect a Bayesian design for this thought experiment and intend to supply probabilities for each of the sources of uncertainty that I have identified in this argument. As we will discuss in more detail in Chapter 7, two likelihoods are required at each stage of reasoning. Suppose that the index i labels an event at one of these stages and index j labels an event at the *next higher stage*. At each stage i two likelihoods are necessary: $P(E_i|E_j)$ and $P(E_i|E_j^c)$. Since there are ten stages in my argument, I will need to supply 20 likelihoods to grade the extent of my uncertainties in determining the force of Connolly's testimony. I have an equation that shows me how to combine these 20 likelihoods in order to determine a likelihood ratio for Connolly's testimony. Recall that the force of evidence in Bayesian terms can be graded by likelihood ratios. I could easily produce 20 likelihoods, but the question is, Would you take any of them seriously?

I have at least made a start in the process of defending any judgments of these likelihoods. In Sections 3.2.3 and 3.3.1 I asserted generalizations in support of each of the ten reasoning stages in my argument linking Connolly's testimony and hypothesis H. But I must now face the issue concerning how strongly these generalizations apply in the particular instance involving Officer Connolly. In short, I must put these generalizations to the test using whatever ancillary evidence I can find that seems to bear upon these generalizations. This is where the trouble starts. From the transcript of the Sacco and Vanzetti trial and from recent accounts of evidence not available during the trial I can find evidence that bears only upon stages 1, 4, and 7 of the argument shown in Figure 3.9. There is a variety of evidence that strongly impeaches Connolly's veracity. Sacco denied any intention of drawing his revolver. There is evidence that Sacco knew he might be in trouble for distributing anarchistic literature (not a criminal offense), but he denied that he had ever committed a crime. So, if I produced 20 Bayesian likelihood judgments regarding the force of Connolly's testimony, you might regard at least 14 of them as having a distinctly fictional quality.

But there are other problems I would face in justifying how the ancillary evidence I have actually gets translated into my specific numerical likelihood judgments. As I indicated in Figure 3.10, in either strengthening or weakening the linkages in arguments from directly relevant evidence such as Connolly's testimony, there may be elaborate arguments necessary in order to justify the relevance, credibility, and force of ancillary evidence. You might not agree that these arguments are sound or that they justify the likelihoods I have assessed when I do have ancillary evidence. Shafer and Tversky argue that subjective probability assessments are always made with reference to *canonical examples* involving chances or sampling operations that seem to fit the situation in which these assessments are required (1985). In short, their claim is that in judging a subjective probability for a unique event, we all naturally base this probability on some imagined enumerative process. This seems to me an unnecessary requirement. I know of no instance in psychophysics in which it has ever been found necessary to suppose that human numerical judgments involve any scales based on canonical examples.

Again, consider Connolly's testimony and the fourteen likelihoods for which I have no specific ancillary evidence to support them. I might say that as far as these likelihoods are concerned I am in a state of *ignorance;* I have no specific evidence bearing upon them. A counterargument is that we are never in a state of total ignorance; we always have at least some background knowledge or evidence to support probabilistic judgments. Let us recall the factor S, which I have labeled "background knowledge." In my present judgment of these twenty likelihoods I suppose that I might have at least some background knowledge S that could support any of them. So I express these likelihoods in the form $P_S(E_i|E_j) = P(E_i|E_jS)$ and $P_S(E_i|E_j^c) = P(E_i|E_j^cS)$. In aleatory situations S has a clear meaning; it is an *advance* listing of all possible outcomes. In relative frequency situations S refers to a relevant sample space also decided in advance. But what does S indicate in the *epistemic* situation involving my judgments concerning the force of Officer Connolly's testimony about a unique or singular event? As Shafer and Srivastava have noted, S in epistemic situations is certainly not specified in advance; nor would I find it easy to specify what elements of my own S are indeed relevant to any of my judgments about these likelihoods (1990, 493).

So it appears that I have constructed an argument bearing on the relevance and credibility of Officer Connolly's testimony that does strongly outrun the evidence I have. If I wished to use this argument as a basis for a detailed or decomposed Bayesian assessment of the inferential force of his testimony, I would face trouble in defending any numerical judgments I made for reasoning stages backed by no ancillary evidence. If I were actually compelled to assess the force of Connolly's testimony, I would also be compelled to consider a simpler argument. I might still employ a Bayesian design to an argument not decomposed in such fine detail. But Shafer offers us another alternative that can be called a *belief function* design. The vocabulary in such a design consists of the same Pascalian probabilities used in a Bayesian design. The difference is that these probabilities can be distributed in a way not sanctioned by the Kolmogorov axioms. Shafer makes use of several different semantics to explain the meaning of numbers chosen from this vocabulary, one of which involves the credibility of witnesses such as person P in my example involving your neighbor and whether he is keeping a dog. At this point I note Shafer's agreement that metaphors drawn from legal experience and scholarship can play a significant role in the study of probabilistic judgment, since they force us to consider the means by which such judgments can be constructed (1986a, 799–801). But the calculus Shafer employs for combining our judgments of evidential support involves, not Bayes's rule, but another called *Dempster's rule*. Our next topic shows how evidential support can be combined to form partial beliefs about collections of hypotheses and how Dempster's rule is appropriate for combining evidential support across different items or bodies of evidence.

5.4.4 Belief Functions and Evidential Support

Numerical assignments of s, such as those in Figure 5.3, indicate the amount of evidential support committed *exactly and only* to various subsets of hypotheses in the power set associated with some frame of discernment. But we have to consider the *total* amount of evidential support committed to any subset of hypotheses. This total amount of evidential support committed to any subset of hypotheses is called a *belief* (Bel). A *belief function* Bel{A}, for any subset A of hypotheses, indicates the total of the evidential support committed to A and to any other subset of hypotheses that is a subset of A. For example, suppose we have the evidential support assignment shown in Figure 5.4, and let A = $\{H_1, H_2\}$. In this case A has three proper subsets: itself, $\{H_1\}$, and $\{H_2\}$. So the total amount of evidential support given to A in this case is $s\{H_1, H_2\} + s\{H_1\} + \{H_2\} = \text{Bel}\{H_1, H_2\} = 0.1 + 0.5 + 0.2 = 0.8$, as indicated in this figure. Since all singletons such as $\{H_1\}$ have only one proper subset, namely themselves, it is clear that $s\{A\} = \text{Bel}\{A\}$ when A is a singleton. Since frame F has, as its proper subsets, itself and all other possible subsets, it is equally clear that $\text{Bel}\{F\} = 1.0$. The vacuous set $\varnothing$ has only itself as a subset and is always given $s\{\varnothing\} = 0$, so $\text{Bel}\{\varnothing\} = 0$.

The basic idea behind Shafer's definition of Bel{A} is that the support committed to any subset A is also committed to any other subset that entails A. For example, since $\{H_1\}$ is a subset of $\{H_1, H_2\}$, we can say that $\{H_1\}$ entails $\{H_1, H_2\}$, and whatever support is committed to $\{H_1\}$ is also committed to $\{H_1, H_2\}$. By such means Bel{A} indicates the total amount of support committed to the hypotheses in A. For some item or body of evidence, whose

Frame F = $\{H_1, H_2, H_3\}$

Power Set of Hypotheses in F							
$\{H_1\}$	$\{H_2\}$	$\{H_3\}$	$\{H_1,H_2\}$	$\{H_1,H_3\}$	$\{H_2,H_3\}$	$\{H_1,H_2,H_3\}$	$\varnothing$
s{ }: 0.5	0.2	0	0.1	0	0.1	0.1	0
Bel{ }: 0.5	0.2	0	0.8	0.5	0.3	1.0	0
Dou{ }: 0.3	0.5	0.8	0	0.2	0.5	0	1.0
Pl{ }: 0.7	0.5	0.2	1.0	0.8	0.5	1.0	0

FIGURE 5.4 Determining belief, doubt, and plausibility from an evidential support assignment.

support we are assigning to hypotheses in frame F, Bel{A} indicates the support given directly to A plus the support given to any other subset of hypotheses that entails A. We might also say that Bel{A} indicates our total belief that the evidence, whose support we are assessing, means that one of the hypotheses in A is true. Belief functions have a variety of interesting properties, the first of which illustrates their possible nonadditivity in the Pascalian sense. In Figure 5.4, if we let $A = \{H_1\}$ and $A^c = \{H_2, H_3\}$, Bel{A} + Bel{A^c} = 0.8 and not 1.0 as would be required in a Pascalian construal. Our probabilistic beliefs, construed in Shafer's terms, are possibly nonadditive for the reason that we are entitled to leave some of the evidential support uncommitted in various ways. Shafer argues that this gives us a more adequate account of the process of forming partial beliefs in probabilistic reasoning. If an inference is construed in Bayesian terms, we have no mechanism for witholding belief when we are not sure about the meaning of our evidence.

The term Bel{A^c} has an important role in Shafer's system for indicating partial beliefs. Consider some subset A of hypotheses in frame F. Suppose we wish to express our *doubt* that the evidence we have means one of the hypotheses in A. In Shafer's terms our doubt about A, Dou{A}, equals Bel{A^c}. In words, our doubt that the evidence means one of the hypotheses in A is equivalent to our belief that this evidence means hypotheses that are incompatible with A. As an example, suppose $A = \{H_1\}$; the subset of hypotheses incompatible with A are those to be found in $A^c = \{H_2, H_3\}$. So our doubt about $\{H_1\}$ is equivalent to our belief in $\{H_2, H_3\}$. In the example shown in Figure 5.4, Dou{H_1} = Bel{H_2, H_3} = 0.3.

The term Bel{A^c} = Dou{A} has additional significance. Since Dou{A}, like any other belief measure, is a number between zero and one, we might think of the measure $[1 - \text{Dou}\{A\}]$ as the degree to which we *fail to doubt* hypotheses in A. Shafer has given two names to the measure $[1 - \text{Dou}\{A\}] = [1 - \text{Bel}\{A^c\}]$; it is called either an *upper probability* or a *plausibility*. In Figure 5.4, for example, the plausibility of $\{H_1\}$, Pl{H_1}, is equal to $1 - \text{Dou}\{H_1\} = 0.7$. The meaning of an upper probability or plausibility can best be illustrated by an example. Consider hypothesis H_1 in Figure 5.4, and note the subsets of frame F in which this hypothesis appears; they are $\{H_1\}$, $\{H_1, H_2\}$, $\{H_1, H_3\}$, and $\{H_1, H_2, H_3\}$. Observe that the singleton $\{H_1\}$ is a subset of each of the other three subsets, each of which may have uncommitted support assigned to them. But new evidence might allow us to move this previously uncommitted support specifically to $\{H_1\}$. In this event there would now be support for $\{H_1\}$ equal to the sum of the support given to $\{H_1\}$ plus any previously uncommitted support assigned to other subsets in which H_1 appears. In this limiting case the total support now given to $\{H_1\}$ would be the sum of the support given $\{H_1\}$ plus the support given any other subsets of which $\{H_1\}$ is a subset. This total is the upper probability or the plausibility of $\{H_1\}$. In the example Pl{H_1} = $s\{H_1\}$ + $s\{H_1, H_2\}$ + $s\{H_1, H_2, H_3\}$ = 0.5 + 0.1 + 0.1 = 0.7. Notice that this is exactly the value of $[1 - \text{Dou}\{H_1\}]$.

Figure 5.4 shows one other property of belief functions that is important in comparing Shafer's and Bayes's approach to capturing partial beliefs. As we have observed, for any subset A of F, Bel{A} indicates the total amount of evidential support actually committed to A and Pl{A} indicates the total amount of support that is or might be committed to A. We might interpret the belief interval [Bel{A}, Pl{A}] as a measure of the extent to which we are uncertain about the meaning of the evidence as far as A is concerned. In the example shown in Figure 5.4, this interval is [0.5, 0.7] for {H$_1$}. I noted that Pl{A} is also called an *upper probability*. For various reasons Shafer cautions us against calling Bel{A} a *lower probability* if the intention is to suggest that this number represents a lower bound on a "true" probability (1990, 475–476). In applications of Pascalian rules to probabilistic inference, intervals of probabilities are sometimes reported rather than exact values. This is often required in epistemic situations in which an exact probability judgment might not be taken seriously. Being uncertain about the meaning of evidence and being imprecise in a probability judgment are not the same things.

Figure 5.5 shows the evidential support assignment given as case 5 in Figure 5.3. Also shown are Bel{A}, Dou{A}, and Pl{A}, for each subset A of frame F = {H$_1$, H$_2$, H$_3$}, based upon this support assignment. First, observe that all evidential support has been committed to the three singletons; no support has in any way been left uncommitted. Shafer refers to the Bel{A} determined in such instances as *Bayesian belief functions*. Belief is certainly additive in every possible case. For example, when A = {H$_1$} and A^c = {H$_2$, H$_3$}, Bel{A} = 0.6 and Bel {Ac} = 0.4. Another interesting fact is that Bel{A} = Pl{A} for every subset A; in other words, our belief interval is zero in every possible case. On Shafer's interpretation, this must indicate that we have no uncertainty in our minds about the meaning of the evidence for which this support assignment was made. This is consistent with the fact that in this case we have not left any evidential support uncommitted; 0.6 was committed exactly and only to {H$_1$}, 0.3 was committed exactly and only to {H$_2$}, and 0.1 was committed exactly and only to {H$_3$}.

In the language of belief functions we finally have a defensible way to represent the concept of *ignorance*. Consider again case 4 in Figure 5.3. In

Frame F = {H$_1$, H$_2$, H$_3$}

Power Set of Hypotheses in F

	{H$_1$}	{H$_2$}	{H$_3$}	{H$_1$,H$_2$}	{H$_1$,H$_3$}	{H$_2$,H$_3$}	{H$_1$,H$_2$,H$_3$}	Ø
s( ):	0.6	0.3	0.1	0	0	0	0	0
Bel( ):	0.6	0.3	0.1	0.9	0.7	0.4	1.0	0
Dou( ):	0.4	0.7	0.9	0.1	0.3	0.6	0	1.0
Pl( ):	0.6	0.3	0.1	0.9	0.7	0.4	1.0	0

FIGURE 5.5 A special case of evidential support assignment and its consequences.

this case $Bel\{H_1, H_2, H_3\} = 1.0$, and Bel for any of the other subsets of hypotheses is zero. Here we are completely noncomittal in assigning evidential support. To be in a state of ignorance can mean that we lack any basis for belief. This is precisely what $Bel\{H_1, H_2, H_3\} = 1.0$ indicates. The belief function approach makes a very useful distinction between *disbelief* and *lack of belief*: $Bel\{A\} = 0$ simply means that the evidence offers no support for A; it does not mean that we disbelieve A. In Section 5.5 we will examine a view in which a similar distinction is made between *lack of proof* and *disproof*.

Finally, Shafer contends that a Bayesian representation of partial beliefs is but a special case of his approach using belief functions. It might be noted, however, that what Shafer terms a Bayesian belief function (as in the example in Figure 5.5) must always begin with support assignments that normalize across mutually exclusive and exhaustive singleton hypotheses. If these support assignments are construed in terms of prior or posterior probabilities, they cannot refer to Bayesian gradations of the weight of evidence. Neither posterior nor prior probabilities alone say anything about the weight of evidence. In Shafer's system there is a relationship between evidential support and evidential weight. In the Bayesian approach, likelihoods and their ratios are used to grade the weight of evidence. Posterior and prior probabilities must normalize in the Bayesian system; there is no such requirement for likelihoods. Consequently we cannot interpret Shafer's evidential support assignments in terms of likelihoods. I note that likelihoods could be normalized to make them conform to Shafer's requirements for evidential support assignment s. However, no self-respecting Bayesian would do so, since normalization would then destroy information about event rareness that is preserved in likelihoods. In Section 7.1.3 I will show just how important is such information in Bayesian assessment of the inferential force of evidence.

5.4.5 Dempster's Rule for Combining Partial Beliefs

Our entitlement to non-Pascalian evidential support assignments in Shafer's system means that we should not expect Bayes's rule to be appropriate for combining partial beliefs graded in terms of belief functions. As we have seen, there is no requirement that $Bel\{A\}$ and $Bel\{A^c\}$ sum to one. But there is a rule appropriate to the combination of partial beliefs indicated by $Bel\{A\}$; it is called *Dempster's rule*, named after the American statistician A. P. Dempster who first saw its essentials and its roots in earlier work (1967, 1968). The roots of this rule in the work of early probabilists I will illustrate by means of two cases involving our running example of an inference about whether or not your neighbor is keeping a dog. One matter of interest to early probabilists concerns what they termed *concurrent* testimony; the testimony of multiple witnesses who report the same event. In Section 3.5.2 I used the term *corroborative* with reference to such testimony. Intuition suggests that our belief in the occurrence of some event should increase as we obtain additional testimony about this event from credible witnesses. As long as our inference from concurrent or corroborative testimony concerns just the event reported in this testimony, we do not encounter the redundancy problems I mentioned in Section 3.5.3.

Your present inference involves possibilities H and H^c, whether or not your neighbor is keeping a dog in his apartment. Suppose you have testimony H^* from person P that H is true. Using the argument illustrated in Figure 5.2, you assigned $s\{H\} = 0.9$ and $s\{H, H^c\} = 0.1$; this leads to $\text{Bel}\{H\} = 0.9$, based on P's testimony and your belief about his credibility. But now another person Q tells you the same thing (H^*), corroborating what P told you. Two judgments are now necessary; one concerns P's credibility and the other concerns the independence of testimony from the two witnesses. Suppose you believe that Q also has a 90% chance of being credible. By the same argument illustrated in Figure 5.2 you assign $s\{H\} = 0.9$ and $s\{H, H^c\} = 0.1$ to Q's testimony. The support assignments for persons P and Q are shown in Figure 5.6a.

We now consider how we should combine your belief about H based on P's testimony ($\text{Bel}_P\{H\}$) with your belief about H based on Q's testimony ($\text{Bel}_Q\{H\}$). The first stage of this process requires a judgment regarding the *independence* of your witnesses P and Q. In assessing P's credibility, you might have supposed that P was a person selected at random from a population 90% of whose members could be deemed credible. This gives you some basis for saying that the chances are 90% that P is credible. You might then suppose that Q has also been selected at random from this same population. Thus you say the chances are 90% that Q is credible. The independence at issue here concerns the selection of these witnesses. If you suppose that the selection of P in no way influenced the probability of selecting Q, you can regard the selection of these witnesses as being independent in the ordinary Pascalian sense of this term. From a sampling point of view, such an assumption would be justified if the size of your hypothetical population were very large. You would not of course even be willing to entertain an independence assumption if you had evidence that P and Q collaborated in any way or that one coerced the other into giving testimony H^*. Recalling the product rule for independent events in ordinary probability, the assumption of independence entitles you to believe that the chances of *both* P and Q being credible are $(0.9)(0.9) = 81\%$.

Recall that if P is credible, his testimony H^* entails H; the chances are 90% that this is so. Thus we have said that P's evidence supports {H} to degree 0.9. The same applies to the testimony from Q. But in each case we have left 0.1 support uncommited among H and H^c. Subsets of hypotheses in some frame of discernment that are assigned nonzero support are called *focal elements*. For each of our two support assignments shown in Figure 5.6a the focal elements are {H} and {H, H^c} for each witness. Our judgment about the independence of P and Q, if appropriate, entitles us to apply the product rule when determining the support assigned to *intersections* of these focal elements. The possible intersections of focal elements for each support assignment are shown in Figure 5.6*a* together with their probabilities under the independence assumption. For example, the intersection of focal elements {H} and {H, H^c} is {H} with probability $s\{H\} \times s\{H, H^c\} = (0.9)(0.1) = 0.09$. Notice that three of the intersections of focal elements result in {H}. Thus the combined support given to {H} is $0.09 + 0.81 + 0.09 = 0.99$; the combined support given to {H, H^c} is 0.01. These combined support assignments are called *orthogonal sums* and are indicated by $s_P \oplus s_Q$ in Figure 5.6*a*.

From these orthogonal sums we can determine the total amount of support committed to hypothesis subsets in terms of the combined belief function

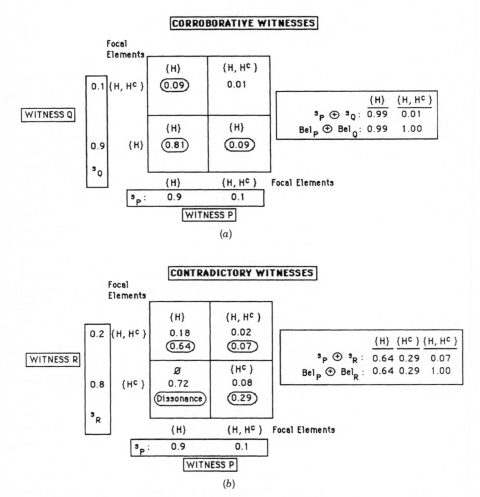

(a)

(b)

FIGURE 5.6 Examples of the use of Dempster's rule. (a) For corroborative evidence. (b) For contradictory evidence.

$Bel_P \oplus Bel_Q$. For $\{H\}$, $Bel_P\{H\} \oplus Bel_Q\{H\} = 0.99$ and $Bel_P\{H, H^c\} \oplus Bel_Q\{H, H^c\} = 0.01$. Dempster's rule is a device for determining orthogonal sums of evidential support assignments and combinations of partial beliefs based upon these sums. The word *orthogonal* comes from the independence assumptions involved in calculating support given to intersections of focal elements. In the present example involving concurrent (corroborative) evidence, our result $Bel_P\{H\} \oplus Bel_Q\{H\} = 0.99$ agrees with a conclusion reached in 1699 by George Hooper. Hooper argued that if n witnesses concurrently testify H*, each of whom has credibility p, the credibility of their joint testimony should be $1 - (1 - p)^n$. In the present case we have two witnesses, each of whom we believe has credibility $p = 0.9$. This gives a credibility of 0.99 to their joint report in agreement with Dempster's rule (Shafer 1986b, 156–157). Thus we see that corroborative testimony about the same event acts to increase our belief that this event did occur.

But we need another case, shown in Figure 5.6b, in order to provide a more complete account of the manner in which Dempster's rule combines partial beliefs. Suppose you continue to believe that the chances are 90% that P is credible in his report H*. But now comes person R who testifies H^{c*}, that your neighbor is not keeping a dog. Suppose you believe that the chances are 80% that R is credible and that the selection of witnesses P and R satisfy the independence assumption mentioned above. How does Dempster's rule cope with this evidential *contradiction*? Recall that our assignment of $s_P\{H\} = 0.9$ is interpreted to mean that there is a 90% chance that P's testimony means that H is true. If P is not credible, with a chance of 10%, this tells us nothing, so we assign $s_P\{H, H^c\} = 0.1$ to indicate our inability to commit this support to either hypothesis. Now here comes R, whom we believe to have a 80% chance of being credible, who tells us that H is not true. If R is credible, his testimony H^{c*} entails or means H^c. If R is not credible, with a chance of 20%, we leave support $s_R\{H, H^c\} = 0.2$ uncommitted. Now we have trouble when we attempt to assign evidential support to the intersection of our focal elements for each witness under the assumption of independence. The intersection of $\{H\}$ and $\{H^c\}$ is empty but, as Figure 5.6b shows, we have assigned support of 0.72 to the vacuous set $\emptyset$ in violation of the rules for such assignment.

The two support assignments $s_P\{H\} = 0.9$ and $s_R\{H^c\} = 0.8$ have given rise to a belief incompatibility when we attempt to combine them. The first assignment says that there is a 90% chance that P's evidence means H; the second says that there is a 80% chance that R's evidence means H^c. What we have in this case is what a psychologist might term *cognitive dissonance*. Even if our independence assumption is valid, we cannot say that there is an 72% chance that H and H^c are both true. Using Dempster's rule, we are first entitled to discard whatever support gets assigned to empty intersections of focal elements, those indicating cognitive dissonance. In the present case this leaves us with 0.18 assigned to $\{H\}$, 0.08 assigned to $\{H^c\}$, and 0.02 assigned to $\{H, H^c\}$.

Another problem now arises, since these combined support assignments do not sum to 1.0 as they must according to the rules for support assignment across a power set. The remedy provided by Dempster's rule is to *renormalize* the combined support assignments for nonempty focal element intersections. This is accomplished by dividing each individual assignment by the quantity $1 - K$, where K is the sum of support assignments given to empty intersections of focal elements. The value $1 - K$ is the sum of support given to nonempty intersections. In our present example we have one empty intersection to which 0.72 support has been assigned, so the quantity $1 - K = 1 - 0.72 = 0.28$. Consequently the combined support for {H} = 0.18/0.28 = 0.64, for {H^c} it is 0.08/0.28 = 0.29, and the combined support for {H, H^c} = 0.02/0.28 = 0.07. These renormalized support assignments are circled in Figure 5.6b. As Shafer explains, this result for contradictory evidence correponds to one given in 1764 by the mathematician J. H. Lambert (1986b, 162). Notice in Figure 5.6b that our resulting belief in either {H} or {H^c} is less than it would be if we had uncontradicted testimony on either hypothesis from a single witness. In short, a contradiction weakens the strength of our belief about either side of a contradiction. Notice also that our belief based upon the less credible witness is weakened more than is our belief based upon the more credible witness.

Dempster's rule for combining partial beliefs based upon two independent items or bodies of evidence E_1^* and E_2^* can be expressed more generally. Suppose we wish to determine the combined support provided by E_1^* and E_2^* for subset C of hypotheses in some frame of discernment. Let A_j be a focal element in the support assignment s_1 provided by E_1^*, and let B_k be a focal element in the support assignment s_2 provided by E_2^*. The combined evidential support for subset C is given by

$$s\{C\} = \frac{\displaystyle\sum_{A_j \cap B_k = C} s_1(A_j)s_2(B_k)}{1 - \displaystyle\sum_{A_j \cap B_k = \emptyset} s_1(A_j)s_2(B_k)}$$

The numerator is the orthogonal sum of support assignments for those focal element intersections equaling subset C. The denominator is a renormalization factor. If there are no empty focal element intersections, the denominator simply equals one. The equation above shows the combined evidential support committed exactly and only to subset C. To determine Bel{C}, we simply add to s{C} the combined support, similarly determined, from all other subsets that are subsets of C.

There was some early dissatisfaction about the manner in which Dempster's rule removes any "cognitive dissonance," but this unrest seems to have dissipated. In Chapter 8 we will consider how a Bayesian account of contradictory evidence produces the same general conclusions that arise through the use of Dempster's rule. The Shafer-Dempster system for expressing and combining partial beliefs has been found useful in many areas of application. Judea Pearl has recently provided a useful account of the distinction between the Bayesian and Shafer-Dempster appproaches to expressing and combining partial beliefs (1988, 571). He notes that in the Bayesian approach a proposition is believable when it is *provably probable*. I have now given many examples of arguments that might be used to justify the calculation of posterior probabilities for hypotheses of interest. But Pearl notes that in the Shafer-Dempster approach a proposition is believable when it is *probably provable*. In my illustrations involving your neighbor's putative dog, we employed probabilistic statements regarding the meaning of the evidence in your attempts to draw a conclusion. We now consider a quite different view of inductive reasoning that also concerns probability and provability.

5.5 THE WEIGHT OF EVIDENCE IN ELIMINATIVE AND VARIATIVE INFERENCE

The belief functions just examined rest on Pascalian probabilities that may be employed in non-Pascalian ways. The view of probability we now examine is definitely not Pascalian in any way. The basic reason is that it does not rest upon any *enumerative* processes of the sort giving rise to the Pascalian calculus of probability. We are now concerned about instances in which we attempt to grade the extent to which some hypothesis survives our best attempts to *eliminate* it on the basis of a *variety* of different evidential tests. I mentioned in Section 2.2.3 that we need a different metric for grading the force of evidence in probabilistic inferences that are eliminative and variative rather than enumerative in nature. In a series of works Jonathan Cohen has provided a system of probabilities he terms *Baconian* to acknowledge their linkage to Bacon's seminal views about the elimination of hypotheses on the basis of experimental tests (e.g., Cohen, L. J., 1977, 1989a). This Baconian system of probabilities rests upon Cohen's earlier work regarding the manner in which hypotheses receive support from suitably performed eliminative experimental tests (Cohen, L. J., 1970). As we will see, Baconian probabilities have only *ordinal* properties; they can be compared one with the other, but they cannot be algebraically combined in any way. Though this may appear to be a disability, it is not, as I will explain as we proceed. Indeed Baconian probabilities force us to consider a variety of very important inferential issues that are either overlooked or slighted in other views of probabilistic inference.

The title of Cohen's major work on Baconian probability is *The Probable and the Provable* (1977). In this work he specifically interprets probability to be a means for grading the *provability* of hypotheses or generalizations we assert about matters of interest (1977, 13–32) . Cohen's view of probabilistic reasoning is pluralistic in nature; different inferential situations require different interpretations of probability (e.g., 1977, 5–32; 1989a, 81–115). In some situations one or more of the various interpretations of a Pascalian probability may be quite appropriate. Alternative interpretations of Pascalian probability arise, Cohen says, because this system provides a syntax but no semantics (1970, 15). In other situations grading the provability of some hypothesis may require probabilities having quite different properties. In particular, Cohen addresses situations in which the probability or provability of some hypothesis can increase only to the extent that we are able to eliminate possible reasons for its invalidity. As I will discuss in some detail in Chapters 7 and 8, a Bayesian view of the force of evidence is very rich in its implications. However, in the same way that rich food can sometimes cause indigestion, a rich system of probability can also cause "intellectual indigestion." Cohen tells us that such indigestion takes the form of various anomalies and paradoxes when Pascalian views are applied in many probabilistic inferences such as those encountered in courts of law and in other contexts (1977, 49–120).

An interpretation of the weight of evidence emerges from Baconian probability that is quite different from any we have considered. Going to the supermarket to purchase some apples, you are not at all surprised to see apples sold by weight, volume, or number; so it is with the force, strength or weight of evidence. We have already observed two different schemes for grading the force of evidence; Cohen offers a third. As we will observe, the weight of evidence in Baconian terms is related in an interesting way both to the number of evidential tests a hypothesis survives and to the number of tests that might have been performed but were not.

A very simple illustration of what is involved in eliminative induction is shown in Figure 5.7. Suppose I assert the hypothesis: "If a thing is an A, then it is also a B." I might have based this hypothesis on several observations of the joint occurrence of A and B (represented by the dots in Figure 5.7). If I intend to convince you of the universality of H, it will not do for me simply to record further instances of the joint occurrence of A and B. In the spirit of Bacon's views on the value of negative instances, I must deliberately try to find some A's that are not also B's (in the shaded area in Figure 5.7).

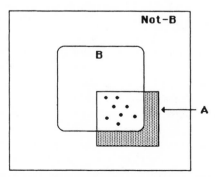

FIGURE 5.7 A simple example of variative and eliminative induction.

So I begin to think of circumstances in which I might observe an A that is not also a B. Thus a pharmacologist interested in showing that drug A is nontoxic to humans (B) must contrive relevant circumstances in which drug A might possibly be toxic. Relevant circumstances might include such matters as dosage level and spacing, interactions with other substances, the physical condition and age of the person taking the drug, and so on. Each circumstance canvased in which drug A remains nontoxic increases our confidence in the generality of the assertion that A is nontoxic to human beings. But we need to be very careful about what qualifies as a *relevant* circumstance or variable for the testing of hypotheses and about the manner in which such testing is performed.

5.5.1 Relevant Variables in Eliminative Induction

As discussed in Chapter 3, an important credential of evidence is its relevance. Efforts to grade the relevance of evidence typically fail; the best we could say in earlier discussion is that evidence is relevant if it has *some* force in changing our probabilistic beliefs about hypotheses of interest. We might grade the inferential force of evidence in various ways without being able to say that we are also grading its relevance. The concept of relevance arises of course in eliminative induction, but it does so in connection with the circumstances or variables employed in efforts to eliminate or falsify hypotheses. Basic to Cohen's view of eliminative induction is what he terms the *method of relevant variables*. This method involves various criteria for assessing the relevance of a variable, criteria for saying that some hypothesis has either passed or failed a test involving a relevant variable, and necessary strategies for the employment of relevant variables.

Cohen's original work on these matters concerned hypothesis testing in the experimental sciences (1970). He has shown how the method of relevant variables incorporates the eliminative methods associated with Mill (1977, 144–157). But the essential idea underlying the method of relevant variables applies in nonexperimental induction as well. In the following example I will introduce some basic features of the method of relevant variables (for a full treatment of this method, see Cohen, L. J., 1970, 1–105; 1977, 121–187; 1989a, 145–175). This example has been contrived to illustrate the basis for Cohen's claim that the degree of support provided hypotheses by evidence in eliminative and ampliative induction can only be graded in ordinal terms. Recall that an ampliative inference is one that goes beyond the content of its premises.

Suppose, as an electronics engineer, that you are required to test the performance of a particular system S in some area of application. From prior experience with similar systems you know that certain variables or factors in this area of application have an influence on whether S will perform as required. If S is entirely novel, we suppose you have some well-supported theoretical basis for determining what these performance-related variables might be. In either case you have some initial basis for saying that the test variables you have identified are relevant to the performance of S in this area of application. Each variable you have chosen has two or more *variants,* states, or levels. To simplify this example, suppose that each variable has just two variants, each of which has the following characteristic. It is known that systems like S often fail in the presence of at least one of the variants of each variable you have identified. For example, suppose that S must function not only at "normal" ambient temperatures but also at high temperatures. You might choose to include a "normal" temperature variant as an *experimental control.* System S will pass the temperature test if it performs under *both* normal ambient and at some high temperature. It will fail this test if it fails under either or both of these two variants. In general, a variable is relevant only if at least one of its variants can serve to eliminate or falsify one or more hypotheses being considered. The variables you choose in testing system S must be independently manipulable. All this means is that the variants you choose for one variable do not force a choice of variants of another variable.

Now suppose that you have identified some number n of independent variables that are similarly relevant as far as the performance of system S is concerned; four of them are listed in Figure 5.8. In addition to temperature you incorporate a normal level and a high level of humidity. The ability of S to withstand shock is also important; many systems are subjected to "drop tests"—to see if they will continue to function if they are dropped on the floor from certain heights. System S must also be able to function in the presence of various levels of electromagnetic interference (EMI). As Figure 5.8 illustrates, you thus have two variants of each variable you have included. In actual practice each of these variables could have any number of variants. For example, you might wish to test whether S also functions properly at low temperatures. In addition to listing these relevant test variables, suppose you have ordered them in terms of their importance. This ordering might involve a judgment on your part, but it might also be implied by an established or canonical procedure for testing systems such as S.

The method by which you implement these relevant variables in testing system S is all-important. It will not do simply to test S on each of them separately. We have to implement a testing sequence in which all combinations of variants are included as we perform additional tests. As Figure 5.8 illustrates, we first test S under each of the temperature variants. At this step we would normally hold other variables at their normal or ambient levels such as, for example, no shock or EMI. Then, incorporating the humidity variable, we test S under all four combinations of the temperature and humidity variants. As the figure shows, your testing sequence involves successively more complex tests as all possible combinations of new relevant variables are incorporated. The reason is that S might fail only under certain combinations of variants. For example, S might fail the high shock test only when temperature and humidity are both at high levels. This is illustrated by the outlined f (failure) in this figure at the third stage of testing. There is another language we can employ to illustrate the nature of your implementation of these relevant variables; this language comes from research on experimental design. Each one of the relevant variables can be termed a *main effect*. In the experiment illustrated in Figure 5.8, you did not test these main effects individually. What you did was to perform a successively more complex *factorial* experiment in which you included all possible combinations of the variants at any level of testing. Such a design is said to be *orthogonal*, and it allows for the examination of all possible *interactions* between the main effects you have included. Thus, for example, it might be said that high temperature and humidity interact with a high shock level to produce the failure you observed.

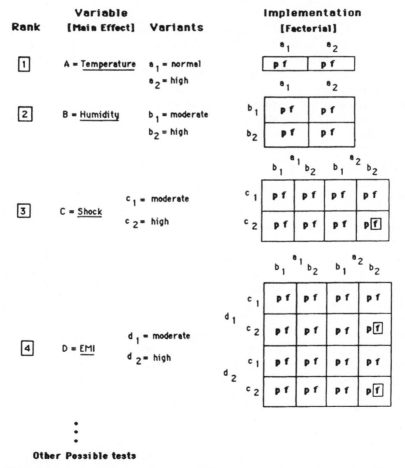

FIGURE 5.8 An illustration of Cohen's method of relevant variables in eliminative and variative induction.

If S fails a certain test at one level, we ordinarily suppose that it will fail this same test when another variable is incorporated. For example, if S fails the high shock test at high levels of temperature and humidity, we might also suppose that it will fail under these same conditions regardless of whether EMI is at some moderate or some high level. This is indicated by the two outlined failures (f) at the fourth level of testing. But we have to be a bit careful here, since it is possible (not necessarily in this example) that an unfavorable test result can be counteracted by some variant at a later stage of testing. This subsequently favorable result might also suggest the presence of a hidden (or confounding) variable that was operating at an earlier stage of testing. So the failure of S at one stage of testing does not always guarantee its subsequent failure at higher levels of testing.

Clearly we obtain more confidence in the capability of system S as it continues to pass successively higher levels of such a testing procedure. In general, we might say that we gain more confidence in some hypothesis as it continues to survive our best efforts to eliminate it by the variative testing illustrated in the present example. Stated in other words, hypothesis H gathers support as it continues to remain unfalsified by successively more varied and thorough tests. An important question concerns how we ought to grade the support provided by inductive procedures such as those you employed in testing system S. In symbols, let $s[H, E]$ indicate the *inductive support* provided hypothesis H, based upon test result E, where E might refer to the results obtained at any level of testing. Suppose that n tests have been performed and that H has passed the first i of them; we indicate this by saying that $s[H, E] = i/n$. This looks like a simple fraction that will always take on values $0 \leq s[H, E] \leq 1.0$. Thus it appears that we might be able to grade evidential support in terms of numbers that resemble ordinary probabilities in the same way Shafer has done. But Cohen says this will not do for the following reasons:

First, it is clear that not all experimental tests are on the same par. In the testing sequence illustrated in Figure 5.8, the tests become successively more complex as well as more thorough. What this means, for example, is that the difference between $4/n$ and $3/n$ is not necessarily the same as the difference between $2/n$ and $1/n$. By itself this rules out $s[H, E]$ having interval or cardinal scale properties (and also ratio properties). Second, there is no obvious way to grade the degree of relevance of the tests being employed any more than there is to grade the relevance of any evidence. In the example the best you can do is to stand your tests in rank order in terms of their perceived importance. Third, there would be considerable difficulty in the meaning of i/n *as a fraction* when it is used grade the support provided to different hypotheses tested under possibly different circumstances. Suppose, for example, that you have a competitor who has produced her version S' of this system; she also performs n tests of S'. Suppose that your version S passes the first three tests out of n you performed and that her version S' passes 4 tests out of the n she performed. These results would not be comparable in any cardinal way if she ordered her eliminative tests differently or employed different tests. Finally, one might propose giving H a grade of $+1$ if it passes a test and a grade of -1 if it fails. Unfortunately, this would indicate the same degree of support to an H that passes two tests and then fails one as it indicates to H' that just passed the first test. In the former case H was subjected to a more thorough test.

Finally, we need to consider the role of the number n of tests performed in eliminative induction. You would never have any assurance that the n tests you performed included all those that could possibly be performed. Suppose, that there is some number N of tests that are possible given the conditions under which system S will operate. Some of these tests might well be more important than the ones you have identified. This casts further suspicion on any possible ratio properties of $s[H, E] = i/n$. The whole point here, as Cohen emphasizes, is that in eliminative induction by the method of relevant variables the best we can do is to say that $s[H, E]$ provides only an *ordinal* measure for grading evidential support. We can only say that one hypothesis is better supported than another but not by how much or by what ratio. Cohen has provided an extensive syntax of properties for this ordinal inductive support grading $s[H, E]$, some of which we will discuss in connection with Baconian probabilities that are implied by his inductive support functions (1970, 216–237).

Not all eliminative induction is based upon a systematic manipulation of relevant variables such as those in the preceding example. We need to extend the idea of relevant variables to eliminative induction in situations that are not experimental in nature. Such extension involves the ideas of *generalizations* and *ancillary evidence* that we have considered repeatedly in connection with the structuring of argument. As an example, consider the top diagram in Figure 5.9. Witness W has testified E^*, that event E occurred. One stage in our inference about whether E did occur concerns whether W *believes* it did occur. In Section 3.2.3 we discussed how this stage concerns W's *veracity*. We would not say that W is truthful in reporting E^* if he did not believe what he tells us about event E. The issue here concerns the extent to which we are entitled to infer that W believes E occurred (E_b) from his testimony E^* that it did. Our inference takes the form: "If E^*, then E_b." To justify this inference, we might assert the veracity-related generalization: "If a person reports the occurrence of an event, then this person believes this event did occur." This generalization or presumption is of course rebuttable in the case of W or any other witness. If we were to infer E_b from E^* just on the basis of this generalization, we would be looked upon as being very credulous; witness W might well be an exception to this generalization. What we can do is to put this generalization to a *variety* of different relevant evidential tests, each one designed to invalidate this generalization as far as W and his present testimony are concerned. The answers we obtain constitute *ancillary evidence* regarding W's veracity and the strength or weakness of our inference of E_b from E^*.

Experience in legal and other affairs supplies us with a list of relevant questions that might be asked regarding how well the above generalization holds in the present case of W and his testimony E*. Six such questions are shown in the top diagram of Figure 5.9. These questions constitute relevant variables in a test of a veracity generalization (Figure 3.8 shows similarly relevant questions regarding other credibility attributes of witnesses). The more of these tests that W passes, the more we are entitled to infer that this veracity generalization holds in the present instance of W and his testimony E*. We might regard the successful passing of tests such as these as amounting to a shrinkage of the shaded area shown in the bottom diagram of Figure 5.9. Each test W passes regarding his veracity eliminates a reason we might have for believing that E* entitles us to infer E_b^c, that W does not believe what he has just told us about E. Each test you made of system S was designed to eliminate reasons why this system would not perform in relevant circumstances. Thus the veracity-related questions we ask about W qualify as relevant variables in our attempts to eliminate reasons why we might believe W is not being truthful.

But we cannot expect to manipulate relevant veracity-related variables in the same way that we manipulated the variables in the systematic testing of

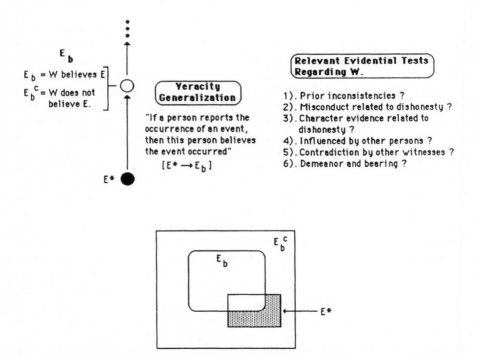

FIGURE 5.9   Eliminative and variative induction applied in a nonexperimental context.

system S. In the first place W has made a specific report about a unique or singular event that either happened or didn't happen; this is one reason why there are no veracity-related statistics. Second, there would almost certainly be argument about the relative importance of the six veracity questions as far as W is concerned. There might also be disagreement about whether W has actually passed or failed any of these veracity-related tests. Though the idea of performing an increasingly thorough factorial test disappears, the essential Baconian idea remains in the testing of generalizations such as the one we have examined. A generalization is supported to the extent that this generalization survives our best attempts to show that it is invalid in the particular instance of concern. Such support can only be graded in ordinal terms; this is even more obvious in the nonexperimental situation shown in Figure 5.9. Our next task is to examine how the grade of evidential support in eliminative induction can be translated into a probability.

5.5.2 Baconian Probability and the Weight of Evidence

To examine the connection between inductive support and Baconian probability in eliminative and variative inference, consider the witness veracity situation in Figure 5.9. Let the Baconian probability that witness W believes event E occurred (E_b), on evidence of his testimony E^*, be expressed as $B(E_b, E^*)$. This certainly resembles a Pascalian posterior probability of the form $P(E_b|E^*)$. However, a different expression for Baconian probabilities is necessary. One reason is that Baconian probabilities have the same ordinal properties as the inductive support functions examined above; they can be compared but cannot be combined algebraically. The Pascalian posterior probability $P(E_b|E^*)$ is *defined* in terms of the ratio of $P(E_bE^*)$ to $P(E^*)$. Since it makes no sense to take ratios or make other algebraic combinations of Baconian probabilities, we should not expect to see any Baconian expressions similar to Bayes's rule or Dempster's rule, both of which require algebraic combination of various ingredients. In addition the mechanism for probabilistic belief revision is quite different in Baconian terms, as we now examine.

To justify an inference of E_b from E^*, we asserted the veracity generalization: "If a person reports the occurrence of an event, then this person believes this event did occur." We may express this generalization symbolically as $E^* \rightarrow E_b$ ("E^* implies E_b"). Our testing of the veracity of W involves obtaining answers to questions, such as those in Figure 5.9, which might possibly invalidate this generalization or presumption in the *particular circumstances* involving witness W. As this generalization passes more tests, as far as W is concerned, we are increasingly confident in asserting that $E^* \rightarrow E_b$, and so we are entitled to say that the grade level of $B(E_b, E^*)$ also increases. Each reason we remove for doubting the veracity of witness W raises the ordinal grade level of $B(E_b, E^*)$ one "notch" higher. Suppose that the veracity generalization $E^* \rightarrow E_b$ has passed the first i tests of the n we intend to perform; in this case $s[E^* \rightarrow E_b] \geq i/n$. We say "greater than or equal to" here, since this generalization might pass further tests we have not yet made. Correspondingly we can also say that $B(E_b, E^*) \geq i/n$.

Cohen has provided an elaborate syntax of properties of Baconian probabilities (1977, 217–244). Here we discuss just a few of them. The ones we examine will allow us to note certain basic features of Baconian probability applied in eliminative and variative induction and what these features have to tell us about the weight of evidence. To begin, let H represent some hypothesis and E^* represent some evidence taken as a basis for inferring H. The Baconian probability $B(H, E^*) \geq i/n$ means that the generalization licensing an inference of H from evidence E^* has been supported through level i in a sequence of n evidential tests involving variables believed to be relevant to the testing of this generalization. It is most important that you do not interpret the symbol (i/n) as a ratio or a fraction. All it asserts is that the first i tests from among n have been favorable to the generalization that links E^* and H.

The first point of distinction between Baconian and Pascalian probabilities involves $B(H, E^*) = 0/n$. A Baconian probability of zero simply indicates *lack of proof* of H and not *disproof* of H, as would be the meaning of the Pascalian probability $P(H|E^*) = 0$. A Baconian probability $B(H, E^*) = N/N$ would indicate full evidential support, assuming that all N possible relevant evidential tests had been performed and that all were favorable to the generalization linking E^* and H. Thus Baconian probabilities exist on a scale ranging from *lack of proof to proof,* rather than on a scale ranging from disproof to proof. In discussing belief functions, we noted how, for some hypothesis subset A, it is possible to revise Bel(A) upward from zero. In other words, it is possible to go from having a lack of belief to having some belief. The same thing happens with Baconian probability; we can go from lack of proof to some proof. Thus, if $B(H, E^*) = 0/n$, this does not mean that H cannot be inferred from E^* on the basis of further evidential tests that we might make. Again, $B(H, E^*) = 0/n$ simply indicates lack of proof and not disproof.

In Pascalian probability we have single-place terms such as $P(H)$ and two-place terms such as $P(H|E^*)$. The first we might usually read as "the *prior probability* of H" (or the probability of H conditional only upon background information S); the second we would read as "the probability of H, given evidence E^*." There are single- and two-place Baconian support functions and probabilities, but their interpretation is quite different. This difference stems from the fact that the following three ordinary probabilistic expressions are not necessarily equivalent: (1) $P(H|E^*) = p$, (2) $P(E^* \rightarrow H) = p$, and (3) $E^* \rightarrow P(H) = p$ (Cohen, L. J., 1977, 30). Taking the first and the third of these expressions, saying "the probability of H, conditional upon evidence E^*, is p" is not necessarily equivalent to saying "given E^*, then the (uncon-

ditional) probability of H is *p*." This distinction becomes important in eliminative induction, so Cohen prefers to label single- and two-place Baconian
probabilities in a somewhat different manner. Single-place Baconian probabilities, such as B(H), are termed *monadic,* and two-place Baconian probabilities, such as B(H, E*), are said to be *dyadic.* As I will now explain, monadic
Baconian probabilities have a different meaning than monadic Pascalian probabilities.

Returning to your eliminative testing of system S, suppose that S passed
the first *i* tests among *n* that are possible. If H represents the hypothesis that
S will perform as required and E* is the report of the results of the tests you
have performed, then you can say that $s[H, E^*] \geq i/n$. This is the interpretation you might draw simply by examining your test results. But some of
your test results may have been erroneous. Perhaps, for example, there was
an error made either in setting the humidity level or in recording the result
for this test. Cohen's approach to eliminative induction accounts for the
necessity of *replicating* the results of testing. Suppose that you repeated your
tests over several times and obtained the same results on each occasion; you
conclude that the test result E* is true or genuine. In this case you are entitled
to make the statement: "If E* is true, then $s[H] \geq i/n$." In such instances
you are said to have *detached* your statement of evidential support for H from
any particular testing sequence. Your confidence in your test procedure now
allows you to talk about the support for H without having to qualify it for
any particular testing result. Thus, you have passed from a dyadic statement
involving $s[H, E^*]$ to a monadic statement $s[H]$ as a result of your confidence
regarding test evidence E*.

The same *detachment* can occur for Baconian probabilities. As an illustration, consider again our inference about whether or not W believes event E
occurred, based upon his testimony that E occurred. Recall that the dyadic
Baconian probability B(E_b, E*) indicates the degree to which the generalization $E^* \rightarrow E_b$ has resisted being falsified by the tests we have made relevant
to W's veracity. Of course we must be concerned about the credibility of this
veracity-related ancillary evidence about W. In Section 3.3 (specifically Figure
3.10) I discussed ancillary evidence and ancillary evidence about ancillary
evidence. Suppose that as far as W is concerned, the veracity generalization
$E^* \rightarrow E_b$ has passed the first *i* tests from among *n* we believe are possible;
in this case we say that $B(E_b, E^*) \geq i/n$. If we have confidence in the results
of the *i* tests that we have thus made of W's veracity, we can detach a belief
in E_b with strength indicated by the monadic Baconian probability $B(E_b) \geq$
i/n, that W does believe what he has testified. In Section 5.5.3 we will discuss
the importance of the concept of belief detachment in applications of Baconian
probabilities to chains of reasoning in cascaded or catenated inference.

Following are several properties of Baconian probabilities for eliminative
and variative induction. Cohen's support functions for experimental testing
have these same properties. Cohen discusses how these properties, as well

as the many others in his entire syntax, are generalizations on the Lewis-Barcan system S-4 of modal logic (1970, 207–237; 1977, 229–244).

1. *Ordinal Properties*. Grading the support evidence provides hypotheses in eliminative and variative inference can only be performed in comparative terms (i.e., they cannot be combined algebraically), as these two properties of monadic and dyadic Baconian probabilities show:

   i. For monadic probabilities: $B(H_1) \geq B(H_2)$ or $B(H_2) \geq B(H_1)$.
      For dyadic probabilities: $B(H_1, E_1^*) \geq B(H_2, E_2^*)$, or $B(H_2, E_2^*) \geq B(H_1, E_1^*)$.

   ii. For monadic probabilities: if $B(H_1) \geq B(H_2)$ and $B(H_2) \geq B(H_3)$, then $B(H_1) \geq B(H_3.)$.
      For dyadic probabilities: if $B(H_1, E_1^*) \geq B(H_2, E_2^*)$ and $B(H_2, E_2^*) \geq B(H_3, E_3^*)$, then $B(H_1, E_1^*) \geq B(H_3, E_3^*)$.

These two properties concern ordinal gradings (property i) that are also transitive in nature (property ii). The manner in which the dyadic properties are stated may, at first sight, seem irregular, since they suggest that we can make comparisons involving different hypotheses and different bodies of evidence. But this is exactly what Baconian probabilities allow us to do. Different hypotheses we entertain in some area of investigation may involve different eliminative evidential tests.

2. *Negation Property*. Pascalian probabilities for complementary events must normalize or sum to one whether they are conditional or unconditional. The negation property for Baconian probability is entirely different.

   iii. For monadic probabilities: if $B(H) > 0$, then $B(H^c) = 0$.
      For dyadic probabilities: if $B(H, E^*) > 0$ and if $B(E^{c*}) = 0$, then $B(H^c, E^*) = 0$.

In the monadic case, if we believe in the credibility or genuineness of evidence E^* and thus detach a belief favoring H, then we must also say that we have no present basis for a detached belief in H^c. We cannot detach simultaneous beliefs about incompatible hypotheses. However, there are instances in which it is entirely appropriate to have $B(H) = B(H^c) = 0$. Before any eliminative tests are performed, we may have no prior basis for assuming H to be more likely than H^c. The zero Baconian probability of these incompatible hypotheses simply says that, as yet, we lack any basis for a proof either way. The dyadic case asserts that if H has survived a certain number of eliminative tests reported in E^*, and if we have no basis for disbelieving these test results, then we also have no basis for a belief in H^c, on this evidence E^*. Thus, according to the method of relevant variables, in eliminative and variative induction evidence cannot support incompatible hypotheses, nor can the same evidence eliminate H and not-H at the same time. It is necessary to remember that a Baconian probability of zero for any hypothesis may be revised upward in light of further eliminative testing.

3. *Conjunction Rule.* In the Pascalian system, according to the general product rule (or chain rule), $P(AB) = P(A)P(B|A)$; if A and B are independent, then $P(AB) = P(A)P(B)$. In the general case this means that for $0 < P(A) < 1.0$ and for $0 < P(B|A) < 1.0$, $P(AB)$ must always be less than either $P(A)$ or $P(B|A)$. In the case of independence, for $0 < P(A) < 1.0$ and $0 < P(B) < 1.0$, $P(AB)$ must always be less than either $P(A)$ or $P(B)$. In The Baconian system the probability of a conjunction is never less than the smallest Baconian probability of either of its conjuncts.

    iv. For monadic probabilities: if $B(H_1) \geq B(H_2)$, then $B(H_1 \cap H_2) = B(H_2)$.
      For dyadic probabilities: if $B(H_1, E^*) \geq B(H_2, E^*)$, then $B(H_1 \cap H_2, E^*) = B(H_2, E^*)$.

Suppose two hypotheses H_1 and H_2 and a test result E^*. According to this test result, H_1 survived four tests and H_2 survived three tests. They have both survived no fewer than three tests. We may refer to Baconian conjunction as a minimization (Min) rule; as we will later observe, this same rule occurs in other views of inductive reasoning.

4. *Disjunction Rule.* The rule for disjunction in Pascalian probabilities asserts that $P(A \cup B) = P(A) + P(B) - P(AB)$. This means that $P(A \cup B) \leq P(A) + P(B)$, with equality when $P(AB) = 0$ (A and B are disjoint). In Baconian terms the disjunction rule is stated:

    v. For monadic probabilities: if $B(H_1) \geq B(H_2)$, then $B(H_1 \cup H_2) \geq B(H_1)$.
      For dyadic probabilities: if $B(H_1, E^*) \geq B(H_2, E^*)$, then $B(H_1 \cup H_2, E^*) \geq B(H_1, E^*)$.

If H_1 survives through five levels of eliminative testing and H_2 survives through four levels of the same testing, then at least one of them has survived through five levels. This rule can also be termed a maximization (Max) rule and, like the Min rule for conjunction, it is a feature of other formal systems for inductive reasoning.

5. *Contraposition.* I am a resident of Vienna, Virginia; this entails that I am also a resident of Fairfax County, Virginia, since Vienna is in Fairfax County. It is also true that, if I am not a resident of Fairfax County, Virginia, then this entails that I am not a resident of Vienna, Virginia. In symbols, $(A \rightarrow B) \rightarrow (B^c \rightarrow A^c)$. In Pascalian probability there is no corresponding requirement that $P(B|A) = P(A^c|B^c)$, but Baconian probabilities are contraposable.

    vi. For dyadic probabilities: $B(H, E^*) = B(E^{c*}, H^c)$.

The Baconian contrapositon property is frequently useful in situations in which we may wish to equate the probability of some H being true, on evidence E*, with the probability of the nonoccurrence of evidence E* if H is not true.

Baconian probabilities thus have non-Pascalian properties under the operations of negation, conjunction, and disjunction. The next question concerns how the *weight of evidence* is graded in Baconian terms. An answer to this question first requires us to examine the thoughts of J. M. Keynes on the *weight of arguments* (1921, 71–78). Keynes appears to have been the first to distinguish between the weight and the probability of an argument. Imagine inferences being performed, using Bayes's rule, in two distinct problem areas. In the first problem area we have a posterior probability of 0.99 for H_1 that is based upon just three items of evidence. In the second problem area we have a posterior probability of 0.99 for H_2 that is based upon 25 items of evidence. Though H_1 and H_2 have the same posterior probability, these probabilities are based upon different amounts of evidence. Keynes argued that grading the *weight* of an argument involves considering the *amount of evidence* upon which some conclusion is based. He records (1921, 71):

> As the relevant evidence at our disposal increases, the magnitude of the probability of the argument may increase or decrease, according as the new knowledge strengthens the unfavorable or the favorable evidence; but *something* seems to have increased in either case,—we have a more substantial basis upon which to rest our conclusion. I express this by saying that an accession of new evidence increases the weight of an argument. New evidence will sometimes decrease the probability of an argument, but it will always increase its "weight."

Thus the argument in the second problem area above has more weight than the one in the first problem area, even though the posterior probabilities are the same in either case. In short, the posterior probabilities in Bayes's rule tell us nothing about how much evidence was considered. Some have rebuked Keynes for his grading the *weight* of evidence in terms of the amount of evidence. I. J. Good notes (1983, 160): "The expression was used by J. M. Keynes (1921, 71) in a less satisfactory sense, to apply to the total bulk of evidence whether any part of it supports or undermines a hypothesis, almost as if he had the weight of the documents in mind." Cohen's assessment of Keynes's work is more charitable. Indeed the Baconian view of the weight of evidence is similar to but not identical to the one of Keynes (Cohen, L. J., 1985, 263–278). The Baconian probability B(H, E*) $\geq i/n$, for a body of evidence E*, indicates several things. First. it records the level i at which hypothesis H has resisted our attempts to invalidate it. In other words, level i indicates the *amount* of uncounteracted favorably relevant evidence that supports H. But it can reveal something else of equal importance.

Suppose, for the moment, that careful deliberation suggests that there are n recognized evidential tests of H that are eliminatively relevant. Our hypothesis H has passed the first i of these tests, so we record B(H, E*) $\geq i/n$. But the difference between i and n reveals how many relevant tests hypothesis H has *not yet passed*. In other words, there are questions yet to be answered as far as the provability of H is concerned. Thus a Baconian probability can give us some idea about the *completeness of coverage* of matters that we believed relevant to the provability of H. If we had confidence in our test results E*, we might detach the monadic probability $B(H) \geq i/n$. If this level seemed acceptable or sufficient, we might say that we have detached a belief that H is true. But, in doing so, we have also to suppose that the remaining $(n - i)$ tests we have not performed will be similarly favorable to H. We might say: "Other things equal (or favorable), H seems to be true." As Cohen tells us, the difference between i and n tells us something about the content of the *ceteris paribus* assumption involved in such belief detachment (1977, 212). If we had performed all n tests and every one was favorable to H, this ceteris paribus assumption would have no content. If we detached a belief in H just on the basis of a generalization underlying H, but no evidential tests of it, this ceteris paribus assumption would have maximum content. The content of such an assumption depends upon the number of relevant questions we leave *unanswered*. In other words, Baconian probabilities tell us something about the length and the strength of the inferential limb on which we find ourselves when we draw conclusions about hypotheses of interest.

5.5.3 Baconian Probability and Chains of Reasoning

Pascalian mechanisms for inference upon inference in a chain of reasoning involve algebraic combinations of probabilities that appear at every link in the chain. Baconian probabilities, being ordinal in nature, cannot be thus combined. In addition, if we apply eliminative and variative induction to the possible events at every stage of reasoning, we see that such induction involves substantively different tests tests at each stage. The reason is that the generalizations being tested at each stage are quite different. Thus, Baconian probabilities are incommensurable from one stage to another (Cohen, L. J., 1970, 268). These points about Baconian probabilities have led some to conclude, quite incorrectly, that there is no possible Baconian analysis of inference upon inference (Wagner, 1979, 1080). Following is a simple illustration of the essentials of a Baconian approach to inference upon inference; I have provided a more extensive analysis elsewhere (Schum 1991, 97–145).

Consider the credibility-related chain of reasoning in Figure 5.10. Suppose that person W has testified E*, that event E occurred. Also suppose we have very good evidence that W made an observation regarding event E and that his present testimony is based neither upon hearsay nor upon an inference from other events. Our task is to draw a conclusion about whether E did occur based upon W's testimony E*. We lay out the argument from E* to {E, Eᶜ} shown in Figure 5.10 in order to marshal our thoughts and our evidence about the three attributes of the credibility of human witnesses discussed in Chapter 3: veracity, objectivity, and observational sensitivity. Recall the var-

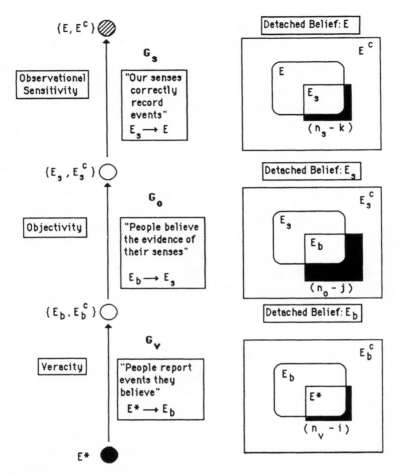

FIGURE 5.10   An example of Baconian credibility assessment.

ious categories of potential evidence, shown in Figure 3.8, that are relevant to the testing of each of these attributes.

The first stage of our inference involves whether W believes that event E occurred $\{E_b, E_b^c\}$, this involves W's *veracity*. Such an inference might be based upon a generalization G_v that reads: " If a person reports an event, then this person believes this event occurred" (elliptically, "people report events they believe"). In symbols this generalization reads: $E^* \rightarrow E_b$. Suppose that there is some number n_v of possible tests of this veracity generalization to see if it does in fact apply to W and his present testimony E^*. These questions are suggested by the general categories of veracity-relevant questions shown in Figure 3.8. Answers to questions such as these supply ancillary evidence about W's veracity. Suppose we have asked i of these questions and that the answers are all favorable to the generalization G_v as far as W is concerned. In Baconian terms, if we have confidence in these answers, we are entitled to *detach* a belief in E_b *at least* at grade level i/n_v. But notice that this detached belief in E_b involves the *ceteris paribus* assumption that the $(n_v - i)$ veracity questions we have not asked will also supply answers that are favorable to G_v as far as W is concerned. In short, our detached belief in E_b involves $(n_v - i)$ reasons for doubt that $E^* \rightarrow E_b$. I have indicated these reasons for doubt by the shaded area in the bottom diagram in Figure 5.10. These are all reasons involving the possibility that E^* might be consistent with E_b^c, that W does not believe event E occurred.

An interesting feature of Baconian probability is that it allows us to detach a belief, if we choose to do so, just on the basis of a generalization and no evidential tests of it. But Cohen's system also provides an assessment of the consequences of doing so. Suppose we give benefit of the doubt to the veracity generalization G_v as far as W is concerned. We perform no eliminative tests to see whether this generalization holds as far as W's testimony is concerned. In this case, giving a grade level of 1 to G_v, we would have a Baconian probability $B(H, E^*) \geq 1/(n_v + 1)$. But notice that our ceteris paribus assumption has maximum content, since there are $(n_v + 1) - 1 = n_v$ questions that remain unanswered about W's veracity. After i successful tests of G_v, when we give it benefit of the doubt, the Baconian grade level would be $B(H, E^*) \geq (i + 1)/(n_v + 1)$.

Suppose we detach a belief in E_b after i successful tests of G_v. This provides a basis for a further *objectivity-related* inference about whether W received sensory evidence of E, $\{E_s, E_s^c\}$. The objectivity-related generalization G_o tested at this stage, as far as W is concerned, might read: "As a result of an observation, if a person believes an event occurred, then this person obtained sensory evidence of this event" (elliptically, "people believe the evidence of their senses"). In symbols, G_o reads: $E_b \rightarrow E_s$. Suppose that W passes j of n_o possible eliminative tests of G_o. If we believe these test results, we can detach a belief in E_s at grade level j/n_o [or at level $(j + 1)/(n_o + 1)$, giving G_o benefit of the doubt]. In such detachment our ceteris paribus assumption has content equal to the $(n_o - j)$ objectivity-related questions we have not answered as far as W is concerned. Perhaps, as Figure 5.10 illustrates by the larger shaded area, we have more unanswered questions about W's objectivity than about his veracity.

Finally, our detached belief in E_s provides a basis for an inference about whether E did occur, $\{E, E^c\}$. This inference involves W's observational sensitivity. An observational sensitivity generalization G_s might read: "If a person's senses give evidence of an event, than this event did occur" (elliptically, "our senses correctly record events"). In symbols, $E_s \rightarrow E$. Suppose that W passes k of n_s eliminative tests of generalization G_s. We detach a belief in E at grade level k/n_s [or at level $(k + 1)/(n_s + 1)$, giving G_s benefit of the doubt]. In such detachment we leave $(n_s - k)$ observational sensitivity questions unanswered.

Thus Baconian analyses of chains of reasoning proceed a stage at a time and involve the detachment of beliefs regarding events at each link in the chain. My analysis in the example above was quite simplified; there are additional details that need to be considered at each stage as far as belief detachment is concerned. The example shows a fortunate instance in which witness W always passed tests. His failure of tests at any level might have forced us to make different belief detachments and to have decided, eventually, that E did not occur, as W reports. A long-standing expectation is that inferences should be weakened as we add links in chains of reasoning. There is a definite Baconian counterpart to this expectation. The number of unanswered questions accumulates as we reason from one stage to another. The detachment of belief at any stage of an inference actually involves consideration of the total number of recognized questions that have not been answered at this stage and at stages lower in the chain of reasoning. In the example we have left unanswered $(n_v - i)$ at the first stage, $[(n_v - i) + (n_o - j)]$ at the second, and $[(n_v - i) + (n_o - j) + (n_s - k)]$ at the third. Thus, for example, our final detachment of a belief that E did occur, based on W's testimony, has a ceteris paribus assumption with content equal to the $[(n_v - i) + (n_o - j) + (n_s - k)]$ questions that have been left unanswered. This content indicates how complete has been our coverage of matters relevant to W's credibility. The more questions we leave unanswered about W's credibility, the less confident we can be in believing what he tells us. In Section 7.1.1, I will return to the Baconian conception of the weakening of chains of reasoning as they are made longer.

5.5.4 Applications of Baconian Probability

Eliminative and variative induction, along lines suggested by the method of relevant variables, requires different methods for grading the weight of evidence than those suggested by the Pascalian calculus. There is no sense in which Jonathan Cohen advocates any displacement of Pascalian probability by Baconian probabilities in all of inductive reasoning. But Cohen does argue that Pascalian analyses, even when appropriate, are often quite incomplete (1989a, 109–114). In Chapter 7 I will present a Bayesian analysis of the inference shown in Figure 5.10. In the process I will show how Bayesian and Baconian analyses of this inference are quite complementary. The Baconian approach makes quite explicit the importance of the *completeness* of evidential coverage in any form of inductive reasoning.

In many areas of application people have a singular aversion to assessing subjective or personal Pascalian probabilities or other related quantities. This aversion has many roots. In some situations subjective assessments, however carefully made, are viewed with suspicion by persons who are to be influenced by these numerical judgments. In other instances recognition of the sheer number of required subjective probabilities in some inference problem leaves many people astonished. There are no judgments of subjective probabilities required in any Baconian analysis, but this does not mean that no subjective judgments are required. Identifying relevant variables, stating appropriate generalizations to be tested, deciding whether a generalization has passed or failed an eliminative test, and indeed assessing the number of tests possible in some episode of eliminative induction all call for judgments of various kinds. Many of these judgments are no less difficult than are the subjective judgments of probabilities having Pascalian properties.

Cohen's ideas about eliminative and variative induction, although originally cast within the context of experimental science, are readily applicable in fields such as law (Cohen, L. J., 1977; 1986, 635–649) and medicine (Cohen, L. J., 1980). In the field of law there has been quite vigorous debate about the degree to which Baconian rather than Pascalian probability accounts for the inferential activities of investigators, advocates, and fact finders (Schum 1979; Tillers and Green 1986, 1988; Tillers 1991). There are doubtless many other fields in which induction often proceeds by variative elimination. Cohen's ideas about the detachment of monadic from dyadic Baconian probabilities may bring to some minds the various default reasoning schemes of interest to persons working on the development of intelligent systems (Reiter 1980). Persons interested in the many difficult probabilistic elements of the inference tasks they perform cannot afford to be innocent of Cohen's work. I will have more to say about Baconian probabilities in later chapters.

5.6   EVIDENCE, INFERENCE, AND IMPRECISION

We have examined the concepts of relevance, credibility, and inferential force in connection with the uncertainty, or with the degree of certainty, we experience in drawing conclusions from evidence. Since 1965 Lotfi Zadeh and his many colleagues have been very successful in convincing everyone that human inference involves another pervasive characteristic: *imprecision*. Of equal importance are the methods they have provided for coping with imprecision or vagueness in a wide variety of situations. Uncertainty and imprecision are not the same, and we might expect any rules for managing imprecision to be different from those involving the management of uncertainty. In various ways we may be quite imprecise in telling others about the extent of our uncertainty. Earlier in Section 4.4.2 we noted Wigmore's imprecise ways for grading the inferential force of evidence. Imprecision abounds in all of probabilistic reasoning; one major source of it concerns vagueness in the language we employ in describing and classifying objects, people, and their characteristics.

Suppose you are asked to estimate the probability that the next person you see has had an appendectomy. People can be precisely classified on this basis, since any one of us either has had or has not had an appendectomy. Access to appropriately obtained medical actuarial records would supply a relative frequency that could form a basis for this probability estimate. Now suppose you are asked to estimate the probability that the next person you see is "old." The obvious problem here concerns what is meant by "old." The next person you see happens to be X, who has just celebrated his 46th birthday; does X belong in the set of "old" persons? What we have in the first of these two examples is the *crisply defined* set of persons who have had an appendectomy. In the second example the set of "old" individuals is not crisply defined; in Zadeh's terms, such a set is *fuzzy* in nature (1965). Fuzzy descriptions such as *old, short, probable,* and *possible* are in common use and of course have different meanings to different people. We may employ a variety of ordinary-language terms in connection with the characteristics of objects, people, and processes. In some cases we may employ additional modifiers that are themselves fuzzy in nature. For example, we might speak of *very old* persons, or persons who are *not very old*. Given the fuzziness of the description "old," we might expect that any assessment of the probability that the next person you see is "old" will also be fuzzy in nature. For example, you might only be able to say something such as "It is *likely* that the next person I see will be *old*."

We can of course use numbers as a basis for classifying things or people. First, consider the appendectomy example, and let A be the set of all persons who have had an appendectomy and A^c = the set of all persons who have not had an appendectomy. An expression called an *indicator function* (I) assigns the numbers zero or one depending upon whether or not some particular element is a member of a set. Thus, for person Y, $I_A(Y) = 1$ if Y has had an appendectomy, and $I_A(Y) = 0$ if Y has not had an appendectomy. The logic employed in such categorization is two valued. Now consider the fuzzy set involving the description *old*. We contemplate whether X, presently age 46, belongs to this fuzzy set. Clearly a two-valued indicator function will not suffice in this case, since the boundary between old and not-old is not precisely defined as in the case of A and A^c. What Zadeh suggests is that we assign a number between zero and one to X that grades the extent to which we believe X, age 46, belongs in the fuzzy set *old*. For this purpose we employ a *membership function* (μ) that takes values in the *entire interval* $[0, 1]$. Thus, for example, if we let B represent the fuzzy set *old*, $\mu_B(46)$ represents the degree to which we believe X, age 46, belongs in the fuzzy set *old*. You might be willing to say, for example, that $\mu_B(46) = 0.55$ to indicate that X is "0.55 old." The logic here is *multivalued,* since μ_B can take on an infinity of possible values. It includes, as a limiting case, the indicator functions for crisply defined sets. But, as we will see, there are several important differences between *fuzzy logic* and *multivalued logic*. Though μ is graded on the interval $[0, 1]$, it is not to be thought of as a probability. Its purpose is to show the grade of membership of some element in a fuzzy set.

Consider the following argument: "If a person is *overworked* and *underpaid,* then she is *probably not very happy* with her job." Every day we hear arguments expressed in such terms. This is an example of what Zadeh has called *fuzzy* or *approximate* reasoning, since it contains the fuzzy elements:

overworked, underpaid, probably, and *not very happy* (1979). The logic applied in such situations is itself fuzzy. Notice in the argument above that both the premises and the conclusion are stated in fuzzy or imprecise terms. The conclusions reached in fuzzy or approximate reasoning are not as definite as those reached using conventional logic. However, fuzzy logic may cover a wider range of actual human reasoning tasks. We have to acknowledge the fact that, on many occasions, any of the ingredients of the inductive arguments we have discussed so far may be fuzzy in nature.

5.6.1 Imprecision and the Ingredients of Inductive Reasoning

In Chapter 4 we discussed arguments constructed from masses of evidence, and we considered various network representations of these arguments. The principal ingredients of arguments are propositions (in the form of hypotheses) at various levels or stages of an argument, directly relevant evidence of various forms, generalizations linking evidence and hypotheses, and ancillary evidence that supports or weakens a generalization. In a network construal of an argument, nodes represent evidence and hypotheses (at various levels) and arcs indicate probabilistic linkages between nodes. Examples are easily identified in which any or all of these argument ingredients are fuzzy in nature.

Taking evidence, first, note in Figure 3.9 that Officer Connolly stated that *on several occasions* Sacco attempted to put his hand under his overcoat despite being warned not to do so. The argument shown in this figure was constructed to show the direct relevance of Connolly's fuzzy testimony. But indirectly relevant or ancillary evidence might be similarly fuzzy in nature. In judging person P's veracity, for example, we might find another person who asserts, "P *usually* tells the truth." Regarding P's observational sensitivity, we might encounter another person who asserts that P has *very good eyesight.* As an example of a fuzzy hypothesis suppose that in the earlier example involving your testing of system S, your hypothesis was that "system S will have *very high reliability.*" In a wide array of disciplines hypotheses are frequently stated in fuzzy terms. Generalizations we assert to license stages of reasoning offer some of the *very best* examples of the omnipresence of imprecision (see how difficult it is to avoid being fuzzy). As I have noted, generalizations form the "glue" that holds our arguments together; often this is fuzzy glue.

In discussing the fuzzy generalizations we so often make, let us begin with Aristotle's assertions that probability refers to what *usually* or *for the most part* happens (see Section 2.2.1). An important element of fuzzy logic is its *dispositional* nature. A disposition refers to statements or propositions that are *usually* but not necessarily always true. In his work on usuality and dispositional logic Zadeh shows us how usuality may be expressed as a fuzzy proportion or probability (1985, 761). Perhaps Aristotle might have agreed with Zadeh's relation between usuality and probability that is shown in Figure 5.11. The curve in this figure shows Zadeh's conjecture about the degree of

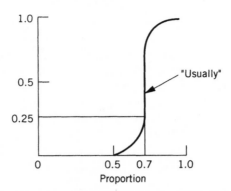

FIGURE 5.11   The fuzzy set "usually" and an example membership function.

membership (μ) various possible proportions have in the fuzzy set *usually*. No proportion less than 0.5 means usually; membership in the fuzzy set *usually* increases, as shown by the function, when proportions increase from 0.5 to 1.0. For example, a proportion of 0.7 might have membership grade $\mu = 0.25$ to indicate that a proportion of 0.7 is 0.25 *usually*. Another way of viewing a fuzzy set is to say that it is *elastic* in nature. The set of persons who have had an appendectomy is not at all elastic; to obtain membership in this set, you must have had an appendectomy. But, as Figure 5.11 shows, the fuzzy set *usually* is one that has been "stretched" in order to accommodate proportion values between 0.5 and 1.0.

Commonsense knowledge may be thought of as a collection of dispositions, things we take to be usually or commonly true. As noted in Section 3.1.6, a cornerstone of our Anglo-American system of settling disputes is the presumed ability of people who serve as jurors to apply their ordinary or commonsense reasoning in reaching a conclusion from evidence about some matter at issue. Legal scholars are quite aware of the importance of generalizations asserted in defense of the relevance of evidence (e.g., Binder and Bergman 1984; Twining and Miers 1982; Anderson and Twining 1991). Generalizations in legal contexts are always dispositional in nature or are asserted in fuzzy terms. I gave a number of examples of such generalizations in Sections 3.1.6 and 3.3.1 in my attempt to structure an argument bearing on the relevance and credibility of Officer Connolly's testimony in the Sacco and Vanzetti case. Notice that I offered several possible fuzzy qualifiers that a person might choose in stating any of these generalizations. Which qualifier a person might choose depends upon her experience. Any membership functions associated with fuzzy terms, such as the one in Figure 5.11, are naturally subjective in nature. Fuzzy logic applied to commonsense reasoning has been studied extensively (e.g., Zadeh 1984).

Finally, we all employ a variety of means for hedging conclusions we assert. Often these hedges are stated verbally and not numerically. We all hear about the prescribed forensic standards of proof in trials at law. In criminal cases the prosecution must prove its case to the standard *beyond reasonable doubt;* in civil cases the standard of proof imposed upon plaintiff is *preponderance of evidence* or *balance of probabilities.* In some civil cases an intermediate standard called *clear and convincing proof* may be imposed. All of these forensic standards of proof are of course fuzzy in nature. Many important evidential terms such as *relevance* are also stated in fuzzy terms. In Section 3.1.1 we noted that Federal Rule of Evidence FRE-401 states that evidence is relevant if it *"has any tendency* to make the existence of any fact that is of consequence to the determination of the action *more probable* or *less probable* than it would be without the evidence." Various attempts have been made in other contexts to identify probability intervals commonly associated with various fuzzy hedges such as very probable, probable, improbable, and very improbable. A notable example is the scale developed by Sherman Kent for use by intelligence analysts to give specific probabilistic referents to verbal hedges they provide in their analyses (Barclay et al. 1977). For example, *almost certainly* and *highly likely* are hedges said to be associated with probabilities above 0.85; *highly unlikely* is associated with probabilities below 0.15. Ward Edwards recently remarked that human ingenuity in finding verbal ways to equivocate will always outdistance any effort to translate these equivocations into numbers (1988, 275–276).

5.6.2 Fuzzy Sets and Fuzzy Logic

There are now thousands of published works on both the theory and application of fuzzy sets and fuzzy reasoning. A recent collection of Zadeh's seminal works is available (Yager et al. 1987), and there are treatises devoted to the essential underpinnings of work in this area (e.g., Dubois and Prade 1980; Klir and Folger 1988). The examples I have used so far indicate that fuzzy logic is multivalued in nature in contrast to the two-valued logic familiar to most of us. But it is clear that fuzzy logic, as proposed by Zadeh and his colleagues, is much more general than other multivalued logics that have been proposed; Klir and Folger provide a survey of alternative multivalued logics (1988, 27–32). Our current interest concerns alternative methods for grading the inferential force of evidence. Following are some elements of fuzzy logic that are important in suggesting how we might grade the fuzzy weight of possibly fuzzy evidence. These elements offer reasons why Zadeh's fuzzy logic offers much more than other multivalued logics.

The concept of a *linguistic variable* is important in fuzzy reasoning. Age is an example of such a variable; its possible values are verbally described states such as very old, old, not very old, young, and very young. We often employ combinations of linguistic variables as predicates. For example, you hear me describe my car as being *old* and *cheap.* So it is of interest to observe how one combines fuzzy predicates according to the operations of intersection, union, and negation. Suppose that the blue book value of a 1984 Ford is $500. Using my subjectively determined membership functions for *old* and *cheap* (as applied to cars), I might say that a 1984 Ford is 0.7 old and one with a value of \$500 is 0.8 cheap. Since old and cheap are both fuzzy sets, so is the intersection of these fuzzy sets. Let A be the fuzzy set of old cars, B be the fuzzy set of cheap cars, and C be the fuzzy set of old *and* cheap cars. In the theory of fuzzy sets, the membership function of a fuzzy intersection or conjunction is always equal to the minimum (Min) of the membership functions for the sets being conjoined. Thus in the example $\mu_C = \text{Min}[\mu_A, \mu_B] = \text{Min}[0.7, 0.8] = 0.7$; I can say that this car is 0.7 *old and cheap*. The rule for the disjunction D of fuzzy sets A and B is $\mu_D = \text{Max}[\mu_A, \mu_B]$, where Max means "the larger of." In the example $\mu_D = \text{Max}[\mu_A, \mu_B] = \text{Max}[0.7, 0.8] = 0.8$. I can say that this car is 0.8 *old or cheap*. The rules for conjunction and disjunction of fuzzy sets are the same as Cohen's rules for Baconian probability. But the rule involving the negation of fuzzy sets is the same as the Pascalian rule of negation. If I say a car is 0.7 *old*, then I must also say that this car is 0.3 *not old*. In general, for any fuzzy set A, $\mu_{A^c} = 1 - \mu_A$.

Fuzzy logic involves predicate modifiers such as *more or less* (recall FRE-401), *very*, and *extremely*. It also involves fuzzy quantifiers such as *most, many, few*, and *several*. For example, we hear: *Most* college students are *young*. Truth values asserted in fuzzy reasoning are also fuzzy in nature. Likewise we may hear, It seems *very true* that most college students are young. I have mentioned that probability assertions are often fuzzy in nature; we employ all sorts of linguistic devices in preference to the assertion of numerical probabilities. Subjective assessments of ordinary probabilities that display any precision are not taken seriously. No meteorologist would seriously assert that the probability of rain tomorrow is 0.875. In some cases interval estimates of probabilities are taken seriously. Zadeh shows us how we may even give interval estimates of membership functions when membership functions themselves are fuzzy sets. These he terms *ultrafuzzy sets*. For example, instead of providing the crisply defined membership function for *usually*, as shown in Figure 5.11, we might instead provide an interval for each membership value. Finally, the theory of fuzzy reasoning allows us to grade membership in fuzzy sets associated with *possibility*. We may wish to assess membership functions associated with such fuzzy terms as *very possible, quite possible, not very possible*, and *almost impossible*.

The essential rules for fuzzy or approximate reasoning have been summarized (e.g., Zadeh 1983, 1984, 1985, 1988; Klir and Folger 1988, 27–33). The Klir and Folger reference also includes a summary of the extraordinary range of applications of fuzzy logic in science and engineering, medicine, business, and other disciplines. Our current interest concerns what fuzzy reasoning has to tell us about the inferential force of evidence.

5.6.3 The Fuzzy Force of Fuzzy Evidence

In this chapter we have considered three different conceptions of the inferential force of evidence. In Pascalian terms we have log likelihood ratio as a gradation of the relative likeliness of evidence under various hypotheses. In Shafer's system of belief functions we have judgments about the degree of support or the weight of evidence for various subsets of hypotheses. In Cohen's system for eliminative and variative induction we have an ordinal gradation of the force of evidence in terms of its completeness of coverage of variables or questions relevant to the possible elimination of hypotheses being considered. But I have also mentioned Wigmore's fuzzy methods for grading the inferential force of evidence (Section 4.4.2). One trouble is that Wigmore gave no hint about which, if any, of these three possible gradations of the force of evidence he might have had in the back of his mind as he made his gradations in fuzzy terms. Did Wigmore think of evidential force in terms of relative likeliness, evidential support, or completeness of evidential coverage? There is no way to tell, and it may not be important anyway. What seems to be important is that we could, if it were necessary, grade the force of evidence in fuzzy terms with reference to any of these other conceptions of evidential force.

In most situations fuzzy or elastic sets are related to scales already in existence for a precise grading of objects, people, qualities, or processes. For example, the linguistic variable age and its variants old, very old, young, very young, and so on, are elastically related to a scale of elapsed time. The linguistic variable *cost*, and its variants, very expensive, expensive, cheap, very cheap, and so on, are related to a dollar scale. As shown in Figure 5.11, the fuzzy set *usually* is related to a proportion or probability scale. The question now is: When someone like Wigmore makes a fuzzy judgment regarding the force, strength, or weight of evidence, to what internal numerical scale should these fuzzy judgments be related? Suppose I say that a certain item or body of evidence has *strong inferential force* in a certain instance. This fuzzy statement, to be quantified, must be related to or "calibrated" with reference to another numerical scale such as the ones just mentioned for *age, cost,* and *usually.* As Figure 5.12 illustrates, we presently have three candidates for such an internal scale.

Figure 5.12a shows two fuzzy judgments of the force of evidence in the case in which these fuzzy judgments are related to or calibrated on a Bayesian log likelihood ratio scale. Suppose I say that some item or body of evidence has strong force on hypothesis H. You ask me what this means, and I first tell you that any likelihood ratio in the interval $[a, c]$ has some *possibility* of being what I mean by "strong force." If a likelihood ratio for some evidence is less than a, I will not say it has strong force on H. If this likelihood ratio exceeds c, I will intensify my judgment and say, for example, that it has *very strong force.* When you press me to tell you how possible are the values in $[a, c]$ of meaning "strong force," I describe a membership function μ that has been scaled to show the value of log likelihood ratio that has the greatest possibility of being what I mean by "strong force." As the membership function shows, my judgment is that a log likelihood ratio having value b has a grade of membership $\mu = 1.0$ in the fuzzy set *strong force.* Thus I say that

(a) **Inferential Force and Relative Likeness [Bayes]**

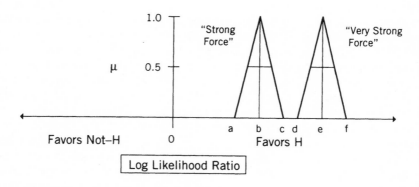

(b) **Inferential Force and Evidential Support [Shafer]**

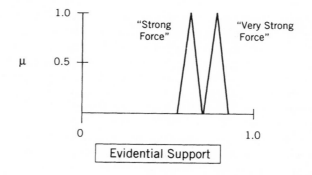

(c) **Inferential Force and Completeness of Coverage [Cohen]**

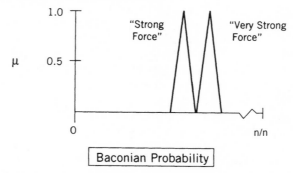

FIGURE 5.12   Three fuzzy gradations of the inferential force of evidence.

a log likelihood ratio equaling b has the *highest possibility* of being what I mean by "strong force" on hypothesis H. My membership function also conveys some idea of my judgmental variability. For example, the horizontal line for $\mu = 0.5$ identifies an interval of log likelihood ratio values all of which I would say have at least 0.5 possibility of meaning "strong force." If I had said the evidence has "very strong" inferential force, I might have described the other membership function shown in Figure 5.12a.

In fairness to Shafer and Cohen, it might be argued that other scales could also be used to calibrate my fuzzy judgments of "strong force," and "very strong force," as shown in Figures 5.12b and 5.12c. Depending upon what I believe the evidence means, and upon whether or not my inference is eliminative in nature, I might be entirely justified in saying that the best representation for my internal scale of evidential force assessment is either Shafer's support/weight assignments (on the [0, 1] interval) or Cohen's Baconian probabilities (on a scale ranging from $0/n$ to n/n). I must emphasize that by Figure 5.12 I am not advocating mixing together any of these formal systems. My purpose has been simply to illustrate that there is more than one possible scale against which fuzzy judgments of the inferential or probative force of evidence might be calibrated. Wigmore advocated fuzzy judgments of the probative force of evidence, but he offered no mechanism for combining these fuzzy judgments within and across arguments based upon a mass of evidence. The fact that there are different possible scales against which such fuzzy judgments may be calibrated only adds to the difficulty. However, my faith in the ingenuity of Zadeh and his many colleagues leads me to assert, in fuzzy terms, that development of such mechanisms is *quite possible*.

Having now examined both structural and force-related concepts at some length, my next task in this discourse is to discuss how these concepts might be combined in our study of the properties of evidence and the many inferential subtleties that such study can reveal. Before I begin this task, I must mention that my coverage of alternative systems of probabilistic reasoning is not exhaustive. There are other systems I might have mentioned that also have useful properties. Examples include the *evidentiary value model* (e.g., Gardenfors, Hansson, and Sahlin 1983) and the theory of *potential surprise* (Shackle 1969). I had to draw a line somewhere; I have drawn it around Bayes, Cohen, Shafer, and Zadeh.

Chapter **6**

The Analysis of Evidential Properties and Subtleties

The structural matters examined in Chapters 3 and 4 are informative about recurrent forms and combinations of evidence, various uses made of evidence, and the process of constructing arguments bearing upon the relevance and credibility of evidence. The alternative conceptions of probabilistic reasoning considered in Chapter 5 show us how we might assess the inferential force of evidence and then combine these assessments in reaching a conclusion. But evidence has many interesting properties, some of which are as inconspicuous as they are important. In many situations we may be quite unaware of important questions we should ask about evidence as we attempt to draw conclusions from it. Capturing this evidential richness and identifying questions to ask about evidence requires an integration of structural and probabilistic concepts. This integration takes place in the analyses I will present in Chapters 7 and 8. The present chapter sets the stage for these analyses by considering how structure and probability are to be linked, what evidential properties and subtleties are of interest, and what analytic methods will be employed.

6.1 COMBINING STRUCTURAL AND PROBABILISTIC CONCEPTS

Persons interested in argument structural matters and those interested in probability have often followed more or less separate paths, often for good reasons. It would have been too much to ask of Wigmore that he also be a probabilist or to ask of Kolmogorov that he also be an evidence scholar. However, as interest developed in complex probabilistic reasoning and how it might be assisted, the necessity for linking structure and probability became obvious. My own work on evidence has been based on the idea that we can learn more about evidence, and about what is required in assessing its inferential force, by casting in probabilistic terms the structural insights of Wigmore and other evidence scholars. Others have seen the necessity of integrating structural and probabilistic ideas. Glenn Shafer has repeatedly emphasized how inattention to structural issues has worked to the disadvantage of probabilists and statisticians (1986a, 1988). In fact he argues that probability is more about structure than it is about numbers (1988, 5–9). In addition persons currently at work on computerizing the inference networks mentioned in Chapter 4 are certainly aware of the linkage between structural and probabilitistic issues.

Some questions about evidence can be answered entirely in structural terms. For example, if asked to describe the essential distinction between contradictory and conflicting evidence, we could make use of structural devices such as the ones shown in Figure 3.13. Similarly questions about the distinction between directly relevant and ancillary evidence can be answered in structural terms. But now suppose someone inquires whether it is always true that secondhand or hearsay evidence about some event has less inferential force than evidence obtained from a primary source (the "horse's mouth") whom we believe to have made a direct observation of this event. An answer to this question requires attention to both probabilistic and structural matters. A long-standing expectation, going back at least to the time of John Locke (see Section 5.1), is that evidence from a secondary source always has weaker inferential force than evidence from a primary source. But there are situations, easily identified, in which secondhand evidence can be more forceful than evidence from a primary source. Indeed hearsay evidence about some event can often be more inferentially valuable than *knowing for sure* that this event did occur. It all depends upon what we know about our sources and whether this knowledge has any inferential value on its own. A wide variety of questions about evidence and its inferential force have answers in which structural and probabilistic considerations are bound together.

6.1.1 Probabilistic Analyses of Evidential Forms and Combinations

The recurrent forms of evidence categorized in Figure 3.11 each have certain recognizable characteristics and play particular roles in probabilistic reasoning. The row dimension of this categorization concerns the nature of the evidence and how a user stands in relation to it. Thus, for example, we have distinctions between various forms of tangible and testimonial evidence. Such distinctions become important in assessing the credibility of evidence. The other dimension concerns the relevance relationship between evidence and the hypotheses at issue in some particular inference. As discussed in Section 3.4 and noted in Figure 3.11, whether evidence has direct or indirect relevance on major hypotheses at issue is always problem specific or argument specific. Recall from Section 3.4 that ancillary evidence bears upon the inferential strength or weakness of directly relevant evidence. Directly relevant evidence can be direct on hypotheses at one stage of argument but only circumstantial on hypotheses at other stages.

The level of detail employed in structuring arguments from evidence directly influences the number of questions that we can generate about evidence. More detailed structuring is equivalent to more detailed inquiry. Consider Figure 3.9 and the argument bearing on the relevance and credibility of Officer Connolly's testimony. Each stage of this argument identifies a potential source of uncertainty and suggests a new question that we might ask about this evidence. The trouble of course is that by such detailed structuring we may raise more questions than we can answer and be required to assess more probabilities than we can justify. This is certainly a troublesome matter in actual inferences, as discussed in Chapter 5. However, in my probabilistic analyses of evidence my intent is simply to illustrate what various views of probability have to say about the inferential force of various forms and combinations of evidence. The specific numbers I will use in such analyses simply provide a means for illustrating the manner in which various formal systems of probability capture often inconspicuous elements of the process of assessing the inferential force of evidence.

One obvious question concerns the extent to which evidential form influences inferential force. We might suppose, for example, that tangible evidence of a certain event is always more forceful on given hypotheses than testimonial evidence about this same event. The argument might be: "I trust my own senses more than I trust the senses of others." However, instances are readily identified in which testimonial evidence about an event can have greater inferential force than tangible evidence about this same event. Different forms of evidence involve different structural considerations and raise different questions. As observed in Section 3.2, questions related to the credibility of tangible evidence differ from those related to the credibility of testimonial evidence. The form taken by an item of evidence in a particular inference does not, by itself, determine its inferential force. Evidence in any of the fifteen categories shown in Figure 3.11 can be weak or strong in its influence upon our probabilistically expressed beliefs about any hypotheses of interest. We need to give special attention to the categories of *ancillary evidence* shown in Figure 3.11.

Another question concerns how we are to grade the force of ancillary (or indirectly relevant) evidence, when such evidence simply strengthens or weakens the force of other evidence that is directly relevant? As noted in Section 4.5.4, we need to show, by argument, why an item of ancillary evidence is indeed relevant and credible in strengthening or weakening the force of other evidence. Thus we are led to the possibility of one inference network being embedded in another, as illustrated in Figures 4.17 and 4.18. The different probabilistic systems we examined in Chapter 5 seem to have different means for incorporating ancillary evidence in assessments of the inferential force of evidence. Here is an example that illustrates some of the distinctions we must make.

First, suppose, as in Figure 6.1a, that evidence E* is directly relevant on major hypotheses {H, Hᶜ}. Suppose that E*, whatever its nature, is just *circumstantial* evidence on {H, Hᶜ}. Even if perfectly credible, E* provides some grounds for, but does not entail, the truth of either H or Hᶜ. In Bayesian terms we can form a likelihood ratio for E* that expresses one way of grading the inferential force of E* on {H, Hᶜ}. Now suppose, as in Figure 6.1b, the same inference from evidence E* to {H, Hᶜ}. The essential difference is that E* now plays an ancillary role. In this case it is evidence F* that is directly relevant but circumstantial evidence on our major hypotheses {G, Gᶜ}. In Bayesian terms we can form a likelihood ratio for F* that expresses its inferential force on {G, Gᶜ}. Suppose that ancillary evidence E* bears unfavorably upon the credibility of evidence F* in the following way: If event H were true, we believe this would reduce the force of F* on hypotheses {G, Gc}. But we do not have direct evidence of H; all we have is circumstantial evidence E* that H occurred. Depending upon its inferential force on H, the ancillary role E* plays in this case is to weaken the inferential force of F* on major hypotheses {G, Gᶜ}.

As an example, suppose that E* and F* are items of testimony; E* is evidence that the source reporting F* lost his glasses the day before he says he observed event F. Even if completely credible, E* would be just circumstantial evidence that the person reporting F* was not wearing glasses (H) when he said he saw F happen. If we knew that H were true, this would tend to weaken the inferential linkage between F* and F and thus reduce the inferential force of F* on {G, Gᶜ}. Using appropriate likelihood ratios, we can give Bayesian gradations of the force of E* on {H, Hᶜ} and the force of F* on {G, Gᶜ}. But we have no means for combining them in any way if we wished to grade the force of *ancillary evidence* E* on *major hypotheses* {G, Gᶜ}. The reason is that the argument from E* to {H, Hᶜ} is embedded in but

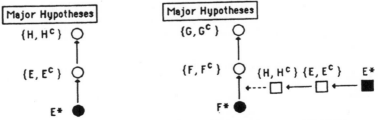

(a) **Direct Relevance of Evidence E***   (b) **Indirect Relevance of Evidence E***

FIGURE 6.1 Illustrating the direct and indirect relevance of evidence.

not linked to the argument from F^* to $\{G, G^c\}$. The best we can say is that our probabilistic belief about H, based on ancillary evidence E^*, somehow affects another belief about the force of evidence F^*. In Ron Howard's terms (see Section 4.5.4), we might say that the inference from E^* to $\{H, H^c\}$ simply provides *evocative* information bearing upon the force of evidence F^*.

But in situations such as the one in Figure 6.1b there are other ways of describing the force of ancillary evidence E^* on major hypotheses $\{G, G^c\}$. On a belief function construal of this situation we would be entitled to regard F^* and E^* as a *body of evidence* that may support $\{G\}$, $\{G^c\}$, and $\{G, G^c\}$ to varying degrees. This body of evidence consists of F^* from one source and E^* from another in which it is the case that E^* tells us something about the extent to which F^* may mean $\{G\}$, $\{G^c\}$, or $\{G, G^c\}$. In a Baconian construal of this situation, it may be the case that H identifies a *relevant variable* in testing an appropriate generalization linking F^* and $\{F, F^c\}$. Evidence E^* simply allows us to determine whether this generalization passed or failed an eliminative test involving whether or not H is true. In the various probabilistic analyses of the inferential force of of evidence I will make it clear what is being assumed about the existence and the role of ancillary evidence.

In Section 3.5 we considered various recurrent *combinations* of two or more evidence items. Distinctions were made between contradictory and conflicting evidence and between corroborative and convergent evidence. In the case of convergent evidence the possibility of evidential synergism was noted; one item of evidence can act to enhance the inferential force of another. Stated another way, the inferential force of two or more evidence items considered jointly can often exceed the inferential force of these items when they are considered separately. We also examined two species of evidential redundancy, corroborative and cumulative, in which one item of evidence can act to reduce the inferential force of another. Evidence combinations provide another rich source of subtleties which, if recognized, can be exploited.

6.1.2   Capturing Evidential Subtleties: The Warp and the Weft of Arguments

As I mentioned in Chapter 4, it very useful to think of an argument from a mass of evidence as a *fabric*. It is quite common to hear a person's arguments described as being "threadbare." Occasionally an inferential network is described as being "sparse" to indicate that arguments captured by the network could be further decomposed. A fabric has both vertical threads (its *warp*) and horizontal threads (its *weft* or *woof*). In the same way complex arguments or inference networks such as the one illustrated in Figure 4.1 have both vertical and horizontal linkages or threads. Both the number and the strength of the warp and weft threads in the fabric of an argument contribute to its overall strength. The structural and the probabilistic concepts we have examined so far contribute to our ability to recognize and exploit a remarkable variety of evidential subtleties whose importance in probabilistic reasoning is so easily overlooked. We first consider some structural concepts and their relation to evidential subtleties.

Given a collection of directly relevant evidence, we have characterized arguments from this evidence to hypotheses of interest as *directed acyclic graphs* (DAGs). All of the structures we considered in Chapter 4 are DAGs. Recall that a DAG is said to be *singly connected* if, for every two nodes on the graph, there is at most one chain of arcs between these two nodes. One major class of evidential subtlety arises in graphs that are *not singly connected*. Pursuing our fabric metaphor, we will observe that for graphs not singly connected we will have the existence of weft threads and/or additional vertical or warp threads. Consider Figure 4.1 again, and observe that there are two chains leading from evidence E* to node **H** and two chains leading from evidence L* to node **K.** In both of these instances we have additional warp threads in our overall argument. In the example shown they involve possible state-dependent credibility of evidence E* and L*. Next observe the lateral or weft linkages labeled 2 and 5. We will later observe that by such linkages or threads we can capture possible evidential synergism and redundancy. As we will see, the weft thread labeled 3 concerns evidential subtleties involving possible interactions among the sources of our evidence G* and J*. As noted in Section 4.5.3, the additional warp and weft threads or linkages in an inference network present some severe computational difficulties when Bayesian analyses are performed. To ignore them, however, is also to ignore evidential subtleties that can, in many cases, have a substantial effect on our beliefs about the inferential force of evidence.

Modern systems of probability are informative about a variety of evidential properties and subtleties. A list of some of the ones we will consider appears in Section 6.2 below. There is a probabilistic concept in the Bayesian view of probabilistic reasoning that, I believe, stands above all others in its importance as far as the capturing of evidential subtleties is concerned. This concept involves the possible *conditional nonindependence* of events appearing at nodes in an argument from evidence. Conditional nonindependence is a very good example of a simple idea that has profound consequences. Weft threads or additional warp threads in the fabric of an argument signal the existence of conditional nonindependencies. As noted in Section 4.5.2, the existence of such nonindependencies requires additional probability assessments. Following is a very simple example that illustrates how powerful this concept can be in influencing an assessment of the inferential force of evidence.

Suppose we "know" that events B and C have occurred, and we wish to assess their inferential force, in Pascalian terms, on hypotheses $\{A, A^c\}$. Also suppose we have some basis for assuming events B and C to be independent, conditional upon A and upon A^c. In network terms we have the structure shown in Figure 6.2a. This judgment of conditional independence means that $P(B|AC) = P(B|A)$, $P(B|A^cC) = P(B|A^c)$, $P(C|AB) = P(C|A)$, and

$P(C|A^cB) = P(C|A^c)$. It also means that $P(BC|A) = P(B|A)P(C|A)$ and $P(BC|A^c) = P(B|A^c)P(C|A^c)$. Suppose that we assess the values $P(B|A) = 0.6$ and $P(B|A^c) = 0.3$. Dividing the first by the second, we obtain the likelihood ratio for B to be $L_B = 2$. For event C we assess the values $P(C|A) = 0.4$, $P(C|A^c) = 0.1$ and determine the likelihood ratio $L_C = 4$. With these four values determined under a judgment of conditional independence, we can also form the likelihood ratio for the joint occurrence of events B and C by observing that $P(BC|A) = P(B|A)P(C|A) = (0.6)(0.4) = 0.24$ and $P(BC|A^c) = P(B|A^c)P(C|A^c) = (0.3)(0.1) = 0.03$. Thus $L_{BC} = (0.24)/(0.03) = 8 = L_B \times L_C$. The value $L_{BC} = 8$ is a Bayesian gradation of the inferential force of the joint occurrence of B and C; it indicates that the joint occurrence of B and C is eight times more probable given A than it is given A^c. We might also, of course, take $\log L_{BC}$ as a measure of the inferential force of B and C together.

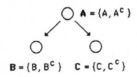

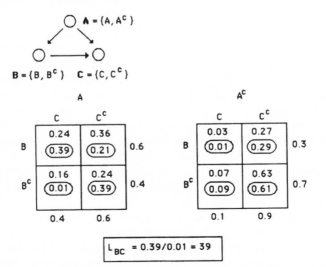

FIGURE 6.2 Illustrating the effects of conditional nonindependence on the inferential force of evidence.

Now suppose that a critic argues that B and C are not independent given A or given A^c. The additional arc shown in the network in Figure 6.2b captures this conditional nonindependence. Notice that this network is not singly connected, since there are two possible chains of arcs from node **A** to node **C**, namely we have added a "weft" thread in the fabric of our argument (the arc connecting nodes **B** and **C**). Our critic does not argue with the probabilistic assessments that we have made for events B and C considered separately. But she argues that the joint occurrence of B and C is more probable under A and less probable under A^c than the values $P(BC|A) = 0.24$ and $P(BC|A^c) = 0.03$ which we determined under our conditional independence assumption. One possible set of values that captures this criticism is shown in the tables in Figure 6.2b. Suppose we now assess $P(BC|A)$ to be 0.39 and $P(BC|A^c)$ to be 0.01. Notice that we have preserved the separate or marginal conditional probabilities originally assessed. Other possible joint conditional probabilities follow from this new assessment; all new assessments are circled in Figure 6.2b. The other values in the tables are joint conditionals under our initial conditional independence assumption. If we now determine the likelihood ratio for the joint occurrence of B and C, we observe that $L_{BC} = P(BC|A)/P(BC|A^c) = 0.39/0.01 = 39$. In this case the force of evidence B and C is nearly five times the value it had, assuming independence of B and C conditional on A and A^c. Taken jointly, events B and C have more inferential force than they do if considered separately. Thus our critic has argued that the conditional nonindependence of events B and C means that they operate synergistically in their bearing upon hypotheses {A, A^c}.

There is another way to illustrate what has happened in this example involving conditional nonindependence. We first assessed the inferential force of B by means of $L_B = P(B|A)/P(B|A^c) = (0.6)/(0.3) = 2$. Now we consider the likelihood ratio for C, given event B. In symbols, $L_{C|B} = P(C|BA)/P(C|BA^c)$. From our assessed values of $P(B|A)$, $P(B|A^c)$, $P(BC|A)$, and $P(BC|A^c)$ we can determine $P(C|BA)$ and $P(C|BA^c)$, since $P(C|BA) = P(BC|A)/P(B|A)$ and $P(C|BA^c) = P(BC|A^c)/P(B|A^c)$. Using the assessments that we have made, $P(C|BA) = (0.39)/(0.60) = 0.65$ and $P(C|BA^c) = (0.01)/(0.3) = 0.033$. So $L_{C|B} = (0.65)/(0.033) = 19.5$. If we compare $L_{C|B}$ with our original assessment L_C, we observe that the inferential force of event C is now nearly five times greater when we take event B into account, in light of the conditional nonindependence of B and C that is captured in our revised assessment. The combined inferential force of B and C is now given by $L_{BC} = L_B \times L_{C|B} = (2)(19.5) = 39$, the same as when we assessed the inferential force of the joint occurrence of B and C.

This example illustrates two major facts about conditional nonindependence: (1) two or more items of evidence, considered jointly, can have more/less inferential force than they do when considered separately, and (2) the inferential force of one item of evidence can be judged greater or smaller in light of other evidence we have. As we proceed, we will examine a variety of situations in which patterns of conditional nonindependence among evidence items and among events in our chains of reasoning alter our beliefs about the inferential force of evidence. The concept of conditional nonindependence is associated with the Pascalian system of probability. The existence of conditional nonindependence can be revealed by examining appropriate relative frequencies, if they are available. In other situations, however, both the existence and the character of a conditional nonindependency are matters requiring subjective judgment.

6.2 SOME INTERESTING EVIDENTIAL PROPERTIES AND SUBTLETIES

I closed Chapter 2 with a comment about the "evidential rocks" I have turned over to see what I could find beneath them. Here is a brief account of the kinds of rocks I have turned over; what I and others have found beneath them forms the subject matter of Chapters 7 and 8. Some of the interesting properties and subtleties of evidence can be revealed by examining single or *isolated* items of evidence and the chains of reasoning linking them to major hypotheses at issue. In actual inferences, however, there is no such thing as a single or isolated item of evidence, so I have to explain my usage of this term. As the Swedish jurist Per Olof Ekelof put it, "What we call a 'piece of evidence' is strictly speaking an evidentiary fact together with auxillary facts attached to it" (1983, 11). In the language that I have used, we may identify a single directly relevant evidence item together with ancillary (auxillary) evidence that supports or weakens the inferential force of the directly relevant item. In short, we always have evidence and evidence about this evidence. But in the analyses to come, I will simply assume the existence of at least some ancillary evidence to support the probabilities that are revealed in chains of reasoning from a single or isolated item of directly relevant evidence. I will identify isolated items of evidence with the understanding that, if they were encountered in actual situations, we would always require ancillary or auxillary evidence to justify any probabilistic judgments necessary in grading the force of this evidence. Other evidential properties and subtleties are revealed in the combinations of evidence such as the ones examined in Section 3.5. It is certainly true that these combinations of evidence also require bodies of ancillary evidence to justify any grading of their inferential force.

6.2.1 Evidence in Isolation

The metaphor of an argument as a chain of reasoning suggests questions such as the following: How does the force of evidence vary with the *number of links* in the chain? If there is to be a *weak link* in a chain of reasoning, does it matter to the inferential force of evidence where in the chain this weak link is located? Some links may involve *rare events;* as far as the force of evidence is concerned, does it matter where rare events are located in a chain of reasoning? Chains of reasoning from a single item of evidence also allow us to examine some very interesting matters associated with the *transitivity* of reasoning. Suppose we believe that evidence E* favors the occurrence of event E and that event E favors the truth of hypothesis H. Does it always follow that evidence E* necessarily favors the truth of H? The answer, in general, is no. There are situations involving patterns of conditional nonindependence of events in reasoning chains in which such inferential transitivity is not guaranteed. As we will observe, different systems of probability give us different views of the conditions necessary for transitive reasoning.

The forms of evidence identified in Figure 3.11 provide rich ground for examining inconspicuous details of probabilistic reasoning. As discussed in Section 3.2, tangible and testimonial evidence require different credibility-related considerations. In Chapter 7 appears an array of analyses of the manner in which the credibility of various species of evidence can influence the inferential force of evidence. It is here that we will encounter, in a new light, the *credibility-testimony* problems of such great interest among early probabilists. Examined carefully, chains of reasoning from tangible evidence, open to our own inspection, seem to have different stages or links than do chains of reasoning from testimonial evidence provided by other persons. Some of these analyses will involve comparisons of the inferential force of tangible and testimonial evidence in the face of variations in the accuracy and authenticity of tangible evidence and variations in the veracity, objectivity, and observational sensitivity of sources of testimonial evidence. Other analyses will show how a wide variety of commonly employed concepts concerning the credibility of evidence and its sources can find expression in formal probabilistic studies of evidence and its inferential force. The issue of conditional nonindependence plays a very important role in these analyses. Many interesting credibility-related subtleties can be captured by means of patterns of conditional nonindependence involving events at various stages of reasoning from tangible or testimonial evidence.

As noted in Figure 3.11, testimonial evidence can either be unequivocal or equivocal (in various ways) regarding the event(s) reported in testimony. First, consider a person who equivocates completely when asked if a certain event occurred. This person responds by saying such things as "I don't know" or "I can't remember." Suppose we suspect that this person does know or can remember, so we regard his equivocation as having at least some inferential force on hypotheses that we are considering. As we will discuss later, it is an interesting exercise to establish an argument showing the relevance of this complete equivocation on hypotheses at issue. But a person may also equivocate in a probabilistic manner by providing a response such as "I believe it 70% likely that event E occurred and 30% likely that E did not occur." The evidence given by this person is a probability distribution assigned across event class $\{E, E^c\}$. We might regard this as *uncertain evidence;* in some modern works it is called *virtual evidence* (Pearl 1988, 44–46; Neapolitan 1990, 230–235, 291–293). There is an interesting history I will mention regarding attempts to represent probabilistically hedged evidence in Bayes's rule.

The length of a chain of reasoning from an item of evidence to hypotheses of interest is increased if the evidence comes to us through a chain of sources. As I have noted, early probabilists were interested in what they termed *successive testimony* passed from one source to another. One species of successive testimony is commonly termed *hearsay evidence*. Such evidence is also said to have been obtained at *secondhand*. The trouble is that we may easily encounter evidence that involves more than two successive sources. It might be more appropriate to refer generically in such cases to *nth-hand evidence*. As we will observe in Chapter 7, the process of establishing the inferential force of nth-hand evidence depends directly upon how finely we choose to decompose the credibility-related foundations for argument from such evidence.

Some interesting inferential issues arise when we pursue the distinction between *positive evidence,* recording the occurrence of an event, and *negative evidence,* recording the nonoccurrence of an event. In the process we will take a closer look at Sherlock Holmes' inferential behavior in the case *Silver Blaze*. An important item of evidence in this case involved a certain dog's not barking. As we will see, Holmes might have drawn the wrong conclusion from this negative evidence. We will also observe that as far as inferential force is concerned, there is no order of preference between positive and negative evidence.

As mentioned in Section 2.1.1, our failure to obtain expected tangible or testimonial evidence can itself be evidence. In short, *missing evidence* can be evidence having significant inferential force on occasion. Tangible evidence can go missing for any number of reasons, some of which are quite benign. Suppose we expect to find a certain document that allegedly records the occurrence of an event of interest to us. The document may not now exist (someone had access to a paper-shredder) or perhaps our failure to find it only means that we are looking in the wrong place. But it might also happen that the document does exist and someone is keeping it from us. Suppose our inference involves whether or not some hypothesis H is true. Let M^* represent evidence expected but missing. As we will discover, it is a challenge to form an argument from M^* to $\{H, H^c\}$ in defense of the relevance and credibility of missing evidence M^*. Certainly no less challenging is the task of constructing an argument showing the relevance of someone's refusal to provide testimonial evidence about a certain event. First, it is necessary to distinguish between *completely equivocal testimony* and *no testimony*. In the former case a person could offer replies such as "I don't know" or "I can't remember" (as discussed above). In the latter case a person simply refuses to say anything at all. I will propose what I regard as plausible arguments in defense of the relevance of missing tangible and testimonial evidence. At the very least these arguments provide some basis for marshaling whatever ancillary evidence we may have that justifies the inferential force of missing evidence.

The analysis of single or isolated items of evidence allows us to consider some evidential distinctions recognized by Jacques Bernoulli in his 1713 treatise *Ars Conjectandi* (The Art of Conjecture). My later analysis of these distinctions, illustrated in Figure 6.3, will rest upon Hacking's account of them (1975, 150–153). The first distinction, shown in Figure 6.3*a*, concerns whether the relation between two propositions or events is one of *necessity* or *contingency*. Case 1 illustrates a situation in which we have conclusive evidence E* that event E occurred, when it is also the case that the occurrence of E makes hypothesis H certain to be true. In other words, E* entails E which, in turn, entails H; or, E is necessarily true because of E* and H is necessarily true because of E. The reasoning here is deductive or demonstrative and not inductive. Case 2 is one in which event E, if true, would entail H. The trouble is that E* provides only inconclusive evidence of E. Stated another way, the relation between E and H is one of necessity, but the relation between E* and E is one of contingency or probability. In this case E* has some probability under both E and E^c; this is represented by the arrow from E* to the line under {E, E^c}. A very good example involves *alibi testimony*. Suppose that H represents the hypothesis that defendant (Def) is *innocent* of committing the assault and battery on or about 3:00 PM on February 20, 1993, in Detroit, Michigan. Event E is the event that Def was in Nashville, Tennessee at 3:00

(a) Bernoulli's Cases of Necessity and Contingency

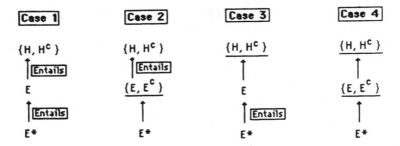

(b) Mixed vs Pure Evidence

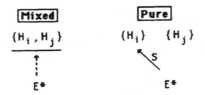

FIGURE 6.3   Bernoulli's evidential distinctions.

on February 20, 1993. Clearly E entails H, since Def cannot have been in Detroit and Nashville at the same time. But we suppose that the witness providing alibi testimony E^* is not perfectly credible, so E^* has some probability under E and also under E^c.

Case 3 in Figure 6.3*a* involves a situation in which we have perfectly credible evidence E^* about an event E that has only a contingent or probabilistic relation to hypotheses {H, H^c}. Perfectly credible sources are hard to find in any context, so this case, like case 1, is rather uninteresting. However, I did note in Section 5.1 Wigmore's discussion of tangible evidence and how courts would regard a juror's observations of a tangible as being conclusive evidence of the existence of this tangible. Case 4 shows the commonly occurring situation in which we have inconclusive evidence about an event that is itself just inconclusive on hypotheses of interest. All of the analyses of single or isolated evidence items in Chapter 7 will involve Bernoulli's case 4; case 2 is discussed in Chapter 8.

But Bernoulli also made a distinction between *pure* and *mixed* evidence; this distinction has assumed additional importance in current work on probabilistic reasoning. Evidence E^* is said to be mixed with respect to hypotheses such as H_i and H_j, if, as shown in Figure 6.3*b*, it seems to be consistent to some degree with the truth of both of these hypotheses. Thus, for example, the present existence of dark clouds would be regarded as mixed evidence on the hypothesis that it will rain in an hour. This evidence has some probability of occurrence under H, that it will rain in an hour, and some probability under H^c, that it will not. Evidence is said to be pure if it supports one hypothesis but says nothing at all about others. In Figure 6.3*b* evidence E^* offers some support (s) to H_i but has no bearing at all on H_j. Suppose that there are several suspects A, B, C, and D in the investigation of a robbery known to have been committed by a single person. Evidence E^* places A near the scene of the robbery at the time it was committed and thus offers support to the hypothesis that A did it. Evidence E^*, however, says nothing at all about whether or not any of the other suspects might have committed the crime. The distinction between pure and mixed evidence is captured in Shafer's system of belief functions. In the example in Figure 5.2 person P's testimony about your neighbor's dog, together with what you believe about his credibility, offers support to H (that your neighbor is keeping a dog) but says nothing at all about H^c (that he is not keeping a dog).

6.2.2   Evidence in Combination

Chapter 8 contains a variety of analyses of evidence items taken in combination. It is true that evidence items can be combined in a virtually unlimited way; I will focus mainly upon the recurrent combinations discussed in Section 3.5. The different conceptions of the force of evidence considered in Chapter 5 each add to our understanding of harmonious evidence, that which is either *corroborative* or *convergent (confirming)* in nature. But convergent evidence can also be *synergistic;* this subtlety can be captured in Pascalian terms by means of a certain pattern of conditional nonindependence. Synergism has two interpretations, as illustrated in the example in Figure 6.2. Two or more items of evidence, considered together, can often have greater inferential force than if these items were considered separately and independently. Synergism also means that one item of evidence can act to enhance the inferential force of another. But there are other situations in which one item of evidence can act to reduce the inferential force of another item. Such instances occur when we have either corroborative or cumulative evidence. In such cases we have the problem of evidential *redundancy* to consider. Here is another evidential subtlety that can be captured by appropriate patterns of conditional nonindependence. Concepts that we borrow from *statistical communications theory* (also called *information theory*) are helpful but not completely adequate in efforts to grade the degree of redundancy of evidence and the degree to which redundancy affects the inferential force of evidence.

Not all evidence is harmonious, so we have to consider situations involving two species of dissonant evidence: *contradictory* or *conflicting*. There are some very interesting subtleties here that we should recognize. For example, behind every instance of contradictory evidence lurks the possibility of evidential redundancy. Suppose that one source reports E*, that event E occurred, and another source reports E^c*, that event E did not occur. We may have ancillary evidence strongly suggesting that the second source is lying, in which case we may be entitled to believe the opposite of what he says. If so, we then have essentially corroborative evidence that is redundant to some degree. One view of the force of contradictory evidence automatically takes the possibility of such redundance into account. Especially interesting, historically and otherwise, are instances in which we have some pattern of corroborative and contradictory evidence about the same event. We may have a situation in which r sources tell us that event E happened and $n - r$ sources tell us that E did not happen. A Pascalian account of the force of the joint report from these n persons or sensing devices shows precisely why it makes no sense to try to resolve this dissonance by counting heads on either side and letting majority rule.

Suppose that person X reports evidence E*, that event E occurred. We ask X how she obtained this information, and she replies: "I observed events C and D, and from these observations I inferred that event E also occurred." In this case X admits to no direct observation of event E, nor has she obtained information about E at secondhand from another source. What she reports is an inference about the occurrence of one event based upon her observation of other events. In legal contexts such evidence is normally termed *opinion evidence*. The rules governing the admissibility of opinion evidence depend upon the witness. Expert witnesses are commonly allowed to express opinions about the occurrence of events but ordinary witnesses are not. Thus, if you appeared as an ordinary witness and testified that I was intoxicated, my counsel would object on grounds that your testimony was an opinion and not the result of direct observation. You would, however, be permitted to testify that I was staggering about and that I had a half-empty whiskey bottle in each hand. The jury might then infer that I was intoxicated if it judged you to be a credible source. There are interesting inferential issues associated with establishing the credibility and force of opinion evidence. One major class of issues concerns the source's credibility regarding the observational basis for an opinion. Another class concerns whether or not anyone could reasonably infer unobserved event E from other observed events C and D. I include opinion evidence as a species of an evidence combination, since opinions or inferences, asserted as evidence, usually rest upon any number of other evidence items.

We have also to consider situations in which the evidence items in recurring combinations take different forms. Thus, for example, we may have items of convergent (and possibly synergistic) evidence, some of which are tangible and others testimonial in form. Analyzing the inferential force of different combinations of evidence, that also differ with respect to form, is a challenging exercise. On close examination, the number of instances in which we draw conclusions from secondhand (or nth-hand) evidence is astounding. We may have certain combinations of secondhand evidence or combinations in which secondhand evidence is mixed with other forms of evidence. One important case concerns the corroboration of hearsay. In such analyses we have to be particularly careful in specifying exactly which argument propositions are being corroborated.

6.3 ANALYTIC OBJECTIVES AND METHODS

The essential objective in the probabilistic analyses in Chapters 7 and 8 is to examine the process of assessing the inferential force of various forms and combinations of evidence and to observe various attributes of evidence that such analyses reveal. In Chapter 5 we examined different ways in which the force of evidence might be graded. Confronted with alternative views of probabilistic reasoning, a frequently asked question is: Which one is to be preferred? In response to such a question I have usually said that this is rather like asking whether you prefer your saw or your hammer. When you wish to cut wood, you prefer your saw; when you wish to pound a nail, you prefer your hammer. The different formal systems of probabilistic reasoning each resonate to different attributes of the very rich process of probabilistic reasoning. In my analyses of evidence I have viewed these different formal systems not as normative guides to life but as heuristics for examining evidence from different perspectives or standpoints. The Pascalian system, together with the Bayesian view of probabilistic reasoning, has been around for many years and has been thoroughly examined. Although they have old roots, the non-Pascalian systems we discussed have just recently been well articulated. Exploration of their properties and uses is now in progress. Thus I will not be able to examine every evidential form and combination from every different extant view of the force of evidence. I fear that such examination, carefully done, would take more than one lifetime.

6.3.1 Asking Questions about Evidence

There are two quite different questions that arise in reasoning from inconclusive evidence. We can ask questions *about our evidence*, and we can ask questions *of our evidence*. Questions about evidence concern its relevance, credibility, and force. The various analyses in Chapters 7 and 8 all assume that the direct relevance of the evidence of concern has been established by arguments made clear in the analyses. But questions we ask of evidence usually involve efforts to generate or discover new evidence or new hypotheses or possibilities. The role of evidence in the process of discovery is a major topic in Chapter 9. Here is an example of a question we might ask about evidence: How important is the rareness or improbability of a reported event in a determination of the inferential force of this report? Formal systems of probabilistic reasoning can give answers to such questions. The trouble is that there are so many different questions that we could ask about our evidence. Can we ever be sure that we are always able to ask all the "right" questions about the evidence whose inferential force we are attempting to assess?

In using various probabilistic systems for the study of evidence, we might entertain the idea of determining expressions that seem to be *general* in nature and then examine *special cases* suggested by the general expressions that we have constructed. If we have determined truly general expressions, we might have some hope of identifying complete sets of questions that we could profitably ask about evidence of any form or combination. There are, for example, allegedly general Bayesian algorithms for what we have termed cascaded, hierarchical, or catenated inference (Kelly and Barclay 1973). The trouble is that such general expressions, though formally impressive, are also unrevealing about matters associated with assessing the inferential force of forms and combinations of evidence. Developing general case expressions for the inferential force of various evidential forms and combinations is very difficult because of the virtually unlimited number of ways in which these forms and combinations of evidence can be linked to hypotheses of interest.

Suppose we wish to study the force of contradictory evidence given by two sources. Figure 6.4a shows just three of the many instances of contradictory evidence that can arise. In the first instance we have a contradiction involving direct evidence about major hypotheses at issue. One source says that H is true, and a second says that H is not true. In the second case we have a contradiction involving whether or not event E occurred, where E is just circumstantial evidence on hypotheses $\{H, H^c\}$. One source says E occurred, and another says it did not. In the third case the contradiction involves an event even more remotely linked to major hypotheses $\{H, H^c\}$. We can, however, develop general expressions for the force of an evidence combi-

(*a*) **Chain Length and Contradictory Evidence**

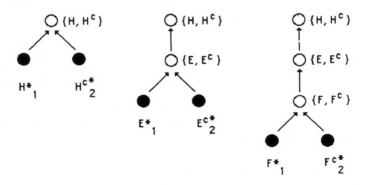

(*b*) **Linkage Patterns**

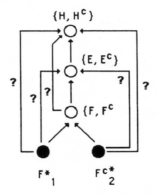

FIGURE 6.4   Examples of possible linkage patterns.

nation (e.g., a contradiction) once we have settled upon a particular relevance argument linking this contradictory evidence with hypotheses of concern. As an example, suppose we begin with the third case of contradiction in Figure 6.4*a*. A likelihood ratio expression for the force of the contradiction F^*, F^{c*} on hypotheses $\{H, H^c\}$ will quickly alert us to the necessity of considering the additional linkages shown in Figure 6.4*b*. Each of the linkages labeled with a question mark identifies possible conditional nonindependencies that we have to consider. Such nonindependencies provide a very rich source of evidential subtleties for us to identify and examine. In many current works on inferential networks and their computational analysis, attempts are made to reduce the number of conditional nonindependencies because of the additional assessment and computational burdens they impose. Rather than reduce these nonindependencies in my own work, I have sought them out because of the evidential subtleties they reveal.

Another approach to identifying questions to ask about evidence involves exploiting the recorded experience and scholarship of persons who have daily commerce with evidence in all of its various forms and combinations. For reasons expressed in Section 2.4, I have found the literature in the field of evidence law to be the richest source of questions to ask about evidence. Answers to such questions are to be found in structural terms, in probabilistic terms, or in some combination of of the two. Thus the questions I will raise about evidence have been suggested by recorded experience as well as by probabilistic expressions.

6.3.2 Methods of Analysis

I have advertised the Pascalian system of probability and the Bayesian approach to inference, based on evidence, as being very rich in implications and applications. But I have also mentioned how the works of Cohen, Shafer, Zadeh, and others show us that such richness can, on occasion, provoke what I termed "intellectual indigestion." In an actual inference task we can often construct very elaborate Bayesian formalizations and then discover that we have little or no basis for justifying assessments of all of the probabilities this formalization reveals. On some occasions we encounter anomalies and paradoxes when an inference is construed in Pascalian terms. On other occasions our inferences are based on imprecise or fuzzy ingredients from which we can hardly justify precise probability assessments. These difficulties acknowledged, I will begin most of my analyses in Chapters 7 and 8 with a Bayesian likelihood ratio formulation for the inferential force of a certain form or pattern of evidence. I know, of course, that application of Bayes's rule requires other ingredients such as prior probabilities or prior odds. For reasons I mentioned in Section 5.3, it is the likelihood and likelihood ratio terms in Bayes's rule that directly concern the inferential force of evidence.

Beginning each evidential analysis in Bayesian terms seems natural for several reasons. Complex inference structures find representation in Bayesian terms, and the concept of conditional nonindependence traps a wide variety of evidential subtleties. Second, Bayes's rule appears in other formal systems that have considerable utility in the study of evidence. It appears in signal detection theory, from which I will borrow several concepts concerning the credibility of sources of evidence. Bayes's rule also appears in statistical communications theory, from which I will borrow concepts useful in the analysis of redundant evidence. In many studies of inference based on evidence Bayes's rule provides a reference point for comparing conclusions reached by other systems of probabilistic reasoning. All of the analyses I will present involve special cases contrived to exhibit certain interesting and important attributes of evidence. Having presented what a Bayesian analysis has to tell us about a particular evidential issue, I will frequently present another analysis of the same evidential situation in terms of belief functions or Baconian probabilities. Thus we will obtain more than one view of the same evidential issue. Not all evidential issues that I will raise find easy expression on all current views of probabilistic reasoning. This is to be expected since, as I have noted above, the alternative formal systems we have discussed resonate to different attributes of probabilistic reasoning and evidence.

In some cases we will be able to identify an interesting evidential property just by examining a likelihood ratio expression. However, such cases are few in number and always involve quite simple situations. The likelihood ratio equations constructed for various evidential patterns can have a very large number of ingredients or variables, too many in fact to allow us to extract meaning from an equation just by staring at it or subjecting it to conventional methods of analysis. Meaning can be coaxed from such complex equations by the process of trying them out with specific numerical ingredients, a process often involving hundreds of calculations. This process is sometimes called *sensitivity analysis;* by such analysis we observe how a complex equation behaves in response to variations in the values of its ingredients. Another way of describing this form of analysis to say that one performs *experiments* with equations. Such experiments are not performed haphazardly but in response to particular questions raised by an equation. For example, in certain situations the terms $P(E^*|E)$ and $P(E^*|E^c)$ appear and are associated with the credibility of the source reporting E^*. Borrowing terms from signal detection theory, I will label $P(E^*|E) = h$ as the probability of a *hit* and $P(E^*|E^c) = f$ as the probability of a *false-positive*. Values of h and f, and occasionally their ratio, can be chosen to illustrate various situations in which the credibility of a source might be low or high. In short, we can tell various evidential "stories" in terms of the probabilistic ingredients of a likelihood ratio equation or in terms of other equations concerning the force of evidence. Sensitivity analysis simply shows how an equation reacts to different evidential stories we can tell.

Most of the conclusions I will report about various forms and combinations of evidence are the result of my having performed hundreds of calculations (or experiments) on many different likelihood ratio equations. This may seem like a mindless activity, even with computer assistance (which I have not always had), but it is not. The reason is that the complexity of most likelihood ratio equations adds excitement; it is not always possible to predict how an equation will react to a certain combination of ingredients. We can tell an evidential "story" and not always be able to predict what the outcome will be. In other forms of empirical research there is always excitement, since one can never be certain about what results one will obtain; the same is true in the empirical study of evidence-related equations. I now alert you to the fact that many of the numerical examples I will discuss in Chapters 7 and 8 will seem quite abstract. Unfortunately, space does not permit me to invent appealing "cover stories" for all of the analyses I will present. There is more to be said about the empirical process of studying formal expressions concerning the inferential force of evidence.

6.3.3 The Science and Technology of Evidence

You may or may not agree with what Israel Zangwill's character Mr. Grodman said about there being a science of evidence and how it is the most difficult of all the sciences (see the quote from *The Big Bow Mystery* in Section 1.3). What is indisputable is that there is an emerging technology for drawing probabilistic conclusions from evidence. There are now several commercially available computer-based systems for performing Bayesian analyses of inference networks. In addition various knowledge-based systems exist that incorporate belief functions and fuzzy probabilities. I know of one computer-based system for eliminative induction that incorporates Baconian probabilities. We might ask whether any of these systems offers hope of advancing the "scientific" study of evidence, its properties, and its subtleties. Regarding Bayesian analyses of the sort I will present in Chapters 7 and 8, I believe the present answer must be negative. It is quite possible to perform sensitivity analyses using current systems for the analysis of Bayes's nets. The trouble is that the algorithms employed by these systems are always buried and are not directly accessible to the user. Thus, when a sensitvity analysis is performed and a result is obtained, it is not always easy to evaluate the significance of this result. In other words, we can tell an evidential story and have a computer-based system supply an outcome. But we will not always be able to observe why this outcome seems sensible.

A very useful and commonly available computer-based tool now exists for the empirical study of equations for the inferential force of evidence; it is called a *spreadsheet*. Using your favorite spreadsheet, you can easily perform your own analyses of evidence in addition to the ones I now present. You can tell evidential stories of interest to you and be able to judge for yourself whether or not an equation produces an intuitive outcome. Using likelihood ratio equations I will provide for particular evidential situations, each new combination of ingredient probabilities identifies a new special case or "story." By studying special cases in addition to the ones I will describe, you may easily turn over "evidential rocks" that have escaped my attention, and in the process you may identify additional evidential subtleties of interest and importance in your own work. This is another way of saying that I do not regard the following analyses as exhaustive in identifying interesting attributes of evidence.

Chapter 7

Analyses of Isolated Items of Evidence

It would be quite difficult to defend the assertion that a certain probabilistic inference has precisely one stage of reasoning from an item of evidence to hypotheses of interest. Someone may easily recognize sources of uncertainty, interposed between the evidence and hypotheses, that we had not considered. For example, suppose we have a direct testimonial assertion H^*, from an eyewitness, that hypothesis H is true. We might argue: If this person is absolutely credible, that settles it, H is true. But someone may suggest that we decompose the inference from H^* to $\{H, H^c\}$ in order to represent uncertainties associated with attributes of this person's credibility. In another case we might be prepared to argue that the known occurrence of event E is related to hypotheses $\{H, H^c\}$ by a single stage. But we have to suppose, as in Bernoulli's case 3 in Figure 6.3, that the credibility of our tangible or testimonial evidence about E is perfect in order to justify a single-stage inference from E to $\{H, H^c\}$. In short, virtually all inferences we encounter are *cascaded* or *catenated,* as Wigmore recognized within the context of law. Such inferences involve reasoning chains having links whose number is determined by the uncertainties we recognize in arguments constructed from evidence to hypotheses of concern. In this chapter our analyses of the inferential force of evidence begin with an examination of chains of reasoning of various lengths.

7.1 EVIDENCE AND SINGLY CONNECTED CHAINS OF REASONING

My first analytic task is to consider Bayesian and Baconian views of several evidential matters that can best be illustrated using uncomplicated chains of reasoning. By "uncomplicated" I refer to chains that are are singly connected;

namely there are no conditional nonindependencies lurking about in our reasoning chain (we will find some later on in Section 7.2). To set the stage for this analysis, we consider the reasoning chains shown in Figure 7.1. The single-stage reasoning chain in this figure involves an inference from the *known occurrence* of event E_1 to hypotheses $\{H, H^c\}$ and corresponds to

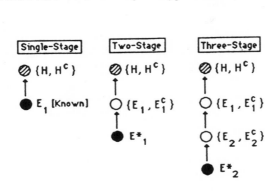

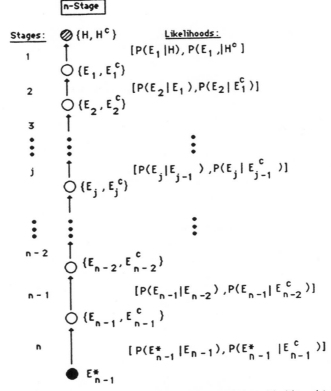

FIGURE 7.1 Singly connected reasoning chains and their likelihood ingredients.

Bernoulli's case 3. Here we suppose the existence of perfectly credible evidence about the occurrence of event E_1. In this case event E_1 provides only some grounds for an inference about hypothesis H; we may have E_1 when H is true but also when it is not. For the two-stage inference suppose that evidence E_1^*, about event E_1, comes from a source whose credibility is not perfect; there is some chance that we may have E_1^* when E_1 did not occur. Our inference in this case corresponds to Bernoulli's case 4 in Figure 6.3. The three-stage chain of reasoning in Figure 7.1 arises if we cannot obtain any direct evidence of E_1. Suppose we can obtain evidence E_2^* about an event E_2 that provides inconclusive grounds for a belief in E_1.

Now consider the n-stage inference in Figure 7.1. The first analyses I will offer rest upon Bayesian likelihood ratios for the inferential force of evidence involving singly connected chains of reasoning of any length. As we will observe, these likelihood ratios require two likelihoods at each stage in a reasoning chain. For a single-stage inference from E_1 to $\{H, H^c\}$, the likelihood ratio for E_1 is $L_{E_1} = P(E_1|H)/P(E_1|H^c)$ provided that $P(E_1|H^c) \neq 0$. In Bayesian terms, this likelihood ratio prescribes the inferential force on hypotheses $\{H, H^c\}$ of the *known occurrence* of E_1. We now consider what happens when we obtain increasingly remote evidence of event E_1.

7.1.1 Reasoning Chain Length and "Inferential Drag"

A common belief is that the force of an item of evidence is diminished in proportion to the number of reasoning stages or sources of uncertainty interposed between the evidence and major hypotheses at issue. I noted in Section 3.3.1 a trial judge's comment that an inference piled on an inference has as much strength as Abraham Lincoln's soup made by boiling the shadow of a pigeon that had already been starved to death. The philosopher Hume said as much in quite different terms in his *Treatise of Human Nature*, as I noted in Section 2.2.5.

Likelihood ratios from Bayes's rule, applied to evidence and chains of reasoning of various lengths, allow us one way of interpreting the effects of reasoning chain length upon the inferential force of evidence. They also illustrate a number of other inferential matters involving chains of reasoning. We first should remind ourselves of the major conditional independence constraint we have so far imposed on the n-stage and singly connected chain of reasoning in Figure 7.1. Observe that the likelihoods shown at each stage involve events conditioned by other events at just the next highest stage and by none other. For later notational convenience I number stages of reasoning from the top (nearest $\{H, H^c\}$), so a higher stage has a lower number. For example, event E_2 is conditioned just by E_1 and E_1^c (and not by H or H^c); evidence E_{n-1}^* is conditioned by just E_{n-1} and E_{n-1}^c and by no other events higher in the chain of reasoning. For this particular n-stage inference, an event at stage j is conditionally independent of events at any stage *at or higher than $j - 2$*, given events at stage $j - 1$. A chain having such properties is called a *Markov chain.* As we proceed, we will observe that the intuitions of the judge and of Hume regarding chain length are essentially but not completely correct for Markov chains of reasoning. When we drop the requirement for singly connected chains of reasoning, their intuitions falter completely.

To illustrate how adding links in a chain of reasoning affects the inferential force of evidence, Peter Tillers and I introduced the concept of *inferential drag* to describe how each link added to a singly connected chain of reasoning puts an additional damper on the force of evidence in changing probabilistic belief about hypotheses of interest (Tillers and Schum 1992, 839). Each new link adds another component of drag. Another colleague, Ray Curts, noted the resemblance between the inferential drag to be described and the similarly additive parasitic drag induced by various forces on an aircraft. Curts and I collaborated on the following development of the concept of inferential drag.

To begin, suppose the single-stage inference in Figure 7.1. Since we know that E_1 has occurred, we can employ the full inferential force of E_1 given by $L_{E_1} = P(E_1|H)/P(E_1|H^c)$. In the following developments let us suppose that $P(E_1|H) > P(E_1|H^c)$; in words, the known occurrence of E_1 favors the occurrence or the truth of H over H^c. In this case there is no drag on our belief revision, since we are certain about the occurrence of E_1. Suppose, instead, we have evidence E_1^*, about E_1, that is not perfectly credible, so we now have the two-stage inference in Figure 7.1. The likelihood ratio for evidence E_1^* on hypotheses $\{H, H^c\}$ is defined as $L_{E_1^*} = P(E_1^*|H)/P(E_1^*|H^c)$. We observe, however, that E_1^* is not directly linked to hypotheses $\{H, H^c\}$ but only indirectly through events $\{E_1, E_1^c\}$. We need to expand the terms in $L_{E_1^*}$ to take account of these intermediate possibilities E_1 and E_1^c.

Taking the term $P(E_1^*|H) = P(E_1^*H)/P(H)$ as an example, we expand the numerator to be $P(E_1^*H) = P(E_1^*E_1H) + P(E_1^*E_1^cH)$. Here is recognition of the fact that we may have evidence E_1^* when event E_1 is true, but we may also have E_1^* when E_1 is not true. Applying the general product rule (or chain rule) to these two joint probabilities, we have $P(E_1^*E_1H) = P(H)P(E_1|H)P(E_1^*|E_1H)$ and $P(E_1^*E_1^cH) = P(H)P(E_1^c|H)P(E_1^*|E_1^cH)$. The term $P(H)$ is isolated in such expansion, and it vanishes when we divide the expanded form of $P(E_1^*H)$ by $P(H)$ to obtain $P(E_1^*|H)$. Thus $P(E_1^*|H) = P(E_1|H)P(E_1^*|E_1H) + P(E_1^c|H)P(E_1^*|E_1^cH)$. We notice that $P(E_1^c|H) = 1 - P(E_1|H)$; then with a bit of algebra we can express $P(E_1^*|H) = P(E_1|H)[P(E_1^*|E_1H) - P(E_1^*|E_1^cH)] + P(E_1^*|E_1^cH)$. By exactly the same development, we obtain $P(E_1^*|H^c) = P(E_1|H^c)[P(E_1^*|E_1H^c) - P(E_1^*|E_1^cH^c)] + P(E_1^*|E_1^cH^c)$.

We will encounter much longer chains of reasoning. In every case the expansion of terms such as $P(E^*|H)$ and $P(E^*|H^c)$ proceeds in exactly the same way as in the simple two-stage expansion just described. The number of terms in an expansion depends upon the number of reasoning stages interposed between E^* and $\{H, H^c\}$.

Since we are presently considering a singly connected chain of reasoning in which an event at one stage is conditioned only by events at the next higher stage, we note the following conditional independencies: $P(E_1^*|E_1H) = P(E_1^*|E_1H^c) = P(E_1^*|E_1)$ and $P(E_1^*|E_1^cH) = P(E_1^*|E_1^cH^c) = P(E_1^*|E_1^c)$. We can now express $P(E_1^*|H) = P(E_1|H)[P(E_1^*|E_1) - P(E_1^*|E_1^c)] + P(E_1^*|E_1^c)$ and $P(E_1^*|H^c) = P(E_1|H^c)[P(E_1^*|E_1) - P(E_1^*|E_1^c)] + P(E_1^*|E_1^c)$, so the likelihood ratio for evidence E_1^* is

$$L_{E_1^*} = \frac{P(E_1|H)[P(E_1^*|E_1) - P(E_1^*|E_1^c)] + P(E_1^*|E_1^c)}{P(E_1|H^c)[P(E_1^*|E_1) - P(E_1^*|E_1^c)] + P(E_1^*|E_1^c)} \qquad (7.1)$$

For developments to follow, we need a simpler notation. Let $P(E_1|H) = a_1$ and $P(E_1|H^c) = b_1$; let $P(E_1^*|E_1) = a_2$ and $P(E_1^*|E_1^c) = b_2$. Equation 7.1 can then be expressed as

$$L_{E_1^*} = \frac{a_1(a_2 - b_2) + b_2}{b_1(a_2 - b_2) + b_2} = \frac{a_1 + [(b_2)/(a_2 - b_2)]}{b_1 + [(b_2)/(a_2 - b_2)]}. \qquad (7.2)$$

Using the right-hand expression in Equation 7.2, we can now identify the source of inferential drag in a two-stage chain of reasoning. This drag is associated with the imperfect credibility of evidence E_1^*. Recall that if we knew for certain that event E_1 had occurred, we would be able to use its full inferential force given by the likelihood ratio $L_{E_1} = a_1/b_1$. Inferential drag (D) is zero for a single-stage inference, so we might express the likelihood ratio for E_1 as $L_{E_1} = (a_1 + D)/(b_1 + D)$, where $D_1 = 0$. A subscript on D identifies the reasoning stage at which it occurs. When we add a second reasoning stage because our evidence E_1^* is not perfectly credible, we induce a drag component on *both* a_1 and b_1 as in Equation 7.2. This component is the quantity $D_2 = D_1 + [b_2/(a_2 - b_2)] = [b_2/(a_2 - b_2)]$, since $D_1 = 0$. As we will observe, drag accumulates recursively as we add reasoning stages.

Drag terms like D_2 have several interesting properties that we will make use of, the first of which is *directionality*. The sign of D_2 indicates the *inferential direction* of the force of evidence E_1^*. Positive values of D_2 mean that E_1^* favors E_1 which, as agreed above, favors H; negative D_2 means that E_1^* favors E_1^c which, according to Pascalian rules, must favor H^c if E_1 favors H. We begin by examining some limiting cases. First, if $b_2 = P(E_1^*|E_1^c)$ were zero, then $D_2 = 0$, in which case $L_{E_1^*} = a_1/b_1 = L_{E_1}$. If we believed that there was no chance that our evidence would tell us that event E_1 occurred when it did not, we are entitled to apply the full inferential force of E_1, as in a single-stage inference from the known occurrence of E_1. Now suppose that $a_2 = P(E_1^*|E)$ were zero, in which case $D_2 = -1.0$. If this were so, $L_{E_1^*} = (a_1 - 1)/(b_1 - 1) = -(1 - a_1)/-(1 - b_1) = P(E_1^c|H)/P(E_1^c|H^c) = L_{E_1^c}$. This is interesting since, if we believed the probability of evidence E_1^* to be zero, if E_1 did occur, then this evidence can only be consistent with the nonoccurrence of E_1, in which case we apply inferential force to E_1^* that favors H^c over H in the ratio $(1 - a_1)/(1 - b_1)$. Taken together, these two limiting cases show us that $(1 - a_1)/(1 - b_1) \le L_{E_1^*} \le a_1/b_1$. In words, this expression says that

$L_{E_1^*}$ is bounded above by the inferential force of knowing E_1 for sure and is bounded below by the inferential force of knowing E_1^c for sure. As we will later observe, there are no such bounds on $L_{E_1^*}$ when we add a direct linkage between E_1^* and hypotheses $\{H, H^c\}$.

Let us suppose that neither a_2 nor b_2 are zero. We will later profit by identifying terms *involving evidence*, such as $a_2 = P(E_1^*|E_1)$, as the probability of a *hit*; our evidence says event E_1 occurred when in fact it did. We will also define evidence terms such as $b_2 = P(E_1^*|E_1^c)$ as the probability of a *false-positive*, the probability that the evidence says event E_1 occurred when it did not. As a third limiting case we need to consider what happens to D_2 as the *difference* between a_2 and b_2 gets smaller. In Figure 7.2 consider the point identified as $a_2 = b_2$ on the a_2 probability scale. For any fixed $b_2 > 0$, as a_2 approaches b_2 from above, D_2 increases positively without bound. As a_2 approaches b_2 from below, D_2 increases negatively without bound. So in this third limiting case we learn that the drag at stage two increases as the difference between hit and false-positive probabilities gets smaller relative to the size of the false-positive probability. As we will later observe, interesting things happen when both hit and false-positive probabilities are both very small. Although the right-hand expression in Equation 7.2 is undefined when $a_2 = b_2$, we can use the middle expression in Equation 7.2 to observe that when $a_2 = b_2$, $L_{E_1^*} = 1.0$, meaning that E_1^* has no inferential force at all. This seems intuitive. If we believe that our evidence E_1^* is just as likely if E_1 occurred as if E_1 did not occur, then this evidence can hardly have any inferential force, since it is uninformative about whether or not E_1 did occur.

Figure 7.2 shows other interesting limits on D_2. These limits show us why there is no value of D_2 that produces negative values of $L_{E_1^*}$. For any fixed value of $0 < b_2 < 1.0$, as a_2 approaches 1.0, D_2 approaches $b_2/(1 - b_2)$, in which case $L_{E_1^*} > 1$ since $b_2/(1 - b_2)$ is always positive. For any fixed value of $b_2 > 0$, as a_2 approaches zero, D_2 approaches -1, in which case $L_{E_1^*} = P(E_1^c|H)/P(E_1^c|H^c) = L_{E_1^c}$. So, when $b_2 > 0$, D_2 takes no values in the interval $-1 < D_2 < b_2/(1 - b_2)$, and as a result $L_{E_1^*}$ is always positive, as we require. Again, as Figure 7.2 illustrates, positive values of D_2 mean that E_1^* favors H, and negative values of D_2 mean that E_1^* favors H^c.

We identify D_2 as the *drag* induced at stage two for the following reasons: Increasingly positive values of D_2 make the numerator and denominator of Equation 7.2 closer together and thus indicate the weakening of the inferential force of E_1^* favoring H. Values of D_2 increasingly less than the value -1 also bring the numerator and denominator of Equation 7.2 closer together. For example, suppose that $a_1 = 0.98$ and $b_1 = 0.01$, which means that the *known occurrence* of E_1 will have a very strong inferential force favoring H over H^c in the ratio 98:1. If D_2 is, say, 1.0, then $L_{E_1^*} = (0.98 + 1)/(0.01 + 1) = 1.96$. With $D_2 = 1.0$, we have a very powerful drag on our opinion revision regarding $\{H, H^c\}$, since the force of evidence E_1^* is $98/1.96 = 50$ times smaller than the force of knowing E_1 for sure. We can express this result in credibility-related terms. For $D_2 = 1$ we have a hit probability $a_2 = P(E^*|E)$ that is

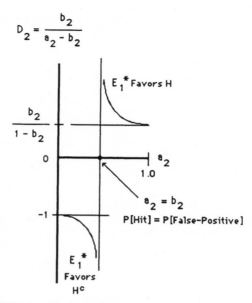

FIGURE 7.2   The bounds on an inferential drag coefficient.

just twice the value of a false-positive probability $b_2 = P(E_1^*|E_1^c)$. This low ratio of hit to false-positive probabilities provides a very substantial drag on our opinion revision regarding $\{H, H^c\}$ based on evidence E_1^*.

Before we proceed with analyses of longer chains of reasoning, there is another characteristic of Equation 7.2 that we will encounter in every Bayesian analysis of the inferential force of evidence. Notice that the term D_2 gets applied to both a_1 and b_1. This result is not as innocuous as it may appear. It alerts us to the fact that in a two-stage inference we need to have *specific values* of a_1 and b_1, and not simply their ratio which is all we would need in a single-stage inference based on the known occurrence of E_1. The significance of this fact is that it identifies a Bayesian mechanism for incorporating information about the *rareness* or *improbability* of the event reported in evidence. Bayes's rule responds to the *difference* as well as to the *ratio* of certain probabilistic ingredients of likelihood ratios, a fact we will explore further in Section 7.1.3.

Now consider the three-stage inference shown in Figure 7.1. In this case we have circumstantial but no direct evidence of event E_1. We now have evidence E_2^* about an event E_1 which, if it occurred, provides just some ground for a belief that E_1 occurred. We will suppose that the credibility of evidence E_2^* is not perfect. What we desire is the likelihood ratio $L_{E_2^*} = P(E_2^*|H)/P(E_2^*|H^c)$. Using the same procedure we followed in formulating

$L_{E_1^*}$, we expand these two conditional probabilities taking, account of intermediate event classes $\{E_2, E_2^c\}$, and $\{E_1, E_1^c\}$. The result is

$$L_{E_2^*} = \frac{a_1 + b_2/(a_2 - b_2) + b_3/[(a_2 - b_2)(a_3 - b_3)]}{b_1 + b_2/(a_2 - b_2) + b_3/[(a_2 - b_2)(a_3 - b_3)]}$$

$$= \frac{a_1 + D_2 + b_3/[(a_2 - b_2)(a_3 - b_3)]}{b_1 + D_2 + b_3/[(a_2 - b_2)(a_3 - b_3)]} \tag{7.3}$$

As in Equation 7.2, $a_1 = P(E_1|H)$ and $b_1 = P(E_1|H^c)$. But at the second stage in the reasoning chain, $a_2 = P(E_2|E_1)$ and $b_2 = P(E_2|E_1^c)$. At the third stage of reasoning, $a_3 = P(E_2^*|E_2)$ and $b_3 = P(E_2^*|E_2^c)$. These last two terms are hit and false-positive probabilities, since they concern evidence E_2^*. Using Figure 7.3, we can now begin to see what is happening to inferential drag as we add reasoning stages. For a single stage of reasoning we had $D_1 = 0$, and for a two-stage inference we had $D_2 = D_1 + [b_2/(a_2 - b_2)] = 0 + [b_2/(a_2 - b_2)]$. We now observe in Equation 7.3 that $D_3 = D_2 + [b_3/(a_2 - b_2)(a_3 - b_3)]$; drag accumulates as we add reasoning stages.

Adding a fourth stage for evidence E_3^* about event E_3 which is inconclusive on E we have

$$L_{E_3^*} = \frac{\begin{array}{l}a_1 + b_2/(a_2 - b_2) + b_3/[(a_2 - b_2)(a_3 - b_3)]\\ + b_4/[(a_2 - b_2)(a_3 - b_3)(a_4 - b_4)]\end{array}}{\begin{array}{l}b_1 + b_2/(a_2 - b_2) + b_3/[(a_2 - b_2)(a_3 - b_3)]\\ + b_4/[(a_2 - b_2)(a_3 - b_3)(a_4 - b_4)]\end{array}}$$

$$= \frac{a_1 + D_3 + b_4/[(a_2 - b_2)(a_3 - b_3)(a_4 - b_4)]}{b_1 + D_3 + b_4/[(a_2 - b_2)(a_3 - b_3)(a_4 - b_4)]}. \tag{7.4}$$

For $L_{E_3^*}$ in Equation 7.4, a_1, a_2, b_1, and b_2 are defined as in Equation 7.2, but now $a_3 = P(E_3|E_2)$, $b_3 = P(E_3|E_2^c)$, $a_4 = P(E_3^*|E_3)$, and $b_4 = P(E_3^*|E_3^c)$. The last two terms are hit and false-positive probabilities for evidence E_3^*.

A general recursive pattern involving inferential drag emerges as shown in Figure 7.3. For an n-stage chain of reasoning based upon evidence E_{n-1}^* about event E_{n-1}, we have

$$L_{E_{n-1}^*} = \frac{a_1 + D_{n-1} + b_n \bigg/ \prod_{i=2}^{n} (a_i - b_i)}{b_1 + D_{n-1} + b_n \bigg/ \prod_{i=2}^{n} (a_i - b_i)} \tag{7.5}$$

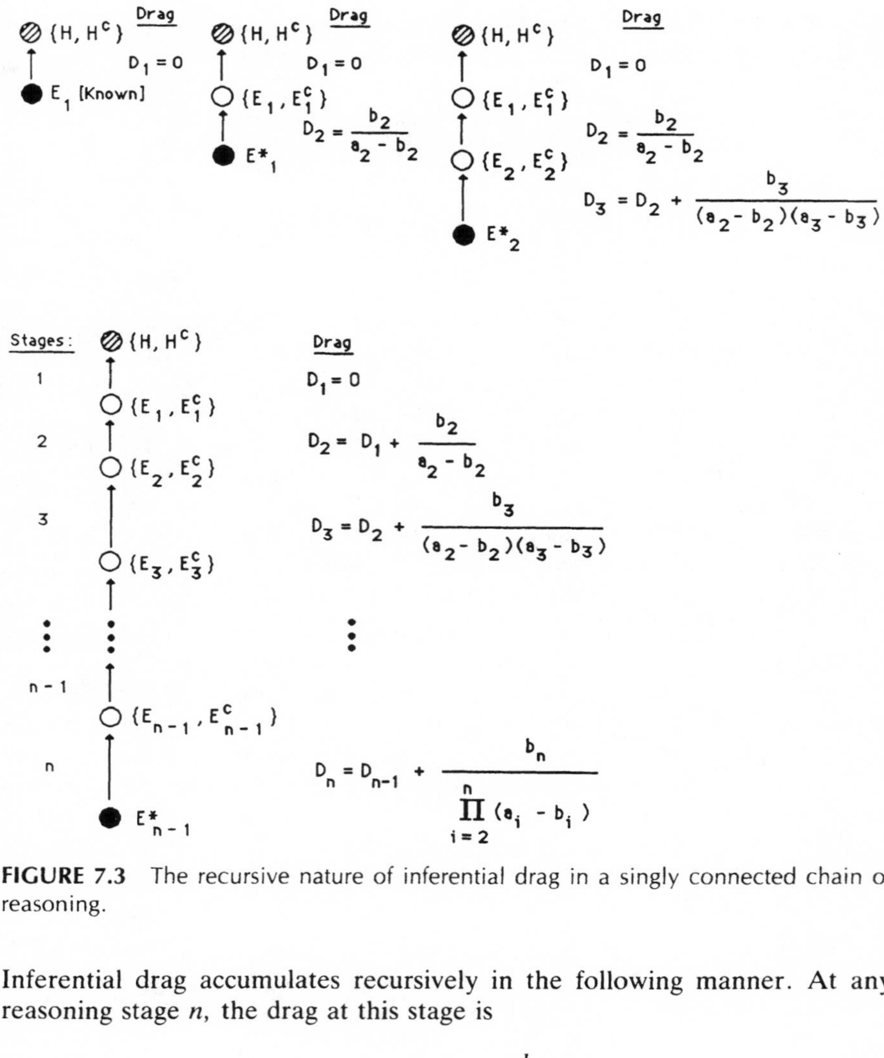

$\oslash \{H, H^c\} \xrightarrow{\text{Drag}}$

$\uparrow \qquad D_1 = 0$

$\bullet E_1 \text{ [Known]}$

$\oslash \{H, H^c\} \xrightarrow{\text{Drag}}$

$\uparrow \qquad D_1 = 0$

$\bigcirc \{E_1, E_1^c\}$

$\uparrow \qquad D_2 = \dfrac{b_2}{a_2 - b_2}$

$\bullet E^*_1$

$\oslash \{H, H^c\} \qquad \xrightarrow{\text{Drag}}$

$\uparrow \qquad\qquad D_1 = 0$

$\bigcirc \{E_1, E_1^c\}$

$\uparrow \qquad\qquad D_2 = \dfrac{b_2}{a_2 - b_2}$

$\bigcirc \{E_2, E_2^c\}$

$\uparrow \qquad\qquad D_3 = D_2 + \dfrac{b_3}{(a_2 - b_2)(a_3 - b_3)}$

$\bullet E^*_2$

Stages:

$\oslash \{H, H^c\} \qquad \xrightarrow{\text{Drag}}$

1 $\qquad \uparrow \qquad\qquad D_1 = 0$

$\bigcirc \{E_1, E_1^c\}$

2 $\qquad \uparrow \qquad\qquad D_2 = D_1 + \dfrac{b_2}{a_2 - b_2}$

$\bigcirc \{E_2, E_2^c\}$

3 $\qquad \uparrow \qquad\qquad D_3 = D_2 + \dfrac{b_3}{(a_2 - b_2)(a_3 - b_3)}$

$\bigcirc \{E_3, E_3^c\}$

$\vdots$

$n-1 \qquad \uparrow$

$\bigcirc \{E_{n-1}, E_{n-1}^c\}$

$n \qquad \uparrow \qquad\qquad D_n = D_{n-1} + \dfrac{b_n}{\prod\limits_{i=2}^{n} (a_i - b_i)}$

$\bullet E^*_{n-1}$

FIGURE 7.3 The recursive nature of inferential drag in a singly connected chain of reasoning.

Inferential drag accumulates recursively in the following manner. At any reasoning stage n, the drag at this stage is

$$D_n = D_{n-1} + \frac{b_n}{\prod\limits_{i=2}^{n} (a_i - b_i)} \tag{7.6}$$

So, we can express $L_{E^*_{n-1}}$ as

$$L_{E^*_{n-1}} = \frac{a_1 + D_n}{b_1 + D_n} \tag{7.7}$$

Equations 7.5, 7.6, and 7.7 are undefined if $a_i = b_i$, for any $i \geq 2$. We can identify D_n as the *drag coefficient* for an n-stage chain of reasoning. It has properties similar to the special case D_2 we identified above. Positive values of D_n mean that evidence E_{n-1}^* at the bottom of the chain favors H; negative values of D_n mean that E_{n-1}^* favors H^c. The larger that D_n is, positively or negatively, the weaker is the inferential force of E_{n-1}^*. Examination of limiting cases of D_n in Equation 7.7 will be useful in our later analyses. First, if D_n is zero, the force of evidence E_{n-1}. cannot exceed the force of knowing E_1 *for sure*, as expressed by the likelihood ratio $L_{E_{n-1}^*} = a_1/b_1 = P(E_1|H)/P(E_1|H^c)$. This special case occurs if $b_j = 0$, for every $j \geq 2$. Another limiting case occurs when $D_n = -1$. In this case we have $L_{E_{n-1}^*} = P(E_1^c|H)/P(E_1^c|H^c)$, the inferential force of knowing *for sure* that E_1 did *not* occur. This special case occurs when the following three conditions hold: (1) $a_j = 0$, for every $j \geq 2$, (2) $b_j = 1$, for every $j \geq 2$, and (3) the number of stages below the first is odd. When the first two of these conditions holds and the number of stages below the first is even, $D_n = 0$ (these conditions can be observed in the special case in Equation 7.4). Thus the force of evidence $L_{E_{n-1}^*}$ is bounded above by the force of knowing E_1 for sure and is bounded below by the force of knowing E_1^c for sure.

We are now in a position to state, in Bayesian terms, how the force of evidence is diminished as we add new links in a singly connected chain of reasoning. At each stage of reasoning, inferential drag is introduced in an amount determined by the likelihoods necessary at this stage. Consider stage j in Figure 7.1 and its two likelihoods: $P(E_j|E_{j-1}) = a_j$ and $P(E_j|E_{j-1}^c) = b_j$. No *additional* inferential drag is induced at this stage only if $b_j = 0$. For $b_j > 0$ the amount of drag induced is determined by the size of b_j and by the difference between a_j and b_j. As the *difference* between the likelihoods at any stage decreases, the drag induced at this stage increases. Once again we note that Bayes's rule responds to likelihood differences as well as to their ratios. If likelihoods a_j and b_j are close together in value, this simply says that the inferential linkage between E_j and events $\{E_{j-1}, E_{j-1}^c\}$ at the next higher stage is not very strong. Further, as Equation 7.6 tells us, the inferential drag induced at stage j is inherited by every stage of reasoning below stage j. Notice, for example, that the difference $(a_2 - b_2)$ appears in all terms in Equation 7.6. Some interesting implications of this fact are discussed in Section 7.1.2.

In a Bayesian view weaknesses in inferential linkages accumulate as linkages are added. As we obtain increasingly remote evidence about an event that we believe to be directly linked to our hypotheses, the force of this evidence diminishes. To this extent the intuitions of the judge mentioned above and of the philosopher Hume are essentially correct. It should be noted, however, that if the inferential linkage at every stage below E_1 were perfect (i.e., every $b_i = 0$ for $i \geq 2$), then the inferential force of evidence E_{n-1}, would be the same as the inferential force of knowing E_1 for sure, since in this case $L_{E_{n-1}^*} = L_{E_1}$. Unfortunately, we are not likely to encounter any n-stage inference in which an event at any stage is conclusive on an event at the next higher stage. This would amount to saying that we have a deductive or demonstrative chain of reasoning from E_{n-1} to E_1. We will have further need of Equations 7.1 through 7.7 regarding inferential drag, since they have a variety of useful properties.

We can give an entirely different analysis of the weakening of progressively longer chains of reasoning. Suppose we adopt the eliminative and variative approach to inference along Baconian lines, as discussed in Section 5.5.3 and illustrated in Figure 5.10. As was mentioned earlier, the major Baconian mechanism for passing from one stage to another in a chain of reasoning involves the testing of generalizations appropriate to each stage and the *detachment of beliefs* based upon the (ancillary) test results we obtain. But unless our testing at each stage is complete in the sense that we have performed all relevant tests, we leave unanswered questions behind at each stage. Consider Figure 7.4, and suppose that at stage n we have performed j of the n_n tests that we believed relevant in justifying an inference from E_{n-1}^* to E_{n-1}. At this stage we have left unanswered $U_n = (n_n - j)$ questions. Figure 7.4 shows the number of questions that we leave unanswered at each stage. The total number of questions we leave unanswered is the sum $\mathbf{U_n}$. As we make a chain of reasoning longer, we tend to leave behind more unanswered questions about the strength of its links, so the force of evidence E_{n-1}^* is, in Baconian terms, naturally weakened.

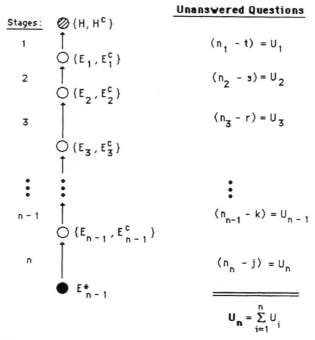

FIGURE 7.4 A Baconian interpretation of the weakening of a chain of reasoning as it is made longer.

We can at this point put a finishing touch on an assessment of the inferential strength of Officer Connolly's testimony in the Sacco and Vanzetti case. Whether we adopt the eight-stage chain of reasoning in Figure 3.5 or the ten-stage chain of reasoning in Figure 3.9, we have to conclude, based upon the virtual absence of ancillary evidence to support most of the links in this chain, that we are out on a very long and very slender limb if we infer, based upon Connolly's testimony, that Sacco had knowledge of guilt. We might easily conclude that, by itself, this testimony has as much strength as Abraham Lincoln's soup made by boiling the shadow of a pigeon already starved to death.

7.1.2 Weak Links in a Chain of Reasoning

If a chain of probabilistic reasoning from an item of evidence to hypotheses $\{H, H^c\}$ is to have a weak link, does it matter to the inferential force of this evidence where in the chain this weak link is located? There is a related question of some importance: Is it preferable to have a weak foundation for a strong argument or a strong foundation for a weak argument? To answer these questions, we first make reference to earlier discussion of argument construction. I noted in Chapter 3 that the direct relevance of an item of evidence on hypotheses, say, $\{H, H^c\}$, must be established by an argument or a chain of reasoning. Then, in the discussion of Figure 4.1, I noted that we could identify different arguments in terms of the event classes at nodes directly linked to hypotheses $\{H, H^c\}$. Thus in Figure 4.1 we have an $A_1 = \{A_1, A_1^c\}$ argument, an $A_2 = \{A_2, A_2^c\}$ argument, and so on. The *foundation* for any of these arguments is provided by the evidence we have and by how it is linked to one of the arguments. For example, in Figure 4.1 we have evidence B^*, C^*, and D^* forming the foundation for argument A_1 according to the linkage patterns illustrated. We will now make use of these ideas in an analysis of the force of evidence in the singly connected chains of reasoning shown in Figure 7.1.

Suppose an E_1 argument whose events $\{E_1, E_1^c\}$ are directly linked to hypotheses of interest $\{H, H^c\}$. The single-stage chain of reasoning in Figure 7.1 rests on the *known occurrence* of event E_1. The inferential force on $\{H, H^c\}$ of knowing E_1 occurred is given, in Bayesian terms, by the likelihood ratio $L_{E_1} = P(E_1|H)/P(E_1|H^c) = a_1/b_1$. But now suppose we do not know that event E_1 occurred but only have evidence for it that is remote to various possible degrees. The evidence we have *about* E_1 forms the *foundation* for our argument based *upon* E_1. As we obtain more remote evidence bearing upon the occurrence of E_1, the foundation for our argument from E_1 to $\{H, H^c\}$ contains more successive stages and, in singly connected chains of reasoning, is generally weaker. So in Equation 7.7 the terms a_1 and b_1 concern the strength of our argument from E_1, and the inferential drag term D_n concerns the strength of the foundation for this argument. The smaller the drag, the stronger is the foundation.

In the singly connected chains of reasoning we are considering, answers to the two related questions mentioned above depend upon whether we think in Bayesian or Baconian terms. Taking the Bayesian view first, a chain of reasoning cannot be any stronger than its weakest link, wherever in the chain this weak link is located. In addition Bayesian analyses of singly connected chains of reasoning show that a strong foundation for a weak argument is not to be preferred over a weak foundation for a strong argument. I will first explore these conclusions analytically and then provide some examples.

Consider Equation 7.5 and the special case of it in Equation 7.4. Because of the recursive nature of the inferential drag coefficient, as we make evidence more remote, a weakness at any stage gets passed along to succeeding stages. Observe in Equation 7.4, for example, that if the ratio $b_2/(a_2 - b_2)$ at the second stage were large, indicating significant inferential drag and a weak link, this drag will be passed along to each successive stage. Thus, having a strong link at a more remote stage cannot overcome the effects of a weak link at an earlier stage. On the other hand, suppose that at the nth stage the likelihood difference $(a_n - b_n)$ were small relative to the size of b_n. This would give rise to substantial inferential drag, since the *product* of the other $(a_i - b_i)$ terms must lie between -1 and $+1$. Thus a large drag at the most remote stage is not overcome by small drag at earlier stages, since drag is additive in nature. Now consider Equation 7.7 in which the terms a_1 and b_1 concern the strength of the E_1 argument and the D_n term concerns the strength of its foundation. If our argument is strong (a_1 and b_1 differ considerably), this does not help the force of evidence E_{n-1}^* unless D_n is very small. On the other hand, a very small D_n does not help if a_1 and b_1 do not differ considerably. Thus, in Bayesian terms, a weak foundation for a strong argument has the same effect in reducing the force of evidence as does a strong foundation for a weak argument.

Consider the two sets of examples shown in parts A and B of Table 7.1. To give an adequate account of the manner in which likelihood ratios justify the conclusions just mentioned, we must consider two conditions concerning the *inferential symmetry* of likelihood assessments. Consider the two likelihoods $P(E_i|E_{i-1})$ and $P(E_i|E_{i-1}^c)$ at any stage i. There is no Pascalian requirement that these two probabilities must normalize or sum to 1.0. However, we are not prevented from assessing likelihoods that do normalize. Normalized likelihoods indicate inferential symmetry in the following sense: Suppose that $P(E_i|E_{i-1}) > P(E_i|E_{i-1}^c)$ so that E_i favors the occurrence of E_{i-1}. If these likelihoods normalize, then E_i^c will favor E_{i-1}^c to exactly the same extent that E_i favors E_{i-1}. For example, suppose that $P(E_i|E_{i-1}) = 0.9$ and $P(E_i|E_{i-1}^c) = 0.1$. By normalization rules, this must mean that $P(E_i^c|E_{i-1}) = 0.1$ and $P(E_i^c|E_{i-1}^c) = 0.9$. Thus E_i favors E_{i-1} in the ratio 9:1, but E_i^c also favors E_{i-1}^c in the ratio 9:1. Nonnormalized likelihoods do not have this symmetry property. Whether we employ normalized or nonnormalized likelihoods does affect the conclusions we reach in our analyses of weak links in chains of reasoning.

TABLE 7.1 A Weak Link Located at Various Points in a Chain of Reasoning

Stage	Likelihoods	A. Nonnormalized Likelihoods				
		Case 1	Case 2	Case 3	Case 4	Case 5
1	$a_1 = P(E_1|H)$	0.9999	0.9999	0.9999	**0.60**	0.9999
	$b_1 = P(E_1|H^c)$	0.0010	0.0010	0.0010	**0.15**	0.0010
2	$a_2 = P(E_2|E_1)$	0.9999	0.9999	**0.60**	0.9999	0.9999
	$b_2 = P(E_2|E_1^c)$	0.0010	0.0010	**0.15**	0.0010	0.0010
3	$a_3 = P(E_3|E_2)$	0.9999	**0.60**	0.9999	0.9999	0.9999
	$b_3 = P(E_3|E_2^c)$	0.0010	**0.15**	0.0010	0.0010	0.0010
4	$a_4 = P(E_3^*|E_3)$	**0.60**	0.9999	0.9999	0.9999	0.9999
	$b_4 = P(E_3^*|E_3^c)$	**0.15**	0.0010	0.0010	0.0010	0.0010
	D_4	0.336	0.337	0.338	0.003	0.0030
	$L_{E_1^*}$	3.963	3.956	3.949	3.941	250.73

Stage	Likelihoods	B. Normalized Likelihoods			
		Case 1	Case 2	Case 3	Case 4
1	$a_1 = P(E_1|H)$	0.99	0.95	0.89	**0.80**
	$b_1 = P(E_1|H^c)$	0.01	0.05	0.11	**0.20**
2	$a_2 = P(E_2|E_1)$	0.89	0.99	**0.80**	0.99
	$b_2 = P(E_2|E_1^c)$	0.11	0.01	**0.20**	0.01
3	$a_3 = P(E_3|E_2)$	0.95	**0.80**	0.95	0.89
	$b_3 = P(E_3|E_2^c)$	0.05	**0.20**	0.05	0.11
4	$a_4 = P(E_3^*|E_3)$	**0.80**	0.89	0.99	0.95
	$b_4 = P(E_3^*|E_3^c)$	**0.20**	0.11	0.01	0.05
	D_4	0.687	0.590	0.445	0.227
	$L_{E_1^*}$	2.406	2.406	2.406	2.406

The five cases shown in part A of Table 7.1 involve a four-stage chain of reasoning; observe that none of the required likelihood pairs at any stage in these five cases normalize. First, consider cases 1 through 4, all of which contain three links that are very strong and one that is weak. The only difference in these cases concerns which of the four links is the weak one. The three strong links in each case are equally strong, each having likelihoods 0.9999 and 0.0010. The weak link in each case, shown in bold type, has likelihoods 0.60 and 0.15. Cases 1 through 3 represent instances in which we have a *weak foundation for a strong argument*. First, an argument concerning {H, H^c}, based on the known occurrence of E_1, would be very strong in each of these cases, since the likelihood ratio L_{E_1} = 999.9. The trouble is that in each of these cases all we have is the remote evidence E_3^* that is linked through three reasoning stages to E_1. In each of these cases one of the links between evidence E_3^* and event E_1 is weak; in other words, we have a *weak foundation for a strong argument*. Using the information in Table 7.1 in Equation 7.4, we obtain the inferential drag coefficient D_4 and the likelihood ratio $L_{E_3^*}$ for cases 1–3. Note that these three $L_{E_3^*}$ values are close but not identical in value. This is a consequence of the fact that the likelihoods in this case do not normalize. Thus, according to Bayes's rule, it matters very little which of the foundation links is the weak one as cases 1–3 illustrate. We also notice that the likelihood ratios in each of these cases is less than the ratio of the "weak link" likelihoods, which equals $0.60/0.15 = 4$. The strength of the entire chain of reasoning in each of these cases does not exceed the strength of their weakest link.

Case 4 in Table 7.1 represents a *strong foundation for a weak argument*. In this case the weak link concerns the argument from E_1 to $\{H, H^c\}$. If we knew for sure that E_1 occurred, its likelihood ratio $L_{E_1} = 0.60/0.15 = 4$. But the foundation linkages from evidence E_3^* to E_1 are all equally strong and are in the ratio 999.9:1. From Equation 7.4 we determine inferential drag $D_4 = 0.003$, which differs considerably from the drag in cases 1–3. We expect this to happen, since the foundation was weak in the first three cases and strong in case 4. However, notice in case 4 that $L_{E_3^*} = 3.941$ and is very close to the values of $L_{E_3^*}$ in cases 1–3. This illustrates a Bayesian indifference between a weak argument based on a strong foundation and a strong argument based on a weak foundation. Case 5 in Table 7.1 shows a strong argument based on a strong foundation; each link in the chain of reasoning in this case is probabilistically very strong. I include it only to show that the intuitions of the trial judge and Hume about the strength of singly connected chains of reasoning were only partially correct. Evidence E_3^* in this case has very substantial inferential force ($L_{E_3^*} = 250.73$), even though it is three stages removed from E_1 and four stages removed from $\{H, H^c\}$.

Now consider the cases in part B of Table 7.1. First, note that the required likelihood pairs normalize at each stage in all four cases; namely there is inferential symmetry at each stage. Also observe that the three strong links in each case are not equally strong as they were in the cases in part A. The weak link in each case in part B has the same ratio of likelihoods as in the cases in part A except that these likelihoods normalize. Cases 1–3 show weak foundations for strong arguments. The foundations in these cases, as those in part A, are rendered weak by the presence of a weak link. Observe that, though the value of D_4 differs in each case, $L_{E_3^*}$ is identical in each case. In case 4 we have a reasonably strong foundation for a weak argument; $L_{E_3^*}$ takes the same value as in the first three cases. For any case shown in part B, the strong links can be permuted in $3! = 6$ ways. Thus, given the four likelihood pairs shown in these examples, there are 24 possible examples I might have given. As easily verified, all 24 cases have exactly the same likelihood ratio. Finally, observe that $L_{E_3^*}$ in each of these four cases is less than the ratio of likelihoods $(0.8/0.2 = 4)$ at the weakest stage.

In Baconian analyses of reasoning chains it does matter where in a chain a weak link is located. Correspondingly a different answer is given to issues concerning the relative strengths of an argument and its foundation. In discussing chains of reasoning, or *inference upon inference*, Jonathan Cohen states: "Proof is something that may depend on what is probably inferable from known facts, but not on what is certainly inferable from probable ones" (1977, 73). In other words, a strong foundation for a weak argument *is preferable* to a weak foundation for a strong argument. The Baconian view on this matter can be illustrated using a different metaphor as in Figure 7.5. When we reason from one stage to another, we go out on an inferential limb whose length and strength depends upon the *favorableness and completeness* of relevant eliminative and variative tests of the generalization that warrants this reasoning stage. The more evidential tests this generalization has passed, the stronger is the inferential limb on which we find ourselves. Thus a belief detached at this stage is well supported to the extent that we have favorable test results and completeness of evidential coverage of matters judged relevant in testing this generalization.

Suppose that, as in Figure 7.5a, my detached belief in E_1 is supported by the strong limb indicated by the thick line. I performed a variety of evidential tests of the generalization linking E_1^* and E_1 and found them to be favorable. But suppose that my tests of the generalization linking E_1 and H are not so complete and not so favorable; that is, this limb is weaker. In this situation I might say that I have a strong foundation for a weaker argument about H based on E_1. Now consider the situation depicted in Figure 7.5b in which the reverse is true. I have a very weak inferential limb (a weak foundation) attempting to support a stout limb (a strong argument). In another work I have noted how a weak inferential limb attempting to support a strong one seems to do so in defiance of gravity (Schum 1991, 122–131). The essential difference between the Bayesian and Baconian accounts of the effects of weak inferential links concerns the issue of ancillary evidential completeness. The Baconian view makes explicit the importance of evidential completeness or sufficiency in reasoning from one stage to another. On the Baconian view,

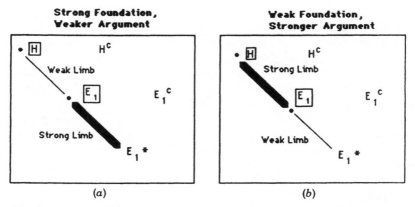

FIGURE 7.5 A Baconian response to the question: Which is preferable, a strong foundation for a weak argument or a weak foundation for a strong argument?

questions left unanswered regarding the foundation of an argument seem more serious than questions left unanswered regarding the argument itself. If we have only weak support for a belief that event E_1 has occurred, then it may matter very little how weak or strong is our argument from E_1 to hypotheses of interest.

7.1.3   Rare Events in a Chain of Reasoning

Consider stage j in the n-stage inference shown in Figure 7.1. At this stage we have the necessary likelihoods $a_j = P(E_j|E_{j-1})$ and $b_j = P(E_j|E_{j-1}^c)$. Suppose you believe that event E_j is quite *improbable*, whether or not E_{j-1} is true. We might then describe event E_j as a *rare event*, at least with respect to the occurrence of events $\{E_{j-1}, E_{j-1}^c\}$. But we also notice that if a_j and b_j are both small, then their difference $(a_j - b_j)$ will also be small. In the preceding section I mentioned that a small difference $(a_j - b_j)$ relative to b_j signifies a *weak link* at reasoning stage j. Thus we might be led to expect that Bayes's rule responds to stages involving rare events in the same way it responds to stages involving weak links. In particular, we might expect that it matters little in singly connected chains of reasoning where in the chain a rare event is located. But such expectation would be quite incorrect. One of the remarkable features of Bayes's rule, applied to chains of reasoning, is that it responds to differences as well as to ratios of pairs of likelihood ingredients. As I will now illustrate, *a link involving a rare event is not necessarily weak*.

Suppose that $a_j = 0.78$ and $b_j = 0.77$, in which case we have $(a_j - b_j) = 0.01$. In a singly connected chain of reasoning a likelihood pair having these values would certainly represent a weak link, causing very substantial inferential drag. In this case the ratio $a_j/b_j = 1.013$. Two large probabilities whose difference is small cannot have a large ratio. But two small probabilities whose difference is necessarily small can have a very large ratio. Consider an event E_j whose likelihoods at stage j are $a_j = 0.0090$ and $b_j = 0.0001$. In this case we have $(a_j - b_j) = 0.0089$ and $a_j/b_j = 90$. To observe the difference between these two cases in Bayesian likelihood ratio expressions, suppose that $j = 2$, so that we have the isolated expression $b_2/(a_2 - b_2)$ as in Equations 7.3 and 7.4. In the first case we have $b_2/(a_2 - b_2) = 0.77/0.01 = 77$, a drag component that would completely destroy the inferential force on $\{H, H^c\}$ of evidence on this chain. In the second case, however, $b_2/(a_2 - b_2) = 0.0001/0.0089 = 0.011$. This represents a very small drag component. Thus, even though these two cases involve similar likelihood *differences*, the force of evidence in each case is quite different. As we now consider, it very much matters to Bayesian gradations of the inferential force of evidence where in a chain of reasoning a rare event is located.

Analytically we first observe that the rareness of an event has no effect on the inferential force of evidence on a singly connected chain of reasoning if this rare event is located at stage n (at the bottom of the chain). To show why this is so, we need to consider another way of expressing the inferential drag coefficient D_n as it was defined in Equation 7.6. In this equation we can factor out only the last term involving a_n and b_n as follows:

$$D_n = D_{n-1} + \frac{b_n}{\prod_{i=2}^{n} (a_i - b_i)} = D_{n-1} + \frac{1}{\prod_{i=2}^{n-1} (a_i - b_i)} \left[\frac{b_n}{a_n - b_n} \right]$$

$$= D_{n-1} + \frac{1}{\prod_{i=2}^{n-1} (a_i - b_i)} \left[\frac{a_n}{b_n} - 1 \right]^{-1}. \tag{7.8}$$

In Equation 7.8 we observe that all we need is the ratio a_n/b_n and not the exact values of a_n and b_n. Thus, for example, the a_n, b_n pairs (0.999, 0.010) and (0.0999, 0.0010) contribute exactly the same amount to D_n. In the latter pair we have a rare event. We need to recall that the terms a_n and b_n always concern the credibility of evidence E_{n-1}^* on which the chain of reasoning is grounded. Earlier we gave these two terms the labels hit (h) and false-positive (f) probabilities, so we can identify the factored term as $[(h/f) - 1]^{-1}$.

It can now be shown more clearly that in a Bayesian interpretation of the inferential force of evidence, it *does* matter where in a chain of reasoning a rare event is located. Table 7.2 provides several examples involving a four-stage chain of reasoning. First compare cases 1 and 5. Observe that in case 1 the probability of evidence E_3^* is ten times smaller, given E_3 and given E_3^c, than it is in case 5. Thus in case 1 we have E_3^* as a rare event. Notice, however, that the ratio $a_4/b_4 = h/f = 99:1$ in both cases. In accordance with the analysis in the paragraph above, we note that the values of D_4 and $L_{E_3^*}$ are the same in both cases. Cases 2 through 4 then show how making a rare event appear at successively higher stages in the reasoning chain does diminish the inferential force of evidence E_{3*}. Thus we may say that using Bayes's

TABLE 7.2 A Rare Event Located at Various Points in a Chain of Reasoning

Stage	Likelihoods	Case 1	Case 2	Case 3	Case 4	Case 5
1	$a_1 = P(E_1\|H)$	0.999	0.999	0.999	**0.0999**	0.999
	$b_1 = P(E_1\|H^c)$	0.010	0.010	0.010	**0.0010**	0.010
2	$a_2 = P(E_2\|E_1)$	0.999	0.999	**0.0999**	0.999	0.999
	$b_2 = P(E_2\|E_1^c)$	0.010	0.010	**0.0010**	0.010	0.010
3	$a_3 = P(E_3\|E_2)$	0.999	**0.0999**	0.999	0.999	0.999
	$b_3 = P(E_3\|E_2^c)$	0.010	**0.0010**	0.010	0.010	0.010
4	$a_4 = P(E_3^*\|E_3)$	**0.0999**	0.999	0.999	0.999	0.999
	$b_4 = P(E_3^*\|E_3^c)$	**0.0010**	0.010	0.010	0.010	0.010
	D_4	0.031	0.124	0.216	0.031	0.031
	$L_{E_3^*}$	25.12	8.38	5.38	4.09	25.12

rule, we would prefer a probable argument on an improbable foundation over an improbable argument on a probable foundation.

Consideration of event rareness is a very important element of Bayesian analyses of the inferential force of evidence. The fact that Bayes's rule responds to differences as well as to ratios of likelihood ingredients has recently given rise to a good-natured debate about whether this fact destroys an important consequence called the *likelihood principle*. Briefly this principle asserts that ". . . *all* the information which the data provide concerning the relative merits of two hypotheses is contained in the likelihood ratio of those hypotheses on the data" (Edwards 1992, 30). In this debate involving Ward Edwards, Bob Winkler, and me, we sorted out the issues within the context of a trial in which Ward is accused of murdering me for having discovered that, in cascaded inference, differences as well as ratios of likelihoods are crucial in Bayesian analyses (Edwards, Schum, and Winkler 1990). Winkler argues that the likelihood principle remains intact. Edwards confesses to my murder, not for my having destroyed the likelihood principle but for emasculating it as far as its practical importance is concerned.

7.1.4 Transitivity in Singly Connected Chains of Reasoning

By the term *transitivity* we refer to a particular relation or association between pairs of entities. In algebra, for example, the relations "greater than" and "equals" are transitive. Thus, if $a > b$ and $b > c$, then $a > c$; if $a = b$ and $b = c$, then $a = c$. Some relations such as "fathered" are naturally *intransitive;* if A fathered B and B fathered C, then A did not father C. On occasion, transitivity is expected but not observed. Consider three football teams A, B, and C. Team A beats B and B beats C, but then C beats A. Human preference and probability judgments are not always transitive. You hear me say that I prefer A to B and that I prefer B to C, but then, intransitively, I assert that I prefer C to A. My judgments of probability would be intransitive if I asserted: $P(A) > P(B)$, $P(B) > P(C)$, but $P(C) > P(A)$. It is of some interest to note conditions under which Bayesian expressions for the inferential force of evidence confer transitivity in chains of reasoning. Jonathan Cohen has noted some anomalies concerning transitivity when inference upon inference in legal matters is construed in Bayesian terms (1977, 68–73); I responded to his concerns in another work (Schum 1979).

Here is a simple example of the transitivity issues of interest to us. Suppose I say that A inferentially favors B over B^c and that B favors C over C^c. Under what conditions does it follow that A then, transitively, favors C over C^c. Certain conditions guarantee transitivity in Bayesian likelihood ratio formulations for the inferential force of evidence. This guarantee depends upon whether a chain of reasoning is singly connected. First, consider the n-stage chain of reasoning in Figure 7.1, supposing that E_{n-1}. favors E_{n-1}, E_{n-1} favors $E_{n-2}, \ldots$, E_3 favors E_2, E_2 favors E_1, and E_1 favors H. We capture this situation probabilistically by saying that $a_j > b_j$ at any reasoning stage j. When this is so, we have the transitive relation in which E_{n-1}^* also favors H. This is easily shown by examining Equations 7.5 through 7.7. If $a_j > b_j$, for every j, then $L_{E_{n-1}^*} > 1$, which means that E_{n-1}^* favors H over H^c. For chains of reasoning that are not singly connected, the conditions for inferential transitivity are not so simple, as we will observe in Section 7.2.2.

7.2 CHAINS OF REASONING AND CONDITIONAL NONINDEPENDENCE

So far we have observed that the strength of a singly connected chain of reasoning, expressed in Bayesian terms, cannot exceed the strength of the chain's weakest link. In discussing Equation 7.7, we also observed how the force of evidence in an n-stage singly connected chain of reasoning is bounded above by the inferential force of knowing for sure that argument event E_1 occurred (at the first stage), and how it is bounded below by the force of knowing for sure that E_1 did not occur. For a chain of reasoning that is not singly connected, we can readily observe that these conclusions regarding the force of evidence no longer apply. When we introduce patterns of conditional nonindependence among events at various stages of reasoning, we add considerable complexity to our analyses; then we also are able to trap a variety of interesting evidential subtleties in the process. The analytic trouble we face is that there are so many patterns of conditional nonindependencies possible among events in an n-stage chain of reasoning. We are thus forced to consider particular cases of reasoning chains, most of which will be quite short. Fortunately we do not need to consider very long chains of reasoning in order to identify many interesting subtleties associated with the task of assessing the inferential force of evidence.

7.2.1 Removing Bounds on the Inferential Force of Evidence

To begin an investigation of evidential force in chains of reasoning that are not singly connected, consider the situation illustrated in Figure 7.6a. First suppose that H_1 and H_2 represent *any two* hypotheses in a mutually exclusive and exhaustive class (in one special case, $H_2 = H_1^c$). Numbering hypotheses simplifies later notation. Events $\{E, E^c\}$ are linked probabilistically to these hypotheses. In particular, suppose that event E favors the occurrence or truth of H_1 over H_2; that is, $P(E|H_1) > P(E|H_2)$. But all we have is evidence E^* which we believe is not perfectly credible. On examining this situation, we also believe that evidence E^* is linked probabilistically not only to events $\{E, E^c\}$ but also directly to either or both of hypotheses H_1 and H_2. Thus we form an additional arc from E^* to $\{H_1, H_2, \ldots\}$, as shown in Figure 7.6a; our reasoning chain is no longer singly connected. In this relatively simple inference from E^* to hypotheses in $\{H_1, H_2, \ldots\}$ there is just one possible additional arc or linkage. But suppose we had no direct evidence of event E.

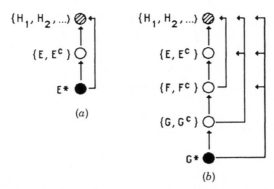

FIGURE 7.6   Additional linkages in a chain of reasoning for possible conditional non-independencies. (a) Illustrating state-dependent credibility. (b) Illustrating state-dependent credibility and other possibilities.

All we have is remote evidence G^* linked to $\{E, E^c\}$ through three reasoning stages, as shown in Figure 7.6b. In this case the number of possible additional arcs increases. Events $\{F, F^c\}$ might be directly linked to any of $\{H_1, H_2, \ldots\}$ as well as to $\{E, E^c\}$. Events $\{G, G^c\}$ might be linked to any of $\{H_1, H_2, \ldots\}$ or to $\{E, E^c\}$ in addition to being linked to $\{F, F^c\}$. Finally, G^* might be linked to any of $\{H_1, H_2, \ldots\}$, $\{E, E^c\}$, and $\{F, F^c\}$ as well as to $\{G, G^c\}$. In this situation there are six possible additional arcs that we need to consider.

The simple case in Figure 7.6a allows us to consider instances in which the inferential force of evidence E^* can exceed the force of knowing event E for sure. Using the expansion process described in Section 7.1.1, we determine the likelihood ratio L_{E^*} to be

$$L_{E^*} = \frac{P(E|H_1)[P(E^*|EH_1) - P(E^*|E^cH_1)] + P(E^*|E^cH_1)}{P(E|H_2)[P(E^*|EH_2) - P(E^*|E^cH_2)] + P(E^*|E^cH_2)} \quad (7.9)$$

In my initial discussion of Pascalian conditional probabilities in Section 2.3.2, I made use of a hybrid notational scheme that I then promised would be useful later on. I can now make good on this promise. The two terms $P(E|H_1)$ and $P(E|H_2)$ prescribe the Bayesian inferential force on hypotheses H_1 and H_2 of knowing E for sure. We must have exact values of these two conditionals and not just their ratio. All of the other terms in Equation 7.9 involve our evidence E^* and the credibility of the source from which it came. Using the hybrid notational scheme for any hypothesis H_k, we can express $P(E^*|EH_k) = P_{H_k}(E^*|E)$ and $P(E^*|E^cH_k) = P_{H_k}(E^*|E^c)$. Staring at these terms for a moment, we see that they are the *hit* and *false-positive* probabilities we identified earlier. Thus $P_{H_k}(E^*|E)$ is a hit probability, conditional upon H_k; $P_{H_k}(E^*|E^c)$ is a false-positive probability, conditional upon H_k. Using a simpler notation, we let $P_{H_k}(E^*|E) = h_k$ and $P_{H_k}(E^*|E^c) = f_k$ for $k = 1, 2$.

With these simplifications Equation 7.9 becomes

$$L_{E^*} = \frac{P(E|H_1)[h_1 - f_1] + f_1}{P(E|H_2)[h_2 - f_2] + f_2} \qquad (7.10)$$

The h and f terms in Equation 7.10 concern the credibility of evidence E^* and its source, since they concern the likeliness of the evidence under assumptions about whether the event reported actually occured. This equation allows for the possibility that credibility is state dependent on either or both of H_1 and H_2. Consider the five cases shown in Table 7.3. In all five cases the *known occurrence* of event E would favor H_1 over H_2 in the ratio 8/1; this is indicated by the likelihoods $P(E|H_1)$ and $P(E|H_2)$. In case 1 we have a situation in which evidence E^* favors H_1 over H_2 more strongly than does the known occurrence of event E. Observe that $L_{E^*} = 12.49 > L_E = 8$. How can this happen? The answer is that what we know about a source of evidence can often be as inferentially valuable as what the evidence itself tells us. We have evidence of event E from a certain source (including our own observation); it may indeed matter what particular source informed us about the occurrence of event E. In case 1 we have a source whose hit probability we believe to be greater assuming H_1 rather than H_2. If grounded on appropriate ancillary evidence about this source, this belief has inferential significance on its own.

There is another way of showing how the behavior of a source of evidence can have inferential value on its own, apart from what the evidence reports. First, suppose for some hypothesis H and for some source i, that $P(E_i^*|EH) = P(E_i^*|E)$. This is an assertion that E_i^* and H are independent, conditional upon E. The equality just stated implies another, namely that $P(H|EE_i^*) = P(H|E)$. This second equality says that the posterior probability of H, given the known occurrence of E, would not change if you then received evidence of E from source i. In short, receiving evidence of E from source i does not add anything. But if $P(E_i^*|EH) \neq P(E_i^*|E)$, then $P(H|EE_i^*) \neq P(H|E)$. This means that receiving evidence about E from source i would

TABLE 7.3   Examples Using Equation 7.10

Ingredients	Case 1	Case 2	Case 3	Case 4	Case 5
$P(E|H_1)$	0.8	0.08	0.008	0.8	0.8
$P(E|H_2)$	0.1	0.01	0.001	0.1	0.1
h_1	0.95	0.95	0.95	0.95	0.02
f_1	0.01	0.01	0.01	0.01	0.001
h_2	0.50	0.50	0.50	0.02	0.95
f_2	0.01	0.01	0.01	0.001	0.01
L_{E^*}	12.49	5.72	1.67	262.76	0.16[a]

[a]Favors H_2.

change your probabilistic belief about H from where it was if you knew for sure that event E occurred. In other words, the report from source *i* has inferential significance in addition to that contained in the event reported.

Cases 2 and 3 involve the same state-dependent credibility as case 1. The difference is that the event reported is made rare by a factor of 10 in case 2 and by a factor of 100 in case 3. Once again, Bayes's rule responds to differences as well as to ratios in its likelihood ingredients. What we gain by the inferentially valuable information we have about the source of evidence of event E is lost if E is a rare event. As L_{E^*} in cases 2 and 3 show, the inferential force of E* no longer exceeds the force of knowing E for sure. Case 4 is an illustration of how much additional force evidence can have in light of inferentially valuable information we have about its source. In this case $h_1 = 0.95$ and $f_1 = 0.01$ indicate that our source is very credible assuming the truth of H_1. However, assuming H_2 to be true, we have an entirely different belief about the credibility of this source. First, notice that the ratio $h_2/f_2 = 20$ indicates our belief that this source's hit to false-positive ratio is quite large. Apparently we believe this source to be quite credible. But we also believe h_2 and f_2 to be very small; what does this mean? If the probability of evidence E* is very small, whether or not the reported event occurred, we must believe the source of this evidence to be *biased against* reporting this event. We might say that given H_2, this source is very unlikely to have reported event E, whether or not E did occur. Such a bias, conditional upon H_2, gives rise to $L_{E^*} = 262.76$, showing that E* is $262.76/8 = 32.85$ times more forceful than knowing E for sure. In another work I have provided even more extravagant examples of the potential inferential force of conditional bias and other attributes of sources of evidence (Schum 1981). Some of this work is described in Section 7.3.1.

Given $P(E|H_1) = 0.8$ and $P(E|H_2) = 0.1$, it follows from Pascalian rules that $P(E^c|H_1) = 0.2$ and $P(E^c|H_2) = 0.9$. From our discussion in Section 7.1, if the chain of reasoning from E* to {H_1, H_2, . . .} were singly connected, the bounds on $L_{E^*} = P(E^*|H_1)/P(E^*|H_2)$ would be $2/9 \le L_{E^*} \le 8$. Recall that when $L_{E^*} < 1$, E* would favor H_2 if E favored H_1. Case 1 illustrated how L_{E^*} can exceed the value 8 (favoring H_1) when the chain of reasoning is not singly connected and when we believe the credibility of a source to be state dependent in a certain way. Case 5 illustrates how we may have $L_{E^*} < L_{E^c} = 2/9$ (favoring H_2) for a chain of reasoning that is not singly connected. We simply reverse the credibility situation in case 4. In case 5 we now have conditional bias on the source's part conditional upon H_1. This leads to $L_{E^*} = 0.16 = 1/6.25 < 2/9$. In Section 7.3 we will examine a variety of other credibility-related matters that influence the force of evidence whether or not chains of reasoning are singly connected.

7.2.2   Transitivity Revisited

In Section 7.1 conclusions were drawn regarding the conditions for transitive reasoning and the location of weak links and rare events in singly connected

TABLE 7.4   Transitivity Expected But Not Justified

Ingredients	Case 1	Case 2
$P(E\|H_1)$	0.55	0.8
$P(E\|H_2)$	0.40	0.1
h_1	0.50	0.02
f_1	0.10	0.001
h_2	0.95	0.95
f_2	0.01	0.01
L_{E^*}	1/2.38	1/6.25

chains of reasoning. It is necessary to examine these conclusions again for a chain of reasoning that is not singly connected. Examine, again, Figure 7.6a, and suppose the following: We believe that evidence E^* inferentially favors E over E^c and that E inferentially favors H_1 over H_2. If this chain of reasoning were singly connected, then we would be quite justified in believing that E^* inferentially favors H_1 over H_2. But, since it is not singly connected, we will be able to identify situations in which E^* inferentially favors E over E^c, E favors H_1 over H_2, but E^* does *not* favor H_1 over H_2.

Table 7.4 gives two examples of transitivity expected but not conferred by Bayes's rule. Both cases make use of Equation 7.10. In case 1 event E favors H_1 over H_2 in the ratio $0.55/0.40 = 1.375$. In addition E^* favors E over E^c under both H_1 and H_2. Observe that $h_1 > f_1$ and that $h_2 > f_2$. We might expect therefore that E^* favors H_1 over H_2. But notice that $L_{E^*} = 1/2.38$, favoring H_2 over H_1. The reason why transitivity, though expected, is not conferred in this case is that the h/f ratio for the source of this evidence is much greater under H_2 than it is under H_1. This evidential subtlety, trapped by conditional nonindependence, is "noticed" by Bayes's rule. Case 2 in Table 7.4 is the same as case 5 in Table 7.3. In this case E favors H_1 over H_2 in the ratio 8/1. As in case 1, $h_1 > f_1$ and $h_2 > f_2$. But this case involves a source whose bias against reporting E^* is conditional upon H_1 being true. The effect is to reverse the direction of the inferential force of E^*. We have $L_{E^*} = 1/6.25$ which, as we observed earlier, is more forceful on H_2 than knowing E^c for sure.

7.3 CREDIBILITY AND THE FORCE OF EVIDENCE

Anyone with a passion for identifying important but subtle elements of probabilistic reasoning can do no better than to focus attention on the relationship between the credibility and the inferential force of evidence. As noted in Chapter 2, this relationship was of interest during the emergence of mathematical probability in the 1600s. Particular interest was then expressed in the credibility of testimonial evidence from human sources, an interest that seems to have lingered at least until the nineteenth century. There is still intermittent discussion of this topic among probabilists (e.g., Zabell 1988). But we have more than testimonial evidence to consider, and as I mentioned throughout Chapter 3, credibility considerations actually form one of the two basic dimensions for categorizing recurrent forms of evidence. In the early and in some of the modern work on probabilistic reasoning, it has been common to grade credibility-related characteristics of an evidence source in probabilistic terms. In the case of testimony, for example, all of the following characteristics have been graded by *single* Pascalian probabilities in the [0, 1] interval: *credibility* (Keynes 1921, 183; Shafer 1986b, 156; Zabell 1988, 332), *reliability* (Keynes 1921, 183), *reliability and accuracy* (Shafer 1986b, 157), and *veracity* or *truthfulness* (Keynes 1921, 180; Zabell 1988, 332). However, if our purpose is to use the Pascalian system and Bayes's rule to inform us about credibility and its influence on the force of evidence, we cannot rely upon single probabilities.

In an example I used in Section 5.4.2 to illustrate the judgmental foundations of Shafer's belief functions, I let a single probability represent the likeliness that your source of evidence was credible in his report about your neighbor keeping a dog in his apartment. Shafer is quite correct in his assertion that, in practice, we must often resort to very simple probability arguments and simple judgments. But my present purpose is to give an account of what different formal systems for probabilistic reasoning can tell us about source credibility and its relation to the inferential force of various forms of evidence. In this account I will not shy away from detailed chains of reasoning constructed in order to capture attributes of the credibility of different forms of evidence and of their sources. In the Bayesian analyses I will present it becomes obvious why the use of *single* probabilities to grade credibility attributes is not satisfactory. I now offer probabilistic analyses of credibility-related issues for different forms of evidence. My discussion of these issues rests upon more elaborate accounts I have provided in other works (Schum 1981a, 1989, 1991).

7.3.1 Tangible Evidence, Credibility, and the Theory of Signal Detection

A person using tangible evidence can examine it directly in order to determine whether the evidence records an event of interest. As I noted in Section 3.2.2, the major attributes of the credibility of tangible evidence are its *authenticity* and *accuracy*. For example, suppose we examine a visible or audible report produced by a mechanical or electronic sensing device to determine whether this report records the occurrence of event E. If it did occur, event E would be important in an inference regarding some collection of hypotheses of interest to us. Let us suppose that this report is authentic; it has not been contrived or altered in any way. As discussed in Section 3.2.2, and illustrated in Figure 3.7b, our own senses are involved in the process of inference from this sensor's report. We might be mistaken in interpreting this sensor report.

We might believe that this report records event E when it does not; we might also believe that the report fails to record E when it does. So, as sensing devices ourselves, we have our own *objectivity* and *observational sensitivity* to consider as Figure 3.7b illustrates. For a start, however, let us focus upon the credibility of a sensing device and not on the credibility of the person who interprets what the sensor reports. Suppose we all agree about whether or not the report from a certain sensor records the occurrence of event E. What is of concern to us is the *accuracy* of the report this sensor provides.

In symbols, let E^* represent the sensor's report of event E, and let E^{c^*} be the sensor's report of the nonoccurrence of event E. As shown in Figure 7.7, there are four possible outcomes or consequences depending upon the sensor's report and upon whether or not event E did occur; we suppose that each of these outcomes has some probability of occurring. The probabilities are (1) $P(E^*|E) = h$ = the probability of a hit (also called a true-positive), (2) $P(E^*|E^c) = f$ = probability of a false-positive, (3) $P(E^{c^*}|E^c) = c$ = the probability of a correct rejection (also called a true-negative), and (4) $P(E^{c^*}|E) = m$ = the probability of a miss. If we suppose these to be Pascalian probabilities, we must have $m = 1 - h$ and $c = 1 - f$. Also shown in Figure 7.7 are *subjective values* (V) that might be placed upon each of the four outcomes of the sensor's report. We suppose that two of these values, V_h and V_c, are positive and that the other two, V_f and V_m, are negative. Finally, suppose that there is some basis for assessing the prior probabilities $P(E)$ and $P(E^c)$ which, under Pascalian assumptions, must sum to 1.0.

Let us suppose that event E represents the occurrence of some information-carrying signal (s) that the sensor has been designed to detect. We might also suppose that signal s, when it occurs, is always presented against a background of noise (n). So the occurrence of event E means that we have $s + n$, a signal of interest has occurred in the omnipresence of noise. When the sensor reports

Actual Occurrence

		E	E^c
Sensor Report	E^*	$h = P(E^*|E)$ V_h (+)	$f = P(E^*|E^c)$ V_f (-)
	E^{c^*}	$m = P(E^{c^*}|E)$ V_m (-)	$c = P(E^{c^*}|E^c)$ V_c (+)

FIGURE 7.7 The four possible outcomes of a sensor report about binary events and an assessment of their consequences.

E*, we interpret this to mean that it has detected the existence of *s* against this noise background. If the sensor reports E^{c*}, we interpret this to mean that the sensor detected only noise and no signal. The theory of signal detection (TSD) provides us with numerous insights concerning the task of assessing the credibility of both tangible evidence from sensors and testimonial evidence from human observers. In another work I have given an account of the manner in which insights from TSD might be used to good advantage in Bayesian approaches to assessing the inferential force of evidence (Schum 1981a). Indeed there is a natural linkage between TSD and Bayes's rule, as I will explain. What follows is a brief account of what TSD has to tell us about hit and false-positive probabilities when they concern the credibility of tangible evidence. In Section 7.3.3 we will consider ideas from TSD with reference to the credibility of human observers who provide testimonial evidence.

One of the fundamental advantages of TSD is that it allows us to keep separate what we know about the *sensitivity* or *detection capacity* of a sensor from what we know about this sensor's *response threshold*. A sensor might be instructed not to respond unless the detected signal energy exceeds some specified threshold level. We suppose that the sensor of interest is not perfect and that signal *s* can vary in its intensity from occasion to occasion. Sometimes the sensor will record the occurrence of *s* when there is only noise, and sometimes it will fail to record the occurrence of *s* when *s* was present. Thus we suppose that both false-positives and misses are possible for this sensor. We will begin by supposing that $h > f$ for the sensor of interest to us. If we observed $f > h$ for a sensor, we might easily suppose that it had been interfered with in some way or was broken. Later on we will consider situations in which $f > h$ for human observers.

A sensor might be designed to take account of the prior likeliness of signal *s* as well as the values that may be placed upon the consequences of the sensor's report, as shown in Figure 7.7. First, suppose that, as in the case of radar detection of hostile aircraft, it is believed that the cost of a miss (V_m) is very high relative to the cost of a false-positive (V_f). So we set the sensor's *response threshold* at a very low value to ensure that the sensor will report the occurrence of *s* under conditions in which detected energy is small and very likely due to the occurrence of noise alone. In such cases we seek to maximize h, but in doing so, we must accept a high value of *f*. We might say in such instances that we have *biased* the sensor in favor of reporting E*, that signal *s* occurred. On the other hand, if the cost of a false-positive were high relative to a miss, we could bias the sensor to minimize false-positives at the expense of minimizing hits. In this case we have set the sensor's response threshold at a high value, one that indicates a bias against reporting E*. In TSD Bayes's rule appears in prescriptions for ideal settings of response thresholds based upon prior probabilities of signal occurrence, evidence about about the sensor's detection capacity, and the values placed on the four consequences shown in Figure 7.7 (Egan 1975, 12–13).

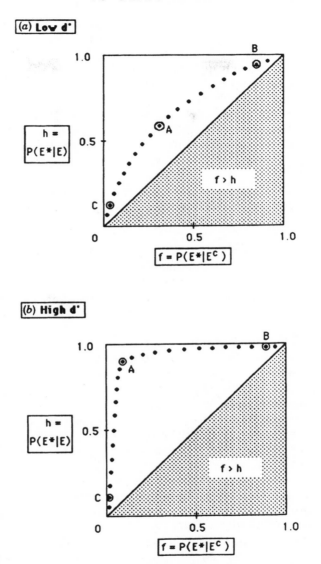

FIGURE 7.8 Two examples of *receiver operating characteristic* curves.

Figure 7.8 illustrates how we may separately consider a source's detection sensitivity and response threshold. What is illustrated in both diagrams is the space of all possible combinations of h and f. In repeated detection trials involving the presence or absence of s, *whose strength is held constant*, a plot of a sensor's h and f values under various conditions would reveal to us information about the sensor's sensitivity and response threshold setting. Let us first consider a sensor's detection sensitivity as indicated in TSD by a measure termed **d'**. Suppose a sensor for which it is true that $h > f$ and for which, regardless of response threshold setting, $(h - f)$ is small and h/f is close to 1.0. This situation is illustrated in Figure 7.8a. Each point on the curve is an h, f combination for a particular response threshold setting, as I will explain momentarily. Curves such as these are called *receiver operating characteristic (ROC) curves*. A sensor having the ROC curve in Figure 7.8a would have a low value of **d'** indicating a low degree of sensitivity. As a limiting case, suppose a situation in which $h = f$ for any response threshold setting. In this case the ROC curve would fall along the positive diagonal and have **d'** $= 0$.

In Figure 7.8b we have a situation in which the following conditions hold: (1) for some response threshold settings the difference $(h - f)$ is large (as at point A in the figure) and (2) for other response threshold settings the difference $(h - f)$ is small, but the ratio h/f is large, as at point C in the figure. In this case we would determine a high value of **d'** indicating that the sensor has considerable detection sensitivity. The manner in which **d'** can be determined from ROC curves, under various assumptions about a sensor's properties, is described by Green and Swets (1966) and by Egan (1975).

By comparing the two **d'** conditions in Figure 7.8, we can now begin to provide a TSD interpretation of the credibility-related matters I have introduced so far only by means of examples. Suppose we fix the sensitivity of a sensor at some **d'** level but vary the response threshold. Effectively we are telling the sensor not to report E* unless the detected energy exceeds some threshold amount. For example, consider a smoke detector that is capable of responding to very small amounts of smoke. You would not enjoy having this sensor in your home if it reported (by means of a loud and raucous sound) every time you lit a match. We might employ a less-sensitive detector, but we might also set the sensor's response threshold so that the sensor does not report unless a certain concentration of smoke is present. First, consider point A in both ROC curves. This point indicates the maximum $(h - f)$ difference on each curve; observe that it is larger for the high **d'** condition. Now consider point B on the two ROC curves. In both instances we have a sensor being biased *in favor of* reporting E*, that the signal was present. The difference between the two situations is that the high **d'** sensor has nearly as high values of h for lower values of f than does the low **d'** sensor. Thus point B for the high **d'** sensor represents a case in which the sensor's high hit rate is negated by the acceptance of a high false-positive rate, perhaps for the reason that a miss is deemed more damaging than a false-positive. As we will observe, as far as the force of evidence E* is concerned, Bayes's rule makes virtually no distinction between the two h, f pairs labeled B in Figure 7.8.

But Bayes's rule does make a distinction between the two h, f pairs labeled C in Figure 7.8. In the low **d'** condition, C is an instance in which we have very small h and f values that also have a small ratio. But in the high **d'** condition we have small h and f values with a large ratio. In either case we have a sensor whose response threshold is set very high in order to minimize the probability of a false-positive at the expense of reducing the probability of a hit. Remembering that Bayes's rule responds to ratios and differences of h and f, the force of evidence E^* for the high $\mathbf{d'}$ condition would be greater than it would be under the low $\mathbf{d'}$ condition. In the discussion of Equation 7.8 for singly connected chains of reasoning, I mentioned that we need only the ratio h/f regarding the credibility of the source of evidence at the bottom of the chain. This ratio is greater for a high $\mathbf{d'}$ sensor than it is for a low $\mathbf{d'}$ sensor.

We can now incorporate ideas from TSD in a Bayesian interpretation of the force of evidence. Consider the singly connected chain of reasoning from sensor evidence E^* to hypotheses $\{H_1, H_2, \ldots\}$ shown in the right-hand diagram of Figure 7.9a. Suppose that event $E = (s + n)$ favors the occurrence of H_1 over H_2. We can express the likelihood ratio for sensor evidence E^* as

$$L_{E^*} = \frac{P(E|H_1)[h - f] + f}{P(E|H_2)[h - f] + f} = \frac{P(E|H_1) + [(h/f) - 1]^{-1}}{P(E|H_2) + [(h/f) - 1]^{-1}} \quad (7.11)$$

Notice that the right-hand expression is not defined when $f = 0$ or when $h = f$. But in such instances we may make use of the middle expression. However, neither expression is defined when both h and f are zero. Equation 7.11 is a special case of Equation 7.10 in which $h_1 = h_2 = h$ and $f_1 = f_2 = f$. These equivalencies result from the singly connected nature of the reasoning chain that we are considering.

An examination of Equation 7.10 and its special case in 7.11 makes apparent why Bayesian gradings of the inferential force of evidence require more than one probability associated with the credibility of the source of the evidence. This requirement is reinforced when we interpret the task of assessing the force of evidence in terms of TSD. If we grade the accuracy of a sensor just in terms of its hit rate $h = P(E^*|E)$, this can be very misleading in absence of information about this sensor's false-positive rate. In any attempt to assess the force of E^*, we must also have the sensor's false-positive rate $f = P(E^*|E^c)$. Indeed the role played by a false-positive rate can often dominate the determination of the force of evidence, as I will illustrate by example. When we later examine the force of testimonial evidence from human sources, we will often need more than just two probabilities.

Let us now examine the ratio h/f to see what it tells us. Suppose that, as in Figure 7.9a, h/f is some number $k > 1.0$. All h, f pairs on the line $h/f = k$ have an equivalent effect on the force of evidence E^*. In the special case we are considering, Bayes's rule responds only to the ratio of h and f and not to their difference. What the line $h/f = k$ shows are combinations of $\mathbf{d'}$ and response threshold setting, all of which have an identical effect on the force of evidence E^*. In other words, $h/f = k$ expresses trade-offs between $\mathbf{d'}$ and response threshold as far as the force of evidence E^* is concerned. For example, consider the two points A and B shown on this line. At point (*a*) **Sensitivity–Response Threshold Tradeoffs**

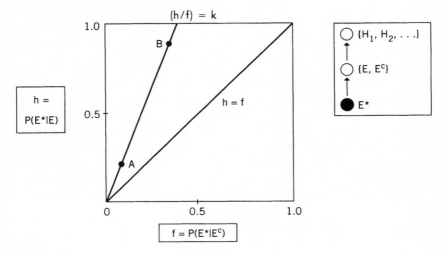

(*b*) **Response Threshold, d*, and the Force of Sensor Evidence.**

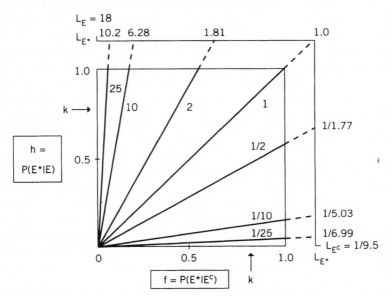

FIGURE 7.9 The *theory of signal detection* and the force of sensor evidence.

A we have a low **d'** sensor with a bias against reporting E*. At point B we have a high **d'** sensor with a slight bias in favor of reporting E*.

In Figure 7.9b appear some numerical examples of the manner in which the ratio h/f affects the value of L_{E^*}. These examples are based upon particular values $P(E|H_1) = 0.90$ and $P(E|H_2) = 0.05$, in which case $L_E = 18$ (favoring H_1). Under Pascalian rules we must then have $P(E^c|H_1) = 0.10$ and $P(E^c|H_2) = 0.95$ so that $L_{E^c} = 1/9.5$ (favoring H_2). If we let f approach zero in the ratio h/f, L_{E^*} approaches $L_E = 18$. If we let h approach zero, L_{E^*} approaches $L_{E^c} = 1/9.5$. The precise manner in which h/f affects the force of evidence may come as a surprise to some persons. We might suppose that if h were, say, 25 times the value of f, this represents a very credible sensor. However, as Figure 7.9b shows, for $h/f = 25$ we have $L_{E^*} = 10.2$ which is just about half of the inferential force of knowing E occurred for sure. An h/f ratio of 10 makes $L_{E^*} = 6.28$, about 1/3 of the inferential force of knowing E for sure.

The theory of signal detectability can also assist us in assessing the force of tangible evidence in cases in which we may believe the sensitivity and/or the response threshold of a sensor to be situation dependent. If this situation happened to be represented by some hypothesis of interest to us, we could exploit this dependence in assessing the inferential force of evidence from a sensor. Consider the reasoning chain at the top of Figure 7.10. In this case we have tangible evidence E* linked not only to events {E, E^c} but also to hypotheses in {H_1, H_2, . . .}. This reasoning chain is not singly connected, and we have either or both of h and f conditional upon either or both of H_1 and H_2, as discussed in connection with Equations 7.9 and 7.10. In Figure 7.10a we have a situation in which a sensor's **d'** is different under H_1 than it is under H_2. In Figure 7.10b we have a high **d'** sensor with a high response threshold setting conditional upon H_2. These are just two of the many possible conditioning patterns involving either or both of **d'** and response threshold setting.

Shown in Table 7.5 are examples of L_{E^*} calculated using Equation 7.10 for situations illustrated in Figure 7.10. Observe that in all five cases $P(E|H_1) = 0.90$ and $P(E|H_2) = 0.05$, so $L_E = 18$. The known occurrence of E favors H_1 over H_2 in the ratio 18/1. Case 1 is an example of the situation illustrated in Figure 7.10a in which **d'** is low if H_1 is true but high if H_2 is true. In this case we have $h_1 = 0.52$ and $f_1 = 0.47$, whose difference is 0.07 and whose ratio is 1.11. These values mark the sensor as having low **d'** in situation H_1. But $h_2 = 0.95$ and $f_2 = 0.01$ with a difference of 0.94 and a ratio of 95, indicating that this sensor is high **d'** in situation H_2. The resulting $L_{E^*} = 9.0$ shows us that E* from a sensor with this pattern of conditional sensitivity has exactly half the inferential force of knowing event E for sure.

The result in case 1 seems unremarkable; however, it may seem quite counterintuitive when it is compared with the result in case 2. In this second case we have the conditioning of **d'** reversed; the sensor is high **d'** when H_1 is true and low **d'** when H_2 is true. The inferential force of E* in case 2 is very

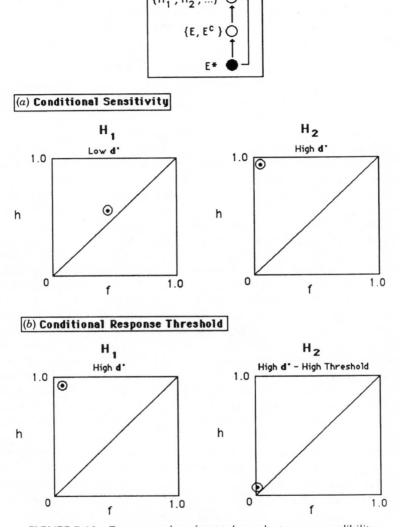

FIGURE 7.10 Two examples of state-dependent sensor credibility.

low, since $L_{E^*} = 1.13$. The question relevant to these two cases is: Why should the low sensitivity of this sensor, conditional upon H_1 in case 1, provide greater inferential force *favoring H_1* than it does when made conditional upon H_2 as in case 2? It might appear that low sensor sensitivity, conditional on H_1, would amount to evidence against H_1. Earlier I promised an example illustrating how a false-positive rate can be a dominating factor in determining Bayesian gradations of the force of evidence; cases 1 and 2 considered together

TABLE 7.5 State-Dependence of d' and Response Threshold

Ingredients	Case 1	Case 2	Case 3	Case 4	Case 5
$P(E|H_1)$	0.90	0.90	0.90	0.90	0.90
$P(E|H_2)$	0.05	0.05	0.05	0.05	0.05
h_1	0.52	0.95	0.95	0.52	0.95
f_1	0.47	0.01	0.01	0.47	0.01
h_2	0.95	0.52	0.95	0.52	0.020
f_2	0.01	0.47	0.01	0.47	0.001
L_{E^*}	9.00	1.89	15.02	1.13	438.97

provide this example. The role played by the false-positive rate in these examples helps explain the results in these two cases.

In case 1 we have the interesting situation in which $P(E^*|H_1)$ depends mainly upon the size of the sensor's *false-positive rate* f_1; the larger is f_1, the larger is $P(E^*|H_1)$. The following limiting case of L_{E^*} in Equation 7.10 closely resembles the situation in case 1. The numerator is $P(E^*|H_1)$ = $P(E|H_1)[h_1 - f_1] + f_1$. Suppose we let $f_1 = h_1$; the result is $P(E^*|H_1) = f_1$. In case 1 we have $P(E^*|H_1) = 0.90[0.52 - 0.47] + 0.47 = 0.515$, which is close to $f_1 = 0.47$. The large size of f_1 in case 1, due to the low **d'** when H_1 is true, is clearly the dominant factor in determining $P(E^*|H_1)$. The denominator in Equation 7.10 is $P(E^*|H_2) = P(E|H_2)[h_2 - f_2] + f_2$. Suppose we let $f_2 = 0$ so that $P(E^*|H_2) = P(E|H_2)h_2$. In case 1 we have a small false-positive rate, conditional upon H_2, and so $P(E^*|H_2) = 0.05[0.95 - 0.01] + 0.01 = 0.057$, which is close in value to $P(E|H_2)h_2 = (0.05)(0.95) = 0.0475$. In this case the low value of f_2, due to the high **d'** when H_2 is true, contributes almost nothing to the size of $P(E^*|H_2)$. In the limiting case, as f_2 approaches zero and h_1 approaches f_1, we have $L_{E^*} = f_1/P(E|H_2)h_2 = 9.89$ which is close to the value of L_{E^*} in Case 1.

But in case 2 it is the denominator in Equation 7.10 that is dominated by a false-positive rate. To approximate the **d'** conditioning in case 2, we let $f_1 = 0$ and $f_2 = h_2$ in Equation 7.10. This corresponds to high **d'** under H_1 and low **d'** under H_2. The result is $L_{E^*} = P(E|H_1)h_1/f_2$. In this limiting case $P(E^*|H_2) = f_2$. Because of the low **d'** and large f_2 in Case 2, L_{E^*} cannot be very large. In the limiting case we have $L_{E^*} = (0.90)(0.95)/(0.45) = 1.9$ which is nearly identical to the value observed in case 2. In summary, the **d'** conditioning patterns illustrated in cases 1 and 2 illustrate how a sensor's false-positive rate can be a dominating factor in determining the inferential force of tangible evidence. Cases 3 and 4 in Table 7.5 simply provide additional reference points for evaluating cases 1 and 2. In cases 3 and 4 the arc connecting E^* with $\{H_1, H_2, \ldots\}$ has been eliminated. In case 3 we have the same high **d'** conditions under both H_1 and H_2; in case 4 the same low **d'** condition appears under both hypotheses.

Case 5 in Table 7.5 is an example of the situation illustrated in Figure 7.10b. In this situation we have a sensor being high **d'**, conditional upon H_1

being true. This sensor is also high **d'** when H_2 is true; the difference is that the response threshold for this sensor has been set at a very high level in situations like H_2. We might suppose, for example, that a false-positive in reporting E^* might be very damaging under conditions represented by H_2. In the numerical example in case 5, $f_2 = 0.001$. If we had knowledge of this bias against reporting E^*, when H_2 was true, a sensor report of E^* would have $438.97/18 = 24.4$ times the inferential force favoring H_1 over H_2 than would the known occurrence of the event the sensor reports. This may seem a preposterous example in most situations involving physical sensors. I have contrived it simply to illustrate the extreme likelihood ratios sanctioned by Bayes's rule and TSD when the sensitivity and response thresholds of a sensor are state dependent in various ways. Even more extreme examples are possible (Schum 1981a, 177–189). What we know, or believe we know, about a source of evidence can be at least as valuable inferentially as the event(s) reported by this source. This is especially true for human sources of testimonial evidence.

7.3.2   Decomposing the Credibility of Testimonial Evidence from Human Sources

In analyses of the force of testimonial evidence from a person, we might be tempted to grade her credibility in terms of hit and false-positive probabilities and proceed as we have just done for tangible evidence. Suppose that a person provides testimony E^*, that event E occurred, where E is directly linked to hypotheses $\{H_1, H_2, \ldots\}$. We might employ Equations 7.10 or 7.11 in analyses of the inferential force of E^* depending upon whether we believed her testimony to be state dependent. Such analyses are useful, but there are several difficulties. First, we might have relative frequencies to support judgments of hit and false-positive probabilities for a mechanical or electronic sensor, but it is very unlikely that we would have such frequencies for human observers or witnesses. For example, relative frequency estimates of $h = P(E^*|E)$ and $f = P(E^*|E^c)$ suppose a replicable situation in which we are able to determine the number of trials when event E occurred and the number of trials when it did not. Such situations do occur in research on human sensory capabilities and limitations, as I will mention later. However, in many important and interesting situations people report the occurrence of unique, singular, or one-of-a-kind events for which no relative frequencies are possible.

Second, as discussed in Section 3.2.3, the credibility of a human source is *multiattribute*. We have at least a person's *veracity, objectivity,* and *observational sensitivity* to consider in assessing this person's credibility. One analytic approach, suggested in Figure 3.6a, is to decompose the reasoning linkage between testimony E^* and events $\{E, E^c\}$ in order to capture these credibility attributes. When we employ this decomposition in Bayesian terms, certain conditional probabilities are associated with each of these three credibility attributes. There will rarely be any relative frequencies to support these conditionals; they have to be judged subjectively on the basis of relevant ancillary evidence. So we need to be specific about what information would provide a reasonable basis for assessing them. Baconian analyses of credibility-related issues, entirely complementary to Bayesian analyses, force us to consider how complete or sufficient is our coverage of ancillary evidence relevant in judgments about a person's veracity, objectivity, and observational sensitivity.

I noted in my opening remarks in Section 7.3 that there has been some vagueness in grading, in probabilistic terms, source credibility or any of its attributes. In the Bayesian analyses of tangible evidence just considered, we noted the need for both hit and false-positive probabilities. A single probability will not suffice to capture the sensitivity and response threshold setting of a sensor. In Bayesian analyses of testimonial evidence in which a credibility-related stage of reasoning is decomposed, we will discover a need for at least six conditional probabilities. There are at least two associated with each of the three credibility attributes mentioned above. The analyses I will offer are quite clear in showing us how easily we can be misled in labeling credibility-related probabilities. For example, we cannot employ $h = P(E^*|E)$ alone or in combination with $f = P(E^*|E^c)$ as a gradation of a person's veracity or truthfulness as suggested on various occasions (e.g, Zabell 1988, 332). The reason is that a person may report E^* when event E did not occur, not because of untruthfulness but because of a sensory failure or a lack of objectivity. Decomposed likelihood ratios for the force of testimonial evidence allow us to capture all three attributes of a human source of evidence.

Consider the two-stage and singly connected chain of reasoning shown in Figure 7.11a. Suppose that E^* is testimonial evidence provided by a witness W. Let us assume that W has based this testimony on a direct observation; that is, W did not learn about E from another source, nor did W infer the occurrence of E based upon observation of other events. In short, E^* is based neither upon hearsay nor opinion based upon other evidence. We wish to employ a Bayesian likelihood ratio to grade the force of evidence E^* on hypotheses H_1 and H_2. Suppose further that we wish to decompose the credibility-related foundation stage, involving an inference from E^* to events {E, E^c}, as shown in Figure 7.11b. I argued in Section 3.2.3 that, for a human source, this decomposition allows us to expose three attributes of W's credibility. Testimony E^* is linked to events {E_b, E_b^c} representing whether W believes what she testified; this linkage involves W's *veracity*. At the next stage we have linkages between {E_b, E_b^c} and {E_s, E_s^c}, whether W's senses gave evidence of the event W believes; this stage of reasoning concerns W's *objectivity*. Finally, this decomposition involves linkages between events {E_s, E_s^c} and events {E, E^c} and concern W's *observational sensitivity*.

Before we proceed with analyses based upon this decomposition of witness credibility, there are several matters that require careful attention. First, the nodes above an evidence node (E^* in the present case) involve event classes whose partitioning is often arbitrary. In the present case I inserted two nodes

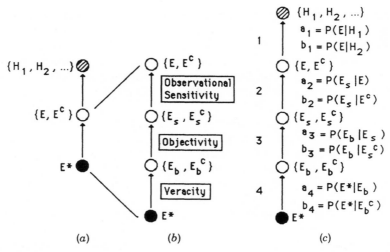

FIGURE 7.11   Decomposing the credibility of a testimonial assertion from a human source.

with associated event classes $\{E_b, E_b^c\}$ and $\{E_s, E_s^c\}$. The event E_b^c means: "W does not believe E happened." Notice that this is not the same thing as saying: "W believes E did not happen" (E_b^c). In assessing W's veracity, we have to consider the possibility that W has no belief about E one way or the other. This might happen if W made up a story about the occurrence of event E or was influenced by someone else into telling us that E occurred. Similarly E_s^c means: "W's senses did not give evidence of E." It does not mean: " W's senses gave evidence of E^c" (E_s^c). We have to allow for the possibility that W's senses gave no evidence about E, in other words, that W made no observation at all. So E_b^c incorporates two possibilities: (1) W believes E did not occur, and (2) W has no belief one way or the other. Similarly E_s^c incorporates the possibilities: (1) W's senses gave evidence of E^c, and (2) W's senses gave no evidence at all about event E.

The credibility-related chain of reasoning in Figure 7.11b invites questions concerning the necessity of the ordering: veracity–objectivity–observational sensitivity. In an observation that W might have made, we suppose the temporal sequence of events to be (1) W's senses gave evidence, (2) W formed beliefs based on this evidence, and then (3) W gave testimony in accordance with or against these beliefs. Since we only have W's testimony and have uncertainty about what W believes and what W's senses recorded, our inference goes in the reverse order from testimony to belief states, from belief states to sensory states, and then from sensory states to possibilities regarding the reported event. It is natural that observational sensitivity forms the top link in this chain. The reason is that since we were not privy to the occurrence or nonoccurrence of E, we have to rely upon W's senses as the primary "interface" with these events. No psychologist would ever believe that a person's testimony E^* is directly linked to her sensory states; indeed this is one of the major messages of TSD applied to human observers. Thus we insert a reasoning stage involving a *commonly overlooked* credibility attribute: How objective was W in her interpretation of the sensory evidence she allegedly obtained? The attributes and their ordering shown in Figures 7.11*b* and *c* seem quite consistent with experience and scholarship in experimental psychology, epistemology, and law, as I have discussed at length in Section 3.2.3 and in other works (Schum 1987, 1992).

Diagram C in Figure 7.11 shows that we now have a four-stage inference from E^* to $\{H_1, H_2, \ldots\}$ when we decompose the credibility-related link in this chain. Have we accounted for all of our uncertainties in this decomposition? The answer of course is *no*. First, we might have been mistaken in hearing W's testimony; she may have said that E did not occur or even that some other event occurred. We could, if sufficiently compulsive, add additional reasoning stages to account for our own objectivity and observational sensitivity, as shown in Figure 3.6*b*. In addition I mentioned in Section 3.2.3 that a person's beliefs are supple or elastic; they may change over time. We might choose to decompose the veracity stage of reasoning further by distinguishing between W's beliefs at the time she gave testimony from the beliefs she might have held at the time she made her (alleged) observation. But we may have other difficulties with the concept of veracity.

In several recent works Jonathan Cohen argues that it is necessary for us to distinguish between what a person *believes* and what he has *accepted* (1989b, 1991, 1992). Cohen proposes that beliefs are formed involuntarily and essentially involve feelings, but what we accept is a matter of choice. New beliefs we acquire increase the range of our feelings. But a new acceptance increases our stock of evidence, which we may then take as premises in further arguments, proofs, or deliberations (1992, 4–5). We may readily accept things that we do not believe or believe things that we do not accept. As a result of sensory evidence, we may involuntarily form certain beliefs which, on Cohen's account, we may later come to accept or reject. Recall that we are now concerned about situations in which person W provides testimony based on an observation. So at the veracity stage we might distinguish between what W might have believed, based on sensory evidence, and what W might have accepted as a result of thinking about this belief for a time. We are then naturally prompted to inquire whether W is telling us what she believes or what she has accepted. It might be argued that untruthfulness involves testimony at variance with what a witness has accepted rather than being at variance with what she believes. To keep matters reasonably simple in my analyses, I will suppose a witness whose beliefs about event E coincide with what she has accepted.

Finally, someone with better knowledge than I possess about human sensory-perceptual activities and their linkages to our belief states might suggest interposing additional reasoning stages between $\{E_b, E_b{}^c\}$ and $\{E_s, E_s{}^c\}$ in my chain of reasoning. As I have repeatedly mentioned, the construction of a chain of reasoning is always subject to alteration made necessary in light of further information. These matters acknowledged, I will confine my present credibility-related analyses of testimonial evidence to the chains of reasoning shown in Figures 7.11*b* and *c*.

Figure 7.11*c* shows the conditional probabilities that we must have at each link if the chain of reasoning is singly connected and if we intend a Bayesian analysis of the force of testimonial evidence E*. At the veracity stage we must judge how probable is W's testimony E*, given that she believes that E occurred and given that she does not believe that E occurred. At the objectivity stage we judge how probable is her belief that E occurred, given that she received sensory evidence of event E and given that she did not receive such evidence. Remember that a person may hold a belief in spite of or counter to the sensory evidence she obtains. At the observational sensitivity stage we must judge the probability of W obtaining sensory evidence of E, given that E did occur and given that E did not occur. At this final credibility-related stage we are essentially inquiring about the quality of the sensory evidence W obtained if, in fact, W made any observation at all. At the final stage of our inference we need to assess how likely event E is, given H_1 and given H_2. By such assessments we judge the inferential force of knowing E for sure. Shown in Figure 3.8 in Section 3.2.3 is an account of the kinds of ancillary evidence that could be used to support or weaken these probability judgments in particular cases; this account rests upon many centuries of experience with human witnesses in our Anglo-American legal system.

Our task is now to determine the manner in which credibility-related likelihood judgments are to be combined in a Bayesian assessment of the inferential force of testimonial evidence E*. The equations involving inferential drag, developed in Section 7.1.1, are very useful in illustrating a Bayesian approach to assessing the force of testimony. There are other equivalent expressions that we will also employ. The various formal expressions we will employ allow us to be more precise in analyses of the credibility-testimony matters of such great concern to early probabilists. In addition they inform us about a variety of matters commonly overlooked in many probabilistic analyses of testimony.

Let us begin by identifying a special case of Equation 7.7 in which we have the four (singly connected) stages of reasoning in Figure 7.11*c*. In this special case, the likelihood ratio for evidence E* is given by

$$L_{E^*} = \frac{a_1 + D_4}{b_1 + D_4} \qquad (7.12)$$

where

$$D_4 = \frac{b_2}{(a_2 - b_2)} + \frac{b_3}{(a_2 - b_2)(a_3 - b_3)} + \frac{b_4}{(a_2 - b_2)(a_3 - b_3)(a_4 - b_4)}$$

The a_i and b_i terms are as defined in Figure 7.11 and concern the veracity (a_4, b_4), objectivity (a_3, b_3), and observational sensitivity (a_2, b_2) of our witness W who has testified E^*. In this case the entire drag on our opinion revision regarding H_1 and H_2, based on testimony E^*, is due to any defects in W's credibility. The drag term D_4 is zero only when $b_2 = b_3 = b_4 = 0$ (recall an earlier assumption that a_i and b_i are not both zero at any reasoning stage i). Thus D_4 is zero only if we believe W would (1) never testify E^* if she did not believe E occurred ($b_4 = 0$), (2) never believe E occurred when her senses told her it did not occur ($b_3 = 0$), and (3) never sense the occurrence of E when E did not occur ($b_2 = 0$). Few human witnesses have these three characteristics, so we have to examine cases that exhibit a variety of imperfections commonly associated with attributes of the credibility of witnesses.

Conclusions reached in Section 7.1 in a general examination of singly connected chains of reasoning also apply when links in a chain concern credibility attributes. In a likelihood ratio construal of the force of evidence, a weak link is devastating regardless of where it is located in a chain of reasoning. Applied to credibility matters, the result is that there is no order of inferential importance or precedence among the attributes veracity, objectivity, and observational sensitivity. A defect in any one of these attributes is equally serious in its effects upon the force of testimony. Thus, for example, any of the results shown for the four-stage inference in Table 7.1 apply when the bottom three stages concern the veracity, objectivity, and observational sensitivity of a witness. In Section 7.1.3 we discussed the effects on the force of evidence of locating a rare event at various links in a chain of reasoning, noting in the process that a link having a rare event is not necessarily weak. Event rareness in credibility-related matters deserves special attention, since it arises as an important element in assessing every attribute of a person's credibility.

It is very common to hear a witness described as being *biased*. Perhaps this witness has some stake in the outcome of deliberations in which he provides testimony. A witness' testimony might be favorable or unfavorable to his interests or to the interests of someone else whom he may either admire or despise. The present analysis makes clear the fact that *there is more than one species of witness bias to be considered*. We need to recognize the possible existence of biases that can be associated with any or all of the attributes: veracity, objectivity, and observational sensitivity. Let us start at the bottom of our four-stage reasoning chain and consider the veracity-related likelihoods: $a_4 = P(E^*|E_b)$ and $b_4 = P(E^*|E_b{}^c)$. On ancillary evidence, we believe witness W to be generally truthful but to have what I will term *testimonial bias*. First, suppose we believe that W's testimony E^* is very improbable, regardless of what she believes; that is, her testimony E^* is a rare event. If so, we may say she is *biased against* giving testimony E^*. In this case we might have $P(E^*|E_b) > P(E^*|E_b{}^c)$ where both are very small. Perhaps the reporting of event E was an extremely painful experience for witness W. On the other hand, we might suppose W's testimony E^* to be very probable, regardless of what she believes. In other words, she is *biased in favor* of giving testimony E*. On evidence, we might suppose that she relishes the act of providing this testimony. In this case we might have $P(E^*|E_b) > P(E^*|E_b^c)$ where both likelihoods are very large.

The same concerns appear at the next stage involving W's objectivity. At this stage we have the likelihoods $a_3 = P(E_b|E_s)$ and $b_3 = P(E_b|E_s^c)$. First suppose that, on evidence, we believe that W would be *biased against* believing that event E occurred; that is, E_b is a rare event. Perhaps she is so averse to the thought of E happening or so little expects E to happen that she would fail to believe even strong sensory evidence that E did occur. In this case we might have $P(E_b|E_s) > P(E_b|E_s^c)$ where both are very small. On the other hand, we might have evidence that W would believe that E occurred regardless of the sensory evidence she obtained in her alleged observation. Perhaps she so strongly wished or expected to observe event E that she would do so regardless of what her senses told her. In this case she is *biased in favor of believing* that E occurred, and we might have $P(E_b|E_s) > P(E_b|E_s^c)$ where both are very large. I have termed these two situations *objectivity biases*.

Finally, our senses may be biased in various ways. Evidence of sensory disabilities that affect response thresholds may lower the probability of a sensory response, whether or not a reported event did occur. In such cases our senses might be *biased against* reporting E; so for witness W we might have $P(E_s|E) > P(E_s|E^c)$ where both are very small. We might also encounter evidence of deception in which case we might believe a witness's senses to have been *biased in favor* of reporting the occurrence of event E, whether or not E did occur. In this case we might have $P(E_s|E) > P(E_s|E^c)$ where both are very large. These two situations involve *sensory biases*. Notice that in Figure 3.8 I have included categories of ancillary evidence bearing upon testimonial, objectivity, and sensory bias.

Table 7.6 gives examples of two general facts about witness bias when we construe the force of evidence in Bayesian terms for singly connected chains

TABLE 7.6   Three Species of Witness Bias

Ingredients	Case 1	Case 2	Case 3	Case 4	Case 5	Case 6
1. $a_1 = P(E|H_1)$	0.90	0.90	0.90	0.90	0.90	0.90
2. $b_1 = P(E|H_2)$	0.05	0.05	0.05	0.05	0.05	0.05
3. $a_2 = P(E_s|E)$	0.95	0.95	0.95	0.95	**0.095**	**0.95**
4. $b_2 = P(E_s|E^c)$	0.01	0.01	0.01	0.01	**0.001**	**0.80**
5. $a_3 = P(E_b|E_s)$	0.95	0.95	**0.095**	**0.95**	0.95	0.95
6. $b_3 = P(E_b|E_s^c)$	0.01	0.01	**0.001**	**0.80**	0.01	0.01
7. $a_4 = P(E^*|E_b)$	**0.095**	**0.95**	0.95	0.95	0.95	0.95
8. $b_4 = P(E^*|E_b^c)$	**0.001**	**0.80**	0.01	0.01	0.01	0.01
D_4		0.034	6.058	0.142	5.760	0.244	5.480
L_{E^*}	11.12	1.14	5.43	1.15	3.89	1.15

of reasoning. In each case L_{E^*} has been determined using Equation 7.4. Those biases that act *in favor of* E^*, E_b, or E_s typically also act to destroy the inferential force of evidence. Biases *against* E^*, E_b, or E_s have a different effect. Six cases are shown in this table. Observe in each case that event E, if it did occur, favors H_1 over H_2 in the ratio 18/1. Cases 1 and 2 concern witnesses whom we believe to be objective and sensitive observers (see the likelihoods in rows 3 through 6) but who also appear to have *testimonial biases* (rows 7 and 8). In case 1 we believe the witness to be very trustworthy, as indicated by the large ratio of the likelihoods in rows 7 and 8. However, both of these likelihoods are very small, indicating our belief that the witness is biased *against* testifying E^*. But this testimonial bias by itself has almost no degrading effect on the force of evidence E^*. Recalling the discussion of Equation 7.8, in a singly connected chain of reasoning Bayes's rule responds only to the ratio and not the difference between likelihoods at the bottom of a chain of reasoning. In case 2, however, we have a witness who, although an objective and sensitive observer, has a distinct bias *in favor of* testifying E^*; notice the large values of a_4 and b_4. The value of testimony from this witness is virtually destroyed ($L_{E^*} = 1.14$), since, on ancillary evidence, we believe that this witness would, with high probability, tell us that event E occurred regardless of what she believed about E.

Cases 3 and 4 involve witnesses who, on evidence, demonstrate an *objectivity* bias. In case 3 the witness is a trustworthy and sensitive observer, but one who appears to have been *biased against* believing event E occurred at the time of her observation. Recalling the discussion, in Section 7.1.3, of the location of rare events in chains of reasoning, it does make a difference where in the chain we locate a rare event. In case 3 the rareness is moved one stage up the chain from where it was located in case 1. The result is that the force of evidence L_{E^*} is decreased over what it is in case 1. In case 4 we have a sensitive and trustworthy witness who, on evidence, appears to have been heavily *biased in favor of* believing that E occurred (notice the large values of a_3 and b_3). The force of evidence from this witness is as effectively destroyed as it was in case 2. Cases 5 and 6 involve *sensory biases*. In case 5 we have a witness whose appropriate sensory modality might have been *biased against* sensing E. The inferential force of E^* is decreased further but not completely destroyed. In case 6, however, the force of evidence E^* is all but completely destroyed because of our belief that the witness' senses would have given evidence of E whether or not it did occur.

All of the examples in Table 7.6 have a common characteristic: At any credibility stage of reasoning we have supposed that $a_i > b_i$. In every example $P(E^*|E_b) > P(E^*|E_b{}^c)$; $P(E_b|E_s) > P(E_b|E_s{}^c)$, and $P(E_s|E) > P(E_s|E^c)$. There is no reason of course why any of these likelihood relations should be assumed for any witness. We might have $a_i < b_i$ at any stage i. As an illustration of some of the very interesting consequences of having $a_i < b_i$ at various stages, consider the simpler chain of reasoning shown in Figure 7.11b. Assume, for the moment, that our major inferential interest concerns only whether or not

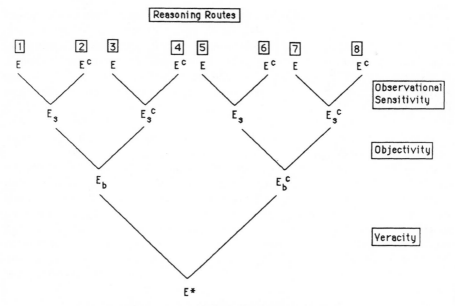

FIGURE 7.12   Credibility-related reasoning routes.

event E occurred, as witness W testifies. Figure 7.12 shows eight possible reasoning routes that we have to consider in our inference about whether event E did in fact occur. Observe that in four of these routes E^* will favor the occurrence of E and that in the other four E^* will favor the nonoccurrence of E. Bayes's rule essentially forces us to consider all of these reasoning routes; this happens during the expansion process described during discussion of Equation 7.1. We may of course believe some of them to be quite improbable. In all of the examples in Table 7.6, E^* favors E_b, E_b favors E_s, and E_s favors E. Thus route 1 in Figure 7.12 seems most likely in these examples.

Examination of other reasoning routes suggests possibilities we might not ordinarily consider. Starting at the top and going downward toward E^*, we identify various situations that may have different explanations. Take route 5, for example; event E happened and was duly recorded by W's senses. But W, against this sensory evidence, did not believe that E occurred. But then she lies by telling us that E did occur. In route 7 event E happened, but W got no sensory evidence of it (perhaps she made no relevant observation as she claims). She does not believe E occured but lies by telling us that E did occur. This route involves the somewhat humorous possibility that W may have made up a story that happens to be true. In either of these cases we may be entitled to conclude that event E occurred even though we received testimony from a lying witness. This possibility is recognized by legal scholars (e.g., Weinstein et al. 1983, 461–462). Case 4 offers the possibility that W, though trustworthy in reporting what she believes, may have hallucinated.

Event E did not happen, and W's senses gave no evidence that it did. Nevertheless, W believes that E occurred. Another possibility is that W so strongly expected or wished E to occur that she believed it did despite the contrary evidence of her senses. Other possibilities suggest themselves in the other routes. How probable any of these routes seem depends entirely upon the nature and amount of ancillary evidence that we have to support judgments of $a_i > b_i$ or $a_i < b_i$ at any credibility stage i.

7.3.3 Testimonial Evidence, Tangible Evidence, and TSD Observers

The likelihood ratio for the force of testimony E^* on events $\{E, E^c\}$ in the singly connected chain of reasoning in Figure 7.11b is $L_{E^*} = P(E^*|E)/P(E^*|E^c)$. Notice that L_{E^*} in this situation is simply a ratio of the hit (h) and false-positive (f) probabilities that we examined in Section 7.3.1 concerning tangible evidence. The difference is that we now wish to decompose h and f to take account of the credibility attributes of a human source. We might consider employing a special case of Equation 7.7 for the three-stage and singly connected chain of reasoning from E^* to $\{E, E^c\}$. In this special case

$$L_{E^*} = \frac{a_1 + [b_2/(a_2 - b_2)] + [b_3/(a_2 - b_2)(a_3 - b_3)]}{b_1 + [b_2/(a_2 - b_2)] + [b_3/(a_2 - b_2)(a_3 - b_3)]} = \frac{h}{f} \quad (7.13)$$

For the chain of reasoning shown in Figure 7.11b, $a_1 = P(E_s|E)$ and $b_1 = P(E_s|E^c)$ concern witness W's observational sensitivity; $a_2 = P(E_b|E_s)$ and $b_2 = P(E_b|E_s^c)$ concern W's objectivity; $a_3 = P(E^*|E_b)$ and $b_3 = P(E^*|E_b^c)$ concern W's veracity.

The trouble with Equation 7.13 is that it provides the *ratio h/f* but does not allow us to determine *exact values* of h and f. Having exact values of these probabilities allows us to establish some interesting relations between the theory of signal detectability (TSD) and the analysis of credibility-testimony issues. Exact values of h and f allow us to make comparisons involving the force of tangible and testimonial evidence. In addition they allow us to represent the behavior of a human subject asked to perform a signal detection task. We can obtain exact values of $h = P(E^*|E)$ and $f = P(E^*|E^c)$ by means of Equations 7.14 and 7.15; the ingredients of these equations are the ones defined in the paragraph above:

$$h = P(E^*|E) = a_1(a_2 - b_2)(a_3 - b_3) + b_2(a_3 - b_3) + b_3 \quad (7.14)$$

and

$$f = P(E^*|E^c) = b_1(a_2 - b_2)(a_3 - b_3) + b_2(a_3 - b_3) + b_3 \quad (7.15)$$

These two equations express the hit and false-positive probabilities for a human source in terms of his veracity, objectivity, and observational sensitivity. Notice that Equation 7.13 is obtained from h and f in Equations 7.14 and 7.15 by taking their ratio and then dividing numerator and denominator by the factor $(a_2 - b_2)(a_3 - b_3)$.

To set the stage for an analysis of the force of testimonial evidence E^* on events $\{E, E^c\}$, consider Figure 7.13. This figure illustrates the decomposition of h and f in terms of human credibility attributes. The pair of likelihoods associated with any of the three credibility attributes can be plotted in the same way that we plotted h and f for a nonhuman sensor. Thus, taking veracity for example, $P(E^*|E_b)$ can be plotted against $P(E^*|E_b{}^c)$. If we have a pair of likelihoods for each credibility attribute, Equations 7.14 and 7.15 show how to combine them in order to determine h and f for this source. By such means we integrate our evidence-justified probabilistic judgments regarding a person's credibility attributes in order to determine h and f, whose ratio prescribes the Bayesian inferential force of this person's testimony on the event testified.

There is now an abundance of empirical research using TSD concepts in studying the detection and recognition behavior of human observers (e.g., Swets 1964; Green and Swets 1966). Such studies involve repeated trials, under various conditions, from which estimates of h and f are obtained for individual observers. From these estimates conclusions are drawn about $\mathbf{d'}$

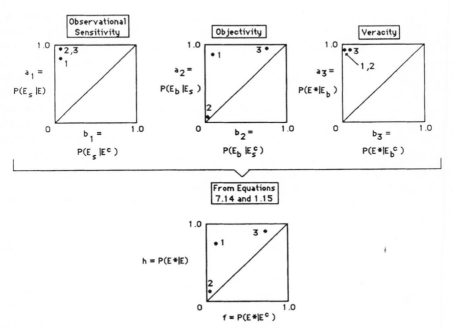

FIGURE 7.13 Calculating the Bayesian force of testimonial evidence from a decomposition of source credibility.

and response threshold settings for human observers. One assumption prevalent in such studies is that human observers will always be truthful in reporting their beliefs. This assumption cannot of course be made outside the laboratory. Equations 14 and 15 simply show us how h and f might be determined for an observer or witness in *nonreplicable* situations when we decompose observer credibility in terms of veracity, objectivity, and observational sensitivity. We will in fact be able to characterize the behavior of a witness giving testimony about a nonreplicable event in the same terms as those used to characterize the behavior of subjects in signal detection experiments.

Shown in Table 7.7 are examples involving the calculation of h, f, and their ratio L_E. from credibility attribute likelihoods in the special case in Figure 7.11*b*. These examples will show us one method for comparing the inferential force of testimonial evidence from a person with tangible evidence provided by a sensor or from an observer who has certain characteristics expressed in TSD terms. The first three cases in Table 7.7 are plotted in Figure 7.13. In case 1 we have a person whose veracity, objectivity, and observational sensitivity we believe to be quite substantial. Likelihood pairs for each of these attributes are plotted as points labeled 1 in the top three diagrams in Figure 7.13. We use these three likelihood pairs in Equations 7.14 and 7.15 to determine $h = 0.69$ and $f = 0.09$, which is shown as point 1 in the bottom plot. Because we have exact values of h and f, we can determine both d' and *response threshold setting* for this person or for a sensor having these h and f values, provided that we are willing to make various (testable) assumptions about the behavior and properties of this observer or sensor. In any comparison of a person with a sensor we would of course be obliged to specify relevant characteristics of the sensor. Persons interested in such comparisons should consult the work of Egan (1975) on the analysis of ROC curves; he discusses a number of assumptions we might make about sensor and observer characteristics. In a previous work I have shown how d', together with various decisional strategies for setting a response threshold, acts to determine the inferential force of evidence in a signal detection task (Schum 1981a).

TABLE 7.7 Values of h and f from Credibility Attribute Likelihoods

Ingredients	Case 1	Case 2	Case 3	Case 4	Case 5	Case 6
$a_1 = P(E_i\|E)$	0.8	0.95	0.95	0.10	0.95	0.01
$b_1 = P(E_s\|E^c)$	0.05	0.05	0.05	0.90	0.01	0.60
$a_2 = P(E_b\|E_s)$	0.9	0.095	0.95	0.20	0.10	0.90
$b_2 = P(E_b\|E_s^c)$	0.05	0.005	0.75	0.70	0.80	0.20
$a_3 = P(E^*\|E_b)$	0.95	0.95	0.95	0.95	0.01	0.10
$b_3 = P(E^*\|E_b^c)$	0.01	0.01	0.05	0.01	0.95	0.80
$h = P(E^*\|E)$	0.69	0.10	0.90	0.62	0.82	0.66
$f = P(E^*\|E^c)$	0.09	0.02	0.73	0.25	0.20	0.37
$L_E. = h/f$	7.67	5.00	1.23	2.48	4.10	1.78

Returning to case 1 in Table 7.7 and Figure 7.13, evidence E* from a person having these credibility credentials has the same inferential force on events {E, E^c} as a TSD sensor or observer having reasonably high sensitivity **d'** and whose response threshold has been set to *minimize maximum error* in terms of false-positives (f) and misses (m). Since we cannot decrease one without increasing the other, an observer (or sensor) adopting this *minimax* threshold setting should attempt to keep $f = m$. Since $m = 1 - h$, this is equivalent to setting $h = 1 - f$, plots of which fall along the *negative diagonal* in the bottom diagram of Figure 7.13. The h, f pair in case 1 falls close to this negative diagonal. In case 2 we have an observationally sensitive and trustworthy witness who also, we believe, is biased against believing that event E happened (note that a_2 and b_2 are both very small but have a large ratio). From the point labeled 2 in the bottom diagram in Figure 7.13, we see that testimony E* from this person has inferential force equivalent to a TSD observer or sensor having a reasonable **d'** but a response threshold setting designed to *minimize false-positives*. Case 3 shows a person who is a sensitive and trustworthy observer but who also appears biased in favor of believing that event E happened. This person's testimony has the same force on {E, E^c} as a TSD observer with reasonable **d'** but whose response threshold is set to *minimize misses* (see the point labeled 3 in the bottom diagram of Figure 7.13).

The remaining cases in Table 7.7, not plotted in Figure 7.13, simply illustrate h and f determination for some of the unusual situations shown as possible in Figure 7.12. In each of these cases we have a witness W whose testimony favors the occurrence of the event she reports, even though attributes of her credibility are made defective in various ways. In an interpretation of the likelihoods used in these examples, it is necessary to note that for any credibility attribute there are two other likelihoods that are obtained by normalization. For example, all cases involve $P(E_s|E)$ and $P(E_s|E^c)$; by required Pascalian normalization, we also have $P(E_s^c|E) = 1 - P(E_s|E)$ and $P(E_s^c|E^c) = 1 - P(E_s|E^c)$. Some of these examples may be more easily interpreted using likelihoods obtained by normalization from the ones given; I have simply listed the likelihoods required by Equations 7.14 and 7.15 to determine h and f.

Case 4 involves route 3 in Figure 7.12. One story we could tell using the numbers in this case is that of deception recognized by a witness. Suppose that E occurred but W's senses were tricked into reporting that it did not occur. Observe that I list $P(E_s|E) = 0.1$. This also means that $P(E_s^c|E) = 0.9$ which corresponds with this part of the story. Perhaps recognizing the possibility of deception, W goes against the evidence of her senses and believes (accepts) that E did occur. Notice that we have $P(E_b|E_s^c) > P(E_b|E_s)$. She then faithfully reports what she believes to us. In a Bayesian construal of the force of W's testimony, we are entitled to believe that it favors the occurrence of event E, even though the evidence of W's senses (our primary "interface" with E or E^c) favors the nonoccurrence of event E. Notice that we have $P(E_s|E^c) > P(E_s|E)$.

Case 5 in Table 7.7 involves reasoning route 5 in Figure 7.12. In this case we can tell a story of a sensitive but nonobjective witness whom we also believe to be a liar. Suppose that E happened and was, with high probability, reported by W's senses; the large ratio of $P(E_s|E)$ to $P(E_s|E^c)$ indicates our confidence in her sensory capabilities. But for some reason W believes E did not occur against this sensory evidence. She then goes against her beliefs about E and tells us that E did occur. If we had ancillary evidence to justify the probability judgments in this example, Bayes's rule says we are entitled to say that her untruthful testimony E* favors the occurrence of event E, in accordance with the sensory evidence we believe she received. Notice, however, that the force of her testimony E* is drastically reduced over the force of knowing for sure that she did receive sensory evidence of event E (which we believe would have been very accurate). Case 6 in Table 7.7 involves reasoning route 7 in Figure 7.12. Here we have the possibility of a witness deceived who then passes another deception along to us. Suppose that event E happened but W's senses, being misled, failed to report its occurrence. Objectively, W does not believe or accept that E occurred but then lies by reporting that event E did occur. Note that, by normalization, $P(E_s^c|E) = 1 - 0.01 = 0.99$, $P(E_b^c|E_s^c) = 1 - 0.2 = 0.8$. Also note that $P(E^*|E_b^c) = 0.8$. Taken together, these likelihoods favor route 7, but only weakly as indicated by $L_{E^*} = 1.78$.

7.3.4 The Force of Testimony in Non-singly Connected Chains of Reasoning

In the preceding discussion of the inferential force of testimony we have assumed the simplest case in which a chain of reasoning, from testimony to major hypotheses or from testimony to the event reported, is singly connected. But there are elements of the credibility-related behavior of human sources of evidence that we cannot capture in simple cases. We may have evidence-justified reasons for believing that attributes of the credibility of a witness are state dependent in ways similar to those we noted for sensors. For example, we might discover that the ability of a radiologist to detect a particular anomaly on X-ray images is better for patients who have tuberculosis than it is for patients who have pneumonia. In this instance the detection behavior of the radiologist has inferential significance on whether a patient has tuberculosis or pheumonia quite apart from the significance of the existence of the anomaly. In other situations we may feel quite justified in believing that a person's veracity, for example, might depend upon situations represented by hypotheses we entertain. In addition we have to consider the possibility of other dependencies involving attributes of a person's credibility. For example, we might wish to consider the possibility that a person's veracity and observational sensitivity are linked in various ways.

Figure 7.14a shows an array of possibilities that Bayesian likelihood ratios force us to consider when we decompose the credibility of a human source. Events at any stage below $\{E, E^c\}$ may be linked to events at stages higher

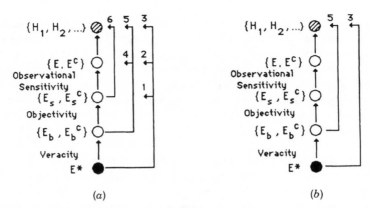

FIGURE 7.14 Possible additional linkages in a decomposition of the credibility of testimonial evidence from a human source.

than the ones immediately above. The arcs labeled 1, 2, and 3 illustrate possible linkages involving E^* to events at stages higher than $\{E_b, E_b^c\}$. Arcs 4 and 5 illustrate possible linkages of events $\{E_b, E_b^c\}$ to events at stages above $\{E_s, E_s^c\}$. Arc 6 shows the possibility of linkages between $\{E_s, E_s^c\}$ and hypotheses $\{H_1, H_2, \ldots\}$. Linkages 1, 2, and 4 concern possible dependencies involving credibility attributes veracity, objectivity, and observational sensitivity. Linkages 3, 5, and 6 concern possible state dependencies involving each of the three credibility attributes. In each of these six possibilties there is potential inferential force on hypotheses $\{H_1, H_2, \ldots\}$ lurking in the behavior of a human source of evidence E^*.

As noted several times earlier, what we know or believe that we know about a human source is at least as valuable inferentially as what the source tells us. To illustrate such situations, I will confine attention to the situation in Figure 7.14*b* in which we have just two of the six additional linkages shown in 7.14*a*. The two linkages I will consider involve state-dependency of a person's objectivity and veracity. As an example of a situation in which such dependencies might occur, suppose we ask person W whether H_1 or H_2 is true. In reply, W says: "I cannot tell you about H_1 or H_2, but I did observe event E." Suppose we recognize that event E, if it occurred, would favor H_1 over H_2. People do not always tell us everything they believe they know. Perhaps W does know whether H_1 or H_2 is true. We might believe, for example, that W would be more likely to lie in his testimony E^* if H_1 were true than if H_2 were true. We capture such possibilities by means of arc 3 in Figure 7.14*b*.

But it is also possible that W's objectivity in observing whether or not E occurred depends upon H_1 or H_2. We might suppose, for example, that the occurrence or truth of H_1, if known or suspected by W, would make him very biased in favor of or against believing that event E occurred, regardless of what his senses reported. Situations like this are captured by means of arc 5 in Figure 7.14b. It is possible, of course, that we might have both situations occurring at the same time. Both W's veracity and objectivity might depend upon whether H_1 or H_2 were true. Let us now examine a likelihood ratio for testimony E^* that captures the possible state-dependency of both objectivity and veracity. In another work I have provided a likelihood ratio expression that captures all of the possible dependencies shown in Figure 7.14a (Schum 1989).

We begin with Equation 7.10, noting that for $i = 1, 2, h_i = P(E^*|EH_i)$ and $f_i = P(E^*|E^cH_i)$. We wish to decompose the linkage between E^* and $\{E, E^c\}$ to take account of person W's veracity, objectivity, and observational sensitivity, as we did using Equations 7.14 and 7.15. Our new problem is that we suppose, as in Figure 7.14b, that E^* is conditioned by events in $\{H_1, H_2, \ldots\}$ in addition to being conditioned by events in $\{E_b, E_b{}^c\}$, and that events in $\{E_b, E_b{}^c\}$ are conditioned by $\{H_1, H_2, \ldots\}$ in addition to being conditioned by events in $\{E_s, E_s{}^c\}$. In this situation we have for $i = 1, 2$,

$$h_i = a[(c_i - d_i)(v_i - w_i)] + d_i(v_i - w_i) + w_i \tag{7.16}$$

and

$$f_i = b[(c_i - d_i)(v_i - w_i)] + d_i(v_i - w_i) + w_i \tag{7.17}$$

where $a = P(E_s|E)$, $b = P(E_s|E^c)$, and for $i = 1, 2$, $c_i = P(E_b|E_sH_i)$, $d_i = P(E_b|E_s{}^cH_i)$, $v_i = P(E^*|E_bH_i)$, and $w_i = P(E^*|E_b{}^cH_i)$.

If we have appropriate ancillary evidence to justify the probabilities shown in Equations 7.16 and 7.17, we can use these equations to determine h_i and f_i and then calculate, by Equation 7.10, the likelihood ratio for testimony E^* on hypotheses H_1 and H_2. Table 7.8 contains six examples of calculations using these three equations. All of these examples illustrate how the behavior of a human source can, by itself, be inferentially interesting. In all six cases the Bayesian inferential force on H_1 and H_2 of knowing event E for sure is given by $L_E = P(E|H_1)/P(E|H_2) = 0.90/0.05 = 18$.

From the likelihood ingredients in case 1 we can tell the following story about a witness who testifies E^*. We believe the witness in this case to be observationally sensitive (see ingredients a and b). We also believe this witness to be objective, whether H_1 or H_2 is true (see ingredients c_1, c_2, d_1, and d_2). We believe this witness would, with high probability, believe that E occurred if he obtained sensory evidence of E and would with only low probability believe that E occurred if his senses did not give evidence of E. We have no evidence that he would believe that E occurred regardless of what his senses told him. But our beliefs about his veracity take the following form. If H_1 were true, he would, with high probability, report E^* if he believed that it occurred and would, with low probability, report E^* if he did not believe that E occurred (see ingredients v_1 and w_1). However, we also believe that, if H_2

TABLE 7.8   Inferentially Interesting Credibility Attributes

Ingredients	Case 1	Case 2	Case 3	Case 4	Case 5	Case 6
1. $P(E\|H_1)$	0.9	0.9	0.9	0.9	0.9	0.9
2. $P(E\|H_2)$	0.05	0.05	0.05	0.05	0.05	0.05
3. $a = P(E_s\|E)$	0.98	0.98	0.98	0.98	0.98	0.98
4. $b = P(E_s\|E^c)$	0.01	0.01	0.01	0.01	0.01	0.01
5. $c_1 = P(E_b\|E_sH_1)$	0.9	0.9	0.9	0.9	0.099	0.95
6. $c_2 = P(E_b\|E_sH_2)$	0.9	0.9	0.099	0.095	0.9	0.98
7. $d_1 = P(E_b\|E_s^cH_1)$	0.05	0.05	0.05	0.75	0.001	0.75
8. $d_2 = P(E_b\|E_s^cH_2)$	0.05	0.05	0.001	0.001	0.05	0.01
9. $v_1 = P(E^*\|E_bH_1)$	0.98	0.95	0.95	0.95	0.095	0.2
10. $v_2 = P(E^*\|E_bH_2)$	0.05	0.09	0.95	0.95	0.95	0.01
11. $w_1 = P(E^*\|E_b^cH_1)$	0.01	0.75	0.01	0.01	0.001	0.9
12. $w_2 = P(E^*\|E_b^cH_2)$	0.01	0.005	0.01	0.01	0.01	0.98
13. h_1 (Eq. 7.16)	0.867	0.927	0.840	0.853	0.010	0.050
14. f_1 (Eq. 7.17)	0.067	0.762	0.065	0.716	0.001	0.374
15. h_2 (Eq. 7.16)	0.045	0.080	0.101	0.098	0.840	0.900
16. f_2 (Eq. 7.17)	0.012	0.010	0.012	0.012	0.065	0.961
17. L_{E^*} (Eq. 7.10)	57.66	67.44	46.35	51.49	0.088^a	0.086^a

[a]Favors H_2.

were true, he would be less truthful and also biased against reporting the occurrence of E (see ingredients v_2 and w_2). Observe in rows 13 to 16 that this person's h/f ratio is much larger if H_1 were true than if H_2 were true. This witness has told us that event E occurred, a report that he would have been loath to provide if H_2 were true. This hypothesis-contingent testimonial bias has inferential force on its own. Observe that L_{E^*} is $57.66/18 = 3.2$ times more forceful in favoring H_1 over H_2 than our knowing for sure that event E occurred.

As far as observational sensitivity and objectivity are concerned, case 2 is identical to case 1. The difference in case 2 is that the pattern of hypothesis-contingent veracity behavior of the witness is quite different. Notice that v_1 and w_1 picture this witness as being very biased in favor of reporting event E if H_1 were true. But if H_2 were true, ingredients v_2 and w_2 picture this witness as being very biased against reporting event E. Notice that h_1 and f_1 are both large but h_2 and f_2 are both very small and not in a large ratio. A Bayesian likelihood ratio for this testimony tells us that it has $67.44/18 = 3.75$ times as much force favoring H_1 over H_2 as does our knowing for sure that event E occurred. In this case we have the hypothesis-contingent dominance of false-positives we discussed in connection with case 1 in Table 7.5.

In cases 3 and 4 the hypothesis-contingent behavior concerns a witness' objectivity. In both of these cases we have observationally sensitive and truthful witnesses. In case 3 we believe the witness reporting E^* to have been strongly biased *against* believing that E occurred if H_2 was also true (see c_2

and d_2). If the witness also knew or suspected H_2 to be true, he might have thought the occurrence of E to be very unlikely, as we have done in setting $P(E|H_2) = 0.05$. Once again, witnesses may have more knowledge or other beliefs that are not reflected in the testimony they provide. The testimony in case 3 favors H_1 over H_2 more strongly than does the known occurrence of event E. In case 4 we have a witness who appears biased *in favor of* believing that E happened if H_1 were true (see c_1 and d_1). Perhaps, if H_1 were true, the thought of E also happening might have been pleasing to the witness, so we think that he might, with strong probability, have believed that E occurred regardless of what his senses recorded. This bias, conditonal upon H_1, acts to increase the Bayesian force of evidence E^* over knowing event E for sure. Case 4 is especially interesting because it shows how a bias against believing some event, if conditional upon some hypothesis we entertain, does not degrade the force of evidence as it does in instances involving singly connected chains of reasoning. Compare the result in case 4 in Table 7.8 with case 3 in Table 7.7.

In cases 5 and 6 in Table 7.8 we consider witnesses whose objectivity and veracity are *both* conditional upon hypotheses H_1 and H_2. In case 5 we believe the witness to be biased against believing event E if H_1 were true (see c_1 and d_1) and also biased against testifying E^* if H_1 were true (see v_1 and w_1). The effect of this double bias is to make h_2/f_2 considerably larger than h_1/f_1. Consequently testimony E^* from this witness favors H_2 over H_1 in the ratio $0.088 = 1/11.36$, even though event E favors H_1 over H_2 in the ratio $18/1$. Notice that E^* in this case has more force on H_2 over H_1 than knowing for sure that E did not occur. The Bayesian force of knowing E^c is $L_{E^c} = 0.10/0.95 = 1/9.5$ favoring H_2 over H_1. In case 6 we have a witness with a bias in favor of believing E if H_1 were true (see c_1 and d_1) whom we also believe is untruthful. But in addition we believe this witness' untruthfulness to be more likely if H_2 were true than if H_1 were true (compare w_2/v_2 with w_1/v_1). Here we have a witness with good observational sensitivity who could easily detect or recognize event E if it occurred. In addition this witness either wants or expects E to be true. But, if we also believe this witness to be lying, we must naturally expect that this witness does not believe E to have occurred. So we feel entitled to believe with some strength the opposite of what he reports. The contingency of this untruthfulness upon H_2 only increases the force of his testimony E^* in a direction opposite to that of the event he reports.

You may regard these examples as preposterous. They certainly involve very strong beliefs as indicated by the extreme likelihoods in each of the examples. My purpose was to provide additional examples of how testimony E^* in non-singly connected chains of reasoning can have value in excess of the value of knowing E or E^c for sure. We can all agree, however, that such strong beliefs *on our part* about attributes of the credibility of the witnesses in these examples must have been justified by equally strong and equally complete credibility-relevant evidence. No one would take extreme probability assessments seriously unless they were backed by compelling evidence. This leads to our next credibility-related topic: the completeness of coverage of matters relevant to assessing the veracity, objectivity, and observational sensitivity of human sources of evidence.

7.3.5 Baconian Credibility Assessment

Discussed in Section 5.5, and illustrated in Figures 5.9 and 5.10, is an eliminative and variative approach to an inference based on testimony when the credibility of a witness has been decomposed into the attributes: veracity, objectivity, and observational sensitivity. I used this inference in Section 5.5 to illustrate elements of Jonathan Cohen's system of Baconian probabilities. Consider Figure 5.10, and note that the inference involves whether or not event E did occur as witness W testifies. We might wish to add other links on this chain of reasoning to show the bearing of events $\{E, E^c\}$ on other hypotheses we might entertain. However, for our present purposes we need only consider an inference from testimony E^* to events $\{E, E^c\}$. Figure 5.10 illustrates how we may detach a belief at each of the three stages of this inference. Belief detachment rests upon eliminative tests of a generalization appropriate to each stage of reasoning. Such testing involves the use of credibility-relevant ancillary evidence (summarized in Figure 3.8) to determine the extent to which each of these generalizations do apply to W and his present testimony E^*. Thus, for witness W, we successively test veracity, objectivity, and observational sensitivity generalizations in reasoning from E^* to events $\{E, E^c\}$.

We have also considered a Bayesian approach to the inference in Figure 5.10. The Bayesian force of evidence E^* on events $\{E, E^c\}$ is given by the values $h = P(E^*|E)$ and $f = P(E^*|E^c)$. In Equations 7.14 and 7.15 we decomposed h and f to incorporate likelihoods associated with credibility attributes: veracity, objectivity, and observational sensitivity. In another work I have illustrated how Bayesian and Baconian approaches to inferences based on testimony are complementary and not at all antagonistic (Schum 1991). We need appropriate generalizations and ancillary evidence to justify judgments of the likelihoods a Bayesian approach requires. It should be clear that relative frequencies are rarely, if ever, available to support these judgments. A Baconian, faced with a chain of reasoning, is concerned about the relevance and completeness or sufficiency of the evidence we have to support our judgments or beliefs regarding events at each stage of reasoning, whether or not it involves credibility issues.

The example of Baconian reasoning in Figure 5.10 shows detached beliefs in the events E_b (W believes that event E occurred), E_s (W received sensory evidence of E), and E. This pattern of belief formation coincides with reasoning route 1 in Figure 7.12. This figure shows that there are seven other reasoning routes or patterns of belief-detachment that are possible. In Baconian terms, which pattern of belief-detachment we adopt depends upon the nature of the ancillary evidence we have. For example, we might believe that on balance the veracity-relevant evidence we have favors event $E_b{}^c$, that W does not believe what he testified. In this case we would then find ourselves on one of routes 5, 6, 7, or 8, depending upon which beliefs we detached at higher stages in this chain of reasoning. Recall from Section 5.5 that the Baconian system of probabilities allows us to grade the length and strength of the inferential limb on which we find ourselves when we detach a belief at any reasoning stage. The length and strength of this limb depends upon how complete has been our coverage of matters we believe relevant in testing the generalization at any stage. The inferential limb is weak to the extent that we have left questions unanswered about whether or not a generalization holds in the present case in which it is being applied.

Suppose we contemplate a Bayesian analysis of the force of testimony E^* from witness W on events $\{E, E^c\}$. In assessing W's credibility in terms of the three attributes we have been considering, suppose we can find no ancillary evidence regarding one or more of these attributes. For example, suppose we have relevant ancillary evidence about W's veracity and observational sensitivity but none at all about W's objectivity in his interpretation of the observation that he allegedly made. We might say that as far as W's objectivity is concerned, we are in a state of ignorance, where this term indicates a lack of evidence or knowledge. If this were so, upon what basis are we to make any judgments about the objectivity likelihoods $P(E_b|E_s)$ and $P(E_b|E_s{}^c)$ that would not be regarded as purely fictional? If we had no basis at all for judging these likelihoods, we would have to regard our chain of reasoning from E^* to $\{E, E^c\}$ to be severed, since we have no basis for passing from events $\{E_b, E_b{}^c\}$ to events $\{E_s, E_s{}^c\}$. In such a case we could draw a conclusion about whether or not W believes that E occurred, but we could never draw a conclusion about whether or not E did occur.

Attempts to proceed by setting $P(E_b|E_s) = P(E_b|E_s{}^c)$ to reflect our ignorance will fail for two reasons. First, giving these two likelihoods the same value completely destroys the force of testimony E^* regardless of the values of the likelihoods for W's veracity and observational sensitivity. Second, these two likelihoods can be set equal in an infinity of different ways, each of which would rest upon specific evidence. However, it might be argued that we are never in a state of true ignorance. In the case of W's objectivity, for example, we have at least some background knowledge about human objectivity or else we would never have been able to assert a generalization such as, "People (usually, often, frequently, etc.) believe the evidence of their senses." We might set $P(E_b|E_s) > P(E_b|E_s{}^c)$ in accordance with giving this generalization the benefit of the doubt in W's case. I note that the Baconian system does allow us to detach a belief in E_s, in absence of relevant ancillary evidence about W's objectivity, by giving this same generalization the benefit of the doubt.

There are still two troubles faced by the Bayesian. First, we might very well set $P(E_b|E_s) > P(E_b|E_s{}^c)$ but not by very much, since the preceding generalization applies to people in general and not to W in particular. Second, we could set $P(E_b|E_s)$ slightly greater than $P(E_b|E_s^c)$ but also in an infinity of ways, each of which supposes we have evidence we do not have. For example, suppose we set $P(E_b|E_s) = 0.09 > P(E_b|E_s^c) = 0.07$. Remember that we have no specific evidence about W's objectivity. But the two likelihoods we have just assessed picture W as being biased against believing that event E happened, an opinion that could only be justified by evidence we do not have. If we set $P(E_b|E_s) = 0.90 > P(E_b|E_s^c) = 0.70$, we picture W as being biased in favor of believing event E occurred, an opinion that would also require evidence that we do not have. If we set $P(E_b|E_s) = 0.55 > P(E_b|E_s^c) = 0.45$, this reflects no particular bias on W's part. But it represents a belief on our part that would also have to be justified by evidence we do not have.

We may differ among ourselves about whether or not total evidential vacuities exist. But it seems obvious that in any assessment of the credibility of a human source of evidence, we will not have evidence about this person's credibility attributes in all of the categories shown in Figure 3.8. What we naturally expect is that we may have more evidence about one attribute than we do about another. The Bayesian view of the task of assessing the force of directly relevant evidence E^* provides us with no methods for grading how complete has been our coverage of evidence relevant to the strength or weakness of each link in a chain of reasoning set up by E^*. But this is precisely what the Baconian system allows us to grade. In testimonial situations in which credibility-related matters are very important, it would do no harm at all to think in Bayesian *and* Baconian terms in assessing the credibility of the person(s) providing us with this testimony.

7.4 SECONDHAND EVIDENCE

Pressed to state what I believe is the form of evidence we most frequently encounter in our daily lives, I suppose I would say it is evidence that we obtain at secondhand. You may recall my earlier comment (Section 6.2.1) that by *secondhand* I really mean *nth hand* to refer to the fact that there may be any number of sources in the chain along which a report about some event has been passed. In some instances all of the sources are people who allegedly pass testimony from one to the other. In other cases the sources are documents or other kinds of tangible evidence. We all hear of "paper trails" in which one document records the existence of information allegedly reported in another. Your passport is a very good example; it alleges the existence of other documents verifying the time and place of your birth. The possible combinations of sources in a chain is endless, as indicated in Figure 7.15. We suppose that there is some *primary source* (the *horse's mouth*, if you like) who/that allegedly recorded the occurrence or nonoccurrence of some event of interest. This primary source could have been a person or some device. So could any of the other *intermediate* sources through which this primary

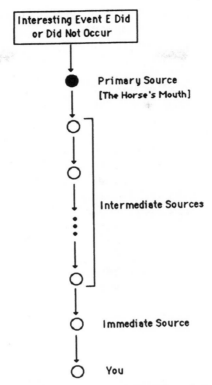

FIGURE 7.15 Evidence obtained through a chain of sources.

record has been passed to the *immediate* source who/that informed you about this event.

Accounts of events reported in newspapers and books, on television, and on the radio all qualify as secondhand evidence unless the person/device doing the reporting is a primary source. We take seriously such reports through a chain of sources if the sources in the chain can be identified, particularly the primary source. The names *rumor* or *gossip* are commonly given to a report whose primary or intermediate sources cannot be identified. It is common knowledge that there are rules governing the admissibility of *hearsay* evidence in court trials. What is not so common knowledge is the array of exclusions to the rule forbidding hearsay (e.g., see Kaplan, Waltz, and Park 1992, 130–351). Debate continues about the extent to which existing hearsay rules make sense (Park 1992).

Suppose that one witness W_2 claims in court that another witness W_1 (not now in court) asserted (to W_2) that event E occurred. As an example, a ship's pilot named Dyer appeared as a witness in the trial of Sir Walter Raleigh, who was accused of being a co-conspirator (along with Lord Cobham) in a plot to kill King James I. At trial Dyer asserted that an (unnamed) Portuguese gentleman had told him in Lisbon that Raleigh and Cobham would cut the king's throat before he was crowned. Raleigh objected: "This is the saying of some wild Jesuit or beggerly priest; but what proof is it against me?" The attorney general replied: "It must perforce arise out of some preceding intelligence, and shows your treason had wings" (Lempert and Saltzburg 1977, 332). Raleigh was convicted on the basis of information having no better status than rumor, since no primary or other intermediate source was ever identfied. The possible existence of other sources was acknowledged in the attorney general's fatuous reply. Rules against hearsay at trial date from the 1600s, largely in response to the recognized injustice in Raleigh's case.

The sixth amendment to the United States Constitution incorporates a confrontation clause allowing the right of a defendant to confront adversary witnesses. Wigmore argued that the purpose of a hearsay rule was to guarantee the right of a defendant to determine, by cross-examination, the credibility credentials of all witnesses against him, something that is difficult to accomplish for witnesses not in court (Wigmore on Evidence, vol. 5, 1974, §1367, 32–36). The following analyses illustrate some of the difficulties inherent in establishing the credibility-related foundations for the inferential force of evidence obtained through a chain of sources. As we have observed, we face interesting and difficult inferential problems even when we have evidence from a primary source. These difficulties are only compounded when we have evidence obtained through a chain of sources. The following analyses rest, to some extent, on others recently provided (Tillers and Schum 1992; Schum 1992). These analyses are also similar in some respects to the one offered by Richard Friedman (1987).

Let us begin with a very simple example of secondhand evidence. This example is simple because we consider just two sources and we do not decompose the credibility of the sources into any specific attributes. Consider the chain of reasoning shown in Figure 7.16. The sources of evidence in this chain of reasoning might be either human or not. What we have is evidence

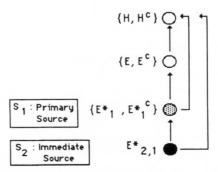

FIGURE 7.16 State-dependent credibility in secondhand evidence.

$E_{2.1}^*$ from an *immediate* source S_2 that a *primary* source S_1 reported the occurrence of event E. Let E_1^* represent the alleged report of event E by S_1 to S_2. The immediacy of S_2 means that we have some direct interface with this source. It could be the testimony of a person to whom we have ready access or some tangible record that we can examine for ourselves. The primacy of S_1 means that to our best current knowledge, S_1 *might have* made some sensory or other record of the occurrence or nonoccurrence of event E. In this situation we are considering S_1 to be the "horse's mouth." Of course we have to entertain the possibility that S_1 made no such recording at all; S_2's report might be entirely fictitious.

In Bayesian terms the force of evidence $E_{2.1}^*$ on hypotheses $\{H, H^c\}$ is given by the likelihood ratio $L_{E_{2.1}^*} = P(E_{2.1}^*|H)/P(E_{2.1}^*|H^c)$. In Figure 7.16 we allow for the fact that our chain of reasoning might not be singly connected; notice the arcs linking $E_{2.1}^*$ and E_1^* directly to $\{H, H^c\}$. First, suppose we eliminate these two arcs and consider a singly connected chain of reasoning from $E_{2.1}^*$ to $\{H, H^c\}$. This gives us a three-stage chain of reasoning, whose likelihood ratio is given by Equation 7.3 in Section 7.1.1. For present purposes we need to change notation a bit. Let $a_1 = P(E|H)$ and $b_1 = P(E|H^c)$, as in Equation 7.3. But now we let $a_2 = P(E_1^*|E) = h_1$ and $b_2 = P(E_1^*|E^c) = f_1$. Similarly we let $a_3 = P(E_{2.1}^*|E_1^*) = h_2$ and $b_3 = P(E_{2.1}^*|E_1^{*c}) = f_2$. Notice here that the event E_1^{*c} means "source S_1 did not report event E to S_2." This includes the possibilities that (1) S_1 reported to S_2 that E did not occur and (2) S_1 made no report to S_2 at all. With these notational changes, we have:

$$L_{E_{2.1}^*} = \frac{a_1 + f_1/[(h_1 - f_1)] + f_2/[(h_1 - f_1)(h_2 - f_2)]}{b_1 + f_1/[(h_1 - f_1)] + f_2/[(h_1 - f_1)(h_2 - f_2)]} \qquad (7.18)$$

As in other cases, the inferential force of knowing event E for sure is given in Bayesian terms by the ratio $L_E = a_1/b_1$. But we do not know E for sure; all we have is evidence of about E that has allegedly passed through two sources. The drag on our opinion revision, based upon $E_{2.1}^*$, depends upon the credibility of the primary source in reporting to the secondary source (indicated by h_1 and f_1) and the credibility of the secondary source in reporting to us (indicated by h_2 and f_2). If we added additional sources in the chain, assuming it is singly connected, we would simply employ Equations 7.5 and 7.6 with $a_i = h_i$ and $b_i = f_i$ for every $i \geq 2$. All of the comments made in Section 7.1 about the location of weak links, rare events, and inferential transitivity apply to Equation 7.18 and to extensions of it just mentioned. In terms of credibility there is no order of precedence between S_1 and S_2; credibility impeachment of either source is equally effective in reducing the force of this secondhand evidence. The rareness of S_2's report to us makes no difference, but the rareness of S_1's alleged report does. Recall from Section 7.1.3 that it does matter to Bayes's rule where in a chain of reasoning a rare event is located. The force of S_2's evidence to us would be reduced if we believed it unlikely that S_1 would have reported the occurrence of E to S_2, whether or not event E did happen. Finally, inferential transitivity is conferred if $h_1 > f_1$ and $h_2 > f_2$. In this case evidence $E_{2,1}^*$ favors the same hypothesis as does event E.

If we suppose that the credibility of either or both of our sources is also dependent upon whether H or H^c is true, we have the additional arcs shown in Figure 7.16. To account for the possibility that the credibilities of both sources are state dependent in this way, we have the more complex likelihood ratio:

$$
L_{E_{2,1}^*} = \frac{a_1(h_{1(H)} - f_{1(H)})(h_{2(H)} - f_{2(H)}) + f_{1(H)}(h_{2(H)} - f_{2(H)}) + f_{2(H)}}{b_1(h_{1(H^c)} - f_{1(H^c)})(h_{2(H^c)} - f_{2(H^c)}) + f_{1(H^c)}(h_{2(H^c)} - f_{2(H^c)}) + f_{2(H^c)}}
$$

$$(7.19)$$

In this case $a_1 = P(E|H)$ and $b_1 = P(E|H^c)$, as in Equation 7.18. But the credibility-related h and f terms for each source have to acknowledge the possible contingency involving H and H^c, and so for S_1 we let $h_{1(H)} = P(E_1^*|EH)$, $f_{1(H)} = P(E_1^*|E^cH)$, $h_{1(H^c)} = P(E_1^*|EH^c)$, and $f_{1(H^c)} = P(E_1^*|E^cH^c)$. For source S_2 we have $h_{2(H)} = P(E_{2,1}^*|E_1^*H)$, $f_{2(H)} = P(E_{2,1}^*|E_1^{*c}H)$, $h_{2(H^c)} = P(E_{2,1}^*|E_1^*H^c)$, and $f_{2(H^c)} = P(E_{2,1}^*|E_1^{*c}H^c)$.

Equation 7.19 allows us to capture situations in which secondhand evidence about event E might have more inferential force on $\{H, H^c\}$ than would our knowing for sure that event E occurred. The value of $L_{E_{2,1}^*}$ in Equation 7.18 cannot exceed the ratio a_1/b_1; there are no such bounds on $L_{E_{2,1}^*}$ in Equation 7.19. I will not provide any numerical examples of Equation 7.19 because you have already observed some of the effects of state-dependent credibility in other examples I have given in Tables 7.5 and 7.8. In addition, transitivity may be expected but not conferred by Equation 7.19, in the manner illustrated in Table 7.4 for Equation 7.10.

I fear that Equations 7.18 and 7.19 may suggest that the task of assessing the force of secondhand evidence is probabilistically uncomplicated, at least when we have just two sources in a chain. But there may be a substantial suppression of uncertainty in these two cases particularly if the sources were people, in which case we would have their veracity, objectivity, and observational sensitivity to consider. Figure 7.17 illustrates a situation in which we choose to decompose the h's and f's in Equation 7.18 to incorporate uncertainties we have about the three credibility attributes of persons S_1 and S_2.

First, observe that both of the chains of reasoning in Figure 7.17 are singly connected. The two chains differ not in length but in the manner in which events are partitioned at each reasoning stage. Chain B contains a certain partitioning of the complemented credibility-related events in chain A. As an example, consider events $\{E_{b,2}, E_{b,2}{}^c\}$ at the bottom stage of chain A. Event $E_{b,2}$ reads: "Source S_2 believes event E happened (as allegedly reported by S_1)." Event $E_{b,2}{}^c$ reads: "Source S_2 does not believe that event E happened (as allegedly reported by S_1)." But there are two possibilities as far as $E_{b,2}{}^c$

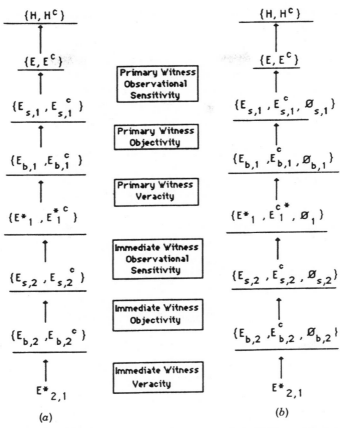

FIGURE 7.17 Secondhand evidence and decomposed credibility-related stages of reasoning.

is concerned. They are shown in chain B as (1) $E^c_{b.2} = S_2$ believes that E did not occur and (2) $\varnothing_{b.2}$, which represents the event that S_2 has no belief one way or the other about event E. It may happen that S_2 made up a story about S_1 telling him that event E happened. Thus $\varnothing_{s.2}$ is the event that S_2 made no sensory observation about what S_1 said, $\varnothing_1$ means that S_1 said nothing to S_2, $\varnothing_{b.1}$ means that S_1 has no belief about E, and $\varnothing_{s.1}$ means that S_1's senses gave no evidence about event E. If we have to rely entirely upon S_2, we have to consider the possibility that S_1 said nothing at all about event E to S_2 and perhaps never even made a relevant observation. Chain B simply includes events that would be associated with this possibility.

    Chain A in Figure 7.17 has seven stages, each involving a binary event class. Thus there are $2^7 = 128$ possible reasoning routes from $E^*_{2.1}$ to H or H^c of the sort we examined in Figure 7.12. In chain B there are many more possibilities because of the finer event partitioning at the credibility-related stages of reasoning; to be exact, there are $4(3^5) = 972$ possible reasoning routes. In either chain, each reasoning route tells a different story about how the hearsay evidence $E_{2,1}^*$ might have originated. Each of these routes identifies a plausible scenario affecting the inferential force of this hearsay. How probable any of them appears will depend entirely upon the ancillary evidence we have to justify the likelihoods required at any reasoning stage.

For the binary event case in chain A the likelihood ratio for hearsay evidence $E_{2,1}^*$ on $\{H, H^c\}$ is simply a seven-stage version of Equation 7.5, whose essential properties we discussed in Section 7.1. A considerably more complex likelihood ratio would result if we adopted the event partitioning shown in chain B. Analytic complexity increases beyond all reasonable bounds in either case when we consider the possible ways in which these chains of reasoning could be non-singly connected. The trouble is that consideration of at least some additional arcs seems necessary on occasion. Suppose we believe that S_2 is lying and in fact never received any word of the occurrence of event E from S_1. It would be entirely appropriate for us to consider why S_2 told us this particular lie instead of others he might have told. Some of the evidence-based reasons we may have for doubting S_2's veracity may have inferential force on whether H or H^c is true.

I have gone to considerable lengths in another work to illustrate how important are Baconian ideas about *evidential completeness* when we have long chains of reasoning such as those in Figure 7.17 (Schum 1992). In the case of hearsay evidence we may or may not have any specific evidence about a primary and other intermediate sources with whom we have no present contact. Absent evidence about the veracity, objectivity, and observational sensitivity of all sources in a chain of hearsay, we could hardly form any settled judgment of the inferential force of this species of evidence. We could, along Baconian lines, reason from one stage to another. This view of cascaded inference would make clear that at many of the reasoning stages we are out on a very slender inferential limb. When these limbs are combined, we are out on a very long *and* slender inferential limb. Assessment of the inferential force of hearsay is yet another situation in which we may have to resort to simpler arguments, as Shafer suggests.

7.5   EQUIVOCAL TESTIMONY

It seems advisable not to underestimate the ability of people to equivocate when it suits them to do so, and even on occasion when it does not. Congressional hearings in recent years have provided a marvelous legacy of imaginative equivocation. The question is, How much inferential force does equivocal testimony have? The first part of an answer to this question involves describing the nature of the equivocation. In my discussion of equivocal testimony in Section 3.4 (see Figure 3.11), I distinguished between two basic forms of equivocation. The first form includes instances in which a person's testimony is not given in the form of a proposition or an event. For example, instead of asserting E*, that event E occurred, or E^{c*}, that event E did not occur, a person provides a probabilistic response to indicate the extent of her uncertainty about which of these events occurred. This person might assert $P^*(E) = 0.7$ and $P^*(E^c) = 0.3$ to indicate that she is 70% sure that E occurred but 30% sure it did not. As I will examine in Section 7.5.1, this form of equivocal evidence has caused problems for Bayesians since Bayes's rule, in its pristine form, requires conditioning of hypotheses by events/propositions and not by a probability distribution such as $P^*(E)$ and $P^*(E^c)$.

In the second species of equivocation a person, asked to tell whether or not some event occurred, responds verbally in a way that I have described as being *completely equivocal*. The person might say: "I don't remember," "I couldn't tell," "I don't know," or "I am not your best witness on this matter." How can such responses have any inferential force when they are taken as evidence in an inference about other matters? The basis for such equivocation having inferential force lies in an examination of what it might mean. On the one hand, the source might be honestly impeaching her own credibility; she does not remember or does not believe she knows whether or not event E occurred. On the other hand, we have to consider the possibility that she does know or remember and is not willing to tell us. In contemporary terms we might say that she is "stonewalling" us. If she is stonewalling, the reasons for it may have inferential force on other matters of concern. As I will mention, the difficulty lies in constructing a plausible argument from a complete equivocation to hypotheses on which this equivocation might be thought directly relevant.

7.5.1 Probabilistic Equivocation, Jeffrey's Rule of Conditioning, and Dodson's MBT

In his discussion of *probability kinematics*, the philosopher Richard Jeffrey offers a Bayesian account of the response made by a person who inspects a piece of cloth by candlelight and who cannot decide what color name to assign to the cloth (1983, 164–165). This person entertains three possibilities, the cloth is green (G), blue (B), or violet (V). First, suppose that before any observation is made, this person has some basis for an original or prior assessment of the probability of each color. The person judges $P^*(G) = 0.3$, $P^*(B) = 0.3$, and $P^*(V) = 0.4$. An observation is now made that results in report **e** from this person's sensory/perceptual apparatus. Suppose that on the basis of this evidence **e**, the person revises his prior probability assessment to the following posterior probability assessment: $P^*(G|e) = 0.7$, $P^*(B|e) = 0.25$, and $P^*(V|e) = 0.05$. The observer cannot be certain about the color of the cloth because of the lighting conditions and any color-sensitivity or other perceptual limitations this person might recognize. Asked to tell what color is the cloth, this person quite reasonably equivocates and reports his judged *distribution* of posterior probabilities across the three color possibilities.

But suppose we wish to use this person's equivocal testimony about the color of the cloth in a further inference about whether hypothesis H or H^c is true. If we contemplate using Bayes's rule, how are we to revise our own prior beliefs about H and H^c, based upon evidence that is not a proposition but a probability distribution? One solution to this difficulty is known as the *Jeffrey rule of conditioning*. As an illustration of this rule, consider Figure 7.18a. Suppose we wish to employ Bayes's rule in an inference about whether or not hypothesis H is true. Event E, if it occurred, would be important but inconclusive evidence favoring H over H^c. Person W is known to have made an observation in the situation in which event E did or did not occur. We ask W whether or not E occurred. In response, W equivocates by giving us two probabilities that he believes represents his own beliefs about the occurrence of E or E^c; they are $P^*(E)$ and $P^*(E^c)$. We notice that they sum to 1.0. Apparently, W is well tutored in conventional probability.

According to Jeffrey's rule, we determine $P(H|W$'s probabilistic report) as follows: We first determine $P(H|E)$, *as if* E did occur; this requires the priors $P(H)$, $P(H^c)$ and the likelihoods $P(E|H)$, $P(E|H^c)$. We then determine $P(H|E^c)$, *as if* E did not occur. This requires the above priors and the likelihoods $P(E^c|H)$ and $P(E^c|H^c)$. The final step involves taking the weighted average of $P(H|E)$ and $P(H|E^c)$, where the weights are W's assessments of the likeliness that he observed E or E^c. Thus, by Jeffrey's rule, we have

$$P(H|W\text{'s probabilistic report}) = P(H|E)P^*(E) + P(H|E^c)P^*(E^c) \quad (7.20)$$

It is quite informative to compare the result of applying Jeffrey's rule with another case in which a witness gives *unequivocal* testimony. As shown in Figure 7.18b, suppose that W reported E^*, that event E occurred. In this case W tells us *unequivocally* that event E occurred. But *we have* uncertainty about W's credibility, which we could express using $h = P(E^*|E)$ and $f =$

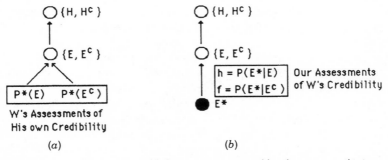

(a)   (b)

FIGURE 7.18 Human source credibility. (a) As assessed by the source. (b) As assessed by the user of the source's evidence.

$P(E^*|E^c)$. We might even decompose these credibility assessments to take account of our beliefs about W's veracity, objectivity, and observational sensitivity. Using h and f, together with priors on H, H^c and likelihoods $P(E|H)$ and $P(E|H^c)$, we could employ Bayes's rule to determine $P(H|E^*)$. The difference between situations A and B in Figure 7.18 involves the question, Who does the credibility assessment of witness W? In the Jeffrey situation in Figure 7.18*a*, W provides an assessment of his own credibility as far as his observation was concerned. He is uncertain about whether his observation was of E or E^c, and he expresses this uncertainty by means of $P^*(E)$ and $P^*(E^c)$. In case B *we* make an assessment of the credibility of W's unequivocal testimony by means of h and f. Schaefer and Borcherding (1973) have noted situations in which cases A and B in Figure 7.18 are formally identical.

Jeffrey's rule in Equation 7.20 has been a source of controversy on several grounds. First, a person can equivocate probabilistically in other ways. Shafer argues that a belief function construal of equivocation problems, such as Jeffrey's color-determination example, offers a more thorough analysis of how the observer might construct his beliefs (1981). Second, the rule in Equation 7.20 is not *path independent*. In applying this belief-updating rule to successive items of testimony, a different result is obtained depending upon the order in which the testimony is incorporated. Other discussions of Jeffrey's rule appear in Diaconis and Zabell (1982, 1986) and Skyrms (1986, 194–198). Pearl (1988, 62–70) discusses Jeffrey's rule in connection with the activation of an inference network by what Pearl terms *virtual evidence*. Such evidence involves what I have termed *probabilistic equivocation*.

While Equation 7.20 is usually associated with Richard Jeffrey, another person, J. D. Dodson (1961), has offered exactly the same rule for belief updating based upon probabilistic equivocation; he referred to it as the *modified Bayes theorem* (MBT). In the 1960s many of us associated this rule with Dodson rather than with Jeffrey. Dodson's rule was criticized at the time for lacking any axiomatic footing. The work of Schaefer and Borcherding, mentioned above, helped to take some of the sting out of this criticism. The lack of path independence of Dodson's rule led Gettys and Willke to devise another version in which this difficulty was removed (1969). But the trouble with the Gettys-Willke formulation is that its conditional independence assumptions are quite devastating in practice. We now examine situations in which people equivocate without resort to probabilistic responses.

7.5.2 Complete Equivocation

Suppose we ask witness W if event E occurred; W responds by saying, "I don't remember." He has other options for complete equivocation, including "I don't know," "I couldn't tell," "I'm not your best witness," and so on. The reason why we are asking W about event E is that we have credible ancillary evidence that W did make a relevant observation in the situation in which E did or did not happen. It is important to note in this case that W does not deny making an observation; if he did, we would have a different inferential problem. We wish to explore the inferential implications of W's current memory lapse as far as event E is concerned. Suppose we believe events E and E^c to be relevant in an inference about $\{H, H^c\}$. Let R^{c*} represent W's testimony that he cannot remember if event E occurred. The first question we face, of fundamental importance, is: How do we establish the relevance of R^{c*} on hypotheses $\{H, H^c\}$? If we have already established the relevance of $\{E, E^c\}$ on hypotheses $\{H, H^c\}$, our remaining task is to establish the relevance of R^{c*} on events $\{E, E^c\}$.

Figure 7.19 illustrates two possible arguments that might be constructed in defense of the relevance of W's complete equivocation R^{c*}. The chain of reasoning shown in Figure 7.19b is a decomposition of the one shown in Figure 7.19a. In either case we first ask the question, Is R^{c*} direct evidence of anything? Witness W tells us that he cannot remember if event E occurred; thus R^{c*} seems to be direct evidence on the event R^c that W, in fact, does not remember if E occurred. But we also have to consider event R, that W does remember if E occurred. One generalization we might assert at this first stage is: "If a person says he does not remember the occurrence of an event, then he (probably, usually, frequently, etc.) does not remember the occurrence of this event." How we proceed at this point depends upon how many uncertainities we wish to trap in our analysis of the force of evidence R^{c*} on $\{E, E^c\}$.

Consider Figure 7.19a and the following generalization: "if, following an observation, a person does not remember observing an event, then this event

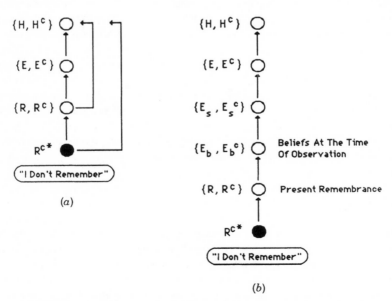

(a)

(b)

FIGURE 7.19   Two examples of a source's complete equivocation.

(probably, frequently, often, etc.) did not occur." Of course this is shakey ground, given what is commonly recognized about the many possible influences on human memory. Time and the interposition of other events are sources of influence; we have to consider how long a time has elapsed since W's observation and our present interrogation of him. Other sources of influence include the possible stake W might have in our present inference regarding hypotheses {H, H^c}, what W expects to gain or lose by testifying, how painful a remembrance of E or E^c might be, and so on. Some of these additional influences we might capture by means of the additional arcs in Figure 7.19a linking R^{c*} and {R, R^c} with {H, H^c}.

The chain of reasoning in Figure 7.19a provides a place to start in an analysis of the force of evidence R^{c*} on hypotheses {H, H^c}. If we believed this chain of reasoning to be singly connected, and we contemplated a Bayesian analysis, we could employ the three-stage version of likelihood ratio shown in Equation 7.3, with $a_1 = P(E|H)$, $b_1 = P(E|H^c)$, $a_2 = P(R|E)$, $b_2 = P(R|E^c)$, $a_3 = P(R^{c*}|R)$, and $b_3 = P(R^{c*}|R^c)$. By such means we determine $L_{R^{c*}}$. If we choose to take account of the additional arcs in Figure 7.19a, $L_{R^{c*}}$ has the same form as in Equation 7.19 (but with likelihood ingredients particular to the events in Figure 7.19a). Observe that the chain of reasoning in Figure 7.19a for complete equivocation is the same as the one in Figure 7.16 for the simplest case of hearsay evidence.

Let us now reconsider what I described as a shakey foundation for linking events {R, R^c} and {E, E^c} in Figure 7.19a. One reason why this foundation is shakey is that Figure 7.19a does not consider specific attributes of W's credibility, about which we may be able to obtain ancillary evidence. Remember that W does not deny making an observation; all he says is that he cannot remember if he observed E. He may hope, by such equivocation, to avoid any charge of untruthfulness, since he has not committed himself to any specific testimony about event E. But we may discover evidence that he recently told someone else that E happened or did not happen. In this case we might be justified in saying that W lied to us by saying that he could not remember what his observation produced. This forces us to broaden our conception of veracity to include instances in which a person's equivocation is in fact "stonewalling." Wigmore tells us that a person lies if he intentionally tries to induce into another's mind a belief that is not in harmony with what this person himself takes to be the truth (Wigmore 1937, 605).

Figure 7.19b shows a possible chain of reasoning from R^{c*} to {H, H^c} that does take account of attributes of W's credibility. To make matters as simple as possible, I have not added any additional arcs (conditional nonindependencies) in Figure 7.19b; we could always do so. In this reasoning chain the linkage between R^{c*} and {R, R^c} concerns W's veracity for reasons mentioned in the paragraph above. But I have to defend the linkage between {R, R^c} and {E_b, E_b^c} and then decide what to label this stage of reasoning in terms of an attribute of W's credibility. First, as shown in the figure, suppose we let E_b represent W's belief, at the time of his observation, that E occurred;

$E_b{}^c$ means that W held no belief, at the time of his observation, that E occurred. Recall the discussion in Section 3.2.3 about how our beliefs are supple or elastic; they may change over time. Events $\{R, R^c\}$ refer to W's present remembrance about event E. Event R = W does presently remember if event E occurred, and R^c = W does not presently remember if event E occurred. One generalization that might plausibly license a linkage between $\{R, R^c\}$ and $\{E_b, E_b{}^c\}$, so defined, reads: "If, following an observation, a person now tells us he cannot remember if an event occurred, then this person (probably, frequently, often, etc) held no belief that this event occurred at the time of his observation."

What attribute of W's credibility have we identified by the linkage of events $\{R, R^c\}$ and $\{E_b, E_b{}^c\}$? This linkage seems to involve remembrance (or not) of things believed or not believed following some previous observation. Following Cohen's argument about beliefs being involuntary feelings, we might say that W simply cannot remember what he felt about E at the time of observation. So we might label this stage as being associated with a *memory* attribute. To do so seems quite in harmony with a view among some jurists that memory is a specific credibility attribute (e.g., Weinstein 1961, 332; Stone 1984, 62–80). In another work I argued that memory is certainly a factor in the attribute I have labeled *objectivity* (Schum 1992, 36–37). But when a witness specifically testifies that he cannot remember whether or not some event occurred, it may be necessary to identify memory as a specific credibility attribute. In Figure 7.19b the reasoning stages from $\{E_b, E_b{}^c\}$ to $\{E_s, E_s{}^c\}$ and from $\{E_s, E_s{}^c\}$ to $\{E, E^c\}$ involve W's objectivity and observational sensitivity, as we have discussed. Anyone who accepts, as plausible, the five-stage chain of reasoning in Figure 7.19b, can determine $L_{R^{c*}}$ using Equations 7.5 and 7.6, with definitions of the likelihoods a_i and b_i made appropriate to the linkages in this chain of reasoning. All of the comments made in Section 7.1 about the force of evidence in singly connected chains of reasoning apply as well to the one illustrated in Figure 7.19b.

As an illustration of the plausibility of the reasoning chain in Figure 7.19b, suppose that W now asserts R^{c*} and we have the following ancillary evidence. First, we have abundant evidence that W is an acute observer. So we have no reason to question his observational sensitivity, and we judge $P(E_s|E) > P(E_s|E^c)$. We also have evidence that W would have been an objective observer and would not have let his wishes or expectations influence his beliefs about what his senses recorded. Consequently we set $P(E_b|E_s) > P(E_b|E_s{}^c)$. We have further evidence, of the sort introduced regarding a witness in the congressional hearings on the Iran-Contra matter, that W has a very good memory; so we set $P(R|E_b) > P(R|E_b{}^c)$. These two likelihoods express our belief that W is more likely to remember the occurrence of E if he believed that it occurred, than if he did not believe it occurred. But suppose we have rather compelling evidence that W's observation of E puts W in an embarrassing situation and is unfavorable to his interests. Further we also have evidence that W told someone else that he observed E (this evidence of course would be hearsay). We might be entitled to judge $P(R^{c*}|R) > P(R^{c*}|R^c)$, in which case we might justify W's memory equivocation as favoring the occurrence of E over E^c, and therefore H over H^c, by an amount that depends upon the likelihoods we have assessed.

7.6 MISSING EVIDENCE

If we say that certain evidence is *missing*, we have obviously expected to observe it in some way or we would not even recognize that it is missing. As I mentioned in Section 3.4, evidence expected but not forthcoming can involve either tangibles or testimony. In some cases we discover for ourselves that evidence is missing; we search records and files or look for an object but cannot find what we expect to find. In other cases we make inquiry of another person who, for reasons good or ill, cannot or will not produce the evidence we require. Does our failure to obtain expected evidence have any inferential force? The answer is yes, provided that we are able to construct a plausible argument from our recognition that it is missing to hypotheses of interest. Here are two examples of the many situations in which evidence is expected but missing.

7.6.1 The Nonproduction of Tangible Evidence

Consider an instance in which we ask someone to produce a tangible item and this person either refuses or is unable to provide it. In our legal system a precedent for drawing an adverse inference from a person's refusal to provide evidence dates from the year 1722 and involves what Wigmore termed "The Case of the Chimney Sweeper's Jewel" (Wigmore on Evidence, vol. 2, 1940, §285, 162). In London in 1722 a chimney sweeper's young apprentice found what he thought to be a jewel in sweepings they had collected. He took this object to a jeweler to have it appraised. The jeweler refused to return it to the boy, whereupon an action for the recovery of the object was filed in court. At trial the jeweler refused to produce the object given him by the boy. The chief justice ruled that unless the jeweler produced the object, the court would rule that the object was a jewel of finest value and award damages accordingly, which it did.

As an illustration of an argument we might construct in defense of the relevance of the nonproduction of tangible evidence, consider the chain of reasoning shown in Figure 7.20. You have taken your car to get an oil change and are astounded to discover that the bill is for $250. The mechanic tells you that your engine had a defective part which, in the interests of your safety, he felt obliged to change. You ask to see the allegedly defective part, and the mechanic testifies M*, that the part has gone missing and he cannot find it. One possibility is M, that the part has indeed been lost or perhaps stolen. Another possibility is M^c, that the part is not missing; the mechanic

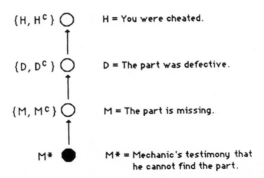

FIGURE 7.20   An example of an inference from the nonproduction of tangible evidence.

knows perfectly well where it is (he has it and intends to install it as a new part in someone else's car). By the argument in The Case of the Chimney Sweeper's Jewel, if M^c were true, you would be entitled to infer event D^c, that your engine part was not defective, and from this infer H, that you were cheated. If you were a Bayesian, you could apply Equation 7.3 in determining L_{M^*} as a gradation of the force of evidence M^* on hypotheses $\{H, H^c\}$.

7.6.2   Silence as Evidence

In many situations people respond with silence when asked to testify about the results of observations they have made. Because of our interest in whether or not event E occurred we ask person W, whom we believe to have made a relevant observation in the situation in which this event occurred or did not. First suppose we ask her directly; she refuses to say anything about event E and does not even equivocate by telling us that she does not remember. We might instead have queried her by mail; she does not answer our letter. Does her *silence* in either instance have any inferential force on whether or not event E did occur and on any further hypotheses on which we believe E to be relevant? Of course this question is of interest to our courts, since we have an assortment of privileges we may invoke to justify a refusal to testify (e.g., Wigmore on Evidence, vol. 8, 1961; Lempert and Saltzburg 1977, 606–766; Zuckerman 1989, 284–342).

In response to an inquiry, silence on someone's part may have many explanations. In the present example perhaps W thought our inquiry about event E to be foolish or impertinent and not deserving a reply. She might have thought it none of our business whether or not event E occurred. Perhaps she never received our letter of inquiry or is incapacitated in some way. It is even possible that she made no relevant observation at all and hesitates to admit it. On the other hand, she may indeed have some belief about E, based on a relevant observation, that she simply refuses to share with us for some reason or another. Suppose we label W's silence about event E as S*. To have any inferential force as evidence on whether or not event E occurred, we must be able to construct a plausible argument from S* to {E, E^c}.

I have never seen a specific argument constructed in defense of a witness's silence. But in our legal system, at least, specific inferences are allowed from a person's silence. The underlying presumption seems to be that a person would testify if she thought what she had to say was in her best interests. Wigmore records: "A *failure to assert* a fact, when it would have been natural to assert it, amounts in effect to an assertion of the non-existence of the fact. This is conceded as a general principle of evidence . . ." (Wigmore on Evidence, vol. 3A, 1970, §1042, 1056). For example, in some situations a person might be expected to contradict the testimony of another. But the person remains silent; what inference can be drawn? Wigmore argues: " Silence, when the assertion of another person would naturally call for a dissent if it were untrue, may be equivalent to an assent to the assertion" (Wigmore on Evidence, vol. 2, 1940, §292, 188).

Here is an attempt to justify silence as having possible inferential force. If you are unconvinced by my argument, you are invited to construct your own. We might begin by entertaining the idea that silence S* is an extreme form of testimonial bias. We might argue that a person who responds with silence might be considered so biased against testifying that some event occurred that she has zero probability of doing so regardless of what she believes about this event. But this idea would produce trouble in any Bayesian analysis of the inferential force of silence. Suppose we set $P(E^*|E_b) = P(E^*|E_b{}^c) = 0$ to indicate this extreme bias. The first trouble is that in a likelihood ratio construal of the force of testimony, we cannot have both of these terms equal to zero, as I mentioned in discussing an earlier analysis. Second, we are supposing that W would testify E*, that event E occurred; she might just as easily testify E^{c*}, that event E did not occur. Given her utter silence, we cannot be sure what her testimony would have been if she had not remained silent. Our analysis of the force of S* must take this uncertainty into account.

One possible analysis, shown in Figure 7.21, takes S* to be direct evidence on events {S, S^c}, where S represents the event that W has nothing to say about event E. This seems plausible, since we could also let S* represent the event that S said nothing about event E (i.e., she was silent). On this interpretation, S^c is the event that W has *something* to say about event E. If S^c were true, this might mean that she would say event E occurred, but it might also mean she would say that E did not occur. To license an inference from S* to {S, S^c}, we might invoke the following generalization: "If a person responds with silence when queried about an event, this person (frequently, often, etc.} does have nothing to say about this event."

Suppose we let $E_?^*$ represent the event that S would say that event E occurred, and let $E_?^{c*}$ be the event that she would say E did not occur. The question marks indicate that either of these testimonies are possible but not actually given. We notice here that the required likelihoods $P(S|E^*)$ and

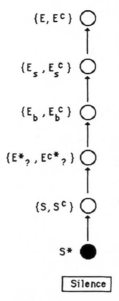

FIGURE 7.21 A chain of reasoning to justify the inferential force of silence on the part of a witness.

$P(S|E_\varsigma^*)$ are not necessarily zero, since W might in truth have nothing to say about the occurrence or nonoccurrence of event E but do so anyway. Suppose she made no relevant observation; she might easily make up a story about observing E or E^c in the hope of pleasing or confusing us. At the next stage we have a connection between her possible testimony and her belief states, and we ask, If W did testify that event E occurred, would this be more likely if she believed E occurred or did not believe that E occurred? We recognize this as a veracity-related question, but we also recognize its subjunctive nature. A generalization we might assert to license reasoning at this stage reads: "If a person does have something to say about an event, then this person (usually, sometimes, frequently, etc.) believes this event to have occurred." The remaining links in the chain of reasoning to events {E, E^c} concern W's objectivity and observational sensitivity, as in other arguments we have constructed from testimony.

On the argument just presented, we have a five-stage singly connected chain of reasoning from S^* to events {E, E^c}; further stages might be added in defense of the relevance of events {E, E^c} on other hypotheses. In a Bayesian analysis of the inferential force of S^* we could determine L_{S^*} using Equations 7.5 and 7.6, provided that we believe this chain to be singly connected. More complex determinations of L_{S^*} can be identified if we add additional arcs to capture conditional nonindependencies we may recognize.

7.6.3 On the Spoliation and Suppression of Evidence

There are many other instances of missing evidence besides to the two I have mentioned: the nonproduction of requested tangible evidence and silence on the part of a witness. We live in the age of the paper-shredder. Another reason why tangible evidence goes missing is that someone has destroyed it or is suppressing its revelation by other means. Evidence that a certain document has been shredded invites the inference that this document contained information unfavorable to the interests of the person(s) who destroyed it. We could, without much difficulty, construct an argument in defense of the relevance of evidence that a document has been destroyed. In any contentious proceeding, whether or not it involves litigation, it is expected that the parties in contention will "filter" the evidence they have discovered in order to present a case or a position that best serves their interests. In this process evidence may be suppressed that is unfavorable to these interests. The entire issue of missing evidence due to spoliation or suppression is now receiving careful attention among legal scholars (Nesson 1991; Nance 1991a, b; Gastwirth 1991).

7.7 ON THE DISCOVERY AND FORCE OF NEGATIVE EVIDENCE

As mentioned in Section 3.2.1, *positive evidence* reports the occurrence of an event, and *negative evidence* reports the nonoccurrence of an event. I know of no view of probabilistic reasoning that gives any preference to positive or to negative evidence as far as inferential force is concerned; one can be as forceful as the other. Consequently it might be thought that there is nothing remarkable about this evidential distinction. But, if we extend the study of evidence to include the means of its discovery, as we will do in Chapter 9, there are some remarkable inferential issues associated with negative evidence. At least Sir Arthur Conan Doyle thought so, since the recognized existence of negative evidence assumed central importance in more than one of his celebrated *Sherlock Holmes* mysteries. So I will begin with a few words about negative evidence and the special problems that are often encountered concerning our awareness of its existence.

Suppose that someone allows you to examine, at your leisure, a photograph or another item of tangible evidence and asks you to list the events this evidence records. This task seems far easier than it would be if you were asked instead to list events this evidence *does not* record. You might give your imagination a free rein and list the nonoccurrence of various events whose actual occurrence in the evidence you are examining would be thought highly unusual or bizzare. For example, suppose that the photograph you are examining was taken in the lobby of a bank during a robbery. On your list of events not recorded in this photo you include the absence of any live elephant. Although factually correct, your inclusion of the absence of an elephant would ordinarily be regarded with humor, at best, unless there was some reason for *expecting* the presence of a live elephant in this particular bank lobby at the time the photograph was taken. In many situations, certainly less unusual than the one just described, we may find it easy to overlook evidence about the nonoccurrence of events whose importance we only appreciate at some later time.

In discussing missing evidence in Section 7.6, I noted that evidence must be expected in order for it to be regarded as missing. There is often a tendency to confuse negative and missing evidence. One reason, perhaps, is that evidence of the nonoccurrence of events often goes unreported even if its existence is recognized. As an example, I cite a tendency common among some scientific journals to accept only those papers reporting positive results, namely results that are in accordance with what was expected or predicted. Reports of negative results, a failure to observe what was expected or predicted, have often been declined on grounds that negative results are uninteresting or simply a consequence of experimental failure of some kind. But in any area of science information about what does not work is frequently as valuable as information about what does. In some situations, usually involving recurrent inferences, a degree of protection against overlooking negative evidence is provided by various procedures for inquiry. For example, in an inquiry regarding a patient's medical history, a physician may use a questionnaire that allows the recording of positive and negative responses to a variety of questions such as, "Are you allergic to any forms of medication?" or "Are you now taking any prescription drugs?" Presumably the physician is equally interested in an answer yes or no to such questions. One trouble is that in many nonrecurrent inferences there are no established procedures for ensuring that positive and negative evidence is recorded. The result is that negative evidence is missing because it was never reported in the first place.

Conan Doyle gave Sherlock Holmes the ability, now legendary, to apprehend both the occurrence and nonoccurrence of events having inferential significance in his criminal investigations. As I will mention further in Chapter 9, Conan Doyle had a living role model for Sherlock Holmes. The same degree of inferential brilliance associated with Sherlock Holmes was also observable in the actual diagnostic behavior of an Edinburgh surgeon named Dr. Joseph Bell. Although there are other instances of the importance of negative evidence scattered throughout the Sherlock Holmes stories, the most celebrated one occurred in a case involving a suspected murder and the theft of a race horse whose name, *Silver Blaze,* gave a title to this mystery. In case you have not read *Silver Blaze,* the following details do not specifically identify the culprit. Holmes used them in combination with other details (or "trifles," as he called them) to solve this mystery.

In the dead of night, someone removed *Silver Blaze* from the stable in which he was kept. A dog also slept in the stables as well as did two grooms who occupied a loft above the stables. When queried the next day, both grooms said they were sound sleepers and heard nothing during the night. During the investigation, Scotland Yard Inspector Gregory (Holmes's foil in this case) asks Holmes (Baring-Gould 1967, Vol. 2, 277):

> Gregory: "Is there any other point to which you would wish to draw my attention?"
>
> Holmes: "To the curious incident of the dog in the night-time."
>
> Gregory: "The dog did nothing in the night-time."
>
> Holmes: "That was the curious incident."

A third person, a stable boy who also slept in the stables, had been drugged with opium in the food he had for supper. Other persons having this same food suffered no ill-effects. Watson asks Holmes who might have had access to the food served to the stable boy. Holmes replies: "Before deciding that question I had grasped the significance of the silence of the dog, for one true inference invariably suggests others." He added: "Obviously, the midnight visitor was someone whom the dog knew well" (Baring-Gould 1967, vol. 2, 280).

A Bayesian, set to the task of determining the force of evidence that the dog did not bark, could raise some potentially embarrassing matters that Holmes did not recognize, or at least neglected to tell us about (through Dr. Watson). In particular, Holmes tells us nothing about the dog who did not bark. As the two analyses shown in Figure 7.22 illustrate, Holmes ought to have known more about the dog before he drew any conclusion about the significance of the dog's not barking. Suppose we let H represent the event that the dog *did* recognize the person who entered the stable and removed the horse; let H^c be the event that the dog *did not* recognize the person who entered the stable and removed the horse. In addition let E represent the event that the dog barked upon seeing the person who entered the stables

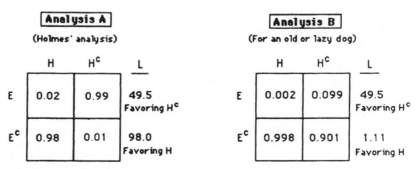

FIGURE 7.22 Two possible interpretations of the force of the negative evidence Sherlock Holmes obtained in the case of *Silver Blaze*.

and E^c be the event that the dog *did not bark* upon seeing the person who entered the stables. What Holmes had essentially is testimonial evidence E^{c*}, that the dog did not bark upon seeing the person who entered the stables. Let us suppose that the sources of evidence about the dog's not barking are perfectly credible, so, in light of earlier discussions, testimony E^{c*} has the same inferential force as knowing event E^c for sure.

Analysis A in Figure 7.22 puts certain probabilities in Holmes's head that seem quite consistent with his stated conclusions. He believes that the dog's not barking is 98 times more probable, asssuming that the dog recognized the person who entered the stable than assuming that the dog did not recognize this person. Perhaps Holmes would have agreed with this assessment of the force of event E^c on $\{H, H^c\}$ in this case. Notice that $P(E^c|H) = 0.98$ means that $P(E|H) = 0.02$ and that $P(E^c|H^c) = 0.01$ means that $P(E|H^c) = 0.99$ under required normalization. This suggests that Holmes also believed the dog's barking would be 49.5 times more probable, assuming that the dog did not recognize the person than assuming that the dog did recognize this person. But, as analysis B illustrates, Holmes should have found out more about the dog. Suppose, for example, that the dog in question was old or lazy and would rarely bark whether or not it recognized persons who entered the stable. We might say in this case that the dog had a distinct bias against barking. Holmes might still believe that the dog's barking is 49.5 times more probable assuming nonrecognition than assuming recognition. But notice in analysis B that making the dog's barking a rare event destroys the inferential force of its not barking. In this case the dog's not barking is just 1.11 times more probable assuming recognition than assuming nonrecognition.

Such is our faith in Sherlock Holmes that we have to suppose he took all of these matters into account but simply neglected to tell Watson that the dog in question was robust and mean and, in any case, one with no discernible bias against barking. My analysis of this case simply affords another example of how Bayesian and other probabilistic analyses of the force of evidence bring to light a variety of important questions we might ask about our evidence and its sources.

7.8 A RETURN TO BERNOULLI'S EVIDENTIAL DISTINCTIONS

In considering the inferential force of individual or isolated items of directly relevant evidence in this chapter, I have focused attention on Bernoulli's case 4 shown in Figure 6.3a. Cases 1 and 3 in this figure are quite uninteresting, since they involve situations in which we are confident, beyond shadow of a doubt, about the credibility of a source of evidence, including our own observations. We have not yet considered case 2 in which we have evidence from a source, not perfectly credible, about an event E whose known occurrence would entail or make necessary some hypothesis that we are entertaining. The best example of this case involves *alibi testimony*. But the necessity for such testimony is established by other directly relevant testimony and thus involves the joint consideration of two or more items of evidence. For this reason I defer discussion of this case to the next chapter, when we examine expressions for the inferential force of two or more items of contradictory evidence.

Shown in Figure 6.3*b* is Bernoulli's distinction between *pure* and *mixed* evidence. This distinction is of particular importance in situations involving assessment of the inferential force of particular combinations of evidence. However, before we proceed to this task, there is one matter concerning the pure versus mixed distinction that should be mentioned in connection with the Bayesian likelihood ratio analyses I offered in this chapter. Recall from Section 6.2.1 that pure evidence is that which may offer some support to one hypothesis but say nothing at all about others. There is no way of capturing this property by means of the likelihood ratios I have constructed for the various chains of reasoning we have considered.

I mentioned at several points that certain likelihoods can take the value zero. We might entertain the thought that a likelihood having zero value indicates that one event says nothing about another, but this cannot be so. For example, we might feel justified in believing, for a certain witness, that $P(E^*|E_b{}^c) = 0$; this witness would not testify E^* if he did not believe E occurred. But this is not to say that E^* says nothing at all about event $E_b{}^c$. Indeed it says that the testimony we have just heard, together with ancillary evidence we have about this person's veracity, make us perfectly confident that this person is not telling us something that he does not believe. The point is simply that ordinary conditional probabilities cannot be used to indicate that one event says nothing about another.

Chapter 8

Analyses of Recurrent Combinations of Evidence

In this chapter structural and probabilistic concepts are integrated in analyses of the inferential force of recurrent combinations of evidence. Earlier I mentioned the metaphor of an argument as a *fabric* having both *warp* and *weft* threads. For the isolated items of evidence examined in Chapter 7, we were only able to consider the strength of vertical or warp threads. As we now consider the inferential force of combinations of evidence we have to give increasing attention to the strength of the lateral or weft threads in our arguments from evidence to hypotheses of interest. Our arguments from combinations of evidence become more complex and we encounter chains of reasoning in which conditional nonindependencies appear among elements of arguments we construct. Figure 8.1 illustrates some of the basic conditioning patterns of interest.

Figure 8.1a shows examples of the linkage patterns we considered in Chapter 7; observe that the two additional arcs added to the chain of reasoning from E^* to $\{H, H^c\}$ go in a vertical direction; they are additional warp threads. In Section 7.2.1 we observed how the addition of arcs such as these can allow the inferential force of evidence E^* to exceed the force of knowing *for sure* that the reported event E did occur. Figure 8.1b shows additional arcs of the sort we must consider when we have a combination of two or more evidence items; such arcs form the weft threads I mentioned. Arc 1 is vertical and is of the sort shown in Figure 8.1a. Arc 2 indicates a probabilistic influence between events at stages in arguments based upon two items of evidence F^* and G^*. Arcs of this nature allow us to capture subtleties associated with the *cumulative redundance* and *synergism* that we discussed in Section 3.5. Arc 3 connects the two items of evidence F^* and G^*. By such an arc we capture subtleties associated with the nonindependence of the evidence items them-

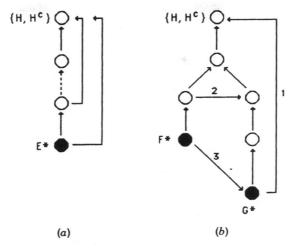

FIGURE 8.1 Examples illustrating the "warp" and the "weft" of arguments based on evidence.

selves. For example, we may have ancillary evidence indicating that the source of evidence F* influenced the source of evidence G*.

As we examine combinations of evidence and more complex arguments, the requirements increase for ancillary evidence to justify probability assessments concerning the force of evidence. In theory, at least, every arc needs to be supported by a plausible generalization backed by ancillary evidence showing the strength or weakness of the generalization in the particular case in which it is being applied. Since my present purpose is simply to show how various formal probability systems operate, I will suppose that such generalizations and ancillary evidence are available to support any actual use of the formalizations I will discuss. My analyses of the inferential force of recurrent combinations of evidence will begin with Bayesian construals of evidential force in terms of likelihood ratios. In some cases I will be able to show how the force of a combination of evidence might be graded in Baconian terms or in terms of belief functions.

8.1 ON THE FORCE OF DISSONANT EVIDENCE

In Section 3.5.1, I gave the labels *contradictory* and *conflicting* to two different species of dissonant evidence. In the process I noted that the evidence in both species is conflicting or at variance as far as the inferential direction of such evidence is concerned. However, it is necessary to preserve the following distinction: In a contradiction we have reports of the occurrence of two mutually exclusive events; they cannot both have occurred. In such cases we naturally look to the credibility of the sources of the evidence; one of the sources must be wrong for some reason. What I have termed *conflicting evidence* involves the reported occurrence of two events that *can occur jointly* but seem to favor different hypotheses or possibilities. We might say that all dissonant evidence is conflicting, but not all conflicting evidence is contradictory.

Assessing the force of conflicting evidence involves difficult philosophical issues. The credibility of the sources of conflicting evidence is certainly an important matter, as in the case of a contradiction. However, there are other matters involving our perceptions of the conflict itself. Suppose that two credible sources report events we believe to be conflicting in their inferential implications. Perhaps our interpretation of the meaning of these events is incorrect. If we had better knowledge of the situation, perhaps we could explain away what now appears to us as evidential conflict. We begin with an analysis of the force of an evidential contradiction involving just two sources; this is the simplest case of dissonant evidence.

8.1.1   Contradictory Evidence

Consider the situation illustrated in Figure 8.2a. We have two sources S_1 and S_2 providing contradictory evidence; S_1 reports E*, that event E occurred, and S_2 reports E^{c*}, that event E did not occur. We could also say in this case that S_1 reports *positive evidence* about E and S_2 reports *negative evidence* of E. Suppose that the occurrence of event E favors hypothesis H over H^c; that is, $P(E|H) > P(E|H^c)$. This simple inference network is not singly connected. Arcs 1 and 2 indicate the state-dependent credibility we discussed in Section 7.2.1. Arc 3 indicates an influence among sources S_1 and S_2. The necessity of incorporating these additional arcs is made evident in an expansion of the likelihood ratio for the joint contradictory evidence E* and E^{c*}. By definition,

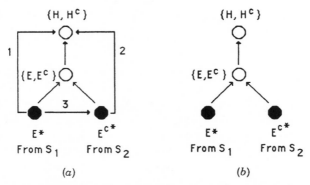

FIGURE 8.2   Linkage patterns for contradictory evidence.

this likelihood ratio is $L_{E^*E^{c^*}} = P(E^*E^{c^*}|H)/P(E^*E^{c^*}|H^c)$. Expanding this likelihood ratio in terms of events $\{E, E^c\}$ yields:

$$L_{E^*E^{c^*}} = \frac{P(E|H)[rt - vx] + vx}{P(E|H^c)[su - wy] + wy} \tag{8.1}$$

where $r = P(E^*|EH)$, $s = P(E^*|EH^c)$; $t = P(E^{c^*}|E^*EH)$, $u = P(E^{c^*}|E^*EH^c)$; $v = P(E^*|E^cH)$, $w = P(E^*|E^cH^c)$; and $x = P(E^{c^*}|E^*E^cH)$, $y = P(E^{c^*}|E^*E^cH^c)$.

Using the hybrid notational scheme introduced earlier, we can simplify discussion of the credibility-related ingredients of Equation 8.1 and also show how a Bayesian likelihood ratio requires consideration of the three additional arcs in Figure 8.2a. First, we can express $r = P(E^*|EH) = P_H(E^*|E)$ and $s = P(E^*|EH^c) = P_{H^c}(E^*|E)$. Thus terms r and s refer to S_1's *hit probability*, conditional upon H and upon H^c. Similarly we can identify S_1's *false-positive* probabilities, conditional on H and on H^c, as $v = P(E^*|E^cH) = P_H(E^*|E^c)$ and $w = P(E^*|E^cH^c) = P_{H^c}(E^*|E^c)$. Thus arc 1 concerns the possibility of a conditioning of S_1's hit and false positive probabilities by either H or H^c. Suppose that there is no ancillary evidence to support these state or hypothesis dependencies; that is, we sever arc 1. Then $r = s = P(E^*|E)$, and $v = w = P(E^*|E^c)$.

Now consider terms $t = P(E^{c^*}|E^*EH)$ and $u = P(E^{c^*}|E^*EH^c)$ regarding S_2's report E^{c^*}. These terms can also be written as $t = P_{E^*H}(E^{c^*}|E)$ and $u = P_{E^*H^c}(E^{c^*}|E)$, and they identify S_2's probability of a *miss*, a report that E did not occur when it did. Our likelihood ratios ask us to consider whether or not this miss probability for S_2 is dependent on either or both of (1) what S_1 reported (E^*) and (2) H and/or H^c. Terms $x = P(E^{c^*}|E^*E^cH)$ and $y = P(E^{c^*}|E^*E^cH^c)$ identify S_2's *correct rejection* (or *true-negative*) probability; that is, S_2 reports the nonoccurrence of E when in fact it did not occur. These probabilities may also be dependent on what S_1 reported and possibly on H and/or H^c. We can express them as $x = P_{E^*H}(E^{c^*}|E^c)$ and $y = P_{E^*H^c}(E^{c^*}|E^c)$. Arc 2 indicates the conditioning of these miss and correct rejection probabilities by H or H^c; arc 3 concerns their conditioning by S_1's report. If arcs 2 and 3 were severed, $t = u = P(E^{c^*}|E)$ and $x = y = P(E^{c^*}|E^c)$.

To illustrate how an evidential contradiction is resolved in Bayesian terms, we begin by considering the situation illustrated in Figure 8.2b. Suppose we have no ancillary evidence to support any of the conditional nonindependencies indicated by arcs 1, 2, or 3. Then for S_1 we would have hit probability $r = s = P(E^*|E) = h_1$ and false positive probability $v = w = P(E^*|E^c) = f_1$. For S_2 we would have miss probability $t = u = P(E^{c^*}|E) = m_2$, and correct rejection probability $x = y = P(E^{c^*}|E^c) = c_2$. Under these conditional independence assumptions, and with these notational changes, we can express

$$L_{E^*E^{c^*}} = \frac{P(E|H)[h_1m_2 - f_1c_2] + f_1c_2}{P(E|H^c)[h_1m_2 - f_1c_2] + f_1c_2} \tag{8.2}$$

With a bit of algebraic manipulation in which we let $K_1 = h_1/f_1$ and $K_2 = c_2/m_2$, we can express

$$L_{E^*E^{c*}} = \frac{P(E|H)[K_1 - K_2] + K_2}{P(E|H^c)[K_1 - K_2] + K_2} = \frac{P(E|H) + [(K_1/K_2) - 1]^{-1}}{P(E|H^c) + [(K_1/K_2) - 1]^{-1}} \quad (8.3)$$

Observe that Equation 8.3 has exactly the same form as Equation 7.11 for a single source. Recalling the discussion of inferential drag in Section 7.1.1, the drag on our opinion revision, based upon contradictory reports about event E from two sources, is given by the term $D = [(K_1/K_2) - 1]^{-1}$. If $K_1 > K_2$, that is, if h_1/f_1 for the source reporting E^* is greater than c_2/m_2 for the source reporting E^{c*}, then the joint contradictory report from these two sources will favor the hypothesis favored by event E, since D will be positive. But, if $K_1 < K_2$, then D is negative and the joint contradictory report will favor the hypothesis favored by event E^c. So the relative size of K_1 and K_2 determines how the contradiction is resolved directionally. Because the inference network shown in Figure 8.2b is singly connected, there are the same bounds on the value of $L_{E^*E^{c*}}$ as those that we discussed in Section 7.1.1 regarding L_{E^*}. The bounds are: $L_{E^c} \leq L_{E^*E^{c*}} \leq L_E$. In this case the joint contradictory evidence can never have inferential force exceeding that of knowing E for sure or knowing E^c for sure.

There are other interesting constraints on $L_{E^*E^{c*}}$ given in Equations 8.2 and 8.3. First, we cannot believe that the sources involved in a contradiction are both perfectly credible. Observe in Equation 8.2 that $L_{E^*E^{c*}}$ is not defined if $f_1 = m_2 = 0$. We would reach an inferential impasse if we believed that S_1 would never report E^* when E did not occur and, at the same time, believed that S_2 would never report E^{c*} when E did occur. The right-hand expression in Equation 8.3 is also undefined if $K_1 = K_2$, that is, if $h_1/f_1 = c_2/m_2$. However, using the equivalent middle expression, we observe that if $K_1 = K_2$, then $L_{E^*E^{c*}} = 1.0$; the joint report has no inferential force at all. Given equivalent credibility of sources on both sides of a contradiction, we are left in a position of maximum uncertainty about whether or not event E did occur. Thus the joint contradictory report allows no basis for opinion revision about hypotheses $\{H, H^c\}$.

Equation 8.3 reveals another interesting subtlety regarding contradictory evidence. Source S_1 reports that event E occurred, and S_2 reports that it did not. Suppose we believe that S_2 is incorrect or untruthful; we believe the opposite of what S_2 says. But the opposite of what S_2 says is exactly what S_1 says, namely that event E occurred. So it appears that we have evidential redundancy to consider. But a Bayesian likelihood ratio automatically accounts for the potential redundancy in this situation. Recall the boundary conditions in this singly connected case: $L_{E^c} \leq L_{E^*E^{c*}} \leq L_E$. There can be no more inferential force in the joint contradictory report E^*E^{c*} than there is in knowing for sure that E occurred or did not occur. If we believed that S_2 were inaccurate or untruthful, then $m_2 > c_2$, in which case $K_2 < 1.0$. As the right-hand term in Equation 8.3 shows, this would simply have the effect of enlarging K_1 for source S_1. Thus S_2's inaccuracy or untruthfulness essentially acts to corroborate S_1's report. In Section 8.4 we will consider other cases of evidential redundancy that Bayes's rule will not automatically capture unless we give it a structural opportunity to do so.

Shown in Table 8.1 are several examples of the manner in which contradictions are resolved in terms of the likelihood ratio in Equation 8.3. These examples bring to light additional characteristics of a Bayesian resolution of evidential contradiction. In the first five cases, the inferential force of knowing for sure that event E occurred is given by $L_E = 0.90/0.05 = 18$, favoring H. Under required normalization, this means that the inferential force of knowing that E did not occur is given by $L_{E^c} = 0.10/0.95 = 1/9.5$, favoring H^c. So these five cases involve the *inferential asymmetry* we discussed earlier; event E is more forceful in favoring H than E^c is in favoring H^c. Cases 6 and 7 involve situations in which knowing E or knowing E^c would be conclusive on hypotheses H and H^c.

In every case three calculations are shown. The first is the likelihood ratio $L_{E \cdot E^{c\cdot}}$, calculated using Equation 8.3, for the joint contradictory report from sources S_1 and S_2. Also included are calculations of $L_{E^\cdot}$, indicating the force of E^* by itself, and $L_{E^{c\cdot}}$, indicating the force of E^{c*} by itself. The calculation of $L_{E^\cdot}$ is made using Equation 7.11. For $L_{E^{c\cdot}}$ this same equation is used with the ratio (m_2/c_2) substituted for (h/f). A comparison of these three likelihood ratios is both necessary and interesting. It is necessary because the conditional independence being assumed in Equation 8.3 needs to be carefully interpreted. It might be supposed that the conditional independence assumptions underlying Equation 8.3 mean that we can determine the inferential force of the joint contradictory report from S_1 and S_2 by multiplying together the likelihood ratios for their separate reports. This is not formally justified,

TABLE 8.1   Resolving Contradictions with Likelihood Ratios

Ingredients	Case 1	Case 2	Case 3	Case 4	Case 5	Case 6	Case 7
$P(E|H)$	0.90	0.90	0.90	0.90	0.90	1.00	0
$P(E|H^c)$	0.05	0.05	0.05	0.05	0.05	0	1.00
h_1	0.98	0.75	0.80	0.98	0.01	0.98	0.98
f_1	0.01	0.25	0.10	0.01	0.98	0.01	0.01
c_2	0.75	0.98	0.60	0.01	0.98	0.75	0.75
m_2	0.25	0.01	0.10	0.98	0.01	0.25	0.25
K_1	98	3	8	98.	0.01	98	98
K_2	3	98	6	0.010	98	3	3
$L_{E \cdot E^{c\cdot}}$	11.42	0.13	1.28	17.96	0.11	32.67	0.03
$L_{E^\cdot}$	15.09	2.55	5.41	15.09	0.11	98	0.01
$L_{E^{c\cdot}}$	0.41	0.11	0.26	15.09	0.11	0.33	3
$L_{E^\cdot} \cdot L_{E^{c\cdot}}$	6.19	0.28	1.41	227.71	0.01	32.67	0.03

however, and the examples will indicate why this is so. These likelihood ratio comparisons are interesting, in part because they provide a more thorough account of Bayesian and belief function analyses of evidential contradictions.

In case 1 we have S_1' s credibility greatly exceeding that of S_2; observe that K_1 is $98/3 = 32.67$ times the value of K_2. The contradiction is resolved in favor of S_1's report E^*; the joint evidence E^* and E^{c*} favors H over H^c in the ratio $L_{E^*E^{c*}} = 11.42$. This value tells us two things. First, the contradictory report from S_2 has taken some of the force out of S_1's report since $L_{E^*E^{c*}} = 11.42 < L_{E^*} = 15.09$. The reason why this contradiction has not taken more force from S_1' s report is that we do not regard S_2 as being all that credible. Second, observe that $L_{E^*E^{c*}} = 11.42$ is not equal to the product $L_{E^*} \cdot L_{E^{c*}} = (15.09)(0.41) = 6.19$. The conditional independence assumptions underlying Equation 8.3 have to be carefully interpreted, a task I will perform as we proceed.

In case 2 I have simply reversed the credibilities of S_1 and S_2 as given in case 1. A likelihood ratio resolves the contradiction in favor of S_2's report since $L_{E^*E^{c*}} = 0.13$ favors H^c over H in the ratio $1/0.13 = 7.69$. Recall that the force of knowing E^c is less than the force of knowing E. Here it is S_1's report that takes some of the force from S_2's report; observe that $L_{E^{c*}} = 0.11$ favors H^c over H in the ratio $1/0.11 = 9.09$. In case 3 the credibility of neither source is very high, so, as expected, the inferential force of their contradictory evidence is small. The contradiction favors H over H^c since S_1's credibility is slightly stronger than S_2's.

Case 4 provides a good example of the redundance issue mentioned above. It allows me to comment further on the nature of the conditional independence assumed in Equation 8.3. First, S_1 has very strong credibility in reporting that event E occurred. But, on ancillary evidence, we believe S_2 is incorrect or untruthful in reporting that E did not occur. In other words, we do not believe the negative evidence this source provides. First, observe that $K_1 = 1/K_2$; that is, $h_1/f_1 = m_2/c_2$. Using Equation 7.11, we determine $L_{E^*} = L_{E^{c*}} = 15.09$. Taken individually, the evidence items on each side of this contradiction favor H over H^c in the same ratio. If we blithely assumed these reports were independent and multiplied these likelihood ratios together, we would (inappropriately) conclude that they jointly favor H over H^c in the ratio $L_{E^*} \cdot L_{E^{c*}} = (15.09)^2 = 227.71$. But Equation 8.3 tells us that the inferential force of this contradiction is $L_{E^*E^{c*}} = 17.96$, just slightly less force than that supplied by knowing event E for sure. What Bayes's rule recognizes, when we give it opportunity to do so, is that evidence items E^* and E^{c*} are *naturally redundant* because they concern events belonging to the *same class*, to {E, E^c}. Case 5 is the same as case 4 with the credibility credentials of S_1 and S_2 reversed. In both cases we would give drastically excessive force to this contradiction by treating these two items of evidence as independent. I will return to this "natural redundancy" in Section 8.4.3.

Cases 6 and 7 allow me to illustrate several matters, the first of which involves Bernoulli's case 2 shown in Figure 6.3 (I will have even more to say about this case later in Section 8.5.1). In case 6 in Table 8.1, suppose that event E, if it did occur, would be conclusive evidence that hypothesis H is true. Event E is certain to occur if H were true, and is impossible if H^c were true. Stated another way, event E is incompatible with H^c, and E^c is incompatible with H. The likelihood ratio L_E is not even defined in this case, since E has infinite force favoring H. The trouble is that we have contradictory evidence about the occurrence of E from two sources, neither of whom/which is perfectly credible. In this example I have made S_1 quite credible and S_2 only weakly credible. The effect of this contradiction is quite interesting when considered in light of the bounds on $L_{E^*} \cdot L_{E^{c*}}$ which, in this case, are $0 \leq L_{E^* \cdot E^{c*}} < \infty$. If we had just S_1's report E^*, its likelihood ratio is $L_{E^*} = 98$. Contradictory evidence from S_2, whose c_2/m_2 ratio is just 3, reduces the force of E^* by a factor of $98/3 = 32.67 = L_{E^* \cdot E^{c*}}$ from Equation 8.3. In case 7, E is now made conclusive on H^c and E^c conclusive on H. The credibility situation is the same as in case 6, and we have $L_{E^* \cdot E^{c*}} = 0.03$. The contradiction favors H^c over H in the ratio $1/0.03 = 33.33$ because of the stronger credibility of S_1.

In Bayesian construals of the force of evidence, likelihood ratios have other bounds besides those provided by knowing E or E^c for sure. In singly-connected chains of reasoning, likelihood ratios for evidence also cannot exceed bounds prescribed by the ratio of likelihoods other than $P(E|H)$ and $P(E|H^c)$. Earlier in Section 7.1.1 we observed that a singly connected chain cannot be any stronger than its weakest link. For example, in Equation 7.11, L_{E^*} cannot exceed the ratio h/f; nor can $L_{E^{c*}}$ exceed the ratio m/c. In case 6, $L_{E^{c*}}$ cannot exceed the ratio $c_2/m_2 = 3$. But now observe in cases 6 and 7 that $L_{E^* \cdot E^{c*}}$ *does equal* the product of L_{E^*} and $L_{E^{c*}}$. Contradictory reports E^* and E^{c*} seem to have become independent in these two cases. If they are "naturally redundant," how can this be so?

Consider Figure 8.2b and imagine that the direction of each of the three arcs has been reversed. All of the cases in Table 8.1 involve the independence of E^* and events in $\{H, H^c\}$, given one of the events in $\{E, E^c\}$; they also involve the independence of E^{c*} and events in $\{H, H^c\}$, given one of the events $\{E, E^c\}$. One way of explaining this pattern of conditional independence is to say that the node $\{E, E^c\}$ blocks the influence of the node $\{H, H^c\}$ on evidence items E^* and E^{c*}. But now in case 6, for example, in which we have E being conclusive on H and E^c being conclusive on H^c, there is no such influence to block, since E essentially "means" H and E^c essentially "means" H^c in this case. Thus $L_{E^* \cdot E^{c*}} = L_{E^*} \cdot L_{E^{c*}}$. Given either E or E^c, evidence items E^* and E^{c*} are independent of $\{H, H^c\}$ in cases 6 and 7. They are also independent of each other, since there is no arc connecting them.

We cannot always assume the pattern of complete conditional independence shown in the inference network in Figure 8.2b, for which Equations 8.2 and 8.3 are appropriate in determining the Bayesian inferential force of a contradiction. The most general expression for trapping all possible conditional nonindependencies is Equation 8.1. But there are some interesting

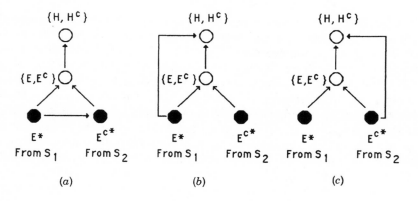

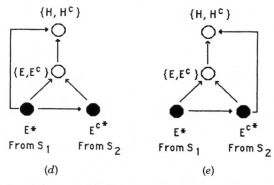

FIGURE 8.3   Special cases of linkage patterns for contradictory evidence.

special cases worthwhile to examine; they are illustrated in Figure 8.3. Suppose, as illustrated in Figure 8.3a, we believe that S_1 has influenced S_2 in some way but in a manner not also contingent upon either H or H^c. In this special case we can express

$$L_{E^*E^{c*}} = \frac{P(E|H)[h_1 m_2 - f_1 c_2] + f_1 c_2}{P(E|H^c)[h_1 m_2 - f_1 c_2] + f_1 c_2}$$

$$= \frac{P(E|H) + [(h_1/f_1)(m_2/c_2) - 1]^{-1}}{P(E|H^c) + [(h_1/f_1)(m_2/c_2) - 1]^{-1}} \tag{8.4}$$

where $h_1 = P(E^*|E)$, $f_1 = P(E^*|E^c)$, $m_2 = P(E^{c*}|EE^*)$, and $c_2 = P(E^{c*}|E^c E^*)$.

First, observe that Equation 8.4 is identical to Equation 8.3, since we could express the product $(h_1/f_1)(m_2/c_2)$ as K_1/K_2, where $K_1 = h_1/f_1$ and $K_2 = c_2/m_2$. The difference is that in Equation 8.3 we defined $m_2 = P(E^{c*}|E)$ and

$c_2 = P(E^{c*}|E^c)$; there was no further conditioning by E^*. The arc connecting E^* and E^{c*} in Figure 8.3a simply indicates that we might wish to alter the miss and correct rejection probabilities for S_2, in light of the fact that S_1 reported E^*. We might believe that $P(E^{c*}|EE^*) \neq P(E^{c*}|E)$ or that $P(E^{c*}|E^cE^*) \neq P(E^{c*}|E^c)$. So the only effect of the conditioning shown in this instance is to allow for revising the drag coefficient applied to $P(E|H)$ and $P(E|H^c)$, as shown in the right-hand expression in Equation 8.4. Notice in Equation 8.4, as well as in Equation 8.3, that we do not need exact values of h_1, f_1, m_2, and c_2; all we need are the ratios h_1/f_1 and m_2/c_2. Finally, the right-hand expression in Equation 8.4 shows us that the likelihood ratio has the bounds $L_{E^c} \leq L_{E \cdot E^c} \leq L_E$. Just believing there to have been some influence of S_1 on S_2 does not allow their contradicting evidence to have more inferential force than knowing E or E^c for sure.

Now consider the inference network shown in Figure 8.3b. In this case we allow for S_1's hit and false-positive probabilities to be dependent on hypotheses H and/or on H^c. Perhaps the behavior of S_1 is itself inferentially interesting. In this case we have the likelihood ratio for the contradiction being

$$L_{E \cdot E^c} = \frac{P(E|H)[h_{1(H)}(m_2/c_2) - f_{1(H)}] + f_{1(H)}}{P(E|H^c)[h_{1(H^c)}(m_2/c_2) - f_{1(H^c)}] + f_{1(H^c)}} \tag{8.5}$$

where $h_{1(H)} = P(E^*|EH)$, $f_{1(H)} = P(E^*|E^cH)$, $h_{1(H^c)} = P(E^*|EH^c)$, $f_{1(H^c)} = P(E^*|E^cH^c)$, $m_2 = P(E^{c*}|E)$ and $c_2 = P(E^{c*}|E^c)$. If, instead, we believed that S_2's miss and correct rejection probabilities were hypothesis-contingent, as in Figure 8.3c, we would have the likelihood ratio

$$L_{E \cdot E^c} = \frac{P(E|H)[(h_1/f_1)m_{2(H)} - c_{2(H)}] + c_{2(H)}}{P(E|H^c)[(h_1/f_1)m_{2(H^c)} - c_{2(H^c)}] + c_{2(H^c)}} \tag{8.6}$$

where $h_1 = P(E^*|E)$, $f_1 = P(E^*|E^c)$, $m_{2(H)} = P(E^{c*}|EH)$, $c_{2(H)} = P(E^{c*}|E^cH)$, $m_{2(H^c)} = P(E^{c*}|EH^c)$, and $c_{2(H^c)} = P(E^{c*}|E^cH^c)$. In the cases captured by Equations 8.5 and 8.6, the inferential force of a contradiction can be greater than the force of knowing E or knowing E^c for sure, as I will illustrate by example.

With a few changes in definitions of likelihood ingredients, Equations 8.5 and 8.6 can also express the Bayesian inferential force of contradictory evidence for the conditioning patterns shown in Figures 8.3d and e. To capture the conditioning of E^{c*} by E^* in Figure 8.3d, we must have $m_2 = P(E^{c*}|EE^*)$ and $c_2 = P(E^{c*}|E^cE^*)$ in Equation 8.5. To capture the conditioning of E^{c*} by E^*; by H, and/or by H^c, we must have $m_{2(HE^*)} = P_{HE^*}(E^{c*}|E)$, $m_{2(H^cE^*)} = P_{H^cE^*}(E^{c*}|E)$, $C_{2(HE^*)} = P_{HE^*}(E^{c*}|E^c)$, and $C_{2(H^cE^*)} = P_{H^cE^*}(E^{c*}|E^c)$. In both cases we may have contradictory evidence about event E that has more inferential force than knowing E or knowing E^c for sure. Table 8.2 contains a

TABLE 8.2 Contradiction and Conditional Nonindependence

Ingredients	A. Equation 8.1			
	Case 1	Case 2	Case 3	Case 4
1. $P(E\|H)$	0.90	0.90	0.90	0.90
2. $P(E\|H^c)$	0.05	0.05	0.05	0.05
3. $r = P(E^*\|EH)$	0.98	0.98	0.01	0.098
4. $v = P(E^*\|E^cH)$	0.01	0.01	0.75	0.001
5. $s = P(E^*\|EH^c)$	0.75	0.098	0.05	0.55
6. $w = P(E^*\|E^cH^c)$	0.05	0.001	0.60	0.45
7. $x = P(E^{c*}\|E^cE^*H)$	0.75	0.75	0.09	0.75
8. $t = P(E^{c*}\|EE^*H)$	0.25	0.25	0.01	0.25
9. $y = P(E^{c*}\|E^cE^*H^c)$	0.95	0.55	0.90	0.95
10. $u = P(E^{c*}\|EE^*H^c)$	0.01	0.40	0.10	0.10
$L_{E^*E^{c*}}$	4.86	81.12	0.013	0.054

Ingredients	B. Equation 8.6			
	Case 1	Case 2	Case 3	Case 4
1. $P(E\|H)$	0.90	0.90	0.90	0.90
2. $P(E\|H^c)$	0.05	0.05	0.05	0.05
3. h_1/f_1	100	100	0.01	0.01
4. $c_{2(H)} = P(E^{c*}\|E^cH)$	0.95	0.01	0.55	0.01
5. $m_{2(H)} = P(E^{c*}\|EH)$	0.75	0.95	0.40	0.98
6. $c_{2(H^c)} = P(E^{c*}\|E^cH^c)$	0.95	0.95	0.75	0.75
7. $m_{2(H^c)} = P(E^{c*}\|EH^c)$	0.01	0.75	0.01	0.01
$L_{E^*E^{c*}}$	70.96	18.38	0.08	0.01

variety of examples involving some of the possible patterns of conditional nonindependence that can be associated with contradicting sources.

In all of the examples in Table 8.2 we have contradictory evidence about an event E whose known occurrence would be 18 times more likely given H than given H^c; the nonoccurrence of E would be 9.5 times more likely given H^c than given H. Part A of this table contains four examples in which we allow for all of the conditional nonindependencies shown in Figure 8.2a. We suppose that the credibilities of both S_1 and S_2 are hypothesis dependent, and we allow for the possibility of some influence among these two sources. In this situation Equation 8.1 tells us that we need assessments of ten likelihoods in order to determine the Bayesian inferential force of contradictory evidence E^* and E^{c*}. In case 1 ingredients r and v picture S_1 as being very credible in reporting event E, if we assumed the truth of H. Ingredients s and w picture S_1 as being somewhat less credible if we assumed the truth of H^c. Ingredients x and t show S_2 as being weakly credible in reporting event E^c, assuming the truth of H; ingredients y and u show S_2 as being strongly credible, if H^c were true. Equation 8.1 tells us that the force of contradictory evidence from two sources having these credibility-related likelihoods favors H over H^c in the ratio $L_{E \cdot E^c \cdot} = 4.86$.

In this and in the other examples in part A of Table 8.2, it is the conditioning of credibility-related ingredients by H and H^c that *may provide* inferential force for a contradiction in excess of knowing E or knowing E^c for sure; it does not do so in Case 1, but it does in the other three cases. We should ask what role is then played by the further conditioning of E^{c*} from S_2 by evidence E^* from S_1. The answer is that, if we believed E^{c*} were not conditioned by E^*, we would still have the hypothesis contingency of ingredients in rows 7–10, but the specific likelihoods would have been different to some degree. For example, we might suppose that $P(E^{c*}|E^cE^*H) = 0.75$ is different from $P(E^{c*}|E^cH)$ and that $P(E^{c*}|EE^*H) = 0.25$ is different from $P(E^{c*}|EH)$.

The credibility-related ingredients in case 2 picture S_1 as being very credible, assuming H; S_1 is also very credible assuming H^c, but with a distinct bias against reporting E^*. Further we believe S_2 to be weakly credible, particularly so assuming H^c. In this case the inferential force of the contradiction, $L_{E \cdot E^c \cdot} = 81.12$, exceeds by a substantial amount the force of knowing event E for sure. In case 3 we believe S_1 to be inaccurate or lying, but more so assuming H than assuming H^c. But we also believe S_2 to be modestly credible with a bias against reporting E^{c*}, assuming the truth of H. In this case the contradiction is resolved in S_2's favor. The contradiction favors H^c over H in the ratio $L_{E \cdot E^c \cdot} = 0.013 = 1/76.92$. This is far in excess of the force of knowing E^c for sure. In case 4, S_1 is pictured as being very credible but having a strong bias against reporting E^*, assuming H. Assuming H^c, we believe S_1 to be only weakly credible. We also have S_2 being weakly credible, assuming H, and slightly more credible assuming H^c. This contradiction is also resolved in favor of H^c and has inferential force $L_{E \cdot E^c \cdot} = 0.054 = 1/18.52$, about twice the force of knowing E^c for sure.

Part B of Table 8.2 shows four examples of the situation illustrated in Figure 8.3c for which Equation 8.6 is appropriate in determining the Bayesian force of the contradictory evidence from S_1 and S_2. Notice in these cases that all we need for S_1 is the ratio $h_1/f_1 = P(E^*|E)/P(E^*|E^c)$. In case 1 we believe S_1 to be very credible, but we also believe S_2's credibility to be contingent on the hypotheses. Assuming H, we believe S_2 would have a strong bias in favor of reporting the nonoccurrence of event E; assuming H^c, we believe S_2 would be quite credible. The contradiction in this case has strong inferential force favoring H, more so than the force of knowing E for sure. In case 2 we strongly believe in the credibility of S_1; we believe S_2 to be inaccurate or lying if H were true and, if H^c were true, strongly biased in favor of reporting that E did not occur. This contradiction has slightly greater force than the force of knowing for sure that event E occurred. In case 3 we believe S_1 to be inaccurate or lying whether or not H is true. We also believe S_2 to be more strongly credible if H were not true. The force of contradictory evidence from these two sources favors H^c in the ratio $0.08 = 1/12.5$; this is stronger than the force of knowing E^c for sure. Finally, in case 4 we again suppose S_1 to be inaccurate or lying, whether or not H is true. We also believe S_2 to be inaccurate or lying if H were true, but credible if H were not true. The contradiction from these possibly lying or inaccurate sources favors H^c over H in the ratio $1/100$.

In Table 8.2 we have eight examples of contradictions involving credibility-related conditional nonindependencies associated with the two sources. Some of the results are more counterintuitive than others. Case 4 in part B of Table 8.2 seems reasonably intuitive. For example, we might believe S_1 to be a liar whether or not H was true, but we believe that the possibility of S_2's lying is contingent on H being true. If H were not true, we regard S_2 as being quite credible. So we side inferentially with S_2's report that E did not occur. Other cases may not be so intuitive unless they are examined very carefully. Bayes's rule often works in strange and wonderous ways; its workings are interesting in part because we do not always obtain answers we expect.

So far, in discussing the inferential force of a contradiction, we have not considered the nature of the evidence we have; evidence items E^* and E^{c*} have been nondescript. We have assumed that both E^* and E^{c*} are direct evidence involving a single reasoning stage linking them to events $\{E, E^c\}$. But now suppose we can be more specific about the nature of two items of contradictory evidence; there are many possibilities as we can observe from the evidence types shown in the rows of Figure 3.11. For example, E^* might be tangible evidence, such as a photograph, and E^{c*} might be testimonial evidence from a person. In another case E^* be testimonial evidence from S_1, who claims to be a primary source, and E^{c*} might be evidence from S_2, who claims to have received this negative evidence at secondhand from another source S_3. Once we identify the nature of the evidence we have, we are naturally concerned about attributes of the credibility of our sources. If we have appropriate ancillary evidence, time, and patience, we might be inclined to decompose the assessments of h and f for S_1 and c and m for S_2. Our probability assessment burden can become quite substantial, as I will illustrate by the situation shown in Figure 8.4.

Suppose that contradictory evidence E^* and E^{c*} are items of *unequivocal testimonial* evidence from two persons S_1 and S_2, both of whom claim to have made a relevant observation concerning event E. Person S_1 says E occurred, and S_2 says it did not. To make matters reasonably simple, suppose we have no ancillary evidence suggesting that S_1 influenced S_2 or that either testimony is in any way contingent upon H or H^c. We wish to employ a Bayesian scheme for determining the inferential force of this joint contradictory testimony. Suppose further that we wish to capture and incorporate specific uncertainties that we have about the veracity, objectivity, and observational sensitivity of both S_1 and S_2. In Figure 8.4 is a decomposition of the situation shown in Figure 8.2b made in order to capture these credibility attributes.

Fortunately, because of the singly connected nature of the inference network in Figure 8.4, we do not need to derive a new expression for the

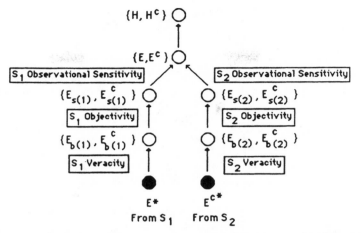

FIGURE 8.4   Decomposing the credibility-related stages of reasoning from contradictory evidence.

likelihood ratio $L_{E \cdot E^{c*}}$. We can join together three equations that we have already discussed. First, Equation 8.3 gives us $L_{E \cdot E^{c*}}$ for the undecomposed case of the contradiction shown in Figure 8.2b. We need $K_1 = h_1/f_1 = P(E^*|E)/P(E^*|E^c)$ for person S_1, and $K_2 = c_2/m_2 = P(E^{c*}|E^c)/P(E^{c*}|E)$ for person S_2. Now Equations 7.16 and 7.17 show us how to determine h_1 and f_1 for source S_1 in the singly connected chain of reasoning from E^* to $\{E, E^c\}$ in Figure 8.4. I now repeat them as

$$h_1 = a[(c - d)(v - w)] + d(v - w) + w \tag{8.7}$$

and

$$f_1 = b[(c - d)(v - w)] + d(v - w) + w \tag{8.8}$$

where $a = P(E_{s(1)}|E)$, $b = P(E_{s(1)}|E^c)$, $c = P(E_{b(1)}|E_{s(1)})$, $d = P(E_{b(1)}|E_{s(1)}{}^c)$, $v = P(E^*|E_{b(1)})$, and $w = P(E^*|E_{b(1)}{}^c)$. Taking the ratio h_1/f_1 yields

$$\frac{h_1}{f_1} = \frac{a + [d/(c - d)] + [w/(c - d)(v - w)]}{b + [d/(c - d)] + [w/(c - d)(v - w)]}$$

$$= \frac{a + d/(c - d) + [1/(c - d)][(v/w) - 1]^{-1}}{b + [d/(c - d)] + [1/(c - d)][(v/w) - 1]^{-1}} \tag{8.9}$$

Since the bottom linkage is that between E^* and $\{E_{b(1)}, E_{b(1)}{}^c\}$, all we need is the ratio v/w.

Similar equations yield the values of c_2 and m_2 for person S_2. They are

$$c_2 = p[(r - s)(t - u)] + s(t - u) + u \qquad (8.10)$$

and

$$m_2 = q[(r - s)(t - u)] + s(t - u) + u \qquad (8.11)$$

where $p = P(E_{s(2)}{}^c|E^c)$, $q = P(E_{s(2)}{}^c|E)$, $r = P(E_{b(2)}{}^c|E_{s(2)}{}^c)$, $s = P(E_{b(2)}{}^c|E_{s(2)})$, $t = P(E^{c*}|E_{b(2)}{}^c)$, and $u = P(E^{c*}|E_{b(2)})$. The ratio c_2/m_2 is

$$
\begin{aligned}
\frac{c_2}{m_2} &= \frac{p + [s/(r - s)] + [u/(r - s)(t - u)]}{q + [s/(r - s)] + [u/(r - s)(t - u)]} \\
&= \frac{p + [s/(r - s)] + [1/(r - s)][(t/u) - 1]^{-1}}{q + [s/(r - s)] + [1/(r - s)][(t/u) - 1]^{-1}}
\end{aligned}
\qquad (8.12)
$$

Observe that all we need at the bottom stage of an inference from E^{c*} to events $\{E, E^c\}$ is the ratio t/u for S_2.

For the singly connected inference network in Figure 8.4 we could determine $L_{E \cdot E^{c*}}$ for this contradiction using Equation 8.3, where $K_1 = h_1/f_1$, as prescribed by Equation 8.9, and $K_2 = c_2/m_2$ as prescribed by Equation 8.12. But this task of determining the decomposed inferential force of a simple case of testimonial contradiction requires evidence-justified assessments of fourteen likelihoods. Such decompositions are certainly informative about what lies below the surface of a contradiction. However, in practice we may not always have ancillary evidence to justify all of the probabilistic judgments a formally decomposed analysis requires. It may be time to consider other ways of assessing the inferential force of contradictory testimony.

Let us return to Glenn Shafer's belief functions and the case of your neighbor's dog presented in Section 5.4. I have already described one belief function analysis of contradictory testimony (see Section 5.4.5 and Figure 5.6b). In this analysis, your hypotheses of interest are $\{H, H^c\}$ whether or not your neighbor is keeping a dog in his apartment (in violation of the rules). You presently have direct contradictory testimony from two witnesses: P reports H* and R reports H^{c*}. You believe that the chances are 90% that P is credible and 80% that R is credible. I discussed Shafer's argument about the meaning of these judgments in Section 5.4.2 and provided an illustration in Figure 5.2. If you had just P's testimony, your evidential support assignment $s_P\{H\} = Bel_P\{H\} = 0.9$ and your $s_P\{H, H^c\} = Bel_P\{H, H^c\} = 0.1$. Recall the argument that if P is not credible (with a 10% chance), this says nothing about $\{H^c\}$. If you had just R's testimony, your $s_R\{H^c\} = Bel_R\{H^c\} = 0.8$ and your $s_R\{H, H^c\} = Bel_R\{H, H^c\} = 0.2$; if R is not credible, this says nothing about $\{H\}$.

As the analysis in Figure 5.6 shows, when we combine these evidential support assignments according to Dempster's rule we can make the following comparisons: (1) $\text{Bel}_P\{H\} \oplus \text{Bel}_R\{H\} = 0.64$ with $\text{Bel}_P\{H\} = 0.9$ and (2) $\text{Bel}_P\{H^c\} \oplus \text{Bel}_R\{H^c\} = 0.29$ with $\text{Bel}_R\{H^c\} = 0.8$ for R. We thus observe two facts about how Dempster's rule resolves a simple contradiction. First, our combined belief about the inferential force of a contradiction favors the side with the greatest credibility, P in this case. Second, notice that this contradiction weakens the strength of our belief about both sides of the contradiction $\{H\}$ and $\{H^c\}$, but it weakens our belief in $\{H^c\}$ more because we believe that R has less credibility than P. As I will now illustrate, Bayes's rule behaves quite similarly in *comparable* situations.

To combine testimonies from P and R according to Dempster's rule, we had to assume that they were independent items of evidence. In Table 8.1 are shown several examples of likelihood ratio for contradictory evidence from sources S_1 and S_2 for the singly connected inference network shown in Figure 8.2 . In these examples we supposed there to be no mutual influence involving S_1 and S_2. The values of $L_{E \cdot E^{c \cdot}}$ shown in each of these examples were calculated using Equation 8.3; first consider cases 1–3. In each of these cases we side inferentially with the source having the largest value of K; recall that $K_1 = h_1/f_1$ and $K_2 = c_2/m_2$. Next observe, by comparing $L_{E \cdot E^{c \cdot}}$ with $L_{E \cdot}$ and $L_{E^{c \cdot}}$, that the side having the smallest value of K has its inferential force weakened the most as a result of the contradiction. For example, in case 1 we have $L_{E \cdot E^{c \cdot}} = 11.42$. This is a far smaller change away from $L_{E \cdot} = 15.09$ than is the change from $L_{E^{c \cdot}} = 0.41 = 1/2.44$ (favoring H^c) to $L_{E \cdot E^{c \cdot}} = 11.42$ (favoring H). Cases 4 and 5 are not comparable, since they involve possibly untruthful sources whose K values are inversely related.

Cases 6 and 7 are comparable to a Dempster rule analysis as you can observe by comparing $L_{E \cdot E^{c \cdot}}$ with $L_{E \cdot}$ and $L_{E^{c \cdot}}$ in each case. In fact these two cases are the ones most comparable with the belief function examples I have provided. The reason involves the entailments in these two cases. In case 6, for example, if E is true, as reported by S_1, this entails H; if E^c is true, as reported by S_2, this entails H^c. In the Shafer examples, P's credibility entails $\{H\}$ and R's credibility entails $\{H^c\}$. As I mentioned in Section 5.4, belief function analyses allow us to draw conclusions from evidence in situations in which more detailed Bayesian analyses might not be accompanied by evidence necessary to justify all of the likelihoods such analyses require. In Table 8.2 I provided examples illustrating how a Bayesian analysis can capture assorted conditional nonindependencies associated with our sources of evidence. But more likelihood assessments are required in these cases, and more ancillary evidence is required to justify these assessments.

A Baconian analysis of a contradiction is certainly possible. As an example, consider Figure 8.4 in which I have decomposed the credibility-related foundation of the arguments from two items of contradictory evidence. Using the variative and eliminative testing procedure I described in Sections 5.5.3 and 7.3.5, we could proceed up both chains from E^* to $\{E, E^c\}$ and from E^{c*} to $\{E, E^c\}$. Our detachment of a belief about E or E^c would be based upon both the favorableness and the completeness with which the credibility-related generalizations for persons S_1 and S_2 survived our best attempts to eliminate them. If the veracity, objectivity, and observational sensitivity generalizations for S_1 best meet these tests, we side with S_1 and believe that event E occurred. If the similar generalizations for S_2 survive the best, we side with S_2 and believe that E did not occur. In either case a Baconian analysis allows us to grade the length and strength of the inferential limb that we find ourselves on when we detach such beliefs. Completeness of evidential coverage is most important in such analyses. We may have more credibility-related evidence about one source than we do another; no analysis of the inferential force of a contradiction should ignore this fact.

8.1.2 Conflicting Evidence

A very simple case of evidential conflict is shown in Figure 8.5a. Source S_1 reports E^*, that event E occurred; source S_2 reports F^*, that event F occurred. For the moment let us not be concerned about the type of evidence we have in this case. Suppose we believe that the occurrence of event E would favor hypothesis H but that the occurrence of event F would favor H^c. On careful analysis we can identify no reason why E and F could not both have occurred or be true. In other words, our belief is that events E and F are not mutually exclusive. In this case we say that evidence items E^* and F^* are in conflict or are at variance in their inferential direction; one points our belief toward H and the other points our belief toward H^c. In Section 3.5.1 I gave two examples of conflicting evidence. In one case two different items of evidence concerned a patient facing heart surgery; one item seemed to favor his survival and the other did not. In another case involving a criminal matter, one item of evidence pointed to defendant's guilt, while a different item pointed to his innocence.

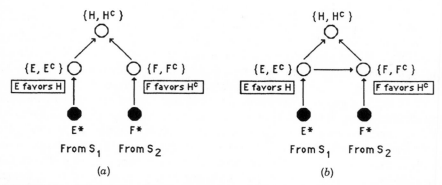

FIGURE 8.5 Evidential conflict. (a) Events reported are conditionally independent. (b) Events reported are conditionally nonindependent.

The fundamental difference between evidential contradiction and conflict is that a contradiction always involves events in *the same* mutually exclusive class, such as events {E, E^c}. Evidential conflict, on the other hand, involves events in *different* classes, such as {E, E^c} and {F, F^c}. It may of course be true that events selected from these different classes are mutually exclusive. For example, it might be true that events E and F cannot occur together. In another case we might believe that E^c and F^c cannot occur together; that is, one or the other of events E and F must have occurred. But such questions have to be established by *empirical* rather than by *formal* means. The mutual exclusivity of E and E^c is settled on logical grounds; we cannot have event E happening and not happening at the same time. These distinctions are quite important in our efforts to resolve evidential dissonance. As I mentioned, an evidential contradiction can only be resolved on credibility-related grounds. The resolution of evidential conflicts, on the other hand, rests on credibility and other grounds as well.

Consider a situation which, to our best current knowledge, is represented by the singly connected inference network in Figure 8.5a. In this case we have no state-dependence of the credibilities of S$_1$ or of S$_2$. In addition we have no basis for a belief that one source influenced the other. Further the absence of an arc between event classes {E, E^c} and {F, F^c} means that we regard events in these classes to be independent, conditional upon H and on H^c. Easily shown in this case is that the likelihood ratio for the joint conflicting report E*F* is given by $L_{E^{\cdot}F^{\cdot}} = L_{E^{\cdot}} \cdot L_{F^{\cdot}}$, where $L_{E^{\cdot}}$ and $L_{F^{\cdot}}$ are each determined by Equation 7.11. Applied in the present case, we have

$$L_{E^{\cdot}} = \frac{P(E|H)(h_1 - f_1) + f_1}{P(E|H^c)(h_1 - f_1) + f_1} \tag{8.13}$$

where $h_1 = P(E^*|E)$ and $f_1 = P(E^*|E^c)$, for S$_1$. For S$_2$'s report we have

$$L_{F^{\cdot}} = \frac{P(F|H)(h_2 - f_2) + f_2}{P(F|H^c)(h_2 - f_2) + f_2} \tag{8.14}$$

where $h_2 = P(F^*|F)$ and $f_2 = P(F^*|F^c)$. Equation 7.11 shows us that Equations 8.13 and 8.14 each have another form in which all we need are the ratios h_1/f_1 and h_2/f_2.

Bayesian conflict resolution in this simplest of cases proceeds as follows: To say that event E favors H over H^c is also to say that $P(E|H) > P(E|H^c)$, or $L_E = P(E|H)/P(E|H^c) > 1$. Our belief that event F favors H^c over H is also to say that $P(F|H) < P(F|H^c)$, or $L_F = P(F|H)/P(F|H^c) < 1$. So, if we knew for sure that events E and F occurred, we would move our belief in the direction of H, if $L_{EF} = L_E L_F > 1$ and in the direction of H^c if $L_{EF} = L_E L_F < 1$. Before we even consider the credibility of the two sources providing us with evidence about events E and F, we might be challenged regarding our interpretation of the inferential directions of knowing event E and knowing event F. Someone might argue that E and F both favor either H or H^c. Someone else might not argue about our assessment of the inferential direction of these two events but argue about the force we have assessed in terms of the magnitudes of L_E and L_F. We might also encounter the argument that events E and F are not independent, as we have claimed. I will return to this challenge momentarily.

In addition to these challenges we recognize that we do not know for sure that events E and F have occurred; all we have is evidence about them from sources S_1 and S_2 whose credibility we cannot assume to be unimpeachable. Suppose, for example, that there is ancillary evidence about S_2's accuracy (if F^* is tangible evidence) or about S_2's veracity, objectivity, or observational sensitivity (if F^* is testimonial evidence). In either case we might have $h_2 < f_2$, in which case S_2's evidence F^* would, according to Equation 8.14, also favor H as does S_1's report E^*. So we could offer an explanation for this apparent conflict on credibility-related grounds, namely that event F did not happen as S_2 reported.

Suppose we adopt the view that nature never generates a true conflict. When we have what we believe to be conflicting evidence, either the evidence itself or our interpretation of it is faulty in some way. I have just given an example of how the evidence itself may be faulty; S_2 reported that event F occurred when in fact it seems very likely that F did not occur. Suppose we concentrate on the possibility of a *faulty explanation* of the inferential direction and force of events E and F. Consider Figure 8.5*b* in which we add an arc indicating the influence of events {E, E^c} on events {F, F^c}. The addition of just this single arc allows us to capture some very interesting issues associated with a Bayesian approach to conflict resolution. This arc indicates that events {F, F^c} are dependent not only upon events {H, H^c} but also upon events {E, E^c}. For example, we may have $P(F|EH) \neq P(F|H)$ and $P(F|EH^c) \neq P(F|E)$. In words, the force of event F on {H, H^c} depends upon event E.

We begin by considering a likelihood ratio $L_{E^*F^*}$ for the joint reports E^* and F^*. As in previous cases we have $L_{E^*F^*} = P(E^*F^*|H)/P(E^*F^*|H^c)$. Using the general product rule (or chain rule), we can also write $L_{E^*F^*}$ as the product $[P(E^*|H)/P(E^*|H^c)][P(F^*|E^*H)/P(F^*|E^*H^c)] = L_{E^*}L_{F^*|E^*}$. The term $L_{F^*|E^*}$ grades the inferential force of evidence F^*, given evidence E^*. As noted above, for the singly connected network in Figure 8.5*a*, we have $L_{E^*F^*} = L_{E^*}L_{F^*}$; the inferential force of F^* is not in any way affected by our knowledge of E^*. But in the situation shown in Figure 8.5*b*, we now need to examine $L_{F^*|E^*}$, since there are reasons why $L_{F^*|E^*} \neq L_{F^*}$. Various reasons can be identified in terms of the conditional nonindependence of events in {E, E^c} and {F, F^c}, given events in {H, H^c}, as discussed in the paragraph above. In such instances we need to be able to determine $L_{E^*F^*} = L_{E^*}L_{F^*|E^*}$. We already have an expression for determining the inferential force of E^* in Figure 8.5*b;* it is given by Equation 8.13. What we do not yet have is an expression for $L_{F^*|E^*}$ appropriate to the conditioning pattern in Figure 8.5*b*.

For the inference network shown in Figure 8.5b the likelihood ratio $L_{F^*|E^*} = P(F^*|E^*H)/P(F^*|E^*H^c)$ has the form

$$L_{F^*|E^*} = \frac{P(E|E^*H)[P(F|EH) - P(F|E^cH)] + P(F|E^cH) + [(h_2/f_2) - 1]^{-1}}{P(E|E^*H^c)[P(F|EH^c) - P(F|E^cH^c)] + P(F|E^cH^c) + [(h_2/f_2) - 1]^{-1}} \tag{8.15}$$

where $h_2 = P(F^*|F)$ and $f_2 = P(F^*|F^c)$. Consider the four likelihoods involving event F. These terms allow us to capture the dependence of the reported event F on events $\{E, E^c\}$ as well as on events $\{H, H^c\}$. But we have two very important terms of a sort we have not yet encountered; they are $P(E|E^*H)$ and $P(E|E^*H^c)$. A determination of L_{E^*} requires assessment of $P(E|H)$ and $P(E|H^c)$. But, in assessing $L_{F^*|E^*}$, we are in a different position, namely we now have evidence E^* to consider. This is made necessary by the arc connecting $\{E, E^c\}$ and $\{F, F^c\}$. Our assessments of the likeliness of event E, under H and H^c, may now be changed as a result of having evidence E^*. The terms $P(E|E^*H)$ and $P(E|E^*H^c)$ are of considerable importance and need to be examined carefully; they will appear again in analyses of the inferential force of redundant evidence.

By definition, $P(E|E^*H) = P(EE^*H)/P(E^*H)$ and $P(E|E^*H^c) = P(EE^*H^c)/P(E^*H^c)$. If we apply the general product rule to the numerator and denominator of these terms, we have $P(E|E^*H) = P(H)P(E|H)P(E^*|EH)/P(H)P(E^*|H) = P(E|H)P(E^*|EH)/P(E^*|H)$. Since in the present instance we have no arc connecting E^* and $\{H, H^c\}$, we have $P(E|E^*H) = P(E|H)P(E^*|E)/P(E^*|H) = P(E|H)h_1/P(E^*|H)$. But by Equation 8.13 we have $P(E^*|H) = P(E|H)[h_1 - f_1] + f_1 = P(E|H)h_1 + P(E^c|H)f_1$, where $f_1 = P(E^*|E^c)$. Putting these equations together, we have

$$P(E|E^*H) = \frac{P(E|H)h_1}{P(E|H)h_1 + P(E^c|H)f_1} \tag{8.16}$$

and

$$P(E|E^*H^c) = \frac{P(E|H^c)h_1}{P(E|H^c)h_1 + P(E^c|H^c)f_1} \tag{8.17}$$

I now wish to use Equations 8.15, 8.16, and 8.17 to illustrate two important facts about Bayesian conflict resolution. The first is that an evidential conflict can be resolved on grounds other than those involving the credibility of the sources of evidence. I will given examples in which we can rule out credibility defects as an explanation of evidential conflict. Second, it is sometimes argued that, when two items or bodies of evidence are in conflict, the effect of each one is diminished by the other (Shafer 1976, 82–86). This may be true of items/bodies of evidence that can be regarded as independent. But it is not a *general* characteristic of conflicting evidence, as my examples will illustrate. Certain forms of nonindependence among conflicting items of evidence can produce Bayesian inferential force assignments in which the force of one item is not only enhanced but directionally altered by other apparently conflicting evidence.

Consider the situation involving event classes $\{E, E^c\}$ and $\{F, F^c\}$ illustrated in Figure 8.6. Suppose we believe that event E, if it did occur, has probability $P(E|H) = 0.8$ and $P(E|H^c) = 0.1$ so that E favors H over H^c in the ratio $L_E = 8$. But we also believe that event F, if it did occur, has probabilities $P(F|H) = 0.1$ and $P(F|H^c) = 0.6$ so that F favors H^c over H in the ratio $L_F = 1/6$. Observe that there are five entries for each of the possible joint occurrences of events in $\{E, E^c\}$ and $\{F, F^c\}$ under both H and H^c. First consider the entries labeled [CI], for *conditonal independence*. Suppose we argue that events E and F are independent, conditional upon H and upon H^c. If we knew that both events E and F occurred, we would have $L_{EF} = L_E L_F = 8/6 = 1.33$ favoring H over H^c. The entries labeled CI in the cells of the two tables in Figure 8.6 show the joint probabilities of events in classes $\{E, E^c\}$ and $\{F, F^c\}$ assuming their independence under H and under H^c. For example, if events E and F are independent, given H, then $P(EF|H) = P(E|H)P(F|H) = (0.8)(0.1) = 0.08$. In this case $L_{EF} = P(EF|H)/P(EF|H^c) = 0.08/0.06 = 1.33 = L_E L_F$, as noted above. I will explain the other four entries in each cell in Figure 8.6 as we proceed.

Suppose we obtain the following evidence: S_1 reports E^*, and S_2 reports F^*. Here we have obtained conflicting evidence, given the assessments we have made for events E and F. On a mass of appropriate ancillary evidence we judge both sources to be very credible. None of this evidence suggests state-dependent credibility for either source, nor does it suggest any mutual

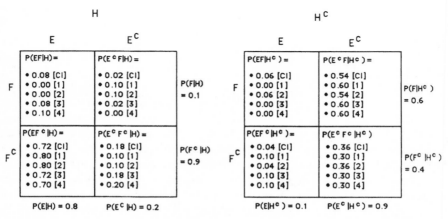

FIGURE 8.6   Conditional nonindependence and apparent evidential conflict: Five examples.

influence between S_1 and S_2. So we are comfortable with the inference network in Figure 8.5a. On our ancillary evidence, we assess the values $h_1 = h_2 = 0.98$ and $f_1 = f_2 = 0.01$. Using these values in combination with the separate likelihoods for events E and F, we employ Equations 8.13 and 8.14 and determine $L_{E^*} = 7.35$ and $L_{F^*} = 0.18$ so that $L_{E^* \cdot F^*} = L_{E^*} \cdot L_{F^*} = 1.32$ favoring H over H^c. Thus the joint evidence E^* and F^* has nearly the same inferential force as knowing E and F for sure.

It is certainly true, so far, that the evidential conflict has weakened the effect of both E^* and F^*. The value $L_{E^* \cdot F^*} = 1.32$ is less than $L_{E^*} = 7.35$ (favoring H). This conflict has certainly weakened the force of F^*, since originally $L_{F^*} = 0.18 = 1/5.56$ (favoring H^c). In this Bayesian analysis we encounter two problems. The first is endemic to certain forms of probabilistic analyses (including Bayesian) and concerns how we can justify any evidence or event as supporting incompatible hypotheses such as {H, H^c}. Recall, for example, that we said that $P(E|H) = 0.8$ and $P(E|H^c) = 0.1$. I will return to this issue a bit later. The second problem concerns the independence assumptions that have led us to believe that our case of conflicting evidence is captured by the inference network in Figure 8.5a. We might have arrived at a different conclusion in resolving this conflict if we had a more informed belief about events E and F and their joint occurrence.

Shown in Table 8.3 are four examples involving arguments that might be made about our analysis so far. These arguments come from critics who claim to be better informed than we are about the joint behavior of event classes {E, E^c} and {F, F^c} under hypotheses {H, H^c}. None of these critics questions our assessments about the *separate* inferential effects of events E and F. But they all argue against our initial assumption that events in classes {E, E^c} and {F, F^c} are independent conditional on hypotheses in {H, H^c}. Recall that this assumption leads to the joint probability values labeled CI in Figure 8.6. So, in this figure let us leave fixed the values $P(E|H) = 0.8$, $P(E|H^c) = 0.1$, $P(F|H) = 0.1$, and $P(F|H^c) = 0.6$. What we will change are the probabilities for the joint occurrence of events in {E, E^c} and {F, F^c}, given H, and given H^c. We will have four critics to contend with; their arguments lead us to the four different joint conditional probabilities numbered 1 through 4 in each cell of Figure 8.6.

As we know from elementary probability, two mutually exclusive events having nonzero probability cannot be independent. Our first critic argues that events E and F cannot occur together whether or not H is true. So we set $P(EF|H) = P(EF|H^c) = 0$. The consequences of this critic's argument are shown by the joint probabilities labeled [1] in Figure 8.6 that are forced when we retain $P(E|H) = 0.8$, $P(E|H^c) = 0.1$, $P(F|H) = 0.1$, and $P(F|H^c) = 0.6$. For example, we must have $P(EF|H) + P(E^cF|H) = P(F|H) = 0.10$. Since we have set $P(EF|H) = 0$, this means that $P(E^cF|H) = 0.1$. So this first critic's argument means that events in {E, E^c} and {F, F^c} are *conditionally nonindependent*, given H and given H^c. The consequences of this critic's argument are shown in case 1 in Table 8.3.

TABLE 8.3   Conflict and Conditional Nonindependence

Ingredients	Case 1	Case 2	Case 3	Case 4
	*A. For Evidence E**			
1. $P(E|H)$	0.8	0.8	0.8	0.8
2. $P(E|H^c)$	0.1	0.1	0.1	0.1
3. $h_1 = P(E^*|E)$	0.98	0.98	0.98	0.98
4. $f_1 = P(E^*|E^c)$	0.01	0.01	0.01	0.01
5. L_{E*}	7.35	7.35	7.35	7.35
	*B. For Evidence F**			
6. $P(E|E^*H)$	0.997	0.997	0.997	0.997
7. $P(E|E^*H^c)$	0.916	0.916	0.916	0.916
8. $P(F|EH)$	0	0	0.10	0.125
9. $P(F|E^cH)$	0.50	0.5	0.10	0
10. $P(F|EH^c)$	0	0.6	0	0
11. $P(F|E^cH^c)$	0.667	0.6	0.67	0.67
12. $h_2 = P(F^*|F)$	0.98	0.98	0.98	0.98
13. $f_2 = P(F^*|F^c)$	0.01	0.01	0.01	0.01
14. $L_{F^*|E^*}$	0.18	0.02	1.66	2.03
15. $L_{E^*} L_{F^*|E^*}$	1.32	0.15	12.20	14.92

Recall that we have two very credible sources reporting the occurrence of conflicting events E and F. This strong credibility is indicated in rows 3, 4, 12, and 13 in Table 8.3. To determine the Bayesian inferential force of their joint report E*F*, we must have $L_{E^*F^*} = L_{E^*} L_{F^*|E^*}$. In case 1, rows 1–4 show the ingredients necessary to determine L_{E^*} for source S_1; we obtain the value $L_{E^*} = 7.35$ shown in row 5 using Equation 8.13. Rows 6–13 show the eight ingredients we need to determine $L_{F^*|E^*}$ using Equation 8.15. All of these ingredients are obtained from our assessments so far. Next we obtain $P(E|E^*H)$ and $P(E|E^*H^c)$ using row 1–4 ingredients (and values resulting from normalization requirements) in Equations 8.16 and 8.17. The ingredients in rows 8–11 are obtained from the joint conditional probabilities labeled (1) in Figure 8.6 as follows: First, $P(F|EH) = P(EF|H)/P(E|H)$. From Figure 8.6 we have $P(EF|H) = 0$ and $P(E|H) = 0.1$, so $P(F|EH) = 0$ in row 8. Similarly in row 9 we have $P(F|E^cH) = P(FE^c|H)/P(E^c|H) = 0.1/0.2 = 0.5$. The other values in rows 10 and 11 are determined in the same way. Given our assessments $h_2 = 0.98$ and $f_2 = 0.01$ (rows 12, 13), we use these eight ingredients to determine $L_{F^*|E^*} = 0.18$ in row 14. The required product $L_{E^*F^*} = L_{E^*} L_{F^*|E^*} = 1.32$ appears in row 15.

This first case of conditonal nonindependence of event classes {E, E^c} and {F, F^c}, given H and given H^c, produces an interesting result. We are entitled to sneer at critic 1, if we wish, since his argument that events E and F cannot happen together produces virtually the same result as did our initial assumption that events in classes {E, E^c} and {F, F^c}, are independent, given H and given H^c. This result is (within rounding) the same as our earlier determination $L_E \cdot L_F \cdot = 1.32$, assuming conditional nonindependence. But we have three other critics to contend with.

The critic in case 2 agrees only partially with our conditional independence assumption and only partly with critic 1. Critic 2 argues that event classes {E, E^c} and {F, F^c} are independent, but only under hypothesis H^c. When hypothesis H is true, she argues that events E and F cannot occur together; partially agreeing with critic 1. In Figure 8.6 the joint conditional probabilities corresponding to her argument are labeled [2]. From these ingredients and from others we have discussed, we determine $L_{F^* | E^*} = 0.02 = 1/50$ favoring H^c. As I promised, the effect of conflicting evidence E* has certainly not degraded the inferential force of conflicting evidence F*. Considered by itself, using Equation 8.14, $L_{F^*} = 0.18 = 1/5.56$ favoring H^c. So, under the pattern of conditional nonindependence suggested by critic 2, the inferential force of F* is *enhanced* by a factor of nearly ten, given *conflicting evidence* E*. Jointly E* and F* have inferential force favoring H^c over H in the ratio $L_{E^*} \cdot L_{F^* | E^*} = (7.35)(0.02) = 0.15 = 1/6.67$. We cannot sneer at critic 2, since the inferential force of conflicting evidence E* and F* has substantial force favoring H^c, whereas, under our initial conditional nonindependence assumption, we determined that the inferential force of this contradictory evidence weakly favored H over H^c.

Now comes critic 3 who argues that critic 2 has matters reversed. Critic 3 argues that events E and F cannot happen together when hypothesis H^c is true and that events in classes {E, E^c} and {F, F^c} are independent, given H. Joint conditional probabilities consistent with critic 3's argument are labeled [3] in Figure 8.6. If critic 3 is correct, there is no conflict at all since both E* and F* favor hypothesis H over H^c. Observe in case 3 that $L_{F^* | E^*} = 1.66$, favors H over H^c, as does $L_{E^*} = 7.35$. On this analysis, evidence E* and F*, considered jointly, has inferential force $L_{E^* \cdot F^*} = 12.2$ favoring H over H^c. Critic 3 gloats over having explained away what we took to be evidential conflict.

Finally, critic 4 argues that no one has yet managed to see the correct way in which the events of concern are related. He agrees with critic 3 that events E and F cannot happen together when H is not true. However, he argues that, when hypothesis H is true, event F cannot occur unless event E occurs. In other words, events F and E^c cannot occur together when H is true. The consequences of this argument are shown by the joint conditional probabilities labeled [4] in Figure 8.6. As case 4 in Table 8.3 shows, critic 4 can also gloat about explaining away what we have taken to be a case of evidential conflict, since in this case evidence F* now also favors H, in light of evidence E*.

In summary, it is not true that the effect of each item of conflicting evidence is *always* weakened by the other. In the examples just provided, if we agreed with any of the arguments given by critics 2, 3, or 4, we could either enhance the value of one evidence item, with knowledge of a conflicting item, or explain away the apparent conflict. But we have still not addressed the concerns of persons who argue that there are problems associated with saying that we have evidence that supports incompatible or inconsistent hypotheses such as {H, H^c}.

Evidential dissonance has been called an "embarrassment" (Shafer 1976, 223–226). The negation property of Baconian probability, discussed in Section 5.5.2, asserts that believable evidence cannot support rival or incompatible hypotheses. There are other arguments that have been made about whether rational persons can, on the basis of any evidence, hold positive beliefs about incompatible hypotheses (e.g., Levi 1980, 11–17). The structural and probabilistic analyses I have provided may not settle any philosophical arguments concerning dissonance. Still they at least allow us to be a bit more precise in discussing evidential dissonance. *Contradictions* in evidence can be explained away entirely on credibility grounds. *Conflicting* evidence, on the other hand, is not so simply explained, since we have at least two sources of dissonance: (1) the evidence may not be entirely credible and (2) our beliefs about the inferential force of the *events reported in the evidence* may not be well-founded.

Any of the analyses of evidential conflict that I have provided could be further decomposed to account for additional sources of uncertainty that are recognized. Additional subtleties arise when the credibility-relevant behavior of the sources of conflicting evidence is state dependent in the manner discussed in Section 8.1.1 for contradictory evidence. In my examples sources S_1 and S_2 have provided what we have judged to be conflicting evidence. Upon closer examination, we could perhaps discover that the behavior of S_2 makes evidence F* favor hypothesis H rather than hypothesis H^c, as we now suppose. If evidence items E* and F* are items of testimony from human sources, we may have evidence to support more specific likelihoods associated with attributes of the credibility of sources S_1 and S_2. In this situation we could decompose our assessments of h and f for these two sources according to Equations 8.7 and 8.8. Such additional assessments place a heavier burden on us to generate ancillary evidence to justify these additional probability judgments.

8.2   ON THE FORCE OF HARMONIOUS EVIDENCE

In a general sense we may say that two or more items of evidence are in harmony when they point in the same inferential direction or favor the same hypothesis. We just observed that there are distinguishable forms of dissonant evidence; so it is with harmonious evidence. We may have two or more evidence items from difference sources, all of which report the *same event*. As I noted in Section 3.5.2, this is one species of evidential *corroboration*. We may, instead, have two or more evidence items, reporting *different* events, all of which we believe favor the same hypothesis. In Section 3.5.2 I referred to such evidence as being *convergent* or *confirming*.

These distinctions are useful in allowing us to make further distinctions between dissonant and harmonious evidence. Both contradiction and corroboration involve events in the same class, such as {E, E^c}. A contradiction arises if one source reports E*, that event E occurred, and the other reports E^{c*}, that event E^c occurred. Corroboration involving two sources arises if both report E* or both report E^{c*}. But both conflict and confirmation (or convergence) involve different event classes, such as {E, E^c} and {F, F^c}. If events E and F are believed to favor different hypotheses, evidence E* and F* are in conflict, as we have just considered. But if events E and F are believed to favor the same hypothesis, then E* and F* are convergent (or confirming). So we might regard contradiction and corroboration as being two sides of one "inferential coin" and confirmation and conflict as being two sides of another.

We have observed how attention to credibility matters alone may settle a contradiction. Two evidence items E* and E^{c*} are contradictory. On the one hand, if we believed the source reporting E^{c*} to be erroneous or lying, then both evidence items are in fact corroborative and favor the same hypothesis (see case 4 in Table 8.1). On the other hand, if we have conflicting evidence E* and F*, involving different events E and F, this conflict can be explained both on credibility grounds as well as on other grounds involving our belief about the inferential implications of events E and F. The same problems arise in assessing the value of *convergent* evidence E* and F* when we believe that events E and F both favor the same hypothesis. One or both of the evidence items might be questioned on credibility grounds. But what if our belief that E and F both favor the same hypothesis is not well-founded? As we will now observe, evidential corroboration raises the topic of evidential *redundance*, a topic that deserves the special attention it receives in Section 8.4. We wish to make sure that we are not getting more than a justifiable amount of "inferential mileage" from our evidence. Evidential convergence, on the other hand, raises the possibility that we may not be getting as much "inferential mileage" from our evidence as it deserves; this problem involves what I have termed evidential *synergism*.

8.2.1 Corroborative Evidence

In Figure 3.14a, I gave illustrations of two different uses of the term *corroboration*. In the first case two sources S$_1$ and S$_2$ both report evidence E*, that event E occurred. In the second case we have one source reporting E*, that event E occurred, and another source providing ancillary evidence favorable to the credibility of the source reporting E*. In the analyses to follow, I will be using the term corroboration as in the first of these two cases. Suppose that sources S$_1$ and S$_2$ both report E*, as shown in Figure 8.7. For the moment we will be unconcerned about the form or type of this evidence; it could be

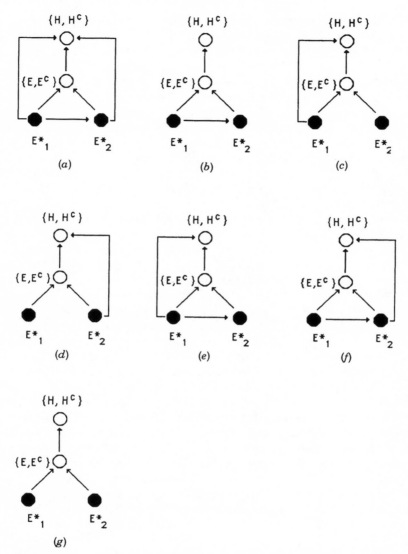

FIGURE 8.7   Special cases of linkage patterns for corroborative evidence.

some kind of tangible evidence or testimonial evidence. Suppose that event E, if it occurred, favors hypothesis H over H^c; in terms of likelihoods, $P(E|H) > P(E|H^c)$.

We contemplate the Bayesian inferential force on $\{H, H^c\}$ of the joint corroborative report E_1^* and E_2^*. We have $L_{E_1^*E_2^*} = P(E_1^*E_2^*|H)/$

$P(E_1^*E_2^*|H^c)$. In its expanded form, we have

$$L_{E_1^*E_2^*} = \frac{P(E|H)[rt - vx] + vx}{P(E|H^c)[su - wy] + wy} \tag{8.18}$$

We can now observe why corroborative and contradictory evidence are two sides of the same inferential coin. As you can see, Equation 8.18 for *corroborative* evidence is exactly the same as Equation 8.1 for *contradictory* evidence. The only difference concerns definition of the terms t, u, x, and y. In Equation 8.18 we have the following definitions:

For S_1,

$$r = P(E_1^*|EH) = P_H(E_1^*|E) = h_{1(H)}$$
$$s = P(E_1^*|EH^c) = P_{H^c}(E_1^*|E) = h_{1(H^c)}$$
$$v = P(E_1^*|E^cH) = P_H(E_1^*|E^c) = f_{1(H)}$$
$$w = P(E_1^*|E^cH^c) = P_{H^c}(E_1^*|E^c) = f_{1(H^c)}$$

For S_2,

$$t = P(E_2^*|EE_1^*H) = P_{E_1^*H}(E_2^*|E) = h_{2(E_1^*H)}$$
$$u = P(E_2^*|EE_1^*H^c) = P_{E_1^*H^c}(E_2^*|E) = h_{2(E_1^*H^c)}$$
$$x = P(E_2^*|E^cE_1^*H) = P_{E_1^*H}(E_2^*|E^c) = f_{2(E_1^*H)}$$
$$y = P(E_2^*|E^cE_1^*H^c) = P_{E_1^*H^c}(E_2^*|E^c) = f_{2(E_1^*H^c)}$$

Equation 8.18 allows for all of the conditional nonindependencies shown in Figure 8.7a. If we have *none* of them, as in Figure 8.7g, we have $r = s = P(E_1^*|E) = h_1$, $v = w = P(E_1^*|E^c) = f_1$, $t = u = P(E_2^*|E) = h_2$, and $x = y = P(E_2^*|E^c) = f_2$. In this case we have

$$L_{E_1^*E_2^*} = \frac{P(E|H)[h_1h_2 - f_1f_2] + f_1f_2}{P(E|H^c)[h_1h_2 - f_1f_2] + f_1f_2}$$

$$= \frac{P(E|H) + [(h_1h_2/f_1f_2) - 1]^{-1}}{P(E|H^c) + [(h_1h_2/f_1f_2) - 1]^{-1}} \tag{8.19}$$

Equation 8.19 can be easily extended to a general situation in which we have n corroborating sources all of whom/which provide the same evidence E^*. In this case we have

$$L_{E_1^*E_2^*\ E_n^*} = \frac{P(E|H) + [\Pi_{i=1}^n (h_i/f_i) - 1]^{-1}}{p(E|H^c) + [\Pi_{i=1}^n (h_i/f_i) - 1]^{-1}} \tag{8.20}$$

Notice that the likelihood ratio in Equation 8.20 is bounded by L_{E^c} and L_E, as in other situations involving singly connected chains of reasoning that we have examined.

Using Equation 8.20, we observe the first of several subtleties associated with evidential corroboration. Suppose that the credibility of none of the n sources is state dependent, and suppose that there is no mutual influence among these sources. In this situation the effect of adding corroborative sources is simply to reduce what I have termed *inferential drag* provided that, for each source i, $h_i > f_i$. For example, suppose a single source reporting E^* for whom/which $h_1 = 0.8$ and $f_1 = 0.1$. The drag term in this case is $[8 - 1]^{-1} = 0.143$. Now let us add another source who also reports E^*. Suppose that this second source has $h_2 = 0.8$ and $f_2 = 0.1$. In this case the drag term is $[64 - 1]^{-1} = 0.016$. Adding just one corroborative report has reduced inferential drag to a significant degree. But now suppose the second source had credibility "credentials" $h_2 = 0.3$ and $f_2 = 0.9$; in other words, we believe this second source to be inaccurate or untruthful. In this case inferential drag is increased, since we now have $[(8)(1/3) - 1]^{-1} = 0.6$, which is considerably greater than the drag for the first source by itself. In a Bayesian sense, corroboration requires that $h_i > f_i$ for every source i.

Various patterns of conditional nonindependence for evidential corroboration are those shown in Figures 8.7a through 8.7f. All of these cases involve just two sources. It should be quite obvious how many possibilities there are for state-dependent credibilities and patterns of mutual influence when we have more than two sources of corroborative evidence. Figure 8.7b illustrates the presence of influence between our two sources but no state-dependent credibility. In this case the only change necessary is to indicate a possible revision of h_2 and f_2, as a result of our having E_1^*. In this case we have $t = u = P_{E_1^*}(E_2^*|E) = h_{2(E_1^*)}$ and $x = y = P_{E_1^*}(E_2^*|E^c) = f_{2(E_1^*)}$. Since neither of these ingredients is further conditioned by H or H^c, Equation 8.19 applies with this notational adjustment. Recall that mutual source influence, by itself, only causes us to revise h_2 and f_2 values over what they might have been if we had not taken this influence into account. Influence among sources, by itself, changes inferential drag but adds no inferential force unless we also have further conditioning of credibility-related ingredients by H and/or by H^c, as illustrated in Figures 8.7a, e, and f.

The cases shown in Figures 8.7c and d involve state-dependent credibilities but no influence among the sources. Taking Figure 8.7c, for example, for S_1 we have

$$r = P(E_1^*|EH) = P_H(E_1^*|E) = h_{1(H)}$$
$$s = P(E_1^*|EH^c) = P_{H^c}(E_1^*|E) = h_{1(H^c)}$$
$$v = P(E_1^*|E^cH) = P_H(E_1^*|E^c) = f_{1(H)}$$
$$w = P(E_1^*|E^cH^c) = P_{H^c}(E_1^*|E^c) = f_{1(H^c)}$$

For S_2, however, we have $r = s = P(E_2^*|E) = h_2$ and $x = y = P(E_2^*|E_c) = f_2$. With these values $L_{E_1^*E_2^*}$ becomes

$$L_{E_1^*E_2^*} = \frac{P(E|H)[h_{1(H)}(h_2/f_2) - f_{1(H)}] + f_{1(H)}}{P(E|H^c)[h_{1(H^c)}(h_2/f_2) - f_{1(H^c)}] + f_{1(H^c)}} \qquad (8.21)$$

Notice that this equation has exactly the same form as Equation 8.5 for a contradiction in which S_1's credibility is state dependent. The only difference is in the ingredients for S_2, who now gives corroborative rather than contradictory evidence. Remember that in situations in which we have state-dependent credibility-related ingredients, there can be more inferential force in evidence about event E than there is in knowing for sure that event E occurred. Thus the likelihood ratio in Equation 8.21 is not bounded by L_{E^c} and L_E, as is Equation 8.20.

As I mentioned in Chapter 6, if you have access to a spreadsheet you may wish to test your intuition against what Bayesian likelihood ratios say is the inferential force of evidence whose forms, combinations, and credibility characteristics you specify. In the case of evidential corroboration there are very many special cases, as shown in Figure 8.7, even for just two sources. Table 8.4 contains several examples involving the use of Equations 8.20 and 8.21. In part A of Table 8.4 we have corroborative evidence from three sources: S_1 = Tom, S_2 = Dick, and S_3 = Harry. We first suppose that the credibility of none of these three sources is state dependent, so we are entitled to make use of Equation 8.20 in determining the inferential force of their joint corroborative report $E_1^*E_2^*E_3^*$. In all cases, if we knew for sure that event E occurred, this knowledge would have inferential force $L_E = 18$, favoring H over H^c.

In case 1, both Tom and Dick are very credible sources, but Harry is not. Suppose that Tom, Dick, and Harry have never had any contact with each other, so there has been no mutual influence among them. By the closeness of Harry's hit and false-positive probabilities, we picture him as someone who might not be able to tell the difference between the occurrence and nonoccurrence of event E. But no matter, Equation 8.20 tells us that because of the very strong credibilities of Tom and Dick, the joint corroborative testimony from these three sources has nearly the same force as knowing event E for sure, since $L_{E_1^*E_2^*E_3^*} = 17.97$. We might also wish to compare this result with the inferential force of each of the separate reports we have from Tom, Dick, and Harry. From Equation 8.13, $L_{E_1^*} = L_{E_2^*} = 15.17$, and $L_{E_3^*} = 1.03$.

Case 2 is based upon a different set of evidence-justified beliefs about Dick and Harry. Suppose, on ancillary evidence, we discovered that Harry, a very accurate observer, intended to report that event E did not occur. However, other ancillary evidence suggests that Dick, hearing of Harry's intention, influenced Harry into corroborating what Tom and Dick would tell us.

TABLE 8.4   Examples of the Inferential Force of Corroborative Evidence

Ingredients	A. Three Corroborating Sources			
	Case 1	Case 2	Case 3	Case 4
$P(E\|H)$	0.90	0.90	0.90	0.90
$P(E\|H^c)$	0.05	0.05	0.05	0.05
$h_1 = P(E_1^*\|E)$	0.98	0.98	0.60	0.60
$f_1 = P(E_1^*\|E^c)$	0.01	0.01	0.20	0.20
$h_2 = P(E_2^*\|E)$	0.98	0.98	0.60	0.60
$f_2 = P(E_2^*\|E^c)$	0.01	0.01	0.20	0.20
$h_3 = P(E_3^*\|E)$	0.51	—	0.60	—
$f_3 = P(E_3^*\|E^c)$	0.49	—	0.20	—
$h_{3(E_2^*)} = P(E_3^*\|EE_2^*)$	—	0.01	—	0.01
$f_{3(E_2^*)} = P(E_3^*\|E^cE_2^*)$	—	0.98	—	0.98
$L_{E_1^*E_2^*E_3^*}$	17.97	15.17	5.86	0.19

Ingredients	B. State-Dependent Credibility			
	Case 1	Case 2	Case 3	Case 4
$P(E\|H)$	0.90	0.90	0.90	0.90
$P(E\|H^c)$	0.05	0.05	0.05	0.05
$h_{1(H)} = P(E_1^*\|EH)$	0.95	0.95	0.95	0.95
$f_{1(H)} = P(E_1^*\|E^cH)$	0.01	0.01	0.01	0.90
$h_{1(H^c)} = P(E_1^*\|EH^c)$	0.60	0.60	0.95	0.98
$f_{1(H^c)} = P(E_1^*\|E^cH^c)$	0.30	0.30	0.90	0.01
$h_2 = P(E_2^*\|E)$	0.98	0.10	0.10	0.98
$f_2 = P(E_2^*\|E^c)$	0.01	0.50	0.50	0.01
$L_{E_1^*E_2^*}$	25.98	0.59	0.20	17.43

So for Harry in this case, suppose we assess $P(E_3^*|EE_2^*) = 0.01$ and $P(E_3^*|E^cE_2^*) = 0.98$. These ingredients are consistent with our belief that Harry is lying in his report. Equation 8.20 still works, since there is no further conditioning of any source's h and f values by H or by H^c. Effectively this ancillary evidence about Dick and Harry allows Equation 8.20 to cancel out the directionally different force of the reports from these two sources. But the overall force of this joint corroborative report has force $L_{E_1^*E_2^*E_3^*} = 15.17$, close to the inferential force of knowing E for sure. This force is preserved by Tom's strong credibility.

In case 3 we picture Tom, Dick, and Harry as being weakly credible sources; the ratio $h/f = 3$ for each source. The force of their joint testimony is degraded of course but is more than twice as strong as the force of a report from just one of them. A report from one of these sources would have force $L = (0.9 + 0.5)/(0.05 + 0.5) = 2.55$. In case 4 we have the same weak credibility of Tom and Dick as in case 3. But in addition we have the same influence of Dick on Harry as in case 2. Our belief is very strong that Harry is lying to us. Equation 8.20 tells us that the joint corroborative report from these three sources now favors H^c over H in the ratio $L_{E_1^*E_2^*E_3^*} = 0.19 = 1/5.26$. Our strong belief that Harry is lying is not overcome by the weak credibility of Tom and Dick.

In part B of Table 8.4 we have just two sources $S_1 = $ Tom and $S_2 = $ Dick. All four cases involve Equation 8.21 and the situation illustrated in Figure 8.7c. Here we have S_1's credibility dependent upon H or upon H^c. Tom and Dick both tell us that event E occurred; the inferential force of knowing that E occurred is the same as in the cases in part A. In case 1 we have a situation in which, on ancillary evidence, we believe Tom's credibility would be very strong if H were true and quite weak if H^c were true. We believe Dick to be a very credible source. Combining the ingredients in this case according to Equation 8.21, we determine that the joint corroborative report in this case has inferential force $L_{E_1^*E_2^*} = 25.98$ in favor of H over H^c. Tom's state-dependent credibility in this case contributes to the inferential force of this joint corroborative report. This corroborative report has inferential force greater than the force of knowing E for sure.

In case 2 we have the same state-dependency of Tom's credibility as in case 1. However, in this case we give the possibility of Dick's being inaccurate or lying a significant probability. The combined effect of Dick's h/f ratio of $1/5$ and the form of Tom's state-dependent credibility is to assign inferential force to their corroborative report that weakly favors H^c over H in the ratio $L_{E_1^*E_2^*} = 0.59 = 1/1.69$. Case 3 is the same as case 2 except that we change the nature of Tom's state-dependent credibility. On appropriate ancillary evidence we believe him to be very credible if H were true but to be very biased in favor of reporting E^* if H^c were true. Notice that $h_{1(H^c)} = 0.95$ and $f_{1(H^c)} = 0.90$. This form of state-dependent credibility on Tom's part, combined with our belief that Dick is lying or inaccurate, causes the inferential force of their corroborative report to favor H^c over H in the ratio $L_{E_1^*E_2^*} = 0.20 = 1/5$. In case 4 we have restored Dick to respectability; we view him as a very credible source. But we give Tom yet a different form of state-dependent credibility. In this case his bias in favor of reporting E^* is contingent on H being true. However, if H were not true, we suppose him to be very credible. The joint report from Tom and Dick in this case has nearly the value of knowing event E for sure. State-dependency of a source's credibility allows but does not guarantee, that the force of evidence about an event can be greater than the force of knowing this event for sure.

My analyses so far show the reason why I have said that contradiction and corroboration are two sides of the same coin. In Bayesian terms, assessing the inferential force of two contradicting sources or two corroborating sources involves the very same general likelihood ratio (Equations 8.1 and 8.18). The only difference involves using correct rejection and miss probabilities for a contradicting source and hit and false-positive probabilities for a corroborating source. In Section 8.3.1 I will use an expanded version of this common equation to determine the inferential force of a pattern of corroborative and contradictory evidence from multiple sources. This equation will show why Bayes's rule argues against the strategy of counting heads on either side in order to resolve a contradiction. Then in Section 8.4.3 I will revisit corroborative evidence to show how Bayes's rule accounts for the natural redundance of such evidence.

When the credibility of no source is state dependent and when $h_i > f_i$, for any source i, the Bayesian inferential force of a corroborative report exceeds the force of any single report in this combination. Cases 1 and 3 in part A of Table 8.4 illustrate this point. In Figure 5.6a I gave an illustration of how Dempster's rule provides essentially the same result. In this example two persons P and Q, each of whom you judge to have a 90% chance of being credible, reported to you that your neighbor was keeping a dog in his apartment. You have no evidence of mutual influence between these persons and so you regard these two reports as independent items of evidence. According to Dempster's rule your combined belief in H (your neighbor is keeping a dog) is $Bel_P \oplus Bel_Q\{H\} = 0.99$, which exceeds $Bel_P\{H\} = Bel_Q\{H\} = 0.9$.

Jonathan Cohen has commented extensively on Baconian and Bayesian accounts of corroboration (and convergence) (1977, 93–115, 277–281). Cohen's comments drew criticism to which he replied (O'Neill 1982; Cohen, L. J., 1981). The Bayesian analyses of corroboration I have just provided differ from the Bayesian analyses presented either by Cohen or by his critic O'Neill. I will first provide what I hope is an accurate portrayal of the essentials of a Baconian approach to evidential corroboration. Then I will mention how my construal of corroboration in Bayesian terms differs from those given by Cohen and O'Neill.

To illustrate a Baconian interpretation of evidential corroboration, I have chosen the decomposition of testimonial credibility already employed to illustrate Baconian belief detachment in a chain of reasoning (see Section 5.5.3 and Figure 5.10). Consider in Figure 8.8 the chain of reasoning from Tom's testimony E_1^* to hypotheses $\{H, H^c\}$. In this case I have, as on other occasions, decomposed the stage of reasoning from E_1^* to $\{E, E^c\}$ in terms of Tom's credibility attributes: veracity, objectivity, and observational sensitivity. Suppose we have good ancillary evidence that Tom did make a relevant observation and that his testimony E_1^* is not based upon hearsay from another source, nor is it an opinion he expresses based upon his observations of other events. In Baconian terms our reasoning from E_1^* to $\{E, E^c\}$ has three stages, at each of which there is a generalization to be tested. The first is a veracity generalization (G_v) linking E^* with $\{E_b, E_b{}^c\}$, whether or not Tom believes E occurred, as he reported. An objectivity generalization (G_o) links $\{E_b, E_b{}^c\}$ with $\{E_s, E_s{}^c\}$, whether or not Tom's senses gave evidence of E. Finally, an observational sensitivity generalization (G_s) links $\{E_s, E_s{}^c\}$ with events $\{E, E^c\}$. In Section 3.2.3 I provided examples of how each of these generalizations might be asserted.

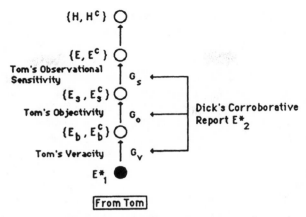

FIGURE 8.8   A Baconian explanation of testimonial corroboration.

The essential Baconian approach to reasoning from E_1^* to $\{E, E^c\}$, through stages $\{E_b, E_b^c\}$ and $\{E_s, E_s^c\}$, involves eliminative and variative testing of each of these generalizations to determine the extent to which they apply in the case of Tom and his present testimony E_1^*. In Figure 3.8 I provided a listing of what hundreds of years of experience by our colleagues in jurisprudence have said are relevant evidential tests of a person's veracity, objectivity, and observational sensitivity. Now let us hear Jonathan Cohen on testimonial corroboration (1977, 278):

> Corroboration and convergence now appear just as two different ways in which probabilities are raised by the favorableness of inductively relevant circumstances. Alongside such factors as a witness's willingness to take an oath, or his demeanor and bearing in the witness box, or his reputed character, one relevant variable for the truth of his testimony is its coherence with other testimony. That is, degree of coherence with other testimony is one relevant variable for the generalization that anything a sworn witness says is true.

Regarding the situation described in Figure 8.8, the generalization Cohen has in mind is one that directly links E_1^* with $\{E, E^c\}$. It might be stated: "If a person says an event happened, then it did happen." As Cohen notes, one test of this generalization applied to Tom concerns the coherence of his testimony E_1^* with other testimony. Enter Dick, who has also testified E_2^*, that event E happened. One way we might view Dick's testimony is simply that it is a favorable result of a relevant test of the generalization that directly links Tom's testimony E_1^* with $\{E, E^c\}$. In other words, we have a favorable result of a test of the coherence of Tom's testimony with other evidence that we have. Suppose we also have Harry's corroborative testimony E_3^*, as in my examples in part A of Table 8.3. Yet we might regard Harry's further corroborative testimony as a replication of Dick's favorable test result concerning the coherence of Tom's testimony with other evidence. We might also argue that Harry's corroboration is a test of the coherence of Dick's testimony with other evidence that we have. Recall that the credibility of all sources is subject to scrutiny.

On this Baconian account of corroboration the testimony of Dick and Harry might be viewed as *ancillary evidence* regarding Tom's credibility. The Baconian result for corroborative evidence is in no way at variance with my Bayesian analyses for singly connected chains of reasoning. Bayesian likelihood ratios simply express our increased confidence in the occurrence of event E by corroborative evidence. This is best shown by an examination of the drag-related product term in Equation 8.20. When we obtain further corroborative evidence of event E from credible sources, the drag on our inference about H, based on event E, decreases, since we are more strongly convinced that E did in fact occur. This is the message conveyed in case 1 in part A of Table 8.4; there is virtually no drag on our opinion revision based upon the event reported corroboratively by Tom, Dick, and Harry. The inferential force of their joint corroborative testimony has nearly the same inferential force as does knowing event E for sure.

My analysis shown in Figure 8.8 differs from Cohen's only by my decomposing his single credibility generalization into three, each of which concerns a particular attribute of a person's credibility. I have performed this decomposition to illustrate what I regard as an important matter concerning testimonial corroboration in either Baconian or Bayesian terms. Notice in Figure 3.8 that one *unspecific* test of a person's credibility involves whether or not there exists *contradictory* testimony. I mentioned in Section 3.2.3 that the existence of contradictory testimony is *unspecific* in credibility impeachment because it does not identify which credibility attribute is being impeached. Thus, for example, if Dick had testified that event E did not occur, we would not know whether this contradiction impeaches Tom's veracity, objectivity, or observational sensitivity. Corroboration and contradiction being two sides of the same coin, when Dick corroborates Tom's testimony we do not know whether this *supports* Tom's veracity, objectivity, or observational sensitivity. This is the message conveyed by Figure 8.8. Dick's corroborative testimony E_2^* is unspecific about which credibility-related generalization (G_v, G_o, or G_s) is being supported in Tom's case.

Cohen's account of the Baconian force of corroborative evidence places great emphasis on the independence of witnesses; the reason is quite obvious. We could not say that Dick's testimony E^* is an appropriate ancillary test result regarding Tom's credibility if Tom influenced what Dick reported. Such influence would destroy the falsification potential of an important test of the coherence of Tom's testimony with other evidence. On a Bayesian view, however, any evidence-justified belief about influence among corroborating sources gets captured by the conditioning of one source's hit and false positive probabilities by another source's report. The four cases in part A of Table 8.4 illustrate how we might change our belief about Harry's hit and false-positive probabilities if we knew that Dick had influenced his testimony. In Bayesian terms, such influence can have inferential force if we also believe it to be conditional upon major hypotheses being considered.

The Bayesian analyses of corroborative evidence mentioned by both Cohen and O'Neill rest upon prior–posterior probability determinations of the sort I mentioned in Section 5.3.1. For reasons noted in Sections 5.3.1 and 5.3.2, I do not believe these analyses put Bayes's rule in its best possible light. By focusing upon likelihood ratio, as a Bayesian gradation of the inferential force of evidence, we are directed to consider specific *likelihoods* associated with stages of reasoning from evidence to hypotheses we entertain. By such means we grade the probabilistic strength or weakness of whatever chain of reasoning we have identified. In such analyses specific judgments of posterior or prior probabilities (or odds) concerning hypotheses are never required. Any conditional nonindependencies among elements of one or more chains of reasoning, made evident by how we have structured a probabilistic argument, can be captured by likelihood ingredients. As I mentioned earlier, my analyses are designed to seek out interesting conditional nonindependencies. By such means we can trap a variety of important evidential subtleties.

8.2.2 Convergent and Possibly Synergistic Evidence

Another species of harmonious evidence concerns reports of two or more *different* events, all of which are believed to favor the same hypothesis. Such evidence is said to be *convergent*. Both structural and probabilistic similarities between convergent evidence and what I have termed conflicting (or divergent) evidence allow us to view these two evidential combinations as being different sides of the same inferential coin. Here are two examples. Evidence that Nicola Sacco was carrying a 32-caliber Colt revolver when he was arrested, and evidence that a 32-caliber bullet was extracted from the body of the slain payroll guard Beradelli, seem to have been convergent in the minds of jurors who voted to convict Sacco. Another example I have shamelessly borrowed from Jonathan Cohen (1977, 101). Evidence that a man has recently had a house built for himself in London and evidence that he has joined an amateur dramatic society in London seem to converge in favoring the hypothesis that he intends to reside in London.

Figure 8.9 shows some structural considerations that influence any analysis of the inferential force of convergent evidence. Suppose that S_1 reports E^*, that event E occurred, and S_2 reports F^*, that event F occurred. Our judgment is that both of these reported events favor hypothesis H over H^c. Considered separately, we would say that $P(E|H) > P(E|H^c)$ and $P(F|H) > P(F|H^c)$ so that L_E and L_F are both greater than 1.0. Our task is to assess the combined inferential force of E^* and F^* on hypotheses $\{H, H^c\}$. Figure 8.9a shows the conditional nonindependence possibilities that we have to consider. These possibilities are made apparent in an expansion of $L_{E \cdot F^*} = P(E^*F^*|H)/P(E^*F^*|H^c)$. The arcs connecting E^* and F^* with $\{H, H^c\}$ concern possibilities

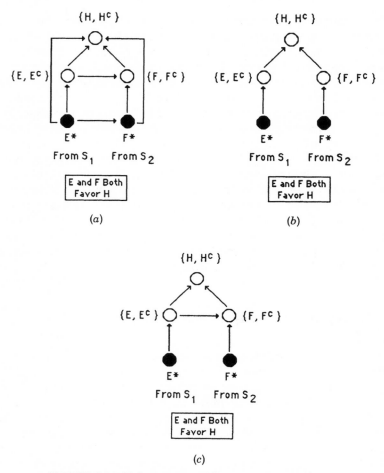

FIGURE 8.9   Linkage patterns for convergent evidence.

of the state dependence of the credibility of sources S_1 and S_2. The arc connecting E^* and F^* concerns possible influence among S_1 and S_2. Finally, the arc connecting events classes {E, E^c} and {F, F^c} indicates that events in these classes may be nonindependent, conditional upon H or upon H^c. In Figure 8.9b these additional arcs have been removed, making the inference network singly connected. In this case it is easily shown that $L_{E^*F^*} = L_{E^*} L_{F^*}$, where L_{E^*} and L_{F^*} are determined by Equations 8.13 and 8.14.

I have already provided many examples of how the state dependence of source credibility can enhance the inferential force of evidence. I have also provided examples showing how influence among sources of evidence acts to change our beliefs about the force of evidence. In my analyses of convergent evidence I wish to focus only upon conditional nonindependence of the events reported in convergent evidence, as illustrated in Figure 8.9c. This will allow me to comment on an interesting subtlety associated with such evidence; I have termed it evidential *synergism* (see Section 3.5.2). Two events, taken together, sometimes have more or less inferential significance than they do when considered separately. If they have *more* significance, we can say that these events operate in a synergistic way; one event seems to enhance the value of another. When one event seems to take some of the inferential significance away from another, we can say that these events are *redundant* to some degree.

To illustrate how a Bayesian likelihood ratio can capture evidential synergism, consider the situation in Figure 8.9c. In a Bayesian gradation of the inferential force of the convergent reports E^* and F^*, we employ the same device used for analyses of conflicting or divergent evidence. First, we express $L_{E \cdot F^*} = L_E \cdot L_{F^* | E^*}$; this allows us to grade the force of E^* and then grade the force of F^*, in light of E^*. Because there is no arc connecting E^* with $\{H, H^c\}$, we determine L_{E^*} by means of Equation 8.13. It is in the formulation of the likelihood ratio $L_{F^* | E^*}$ that we capture any possible synergistic influence of event E on event F. Observe that Figure 8.9c and Figure 8.5b (for conflicting or divergent evidence) are structurally identical. The likelihood ratio $L_{F^* | E^*}$ is identical in each of these cases; it is given as Equation 8.15, which I now repeat:

$$
L_{F^* | E^*} = \frac{
\begin{array}{c}
P(E | E^* H)[P(F | EH) - P(F | E^c H)] \\
+ P(F | E^c H) + [(h_2/f_2) - 1]^{-1}
\end{array}
}{
\begin{array}{c}
P(E | E^* H^c)[P(F | EH^c) - P(F | E^c H^c)] \\
+ P(F | E^c H^c) + [(h_2/f_2) - 1]^{-1}
\end{array}
} \tag{8.22}
$$

Equation 8.22 has three classes of terms which, together, determine the extent of any synergistic influence of evidence E^* on evidence F^*. Here is a brief summary. The terms involving event F will, as I will illustrate, allow knowing event E to enhance the value of knowing event F. The trouble of course is that we do not know events E and F for sure. All we have is evidence about their occurrence from two sources whose credibility may be impeachable. The two terms involving event E we have already encountered in connection with conflicting evidence. We have to determine how likely is event E, under H and under H^c, now that we have evidence of its occurrence from source S_1, whose credibility credentials we have established by means of $h_1 = P(E^* | E)$ and $f_1 = P(E^* | E^c)$. The remaining terms, $h_2 = P(F^* | F)$ and $f_2 = P(F^* | F^c)$, concern the credibility of S_2.

We need to focus attention on the four terms involving event F. It is through these four terms that we can capture situations in which knowledge of event E would enhance the inferential significance on $\{H, H^c\}$ of knowing event F. These four terms give rise to the following question: Would knowing that event E occurred or did not occur influence the probability of event F, either when H is true or when H is not true? We first say no to this question, and we have $P(F|EH) = P(F|E^cH) = P(F|H)$ and $P(F|EH^c) = P(F|E^cH^c) = P(F|H^c)$. Then $L_{F^*|E^*} = L_{F^*}$, as given by Equation 8.14. These equalities say that event classes $\{E, E^c\}$ and $\{F, F^c\}$ are independent, conditional upon H and upon H^c. There can be no inferential synergism when this is so.

I have remarked several times that Bayes's rule responds to differences as well as to ratios in likelihood ratio gradations of the inferential force of evidence. It is by such means that Bayes's rule captures a variety of subtleties, including evidential synergism. Notice in the situation described in the previous paragraph that $L_{F|E} = P(F|EH)/P(F|EH^c) = P(F|H)/P(F|H^c) = L_F$ and $L_{F|E^c} = P(F|E^cH)/P(F|E^cH^c) = P(F|H)/P(F|H^c) = L_F$. Knowing that event E did or did not occur does not change the inferential force of knowing F. Synergistic effects involving E and F can only occur when $[P(F|EH) - P(F|E^cH)] \neq 0$, or when $[P(F|EH^c) - P(F|E^cH^c)] \neq 0$. It is easily shown that the condition $P(F|EH) \neq P(F|E^cH)$ implies that $P(F|EH) \neq P(F|H)$. Similarly $P(F|EH^c) \neq P(F|E^cH^c)$ implies that $P(F|EH^c) \neq P(F|H^c)$. Such cases will allow $L_{F|E} \neq L_F$, an indication that knowing E changes the inferential force of knowing F.

Suppose we wish to make $L_{F|E} = P(F|EH)/P(F|EH^c) > L_F = P(F|H)/P(F|H^c)$. This is accomplished of course by making $P(F|EH) > P(F|H)$, $P(F|EH^c) < P(F|H^c)$, or both. But, as Equation 8.22 shows, we have also to take into account $P(F|E^cH)$ and $P(F|E^cH^c)$. In its wisdom in this case, Bayes's rule recognizes that we do not know for sure that event E occurred simply because we received a report of its occurrence from S_1. Figure 8.10 contains a numerical example from which we can determine values of $P(F|EH)$, $P(F|EH^c)$, $P(F|E^cH)$, and $P(F|E^cH^c)$ that demonstrate a synergistic effect of events E and F. In Figure 8.10a we consider events E and F separately, noting that $L_E = 7/2$ and $L_F = 2$. If we considered these events to be independent, conditional on H and on H^c, the combined force of knowing events E and F for sure would be $L_{EF} = L_E L_F = 7$.

Figure 8.10b offers an illustration of how we may alter the inferential significance of E and F, taken together, without changing the inferential significance of either E or F when they are considered separately. Shown in each cell of the two tables in this figure are two joint conditional probabilities. The first, labeled CI (for conditional independence) arises under the assumption that events E and F are independent, conditional on H and on H^c. For example, $P(EF|H) = P(E|H)P(F|H) = (0.7)(0.6) = 0.42$. The second joint conditional probability in each cell arises as a result of the following judgments:

Suppose we have grounds for believing that the occurrence of E and F together would be made more likely if H were true and less likely if H were not true than this joint occurrence would be if we assumed conditional independence. In other words, the joint behavior of E and F is not independent of H or H^c. One set of joint conditional probabilities, consistent with our beliefs about $P(E|H)$ and $P(E|H^c)$ separately, are the values $P(EF|H) = 0.58$ and $P(EF|H^c) = 0.01$. Observe that we have raised the joint probability of

(a) Events E and F Considered Separately

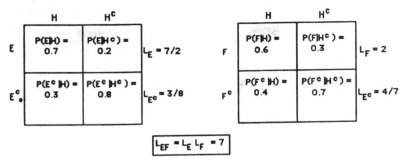

$$L_{EF} = L_E L_F = 7$$

(b) Events E and F Considered Together

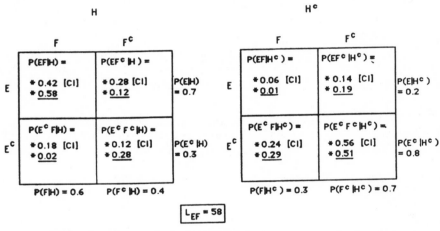

$$L_{EF} = 58$$

FIGURE 8.10 An example of evidential convergence and synergism.

E and F when H is true and lowered it when H^c is true. When E and F are believed to be independent conditional on H and on H^c, $L_{EF} = P(EF|H)/P(EF|H^c) = 0.42/0.06 = 7$ (in accordance with the result in Figure 8.10a). However, in light of our judgment about the *conditional nonindependence* of E and F, under H and under H^c we have $L_{EF} = P(EF|H)/P(EF|H^c) = 0.58/0.01 = 58$. Thus the conditional nonindependence in this case has raised the inferential force of knowing E and F by a factor of $58/7 = 8.29$.

So far we have been behaving as if we could know events E and F for sure. But all we have is evidence about their joint occurrence from sources S_1 and S_2, whom/which we believe not to be perfectly credible. We decide to determine $L_{E^*F^*} = L_{E^*} \cdot L_{F^*|E^*}$, making use of Equation 8.13 to calculate L_{E^*} and Equation 8.22 to calculate $L_{F^*|E^*}$. To calculate L_{E^*}, we have $P(E|H) = 0.7$ and $P(E|H^c) = 0.2$ from Figure 8.10. But we must also have

$h_1 = P(E^*|E)$ and $f_1 = P(E^*|E^c)$. If we have these assessments, then we can also calculate $P(E|E^*|H)$ and $P(E|E^*H^c)$ according to Equations 8.16 and 8.17; these are the first two ingredients required in Equation 8.22 for $L_{F^*|E^*}$. The four likelihoods involving event F in Equation 8.22 we determine from Figure 8.10*b* as follows:

$$P(F|EH) = P(EF|H)/P(E|H) = 0.58/0.70 = 0.83$$
$$P(F|E^cH) = P(E^cF|H)/P(E^c|H) = 0.02/0.30 = 0.07$$
$$P(F|EH^c) = P(EF|H^c)/P(E|H^c) = 0.01/0.20 = 0.05$$
$$P(F|E^cH^c) = P(E^cF^c|H)/P(E^c|H) = 0.29/0.80 = 0.36$$

To complete our calculation of $L_{F^*|E^*}$, we must also have $h_2 = P(F^*|F)$ and $f_2 = P(F^*|F^c)$.

The six examples in Table 8.5 show how any exploitation of the inferential synergism of events E and F, as shown in Figure 8.10*b*, depends entirely upon the credibility of sources S_1 and S_2. Each of the six examples rests upon a different set of judgments regarding the hit and false-positive probabilities for S_1 and S_2. Notice that the six likelihood ingredients $P(E|H)$, $P(E|H^c)$,

TABLE 8.5 Evidential Synergism

Ingredients	Case 1	Case 2	Case 3	Case 4	Case 5	Case 6
*A. For Evidence E**						
1. $P(E|H)$	0.7	0.7	0.7	0.7	0.7	0.7
2. $P(E|H^c)$	0.2	0.2	0.2	0.2	0.2	0.2
3. $h_1 = P(E^*|E)$	0.98	0.05	0.98	0.05	0.98	0.80
4. $f_1 = P(E^*|E^c)$	0.01	0.50	0.01	0.50	0.90	0.05
5. L_{E^*}	3.38	0.45	3.38	0.45	1.04	2.87
*B. For Evidence F**						
6. $P(E|E^*H)$	0.996	0.189	0.996	0.189	0.718	0.974
7. $P(E|E^*H^c)$	0.961	0.024	0.961	0.024	0.214	0.800
8. $P(F|EH)$	0.83	0.83	0.83	0.83	0.83	0.83
9. $P(F|E^cH)$	0.07	0.07	0.07	0.07	0.07	0.07
10. $P(F|EH^c)$	0.05	0.05	0.05	0.05	0.05	0.05
11. $P(F|E^cH^c)$	0.36	0.36	0.36	0.36	0.36	0.36
12. $h_2 = P(F^*|F)$	0.98	0.98	0.05	0.05	0.98	0.80
13. $f_2 = P(F^*|F^c)$	0.01	0.01	0.50	0.50	0.01	0.05
14. $L_{F^*|E^*}$	11.56	0.62	0.27	1.18	2.06	4.91
15. $L_{E^*F^*} = L_{E^*}·L_{F^*|E^*}$	39.08	0.28	0.91	0.53	2.14	14.09
16. L_{F^*}	1.97	1.97	0.63	0.63	1.97	1.82
17. $L_{E^*F^*} = L_{E^*}·L_{F^*}$	6.65	0.89	2.13	0.28	2.05	5.22

$P(F|EH)$, $P(F|E^cH)$, $P(F|EH^c)$, and $P(F|E^cH^c)$ remain the same in all of these cases. In case 1 we suppose that both S_1 and S_2 are very credible sources; the h/f ratio for each source is 98. The result is that we are able to exploit much of the synergism involving events E and F in our assessments of the force of evidence E^* and F^*. By comparing the results in rows 14 and 16, we notice that $L_{F^*|E} = 11.56$ is 5.87 times the value $L_{F^*} = 1.97$. In words, in light of evidence E^* the inferential force of F^* has been enhanced by a factor of 5.87. Comparing rows 15 and 17 shows that the joint force of E^* and F^* has been enhanced by this same factor.

What a Bayesian likelihood ratio can capture in the way of evidential enhancement for credible sources, it abruptly releases for sources whose credibility we have impeached. Case 2 shows an instance in which we believe ancillary evidence acts to impeach the credibility of S_1 reporting E^*. However we believe S_2, reporting F^*, to be very credible as in case 1. In terms of signal detection theory the values $h_1 = 0.05$ and $f_1 = 0.50$ depict S_1 as being a reasonably accurate source who/that is either confused, nonobjective, or untruthful. Careful examination of the likelihood ingredients of this example will allow us to explain what appears to be the surprising result in row 14, namely that F^*, in light of E^*, favors H^c over H despite S_2's strong credibility in reporting an event F that favors H over H^c. This explanation requires several stages.

First, in part A of Table 8.5 we observe that $L_{E^*} = 0.45 = 1/2.22$ favors H^c over H. This is quite close to the inferential force of knowing for sure that E *did not* occur, counter to what S_1 reports. The inferential force of knowing E^c is given by $L_{E^c} = P(E^c|H)/P(E^c|H^c) = 0.3/0.8 = 1/2.67$ favoring H^c over H. Using Equations 8.16 and 8.17, we next determine new likelihoods for event E, in light of S_1's report E^*, which we believe to be inaccurate, nonobjective, or untruthful. The likelihoods are $P(E|E^*H) = 0.189$ and $P(E|E^*H^c) = 0.024$, as shown in rows 6 and 7. For singly connected chains of reasoning when $P(E|H) > P(E|H^c)$, it is easily shown that $P(E|E^*H) \geq P(E|E^*H^c)$. Observe that the probability of E, given H or given H^c, has been reduced by S_1's report E^*, since originally we had $P(E|H) = 0.7$ and $P(E|H^c) = 0.2$. By required normalization, $P(E^c|E^*H) = 0.811$ and $P(E^c|E^*H^c) = 0.976$. As a result of S_1's report E^* we are entitled to raise the probability of E^c, given H and given H^c. Before we had S_1's report, $P(E^c|H) = 0.3$ and $P(E^c|H^c) = 0.8$.

At this point we might tentatively entertain the belief that event E did not happen. So, let us consult Figure 8.10*b* to consider the combined inferential force of knowing that events E^c and F occurred. As shown in this figure, $P(E^cF|H) = 0.02$ and $P(E^cF|H^c) = 0.29$. If we knew for sure that event E did not occur, but event F did, this would favor H^c over H in the ratio $1/14.5$. Notice that this exceeds the force of E^c and F *taken separately*, since $L_{E^cF} = L_{E^c}L_F = (3/8)(2) = 0.75 = 1/1.33$ favoring H^c over H. So event E^c has a synergistic effect on event F, which can be illustrated another way. As we have already determined, $P(F|E^cH) = 0.07$ and $P(F|E^cH^c) = 0.36$. So

$L_{F|E^c} = 0.07/0.36 = 1/5.14$ favors H^c over H. By itself event F favored H over H^c in the ratio 2/1. If we knew that event E *did not* occur, this would change both the inferential *direction* and *force* of knowing that event F occurred.

Finally, as rows 12 and 13 in case 2 indicate, we believe S_2 to be strongly credible in reporting the occurrence of event F. As a result of our strong beliefs that S_1 was not credible in his report of event E, we should now expect S_2's report F^* to favor H^c over H, in accordance with the arguments in the preceeding paragraph. In row 14, $L_{F^*|E^*} = 0.62 = 1.61$, favoring H^c over H. Considered by itself, the force of F^* is $L_{F^*} = 1.97$, *favoring H over H^c*. So the evidential synergism in this case involving one source, whom we believe inaccurate, nonobjective, or untruthful, acts to change the inferential direction and force of another item of evidence provided by a credible source. Comparing rows 15 and 17, we note that E^* and F^* *considered together* have 3.18 times their inferential force, favoring H^c over H, than they do if considered separately.

In case 3 we simply reverse the credibility credentials of S_1 and S_2 from what they were in case 2. Source S_2's credibility has been impeached by ancillary evidence, so we are inclined to believe that the report F^* favors the nonoccurrence of event F. Notice that in Figure 8.10*b* the known occurrence of events E and F^c favors H^c over H in the ratio $0.12/0.19 = 0.63 = 1/1.58$. Knowing event E does not enhance the inferential force of knowing event F^c to any great extent. Thus we are not surprised to learn in row 14 that F^* now favors H^c over H in the ratio $L_{F^*|E^*} = 0.27 = 1/3.7$. This is just 2.33 times the force of F^* by itself, since $L_{F^*} = 0.63 = 1/1.59$. Case 4 involves two perverse sources, S_1 and S_2, whose credibility has been equally impeached by ancillary evidence. Not much evidential enhancement takes place in this case. However, as rows 14 and 16 show, the effect of evidence E^* has been to reverse the inferential direction of F^*. Evidence F^*, by itself, has very little force favoring H^c over H. As a result of E^* it has even less force favoring H over H^c.

In case 5 we have no opportunity to exploit the synergism involving events E and F because of S_1's credibility. The values $h_1 = 0.98$ and $f_1 = 0.90$ indicate a source who is nearly as likely to provide report E^* whether or not event E occurred. The very strong credibility of S_2 does not help in this case. Observe in rows 14 and 16 that taking E^* into account has very little influence on the inferential force of F^*. Finally, in case 6 we have a somewhat less extreme example of evidential synergism than in case 1. In case 6 I have given both S_1 and S_2 an h/f ratio of 16/1 rather than 98/1, as in case 1. The inferential force of F^* is just slightly enhanced by evidence E^*, even though the common h/f ratio of 16 for sources S_1 and S_2 might seem to be substantial. As these six cases illustrate, the conditional nonindependence of events reported in evidence can act in subtle and often mysterious ways. There is more to come in Section 8.4 when we examine evidential redundancy.

My analyses of evidential dissonance and harmony have been restricted to evidence whose direct relevance on hypotheses of interest can be established by a plausible chain of reasoning. It is certainly true of course that ancillary evidence can exhibit these same characteristics. Suppose that S_1 reports evidence E^*, that event E occurred. We establish a chain of reasoning from events $\{E, E^c\}$ to hypotheses $\{H, H^c\}$ in defense of the relevance of E^*. We first consider the credibility-related foundation for this argument involving the linkage between E^* and events $\{E, E^c\}$. We might easily have any pattern of dissonance or harmony among sources of ancillary evidence bearing upon S_1's credibility. For example, sources S_2 and S_3 might contradict each other about whether or not S_1 was wearing his corrective lenses at the time of his alleged observation of events $\{E, E^c\}$. Instead, they might give corroborative evidence about S_1 wearing or not wearing his glasses. Other sources S_4 and S_5 might give either conflicting or convergent evidence about S_1's credibility. In one case S_4 says that S_1's veracity is the envy of his community. But S_5 gives conflicting evidence that S_1 was influenced by another person into telling us that event E occurred. But their evidence regarding S_1's veracity could also be convergent. Finally, we might have similar patterns of dissonant or harmonious evidence regarding any stage of the inferential linkage between events $\{E, E^c\}$ and hypotheses $\{H, H^c\}$.

8.3 PATTERNS OF EVIDENTIAL HARMONY AND DISSONANCE

Patterns of evidential contradiction and corroboration as well as patterns of conflict and convergence can be observed. In some cases we might have mixtures of all of these recognizable combinations of evidence. The structural and probabilistic concepts we have examined allow me to comment on several inferential issues that have been of interest for a very long time. The first involves the once-employed strategy of counting heads on either side of an evidential dispute in order to reach a settlement.

8.3.1 Corroboration and Contradiction: Shall We Count Heads?

In Section 5.1 I made brief mention of methods for grading the force of evidence in terms of numbers of witnesses. As I noted, the counting of witnesses on either side of a matter in dispute seems to have had a biblical origin. Reliance upon numbers of witnesses persisted in continental Europe until the 1800s. Wigmore tells us that even Napolean was offended by such reliance; as Napolean asserted: "Thus one honorable man by his testimony could not prove a single rascal guilty; though two rascals by their testimony could prove an honorable man guilty" (Wigmore on Evidence, vol. 7, 1940, §2033, 256). Vestiges of this numerical system exist to the present time; you might be required to have more than one person witness your will or other legal document. One trouble with counting heads on either side of a dispute is that it assumes all witnesses have equal credibility. On such an assumption the testimony of two rascals could outweigh the testimony of one honorable man as in Napolean's time. Our modern legal system takes a different position on the issue of numbers of witnesses. Three major elements of this position are (1) credibility does not depend upon numbers of witnesses, (2) the testimony of a single witness may suffice as evidence, and (3) the testimony of any *uncontradicted* witness need not necessarily be believed (Wigmore on Evidence, vol. 7, 1940, §2034, 259–261). I will now show how a Bayesian likelihood ratio construal of the inferential force of corroborative and contradictory testimony from any number of witnesses corresponds exactly with this current legal position.

Consider the situation shown in Figure 8.11. Some number r of sources report E*, that event E occurred; their evidence is corroborative. But we also have a number $(n - r)$ of sources reporting E^{c*}, that event E did not occur. Their reports E^{c*} are corroborative, but they are also contradictory to the r reports of E*. Suppose that $P(E|H) > P(E|H^c)$ so that under the required normalization $P(E^c|H) < P(E^c|H^c)$. Observe that the inference network in Figure 8.11 is singly connected. For the moment let us suppose that the credibility of no source is state-dependent and that there are no patterns of influence among these n sources.

Let J represent the joint report from these n sources. In symbols, $J = \cap_{i=1}^{r} E_i^* \cap_{i=r+1}^{n} E_i^{c*}$. What we wish to determine is the inferential force of J on hypotheses H and H^c. In Bayesian terms this is indicated by $L_J = P(J|H)/P(J|H^c)$. If we expand these two likelihoods in terms of events $\{E, E^c\}$, we can express:

$$L_J = \frac{P(E|H)[A_{E^*} - A_{E^{c*}}] + A_{E^{c*}}}{P(E|H^c)[A_{E^*} - A_{E^{c*}}] + A_{E^{c*}}}$$

$$= \frac{P(E|H) + [(A_{E^*}/A_{E^{c*}}) - 1]^{-1}}{P(E|H^c) + [(A_{E^*}/A_{E^{c*}}) - 1]^{-1}} \qquad (8.23)$$

where,

$$A_{E^*} = \prod_{i=1}^{r} \frac{h_i}{f_i}; \quad A_{E^{c*}} = \prod_{i=r+1}^{n} \frac{c_i}{m_i}$$

As in our previous discussions, h_i and f_i are hit and false-positive probabilities for sources reporting E*, and c_i and m_i are correct-rejection and miss probabilities for sources reporting E^{c*}.

The analysis of the force of L_J on $\{H, H^c\}$ can proceed in terms of inferential drag as introduced in Section 7.1.1. The term $[(A_{E^*}/A_{E^{c*}}) - 1]^{-1}$ represents the drag on our opinion revision about $\{H, H^c\}$, resulting from what we know about the aggregate credibility (A) on each side of a contradiction about events E and E^c. The term A_{E^*} indicates the aggregate credibility of the r sources reporting that E occurred; $A_{E^{c*}}$ grades the aggregate credibility of the $(n - r)$ sources reporting that E did not occur. As in previous singly connected cases we have examined, $L_{E^c} \leq L_J \leq L_E$. The directionality of L_J is determined

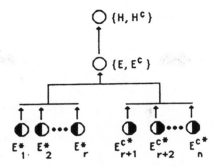

FIGURE 8.11 Corroborative and contradictory evidence from multiple sources.

by the relative sizes of $A_{E^.}$ and $A_{E^{c.}}$. If $A_{E^.} > A_{E^{c.}}$, then $L_J > 1.0$, and J favors H over H^c (if E favors H over H^c, as we have supposed). If $A_{E^.} < A_{E^{c.}}$, then $L_J < 0$, and J favors H^c over H. If $A_{E^.} = A_{E^{c.}}$, then only the middle expression of Equation 8.23 is defined, and $L_J = 1.0$.

Napolean, as well as Wigmore, would have been pleased by the inferential force as determined by Equation 8.23, since it clearly shows that the number of sources on either side of a contradiction is not the determining factor. What matters is the *aggregate credibility* on either side. For example, Tom and Dick (rascals, we believe) both report an event E that favors hypothesis H over H^c. But Harry (an honest person) reports that E did not occur. For Tom we judge $h_1/f_1 = 3$, and for Dick we judge $h_2/f_2 = 5$. In this case we have $A_{E^.} = 15$. But, for Harry we judge $c_3/m_3 = A_{E^{c.}} = 90$. So we side inferentially with Harry's report E^{c*}, since $[(A_{E^.}/A_{E^{c.}}) - 1]^{-1} = [(15/90) - 1]^{-1} = -1.2$. A majority does not necessarily rule in a Bayesian resolution of evidential contradiction. Majority will rule only if the majority has greater credibility than the minority.

Wigmore's other two points about credibility and numbers of witnesses are easily satisfied. First, that the testimony of a single witness may suffice as evidence is easily justified by a likelihood ratio construal of the force of testimony. As noted in Section 7.2.1 and elsewhere, testimony from a single witness can even, in some instances, have greater inferential force than knowing for sure that the event testified did occur. Second, Figure 3.8 shows the array of grounds for impeaching the credibility of a witness. The presence of contradictory evidence is only one such ground, and it is very unspecific. Its existence does not tell us what attribute of a witness's credibility is being impeached. So the fact that there is no contradictory evidence does not mean that we should accept as true an event reported by any source, human or otherwise.

The situation illustrated in Figure 8.11 and captured by Equation 8.23 is the simplest case imaginable of multiple source corroboration and contradiction. In many situations we might have mixtures of corroborative tangible and testimonial evidence on either side of a contradiction. Further some of the evidence on one side or the other may have been obtained at secondhand or might be the expression of an opinion or inference drawn from observations about other events; the possibilities are endless. But any particular combination of recognized forms of corroborative and contradictory evidence can be captured in an appropriately structured inference network.

The difficulty in formulating likelihood ratio expressions for a "goulash" of different forms of corroborative and contradictory evidence depends primarily upon the conditional nonindependencies we trap structurally and then attempt to capture probabilistically on the basis of relevant ancillary evidence. This difficulty also depends upon how minutely we wish to decompose the credibility-related links in the chains of reasoning we have identified. For sources whose credibility is state dependent, Equation 8.23 can easily be revised along lines suggested by Equation 8.6 for a contradiction involving just two sources. If there are patterns of influence among the sources on either side of a multisource contradiction, the h and f or the c and m ingredients for nonindependent sources can be revised along lines discussed in Section 8.2.1 and illustrated in part A of Table 8.4. Finally, given time, appropriate ancillary evidence, and the inclination to do so, we could decompose the credibility of any human source in terms of veracity, objectivity, and observational sensitivity and make use of Equations 8.7, 8.8, 8.10, and 8.11 to determine h and f, or c and m, for any of our sources.

8.3.2   Contradiction Embedded in Conflict

Alone, evidential contradiction or conflict involves difficult judgmental issues, but we frequently encounter them together. The historian can easily find contradictory documentary evidence about each of two events having conflicting inferential implications. At trial there may be contradictory testimony about two events, one of which favors the defendant's innocence and the other his guilt. The formal difficulty of assessing the inferential force of a contradiction embedded in conflict depends, as expected, upon the conditional nonindependencies we recognize among elements of the argument we construct. Shown in Figure 8.12 is a pattern of evidential conflict, corroboration, and contradiction, *all at the same time*. From r sources we obtain evidence that event E, favoring hypothesis H, occurred, but $(n - r)$ sources report the nonoccurrence of event E. In addition we have k sources reporting the occurrence of event F, favoring H^c, and $(t - k)$ sources reporting that event F did not occur. This pattern of corroboration, contradiction, and conflict could be made much more difficult if we believed that the credibility of some or all of the sources were state dependent. In addition various patterns of influence are possible among the sources of this evidence.

In Figure 8.12 we have $(n + t)$ items of evidence from sources who/that might be grouped in two "camps." In the first camp are the r sources giving positive evidence about E and the $(t - k)$ sources who give negative evidence about event F. All of these $(r + t - k)$ evidence items favor H over H^c.

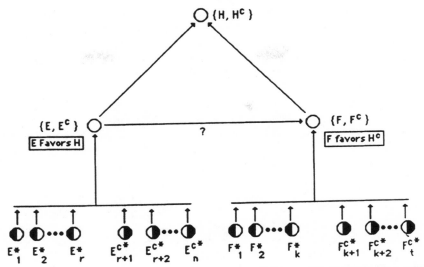

FIGURE 8.12 An example of evidential contradiction embedded in evidential conflict.

Recall that as a consequence of required Pascalian normalization, if F favors H^c over H, then F^c must favor H over H^c. So the negative evidence about event F from $(t - k)$ sources favors H over H^c. In the other camp we have $(n - r)$ sources reporting negative evidence about E and the k sources reporting positive evidence about F. All of these $(n + k - r)$ evidence items favor H^c over H. Intuition suggests that the direction and force of the $(n + t)$ items of evidence on hypotheses {H, H^c} should depend in part upon the aggregate credibility in either camp.

There are of course other ingredients that determine the inferential force of the aggregate evidence from these $(n + t)$ sources. One concerns possible conditional nonindependence involving event classes {E, E^c} and {F, F^c}. One possibility, discussed in Section 8.1.2, is that the conflict we perceive between events E and F is only apparent and can be made to vanish when we consider the joint occurrence of events from these two classes. As illustrated by cases 3 and 4 in part B of Table 8.3, a subtle conditional nonindependency involving E and F may suggest that the events are actually directionally consistent when considered jointly but not when they are considered separately.

The aggregate inferential force of the combined evidence in Figure 8.12 is also determined by the *rareness* of events E and F. Again, we have to keep in mind several interesting facts about event rareness. Suppose, for example, that $P(E|H)$ and $P(E|H^c)$ are both very small so that their difference is also very small. Their ratio, however, can be very large, a consequence "noticed" in a Bayesian likelihood ratio. In addition, if $P(E|H)$ and $P(E|H^c)$ are both very small (whatever their ratio), then $P(E^c|H)$ and $P(E^c|H^c)$ will, under required normalization, both be large. In short, if an event is rare under both

H and H^c, then its nonoccurrence cannot have much much inferential force on {H, H^c}. An example appears in Figure 7.2.2b regarding the dog's not barking in the Sherlock Holmes mystery *Silver Blaze*.

Suppose we sever the arc connecting event classes {E, E^c} and {F, F^c} by assuming that events in classes {E, E^c} and {F, F^c} are independent, conditional upon H and H^c. What we wish to determine is a likelihood ratio expression for the inferential force of the $(n + t)$ items of apparently conflicting as well as corroborative and contradictory evidence. Let T represent the totality or aggregate of all $(n + t)$ items of evidence; in symbols:

$$T = \bigcap_{i=1}^{r} E_i^* \; \bigcap_{i=r+1}^{n} E_i^{c^*} \; \bigcap_{j=1}^{k} F_j^* \; \bigcap_{j=k+1}^{t} F_j^{c^*}$$

What we wish to determine is $L_T = P(T|H)/P(T|H^c)$. We first partition T into two classes, one consisting of the evidence about events {E, E^c} and the other evidence about {F, F^c}. Let $E = \bigcap_{i=1}^{r} E_i^* \bigcap_{i=r+1}^{n} E_i^{c^*}$ and $\Phi = \bigcap_{j=1}^{k} F_j^* \bigcap_{j=k+1}^{t} F_j^{c^*}$ so that $T = E\Phi$. If events in classes {E, E^c} and {F, F^c} are independent, conditional on H and on H^c, $L_T = L_{E\Phi} = L_E L_\Phi$. Notice that E represents the n corroborative and contradictory evidence items regarding events E and E^c; Φ represents the t corroborative and contradictory evidence items that we have about events {F, F^c}.

We have already considered an equation appropriate to determining both L_E and L_Φ for a pattern of corroborative and contradictory evidence about the same event; it is Equation 8.23. I repeat it here twice with notational modifications making it appropriate to evidence in classes E and Φ:

$$L_E = \frac{P(E|H)[A_{E^*} - A_{E^{c^*}}] + A_{E^{c^*}}}{P(E|H^c)[A_{E^*} - A_{E^{c^*}}] + A_{E^{c^*}}}$$

$$= \frac{P(E|H) + [(A_{E^*}/A_{E^{c^*}}) - 1]^{-1}}{P(E|H^c) + [A_{E^*}/A_{E^{c^*}}) - 1]^{-1}} \qquad (8.24)$$

where

$$A_{E^*} = \prod_{i=1}^{r} \frac{h_i}{f_i}; \; A_{E^{c^*}} = \prod_{i=r+1}^{n} \frac{c_i}{m_i}$$

and

$$L_\Phi = \frac{P(F|H)[B_{F^*} - B_{F^{c^*}}] + B_{F^{c^*}}}{P(F|H^c)[B_{F^*} - B_{F^{c^*}}] + B_{F^{c^*}}} = \frac{P(F|H) + [(B_{F^*}/B_{F^{c^*}}) - 1]^{-1}}{P(F|H^c) + [B_{F^*}/B_{F^{c^*}}) - 1]^{-1}} \qquad (8.25)$$

where

$$B_{F^*} = \prod_{j=1}^{k} \frac{h_j}{f_j}; \; B_{F^{c^*}} = \prod_{j=k+1}^{t} \frac{c_j}{m_j}$$

To examine how evidential dissonance involving both contradiction and conflict can be resolved in Bayesian terms, we must consider the credibility-related credentials of sources in the opposing camps. Recall that in singly connected chains of reasoning all we need are ratios such as h/f and c/m and not the exact values of these likelihoods. In the "H-camp" we first have the r sources reporting E^*; their aggregate hit to false-positive ratio is given by the term A_{E^*} in Equation 8.24. Also in this same camp are the $(t - k)$ sources reporting F^{c^*}; their aggregate correct-rejection to miss ratio is given by the term $B_{F^{c^*}}$ in Equation 8.25. We might say that the "H-camp" consists of the E "assenters" and the F "dissenters." In the "H^c-camp" we have the aggregate hit to false-positive ratio B_{F^*} for the k sources reporting F^* and the aggregate correct-rejection to miss ratio $A_{E^{c^*}}$ for the $(n - r)$ sources reporting E^{c^*}. In other words, the "H^c-camp" consists of the F assenters and the E dissenters. The numerical examples shown in Table 8.6 illustrate what is involved in resolving the complex evidential dissonance in this situation.

In case 1 we have a situation in which event E, if known, has exactly the same force favoring H over H^c as event F, if known, has in favoring H^c over H. In this case $L_E = 18$ and $L_F = 1/18$. Thus, assuming events E and F to be independent conditional on H and on H^c, $L_{EF} = L_E L_F = 1$. If we knew that events E and F both occurred, their inferential forces would cancel out. But we also have more credibility in the "H-camp" than in the "H^c-camp"; observe that the F-dissenters have $B_{F^{c^*}} > A_{E^{c^*}}$ for the E dissenters. The result, shown in row 11, is that we side inferentially with the "H-camp" since $L_T = 3.38$ favors H over H^c. In this case credibility considerations alone resolve the evidential dissonance.

The only change in case 2 is that we have made event E rare under H and under H^c. Notice that event E, if known, still has $L_E = 18$, favoring H over H^c. But, as mentioned several times, Bayes's rule will also respond to the small difference $P(E|H) - P(E|H^c) = 0.085$. Even though the credibility

TABLE 8.6 Contradiction Embedded In Conflict

Ingredients	Case 1	Case 2	Case 3	Case 4	Case 5	Case 6	Case 7
1. $P(E|H)$	0.90	0.09	0.90	0.09	0.90	0.90	0.90
2. $P(E|H^c)$	0.05	0.005	0.05	0.005	0.05	0.05	0.05
3. A_{E^*}	90	90	90	90	90	10	90
4. $A_{E^{c^*}}$	8	8	8	8	8	90	10
5. $L_{E^* E^{c^*}} = L_E$	6.76	1.83	6.76	1.83	6.76	0.21	5.86
6. $P(F|H)$	0.05	0.05	0.005	0.005	0.10	0.10	0.10
7. $P(F|H^c)$	0.90	0.90	0.09	0.09	0.80	0.80	0.80
8. B_{F^*}	90	90	90	90	999	999	10
9. $B_{F^{c^*}}$	40	40	40	40	10	10	999
10. $L_{F^* F^{c^*}} = L_\Phi$	0.50	0.50	0.90	0.90	0.14	0.14	4.33
11. $L_T = L_E L_\Phi$	3.38	0.92	6.08	1.65	0.94	0.03	25.37

ratio $A_{E^*}/A_{E^{c^*}}$ for evidence about events $\{E, E^c\}$ is larger than the ratio $B_{F^*}/B_{F^{c^*}}$ for evidence about events $\{F, F^c\}$, this larger credibility-related ratio is not enough to overcome the rareness of event E. Stated differently, the greater credibility in the "H-camp" (indicated by A_{E^*} and $B_{F^{c^*}}$) is not enough to overcome the rareness of event E under H and under H^c. The result is that the combined evidence T slightly favors H^c over H in the ratio $0.92 = 1/1.09$.

Case 3 and case 1 are identical except for the fact that we have now made event F (instead of event E) rare under H and under H^c. Notice that $L_F = 1/18$ if we knew event F for sure. However, we also know that the credibility in the "H-camp" exceeds that in the "H^c-camp," and so we should not be surprised to discover in row 11 that combined evidence T favors H over H^c. The rareness of event F, together with the small ratio $B_{F^*}/B_{F^{c^*}}$, destroys the inferential force of contradictory evidence about event F. In case 4 the source credibility credentials are the same as in the previous three cases, but we have made events E and F both improbable under H and under H^c. The larger "H-camp" credibility wins the day, so we have combined evidence T favoring H over H^c, though not by very much (in the ratio 1.65). In case 5 neither event E nor event F is rare. However, we have decreased the inferential force of knowing event F; in this case $L_F = 1/8$. But we have also increased the credibility of the F-assenters and decreased the credibility of the F-dissenters; observe that $B_{F^*}/B_{F^{c^*}} = 99.9$. In this case we side inferentially by a slight amount with the "H^c-camp" because of its greater credibility, even though event F is less forceful.

Case 6 is the same as case 5 except that we have given the E-dissenters greater credibility credentials than the E-assenters; notice that $A_{E^{c^*}} > A_{E^*}$. This also makes the credibility in the "H^c-camp" strongly predominant, so the combined evidence T favors H^c over H, here by a substantial amount since $L_T = 0.03 = 1/33.33$. In case 7 we have the F-dissenters having much stronger credibility credentials than the F-assenters; $B_{F^{c^*}}$ is 99.9 times larger than B_{F^*}. The result is reversed over case 6 and T now favors H over H^c by a substantial amount.

In none of these cases, nor in any others that can be contrived, does there need to be made mention of the number of sources on either side of the matters in contention. In the present situation involving contradictions buried in conflict, what counts is the the aggregate credibility of sources in the two opposing "camps." The absence of state-dependent credibility of any source in these cases means that L_T is bounded in its value. The bounds depend upon four likelihood ratios for the *known* occurrence of events in classes $\{E, E^c\}$ and $\{F, F^c\}$. The four likelihood ratios are L_{EF}, L_{E^cF}, L_{EF^c}, and $L_{E^cF^c}$. For combined evidence T, L_T cannot exceed in value the largest of these four ratios favoring H or exceed the largest of these four ratios favoring H^c. These same bounds also apply when we have patterns of influence among sources in either "camp" provided that such influence is not also conditional upon H or H^c. Finally, the possible conditional nonindependence of events in classes

{E, E^c} and {F, F^c}, given either H or H^c, gives rise to further inferential subtleties such as those we examined in Section 8.1.2 for evidential conflict alone.

8.4 THE TWO FACES ON EVIDENTIAL REDUNDANCE

In Section 8.2.2 we examined the synergism in which one item of evidence seems to *enhance* the inferential force of another. We now consider situations in which one item of evidence may seem to *diminish* the inferential force of other evidence. We might say that a current item of evidence seems *redundant*, to some degree, with other evidence we have considered. As I mentioned in Section 3.5.3, there are two distinct species of redundant evidence that can be identified. In one case we have two or more sources reporting the same event; they provide corroborative evidence. Their reports are to some degree *corroboratively redundant*, since they concern the *same event*. But there are other situations in which two sources report *different* or *distinct events*, but we believe that the occurrence of one of these events would act to diminish the inferential force of the other event. In a legal context such evidence is said to be cumulative. I will refer to these situations as involving *cumulative redundance*.

Of all the evidential subtleties I have examined, evidential redundance requires the most careful distinctions and analyses. One important matter concerns the locus of redundance. As I will explain, redundance is a property of the events reported in evidence and not necessarily of the evidence itself. Examples are easily contrived in which the events reported in evidence are quite redundant, but evidence about these events is not redundant. In any context in which the term is applied, redundance is a mixed blessing. We are all very happy that aircraft are designed to have redundant control systems; if one fails there is a backup. But such increased protection is costly. In probabilistic reasoning redundant evidence can offer greater assurance of the occurrence of events of interest. But there is an accompanying risk that such evidence may be doublecounted or overvalued. So there are two faces on evidential redundance. The formal process I will describe gives us a good look at both faces.

8.4.1 Redundance in Discourse and in Communication

A parade of witnesses appears at trial; all are prepared to swear on oath that poor Tom, the defendant, was at the scene of the crime shortly after it was committed. The witnesses begin to testify in succession. At some point either the judge or Tom's counsel will say: "That's enough corroboration, you've made your point." In another situation one witness asserts that Tom was at the scene, a second asserts that Tom's car was at the scene, a third asserts that Tom's coat was found at the scene, and yet another shows fingerprints found at the scene and testifies that they belong to Tom. At some point there will be objection made to the cumulative nature of this evidence.

In either situation we have evidence that begins to be repetitious, super-fluous, overflowing, and perhaps inessential. This assumes of course that the sources of the evidence are credible. How redundant we believe is the testimony of the second witness who reports Tom's presence at the scene of the crime depends upon how credible we believe was the first witness who made this same assertion. If, on ancillary evidence, we believe the first witness could not have recognized Tom, then the testimony of the second witness may have some value, depending upon his credibility. If, based on one witness's testimony, we believe that Tom himself was at the scene of the crime, is there any further inferential value in knowing that Tom's car, coat, or fingerprints were also at the scene of the crime? In either situation we *may* conclude that further evidence does not supply any additional information having inferential force.

One virtue of Bayesian analyses of the inferential force of evidence is that we are able to import relevant ideas from other formal systems that have the same Pascalian basis as does Bayes's rule. I mentioned in Sections 7.3.1 and 7.3.3 how ideas from signal detection theory are useful in analyses of source credibility in relation to the inferential force of evidence. In Section 5.3.1 I mentioned how ideas from statistical communications theory (or information theory) allow us one way to grade the inferential force of evidence. I now wish to draw again upon this theory for guidance about how we might grade redundance in probabilistic inference. As it happens, there is a measure of redundance in statistical communications theory that suggests a measure of the redundance of the events reported in evidence.

Suppose that $X = \{x_1, x_2, \ldots, x_n\}$ represents an array of messages that might be transmitted by some communications system. The celebrated Shannon-Weaver formula (1949) allows us to determine the *average uncertainty* $U(X)$ associated with this message array, where

$$U(X) = -\sum_{i=1}^{n} P(x_i)\log_2 P(x_i) \tag{8.26}$$

We suppose that $P(x_i) > 0$ for any message x_i. The value of $U(X)$ depends upon the number of possible messages that might be transmitted and upon the probability distribution assigned across the possible messages. It is easily shown that $U(X)$ has a maximum when all x_i have the same probability, namely $1/n$. We label this maximum value as $U(X)_{\mathrm{max}}$. But the messages in some actual array need not all be equally probable; any probability distribution across the n messages is possible except ones assigning zero probability to any message. Let $U(X)_{\mathrm{act}}$ refer to the *actual average uncertainty* associated with the probability distribution for some message array.

In statistical communications theory redundance R is commonly defined as

$$R = \frac{U(X)_{\text{max}} - U(X)_{\text{act}}}{U(X)_{\text{max}}} = 1 - \frac{U(X)_{\text{act}}}{U(X)_{\text{max}}} \tag{8.27}$$

The ratio $U(X)_{\text{act}}/U(X)_{\text{max}}$ is called the *relative uncertainty* in some message array. Suppose that $U(X)_{\text{act}} = U(X)_{\text{max}}$; in this case there is maximum uncertainty about which message will be sent, so $R = 0$. If transmissions have zero redundancy then they are also maximally informative in the sense that we have no basis for expecting any particular message. Now suppose we let $U(X)_{\text{act}}$ approach zero, in which case R approaches 1.0. In this case there is one message that gets transmitted with great frequency. When we receive this message on any occasion it conveys very little information, since we have heard it over and over again and might easily predict its occurrence on other occasions. From Equations 8.26 and 8.27 we can see that the redundance measure has bounds $0 \leq R < 1.0$.

As I mentioned in Section 3.5.3, redundance reduces the effective capacity of any communication channel. With redundance, transmission time is committed to the sending of messages having low information content. At the same time, however, some redundance is beneficial if it is necessary to ensure that some message will be received. For example, the same message may be sent several times in communications between an aircraft pilot and a tower controller. In Section 8.2.1 I mentioned briefly how a Bayesian likelihood ratio automatically accounts for the natural redundance of repetitive or corroborative evidence in singly connected chains of reasoning. Equation 8.27 supplies an idea about how we might measure the inferential redundance of events reported in either corroborative or cumulative evidence.

8.4.2 Redundance and Evidence

As a point of departure for discussion of how Equation 8.27 suggests a measure of redundance in probabilistic reasoning based on evidence, consider the simple inference network shown in Figure 8.13. Notice that this network does not yet involve any evidence. It simply shows how three event classes {H,

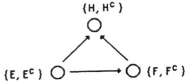

FIGURE 8.13   An inference structure to illustrate the calculation of event redundance.

H^c}, {E, E^c}, and {F, F^c} are related probabilistically. Recall that somewhat obstinately and in defiance of some current customs, I draw the direction of arcs on a network to indicate the direction of reasoning. On this interpretation, what Figure 8.27 shows is that events {E, E^c} bear upon {H, H^c} and also upon {F, F^c}. This network is not singly connected; events {F, F^c} are linked to events in classes {E, E^c} and {H, H^c}. In other words, events in class {F, F^c} are not independent of events in class {E, E^c}, given an event in {H, H^c}. For example, we have $P(F|EH) \neq P(F|H)$ and $P(F|EH^c) \neq P(F|H^c)$. We form two likelihood ratios, $L_F = P(F|H)/P(F|H^c)$ and $L_{F|E} = P(F|EH)/P(F|EH^c)$, and consider the expression

$$R_{F|E} = \frac{\log L_F - \log L_{F|E}}{\log L_F} = 1 - \frac{\log L_{F|E}}{\log L_F} \qquad (8.28)$$

where we assume that $L_F \neq 1$, so that $\log L_F \neq 0$.

Suppose that the conditional nonindependence of events E and F takes the following form: Event E, if it did occur, would act to make the probability of F be the same or nearly the same, given H or given H^c. In symbols $P(F|EH) \approx P(F|EH^c)$. Then $L_{F|E}$ will be close to 1.0, and $\log L_{F|E}$ close to zero. But suppose we believed that if we ignored event E, L_F is much greater than 1.0; that is, $P(F|H)$ is much greater than $P(F|H^c)$. In the limiting case, suppose that $P(F|EH) = P(F|EH^c)$ so that $L_{F|E} = 1.0$. Applying Equation 8.28 to this situation, we have $R_{F|E} = 1.0$. In words, if we knew event E occurred, then event F would no longer have any inferential force on hypotheses {H, H^c}; stated differently, event F is inferentially redundant now that we know E. At the other extreme, suppose we sever the arc between event classes {E, E^c} and {F, F^c} in Figure 8.13. In this case we have $P(F|EH) = P(F|H)$ and $P(F|EH^c) = P(F|H)$, in which $L_{F|E} = L_F$. In Equation 8.28 we would then have $R_{F|E} = 0$. If events E and F are independent, conditional on H and on H^c, then they have zero redundance. The inferential force of F on {H, H^c} is in no way reduced by our knowledge of E.

Measures R, for transmission redundance, and $R_{F|E}$, for inferential redundance, have a similar form. But the bounds on $R_{F|E}$, as defined in Equation 8.28, are different and have to be examined carefully. In fact we will have to make some definite restrictions on $L_{F|E}$ and L_F for $R_{F|E}$ to make sense as a measure of the redundance of events reported in evidence. First, since $U(X)_{act}$ can never exceed $U(X)_{max}$, R can never be less than zero. But for two events E and F, suppose that $L_{F|E} > L_F$; this is a condition we encountered while discussing evidential *synergism*. In such cases knowledge of E *enhances* (rather than diminishes) the inferential force of F. We would then have negative values of $R_{F|E}$. In fact, since $L_{F|E}$ can exceed L_F to any degree, $R_{F|E}$ actually has no lower bound. It might be awkward to say that evidential synergism is "negative redundance."

There is another problem concerning the upper bound on $R_{F|E}$. Since $U(X)$ measures are always positive, R cannot exceed the value 1.0. As we observed above, $R_{F|E} = 1.0$ when $L_{F|E} = 1.0$; that is, E completely destroys the value of F. The trouble is that event E can do more than just diminish the inferential force of event F; it can also induce a directional change in F. We may have $L_F > 1$ (favoring H) but then have $L_{F|E} < 1$ (favoring H^c). Since we are taking logs of L_F and $L_{F|E}$ in Equation 8.28, log $L_{F|E}$ will be negative for $L_{F|E} < 1$, so $R_{F|E}$ can be greater than 1.0. If we collect these assorted facts, we can identify constraints on L_F and $L_{F|E}$ that allow $R_{F|E}$ to make sense as a measure of the redundance in events reported in evidence.

The two diagrams in Figure 8.14 allow us to observe what $R_{F|E}$, as given in Equation 8.28, actually indicates throughout its range of possible values. First, event F, considered alone or with knowledge of event E, can favor H over H^c. In this case $L_F = P(F|H)/P(F|H^c) > 1$, and $L_{F|E} = P(F|EH)/P(F|EH^c) > 1$. This condition is shown in Figure 8.14a. Observe that $R_{F|E}$ grades the redundance of event F only when $1 \leq L_{F|E} \leq L_F$. Knowing E reduces the force of event F but does not change the inferential direction of F. In other words, E makes F redundant to the extent that $L_{F|E}$ approaches one *from above*. If the direction of F is changed with knowledge of E, then $L_{F|E} < 1$ and $R_{F|E} > 1$, as noted above. We would not say that knowledge of event E made F redundant if this were so. If the effect upon F of knowing

(a) **F favors H Over H^c**

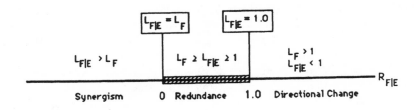

(b) **F Favors H^c Over H**

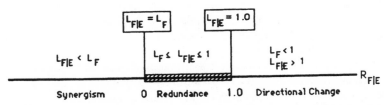

FIGURE 8.14   The measure $R_{F|E}$ and its intervals for grading event redundance.

E were to make $L_{F|E} > L_F$, then event E exerts a synergistic effect on F and $R_{F|E} < 0$; E certainly does not make F redundant in this case either. In summary, when F favors H over H^c and when $1 \leq L_{F|E} \leq L_F$, then $0 \leq R_{F|E} \leq 1$ and $R_{F|E}$ has properties similar to R in communications theory.

But event F could instead favor H^c over H, in which case we have $L_F = P(F|H)/P(F|H^c) < 1$ and $L_{F|E} = P(F|EH)/P(F|EH^c) < 1$. This condition is shown in of Figure 8.14b. In this case E will render F redundant to the extent that knowing E makes $L_{F|E}$ approach one *from below*. Thus, when $L_F \leq L_{F|E} \leq 1$, then $0 \leq R_{F|E} \leq 1$ and $R_{F|E}$ grades event redundance. But when $L_{F|E} > 1$, $R_{F|E} > 1$ indicates an inferential direction change, and when $L_{F|E} < L_F$, then $R_{F|E} < 0$ indicates a synergistic effect of E upon F.

In summary, $R_{F|E}$, unlike R in statistical communications theory, grades more than redundance. However, when we restrict attention to values of L_F and $L_{F|E}$ in the "redundance" intervals shown in Figure 8.14, $R_{F|E}$ has quite useful and informative properties. Events that are conditionally independent, given some hypothesis, cannot be redundant in inferences about this hypothesis, based on these events. Events that are conditionally nonindependent, given some hypothesis, are maximally redundant if knowledge of one event acts to dissolve the inferential force of another.

There is a special case of Equation 8.28 that we need to examine. As shown in this equation, $R_{F|E}$ grades what I have termed cumulative redundance since E and F are two *different* events, one of which may reduce the inferential force of another. The special case of Equation 8.28 concerns the natural redundance of corroborative or repetitive evidence. Let us suppose that two sources report that event E occurred. Momentarily, let us suppose that we have two events here, E and E. So, to determine $R_{E|E}$ by Equation 8.28, we need $L_E = P(E|H)/P(E|H^c)$ and $L_{E|E} = P(E|EH)/P(E|EH^c)$. But since E and E are the same events, $P(E|EH) = 1 = P(E|EH^c)$, so $L_{E|E} = 1$ regardless of what L_E is. This makes $R_{E|E} = 1$, as we expect. The events reported in corroborative evidence are naturally perfectly redundant, since they are all the same. This seemingly trivial result does have some explanatory value, as I will later mention. There is a case of perfect or natural redundance in the *cumulative* case which I will identify in Section 8.4.4.

Our next task is to examine the relationship between *event* redundance and *evidential* redundance. I will argue that event redundance is a necessary but not a sufficient condition for evidential redundance. In Figure 8.15 we now have evidence E* and F* about events E and F. Arc 1 indicates that E and F are nonindependent, conditional on H and on H^c. Suppose that the nature of this conditional nonindependence is such that the inferential force on {H, H^c} of event F is destroyed (or nearly so) if we also knew that event E occurred. In other words, whatever L_F is, $L_{F|E}$ is close to or equal to 1.0. The question is, Does the redundance of events E and F mean that, whatever L_{F^*} is, $L_{F^*|E^*}$ will also be close to or equal to 1.0? The answer is no for the following reasons: First, a report of E* from a source does not entail that

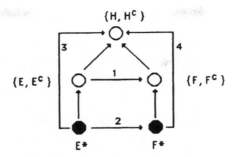

FIGURE 8.15 Possible linkages for a special case of cumulative evidence.

event E actually occurred. We have some uncertainty about event E to the extent that the source of E* is credible. Perhaps E did not occur, in which case we also have to inquire whether or not event F would be rendered redundant by the *nonoccurrence* of event E. In addition, based on evidence F*, we are not certain about the occurrence of event F either; perhaps event F did not occur.

A second reason why event redundance does not entail evidential redundance concerns arc 4 in Figure 8.15. Event F may be completely redundant in light of event E, but we may have ancillary evidence about the source of evidence F*, indicating that the credibility of this source depends upon H or upon H^c. As we have observed on several occasions, this state-dependent credibility may itself supply inferential force to F* on hypotheses {H, H^c}. It may happen, for example, that $L_{F^*|E^*}$ greatly exceeds L_{F^*}, even though events E and F are completely redundant. In addition the presence of arc 3 indicates state dependence of the credibility of the source of E*. Perhaps the force of evidence E* depends not so much upon events {E, E^c} as it does upon hypotheses {H, H^c}. The essential problem here is that, even when events E and F are completely redundant, $L_{F^*|E^*}$ can take on virtually any value relative to L_{F^*} if these credibility-related conditional nonindependencies truly exist.

So event redundance is not a sufficient condition for evidential redundance. Is it a necessary condition? The answer is yes. Suppose that in Figure 8.15 we sever arc 1 and eliminate the possibility of any redundance of events E and F. The question is, Can E* and F* be redundant in such cases? It is certainly the case that we may still have $L_{F^*|E^*}$ close to 1.0, regardless of L_{F^*}. For example, suppose that, as arc 2 indicates, the source of E* influenced the source of F* in such a way that we believe that F* no longer has any inferential force, given E*. In symbols, whatever L_{F^*} is, $L_{F^*|E^*}$ is very close to 1.0. But this devastation of the force of F* in light of E* is a credibility-related matter having nothing to do with redundance. We might easily have such devastation even if our belief was that E enhanced the inferential force of event F. In short, evidential redundance requires but does not ensure event redundance.

One consequence of matters just discussed is that Equation 8.28 applied to evidence E* and F* would be quite unsatisfactory as a measure of evidential redundance. However, there are other measures of evidential redundance that are quite informative. In further discussion of event and evidential redundance we also must consider the *rareness* of redundant events about which we may have possibly nonredundant evidence. We now consider what Bayesian likelihood ratios have to tell us about the force of evidence about events we believe to be inferentially redundant.

8.4.3 The Force of Corroboratively Redundant Evidence

I begin by considering corroborative or repetitive evidence, since certain evidential subtleties are most easily demonstrated in this case. In Section 8.2.1 I gave attention to the problem of determining the inferential force of the *joint report* of the occurrence of an event from n sources. Equations 8.18 through 8.21 provide likelihood ratio expressions for the force of corroborative evidence under various conditions. In light of our current discussion of event and evidential redundance, it is profitable to examine the inferential force of corroborative evidence in another way. Bayesian likelihood ratios are quite informative about the extent to which a second report of the same event has inferential force. These likelihood ratios suggest the metaphor of a "well" in describing how much inferential force remains (in the "well") for a second report of an event, given that this same event has already been reported by another source. As we will observe, however, this "well" has somewhat curious properties.

To begin, consider the singly connected inference network shown in Figure 8.7g. We have two sources S_1 and S_2 who/that both report E*, that event E occurred. We believe that knowledge of event E would be relevant and forceful in an inference about hypotheses $\{H, H^c\}$; suppose that $P(E|H) > P(E|H^c)$ so that $L_E > 1$. As mentioned above, the events they report are naturally completely redundant, since they are the same event. Suppose we consider the reports E_1^* and E_2^* in succession. In Bayesian terms the force of E_1^* on $\{H, H^c\}$ is given, as already discussed, by

$$L_{E_1^*} = \frac{P(E|H)[h_1 - f_1] + f_1}{P(E|H^c)[h_1 - f_1] + f_1} = \frac{P(E|H) + [(h_1/f_2) - 1]^{-1}}{P(E|H^c) + [(h_1/f_1) - 1]^{-1}} \quad (8.29)$$

where $h_1 = P(E_1^*|E)$ and $f_1 = P(E^*|E^c)$ for S_1.

Now comes S_2 who reports E_2^*. How much inferential force does this second report of event E have? In answering this question, we cannot ignore the fact that we already have evidence E_1^*. To do so would invite the *double-counting* of this evidence, since there is only one event E of concern. So we have to consider the inferential force on $\{H, H^c\}$ of E_2^*, in light of E_1^*. In Bayesian terms this force is given by $L_{E_2^*|E_1^*} = P(E_2^*|E_1^*H)/P(E_2^*|E_1^*H^c)$. In its expanded form, this likelihood ratio is

$$L_{E_2^*|E_1^*} = \frac{P(E|E_1^*H)[h_2 - f_2] + f_2}{P(E|E_1^*H^c)[h_2 - f_2] + f_2}$$

$$= \frac{P(E|E_1^*H) + [(h_2/f_2) - 1]^{-1}}{P(E|E_1^*H^c) + [h_2/f_2) - 1]^{-1}} \qquad (8.30)$$

where $h_2 = P(E_2^*|E)$ and $f_2 = P(E_2^*|E^c)$, for S_2. Equations 8.29 and 8.30 have the forms shown because we are now supposing, as in Figure 8.7g, that the credibility of neither source is state dependent and that there is no influence among these sources.

Equations 8.29 and 8.30 have exactly the same form but different ingredients. In 8.29 we have credibility-related ingredients for S_1 and in 8.30 the credibility ingredients are for S_2. But the major difference involves the ingredients $P(E|H)$ and $P(E|H^c)$ for L_{E^*} and the ingredients $P(E|E_1^*H)$ and $P(E|E_1^*H^c)$ for $L_{E_2^*|E_2^*}$; here is where the idea of a "well" of inferential force is suggested. As shown earlier in Equations 8.16 and 8.17,

$$P(E|E_1^*H) = \frac{P(E|H)h_1}{P(E|H)h_1 + P(E^c|H)f_1}$$

$$P(E|E_1^*H^c) = \frac{P(E|H^c)h_1}{P(E|H^c)h_1 + P(E^c|H^c)f_1}$$

At various points we will need to consider the ratio of these two likelihoods $L_{E|E_1^*} = P(E|E_1^*H)/P(E|E_1^*H^c)$.

To demonstrate how $L_{E|E_1^*}$ indicates the amount of inferential force remaining in the "well" after we receive report E_1^*, we first consider some limiting cases. First, suppose we believe that $f_1 = 0$, that S_1 would never report that event E occurred unless it did. In this case, we see that $P(E|E_1^*H) = P(E|E_1^*H^c) = 1.0$, so in Equation 8.30 the second report of event E has no inferential force at all. In this case $L_{E_2^*E_1^*} = 1.0$ indicates that the second report of event E is completely redundant. Also observe in Equation 8.29 that if $f_1 = 0$, then $L_{E^*} = L_E$; that is, all the force of knowing E for sure gets applied to E_1^*. Stated another way, there is no force remaining in the "well" for E_2^*.

On the other hand, suppose that $h_1 = f_1$, an indication that S_1, among other possibilities, could not tell the difference betwen E and E^c. In this case we observe that $P(E|E_1^*H) = P(E|H)$ and $P(E|E_1^*H^c) = P(E|H^c)$. In this case the full inferential force of event E is available for application to E_2^*, depending upon how credible is S_2. In short, if $h_1 = f_1$, then E_2^* is not at all redundant with E_1^*. There is another limiting case of interest. Suppose that $h_1 = 0$; we somehow believe that S_1 would never report E^* if event E did occur. This makes $P(E|E_1^*H) = P(E|E_1^*H^c) = 0$ so that $L_{E_2^*|E_1^*} = 1.0$. Why should this extreme belief about the credibility of S_1 make S_2's report inferentially valueless? The answer is given in Equation 8.29. If we believed that $h_1 = 0$, we would also believe that E did *not* occur. In this case, as Equation 8.29 shows, $L_{E_1^*} = L_{E^c}$. This extreme belief about S_1 allows us to use up all of the inferential force of knowing for sure that E did *not* occur. Thus we might say that S_2's report is *irrelevant* instead of saying that it is completely redundant.

Figure 8.16 illustrates the "well" of inferential force we have been considering. Let us first suppose, as in Figure 8.16a, that $h_1 \geq f_1$, where neither have values zero or one. Before we receive S_1's report, we consider L_E, the inferential force of knowing event E for sure. This force is indicated by the level of the left-hand well. Now, in light of our first report E_1^*, we draw off

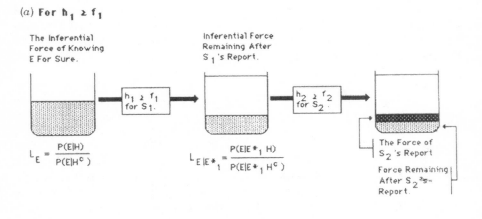

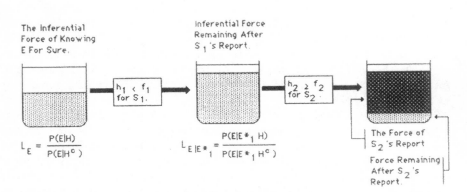

FIGURE 8.16 Corroborative evidence and a "well" of inferential force.

some of this force depending upon how many times greater h_1 is than f_1; the larger the ratio h_1/f_1, the more inferential force we draw from the well. How much force remains is shown by the middle well and indicated by $L_{E|E_1^*}$. We can potentially apply the force in the middle well to E_2^* in an amount depending upon the credibility of S_2. How much is left over as a potential for even more corroborative reports of event E depends on S_2's credibility; this remaining force is shown in the right-hand well.

But, when $h_1 < f_1$, a curious thing happens to the level of inferential force in the well as a result of S_1's report E_1^*; *the well gets fuller*, as shown in Figure 8.16b. As I noted earlier, if E_1^* is conditioned only by events {E, E^c} and if $P(E|H) > P(E|H^c)$, then $P(E|E_1^*H) \geq P(E|E_1^*H^c)$; or $L_{E|E_1^*} \geq 1$. We need to examine what happens to the ratio $L_{E|E_1^*}$, as h_1 and f_1 take on different values. First, as already noted, when $f_1 = 0$, then $L_{E|E_1^*} = 1$. It is also true that when $h_1 = f_1$, then $L_{E|E_1^*} = L_E$. In fact it is easily shown that if $h_1 > f_1$, then $L_{E|E_1^*} < L_E$, and that if $h_1 < f_1$, then $L_{E|E_1^*} > L_E$. So, if we believed the source of the first report of event E was untruthful, unobjective, or inaccurate, there is more potential inferential force in the well, given by $L_{E|E_1^*}$, than that provided by the *known* occurrence of event E. Is this counterintuitive? To answer this question, we must consider again the bounds on likelihood ratio for the joint corroborative evidence that we are considering.

In the singly connected inference network of Figure 8.7g, the force of the corroborative evidence $E_1^*E_2^*$ has bounds $L_{E^c} \leq L_{E_1^*E_2^*} \leq L_E$, as we discussed earlier. We can also express $L_{E_1^*E_2^*}$, using the general product rule for conditionals, as $L_{E_1^*}L_{E_2^*|E_1^*}$. Suppose we believe that $h_1 < f_1$ for S_1 so that $L_{E_1^*} < 1$, meaning that E_1^* favors H^c over H. The condition $h_1 < f_1$ also implies that $L_{E|E_1^*} > L_E$. So, as Equation 8.30 shows, if S_2 were perfectly credible, then $L_{E_2^*|E_1^*}$ is close to $L_{E|E_1^*}$ which is greater than L_E. Along comes S_2, whose credibility we believe to be virtually unimpeachable. From Equation 8.30 we observe that $L_{E_2^*|E_1^*}$ can approach L_E in value only if $L_{E|E_1^*} > L_E$. Stated in words, as a result of S_1's report, which we believe to be not so credible, our minds are led in the direction of H^c over H. To move our minds in the opposite direction by the maximum amount allowed by L_E, $L_{E|E_1^*}$ must be greater than L_E, which is precisely what a likelihood ratio construal says will happen when $h_1 < f_1$.

Our story about the well of inferential force left behind by S_1 is not yet complete; there is another curious feature of this well that concerns *event rareness*. As we have discussed, likelihood ratio construals of the force of evidence are sensitive to differences as well as to ratios of likelihood ingredients. By such means they capture subtleties associated with event rareness. In analyses of the force of corroboratively redundant evidence we have two sources of event rareness to consider: (1) Initially how rare is event E under H and under H^c? and (2) How rare is event E, under H and under H^c, now in light of our first report E_1^*? Regarding the first question I note that its answer would of course depend upon whatever background knowledge or ancillary evidence we had to support the judgment that $P(E|H)$ and $P(E|H^c)$

are both small values. The relation between rare events and corroboration is an important one that we need to examine carefully.

First, recall that $L_E = P(E|H)/P(E|H^c)$ can be very large, even though the values of $P(E|H)$ and $P(E|H^c)$ are both very small. Suppose that $S_1 =$ Tom and $S_2 =$ Dick. Tom tells us about the occurrence of an event E which we believe to be very improbable under H and under H^c, but we also believe that L_E is quite large. While we consider Tom to be very credible, the event he reports is so rare that, according to Equation 8.29, we cannot assign it much inferential force. We say to ourselves, "Tom's testimony wants corroboration"; then we ask Dick, who also says that event E occurred. We believe Dick to be a very credible source. Despite Tom's strong credibility, there is still abundant force left in the well, since, because of the rareness of the event in question, we did not use very much of it on the basis of Tom's testimony. But, as I will show by example, the force of Dick's corroborative testimony will now be quite strong, much stronger in fact than if we had considered his testimony alone.

We have still another source of event rareness to consider, and it involves how evidence E_1^* influences the rareness of event E under H and H^c. Consider Tom and Dick again, and suppose that ancillary evidence mounts that Tom is not only untrustworthy but also unobjective and a very poor observer. Suppose that for Tom, $h_{Tom} < f_{Tom}$. As we make this ratio smaller and smaller, $P(E|E_{Tom}^*H)$ gets much larger than $P(E|E_{Tom}^*H^c)$. As we discussed above, for $f_1 > h_1$, $L_{E|E_1^*} > L_E$. But, what also happens is that both $P(E|E_{Tom}^*H)$ and $P(E|E_{Tom}^*H^c)$ get ever smaller. In short E becomes increasingly improbable, under both H and H^c, to the extent that we believe Tom to be untruthful, unobjective, or inaccurate. The result is that there is more inferential force that can be applied to Dick's corroborative report, if he is credible. Event E is now rare in light of Tom's report of E, which we do not regard as credible. The result is that Dick's corroboration has less force because of the rareness of E, made evident by how little trust we place in Tom's initial report of E.

The examples in Table 8.7 illustrate some of the points just made about the force of corroboratively redundant evidence. The first three cases illustrate rareness issues associated with the event E being corroboratively reported. In all three cases observe that $L_E = 18$. In case 1 we have the first report E_1^* from a very credible source S_1, as indicated by the h_1 and f_1 values in rows 3 and 4. As a result we assign $L_{E_1^*} = 15.09$, using Equation 8.29. Rows 6 and 7 show that as a result of S_1's very credible report, there is not much force remaining in the well for application to S_2's report; we have $L_{E|E_1^*} = 0.99/0.83 = 1.19$. Now comes S_2 making the same report who has the same strong credibility credentials as S_1. Applying Equation 8.30 to S_2's report, we have $L_{E_2^*|E_1^*} = 1.19$ in row 10 which, within rounding, exhausts nearly all of the remaining force in event E. Row 11 shows the force we would have assigned S_2's report if we ignored E_1^* and thus would have double-counted the redundant corroborative evidence in this case. Row 12 shows $L_{E_1^*E_2^*} = L_{E_1^*}L_{E_2^*|E_1^*} = 17.96$, nearly the same force as knowing event E for sure.

TABLE 8.7   Redundance and Corroborative Evidence

Ingredients	Case 1	Case 2	Case 3	Case 4	Case 5	Case 6
1. $P(E\|H)$	0.90	0.09	0.0090	0.90	0.90	0.90
2. $P(E\|H^c)$	0.05	0.005	0.0005	0.05	0.05	0.05
3. h_1	0.98	0.98	0.98	0.20	0.01	0.98
4. f_1	0.01	0.01	0.01	0.90	0.85	0.01
5. $L_{E_1^*}$	15.09	6.55	1.79	0.31	0.12	15.09
6. $P(E\|E_1^*H)$	0.99	0.91	0.47	0.667	0.0957	0.999
7. $P(E\|E_1^*H^c)$	0.83	0.33	0.05	0.011	0.0006	0.838
8. h_2	0.98	0.98	0.98	0.98	0.98	0.20
9. f_2	0.01	0.01	0.01	0.01	0.01	0.90
10. $L_{E_2^*\|E_1^*}$	1.19	2.69	8.44	30.95	9.70	0.64
11. $L_{E_2^*}$	15.09	6.55	1.79	15.09	15.09	0.31
12. $L_{E_1^*}L_{E_2^*\|E_1^*}$	17.96	17.62	15.11	9.59	1.16	9.66

In cases 2 and 3 we continue to have two sources with equally strong credibility credentials. The difference is that we make event E a rare event in these two cases. Notice that L_E still equals 18 in both of these cases, but in case 2 E is 10 times less probable under H and under H^c than in case 1. In case 3, E is 100 times less probable under H and under H^c than in case 1. Observe in rows 5 and 10 that the force of E_1^* decreases across these two cases, but the force of E_2^* increases. The reason is that, because of the rareness of E, the force of the first report of E is decreased, and more force is available in the well for application to the second report of E. In case 2, row 11 shows that we would still overvalue E_2^* if we ignored E_1^*. But in case 3 an interesting thing happens showing that a second and redundant report is not always overvalued if the first report is ignored. In row 10, Equation 8.30 says the inferential force of E_2^*, given E_1^*, is 8.44. In terms of Equation 8.29, S_2's report, considered by itself, yields a force of just 1.79, the same as the force of S_1's report. One way to describe what has happened is to say that the report from the first source about a rare event "takes the hit" as far as the rareness of this event is concerned. The report from the second source then takes less of a hit. By ignoring the first source's report, the second report is thus made to take the same strong hit as the first report.

Cases 4 and 5 illustrate the situation shown in Figure 8.16b in which the report E_1^* and S_1's credibility add force to the well. In case 4, as rows 3 and 4 indicate, S_1's credibility credentials are not so strong; we believe that $f_1 > h_1$ in the ratio 9/2. As a result of E_1^*, our beliefs are led toward H^c over H in the ratio $L_{E_1^*} = 0.31 = 1/3.22$. Notice that in rows 6 and 7 the potential force available for S_2's report is now $L_{E\|E_1^*} = 0.667/0.011 = 60.64$. The well now contains $60.64/18 = 3.37$ times as much force as it contained before we obtained E_1^*. Since S_2 is a very credible source, $L_{E_2^*\|E_1^*} = 30.95$, nearly twice the force E_2^* would have if we ignored E_1^*.

In case 5 appears an additional subtlety. We now make S_1's credibility credentials much weaker than in case 4; we now have $f_1 > h_1$ in the ratio $85/1$. As a result of E_1^*, our beliefs are led quite strongly in the direction of H^c over H in the ratio $L_{E_1^*} = 0.12 = 1/8.33$. Consequently there is now substantial force in the well for S_2, as indicated by $L_{E|E_1^*} = 0.0957/0.0006 = 159.5$. This is $159.5/18 = 8.86$ times the force of knowing E for sure. The trouble, as you can see, is that S_1's report and credibility credentials have now made us believe that E is a rare event under H and under H^c. Even S_2's strong credibility credentials (rows 8 and 9) cannot capture all of the additional force in the well. In case 5 we have another instance in which ignoring the first of two corroborative reports does not result in overvaluing the evidence. As row 11 shows, E_2^* would have considerably more force if we ignored E_1^*. Finally, notice in row 12 that the combined force of E_1^* and E_2^*, as given by Equations 8.29 and 8.30, is very weak in this case. We have two reports of the occurrence of E; one from a highly probable liar and one from a very credible source. Thus we are virtually back where we started before we received this corroborative evidence.

In case 6 we make S_1's credibility credentials strong and S_2's credibility credentials quite weak. There is not much force remaining in the well for S_2. In addition we believe that $f_2 > h_2$ for S_2. Here we have yet another instance in which ignoring E_1^* would not cause us to overvalue E_2^*. As a result of S_2's weak credibility credentials, we would move our beliefs even more strongly in the direction of H^c over H if we ignored E_1^*.

As Figure 8.7 shows, there are many special cases of corroborative evidential redundance made necessary by the various possibilities involving patterns of state- or hypothesis-dependent source credibility as well as influences among sources. I cannot present analyses of all of them. I have chosen the situation in Figure 8.7d for analysis since it provides another kind of instance in which we may have nonredundant evidence about redundant events. Suppose that as this figure suggests, the hit and/or false-positive probabilities for S_2 depend upon H and or H^c. Then we need to identify $h_{2(H)} = P(E_2^*|EH)$, $h_{2(H^c)} = P(E_2^*|EH^c)$, $f_{2(H)} = P(E_2^*|E^cH)$, and $f_{2(H^c)} = P(E_2^*|E^cH^c)$. In this case we have

$$L_{E_2^*|E_1^*} = \frac{P(E|E_1^*H)[h_{2(H)} - f_{2(H)}] + f_{2(H)}}{P(E|E_1^*H^c)[h_{2(H^c)} - f_{2(H^c)}] + f_{2(H^c)}} \tag{8.31}$$

We do not need to make any changes in Equation 8.29 for $L_{E_1^*}$, or in the equations for $P(E|E_1^*H)$ and $P(E|E_1^*H^c)$, since we are not supposing S_1's credibility to be additionally dependent on H or H^c.

Table 8.8 contains examples of some of the evidential subtleties revealed by Equation 8.31. All of these examples involve situations in which we may be justified, by appropriate ancillary evidence, in believing that the hit and false-positive probabilities for S_2 are dependent, in various ways, upon H or H^c. In some of these examples rather extreme results occur that may seem

TABLE 8.8 Corroboration and Conditional Nonindependence

Ingredients	Case 1	Case 2	Case 3	Case 4	Case 5	Case 6
1. $P(E|H)$	0.90	0.090	0.0090	0.0090	0.90	0.0090
2. $P(E|H^c)$	0.05	0.005	0.0005	0.0005	0.05	0.0005
3. h_1	0.98	0.98	0.98	0.20	0.98	0.98
4. f_1	0.01	0.01	0.01	0.90	0.01	0.01
5. $L_{E_1^*}$	15.09	6.55	1.79	0.99	15.09	1.79
6. $P(E|E_1^*H)$	0.999	0.906	0.471	0.0020	0.999	0.471
7. $P(E|E_1^*H^c)$	0.838	0.330	0.046	0.0001	0.838	0.047
8. $h_{2(H)}$	0.98	0.98	0.98	0.98	0.05	0.05
9. $f_{2(H)}$	0.78	0.78	0.78	0.78	0.90	0.90
10. $h_{2(H^c)}$	0.05	0.05	0.05	0.05	0.98	0.98
11. $f_{2(H^c)}$	0.01	0.01	0.01	0.01	0.01	0.01
12. $L_{E_2^*|E_1^*}$	22.52	41.44	73.65	78.00	0.06	9.03
13. $L_{E_2^*}$	80.00	78.23	78.02	78.02	2.31	85.11
14. $L_{E_1^*}L_{E_2^*|E_1^*}$	339.8	271.4	131.8	77.22	0.91	16.16

counterintuitive. On several occasions I have had to explain what appeared to be anomalous results when a Bayesian scheme for grading the force of evidence is employed. One such occasion involved an exchange between Duncan Luce and me on the matter of corroborative evidence from multiple sources (Schum 1980, 1981a, 189–193; Luce 1980). My present task is to explain, using Equations 8.29 and 8.31, why corroborative evidence may not only be nonredundant but may also have very strong inferential force.

In case 1 we have S_1 being very credible, so we determine $L_{E_1^*} = 15.09$ by Equation 8.29. This is nearly the same force the known occurrence of E would have ($L_E = 18$). As rows 6 and 7 show, there is not much force left in the well for us to apply to S_2's corroborative report. What Equation 8.31 tells us, however, is that the evidence we may have about S_2 can add more force to the well. Suppose we have ancillary evidence that suggests the following behavior on the part of S_2: If H were true, S_2's report E_2^* would be very likely whether or not event E did occur. We might believe, for example, that S_2 is biased *in favor of* reporting event E if H were true. This is indicated by the high values of $h_{2(H)}$ and $f_{2(H)}$ in rows 8 and 9. However, we also believe that if H^c were true, S_2 would be biased against reporting event E. This is indicated by the small values $h_{2(H^c)}$ and $f_{2(H^c)}$ in rows 10 and 11.

The result in case 1, shown in row 12, is that, even accounting for a prior report of the same event from a strongly credible source, E_2^* has greater inferential force ($L_{E_2^*|E_1^*} = 22.52$) than does the known occurrence of event E. As you can see, it has more force than E_1^*. In this case E_2^* is hardly redundant with E_1^*, even though the same event is reported in both items of evidence. But row 13 shows that if we had ignored E_1^*, the force of E_2^* would have been much greater ($L_{E_2^*} = 80.0$). When we examine the combined inferential force of E_1^* and E_2^* (row 14), we find that it is $339.8/18 = 18.9$ times the force of knowing event E for sure. In short, what we believe about the state or hypothesis dependence of S_2's credibility does itself have strong inferential force.

In cases 2 and 3 everything remains the same as in case 1 except that we make event E rarer, under H and under H^c. The force of E_1^* declines (row 5), but the force of E_2^* increases (row 12), as in cases 2 and 3 in Table 8.7. What has happened as a result of making E a rarer event is that there is more force in the well in addition to that supplied by the hypothesis-dependent credibility of S_2. The additional force in the well is indicated by comparing the ratios $P(E|E_1^*H)/P(E|E_1^*H^c)$ in each case (rows 6 and 7). The ratios are $0.999/0.838 = 1.19$ (case 1), $0.906/0.330 = 2.75$ (case 2), and $0.471/0.046 = 10.24$ (case 3). But, as row 14 shows, the decrease in the force of E_1^*, as the rareness of E is made greater, is larger than the increase in the force of E_2^*, given E_1^*. The result is that the force of the combined evidence decreases.

In case 4 we retain the rareness of event E as in case 3. A report of the occurrence of this event is given us by S_1, whose credibility credentials are weak. We may believe S_1 to be untruthful, unobjective, or inaccurate (see rows 3 and 4). Considered by itself, this first report E_1^*, has virtually no inferential force (row 5). There is considerable inferential force left in the well as indicated by the ratio of the ingredients in rows 6 and 7; observe that there is more force in the well in this case than in case 3. However, E is still a rare event under H and H^c, given E_1^*. But the hypothesis-dependent hit and false-positive probabilities for S_2 add force to this well. So as Equation 8.31 provides, the force of E_2^* is very strong ($L_{E_2^*E_1^*} = 78.0$) and is greater by a factor of 4.33 than the force of knowing event E for sure. But the combined force of E_1^* and E_2^* is less than in previous cases because of the lack of credibility on the part of S_1.

In case 5 we restore the credibility of S_1 and remove the rareness of event E. But we change the nature of the hypothesis-dependent credibility of S_2. In this case we have S_2 being untruthful, unobjective, or inaccurate, if H is true, but very credible if H^c is true. Though there is virtually no inferential force left in the well after S_1's credible report (rows 6 and 7), some is created by the hypothesis-dependent credibility of S_2. The force that is created is directionally different, since, as shown in row 12, $L_{E_2^*E_1^*} = 0.06$, which favors H^c over H in the ratio $1/0.06 = 16.67$. Thus the force of E_2^*, given E_1^*, has more force favoring H^c than does knowing for sure that E did not occur ($L_{E^c} = 0.10/0.95 = 1/9.5$). In row 14 we observe that the strong credibility of the first source is canceled out by the hypothesis-dependent credibility of the second source. Their joint corroborative report is virtually worthless.

Case 6 is the same as case 5 except that we again make E very improbable under H and H^c. Changing this single ingredient produces some profound changes (over case 5) in the inferential direction and force of the corroborative evidence. First, as in case 5, S_1 is a very credible source, but the event reported is very rare, given H and given H^c. A single report of this event has very little inferential force (row 5). One consequence is that there is now significant force in the well (rows 6 and 7) to apply to the corroborative evidence from S_2 if S_2 is credible. The trouble, however, is that S_2's credibility is hypothesis dependent in a manner we have already encountered. In Section 7.3.1, in Table 7.5, I gave examples of situations in which a source's false-positive probabilility can dominate in determining the inferential force of evidence. In case 6 in Table 8.8 we have such a situation. Observe that $f_{2(H)}$ is 90 times the value of $f_{2(H^c)}$. If justified by ancillary evidence, this hypothesis contingency adds inferential force favoring H over H^c to S_2's report, over and above what is already in the well. There was almost no force in the well in case 5. But, as row 13 shows, if we ignored the fact that we already have E_1^* from a credible source, we would assign E_2^* much greater force, in the ratio 85.11/ 9.03 = 9.43. In short, S_1's strong credibility softens the impact of the particular hypothesis-dependent credibility of S_2.

The twelve numerical examples in Tables 8.7 and 8.8 illustrate a variety of subtleties buried just below the surface of corroborative or repetitive evidence. Some involve source credibility, and others involve evidence about improbable events. Since I could not provide examples of all of the credibility-related contingencies in Figure 8.7, there are other subtleties that can be identified and exploited. Even more can be identified if we take the trouble to decompose credibility-related stages of reasoning. In the case of testimonial evidence, for example, such decomposition exposes uncertainties associated with the veracity, objectivity, and observational sensitivity of our sources.

8.4.4 The Force of Cumulatively Redundant Evidence

Cumulative evidence involves reports of different events; but we may believe the known occurrence of one event tends to make the known occurrence of other events inferentially redundant. In the corroborative cases just examined, we observed that the events reported are naturally redundant, though corroborative evidence need not be redundant. The same thing happens in the cumulative cases; we may have nonredundant evidence about redundant events. Structural considerations are all-important in our efforts to capture cumulative redundance. Here is an example that identifies a situation in which different cumulative events are also completely or "naturally" redundant, as is the event reported repetitively in corroborative evidence.

Suppose that witness Tom tells us he saw defendant Dick at the scene of the crime. Then comes witness Harry who tells us that he found Dick's coat at the scene of the crime. Suppose we believe that Tom is perfectly credible and thus believe that Dick was definitely at the scene of the crime. Suppose that Harry is also perfectly credible, so we believe Dick's coat was also at the scene. But our subsequently knowing that Dick's coat was at the scene adds nothing to what we already know. The reason is that we might take Dick's coat being at the scene as just circumstantial evidence that Dick was there; we already believe that he was. But suppose, instead, that on ancillary evidence we believe it very likely that Tom may have confused Dick with someone else. In this case Harry's testimony about the coat assumes an importance it did not have under the assumption that Tom is perfectly credible. Harry of course might not be completely credible either.

In Figure 8.13 I posed a certain inference network in order to illustrate how we might grade, according to Equation 8.28, the degree of inferential redundance in two different but cumulative events E and F. The key element in this gradation involved a particular form of conditional nonindependence of these events. As you recall, suppose that event E acts to make F's probability the same or nearly the same under H and H^c. This conditional nonindependence was captured by the arc connecting event classes {E, E^c} and {F, F^c} in Figure 8.13. But in the Tom, Dick, and Harry hypothetical we will have to consider a different structure, since, as we just noted, Dick's coat being at the scene (F) would be just circumstantial evidence that Dick was there himself (E). The possible networks we have in this situation are shown in Figure 8.17. The two networks result from different judgments that we might make about the significance of Dick's coat being at the scene.

Suppose, as in Figure 8.17a, we regard Dick's coat at the scene of the crime (F) as being just circumstantial evidence on events {E, E^c}, whether or not Dick was there himself. This chain of reasoning is singly connected, as you observe. To begin, suppose that Tom and Harry are perfectly credible witnesses, so we believe with confidence that events E and F have occurred. In this case we take E^* as equivalent to E and F^* as equivalent to F. On the structure we have in Figure 8.17a, event F is *perfectly redundant*, given event E, for the following reason: We first form the likelihood ratio $L_{F|E} = P(F|EH)/P(F|EH^c)$. Since the network is singly connected and F is independent of H and H^c, given E, we have $L_{F|E} = P(F|E)/P(F|E) = 1.0$. We now form the likelihood ratio $L_F = P(F|H)/P(F|H^c)$. Expanding these two likelihoods in terms of events {E, E^c}, we have

$$L_F = \frac{P(E|H)[P(F|E) - P(F|E^c)] + P(F|E^c)}{P(E|H^c)[P(F|E) - P(F|E^c)] + P(F|E^c)} \qquad (8.32)$$

Now L_F is not zero unless both $P(E|H) = 0$ and $P(F|E^c) = 0$. Judgments of a zero value for both of these conditionals would not make any sense. The first would say that there is no chance that Dick would be at the scene of the crime if he did it; the second would say that there is no chance of Dick's coat being at the scene if Dick was not there himself. So we may regard $L_F > 1.0$, since we might naturally believe that $P(E|H) > P(E|H^c)$ and $P(F|E) > P(F|E^c)$. From Equation 8.28 for $R_{F|E}$, we see that events E and F are completely redundant in this case, since we have $L_{F|E} = 1$ and $L_F > 1$. Thus, if the known occurrence of F is just circumstantial evidence on events {E, E^c}, as in Figure 8.17a, then $R_{F|E} = 1$; knowing E makes F completely redundant.

(a) Conditional Independence

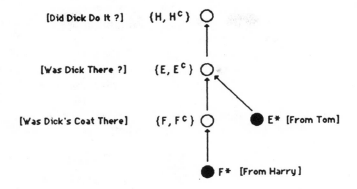

(b) Conditonal Nonindependence

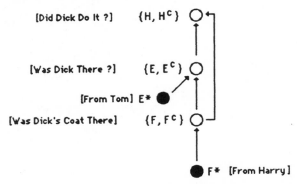

FIGURE 8.17 Two cases of "naturally" redundant cumulative evidence.

But our analysis so far involves a particular conditional independence judg-ment on our part. We have been assuming that Dick's coat being at the scene depends only upon whether Dick was there himself and not on whether he committed the crime {H, H^c}. Suppose that someone produces evidence that Dick rarely forgets anything unless he is under duress. Having committed a crime may certainly be stressful, so we might judge that $P(F|EH) \neq P(F|E)$. To capture such situations we add the arc shown in Figure 8.17*b* connecting event classes {F, F^c} and {H, H^c}. If we rearrange the nodes in this network you will see that it has the same basic structure as the network in Figure 8.15 with arcs 2, 3, and 4 removed. Indeed the networks in Figures 8.15 and 8.17*b* can be made formally the same if we add arcs to Figure 8.17*b*, indicating hypothesis-dependent credibility for Tom and Harry, and add another arc to indicate some influence among them. The formal process we now examine allows us to capture the two basic cases of cumulative redundancy that we have examined so far.

We begin by removing the implausible assumption of perfect credibility of our sources of evidence about events E and F. Doing so requires us to distinguish between E* and E and between F* and F. To illustrate matters influencing the redundancy of cumulative evidence, we need the likelihood ratios $L_{F^*|E^*}$ and L_{F^*}. The first expression concerns the force of F*, in light of E*; the second considers the force of F* taken by itself. We first determine these expressions for the situation illustrated in Figure 8.17a for which $R_{F|E} = 1$. Ignoring evidence E*, $L_{F^*} = P(F^*|H)/P(F^*|H^c)$ can be expressed as

$$L_{F^*} = \frac{P(E|H)[P(F|E) - P(F|E^c)](h_2 - f_2) + P(F|E^c)(h_2 - f_2) + f_2}{P(E|H^c)[P(F|E) - P(F|E^c)](h_2 - f_2) + P(F|E^c)(h_2 - f_2) + f_2}$$

(8.33)

where $h_2 = P(F^*|F)$ and $f_2 = P(F^*|F^c)$. In this singly connected reasoning chain from F* to {H, H^c}, the force of evidence F* on {H, H^c} depends upon differences between and ratios of the ingredients: $P(E|H)$ and $P(E|H^c)$, $P(F|E)$ and $P(F|E^c)$, and h_2 and f_2.

If we now consider F* in light of E*, we have $L_{F^*|E^*} = P(F^*|E^*H)/P(F^*|E^*H^c)$, which, in its expanded form is

$$L_{F^*|E^*} = \frac{P(E|E^*H)[P(F|E) - P(F|E^c)](h_2 - f_2) + P(F|E^c)(h_2 - f_2) + f_2}{P(E|E^*H^c)[P(F|E) - P(F|E^c)](h_2 - f_2) + P(F|E^c)(h_2 - f_2) + f_2}$$

(8.34)

As you observe, the only difference between $L_{F^*|E^*}$ and L_{F^*} involves likelihoods of event E. In the present case event F is completely redundant given event E. Equation 8.32 considers the force of the known occurrence of F, Equation 8.33 concerns the force of fallible evidence F* about event F, but Equation 8.34 concerns the force of F*, given evidence E* about event E. In this case we must consider, as in the corroborative cases, how much force remains in the "E-well," given evidence E*. This is indicated by the likelihoods $P(E|E^*H)$ and $P(E|E^*H^c)$ in Equation 8.34. As we examined in the corroborative cases, these likelihoods depend not only upon $P(E|H)$ and $P(E|H^c)$ but also upon $h_1 = P(E^*|E)$ and $f_1 = P(E^*|E^c)$. As the examples shown in Table 8.9 will illustrate, evidence F* can be nonredundant, given E*, even though event F is completely redundant, given E.

Analyses involving Equations 8.33 and 8.34 are quite important. The reason is that because they concern *different* events, evidence E* and F* may be quite easy to overvalue. The event redundancy inherent in Figure 8.17a may not be quite so obvious as the inherent redundancy of events reported in corroborative evidence. As the following examples illustrate, we can easily

TABLE 8.9   Redundance of Cumulative Evidence when $R_{F|E} = 1.0$

Ingredients	Case 1	Case 2	Case 3	Case 4	Case 5	Case 6
1. $P(E|H)$	0.90	0.90	0.0090	0.90	0.90	0.90
2. $P(E|H^c)$	0.05	0.05	0.0005	0.05	0.05	0.05
3. h_1	0.95	0.50	0.95	0.50	0.05	0.05
4. f_1	0.01	0.25	0.01	0.25	0.90	0.90
5. $L_{E^\bullet}$	15.02	1.81	1.76	1.81	0.16	0.16
6. $P(E|E^*H)$	0.999	0.947	0.463	0.947	0.333	0.333
7. $P(E|E^*H^c)$	0.833	0.095	0.045	0.095	0.003	0.003
8. $P(F|E)$	0.92	0.92	0.92	0.0095	0.80	0.80
9. $P(F|E^c)$	0.12	0.12	0.12	0.0001	0.05	0.05
10. h_2	0.95	0.95	0.95	0.95	0.95	0.05
11. f_2	0.01	0.01	0.01	0.01	0.01	0.90
12. $L_{F^*|E^\bullet}$ (Eq. 8.34)	1.17	4.30	3.00	1.69	4.94	0.75
13. $L_{F^\bullet}$ (Eq. 8.33)	4.99	4.99	1.05	1.71	7.50	0.34
14. $r = L_{F^\bullet}/L_{F^\bullet|E^\bullet}$	4.26	1.16	0.35	1.01	1.52	0.45

determine how much we would have overvalued evidence F* if we ignored evidence E*. However, we will see that it is also possible to *undervalue* cumulative evidence about redundant events.

In case 1 in Table 8.9, event E, having $L_E = 18$ favoring H over H^c, is reported by a very credible source S_1 (rows 3 and 4). The force of E* on {H, H^c} is thus strong and favors H over H^c in the ratio $L_{E^\bullet} = 15.02$. As rows 6 and 7 indicate, there is not much force, regarding event E, remaining in the well; $L_{E|E^\bullet} = 0.999/0.833 = 1.20$. Now comes S_2 who reports F* about event F whose known occurrence would be just circumstantial evidence on events {E, E^c}. Suppose, as in rows 8 and 9, that F favors E over E^c in the ratio $0.92/0.12 = 7.67$. In rows 10 and 11 we see that S_2 is also a very credible source. But S_2's report F* cannot have very much force on {H, H^c}, since we have already exhausted nearly all of the force in event E, about which F* is just circumstantial evidence. In row 12 we see that $L_{F^*|E^\bullet} = 1.17$; F* has almost no inferential force at all. But suppose we had ignored evidence E* as we were determining the force of F*. According to Equation 8.33, the force of F* on {H, H^c}, considered by itself is $L_{F^\bullet} = 4.99$. If we had ignored E* we would overvalue F* by a factor of $r = 4.26$, as shown in row 14.

In case 2 everything remains the same as in case 1 except that we now make S_1 only weakly credible (rows 3 and 4). Considerable E force now remains in the well as shown in rows 6 and 7 by the ratio $L_{E^\bullet|E} = 0.947/0.095 = 9.97$. In this case S_2's circumstantial evidence about the occurrence of E can have value, since we regard S_1's more direct evidence of E as weakly credible. The value $L_{F^*|E^\bullet} = 4.30$ in row 12 is nearly the same as $L_{F^\bullet}$, ignoring E*. If we had ignored E*, we would overvalue F* only in the ratio $r = 1.16$.

In case 3 event rareness rears its peculiar head. Suppose we believe event E to be very improbable, given H or given H^c, as in rows 1 and 2. A report of this rare event cannot have much force on {H, H^c}, even if reported by a very credible source, as S$_1$ is in this case. Considerable E force remains in the well, since $L_{E|E^*}$ = 0.463/0.045 = 10.29. Now comes a very credible source S$_2$ who provides reasonably forceful circumstantial evidence F* about the occurrence of event E. In this case F* does have force on {H, H^c} in light of E* in the ratio $L_{F^*|E^*}$ = 3.0. But now observe in row 13 that, if we had ignored E*, F* would have virtually no force on {H, H^c}. In short, had we ignored E*, we would have *undervalued* F* in the ratio 0.35 = 1/2.86, even though event F is perfectly redundant on {H, H^c}, given event E. According to a Bayesian construal of this situation, evidence E* about event E does not have much force on its own, but it acts to enhance the force of circumstantial evidence F* about event E.

In case 4 several things happen at the same time. First, a not very credible S$_1$ reports the occurrence of an event having strong force on H over H^c. The force of this evidence, however, is very weak; L_{E^*} = 1.81. Much E force remains in the well for S$_2$, a strongly credible source, who reports an event F that strongly favors E over E^c in the ratio 95/1. The trouble, as you can see in rows 8 and 9, is that we believe event F to be very improbable whether or not E is true. Consequently F* has not much force on {H, H^c} because of the rareness of the linkage between F and {E, E^c}. As rows 13 and 14 indicate, the force of F* on {H, H^c} is virtually the same whether or not we ignore evidence E*.

In case 5 event E, if it occurred, strongly favors H over H^c in the ratio L_E = 18. But on ancillary evidence we believe S$_1$, reporting E*, to be in-accurate, unobjective, or untruthful. Thus evidence E*, on a Bayesian con-strual, favors H^c over H (in this case in the ratio L_{E^*} = 0.16 = 1/6.25). As rows 6 and 7 show, there is abundant E force for application to S$_2$'s evidence F*. Here we have the same situation we encountered in the corroborative case, namely $L_{E|E^*}$ > L_E for a source of evidence E* who/that is weakly credible. Note in rows 6 and 7 that $L_{E|E^*}$ = 0.333/0.003 = 111. So $L_{E|E^*}$ is 111/18 = 6.17 times larger than L_E. A strongly credible S$_2$ (rows 10 and 11) reports the occurrence of event F that is srongly circumstantial evidence of E [$P(F|E)/P(F|E^c)$ = 0.80/0.05 = 16]. In this case, even though event F is completely redundant on {H, H^c}, given event E, $L_{F^*|E^*}$ favors H over H^c in the ratio 4.94. But, as rows 13 and 14 show, we would overvalue F* if we ignored E*, even though we believe the source of evidence E* to be lying, unobjective, or inaccurate. Case 6 is the same as case 5 except that we have made a liar out of S$_2$ as well. Here is another case in which we would *undervalue* evidence F* if we ignored E*.

The six cases in Table 8.9 show that there are abundant evidential subtleties to be observed in cumulative and possibly redundant evidence, even when we have no recognized conditional nonindependencies among events and evidence on a chain of reasoning. My final analytic task is to describe a situation in which redundance arises because of a particular form of conditional nonindependence between two events E and F, given hypotheses {H, H^c}. Consider the situation shown in Figure 8.15 in which arc 1 indicates that events {E, E^c} and {F, F^c} are not independent, conditional on hypotheses {H, H^c}. Suppose that the nature of the nonindependence of event classes {E, E^c} and {F, F^c} takes the following form: If event E is true, this would virtually destroy the force of event F on hypotheses {H, H^c}; in other words, whatever L_F is, $L_{F|E} = P(F|EH)/P(F|EH^c)$ is close to 1.0. Equation 8.28 for $R_{F|E}$ shows us how we may grade the redundance of E and F in this case. The present case differs from the one captured by Equations 8.33 and 8.34, since E and F were naturally redundant and $R_{F|E} = 1$. We now consider situations in which E and F may be cumulatively redundant but not naturally or completely so.

I cannot present analyses of all the possible special cases revealed in Figure 8.15; the one I have chosen is shown in Figure 8.18. In this case we allow for two conditional nonindependencies: (1) the redundance involving events E and F and (2) state or hypothesis dependence of source S_2 reporting the occurrence of event F. To explore redundance matters in the network shown in Figure 8.18, we need the two likelihood ratios $L_{F^*|E^*} = P(F^*|E^*H)/P(F^*|E^*H^c)$ and $L_{F^*} = P(F^*|H)/P(F^*|H^c)$. If we ignore E* and E completely, the force of evidence F* on hypotheses {H, H^c} is given by

$$L_{F^*} = \frac{P(F|H)[h_{2(H)} - f_{2(H)}] + f_{2(H)}}{P(F|H^c)[h_{2(H^c)} - f_{2(H^c)}] + f_{2(H^c)}} \tag{8.35}$$

where $h_{2(H)} = P(F^*|FH)$, $h_{2(H^c)} = P(F^*|FH^c)$, $f_{2(H)} = P(F^*|F^cH)$, and $f_{2(H^c)} = P(F^*|F^cH^c)$. These conditionals allow us to capture the state-dependence of S_2's hit and false-positive probabilities.

But, if we now consider F* in light of E*, we have

$$L_{F^*|E^*} = \frac{a(c - e)(h_{2(H)} - f_{2(H)}) + e(h_{2(H)} - f_{2(H)}) + f_{2(H)}}{b(d - g)(h_{2(H^c)} - f_{2(H^c)}) + g(h_{2(H^c)} - f_{2(H^c)}) + f_{2(H^c)}} \tag{8.36}$$

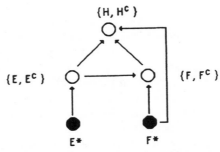

FIGURE 8.18 A special case of cumulative redundance.

where

$$a = P(E|E^*H), \quad b = P(E|E^*H^c)$$
$$c = P(F|EH), \quad d = P(F|EH^c)$$
$$e = P(F|E^cH), \quad g = P(F|E^cH^c)$$

and where the credibility-related ingredients h and f are defined as in Equation 8.35. Here is a summary of the significance of these ingredients. Likelihoods a and b tell us how much E force on {H, H^c} remains in the well, in light of S_1's report E*. Ingredients c, d, e, and g concern how the force of event F, on hypotheses H and H^c, depends upon events E and E^c. I will make the form of this dependence one in which event F is rendered redundant to some degree, given E and possibly given E^c. The h and f ingredients concern the hypothesis-dependent credibility of S_2 reporting F*.

To set the stage for numerical examples of the workings of Equation 8.36, consider the situation shown in Figure 8.19. In Figure 8.19a we have judgments we might have made about the inferential force of the known occurrence of events E and F when they are considered separately. Both events favor H over H^c; $L_E = P(E|H)/P(E|H^c) = 18$, and $L_F = P(F|H)/P(F|H^c) = 8.5$. If E and F were independent, conditional upon H and upon H^c, their joint inferential force on {H, H^c} is $L_{EF} = L_E L_F = (18)(8.5) = 153$. But suppose we believe that these events are nonindependent, conditional upon both H and upon H^c. Our judgment about this nonindependence takes the form shown in the two tables in Figure 8.19b. Considered jointly, we assess the likelihoods $P(EF|H) = 0.80$ and $P(EF|H^c) = 0.03$ so that $L_{EF} = P(EF|H)/P(EF|H^c) = 26.67$. Considered jointly, these two events have much less inferential force on {H, H^c} than they do if considered separately. We judge that events E and F are cumulatively redundant to some degree.

To determine just how redundant F would be if we already knew that E occurred, we decide to apply Equation 8.28; we need L_F and $L_{F|E}$ in order to do so. We already know $L_F = 8.5$, from Figure 8.19a. We determine $L_{F|E} = P(F|EH)/P(F|EH^c)$ from our judgments in Figure 8.19b; $P(F|EH) = P(EF|H)/P(E|H) = 0.8/0.9 = 0.89$, and $P(F|EH^c) = P(EF|H^c)/P(E|H^c) = 0.3/0.5 = 0.6$. So $L_{F|E} = 1.48$. From Equation 8.28 we determine $R_{F|E} = 0.82$. So, according to our judgments in Figure 8.19b, event F is 0.82 redundant on {H, H^c} once we also know E. F might also be redundant to some degree if we knew E^c instead of E. From our judgments we determine $P(F|E^cH) = P(E^cF|H)/P(E^c|H) = 0.05/0.10 = 0.50$ and $P(F|E^cH^c) = P(E^cF|H^c)/P(E^c|H^c) = 0.07/0.95 = 0.07$. From these likelihoods we determine $L_{F|E^c} = 7.14$ and $R_{F|E^c} = 0.08$. Knowing that E did not occur does not make F redundant in this example, though it might in other cases, even when E also makes F redundant.

Table 8.10 contains six examples based upon the information in Figure 8.19b. Observe in rows 8–11 that the four likelihoods of event F are the same in all of these examples. From what we have just determined, $R_{F|E} = 0.82$

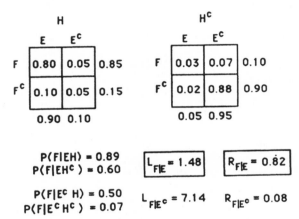

FIGURE 8.19 Cumulative redundancy and conditional nonindependence: An example.

in all of these examples. What makes these six examples differ is just the credibility of the sources of evidence E* and F*. Evidence F* will, to some degree, be redundant with E* in the first three cases. In the last three cases F* will not be redundant with E*, even though F is 0.82 redundant, given E. We now have additional instances in which events may be redundant but evidence about these events nonredundant.

Case 1 forms a baseline for evaluating the other five cases. In case 1 the sources of evidence E* and F* are both very credible. In addition the credibility of neither source is state dependent. From rows 16, 19, and 20 we observe that L_{F^*} is 3.12 times the value of $L_{F^*|E^*}$; we would overvalue F* by this factor if we ignored E*. If we knew for sure that E and F both occurred, Figure 8.19 shows that $L_F/L_{F|E} = 8.5/1.48 = 5.74$. In this limiting case we would overvalue F by a factor of 5.74 if we ignored event E and the fact that $R_{F|E} = 0.82$.

In case 2 we introduce the following state dependence of the credibility of S_2 reporting F*. From rows 12–15 we observe that if H were true, S_2's hit

TABLE 8.10   Cumulative Redundance and Conditional Nonindependence

Ingredients	Case 1	Case 2	Case 3	Case 4	Case 5	Case 6
1. $P(E|H)$	0.90	0.90	0.90	0.90	0.90	0.90
2. $P(E|H^c)$	0.05	0.05	0.05	0.05	0.05	0.05
3. h_1	0.98	0.98	0.98	0.50	0.98	0.01
4. f_1	0.01	0.01	0.01	0.25	0.01	0.98
5. L_{E^*}	15.09	15.09	15.09	1.81	15.09	0.11
6. $P(E|E^*H)$	0.999	0.999	0.999	0.973	0.999	0.1552
7. $P(E|E^*H^c)$	0.838	0.838	0.838	0.095	0.838	0.0005
8. $P(F|EH)$	0.89	0.89	0.89	0.89	0.89	0.89
9. $P(F|E^cH)$	0.50	0.50	0.50	0.50	0.50	0.50
10. $P(F|EH^c)$	0.60	0.60	0.60	0.60	0.60	0.60
11. $P(F|E^cH^c)$	0.07	0.07	0.07	0.07	0.07	0.07
12. $h_{2(H)}$	0.98	0.75	0.98	0.98	0.98	0.98
13. $f_{2(H)}$	0.01	0.60	0.90	0.01	0.90	0.90
14. $h_{2(H^c)}$	0.98	0.98	0.05	0.98	0.01	0.05
15. $f_{2(H^c)}$	0.01	0.01	0.01	0.01	0.98	0.01
16. $L_{F^*|E^*}$ (Eq. 8.36)	1.72	1.44	31.75	6.62	2.02	73.75
17. $P(F|H)$	0.85	0.85	0.85	0.85	0.85	0.85
18. $P(F|H^c)$	0.15	0.15	0.15	0.15	0.15	0.15
19. L_{F^*} (Eq. 8.35)	5.37	4.67	60.50	5.37	1.16	60.50
20. $r = L_{F^*}/L_{F^*|E^*}$	3.12	3.24	1.91	0.81	0.57	0.82

and false-positive probabilities are both quite large. Recall that this indicates a bias favoring the report of E*. But, if H were not true, we believe that S_2 would be very credible. As in case 1, we believe S_1 to be very credible. In case 2, $L_{F^*|E^*}$ is reduced over case 1, but so is L_{F^*} (row 19). The result is that F* is still redundant with E*, since L_{F^*} exceeds the value of $L_{F^*|E^*}$ in the ratio 3.24. For S_2 in case 3 we have very high hit and false-positive probabilities when H is true; if H were not true, we have very low hit and false positives for S_2. Recall that this reflects a bias against reporting F*. If justified by appropriate ancillary evidence, such state-dependent credibility would greatly enhance the force of F*. In row 16, $L_{F^*|E^*}$ = 31.75. This seems to be an extreme result, since, if we knew for sure that events E and F occurred, $L_{F|E}$ = 1.48. But, as shown in row 19, the state-dependent credibility for S_2 also drastically increases the force of L_{F^*}. The result is that F* is not nearly as redundant with E* as in cases 1 and 2.

Case 4, 5, and 6 all represent situations in which we would not overvalue F* if we ignored E*, even though events E and F are redundant to degree 0.82. In case 4 this is achieved simply by reducing the credibility of S_1 (rows 3 and 4). As rows 6 and 7 indicate, there is now substantial force remaining in the E well that Equation 8.36 can incorporate, since S_2's credibility is very strong and is not state dependent. As rows 16, 19, and 20 indicate, there is more force in F* if we take E* into account than there is if we ignore E*. In case 5 we have made S_1 very credible but have made S_2's credibility state dependent in a way that reduces rather than enhances the force of F* whether or not we take E* into account. As shown in rows 16, 19, and 20, both L_{F^*} and $L_{F^*|E^*}$ are quite small (favoring H over H^c), but $L_{F^*|E^*}$ is the larger of the two.

Finally, in case 6 we have two sources with rather interesting credibility credentials. On ancillary evidence we strongly believe S_1 to be untruthful, unobjective, or inaccurate. But S_2's hit and false-positive probabilities depend upon whether nor not H is true. We have ancillary evidence that S_2 would be biased in favor of reporting F* if H were true, and biased against reporting F* if H were not true. The remaining E force in the well (rows 6 and 7) and the force added by the state-dependent credibility of S_2 combine to make the force of F* very large if we take E* into account (row 16). But, as row 20 indicates, the force of F*, ignoring E*, is also substantial in this case.

I advertised Section 8.2 as being concerned about the two faces commonly placed on evidential redundance. One face, benign in appearance, concerns verification of the occurrence of relevant events as well as verification of their inferential consistency. The other face, not always so benign, shows the possibility of double-counting or overvaluing evidence. The assorted likelihood ratio equations I have presented in the corroborative and cumulative cases of redundance have shown both of these faces. In addition they have brought to our attention the fact that the second face need not always appear on either cumulative or corroborative evidence. We may, in some cases, risk *undervaluing* either corroborative or cumulative evidence.

I believe the most important element of the probabilistic analyses that I have presented concerns identifying the locus of redundance. In either the corroborative or cumulative cases, redundance is a property of the events reported in evidence and not necessarily a property of the evidence itself. As we have now observed in numerous examples, the credibility of our sources of evidence and the rareness of the reported events govern the extent to which evidence about redundant events will also be redundant. I have identified two cases involving what I termed the *natural redundance* of reported events. In either case the R measure I imported from statistical communications theory takes a value of 1.0. In the corroborative case the same event gets reported on two or more occasions, so the "natural" event redundance is obvious. Less obvious is the natural redundance in situations in which one event is simply circumstantial on another event. In other cases the measure $R_{F|E}$ allows us to grade the extent of partial redundance of events E and F, as we just observed.

In numerous examples I have shown how a second source, if credible, can use some of the inferential force remaining in a "well" if the first source is not so credible. This is how the benign face involving verfication appears in my equations. If an event reported by the first source is improbable, or if the credibility credentials of a second source are inferentially interesting on their own, then the second source can effectively add additional inferential force to this "well." In all of the Bayesian construals of inferential force I have provided in Chapters 7 and 8, the concept of conditional nonindependence provides a mechanism for trapping a wide assortment of evidential subtleties; evidential redundance is an especially interesting case.

8.5 OTHER RECURRENT COMBINATIONS OF EVIDENCE

Various forms of evidence can be combined in an unlimited number of ways. In the first four sections of this chapter I have identified only the most basic combinations of evidence that are recurrent. There are other recurrent evidence combinations that deserve at least some mention; I will consider just two. The first is a special case of *contradictory* evidence examined in Section 8.1.1. This special case turns out to involve one of the four cases Bernoulli identified regarding either the necessity or contingency of inferential linkages between evidence and hypotheses. Consider Bernoulli's case 2 in Figure 6.3. First, we have a relation of necessity between E and H. This simply means that H^c and E are incompatible; E entails that H^c is not true, so we conclude that H is true. Then we have a contingent or probabilistic relation between evidence E^* and events $\{E, E^c\}$. We do not know for sure that event E is true, since E^* has some probability given E and given E^c. In other words, $h = P(E^*|E) < 1.0$ and $f = P(E^*|E^c) > 0$. As we will discuss briefly, an important example of this situation involves *alibi evidence*.

As I mentioned in Section 3.4 and summarized in Figure 3.11, there are three basic ways in which a person could have obtained the evidence she now reports: (1) by her own direct observations, (2) at secondhand from another source, or (3) as a result of an inference or an *opinion* based on evidence, of one form or another, *about events other than those she now testifies*. In many different situations we take, as evidence, the opinions or the inferences of other persons that do not arise as a result of any direct observations these persons might have made. In all of these situations we have combinations of evidence to consider. There are some postively frightening inferential problems that arise when we attempt to assess the inferential force of opinion evidence.

8.5.1 Contradictions, Entailments, and Alibis

Tom, Dick, and Harry appear for the final time in this discourse. This time poor Tom is accused of assault and battery on the victim (Vic) and now stands trial. Tom pleads innocence, and Vic admits that he never saw his assailant, since he was mugged in a dark alley. Could Tom have had the opportunity to commit this crime? "Yes," says Dick, who testifies that he saw Tom running away from the scene of the crime just moments after it was committed. The crime was committed in Fairfax, Virginia, on Wednesday, May 12, 1993, at around 1:30 AM. Suppose that Dick is correct in his assertion that Tom was running away from the scene at this time. This certainly does not entail that Tom committed the crime. Tom might argue that he was in fact running away from the person who actually mugged Vic. So we regard Dick's evidence as just circumstantial on the hypothesis that Tom committed the crime. But we now hear from Harry who asserts that, between 12:30 and 1:30 AM on Wednesday, May 12, 1993, he was having a quiet drink with Tom at a bar in Front Royal, Virginia, about 60 miles from the scene. If true, Harry's assertion is incompatible with the hypothesis that Tom committed the crime. Tom cannot have been in Fairfax and in Front Royal at the same time. Harry's assertion, if true, entails that Tom did not commit the crime.

The events that Dick and Harry report are mutually exclusive, so their testimonies are *contradictory*. But these events are certainly not exhaustive; think of all the other places Tom might have been if he was neither in Fairfax nor Front Royal. To treat the problem of assessing the force of this contradiction in terms we have already employed, consider the two events E: Tom was at the scene at the time of the crime and E^c: Tom was not at the scene at the time of the crime. If we further let H = Tom committed the crime as charged, and H^c = Tom did not commit the crime as charged, we see that H and E^c are incompatible. In other words, $HE^c = \emptyset$, so $P(HE^c) = 0$. This means of course that for $P(E^c) > 0$, $P(H|E^c) = 0$, and for $P(H) > 0$, $P(E^c|H) = 0$. Thus we can immediately identify two likelihoods that follow from Pascalian rules; $P(E|H) = 1.0$ and $P(E^c|H) = 0$. If Tom committed the crime of assault and battery, he must have been at the scene. But if Tom did not commit the crime, there is some chance that he could have been at the scene. In other words, $P(E|H^c) > 0$. This also means, under Pascalian rules, that $P(E^c|H^c) < 1.0$.

We hear evidence bearing upon the credibility of witnesses Dick and Harry and now contemplate the inferential force of their contradictory testimony. In Section 8.1.1 we examined Bayesian and other construals of the joint inferential force of contradictory evidence from two sources. In the case of a contradiction involving an alibi, it is more informative to examine the separate force of each item of testimony. Let E = Tom was at the scene of the crime when it was committed, and E^c = Tom was not at the scene of the crime at the time it was committed. Let S_1 = Dick and S_2 = Harry so that $E_1^* $ = Dick's report of E and E_2^{c*} = Harry's report of E^c. Finally, let H = Tom committed the crime as charged and H^c = Tom did not commit the crime as charged. We need two likelihood ratios $L_{E_1^*}$ for Dick and $L_{E_2^{c*}|E_1^*}$ for Harry. We cannot of course ignore Dick's testimony placing Tom at the scene when we evaluate Harry's testimony providing an alibi for Tom. If we allow for the credibilities of Dick and Harry to be dependent on H or on H^c but also suppose that they had no influence on each other, we have the situation illustrated in Figure 8.2*a* with arc 3 removed.

For Dick's testimony $L_{E_1^*}$ is simply a special case of Equation 7.9 with $P(E|H) = 1$. Recall that, if Tom did it, he is certain to have been at the scene. So we have

$$L_{E_1^*} = \frac{h_{1(H)}}{P(E|H^c)[h_{1(H^c)} - f_{1(H^c)}] + f_{1(H^c)}} \qquad (8.37)$$

where $h_{1(H)} = P(E_1^*|EH)$, $h_{1(H^c)} = P(E_1^*|EH^c)$, and $f_{1(H^c)} = P(E_1^*|E^cH^c)$. For Harry's testimony E_2^{c*}, in light of Dick's testimony, we have to recall that $P(E^c|H) = 0$; if Tom did it, he cannot have been elsewhere. If we expand $L_{E_2^{c*}|E_1^*} = P(E_2^{c*}|E_1^*H)/P(E_2^{c*}|E_1^*H^c)$, noting that $HE^c = \varnothing$, we obtain

$$L_{E_2^{c*}|E_1^*} = \frac{m_{2(H)}}{P(E^c|E_1^*H^c)[c_{2(H^c)} - m_{2(H^c)}] + m_{2(H^c)}} \qquad (8.38)$$

where $m_{2(H)} = P(E_2^{c*}|EH)$, $c_{2(H^c)} = P(E_2^{c*}|E^cH^c)$, and $m_{2(H^c)} = P(E_2^{c*}|EH^c)$.

Dick's testimony E_1^* says that Tom had opportunity to commit the crime. The force of his testimony depends, as Equation 8.37 shows, upon his hit and false-positive probabilities and upon how likely it is that Tom was at the scene if he did not commit the crime. The inferential force of Harry's contradictory assertion E_2^{c*}, providing an alibi for Tom, depends not only upon Harry's correct-rejection and miss probabilities but also upon Dick's credibility. Here we have the interesting feature of alibi evidence. Even though we suppose that Dick and Harry have not influenced each other's testimony, the force of Harry's testimony depends in part upon Dick's credibility. This is revealed in the term $P(E^c|E_1^*H^c)$. This interesting term resembles the terms we encountered in corroborative evidence that prescribed how much force was left in a "well" after the first report of an event. In the present case we can determine

$$P(E^c|E_1^*H^c) = \frac{P(E^c|H^c)f_{1(H^c)}}{P(E^c|H^c)f_{1(H^c)} + P(E|H^c)h_{1(H^c)}} \qquad (8.39)$$

In the case of corroborative evidence we observed how the force of a second report of the same event depends upon the credibility of the source of the first report of this event. As I noted earlier, corroboration and contradiction are two sides of the same coin. The force of Harry's contradiction, and alibi for Tom, depends in part on the credibility of Dick's establishing that Tom had opportunity to commit the crime. The less we are convinced that Tom had opportunity in the first place the more forceful can be the specific alibi that Harry provides. In another work I have provided extensive numerical examples of the workings of Equations 8.37–8.39 for alibi evidence (Schum 1981b).

8.5.2 The Inferential Force of Opinion Evidence

A fitting place for me to end this discussion of the force of combinations of evidence is with evidence in the form of inferences or opinions from other persons. There are issues involved in assessing the force of opinion evidence that are as difficult as they are interesting. Since we so commonly traffic in opinion evidence, it seems appropriate to examine some of the major inferential difficulties associated with such evidence. Adrian Zuckerman has recently provided an elegant assessment of opinion evidence within the context of law that, I believe, has relevance in other disciplines as well (1989, 59–71). In legal matters there are special rules of evidence that apply to expert witnesses who are allowed to express opinions about matters at issue (Federal Rules of Evidence 701–706; Mueller and Kirkpatrick 1988, 107–118).

The first difficulty is that it can be argued that *all* testimonial evidence from a person involves an opinion or an inference, even if we know for sure that this person made a direct observation of the event(s) he reports. Indeed my analysis of the credibility of human observers in Section 3.2.3 supposes that a person's testimony about some observed event rests upon an inference this person made based upon sensory evidence obtained during the observation. Thus even though we might say that this testimony is based upon a "firsthand" observation, there was an inference drawn or an opinion formed from this observation unless, unrealistically, we supposed the observer to possess an infinitely accurate sensory apparatus together with a mechanism for arriving at beliefs based only upon this perfect sensory evidence. Such a state of affairs hardly characterizes human observers any of us know.

In some cases we instantly recognize a person's assertion as mere opinion, even though we may also believe this assertion to be based upon a firsthand observation. Suppose I assert that X was intoxicated last night in a well-known restaurant. You object, saying that this is mere opinion and not a specific statement of what I observed. I then tell you that X was moving about erratically and was making a fool of himself. Again you object, saying that each of these descriptions calls for a conclusion on my part. I then say "I saw X fall out of his chair, bump into two waiters on the way to the men's room, spill his drink down the back of a person at the next table, and then pass out during the dessert course." Now satisfied with the specificity of my testimony, you proceed to draw your own conclusion about whether or not X was intoxicated last night.

Acknowledging the inferential component of all testimonial evidence, I wish to consider opinion evidence that *does not rest* upon any firsthand observation of the event(s) reported in a person's testimony. Here is an abstract example. Anne tells us that event E occurred; we have an interest in her assertion, since we believe the occurrence of E would be relevant in our inference about whether or not hypothesis H is true. We ask her how she knows that E occurred; specifically we ask her if she observed event E. She says she did not observe E directly but inferred that E occurred on the basis of other information she has. She admits that her testimony about the occurrence of E is an inference or an opinion. We then inquire about the basis for her present opinion about E. She replies: "I saw A and B happen, Mary told me that she saw event C happen, and Joe told me that he read in the newpaper yesterday that D happened; so I concluded that event E also happened." How are we to grade the force on our hypotheses of interest $\{H, H^c\}$ of Anne's opinion evidence about the occurrence of event E?

Our first problem appears to be entirely structural in nature and involves whether we would believe, as Anne does, that events A, B, C, and D are relevant in an inference about event E. We might ask Anne to chart an inference network showing the chains of reasoning she believes link these four events to events $\{E, E^c\}$. Presumably we are already prepared to construct a relevance argument from events $\{E, E^c\}$ to hypotheses $\{H, H^c\}$. While she constructs her arguments, we ponder what kind of evidence she says she has about events A, B, C, and D. This will inform us about relevant credibility matters we will have to consider.

Anne claims to have observed events A and B directly, so we have her veracity, objectivity, and observational sensitivity to consider regarding each of these events. We note that she might be more credible in reporting about event A than she is about event B. But her evidence about event C comes at secondhand from Mary who claims to have made a direct observation. So we have Mary's credibility credentials to ponder as well as Anne's as far as this hearsay evidence is concerned. But then we also have Joe's mention of the news account he saw regarding event D. We can check this newspaper for ourselves to see if Joe's account is correct. But then we also have the credibility of the news source(s) to consider if indeed we are able to determine the exact source(s) of evidence about the occurrence of event D.

Anne is now finished constructing her argument from events A, B, C, and D to events $\{E, E^c\}$. We may or may not agree that all elements of her arguments are plausible or cogent. We might believe that one or more of these events are not relevant on whether or not E occurred. We might also be led to construct different arguments from these four events and, in the process, note avenues of influence among them that Anne did not discern. Perhaps, for example, A and B are cumulatively redundant, or perhaps events C and D are synergistic in their effects upon whether or not E occurred. Suppose we agree upon an inference network that connects evidence about events A, B, C and D through events $\{E, E^c\}$ to our hypotheses $\{H, H^c\}$. If we had the interest, time, resources, and appropriate ancillary evidence, we could subject this argument to probabilistic analyses of the sort I have identified in this chapter or to the current inference network approaches I mentioned in Section 4.5. By such means we could have Bayesian or Baconian gradations of the force of Anne's opinion evidence. One alternative to the compulsive exercise I have just outlined is of course to try to find somone who made a firsthand observation of event E.

We would not, obviously, consider such exercises for every item of opinion evidence we receive. Part of the reason involves the fact that so many of our daily inferences are based upon the opinions of others formed under conditions not unlike those I posed in the above example. But I wish to defend at least the structural elements of this process. As we will observe in the next chapter, being compulsive about the structural tasks required in probabilistic reasoning has distinct heuristic benefits. We may be led by the performance of such tasks to discern or discover new forms of evidence we might well consider or to discern entirely new hypotheses.

Chapter 9

Discovery and the Generation of Evidence

We have now examined, at some length, matters concerning the relevance, credibility, and force of various forms and combinations of evidence. All of these matters bear upon the process of drawing conclusions from evidence. In some works this process is termed *justification,* and it concerns the means by which we can defend or justify the conclusions we reach from the evidence at hand (Salmon 1984, 10–14). In other works the process of drawing conclusions from evidence is said to involve matters of *graded justification* or *proof,* where it is carefully noted that because of the incomplete and inconclusive nature of the evidence we have, such proof can only be *tentative* or probabilistic in nature (Wigmore 1937; Cohen 1989a, 4–13). In the discussion so far I have assumed the existence of certain forms and combinations of evidence, the existence of hypotheses or possible conclusions, and the existence of arguments linking evidence and hypotheses. I did so in order to illustrate what various formal systems of probabilistic reasoning have to tell us about the process of *asking questions about evidence* in order to establish its relevance, credibility, and inferential force on conclusions we entertain. But there are equally important and interesting questions concerning where evidence, hypotheses, and arguments come from in the first place. These questions involve the process of *discovery* in which evidence, hypotheses, and arguments linking them are generated. Among other things, this process involves *asking questions of evidence.*

Logicians, probabilists, and others have provided us with canons, prescriptions, or logics for justification or proof. What about discovery? Can there be a logic of discovery and, if so, what might it involve? One ingredient the process of discovery requires is the exercise of *imaginative reasoning.* If we are not already supplied with possible conclusions, evidence, and arguments linking them (an unlikely possibility outside the classroom), it is natural to suppose that these inferential ingredients emerge only as a result of someone's imagining, inventing, creating, or discovering them. But such intellectual processes seem, at least to some persons, to be subjects for investigation by psychologists rather than by logicians or probabilists. There are differing views on this matter, as we will observe. The literature on imaginative, creative, or inventive thought is now as diverse as it is extensive. Because probabilistic reasoning tasks are often embedded within choice or decision tasks, there are other demands placed on our imaginative reasoning skills. Few decision tasks arise in which possible *options* or *choices* and their possible *consequences* are immediately obvious; they have to be generated or discovered as well.

There is some research on the topics of hypothesis generation and option generation. So you might believe that we could discuss the topic of evidence generation by itself. However, the process of discovery underlying probabilistic reasoning is a *seamless* activity involving the generation of hypotheses, evidence, and arguments. For example, in the discovery process that precedes or accompanies probabilistic reasoning, we often have hypotheses in search of evidence at the same time as we have evidence in search of hypotheses. All is not revealed to us or is on record at the moment we begin the task of trying to draw a conclusion about matters of interest. In many contexts discovery involves much more than just a search through records or thoughts that we already have. We might not yet have asked appropriate or important questions whose answers will lead us to generate new evidence and to discern new possibilities. Not all imaginative efforts will bear fruit, so we have to attend to matters involving the *efficiency* of discovery-related processes. My view is that efficient means for both *search* and *inquiry* are necessary in productive discovery-related activities.

There is one evidence-related matter that I believe to be of vital importance in discovery, and I will dwell upon it in this chapter. I believe that the degree of success we enjoy in generating important new hypotheses and new evidence depends to a great extent upon how well we have *marshaled* or organized the thoughts and evidence that we already have. As I proceed, I hope to dispel any notion that the study of evidence marshaling or organization is devoid of any theoretical significance as far as discovery and probabilistic reasoning are concerned. Juxtaposing or arranging our thoughts and our evidence in different ways reveals different evidential distinctions that may have heuristic value in generating new possibilities and evidence. I will illustrate the heuristic merit in each of several different ways of marshaling thought and evidence. Discovery requires a variety of intellectual tasks and is a process that unfolds over time. It appears that there is no single way of marshaling thought and evidence that meets the requirements of all of these tasks. I will describe a linked network of different evidence-marshaling operations, each of which offers heuristic guides to further inquiry or investigation. In short, we need methods of marshaling existing thought and evidence that act to stimulate the generation of new questions that we might ask *of the evidence we already have.*

9.1   DISCOVERY IN VARIOUS CONTEXTS

One trouble we might just as well face before we proceed is that the term *discovery* suggests different processes to different persons, depending upon the context or discipline within which they labor. Hearing the term "discovery," a scientist might associate this word with the often sudden inspiration that accompanies the generation of a new or revised theory that could account for certain phenomena not explainable by theories she now entertains. An attorney hearing this same term might bring to mind various legally sanctioned coersive measures by which he can obtain evidence from his opponent. A police investigator may associate the term discovery with the process of determining whether or not a criminal act has been committed and, if so, who is responsible. A software engineer might think of various tasks that might be performed in an effort to discover what a client truly wants a finished computer software system to accomplish. The historian might associate this term with the finding of a document or object that suggests a radically new interpretation of some past event.

However, despite these contextual differences, there are some basic similarities. All of the persons just mentioned traffic in ideas and must reach certain conclusions based on the evidence they gather. All are concerned in various ways about generating new ideas or possibilities as well as generating new evidential tests of these possibilities. One point of difference between one context and another concerns how discovery-related activities are integrated with other intellectual activities, two of which are justification/proof and choice. Before we examine contextual differences involving these three activities, a word is necessary about distinctions that have been made between discovery and justification or proof.

9.1.1   Discovery and Justification

The distinction between imagining a possible conclusion and showing why this conclusion follows from evidence was appreciated many centuries ago. Closer to our own time, this distinction was an issue in arguments between the philosophers John Stuart Mill (1806–1873) and William Whewell (1794–1866). Mill had criticized Whewell's (1847) ideas about a logic for discovery on the ground that discovery cannot be cast in terms of rules. In turn Whewell criticized Mill's (1865) inductive methods on the ground that they only allow us to justify what has already been discovered. It appears that Whewell had the better of this argument; in any case he was able to produce abundant historical evidence of the importance of invention or discovery in science that Mill was not able to refute (Cohen 1989a, 10–11). As I noted earlier, Mill allowed that his inductive methods at least involved proof or justification but not discovery. Since Mill's day the distinction between discovery and induction has troubled many logicians and philosophers of science.

Some philosophers have seemed quite content to commit the study of discovery to others such as psychologists. Reichenbach advised that we not confuse discovery with justification. As he remarked (1968, 231):

> The act of discovery escapes logical analysis; there are no logical rules in terms of which a "discovery machine" could be constructed that would take over the creative function of a genius. But it is not the logician's task to account for scientific discoveries; all he can do is to analyze the relation between given facts and a theory presented to him with the claim that it explains these facts. In other words, logic is concerned only with the context of justification. And the justification of a theory in terms of observational data is the subject of the theory of induction.

In a similar vein Popper called for an "elimination of psychologism" from scientific inference. As he remarked (1968, 31):

> The initial stage, the act of conceiving or inventing a theory, seems to me neither to call for logical analysis nor to be susceptible of it. The question how it happens that a new idea occurs to a man—whether it is a musical theme, a dramatic conflict, or a scientific theory—may be of interest to empirical psychology; but it is irrelevant to the analysis of scientific knowledge.

Other philosophers and logicians appreciate the distinction between discovery and justification or proof but seem quite troubled by the thought that logic has no place in analyses of discovery, as Popper suggested. Wesley Salmon, for one, has argued that this puts logic in the position of being able to offer help only when the original creative work is done. He notes: "According to the received opinion, logical analysis can only be used for the dissection of scientific corpses, but it cannot have any role in living, growing science" (1979, 111–112). But Salmon, risking identification with psychology, has obviously done considerable thinking about the process of discovery. He notes that discovery and justification are intertwined activities and may have common elements. He also notes that discovery does not end with the generation of a hypothesis but also involves the generation of evidence and the construction of arguments linking evidence and hypotheses (1970, 71–73).

I mentioned that in discovery-related activities we often have hypotheses searching for evidence at the same time we have evidence searching for hypotheses. Salmon agrees, and sounding very much like a psychologist, he describes how discovery does not always proceed in logical steps. As he says, "Our minds wander, we daydream, reveries intrude, irrelevant free associations occur, and blind alleys are followed" (1984, 13). This description (to which I will later refer) provides one basis for Salmon's belief that there will be no mechanical way of generating true explanatory hypotheses, the hope for which he describes as a "fantastic rationalistic dream" (1979, 112). Part of the difficulty is that we often have no way of knowing for sure when we have a "true" hypothesis. Still Salmon does allow that there are certain stages in discovery that may be followed, though not in any necessary temporal order. The stages are (1) generating a hypothesis, (2) considering its plausibility, and (3) testing the hypothesis (1979, 114). The matter of *plausibility* leads us to the thoughts of others who offer somewhat greater hope for a logic of discovery.

We have already encountered the work of Charles Sanders Peirce in Section 5.3 during discussion of how the inferential force of evidence might be graded. Peirce's works on discovery-related matters are of sufficient importance that I devote two later sections to them (Sections 9.2.1 and 9.3.1). Peirce was convinced that new ideas could never be discovered by means of deductive or inductive reasoning. Deductive reasoning provides a means for demonstrating that a conclusion is *necessarily* true. As noted in Section 2.2.1, the price paid for necessity is vacuity, since the content of the conclusion of a deductive argument is already present in its premises. Inductive reasoning allows us to assert that a certain conclusion is *probably* true. But, as Whewell pointed out, such reasoning involves the justification or graded proof of a conclusion that has already been generated or discovered by other means. Peirce believed that there is a third form of reasoning to which he gave the names *abduction, retroduction,* or *hypothesis.* By such reasoning, he argued, we may show that a certain conclusion is *plausibly* or *possibly* true. In Section 9.2.1 I will examine abduction in some detail. One reason is that this term is currently in widespread use and has been given various meanings.

One person who has taken seriously Peirce's thoughts on discovery is Norwood Russell Hanson, whose work *Patterns of Discovery* (1958) has been quite influential. In another work Hanson brought Peirce back to life and contemplated how easily Peirce would lose an audience of contemporary philosophers regarding the possibility of a logic of discovery. Hanson says: ". . . for the very words 'logic of discovery' seem not to fit together; at their very mention philosophers scurry for cover, they claw the auditorium walls, or chew the college carpets in sophisticated, seething incredulity and disdain" (1965, 42).

Within the context of science at least, Hanson tells us that a logic of discovery should concern itself with reasoning processes actually used during discovery. To a psychologist, such a logic would then be *descriptive* rather than *prescriptive* (or *normative*). Hanson notes that scientists rarely encounter already-constructed lists of hypotheses whose consequences they are required to draw up. Rather, he says, they encounter certain anomalies and desire explanations of them. Hanson suggests that in an episode of discovery, reasoning proceeds retroductively, *from an anomaly,* to the delineation of a *kind* of hypothesis that fits into an organized *pattern* of concepts (1965, 50–51). We might, in modern terms, characterize retroduction as a species of "bottom-up" reasoning from an observed anomaly to some plausible or possible explanation of it. But in 1965 Hanson used the very modern term *inference network* with reference to retroduction; we have already encountered this term in connection with justification or proof.

Having noted that retroduction involves finding an explanation for anomaly x, Hanson then discusses the explanation itself. As he says (1965, 48–49):

> . . . if the finished explanation of x exfoliates quasideductively from "high level hypotheses" down through a theoretical inference-network, terminating ultimately in a "low level" description of x—then something resembling that same inference network must have been traversed by the scientist who, when perplexed by x, did seek to "explain it" by reasoning his way (and x's) back up into a "control-tower" of unchallengeable commitments. The x is rendered nonanomalous when set "as a matter of course" (Peirce's favorite phrase) into the framework of what was initially given as clearly understood.

I will return to Hanson's *inference network* explanation of abduction or retroduction in Section 9.2.1. One matter of later interest to us concerns the difference, if any, between induction and abduction/retroduction. Hanson has characterized retroduction as a "bottom-up" process, from an anomaly to some possible conclusion or explanation. But induction is also characterized in these same terms.

Peirce's work has attracted considerable attention among persons in disciplines other than philosophy and logic. It is fair to say that the idea of a logic of discovery does not cause every philosopher to claw the walls or chew the carpets. Indeed, as we will later discuss, some persons believe that normative or prescriptive rules for discovery are possible, at least in some contexts. But it is one thing to characterize the process of discovery, as Peirce, Hanson, and others have attempted to do, and quite another to demonstrate to others how they might enhance their discovery-related activities in the wide assortment of contexts in which the imaginative reasoning underlying discovery is absolutely essential. To begin discussion of this matter, we must leave philosophy and logic for the moment.

9.1.2 More on Cycles of Discovery, Proof, and Choice

It seems clear that the imaginative reasoning leading to the generation of a possible conclusion is bound together with the evidential and argumentational justification of this conclusion. As Salmon remarked, ". . . discovery is a process involving frequent interplay between unfettered imaginative creativity and critical evaluation" (1979, 140). But discovery and justification or proof are themselves bound together with other activities in many different contexts. This is one reason why I asserted in Section 1.1 that human inference tasks in most natural settings involve *mixtures* of different forms of reasoning and required judgments. As I noted in Section 4.2.1, one activity with which discovery and proof often find themselves naturally associated is *choice*. Engineers, auditors, attorneys, physicians, and many other persons routinely encounter discovery and proof tasks not just for the purpose of drawing conclusions about interesting phenomena. They must use these conclusions, however hedged probabilistically, as part of the process of making decisions of interest to clients and to themselves. In addition, as I noted earlier, there may be more than one person involved in such activities, each of whom has a particular judgmental role to play.

Choice-related matters enter our discussion of discovery for reasons other than the one just noted. In most contexts the process of discovering hypotheses and evidence involves the expenditure of time and resources. Consider a police investigator attempting to discover the person(s) who commited a criminal act. As discovery proceeds, this investigator might have any number of potential "leads" that can be followed, some of which will surely be the "blind alleys" that Salmon mentioned. Given unlimited time and resources, the investigator might follow all leads, or investigative paths, that are discovered. But time and resources are usually limited, so police investigators, in common with many other persons performing discovery-related activities, have choices to make about what investigative paths they will follow. In some contexts the discovery of hypotheses and evidence must cease at some point or no actions will be taken, in which case patients will die, and clients as well as battles will be lost.

It comes as no surprise that persons working in different contexts experience different mixtures of discovery, proof, and choice. One result is that there is often disappointment associated with attempts to implement various schemes for assisting inference and choice invented by others who, unfortunately on many occasions, have little or no awareness of the particular way in which discovery, proof, and choice are bound together in the context of interest. Some schemes for assistance might suppose, for example, that discovery activities will always precede the application of methods for inductive justification. Figure 9.1 illustrates two quite different situations involving the discovery of hypotheses, evidence, and arguments linking them.

(*a*) **Legal Contexts**

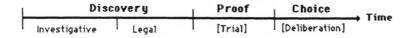

(*b*) **Other Contexts**

FIGURE 9.1 Cycles of discovery, proof, and choice in various contexts.

Figure 9.1*a* shows a situation, often encounted in legal affairs, in which the process of discovery must cease at some point. In another work I have added some important qualifications to this depiction of a well-ordered sequence: discovery–proof–choice (Schum 1986). The point of this example is simply to show one instance (there are others) in which discovery terminates at some point, whereupon there is an episode of proof or justification followed by an episode of deliberation and choice. In legal affairs two forms of discovery can be discerned. The first, labeled *investigative,* concerns the activities of persons such as police investigators who have the task of determining whether a crime has been committed and, if so, who they believe is responsible. The discovery labeled *legal* concerns the process I mentioned earlier in which attorneys for one side attempt to obtain evidence held by the other. Proof or justification takes place at trial, or some other form of settlement if the matter does not come to trial. If there is a trial, then follows an episode in which fact finders (jurors or the judge) deliberate on the hypotheses, the evidence, and the arguments in reaching a verdict and choosing some form of penalty or settlement. This situation is definitely one in which there are many actors who play different inferential and decisional roles throughout the discovery–proof–choice sequence.

Figure 9.1*b* illustrates those instances in which the process of discovery is ceaseless. In engineering, scientific and historical research, as well as in areas such as military intelligence, discovery is ongoing; new hypotheses and evidence are being generated all the time. As discovery proceeds, there may be any number of cycles of proof (in some forum) and choice. In science and engineering such choices may involve possible directions for further research or development. In military contexts the choices might include such matters as deciding what to do about some situation that appears, on evidence, to be threatening in some way. In these situations, as in legal affairs, there may be many persons involved in discovery as well as in proof and choice.

In both of the situations illustrated in Figure 9.1, it is to be expected that different mixtures of deductive, inductive, and abductive or retroductive reasoning are discernible in different contexts. The particular mixtures encountered by auditors investigating whether or not there are material misstatements in the financial records of some client may not be the same as those encountered by persons engaged in medical research or in criminal investigations. Discovery, proof, and choice activities, and the reasoning and judgments they entail, can be discerned in all of these contexts but in different mixtures or combinations.

9.1.3 The Temporal Elements of Discovery

One of the most important but frequently overlooked characteristics of discovery is that it is a process having several temporal elements. The first element concerns the fact that discovery-related activities often concern processes that are nonstationary and that unfold over time. Imagine the inferential tasks faced by a psychiatrist, clinical psychologist, or social worker attempting to draw conclusions about the nature of a patient's behavioral disorder (if there is one) and the possible cause(s) of it. The patient surely changes in some ways as a result of his encounters with any of these persons. In addition the patient continues to live in a changing world in which new difficulties may be encountered every day. Attempts to infer the intentions of some potential foreign adversary are complicated by the fact that this adversary may change intentions any number of times during efforts to infer what they might be. In short, interesting parts of the world change as we are in the process of trying to understand them. This is one matter that may separate discovery, as it is viewed by a philosopher of science, from discovery, as it is viewed by a psychiatrist or a military analyst. The laws of physics may always have held and will continue to do so. Laws governing various aspects of human behavior may not be quite so stationary.

The second temporal element of importance concerns the process of discovery itself. The "playing field" of discovery is certainly not level across all contexts in which it is necessary. The physicist or chemist hoping to provide a more satisfactory or complete account of some phenomenon has at hand an already-existing stock of relevant knowledge to draw upon. Perhaps this more satisfactory explanation lurks within this existing stock of knowledge and can be inferred from it in some way. Although it is true that the experienced criminal investigator or auditor has stocks of background knowledge relevant to matters she is asked to investigate, she may be forced to start from a position of vacuity as far as the *particular* details of the matter she has just begun to investigate. In some cases, specific possible conclusions may be apparent at the outset; a person leaves behind fingerprints linking him with the crime. But in other cases it may be necessary to ask many questions and gather much information before any specific (or refined) hypothesis can be entertained.

The temporal course of discovery itself is just one reason why I will argue in Section 9.2.3 that discovery involves more than just search through what we already have at hand. If we do not ask appropriate or important questions enroute during the discovery process, we may never even have at hand combinations of information from which we may, retroductively, generate possibilities or hypotheses that have some chance of being "true." So the role of *inquiry* is at least as important as the role of *search* in discovery-related activities in many contexts. If we do not ask the "right" questions, some of which may be quite impertinent, we may stand little chance of generating useful or important possibilities.

Another temporal element of discovery involves the order in which events of interest might have occurred. As I mentioned in Section 5.2.1, the temporal ordering of events has inferential significance on its own. One trouble is that we may not be certain about the order in which events of interest actually occurred. The pilot of an aircraft has a checklist that, among other things, prescribes the order in which various control and power settings are to be made prior to takeoff. The investigation of an aircraft accident may provide only inconclusive evidence about whether these settings were made in the proper sequence. Possible orderings of events are themselves hypotheses; different orderings may suggest different explanatory hypotheses. Though it requires no extraordinary imaginative powers to stand evidence items in different temporal orderings, such exercises frequently have considerable heuristic value in generating new hypotheses and new evidence, as I will mention again in Section 9.4.

9.1.4 Discovery, Standpoint, and Frames of Discernment

In Chapters 3 and 4 I drew upon the work of the legal evidence scholars Anderson and Twining on the importance of declaring one's *standpoint* in matters concerning the structuring of argument from evidence to the major conclusions being entertained. Then in Section 4.5.5 I mentioned how the ideas of Anderson and Twining mingle with those of Glenn Shafer in his discussion of *frames of discernment* of hypotheses and how any such frame may submit to various mutations during the course of work on an inference problem. It should not be thought that the related ideas of standpoint and frames of discernment are relevant only to the process of justification or proof; they apply equally to the process of discovery.

In the case of standpoint, the role a person is playing, the stage of discovery this person is in, and the objectives this person may be pursuing all combine to influence what questions this person will ask and, consequently, what hypotheses and evidence this person will generate. It is no source of wonder that different persons having different standpoints or perspectives will tend to generate different hypotheses and evidence regarding the same phenomena or events of interest. Shafer emphasizes that the construction of a frame of discernment is a creative act (1976, 285). Hypotheses that we may generate, revise, or refine depend upon the nature and amount of the evidence we have (as I illustrated in Figure 4.19). In turn, the nature of the hypotheses we discern influences new potential categories of evidence that we may attempt to discover.

There are many works available on the behavioral characteristics of persons whose discoveries have been judged to be exemplary (e.g., Koestler 1964, 674–702; Sternberg 1988; Boden 1991). The discovery-related behavior of the fictional character Sherlock Holmes is well-known and is often taken as a model for such behavior. Salmon lists the following attributes Conan Doyle gave Holmes: keen curiosity, high native intelligence, a fertile imagination, acute powers of perception, a wealth of general information, and extreme ingenuity (1984, 13). Salmon goes on to say that no set of rules can provide a substitute for these abilities; if they existed, we would then have the basis for a logic of discovery. But there is a very interesting connection between Peirce's thoughts on abduction/retroduction and Sherlock Holmes that I will now begin to explore.

9.2 DISCOVERY AND IMAGINATIVE REASONING

Acknowledging the long history of interest in the process of discovery and the imaginative reasoning it entails, I will begin with Peirce's thoughts on the subject. As I mentioned, Peirce believed there to be another form of reasoning by which new ideas come into existence. At various points in his many writings on the topic he used the terms abduction, retroduction, and hypothesis with reference to the generation of new ideas. Unfortunately, Peirce was occasionally vague about the meaning of these terms. The term *abduction* is now in current use among many persons interested in various elements of the process of discovery. There is still substantial vagueness about the meaning attached to this term across the various disciplines in which it is employed. It seems a good idea to begin by hearing from Peirce himself on the topic of discovery, imaginative reasoning, and abduction.

9.2.1 Peirce and Others on Abduction, Retroduction, and Hypothesis

In his second Cambridge Conference Lecture, February 14, 1898, on the topic: *Types of Reasoning,* Peirce makes reference to a logical figure or form of reasoning he traces back to Aristotle (Peirce 1898, Ketner ed., 1992, 140–141). This form of reasoning Peirce called *adopting a hypothesis for the sake of its explanation of known facts.* Peirce expressed this form of reasoning syllogistically as (1898, 140):

If μ were true, π, π', and π'' would follow as miscellaneous consequences.

But π, π', and π'' are in fact true;

Therefore, provisionally, we may suppose that μ is true.

Peirce then tells us that Aristotle appears to have used the term $\alpha\pi\alpha\gamma\omega\gamma\eta$ (apagoge) with reference to this form of reasoning. But Peirce believed this term was wrongly translated as *abduction,* which, from the Latin, has the meaning "leading away from." Peirce proposed that a more appropriate translation of apagoge is *reduction* or *retroduction* (from the Latin, "leading back"). The word *induction* means, from the Latin, "leading toward." There is some confusion here. My colleague and scholar of Aristotle's work, Walter Wehrle, assures me that the correct translation of apagoge is *abduction* and that the Greek $\alpha\nu\alpha\gamma\omega\gamma\eta$ (anagoge) is the exact equivalent of *re[tro]duction.*

Terminological confusion aside, we have no hint from Peirce so far about where hypothesis μ came from in order for it to be an explanation of observed facts π, π', and π''. In another work he begins to tell us something about the origin of explanatory hypotheses. As Peirce relates (1901, on *Abduction and Induction,* Buchler ed., 1955, 150–156):

The first starting of a hypothesis and the entertaining of it, whether as a simple interrogation or with any degree of confidence, is an inferential step I call *abduction* [or *retroduction*]. This will include a preference for any one hypothesis over others which would equally explain the facts, so long as this preference is not based upon any previous knowledge bearing upon the truth of the hypotheses, nor on any testing of any of the hypotheses, after having admitted them on probation. I call all such inference by the peculiar name, *abduction*, because its legitimacy depends upon altogether different principles from those of other kinds of inference.

Thus, for Peirce, hypotheses are often generated in the form of questions, later to be answered by experiment. Referring to the above syllogism, he goes on to explain more about the form of reasoning he has in mind when using the term abduction. He states (1901, 151):

Long before I first classed abduction as a form of inference it was recognized by logicians that the operation of adopting an explanatory hypothesis—which is just what abduction is—was subject to certain conditions. Namely, the hypothesis cannot be admitted, even as a hypothesis, unless it be supposed that it would account for the facts or some of them. The form of the inference, therefore, is this:

The surprising fact, C, is observed;
But if A were true, C would be a matter of course,
Hence, there is reason to suspect that A is true.

But we have to search even further through Peirce's work in order to obtain some idea about what Peirce had in mind as far as the behavioral mechanisms involved in abduction. In fact Peirce had trouble distinguishing between abduction and a perceptual judgment. As he noted (1903, Buchler ed., 1955, 304):

. . . Abductive inference shades into perceptual judgment without any sharp line of demarcation between them; or, in other words, our first premises, the perceptual judgments, are to be regarded as an extreme case of abductive inferences, from which they differ in being absolutely beyond criticism. The abductive suggestion comes to us like a flash. It is an act of *insight*, although of extremely fallible insight. It is true that the different elements of the hypothesis were in our minds before; but it is the idea of putting together what we had never before dreamed of putting together which flashes the new suggestion before our contemplation.

Little wonder that Peirce's ideas about discovery and abduction caused some philosophers to crawl auditorium walls and chew college carpets. How do we form a logic of perceptual judgment and flashes of insight? Many others have recorded instances in which celebrated new ideas or insights came in a flash, often under unusual circumstances (Koestler 1964, 101–120; Penrose 1989, 418–423; Briggs and Peat 1989, 191–200; Boden 1991, 15–28). In several of Peirce's works he draws distinctions between deduction, induction, and abduction. In an article for the *Popular Science Monthly,* August 1878, 470–482 (in Houser and Kloesel 1992, 186–199), he tells us that all inference is either *analytic* (deductive) or *synthetic,* and he distinguishes two forms of synthetic inference: induction and hypothesis. I will return in Section 9.3.1 to Peirce's view of hypothesis as a form of synthetic reasoning; Sherlock Holmes had a different view. Regarding hypothesis (abduction) Peirce tells us: "Hypothesis is where we find some very curious circumstance, which would be explained by supposition that it was a case of a certain general rule, and thereupon adopt that supposition. Or, where we find that in certain respects two objects have a strong resemblance, and infer that they resemble one another strongly in other respects" (Houser and Kloesel 1992, 189).

Though he distinguished between induction and hypothesis (abduction), Peirce allowed that much of scientific inference involved *mixtures* of these two forms of reasoning (Houser and Kloesel 1992, 197). Peirce's analysis on this point correponds with our observations of the cycles of discovery, proof, and choice in various contexts, as I described by means of Figure 9.1. Another distinction among Peirce's terms has been quite important in my attempts to relate his ideas to the task of *generating new evidence;* this distinction involves the terms abduction and retroduction. The thoughts of the philosophers Nicholas Rescher (1978) and Richard Tursman (1987) become important at this point. First, Rescher argues that by the term *abduction,* Peirce referred to the task of *projecting plausible hypotheses* based upon educated guesswork. By the term *retroduction,* Peirce referred to the *eliminative testing of hypotheses* so generated or conjectured (1978, 8). I will later return to Rescher's important thoughts regarding the economics or the efficiency of abductive-retroductive activities during discovery.

Everyone is entitled to have a go at representing the discovery-related processes of interest to Peirce and others. Shown in Figure 9.2 is one rendition of the abductive-retroductive process; it combines the thoughts from Peirce with ideas from Rescher, Tursman, and Hanson. Suppose, at the moment, that you have a body of evidence and a collection of hypotheses $\{H_1, H_2, \ldots, H_n\}$ as possible explanations for this body of evidence. Then, as shown in Figure 9.2a, you obtain an item of evidence E^* that is not explainable by any of the n hypotheses you are currently considering. We might say that E^* is an *anomaly* as far as any of these hypotheses are concerned. One strategy is to try to sweep E^* under the rug. After all, an anomaly here and there might not necessarily be devastating to any hypothesis we entertain (Cohen 1977, 162–166). But the existence of E^* troubles you; in any case its existence has been registered somewhere in your mind, whereupon mental activity, of the sort we would all like to understand, is set in motion.

As so often happens, at some later time while you are occupied by other matters (e.g., mowing the lawn or traveling), your mind chooses to inform you that it has generated a possible explanation for E^*. The subjective experience resembles the "flash of insight" mentioned by Peirce and so many others. You now are able to perceive that new hypothesis H_{n+1} could account

(*a*) **Abduction: Generating a New Hypothesis**

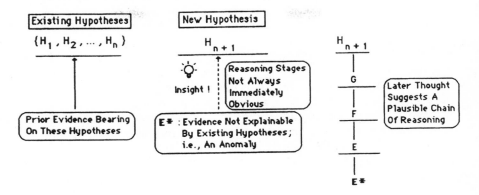

(*b*) **Retroduction and the Testing of a Generated Hypothesis**

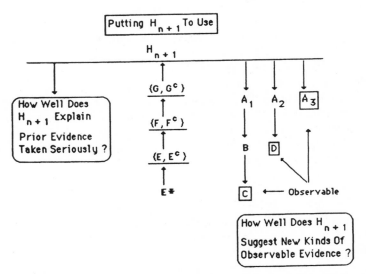

FIGURE 9.2 An interpretation of Peirce's abduction and retroduction.

for the embarrassing anomaly E^*. At the precise moment of insight or even shortly thereafter, you might have some trouble connecting E^* and H_{n+1} by a specific chain of reasoning or argument. But after further thought you begin to form what you regard as a plausible argument linking E^* and H_{n+1}. In other words, you are constructing part of the *inference network* described by Hanson (see Section 9.1.1). As the figure shows, you might say: If E did occur, as reported in evidence E^*, then F could be true; if F is true, then G might follow; and if G is true, then H_{n+1} might be true. Notice in Figure 9.2a that I have made the reasoning chain from E^* to H_{n+1} nondirectional. To explain the insight, we might just as easily have reasoned top-down from H_{n+1} to E.

So you now have a new hypothesis or idea that you have generated, projected, or abducted from anomaly E^*. This new hypothesis might be ridiculed by others if the only thing it explained was this anomaly. You already have other evidence, some of which you may take very seriously. You begin to put this new hypothesis to work according to the retroductive process Rescher described. This process could be the eliminative (Baconian) process Rescher described, or it might proceed in accordance with other inductive methods I have described. First, you might determine, as in Figure 9.2b, the extent to which new hypothesis H_{n+1} accounts for the other evidence you take seriously. In addition, and of great importance, you ask yourself whether this new hypothesis allows you to *generate new evidence*. You might say: "If H_{n+1} were true, then A_1, A_2, and A_3 might have occurred (or will occur) ." But perhaps only A_3 is directly observable; further inferential steps might be necessary (as the figure shows) in order to obtain observable evidence about A_1 and A_2.

This is a good point to return to arguments about the distinction between abduction and induction. As shown in Figure 9.2a, you generated H_{n+1}, from the bottom up, based on evidence E^*. Was this an *inductive* or an *abductive* step? Some believe there to be no sharp distinction between the two (Hacking 1975, 75–76). For others, however, the distinction seems quite clear, in part because there seem to be quite different evaluative criteria for induction and abduction. The philosopher Isaac Levi argues in several of his works that in inductive reasoning we seek to avoid the error of drawing the wrong conclusion from evidence. However, in abductive reasoning we seek not to avoid error but to generate hypotheses that have what he terms "informational virtue" (1983, 41–50; 1984, 92–96, 120–122; 1991, 77–78, 172). Figure 9.2b illustrates some of the "virtues" of H_{n+1} in suggesting new phenomena and, perhaps, in better explaining those we already know about. In Section 2.2.1 I mentioned that *ampliative* inferences extend our present knowledge. Levi cautions that abduction and the generation of a new hypothesis is not necessarily ampliative in this sense because it represents the formation of a conjecture and not a revision in the state of our full beliefs (1991, 172 n.6).

There is one characteristic of the situation in Figure 9.2a that needs further discussion in light of the work of Glenn Shafer on the mutation of hypotheses. The trouble with the situation illustrated in this figure is that it takes no account of instances in which the hypotheses we entertain may exist at *different levels of refinement*. Stated differently, some of the hypotheses we entertain may be quite specific (or refined), while others more vague, imprecise, or diffuse. Shown in Figure 9.3 is a hierarchy of hypotheses at different levels of refinement. Hypotheses farther down in the hierarchy are more refined or specific. What this figure illustrates is simply that from new (and possibly anomalous) evidence E^* we might generate a new or revised hypothesis at

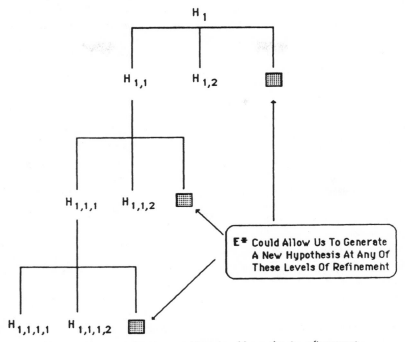

FIGURE 9.3   Abduction and levels of hypothesis refinement.

any level of refinement. In other words, our abductive insight, stimulated by
E*, might not always result in a precisely defined new hypothesis. In part this
depends upon the nature of **E*** and how precisely it allows us to focus on
some possibility or hypothesis. But, even if vague in some respects, a new
hypothesis may still have "informational virtue" or be useful in generating
new observable phenomena.

9.2.2 Abduction, Retroduction, Inference Networks, and the Generation of New Evidence

By examining the purely structural ideas in Figure 9.2, we gain at least some
initial insights about the discovery or generation of new kinds of evidence.
The process shown in this figure involves both "bottom-up" and "top-down"
reasoning. Starting with anomaly **E***, we had evidence searching for an explanation (or hypothesis). Insight, as a result of mental processes no one
understands with any completeness, supplied us an explanation in the form
of H_{n+1}. But now, as I described above, we have a new hypothesis in search
of additional evidence. Remember that H_{n+1} would not be taken seriously,
however plausible the argument linking **E*** and H_{n+1}, if it only explained **E***.
To describe what may happen during this "bottom-up" and "top-down" process as it concerns the generation of evidence, I will expand upon Hanson's
inference network ideas mentioned in Section 9.1.1.

Using Hanson's terms, an explanation of E^* by H_{n+1} "exfoliates quasi-deductively" (top-down) from H_{n+1}. Hanson argues that this same inference network must have been traversed (bottom-up) during the generation of H_{n+1} in the first place. This I illustrated by the chain of reasoning E^*–E–F–G–H_{n+1} in Figure 9.2a. Perhaps, as indicated in this figure, this chain of reasoning was not immediately obvious during the "flash of insight" about H_{n+1} but only became apparent some time later. But now, as Figure 9.2b illustrates, the inference network at issue has become more extensive, since we may reason that H_{n+1} could explain some new observable phenomena as well (C, D, and A_3 in Figure 9.2b). Thus we have generated three new lines of evidence relevant on H_{n+1} and possibly on our other hypotheses as well. So the "quasi-deductive exfoliation" of H_{n+1} becomes more extensive as we begin to put H_{n+1} to use. It becomes even more extensive when we also take on the task of showing the extent to which H_{n+1} explains evidence taken seriously *before* we generated H_{n+1} from E^*.

But there are additional sources of new evidence latent in the process illustrated in Figure 9.2b. I have mentioned that the act of laying out an argument from evidence to hypotheses has merit in identifying new evidence possibly more forceful than what we already have. In Figure 9.2a we have the argument: E^*–E–F–G–H_{n+1}. We currently have evidence E^* about event E but none so far about events F and G. If events F and G are observable, evidence about them would, if credible, be more forceful than evidence E^*, since events F and G are more direct (than E) on H_{n+1}. The chain of reasoning linking E^* and H_{n+1} in Figure 9.2 acknowledges two things. The first is that evidence E^* is only inconclusive on event E; perhaps E did not occur as reported in this evidence. The second is that we presently do not have any evidence about whether or not events F and G occurred. But now, at least, we are stimulated to gather it if we can.

So, putting everything together, H_{n+1} and the processes involved in its generation have allowed us to identify potential evidence about events C, D, A_3, F, and G. But there is more evidence generation to come. All of the potential evidence just listed is what I have termed *directly relevant,* since it can be linked to H_{n+1} by a chain of reasoning. Having some basis in argument for defending the relevance of this potential evidence, we are now stimulated to generate *ancillary evidence* regarding the strength or weakness of each of the links in the chains of reasoning identified by the "exfoliation" of new hypothesis H_{n+1}. Unfortunately, it is one thing to diagram processes such as abduction, retroduction, and the generation of evidence but quite another to recommend how such processes might be effectively enhanced in our everyday inference tasks. Such recommendations rest on other related ideas.

9.2.3 Search, Inquiry, and Heuristics

Ideas and information accumulate, often at a very rapid rate, as the process of discovery unfolds over time. By some means, frequently but not always using computer facilities, we record our ideas and the information we gather. How are we to make use of our expanding idea and information base in order to imagine new hypotheses and new evidence? Suppose that the hypotheses we are currently considering are either incomplete (we recognize that there are other possibilities) or are too vague or undifferentiated to be useful. If we are thinking in terms of inference networks, we might say that our emerging network is currently far too "sparse." In a word, we recognize that the process of discovery must continue. One strategy, easily rejected, for using our idea and information base is to attempt to search through *everything* we have in the hope of finding *something* of value to us in generating new hypotheses and evidence. Such a strategy is not only *inefficient*, it is also *impossible*, as I will discuss in more detail in Section 9.4.1. It would certainly help matters if we knew what to search for. Stated differently, we could proceed more productively if we only knew what questions to ask.

As I have mentioned, we ask questions *about* our existing evidence in order to establish its relevance, credibility, and inferential force during the process of justification or proof of hypotheses we now entertain. But we also have to ask questions *of* our existing evidence in order to generate new hypotheses and new evidence. As I noted in Section 9.2.1, Peirce emphasized that hypotheses are frequently entertained interrogatively or in response to questions we ask. The abductive process in Figure 9.2a may have been set in motion in response to an inquiry about what would explain anomaly E^*. Such a process would never have been initiated if we did not have E^* in the first place; I made no mention at all about where this evidence came from. The questions we ask flow from ideas and information we already have. Perhaps we do not yet have the ideas and information at hand that would allow us to ask the most important questions we should be asking. Our hope is that the other questions that we ask will supply answers leading us to these more important questions. The process of inquiry feeds on itself.

Suppose a conclusion you have drawn in your work turns out to be verifiably wrong and that what actually happened, call it H_t, you never even entertained as a possibility. In hindsight, you now berate yourself for never having generated or "abducted" H_t at any stage of your very careful deliberation. A hindsight critic might easily say: "You did not ask the right questions." But suppose that an equally careful postmortem examination of your base of ideas and information provides no clues for the generation of H_t by anyone else including this hindsight critic. All the elegant search strategies that might have been employed on your idea and information base would not have resulted in the generation of H_t. Your information base was simply incomplete. Even the most careful episodes of investigation or discovery miscarry; patients die of unsuspected ailments, and people are convicted of crimes they did not commit.

Though there is no discovery process presently imaginable whose employment would guarantee eventual convergence to "the truth" in all inferential matters, we might easily suppose that more efficient methods for search and inquiry would greatly assist us during the task of discovery as it is performed in so many different contexts. One important concept employed in such efforts is the idea of a *heuristic,* yet another term employed by Peirce. The term heuristic is commonly used with reference to any device we employ to facilitate intellectual activities such discovery, problem-solving, and learning. Often it is said that a heuristic is a "rule of thumb" that a person might employ in the absence of any rules suggested by a formal analysis of a task. Certain tasks, such as evaluating the force of existing evidence on hypotheses already entertained, submit to various formal analyses, as discussed in Chapters 5 through 8. But discovery-related tasks have not, as yet, submitted to any formal analysis that would apply across the many contexts in which discovery and the exercise of imagination are natural requirements. Lacking formal rules for discovery, we resort to various heuristics.

The works of the mathematician George Pólya have been very influential on the study and employment of heuristics (1945, 1954a, b). In his much-cited work, *How To Solve It,* he tells us that: "Heuristic reasoning is reasoning not regarded as final and strict but as provisional and plausible only, whose purpose is to discover the solution of the present problem" (1945, 113 in 1973 ed.). He goes on to mention that heuristics serve as "scaffolding" in the construction of mathematical proof and that, although necessary, heuristic reasoning should not be confused with rigorous proof.

One of Pólya's associates, the philosopher Imre Lakatos, proposed that we grade the success of any scientific "research program" in terms of its heuristic power in generating new ideas (1980a, b). For Lakatos, a scientific research program consists of major and auxilliary hypotheses (theories) plus a stock of heuristic problem solving methods. As Lakatos noted (1980a, 52): "We may appraise research programmes, even after their elimination, for their *heuristic power:* how many new facts did they produce, how great was their capacity to explain their refutations in the course of their growth?" Research programs that account for already-observed facts but also generate new ones Lakatos called *progressive;* others that do not continue to generate new facts he termed *regressive.* So the term heuristic has also been used to grade the potential of hypotheses in generating new facts (or possible new evidence). This brings to mind Levi's criterion for grading the abduction of a new hypothesis in terms of its "informational virtue." In Figure 9.2b the heuristic power of new hypothesis H_{n+1} is to be graded in terms of the extent to which it generates new observable kinds of evidence such as C, D, and A_3.

In the literature in artificial intelligence (hereafter AI), abduction is frequently defined as *inference to the best explanation* (Peng and Reggia 1987, Neapolitan 1990, 318–319). The trouble with this definition is that it mixes discovery and justification together and thus begs a question. Which explanation is "best" involves *inductive* processes associated with establishing the relevance, credibility, and force of evidence on all hypotheses being entertained. As Peirce and Levi noted, the criteria for abduction simply concern plausibility and information virtue. When we have that flash of *abductive* insight which Peirce described, we have not yet established that our newly generated explanation is best. Inference "to the best explanation" seems to involve the abductive and retroductive steps Rescher described, as illustrated in Figures 9.2*a* and 9.2*b*. But Peirce did note that any inductive testing of a hypothesis frequently involves a certain amount of guesswork; he described such activity as *abductory induction* (1901, Buchler collection, 1955, 152–153).

Followers of the impressive progress made by our colleagues in the field of AI cannot fail to see the influence of Pólya and Lakatos on the matter of problem solving and heuristics. Many tasks we routinely perform are construed in AI as exercises in problem solving, even the task of discovery. One justly acclaimed work in AI on scientific discovery is that of Langley, Simon, Bradshaw, and Zytkow (1987). In this work the authors describe several computer-based systems designed to discover empirical laws. Various iterations of one such system, called BACON, have generated a wide variety of quantitative empirical laws such as Boyle's law on gas pressure, Kepler's third law, and Ohm's law. For Langley and his coworkers scientific discovery is construed as an exercise in *problem solving* in which a key role is played by various heuristic methods for search. What BACON does is to use a variety of quantitative search heuristics in order to discover patterns of invariance among sets of numerical data. Such discovery is said to be "data-driven" and it resembles processes (and heuristics) that they attribute to Francis Bacon for discovering general laws from collections of empirical data (1987, 14).

Langley et al. (1987, 37–62) take a decidedly different position than Reichenbach and Popper (see Section 9.1.1) on the possibility of a logic of scientific discovery. Though they make no claim that they are presently enroute to generating such a logic, Langley et al. view their work as a "progress report" on efforts to better understand the process of discovery. Many other works in AI on heuristics and search could be mentioned, including Douglas Lenat's system EURISKO for generating heuristics (1981, 1983). Lenat views heuristics as compiled hindsights and sees no reason why we should not use heuristic methods to determine what heuristic methods we should employ next in some episode of problem solving. Discovery-related work in AI is summarized, quite enthusiastically, by Margaret Boden (1990, see especially ch. 8). But not all persons in AI are equally enthusiastic about the extent to which work on systems like BACON have captured the intellectual processes requisite in scientific discovery (e.g., see Holland et al. 1989, 320–342).

I have not found equating discovery with problem solving to be necessarily compelling in all contexts in which the discovery of new hypotheses and evidence is required. The term "problem solving" suggests that there is a solution "out there"; all we have to do is to find it. In science and engineering we have recourse to empirical tests to observe whether conjectures, hypotheses, or guesses are correct, in which case we might say that a problem has been solved. But what about discovery as problem solving in areas such as law, auditing, history, and military intelligence analysis? In such areas, how do we ever determine for sure that problems are solved, except in the very short run?

In the case of Sacco and Vanzetti the prosecutor, Frederick G. Katzmann, might certainly have agreed that *his problem* had been solved when the jury returned a guilty verdict and when this verdict resisted subsequent attempts to have it overturned. But the problem of determining whether Sacco and/ or Vanzetti were truly guilty of the crime for which they were charged remains to this day and may never be "solved" to everyone's satisfaction. Is it fair to say that the discovery efforts of an auditor have resulted in a solved problem when this auditor certifies a client's financial statement as being free of material misstatement? In the mind of the auditor it might, at least temporarily, be viewed as solved, since she can now collect a fee and go on to another assignment. But, upon further deliberation, this auditor may contemplate questions she did not ask and data she did not examine and so question whether there has been any real problem solving. The historian interested in whether Mary Queen of Scots was at least witting, and possibly a participant, in the murder of her husband Lord Darnley might not be willing to view further discovery on this issue as problem-*solving* activity.

There is much more involved in productive discovery than just the generation of novel ideas. A murder has been committed outside a bowling alley in Toledo, Ohio. The investigation proceeds at a very slow pace; citizens and the press become restive. In a flash of insight a detective suggests that the culprit might have been the Archbishop of Canterbury. This is certainly a novel hypothesis. Asked to show what existing evidence suggests this possibility, the detective mentions evidence that a person in clerical garb was seen in the vicinity of the crime at the time it was committed. When asked to produce a chain of reasoning that would link this evidence with the hypothesis that His Grace committed the crime, the detective can produce none that meets even the weakest standard of *plausibility*. In his analysis of Peirce's work on scientific discovery, Rescher argues that the most frequently overlooked element of Peirce's thinking was his emphasis on the *economy of research* and that the major ingredient influencing this economy is a scientist's sense or instinct of what is *plausible* (1978, 41–91).

As Rescher puts it: "To this idea of the economy of research—of cost-benefit analysis in inductive inquiry and reasoning—Peirce gave as central a place in his methodology of science as words can imagine to assign. Yet no other part of this great man's philosophizing has fallen on stonier ground" (1978, 72). Rescher mentions how considerations of plausibility provide guidance in the conduct of inquiry and that our sense or instinct of what seems plausible has developed as a result of our evolution. In other words, we are products of the same processes being investigated in science. This same idea is reflected in Rescher's views on the concept of *rationality* (1988, 176–190). A sense of what seems plausible is also called "commonsense." As I noted earlier, our legal system supposes that ordinary persons come with a stock of "commonsense wisdom" in the form of generalizations that they can apply in their role of fact finders in trials at law.

Rescher then summarizes Peirce's ideas on the costs and benefits of pursuing inquiry regarding some hypothesis. On the benefits side may be listed such considerations as closeness of fit to data, explanatory value, novelty, simplicity, accuracy of detail, precision, parsimony, concordance with other accepted theories, even antecedent likelihood and intuitive appeal. On the cost side we have time, effort, energy, and money necessary to pursue any further discovery stimulated by some hypothesis (1978, 68–69). Such considerations, Rescher says, are necessary in decisions about which hypotheses ". . . merit immediate checking, which can be put off until tomorrow, and which can wait until Niagra runs dry" (1978, 66). The hypothesis that the Archbishop of Canterbury committed the murder in Toledo, Ohio, has only novelty going for it and thus is one that might be postponed until Niagra runs dry.

I noted Peirce's suggestion that new hypotheses are often obtained in answer to questions that are asked. The asking of questions, or the process of *inquiry* or *interrogation*, has itself received considerable attention from philosophers and others. One person whose work I will draw upon further as we proceed is Jaakko Hintikka (Hintikka and Hintikka 1983; Hintikka 1983; Hintikka and Bachman 1991; Hintikka 1992). Hintikka argues that discovery and the inductive process of justification can be construed in terms of what he terms the *interrogative model of inquiry*. In this model the scientist or other investigator plays a game against nature having the following stages. The investigator begins with some theoretical premise from which a conclusion is to be drawn. At each stage of this game the investigator has a choice between a *deductive move*, in which a conclusion is drawn from what the investigator has at hand, and an *interrogative move*, in which the investigator puts a question to nature and records the answer, if one is given. Such answers provide new premises upon which to base similar move decisions at succeeding stages. As I will mention in Section 9.3.1, Hintikka argues that the abduction, as described by Peirce and as practiced by Sherlock Holmes, can be construed in terms of this interrogative model.

9.2.4 Argument Structuring, Probabilities, and Heuristics

I believe the asking of questions *about evidence* and the asking of questions *of evidence* are related activities. For example, questions we ask *about* the credibility of the source of a certain item of evidence may, in turn, stimulate questions leading to the generation of a new hypothesis or possibility. In response to questions about a source's veracity we obtain answers suggesting that this source is untruthful. Then, asking questions *of* this damaging veracity-relevant evidence, we may be further led to inquire why this person should wish to deceive us about this particular matter. Answers to such questions might lead us to generate a major hypothesis that we had not previously entertained. One of the distinct virtues of careful argument structuring, as a Wigmore diagram or as an inference network, is that we identify sources of uncertainty which we believe to be lurking between our evidence and our hypotheses. As Glenn Shafer has emphasized, the construction of any probability argument is a creative exercise. My first point is that argument structuring can have distinct heuristic merit in generating new questions *of and about* the evidence we have. It all depends upon how *plausible* are the arguments we construct.

In Chapter 3 I went to some length to illustrate how generalizations are required to license or warrant connections between one link and another in a chain of reasoning (or between one node and another in an inference network). In many instances, such as in law, these generalizations are matters of the "common sense" mentioned by Peirce and in legal treatises. In other instances, such as in science and engineering, generalizations may be based on a stock of existing knowledge about the phenomenon of concern. In any case, the plausibility of such generalizations is a matter of natural concern. You may or may not have agreed that all of the generalizations I invoked in defense of the relevance of Officer Connolly's testimony in the Sacco and Vanzetti case (Section 3.1.6) were plausible. There is no general standard according to which we may grade the plausibility of generalizations that we may assert. One reason why the process of argument construction seems to be an art form is that there are no rules showing us which generalizations to invoke as we attempt to link evidence to hypotheses.

The testing of a generalization to see if it holds in some present case requires evidence, in some cases of a statistical nature if the processes of interest are frequentistic in nature. If they are not, then we have to ask a variety of different questions whose answers may tell us whether or not this generalization may hold in the present case in which it is being invoked. Thus the invoking and the testing of generalizations that license stages of reasoning are also heuristic exercises in the generation of new evidence. The fact that the evidence used to test a generalization is ancillary in nature does not mean that it is uninteresting or unimportant. As I noted above, ancillary evidence may lead to the generation of new hypotheses.

As far as the generation of new evidence is concerned, I believe a process or activity can be said to have heuristic merit if it is useful in generating questions either of or about existing evidence. Consider the various probabilistic strategies for assessing the inferential force of evidence discussed in Chapter 5 and applied in Chapters 7 and 8. It might usually be supposed that probabilistic theories only concern justificiation (or proof) and not discovery. It is certainly true that Bayesian, Baconian, Shaferian, or fuzzy reasoning systems are not theories of discovery. Nothing is said in any of these formal theories about where new hypotheses come from. At the same time, however, I believe that they do have certain heuristic merit in generating questions that we might profitably ask about the evidence before us.

Bayesian likelihood ratios for the inferential force of various forms and combinations of evidence (Chapters 7 and 8) are certainly informative about the various kinds of questions that we need to ask about evidence. For example, these ratios ask us to judge how rare are events at various stages of reasoning; we suppose that any defense of rareness judgments rests upon background information that we could be asked to supply. Bayesian likelihood ratios also alert us to the fact that what we believe about some source of evidence can be at least as interesting inferentially as the event(s) reported in the evidence. Thus we are led to inquire whether any attribute of a source's credibility is state dependent. These likelihood ratios are also important in generating questions regarding other evidential subtleties associated with such factors as synergism and redundancy. We need to inquire about the extent to which the force of one item of evidence may be influenced by other evidence we have.

The Baconian system of evidential weight assessment makes us constantly aware of a fundamental consideration: What questions have we not yet asked in the process of testing the generalizations that license links in the chains of reasoning we identify? As the process of discovery proceeds, certain possibilities are eliminated and others are retained. If a definite conclusion is required, we may accept one possibility in preference to others. The possibility or hypothesis we accept is the one that has resisted our best efforts to eliminate any of our hypotheses on the basis of a variety of different evidential tests. But the elimination of hypotheses is a serious matter. Suppose we eliminate some hypothesis that later turns out to be the one we should have accepted. Critics will say that we have snatched defeat from the jaws of victory; we had "the truth" and let it slip away. So, in the process of hypothesis elimination, we have to rule out as many factors as we can for keeping some hypothesis "alive."

The system of belief functions devised by Glenn Shafer makes us attentive to the fact that our hypotheses themselves may change as we discover new evidence. Some evidence allows us to refine hypotheses or make them more specific; other evidence may force us to retreat to a coarser level of hypothesis discernment. As I illustrated in Figure 9.3, a new hypothesis can be generated at any level of refinement. Hypotheses at any level may be heuristically valuable in generating new evidence and new possibilities. Finally, the work on fuzzy reasoning alerts us to the nature of the evidence we will often discover. Testimonial evidence that a witness has "weak eyesight" or who "frequently lies" is fuzzy in nature and prompts us to obtain more precise evidence if we can.

9.2.5 Discovery and Chaos

In Section 9.1.1 I mentioned Salmon's argument that discovery does not always proceed in logical steps. On his account discovery often involves a person whose wandering mental activity consists of daydreams, reveries, and irrelevant free associations; such mental wanderings frequently take an investigator down blind alleys. On the surface at least (or at a conscious level), mental activities during discovery frequently seem disorganized or unsystematic. In fact we might say, as others have done, that they are often *chaotic* in nature. The study of apparently chaotic processes, in which "islands of order" are often revealed, is now being pursued by researchers in many different disciplines. Chaotic processes of current interest include complex phenomena such as weather patterns, turbulence in fluids, cosmic events, economic trends, cardiac arrhythmias, and population dynamics in different species of plants and animals. There are many published works in this area; some are quite technical (e.g., Mandelbrodt 1983; Barnsley 1988), while others are generally readable (Gleick 1987; Briggs and Peat 1989; Stewart 1989; Kellert 1993). Ideas from the study of chaotic processes are interesting and at least descriptively useful in discussions of complex mental activities such as the process of discovery.

One idea is that the "flashes of insight," so commonly described as accompanying episodes of discovery, result from observations or thoughts that fall at the intersection of two different frames of reference. At several points I have discussed a person's frame of reference in terms of the Anderson and Twining concerns about standpoint and in terms of Shafer's idea of frames of discernment. In his work *The Act of Creation*, Arthur Koestler tells us that creative insights often occur as a result of what he termed the *bisociation* of different frames of reference (1964, 32–97). Trapped in one frame of reference, a solution we are seeking eludes us because it exists on a *different* frame of reference. But some question or observation can serve to put us at an intersection with this different frame of reference. Recently Koestler's ideas about flashes of insight have been cast in terms used in the study of chaotic processes (Briggs and Peat 1989, 192–194).

As an illustration of a chaos interpretation of flashes of insight in terms of bisociation, or the shifting from one frame of reference to another, consider the situation shown in Figure 9.4. Suppose in a homicide investigation it is definitely believed that the victim's death was the result of a criminal act. The deceased was found in a pool of blood and died of head injuries that could not have been self-inflicted or the result of accident. In addition a small quantity of cocaine was found on the deceased and a much larger quantity (too large for his own personal use) was found in the victim's house. At the moment police investigators believe that the victim was both a user and a pusher of narcotics. Their major suspicion is that the victim died as a result of a drug deal gone sour. We might say that their beliefs now exist on the "narcotics frame" shown in Figure 9.4. They begin their search and inquiry processes under the assumption that someone connected with traffic in narcotics killed this victim.

Using terms suggested by Briggs and Peat, we can give a chaos account of what now happens. Let point A in Figure 9.4, called an *attractor,* represent the narcotics evidence that the investigators now have. They observed this

Gambling Frame

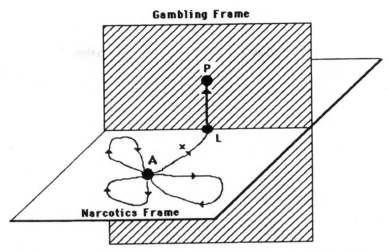

FIGURE 9.4   Abduction and chaos (after Koestler, A., 1964, 107).

evidence themselves and have confidence in its credibility. Their subsequent investigations involving search and inquiry take them on the various paths (all blind alleys) indicated by the wandering lines with arrows on the narcotics frame. What they are attempting to discover is the target possibility P, which represents the person(s) who committed the homicide. Briggs and Peat tell us that these wanderings resemble the *limit cycles* observable in chaotic processes. A limit cycle is any form of recurrent, regular, or cyclical behavior of a physical or mental process. Observe that all but one of the paths come back to A. All of the paths that come back to A reflect the investigators' present belief that the homicide must have been caused by someone in the narcotics trade (either a customer of the victim or one of his suppliers).

The trouble is that P does not lie on the narcotics frame of reference. What happens now can be described in several different ways, one of which is suggested by chaos theory. On one wandering, shown by the path marked x on the narcotics frame, an investigator makes inquiry associated with the victim's traffic in narcotics and the money he presumably made as a result. Bank records, obtained under a subpoena, indicate that he deposited sums of money in amounts not consistent with the salary he earned in his legal job. But these records also indicate that he regularly withdrew large sums of money and that his account presently shows a deficit. It is at this point that the investigator asks a question, which we will later describe (in Hintikka's terms) as being *strategically right*. "What did the victim do with all the money he made in the traffic of narcotics?" Upon further inquiry, the investigator discovers that the victim was a regular gambler and had recently lost large sums of money.

The answer to this strategically correct question is shown as point L in Figure 9.4. In chaos terms it may be described as a *bifurcation,* a point that lies at the intersection of two frames of reference. In chaos theory some bifurcations lead to order, and some lead to further chaos. As Briggs and Peat put it: "At a critical point in this bubbling of thoughts, a bifurcation is reached where a small piece of information or a trivial observation . . . becomes amplified, causing thought to branch to a new frame of reference—a plane that contains the target" (1989, 193). To bring this example to a close, suppose that from L the investigators now shift their frame of reference to the "gambling frame" in Figure 9.4. Eventually they discover P, a person associated with gambling but not narcotics, who later confesses to the crime. In actual episodes of discovery, however, we may encounter many such frame-of-reference bifurcations and be required to shift our frame of reference many times before we experience any flash of insight that leads to the possibility we seek.

9.3 EVIDENCE, SIGNS, AND SEMIOTICS

In my attempt in Section 2.1.1 to find a definition of evidence I made reference to Ian Hacking's argument that, prior to the 1600s, progress in understanding inductive inference was retarded because there was no conception of evidence that included *things that could point to other things.* If Hacking's analysis is correct, before the 1600s evidence was considered only in terms of authoritative records or testimony. If we expand just a bit on Hacking's idea, we can easily interpret any mixture of deductive, inductive, and abductive reasoning encountered in any natural context as an exercise in discovering and interpreting the signs of nature. Whether in science and engineering, accident or criminal investigation, medical diagnosis, historical research, auditing, or any area in which we draw conclusions about hypotheses generated from discovered evidence, the essential task becomes one of trying to correctly read the signs provided by nature.

There is a science of signs, called *semiotics* (there are variations in the spelling of this term, as I will mention). One of the matters making this such a difficult science is that there are so many different kinds of signs conveying so many different kinds of meaning. The words a person utters in testimony are signs of this person's thoughts. The printed words recording the pronouncements of Aristotle, St. Augustine, Galen, or Hippocrates are signs of thoughts allegedly held by these figures of authority as they read the signs of nature. The can of dog food in your neighbor's kitchen is a sign of the presence of a dog. The clothes you wear and the expressions on your face are signs as well. In fact, any of the forms of evidence that I listed in Figure 3.11 are easily construed as signs of one kind or another. From this list one might expect there to have been a regular traffic in ideas between scholars of evidence in law, philosophy, and probability and scholars of signs in the field of semiotics. However, few such associations are to be found, a misfortune I believe. Scholars of evidence and semioticians frequently labor in the same vineyards.

One point of contact between persons in these areas involves the writings of Sir Arthur Conan Doyle and his celebrated *fictional* character Sherlock Holmes. I have set off the word fictional because, for all intents and purposes, Holmes might just as well have been alive. One indication is the array of journals and other works in which Holmes's attitude and his cases are subjected to analyses whose detail represents more than just good-humored or playful study. Among the periodicals are *The Sherlock Holmes Journal, The Baker Street Journal, Baker Street Studies, The Baker Street Gasogene, and Sherlockian Studies.* The full array of scholarship on the details of Holmes and his cases can best be observed in the wide range of entries in the 18-page (three columns per page) bibliography in volume 2 of the Baring-Gould *Annotated Sherlock Holmes* (1967, vol. 2, 807–824). The topic of discovery is a very natural place to bring together evidence scholars and semioticians since, as it turns out, there is more than just a superficial connection between the thoughts of Peirce on abduction and the discovery methods of Sherlock Holmes.

9.3.1 Conan Doyle, Bell, Holmes, and Peirce

It has recently been remarked that Sherlock Holmes ". . . will prove to be one of the most remarkable phenomena of the creative impulse" (Lellenberg 1987, 4). This particular impulse belonged to Sir Arthur Conan Doyle (1859–1930). Conan Doyle spent his childhood in Edinburgh, was sent off to a Jesuit boarding school (Stoneyhurst) in England, and in 1881 received a medical degree from the University of Edinburgh. While in medical school Conan Doyle encountered Dr. Joseph Bell (1837–1911), professor of surgery at the Royal Infirmary, Edinburgh, and (in 1887) president of the Royal College of Surgeons of Edinburgh. If Conan Doyle needed a model for Sherlock Holmes, he could hardly have found a better one than Dr. Bell. Bell's observational and diagnostic abilities were, charitably, extraordinary. There are many recorded instances in which Bell drew correct accurate and detailed conclusions about the illness, occupation, habits, and many other behavioral and physical characteristics of patients on the basis of observations of matters commonly overlooked by others (e.g., Liebow 1982, especially 125–149; Hall 1977, 70–90). The observational and inferential feats of Bell and Sherlock Holmes are very similar.

There are many biographies of Conan Doyle (e.g., Carr 1949; Hall 1977; Lellenberg 1987 [a collection of thirteen biographical sketches]) and of Dr. Joe Bell (Liebow 1982). One lingering controversy concerns the extent to which Conan Doyle patterned Sherlock Holmes after Dr. Bell. In some works the influence of Bell on Sherlock Holmes is given prominence (Liebow 1982; Sebeok and Umiker-Sebeok 1983, 30–38). Indeed Conan Doyle himself mentions the influence of Bell (Sebeok and Umiker-Sebeok 1983, 30–31). In other works, however, the view that Bell was the prototype for Sherlock Holmes is not unqualified (Hall 1977, 70–90; Truzzi 1983, 58). It is recorded that Conan Doyle's son Adrian was quite impressed with his father's inferential capabilities; perhaps Sir Arthur's own observational and inferential skills were often reflected in Sherlock Holmes (Costello 1991, 7–11). Costello notes that Conan Doyle was himself a consulting detective and summarizes twenty-eight cases that Conan Doyle either investigated or commented upon. One in particular was the Sacco and Vanzetti case I have mentioned several times. Conan Doyle believed that the evidence showed that Sacco and Vanzetti were executed not as murderers but as anarchists (Costello 1991, 214–217).

Who or what provided Conan Doyle with the inspiration for the character Sherlock Holmes is not an issue in our present discussion of discovery. What does matter, however, is that there an especially interesting kinship involving the investigative methods of Sherlock Holmes and the abductive reasoning described by Peirce. For insight about this connection we turn first to a work of the semioticians Umberto Eco and Thomas Sebeok entitled *The Sign of Three: Dupin, Holmes, Peirce* (1983). This work is a collection of ten essays all of which concern the process of discovery, abduction, and the investigative methods employed by Holmes and by C. Auguste Dupin (a character in the detective stories of Edgar Allen Poe). In the preface to this work Eco and Sebeok tell us how, often quite by chance, they became aware of the works of scholars in various parts of the world, all of whom had a common interest in Holmes, Peirce, and the process of abduction. The authors further tell us of their hope that *The Sign of Three* will be of interest not only to fans of Sherlock Holmes but will also be important in logic, epistemology, and the philosophy of science. To this I add that, for anyone interested in the study of evidence and its discovery, this work is a feast!

There is little if any evidence that Conan Doyle was aware of Peirce's work on abduction; although it seems likely that Peirce might at least have heard about the early Sherlock Holmes stories (Sebeok and Umiker-Sebeok 1983, 50, n.11). In their offering in *The Sign of Three* (ch. 2) the Sebeoks provide an interesting comparison between Peirce, as detective, and Holmes, as semiotician. In this comparison it emerges that both Peirce and Holmes apply abductive reasoning in solving their cases. In 1879 Peirce took a steamer from Boston to New York. As he left the steamer on his arrival in New York, he realized that he had left behind an overcoat and an expensive Tiffany watch. When he returned to his room to retrieve them, they were missing. Peirce describes the abductive means by which he succeeded in identifying one of the ship's waiters who had in fact stolen these articles (Sebeok and Umiker-Sebeok 1983, 11–19).

I mentioned earlier that Peirce's work on abduction (or retroduction/hypothesis) is subject to different interpretations. Recall in Section 9.2.1 my mention of Rescher's argument that abduction involves the generation of a new hypothesis but retroduction involves the testing of a generated hypothesis (see Figure 9.2). In their chapter the Sebeoks's make reference to passages in several of Holmes's cases that provide a connection between Holmes and Peirce on the matter of discovery; here are just two examples. In the case *A Study in Scarlet* Holmes is attempting to describe to Watson the means by which he was able to solve the case in just three days. In the process, Holmes says (Baring-Gould 1967, vol. 1, 231):

> In solving a problem of this sort, the grand thing is to be able to reason backwards. That is a very useful accomplishment, and a very easy one, but people do not practise it much. In the everyday affairs of life it is more useful to reason forwards, and so the other comes to be neglected. There are fifty who can reason synthetically for one who can reason analytically.

Watson confesses that he does not understand; Holmes continues:

> I hardly expected that you would. Let me see if I can make it clearer. Most people, if you describe a train of events to them, will tell you what the result would be. They can put those events together in their minds, and argue from them that something will come to pass. There are few people, however, who, if you told them a result, would be able to evolve from their own inner consciousness what the steps were which led up to that result. This power is what I mean when I talk of reasoning backwards or analytically.

The Sebeoks's interpret Holmes's *backward reasoning* to be Peirce's *retroduction* (1983, 39). But, as I mentioned briefly in Section 9.2.1, Peirce specifically referred to abduction/retroduction as being synthetic in nature. For Holmes (i.e., Conan Doyle) analysis or "backward reasoning" involves finding an explanation for some observed result.

In another case, *The Five Orange Pips*, Holmes tells Watson (Baring-Gould 1967, vol. 1, 398):

> The ideal reasoner . . . would, when he has once been shown a single fact in all its bearings, deduce from it not only all the chain of events which led up to it, but also all the results which would follow from it.

This description certainly brings to mind the bottom-up and top-down reasoning illustrated in Figure 9.2.

Not all of the papers collected in the *Sign of Three* are in agreement about the nature of the discovery processes employed by Sherlock Holmes. Two of the ten chapters in *The Sign of Three* were provided by the logicians Jaakko and Merrill Hintikka. In the first of these chapters (1983, ch. 7, 154–169) the Hintikkas argue that Holmes's inferential feats involved the interplay of careful observations, deductions, and the asking of *strategically right* questions. In the next chapter Jaakko Hintikka defines a strategically right question to be one ". . . whose answers are likely to be most informative and to open up further lines of successful questioning" (1983, ch. 8, 170). In these chapters we have a construal of Holmes's discovery methods in terms of the interrogative model of inquiry I mentioned in Section 9.2.3. At any stage of inquiry in a game against nature, a person has a choice between a deductive move based upon what is at hand and an inquiry move in which the person puts a question to nature. Citing several passages from Holmes's cases, the Hintikkas argue that Sherlock Holmes was particularly adept at playing this interrogative game.

There is another interesting element of the Hintikkas's work that bears upon a feature of the abductive process I described in Figure 9.2*a*. As this diagram shows, a new possibility suddenly occurs to us (in a flash of insight), and we may, at the time, have no immediate conscious awareness of the stages by which this possibility was generated. The Hintikkas describe a passage from *A Study in Scarlet* involving Holmes's first meeting with Watson. Holmes has just been introduced to Watson and remarks upon Watson's having been in Afghanistan; Watson is astonished by Holmes's correct perception. Later, remarking on this accurate perception, Watson says that Holmes must have been previously informed. Holmes replies (Baring-Gould 1967, vol 1, 160):

> Nothing of the sort. I *knew* you came from Afghanistan. From long habit the train of thoughts ran so swiftly through my mind that I arrived at the conclusion without being conscious of intermediate steps. There were such steps, however.

Holmes then makes explicit to Watson the chains of reasoning he earlier employed without conscious awareness.

Having an interest in such matters, the Hintikkas tell us that chains of reasoning from background information, to evidence, and then to conclusions can be "completely unconscious" (1983, 162). They go on to say that the question is ". . . whether the allegedly unconscious steps of reasoning are traversed so quickly as to escape active attention or whether they are sometimes truly accessible to conscious reflexion and built right into one's unedited sense impressions." The Hintikkas prefers the latter explanation and add (1983, 164): "At other times, we seem to be presented with a complete reasoner who can in his mind run so swiftly through a long series of intermediate steps, following rules of deduction, that he himself need not be immediately conscious of them."

Others have taken an interest in mental phenomena that seem to reside below the surface of our awareness. In his 1866 *Treatise on Physiological Optics,* the physicist Hermann von Helmholtz introduced the term *unconscious inference* to explain certain attributes of our sensory-perceptual experiences (a relevant exerpt appears in Warren and Warren 1968, 171–203). Helmholtz's thoughts on such matters have been much discussed and have formed a source of controversy among psychologists (e.g., Boring 1942, 264; 1950, 308–311; 1963, 13–14; Warren and Warren 1968, 17–18; Kaufman 1974, 13–14). Here, briefly, is the essence of Helmholtz's concept of unconscious inference. When we observe an object and its various properties such as size, shape, distance, and color, our sensory experience seems immediate. However, given what we know about such matters as the geometry of vision, there must have been some "mental calculations" performed in order for us to perceive this object. In other words, there must have been some processing steps interposed between the arrival of visual stimuli from this object and our subsequent awareness of its size, shape, distance, and so forth. Helmholtz referred to these processing stages as inferences about which we have no conscious awareness. There has been some discussion about what sorts of "mental calculations" our perceptions might involve (Kaufman 1974, 349).

But there seems to be a difference between Holmes's being able, after the fact, to reconstruct the stages of his inference for the amazement of Watson and our being able to reconstruct the stages by which we perceive some object. My friend Carl Harris just walked into my office, and I see him instantly in three dimensions, in perfect focus, right side up, and in living color. Try as I might, I cannot bring to my conscious awareness the processing stages (or mental calculations) by means of which I obtained this virtually immediate perception. The reader interested in further discussion of mental processes associated with imaginative discovery and other activities that seem to lie below the surface of our awareness should consult *The Emperor's New Mind* (Penrose 1989, particularly chs. 9 and 10).

9.3.2 Umberto Eco, William of Baskerville, and Peirce's Abduction

Regarding the processes of discovery, imaginative reasoning, and abduction, others besides Conan Doyle have had remarkably creative impulses; one such person is the semiotician, medieval scholar, and novelist Umberto Eco. Many persons first hear about Eco in connection with his best-selling novels: *The Name of the Rose* (1986a) and *Foucault's Pendulum* (1988). But his works on semiotics and abduction are also "best-sellers" among persons interested in these matters (e.g., 1979a, b, 1986b, 1990, and of course his 1983 work with Sebeok: *The Sign of Three*). In the *Name of the Rose* Eco describes the investigative exploits of a learned medieval Franciscan monk, Brother William of Baskerville. Among the things being investigated by Brother William is a series of gruesome murders that take place in a certain abbey in Italy. Brother William's investigative methods and talents are described for us by his disciple, the novice Benedictine monk Brother Adso of Melk. Holmes had his Watson, William of Baskerville had his Adso.

At one point in the exploits of Sherlock Holmes, Conan Doyle brought an end to Sherlock Holmes, or so it seemed. In *The Final Problem* (Baring-Gould 1967, vol. 2, 301–318) Holmes and his arch-enemy, the villain Moriarty, fall from a mountain precipice, locked together in mortal combat, into a "dreadful cauldron of swirling water and seething foam" of a river in Switzerland. Partly in response to enraged readers, Holmes is resuscitated to fight other battles against the forces of evil. Unfortunately, we shall probably never hear more of brother William's investigative exploits, since Adso tells us that he died of the plague. As the *Name of the Rose* begins, Brothers William and

Adso have arrived in the vicinity of the abbey in which the murders subsequently take place. They are greeted by several brothers from the abbey, whereupon Brother William extends his appreciation to them for interrupting their search for a horse whose characteristics, name (Brunellus), and present location he proceeds to describe with perfect accuracy. Everyone is astonished in much the same way as Edinburgh medical students and Watson were astonished at the inferential feats of Dr. Joseph Bell and Sherlock Holmes.

Adso, of course, wishes to know how Brother William could have obtained such knowledge. Brother William replies (1986a, 18–19):

> "My good Adso," my master said, "during our whole journey I have been teaching you to recognize the evidence through which the world speaks to us like a great book. Alanus de Insulis said that
>
> *omnis mundi creatura*
> *quasi liber et pictura*
> *nobis est in speculum*
>
> and he was thinking of the endless array of symbols with which God, throught His creatures, speaks to us of the eternal life. But the universe is even more talkative than Alanus thought, and it speaks to us not only of ultimate things (which it always does in an obscure fashion), but also of closer things, and then it speaks quite clearly."

Such is the depth of Eco's scholarship that readers of *The Name of the Rose* might wish they had access to some reference source that identifies the many real-life characters who enter and exit and that provides translations of the many Latin passages that appear. There is such a reference source, it is called: *The Key to The Name of the Rose* (Haft, White and White 1987). From this key we learn that Alanus de Insulis (c. 1115–1202) was a French theologian who, among other things, used mathematics to try to prove the truth of doctrines he expressed in a work *The Art of the Catholic Faith*. The translation provided of the above Latin passage is "every creature of the world, like a picture and a book, appears to us as a mirror."

We might argue with Brother William's assessment of the clarity with which nature speaks to us about "closer things." You may recall from Section 1.3 the passage from Israel Zangwill's work *The Big Bow Mystery* that Wigmore used to begin his *Science of Judicial Proof*. The character, Mr. Grodman, says (in all reverence) that in appraising the value of evidence or the trails left by the Creator, we have to keep ourselves from being baffled by the myriad of red herrings the Creator has drawn across our paths. Both Conan Doyle and Eco had the luxury of being able to make things turn out just right for Sherlock Holmes and Brother William. However, the startling conclusions drawn by Dr. Joseph Bell, in real life, were not always accurate (Sebeok and Umiker-Sebeok 1983, 31). The signs of nature, as evidence, are always incomplete and inconclusive, and come to us from sources (including our own observations) having any possible gradation of credibility.

We have taken a sample of Eco, as novelist; here is a sample of Eco as semiotician and logician. Eco (1983; 1979a, 131–133; 1986b, 39–43), along with others (e.g., Bonfantini and Proni 1983), argues that there is more than one species of abduction to consider and that any species of abduction, as well as deduction and induction, involves the interpretation of signs. As Eco notes (1986b, 40), "Abduction is, therefore, the tentative and hazardous tracing of a system of signification rules which will allow the sign to acquire its meaning." We might here recall Hanson's explanation of retroduction in terms of inference networks. Chains of reasoning link a sign (or observable evidence) with hypotheses concerning its meaning. An important question raised by Eco, Bonfantini, and Proni, concerns whether the abduction performed, for example, by a criminal investigator is necessarily the same as the abduction performed by a scientist. The answer seems to be that there are discernible differences in abduction, as practiced in different contexts, representing the following ascending levels of originality or creativity:

One form of abduction, said to be *overcoded* or a *hypothesis*, exists when we use some already-established law or convention, automatically or quasi-automatically, as a basis for explaining a sign. As an example, Eco (1979a, 133) cites an experience described by Peirce. On a visit to a certain province in Turkey, Peirce observed a man on horseback surrounded by four men who were holding a canopy over his head. Peirce thought that only the governor of the province would be so honored, so he inferred that the man on horseback was the governor. The preexisting law or convention that Peirce invoked to explain his observation on this particular occasion was one stating that a canopy being held over someone's head is a sign of honor. A notch higher we have what Eco terms *undercoded abduction*. In such instances the selection of an explanation for a sign is made from an array of possible known explanations. An example given by Eco (1986b, 42) is Kepler's choice of an ellipse to explain his observations of the orbit of Mars. He had a choice of course from among other closed geometric curves.

At the next level we have *creative abduction* in which an explanation for a sign or pattern of signs has to be invented, there being no ready stock of possible explanations. This is where real guesswork comes in, of exactly the sort encountered by a criminal investigator. In both overcoded and undercoded abductions there are ". . . preexisting explanations of the same kind that have already proven to be plausible in other cases. In other words, in over- and undercoded abductions one uses explanations that already held for different results. In creative abductions one is not sure that the explanation one has selected is a 'reasonable' one" (Eco 1986b, 43).

Eco also tells us of instances involving what he terms *meta-abductions* (1983, 220). Such abductions occur in contexts, such as criminal investigation, in which an investigator may have to act upon or accept an abduction without being able to test the validity of all stages of reasoning from sign to explanation. Of course such acceptance involves many risks. Here we have one major difference between the scientist and the detective. As Eco notes, "Detectives are rewarded by society for their impudence in betting by metaab-duction, whereas scientists are socially rewarded for their patience in testing their abductions" (1983, 220). Thus Eco has brought us a step closer to understanding what may be involved in discovery and the imaginative reasoning it involves. In different contexts the new hypothesis or explanation H_{n+1} in Figure 9.2 may have been suggested by our mind's rumination over explanations that have worked on other occasions but it might also have been somehow creatively imagined.

9.3.3   Semiotics and the Classification of Evidence

In Chapter 3 (Section 3.4, Figure 3.11) I provided a two-dimensional classification of recurrent forms of evidence. One dimension concerns how a person stands in relation to an item of evidence and raises questions about its credibility. The other dimension concerns how an item of evidence seems to bear upon hypotheses of interest and raises questions about its relevance. This categorization scheme allowed us to examine a variety of matters influencing the inferential force of evidence, as discussed in Chapter 7. So the classification of recurrent forms of evidence in Figure 3.11 has an *inferential basis* and involves only argument structural matters. Indeed I advertised that one virtue of careful argument structuring is that it allows us to discern recurrent forms of evidence. As far as evidence is concerned, no classification scheme will satisfy everyone. I did mention in Section 3.4 how we can easily have evidence involving mixtures of the various evidential forms I identified. For example, we may encounter testimony, given at secondhand, about the existence of a tangible object or a document.

But there are other problems with the evidence classification scheme I presented. Some will argue that it is *substance blind,* and indeed it is. In discussing the inferential force of testimonial evidence, for example, it matters very little what is the substantive content of testimony as long as we can sort out stages of reasoning bearing on its credibility and its relevance to hypotheses of interest. I even claimed substance-blindness to be a distinct virtue of the scheme that I presented, since there apparently are no limits on the substantive varieties of evidence. But others can justifiably argue that my classification scheme does not allow us to make all interesting and important evidential distinctions, particularly if we interpret evidence in terms of *signs*.

Semiotics (spelled *semeiotics* by Peirce), as the study or science of signs, seems to be a discipline that is certainly not substance blind as far as evidence is concerned. Indeed the layperson encountering the literature in this area may easily conclude that it is the study of *everything* that might be construed as evidence as well as study of the process of giving meaning to evidence. Semiotics essentially is the study of *communicative processes of any kind* and thus involves signs, symbols, and codes of various sorts as well as the means by which they are produced and interpreted. As Brother William said to Brother Adso, the world speaks to us, through evidence, like a great book.

How many pages there must be in this book; semioticians seem bent on trying to find out how many there are.

Eco goes even farther in suggesting that semiotics studies the whole of culture (1979a, 6). He notes that this grandiose aim may give the impression of an arrogant "imperialism." As he notes, "When a discipline defines 'everything' as its proper object, and therefore declares itself as concerned with the entire universe (and nothing else) it's playing a risky game" (1979a, 7). Eco does go on to set certain boundaries on semiotics, but he also provides the following listing of nineteen categories of contemporary research in semiotics:

1. *Zoosemiotics.* Study of the communicative behavior of nonhuman species.
2. *Olfactory signs.* Study of the codes of scents.
3. *Tactile communication.* Study of codified human behavior such as kissing or embracing.
4. *Codes of taste.* Study of preferences.
5. *Paralinguistics.* Study of nonverbal communications.
6. *Medical semiotics.*
7. *Kinesics.* Study of codes conveyed by gestures.
8. *Musical codes.*
9. *Formalized languages.* Such as technical terms in algebra and chemistry.
10. *Written languages, unknown alphabets, and secret codes.* (cryptology).
11. *Natural languages.*
12. *Visual communications.*
13. *Systems of objects.* Study of objects as communicative devices.
14. *Plot structures in works of literature of any kind.*
15. *Text theory.*
16. *Cultural codes.* Study of behavioral and value systems.
17. *Aesthetic texts.*
18. *Mass communication.*
19. *Rhetoric.* Study of the persuasiveness of signs.

In a book of semiotics of so many pages, is there an overall "plot" to the story it tells? Eco provides a very interesting answer (1979a, 6–7). Semiotics concerns *everything* that can be taken as a sign; in turn a sign is that which can be substituted for something else. The trouble is that this "something else" does not necessarily exist nor actually appear at the moment when we perceive a sign. We should again recall Mr. Grodman's comment about the many red herrings the Creator places in our paths. Eco concludes that ". . . *semiotics is in principle the discipline studying everything which can be used in order to lie. If something cannot be used to tell a lie, conversely it cannot be used to tell the truth: it cannot be used 'to tell' at all*" (1979a, 7). Thus

Eco concludes that a "theory of the lie" should be taken as a fairly comprehensive program for general semiotics.

We know that Eco tells a good story. But perhaps his somewhat sportive plot for the story of semiotics might not be the one chosen by others in this field. In any case the field of semiotics has an interesting history, a few details of which I now offer. More complete historical accounts appear in the works of Deely (1986, 5–34; 1990, 105–124) and Sebeok (1986, 35–42, 255–263); tutorial works of interest are those by Deely (1990) and Sebeok (1991). It seems that John Locke first coined the name now given to this science of signs. In his *Essay Concerning Human Understanding* (1689), Locke divides the whole field of human inquiry into three divisions, one of which he labels with the Greek word *semeiotike* (reading of signs). This division concerns ". . . the Nature of Signs, the mind makes use of for the understanding of Things, or conveying its Knowledge to others" (ch. 21, 720–721, Nidditch ed., 1991). Locke goes on to say that ideas are the things our minds contemplate and that we need to have some ability to communicate them, since one person's ideas are not open to view by others. The means we employ are articulate sounds, or spoken words. Thus ideas and words form the great "instruments of knowledge."

The mathematician J. H. Lambert, whose name is mentioned in connection with the development of Shafer's belief functions, did in 1764 write a work entitled *Semiotic, or the Doctrine of the Signification of Thoughts and Things* (Sebeok 1986, 256). However, the development of modern semiotics is usually associated with two names: Ferdinand de Saussure (1857–1913) and Charles Sanders Peirce. Saussure, also recognized as the founder of modern linguistics, describes *semiology* as the science of the life of signs within society. Peirce's writings on semeiotics are extensive, and there are collections of his works bearing upon signs (e.g., Hoopes 1991). Peirce gave many definitions of the word *sign* (from the Latin *signum*, meaning a mark or token). Traditionally, the word sign is defined in terms of the Latin phrase *aliquid stat pro aliquo*, meaning "something that stands for something else." One interpretation Peirce gave seems particularly appropriate to our discussions of the chains of reasoning linking evidence and hypotheses (or explanations). Peirce described a sign as: "Anything which determines something else (its *interpretant*) to refer to an object to which itself refers (its *object*) in the same way, the interpretant becoming a sign, and so on *ad infinitum*" (Hoopes 1991, 239–240). In other words, a sign is something that stands for something else (its object) in such a way as to generate another sign (its interpretant). This definition asserts that we may have chains of signs. Peirce also emphasized that there is to be some physical connection between every sign and its object (Hoopes 1991, 141–143).

In Chapter 3 we spent some time discussing the concept of relevance using the testimony of Officer Connolly in the Sacco and Vanzetti case. Let us suppose for the moment that the event in Connolly's testimony actually occurred (it probably did not). Connolly testified that Sacco attempted on several occasions to put his hand under his overcoat in spite of being warned not to do so (Sacco was in fact carrying a 32-caliber Colt revolver). The arresting officers allegedly took this gesture (a sign) as threatening and one the prosecution alleged was a sign of Sacco's consciousness of guilt in the murder for which he was charged. The relevance argument I provided in Figure 3.5 might be construed as chain of conjectural signs leading to this explanation. At least Judge Webster Thayer took Sacco's alleged gesture as a sign of his consciousness of guilt, since he mentioned it in his charge to the jury. He obviously did not consider how many intermediate conjectural "signs" are necessary in order to make this connection.

As an example of interesting evidential distinctions made by semioticians, I will mention those drawn by Eco between *imprints, symptoms, and clues* (1983, 210–212). I have mentioned Wigmore's categorization of evidence as being *prospectant, concomitant, or retospectant* with reference to the time some legally interesting events took place. One species of retrospectant evidence Wigmore called *trace evidence*. Footprints or fingerprints are signs that someone has been at a particular location. Eco tells us that the interpretation of any imprint involves correlating it with some physical cause. He also tells us that imprints are the most elementary kinds of sign-production. Persons leaving fingerprints or footprints behind do not ordinarily do so with the intention of producing signs. They are taken as signs by someone else who observes them.

Symptoms, on the other hand, refer to physical events that, as Eco says, refer back to a class of their possible causes as when, for example, we take red spots on the face of a child to mean that this child has measles. The distinction between imprints and symptoms, Eco says, is one involving the correspondence between a sign and its explanation. For example, the shape of a footprint is a projection from the imprinting object (a foot or a shoe). There is not such a projection between measles and red spots. Additional semiotic analyses of medical symptoms are to be found in the work of Baer (1986, 140–152). Clues, says Eco, are objects left by an agent in places where this agent did something, it being the case that we recognize a link between the clue and the presence of the agent. Here is another example of Wigmore's retrospectant evidence. A person who commits a crime often leaves behind objects linking him or her with the crime. Eco tells us of an interesting difference between symptoms and clues. Interpreting symptoms involves making reference to recorded instances of a *necessary* connection between effects and causes such as when we infer measles to be a cause of the red spots. Clues, on the other hand, only indicate a *possible* past contiguity between the owner of an object and the presence of the owner in some location. Eco tells us that this distinction helps account for the fact that a crime novel usually makes more interesting reading than does the detection of pneumonia. I mentioned earlier in Chapter 2 that our courts must be prepared to assess the relevance, credibility and inferential force of any substantive kind of evidence; semioticians seem to have a similar task.

Finally, the historian's use of documentary evidence (of endless substantive variety), as signs of past events and situations, has not escaped the attention of semioticians (e.g., Williams 1986, 217–223). Documents, as signs, do not record the whole of the experiences to which they are judged to relate. For this reason historians frequently find it necessary to create probable truths from relationships that exist between various kinds of documentary evidence. Williams argues that semiotics can help historians clarify distinctions between fact and fancy as they concern relations between words and ideas. We might say that historians create stories or scenarios in their attempt to explain past events. A story or a scenario contains some mixture of fact and fancy. There is work in semiotics on the telling of stories. In Section 9.4 I will again discuss the heuristic importance of constructing scenarios. Historians certainly acknowledge that history is written from the signs or "tracks" left behind by others. As Bloch noted (1953, 55): "Whether it is the bones immured in the Syrian fortifications, a word whose form or use reveals a custom, a narrative written by the witness of some scene, ancient or modern, what do we mean by document, if it is not a 'track', as it were—the mark, perceptible to the senses, which some phenomenon, in itself inaccessible, has left behind."

9.3.4 Peirce, Eco, and the "Colligation" of Ideas

I will draw upon Peirce and Eco a final time before discussing the interesting and vital task of marshaling thought and evidence during the process of discovery. Peirce seems to have had a ready term for nearly everything including the marshaling of thought and evidence. The term he employed was *colligation*. The word colligation comes from the Latin *colligare*, meaning to combine or bring together. Peirce defined colligation as ". . . the binding together of facts by means of a general description or hypothesis which applies to them all" (Tursman 1987, 19). Peirce argued that colligations occur in preparation for discovery as well as during the process of discovery itself. The likelihood of our having appropriate ideas at hand is increased as we bring together ideas from as many different disciplines as possible. Tursman gives examples of the sorts of colligations Peirce described in scientific discovery.

The importance of the process of colligating or marshaling thought and evidence cannot be overstated. It has the same degree of importance in inductive and in abductive inference. As far as induction is concerned, imagine that in your role as juror, you have heard testimony from a witness who reports an event whose actual occurrence is positively vital to the prosecution's case. Following this testimony, the defense makes every effort to impeach the credibility of this witness. When its turn comes, the prosecution makes every effort to rehabilitate this witness's credibility. What you now have heard is a very large collection of evidence about this witness, some of it favorable to his credibility and some not. What impresses you most is the *variety* of different matters this evidence concerns. How do you possibly make sense out of this jumble of different evidence in trying to decide whether to believe that the event testified by this witness actually occurred?

It might help if someone pointed out to you that there are recognizable attributes of a witness's credibility: veracity, objectivity, and observational sensitivity. It would also help of course if someone provided you with the time and the means for marshaling the evidence in this jumble under each of these attributes. At the very least this would prevent you from taking evidence that bears upon a witness's objectivity as either impeaching or supporting his veracity. So the argument structuring methods we have discussed supply one basis for the colligation or marshaling of thought and evidence during the inductive process of assessing the credibility and force of evidence.

In many situations, too numerous to mention, we hear the following comment made as a result of some inferential miscarriage: "We had all the facts, we just did not put them together in ways our hindsight now suggests would have been more appropriate." Perhaps this miscarriage involved a certain possibility turning out to be true when it was never generated, discovered, or "abducted" in the first place. As Peirce noted, the colligation or marshaling of thought and evidence is vital during the process of discovery. Eco's two novels *The Name of the Rose* and *Foucault's Pendulum* provide marvelous examples of very complex discovery. In *Foucault's Pendulum* Eco seems to take pity on a certain character who faced some of the problems that I will address in just a moment. Eco has this character tell us (*Foucault's Pendulum*, 1988, 225):

> Still, I was accumulating experience and information, and I never threw anything away. I kept files on everything. I didn't think to use a computer . . . . Instead, I had cross-referenced index cards. Nebulae, LaPlace; Laplace, Kant; Kant, Konigsberg; theorems of topology. . . . It was a little like that game where you go from sausage to Plato in five steps, by association of ideas. Let's see: sausage, pig bristle, paintbrush, Mannerism, Idea, Plato. Even the sloppiest manuscript would bring twenty new cards to my hoard. I had a strict rule, which I think the secret services follow, too: No piece of information is superior to any other Power lies in having them all on file and then finding the connections. There are always connections; you have only to want to find them.

I could not possibly find a better introduction to the following discussion about the many virtues of having a variety of means at our disposal for colligating or marshaling our thoughts and our evidence. A vital element in discovery is, as Eco's character tells us, the discovery of connections or associations between various thoughts and evidence that we have, some of which may appear to be trivial or unimportant when we examine them in isolation.

9.4 STRATEGIES FOR MARSHALING THOUGHT AND EVIDENCE DURING DISCOVERY

A study of how to colligate, marshal, or organize things might appear to be a pedestrian undertaking. This would certainly be true if what is being organized are the clothes in a closet, tools in a workshop, or books on a shelf. Study of such tasks within the context of induction and abduction takes on a level of interest and significance it may not have in other contexts. During the inductive processes of assessing the relevance, credibility, and force of evidence, the manner in which we have marshaled our thoughts and evidence is altogether crucial. I just mentioned one example involving the task of credibility assessment. There are many other points in probabilistic reasoning at which thought and evidence marshaling is important. In Chapter 8 I discussed the task of assessing the force of different recurrent combinations of evidence. Some of these evidential combinations might not even have been recognized unless we had organized our evidence in certain ways. For example, unless we had juxtaposed our evidence in a particular way, we might not have recognized that two items of evidence are redundant to some degree, are inferentially synergistic, or are in apparent conflict. All of our studies of recurrent evidence combinations in Chapter 8 assumed that evidence has been marshaled or organized in ways that reveal these combinations.

Our present interest is in the process of discovery in which new hypotheses and evidence are generated. We already have Peirce's and Eco's word that the colligation of ideas and evidence is important in discovery. The jurist Wigmore also devoted attention to evidence marshaling issues in his *Science of Judicial Proof* (1937, 994–1003). He argued that his analytic and synthetic methods are just as important to the discovery-related activities of a detective as they are to the argument-structuring activities of an attorney preparing for trial. As I proceed, I will mention an interesting scheme Wigmore proposed for marshaling a mass of evidence during the process of discovery in order to generate the probanda (matters to be proved) in criminal and other cases.

For the past five years Peter Tillers and I have been at work on the study of strategies for marshaling evidence that might be of assistance in the process of discovery as well as in the processes of proof and choice. I will tell you briefly about this research as it concerns the process of discovery; we have recently provided more extensive accounts of this work, which is still in progress (Tillers and Schum 1988, 1991; Schum and Tillers 1989, 1991). To set the stage for this discussion, suppose that you are attempting to generate hypotheses and evidence in some inference task of importance to you. So far you have collected a mass of information and are now in the process of asking questions of it in order to generate possibilities in addition to those that you already entertain. You have access to a computer for the storage and retrieval of the information that you have gathered so far. It would be very nice to have a computer with the following capability.

You make an inquiry of your computer system. You ask the computer to provide you with all the information you have that has a certain property; let's call it X. You believe that this collection or combination of information might be suggestive of new hypotheses and new evidence. The computer responds with a printed message that says (somewhat impertinently): "I noted the inquiry you just made. In light of the information I now have in storage,

I suggest that you are asking the wrong question. My recommendation is that you ask for data that have properties Y and Z which, together, suggest the plausibility of H_{n+1}, a possibility you have not yet considered." Sad to say, no computer having this capability presently exists, nor is one likely to appear in the foreseeable future. In lieu of a system that is this "smart," we might inquire about other feasible heuristically valuable functions that we might expect a computer to be able to perform. Here is a brief account of our current efforts to develop a computer-assisted evidence marshaling systems that acknowledge the various ideas that we have discussed so far in Chapter 9.

9.4.1 Discovery and Its Many Evidence Marshaling Requirements

In Section 9.1 I mentioned that the process of discovery may be viewed differently in different contexts, is mixed with other activities, is played out over time, and depends upon the standpoints of the investigators. I add to this list the fact that in most contexts no two episodes of discovery are the same. In going from one problem to another, the engineer, historian, auditor, or criminal investigator may generate plausible hypotheses at different times as discovery proceeds. For example, in some cases we may be fortunate in having a datum that immediately suggests a plausible hypothesis (e.g., finding a fingerprint at the scene of a crime). In other cases extensive inquiry and the gathering of information may be required before we can even begin to generate hypotheses with any degree of precision. Perhaps, we are initially able to generate only imprecise, vague, undifferentiated, or coarse (Shafer's term) hypotheses. For example, the evidence presently at hand suggests only that the robber was a young white male about thirty years of age. There are many males who fit this coarse description; refinement of this possibility requires further inquiry.

As discovery proceeds, information or data accumulate, often at a very rapid rate. There may be as many different strategies for keeping track of new information as there are persons who engage in the process of discovery. Eco's character in *Foucault's Pendulum* used cross-referenced index cards; so do many other persons. We also take notes, construct outlines, and use many other devices including computers to keep track of our thoughts and evidence as discovery proceeds. In many cases we easily become swamped with data and are frustrated because we know that some of them will be useless and will never lead us to what possibilities we ought to consider. The trouble is that, lacking clairvoyance, we cannot now tell which data we ought to keep at hand and which we can comfortably discard; only hindsight can supply such answers. So in lieu of access to a clairvoyant we have no choice but to keep everything that we find. As Eco's character reminds us, we need to find connections among our data; they are there, all we need to do is to find them. This is where the real trouble starts.

Our colleagues in the field of artificial intelligence are certainly correct about the need for search strategies that are heuristically valuable in generating new ideas and evidence. In fact, searching for connections among data and ideas that we have recorded is precisely where imagination is required. Here are some examples that illustrate the difficulties that we face and why it is simply impossible to *search through everything in the hope of finding something,* even if it makes sense to do so. Suppose that you presently have n items of data in whatever records you are now keeping. Following Eco's advice, you attempt to find connections among these data and so begin to examine various *combinations* of these data. Unless you were imaginative in doing so, you would face a task having the following dimensions: For n data there are $2^n - (n + 1)$ possible combinations of two or more data taken together. Suppose that you have just fifty items of data on record at this point. You would then have $1.1259(10)^{15}$ possible combinations of data to search through; for 100 items the number of possible combinations is $1.2677(10)^{30}$. In discovery efforts in some contexts we may easily have *thousands* of data on record. The exponential nature of our search problem demands that we apply some imaginative search strategies.

Of course not all combinations of data will be equally informative; the trick is to find ones that are. This is where the process of inquiry and the asking of questions of our accumulated data become so important. Our hope is to be able to ask the *strategically right* questions that J. Hintikka mentions. I recall a point made by two legal scholars David Binder and Paul Bergman in their work *Fact Investigation: From Hypothesis to Proof* (1984). In the preface to this work (p. xvii) they mention how law students are rarely given any preparation for the tasks of gathering, analyzing, and using evidence. As they note, "Thus, many students may be excused for graduating from law school thinking that facts are like starving trout, ready to be reeled in at the drop of a question or two." Heuristically important combinations of data are most assuredly not like starving trout; we may need to ask a variety of different questions in order to reel them in. Again, information bases in most areas are not static; we add new data all the time. At any moment we have no guarantee that we have what we need. This is why discovery so frequently involves more than search. In the next section I will mention some ways of organizing combinations of data that can be heuristically important in generating questions to ask of our data.

Recall Peirce's comment about how a new hypothesis is often generated interrogatively. Suppose that some combination of data (or even possibly a single datum) suggests a possibility or hypothesis at some level of refinement. Now we have a colligational, marshaling, or organizing principle at hand. Using one metaphor, we might look upon this hypothesis as a magnet; let us see how many of our existing data it will attract (or possibly repel). Using Binder and Bergman's metaphor, this hypothesis is now a baited hook or a net; let us see how many new evidential fish we might catch with it. In this connection we can note a quotation Popper used to introduce his *Logic of*

Scientific Discovery (1968). The quote is: "Theories are nets: only he who casts will catch." The hypothesis we have just generated might also be described as a guess. Readers of Sherlock Holmes stories know that he frequently sneered at guessing. In *The Sign of The Four* he says: "I never guess. It is a destructive habit—destructive to the logical faculty" (Baring-Gould 1967, vol. 1, 614). In *A Study in Scarlet* he says: "It is a capital mistake to theorize before you have all the evidence. It biases the judgment" (Baring-Gould 1967, vol. 1, 166). Holmes cannot have taken himself too seriously in this matter. Absent some preliminary guesses, he would never have been able to decide where to begin looking for the clues he so effectively used in his investigations. In fact in *The Adventure of the Sussex Vampire* he says: "One forms provisional theories and waits for time or fuller knowledge to explode them. A bad habit, . . . but human nature is weak" (Baring-Gould 1967, vol. 2, 467–468).

As discovery proceeds, we may come to entertain any number of hypotheses at various levels of refinement. Some will appear more promising than others; some we may even be willing to eliminate. For reasons I discussed earlier, we have to be careful during the process of elimination lest we snatch defeat from the jaws of victory. Careful evidence marshaling under a hypothesis that is a candidate for elimination can help us decide whether we have eliminated all of the reasons why we should be keeping this possibility alive.

As evidence is generated and we are able to refine some hypothesis, the hypothesis itself begins to resemble or at least to suggest a story, a scenario, or a narrative. In other words, a refined hypothesis becomes more specific or detailed and therefore more extensive. It begins to have an explanatory flavor. Discernible differences between stories, scenarios, and narratives have been recognized (Twining 1990, 219–261). Stories are told and scenarios or narratives are constructed for many different purposes. Some purposes involve persuasion as when, for example, an attorney tells a story summarizing her case. The stories or scenarios I now have in mind are constructed *for heuristic purposes only* during the process of discovery. In the act of refining some hypothesis by making it incorporate evidence we take seriously, we try not to outrun what evidence we have. But in the construction of a scenario this hypothesis suggests, we do outrun our present evidence; indeed this is the source of its heuristic value.

A scenario we construct, or a story we tell, involves some mixture of fact and fancy. Our scenario will consist of evidence items that we take seriously; these items are usually arranged in a temporal sequence so that possible causal or other explanatory connections might be revealed. But there will be natural gaps in our scenario which we attempt to fill by guessing that certain events have happened that provide the coherence and completeness that our scenario or story presently lacks. As I mentioned in Section 4.6.1 and illustrated in Figure 4.20, each new "gap-filler" or hypothesized event that we so identify becomes a new category of potential evidence we might observe. The heuristic merit of telling stories cannot be oversold. Suppose we make inquiries suggested by the "gap-fillers" that we have identified. It may be true that we may have to alter our story or scenario depending upon what we observe. It may also be true that the evidence we initially took seriously is not credible after all. Special evidence marshaling may be required as we ask and answer questions *about* our evidence and its credibility.

Suppose we reach a stage in discovery at which we believe some hypothesis or theory, and the "story it tells," is one to which we can commit our beliefs (at least to some level of probabilistic acceptance). Now we do have a problem of persuasion on our hands. Perhaps, as in legal contexts, there are various points or elements of our theory that need to be established before anyone will accept it at some level of probability. One trouble is that many different plausible stories might be told in explanation of the same set of evidence. This is one reason why there are trials at law. The defense and prosecution will tell different stories even if they agree upon the "facts" reported in the evidence. More likely however, they will disagree about what the facts actually are. How does one go about the process of persuading others of the truth of the story one tells based upon a mass of evidence? It is at this stage that the process of discovery begins to blend with processes of proof or justification. We begin to construct often elaborate arguments in defense of the stories we have to tell. This is where all of the argument structural matters we discussed in Chapters 3 and 4 become so important.

The matters I have just discussed make it quite apparent that we cannot expect any single method of marshaling or colligating evidence and ideas to satisfy all of the combined requisites of discovery, proof, and choice. We may have to marshal our thoughts and evidence in several different ways, even during the process of discovery in which we are trying to generate hypotheses that we may subsequently be willing to defend. Following is a brief account of a network of different marshaling strategies that Tillers and I believe has heuristic merit in furthering the process of inquiry. At the very least it summarizes different ways in which we might colligate or marshal our thoughts and evidence as the process of discovery lurches forward.

9.4.2 A Network of Evidence Marshaling Operations for Discovery

Shown in Figure 9.5 is a collection of different evidence marshaling operations arranged in the form of a network. The operations themselves are shown by icons representing a stack of cards. But the stacks and the cards in our network are electronic. Tillers and I have constructed a computer-based prototype of this marshaling network using a system called Hypercard© (Claris Corporation). This system allows one to design stacks of cards that perform different functions. In our case the different functions are simply different ways of marshaling evidence and ideas. The Hypercard system also allows one to establish linkages among cards in the same stack, among cards in different

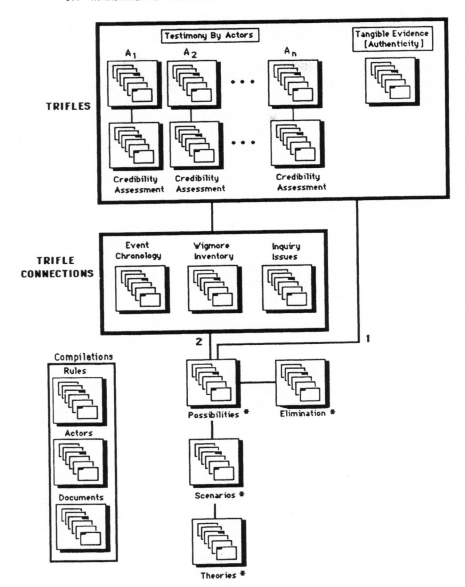

FIGURE 9.5 A network of evidence-marshaling operations for use during the process of investigation or discovery.

stacks, and among different stacks themselves. This linkage capability allows very rapid navigation from one evidence item or idea to another or from one part of the network to another. Our stacks have various indexes that facilitate this process. Thus we have electronic means for establishing connections between various existing thoughts and evidence as discovery proceeds.

In episodes of discovery it is necessary to try to keep many things in mind at the same time. Most people find this to be quite impossible, especially in light of the fact that we need to juxtapose or arrange our thoughts and evidence in different ways in order to perceive connections among them and to note different evidential distinctions that these connections may reveal. As I mentioned in Chapter 4, this was one argument Wigmore used for applying his analytic and synthetic means for charting a mass of evidence in preparation for the process of proof. The network shown in Figure 9.5 at least allows us to keep at hand many things, differently juxtaposed, even if it does not allow us to keep many things in mind all at the same time. This system also allows for the construction of *audit trails* of our intellectual activities as the process of discovery unfolds. By such means we can maintain a temporally sequenced account of what questions we asked, what evidence we obtained, and what possibilities we discerned at various stages of the discovery process. Apart from their pedagogical value, such audit trails may assist in diffusing hindsight critics who will, if discovery efforts miscarry, be quick to point out what they might have done. If this audit trail reveals that we asked "strategically right" or at least sensible questions during discovery, others may not have been able to do any better (except in hindsight).

My account of the network in Figure 9.5 begins with Sherlock Holmes. In *The Boscombe Valley Mystery* Holmes matches wits with his foil, the bumbling Inspector Lestrade from Scotland Yard. Holmes tells Watson (Baring-Gould 1967, vol. 2, 148): "By an examination of the ground I gained the trifling details which I gave to that imbecile Lestrade, as to the personality of the criminal." Watson replies: "But how did you gain them?" Holmes answers: "You know my method. It is founded upon the observance of trifles." The *trifles* of interest in any area of discovery refer to any kind of datum that arises during the investigation. In substance-blind terms, this datum may have any of the forms shown in the rows of Figure 3.11; it may be a tangible object or an item from a document, an item of testimony, something expected but missing, or something drawn from an authoritative record of some kind. In semiotic terms, a trifle is any kind of sign. A trifle may of course be any of the imprints, symptoms, or clues mentioned by Eco. Notice that I did not use the words "relevant datum" in defining trifle. At the moment we observe it, we may have no way of knowing yet whether or not this datum will become evidence relevant to any hypothesis that we generate. Indeed it is from observations of trifles that hypotheses are generated in the first place. This is precisely why we are advised to record all of the trifles that we observe, as did Eco's character in *Foucault's Pendulum*. Conan Doyle simply gave Holmes a prodigious memory for trifles.

How should we marshal or organize trifles? One approach, shown at the top of Figure 9.5, is to keep separate track of tangible and testimonial evidence. Remember from Sections 3.2.2 and 3.2.3 that different issues arise in assessing the credibility of these two forms of evidence. When issues of authenticity and accuracy or reliability arise for tangible evidence, we need to examine such matters as the chain of custody through which some tangible trifle has passed, as mentioned in Section 3.2.2. Eco has recently given a very thorough account of matters involved in detecting fakes and forgeries of objects and documents (1990, 174–202). For testimonial evidence we need to examine at least the veracity, objectivity, and observational sensitivity of human sources from which such evidence comes.

As Figure 9.5 shows, we might marshal testimonial trifles according to the "actors" or sources from which testimony comes. The "actor" stacks labeled $A_1, A_2, \ldots, A_n$ have several characteristics. First, they make separate record of information *from* an actor and information *about* an actor. Information from an actor is what some person tells us; information about an actor concerns his credibility as far as what he just told us. Recall our many discussions in Chapters 3, 7, and 8 about how the credibility-relevant behavior of an actor can be at least as interesting as what this actor tells us. The stacks we have designed also allow us to record how an actor came into possession of the information he reports; namely whether the information was obtained from firsthand observation, obtained from another actor or source, or simply inferred from other observations or information. By such means we identify an actor's report as testimony based on direct observation, hearsay, or an opinion or inference. These stacks also allow us to record how an actor came to provide a testimonial trifle: Was it given in response to our inquiry or volunteered? A volunteered testimonial trifle may raise some particularly interesting discovery matters if we believe the actor to be untruthful. Of course one or more of the actors might be the investigators themselves. Thus one or more of the actor stacks might be termed "investigator" stacks in which such persons record their own personal observations.

There are two interesting and rather difficult decisions required in recording testimonial trifles. The first concerns how the testimony was given. An actor may report to us in a face-to-face encounter during which we make some record (written or electronic) of what this actor reported. But we might also take as a testimonial trifle an assertion allegedly made by an actor in a document of any kind. The records that we have in either case are tangible in the sense that we can go over them time and again in attempts to extract meaning. Should we record such records as testimonial or tangible evidence? One argument is that it may make very little difference as long as we have the testimonial trifle on record and can recall it readily. The other decision concerns the *granularity* of a testimonial trifle. When a person gives testimony orally or by some recorded means it may be quite extensive and detailed. Tangible objects themselves may have many attributes or details. Which ones and how many of these details should we record? In other words, how minutely should we *parse* some testimonial assertion or description of an object? This seems a purely judgmental matter whose resolution depends upon the experience and insight of the investigator(s). The problem is quite obvious. Recording too many details clutters the system; recording too few puts discovery at hazard. Again, not being clairvoyant, we cannot tell which trifles or details will subsequently be of any later importance to us.

Below each actor stack appears another labeled *credibility assessment.* These stacks are designed to allow the marshaling of evidence that we have obtained *about* an actor concerning his/her veracity, objectivity, and observational sensitivity. The stack labeled *tangible evidence* allows for similar marshaling of evidence that we have about the authenticity, accuracy, or reliability of each item of tangible evidence that we record. The cards in every one of these trifle stacks contain special places for the recording of questions that we raise about any trifle or its credibility. The cards also allow us to record any thoughts we might have about the possible meaning of a trifle, its possible connections with other trifles, and what new possible trifles we might try to observe or obtain. In fact allowance for the recording of our questions and our thoughts is a feature of every stack shown in Figure 9.5. One of the major purposes of this evidence-marshaling system is to stimulate the process of inquiry in which we ask questions of and about the trifles we observe as well as about their emerging implications for discovery, proof, and choice.

In some cases a single trifle, together with the questions it suggests, can allow us to generate a possibility (or hypothesis) at some level of refinement. As mentioned above, one trifle can suggest the existence of other possible trifles that we might try to observe or collect. I have already mentioned instances in which certain forms of trace evidence, such as a fingerprint, may allow us to generate a possibility. The generation of a possibility from a single trifle can occur along path 1 in Figure 9.5. We might then generate a possibility from some combination of trifles that we obtain from a single source or actor. I note that there are situations in which an episode of discovery might begin with certain possibilities already apparent. For example, a valuable Ming vase is reported stolen from a locked vault. The first thing discovered is that exactly three persons had access and keys to this vault; so we have some specific possibilities at the outset. But in most episodes of discovery we may not have the luxury of any possibilities either already provided or generated by a single trifle or trifles from a single source. Possibilities lurk in *combinations* of the trifles that we have begun to observe and collect from different sources including our own observations. This is where the heuristic fun begins.

The next level of the system, labeled *trifle connections*, consists of various stacks that allow us to form various combinations of trifles *from different actors or sources.* Each of the three stacks I have shown are based upon heuristics that we could routinely employ. There are many such heuristics, some of which might be useful only in particular situations. The ones I will now describe have, I believe, quite general utility.

The first stack, labeled *event chronology,* is self-explanatory. In many situations the first thing we might think of doing is to arrange trifles that are "time-stamped" in the order in which we believe the event(s) revealed in these trifles actually occurred. In discovery in many contexts this is one of the very first tasks an investigator might think of performing. The trouble is that depending on context, we have to form several or many different event chronologies. A single chronological ordering of *all* of our accumulated trifles might not be particularly revealing. However many chronologies we decide to form, and to connect in various ways, they can have distinct heuristic value in suggesting what possibilities and new information we might try to gather. The event chronology stacks we have designed allow a person to move forward or backward through time and events at any pace. This dynamic quality seems to enhance the heuristic merit of such orderings. These stacks also allow us to assess the extent of our uncertainty about the actual order in which events recorded in our trifles may have occurred.

Another temporally based set of heuristics for discovery comes from the work of Wigmore (1937, 994–1003). In this work Wigmore first describes what he calls an *evidence-clues inventory*. Inference in many contexts concerns possible explanations for events that we believe to have happened in the past; the fields of law, accident investigation, history, medicine, clinical psychology, and auditing supply examples. Suppose we believe the target event(s) whose explanation we seek occurred at some time (or time interval) in the past. Our Wigmore stacks allow us to classify trifles, and the events they suggest, into three categories: (1) *prospectant events* or those occurring before or leading up to the target event(s), (2) *concomitant events* or those occurring at or near the time of the target event(s), and (3) retrospectant events or those occurring after the target events. This method of marshaling trifles goes far beyond being simply a coarse temporal classification.

As Wigmore explains, data in any of the categories: prospectant, concomitant, or retrospectant often have identifiable properties. For example, in a legal context prospectant data may concern such matters as character, motives, intentions, habits, and customs. Some concomitant data concern such matters as opportunity; others are associated with the means by which some action may have occurred. Retrospectant data concern various kinds of trace evidence that can be either physical (e.g., fingerprints, footprints, or objects left behind) or mental (e.g., as the consciousness of guilt I mentioned in discussing Officer Connollly's testimony in the Sacco and Vanzetti case). In short, these categories provide us with certain heuristic hooks on which to hang some of our accumulating trifles. But Wigmore goes even farther, he supplies us with some specific questions to ask about the data falling in each of these categories. Answers to these questions can generate new potential evidence as well as new hypotheses.

In addition to an evidence-clues inventory Wigmore provides what he terms a *progress chart of indications*. These charts resemble the ones that I mentioned in Section 4.4.2 (Figure 4.8) while discussing his analytic and synthetic evidence-charting methods. By a progress chart of indications we begin to form the outlines (in graphic or network form) of an argument that we might make regarding how some combination of trifles begins to suggest a new possibility or hypothesis. Wigmore never uses the term *heuristic,* but the methods he advocates have enormous heuristic power available to anyone willing to use them. Our *Wigmore Inventory* stacks incorporate all of his heuristics for combining trifles and generating new inquiry. Though Wigmore tended to think of discovery problems encountered in legal contexts, his methods can be easily adapted for use in other contexts.

The third trifle connection stack in Figure 9.5 is labeled *inquiry issues,* and it acknowledges the temporal nature of the process of discovery. During the process of discovery we naturally have our minds fixed on hypotheses or explanations of major interest to us. But as the process of discovery unfolds over time and our inquiry and trifle collection proceeds, we naturally encounter other interesting matters that require explanation on their own. Very often, as this stack allows us to acknowledge, answering subsidiary questions raised during discovery can lead us to the generation of new evidence as well as to the generation of major hypotheses of interest to us; here is an elaboration of an example I introduced in Section 4.5.5.

Suppose that during the investigation of a possible homicide we make the following observations:

1. The victim had a small quantity of cocaine in his possession.
2. The victim had no wallet in his possession.
3. Though the victim's body was found in his garage, there were fresh bloodstains in a sink in his house.

These are examples of trifles we might duly record. Naturally such trifles raise in our minds a number of questions: (1) Was the victim a user or a pusher of narcotics, or both? (2) Was the victim's wallet stolen? (3) Where was the victim at the time he died? Answers to such questions may not lead us instantly to any clear conclusions about whether a crime was committed and, if so, who committed it. But they may easily put us on an investigative track that does lead to important conclusions. As I mentioned earlier, the process of inquiry feeds on itself; one question leads to another.

These questions serve another function; they supply new hooks on which to hang other existing trifles that we may already have. In answering these questions, we may be able to colligate or marshal existing trifles under these question areas. In addition they give us hooks upon which to hang further related trifles that we may gather in the future. The major argument underlying our *inquiry issues* stacks is that we cannot always immediately obtain answers to the ultimate questions that we might ask, How did this person die, and if it was homicide, who killed him? This stack allows us to marshal all the trifles that bear upon specific, but ancillary, questions that arise during discovery. Any new trifle that seems to bear upon a question or issue, thus identified, finds a natural home.

But our *inquiry issues* stacks have another important feature. We might easily suppose that questions raised during inquiry have possible linkages.

Our system allows us to form ready linkages among different inquiry issues and their associated trifles. By such means we become attuned to the fact that there may be very subtle processes at work whose interactions or non-independencies we should be willing to investigate. For example, one possibility is that the victim was killed during a narcotics deal gone sour and that the murderer tried to cover his tracks by making the homicide appear to be associated with a robbery.

Using marshaling methods such as the three *trifle connection* stacks that I have just described, we may eventually be able to generate possibilities at some *level of refinement*. The generation of possibilities from *combinations* of trifles from different actors or sources is indicated by link 2 in Figure 9.5. The possibility that the victim was killed as a result of a drug deal gone sour is quite vague or coarse. But our discovery hook is now baited; armed with this generated possibility we can begin to search for other trifles that may be associated with the victim's narcotics connections. In other words, we begin to put even this vague hypothesis to work in the manner shown in Figure 9.2b. Does this vague possibility help us to explain any existing trifles that we have and does it suggest any new data that we should try to gather?

Notice the asterisk on the *possibilities* stack in Figure 9.5. As discovery proceeds, we may have any number of hypotheses at any level of refinement. That is, some hypotheses may be very specific or refined, while others may be quite unspecific or coarse. We need a stack for each possibility we discern, regardless of its level of refinement. As an example, consider the hierarchy of hypotheses shown in Figure 4.19. Suppose we have ruled out natural causes, suicide, and accident as possibilities concerning the death of the victim mentioned above. We believe that his death was the result of a criminal act (H_4). At the moment we have four hypotheses "alive," at different levels of refinement. The first is $H_{4.1}$, that the victim was assaulted during a robbery. At this same level is $H_{4.3}$, that the victim was assaulted but not robbed (he was not carrying his wallet at the time he was slain). But we also have the more specific hypothesis $H_{4.2.1}$, that the victim, a *user* of narcotics, was assaulted during a drug deal gone sour, where the assault was made to appear a concomitant of robbery. Finally, we have an even more refined hypothesis $H_{4.2.2.1}$, that the victim, a *pusher* of narcotics, was assaulted by a white male during a drug deal gone sour, where the assault was made to appear a concomitant of robbery. Notice that $H_{4.2.2.1}$ is more detailed than $H_{4.2.2}$.

Our possibilities stacks allow us to marshal *evidence* for and against possibilities or hypotheses at any level of refinement. I have now used the term *evidence* rather than *data* (or *trifles*), since data become evidence when their relevance to some hypothesis can be defended (by argument). Some of the evidence marshaled under a possibility may be directly relevant to this possibility; others may be only indirectly relevant or ancillary in nature. Additional directly relevant evidence we generate under some possibility, if credible, allows us to refine this possibility. For example, $H_{4.2.2.1}$ might be put to futher use and be subsequently refined in light of additional evidence it suggests. If this happens, $H_{4.2.2.1}$ gets "pushed further down" in our possibilities hierarchy.

To pursue the situation in Figure 4.19, suppose that the following melancholy sequence of events takes place. As discovery proceeds, a criminal investigator refines $H_{4.2.2.1}$ to the point that it includes a particular person and many other details. Its further refinement might read: "Harry Jones, a major supplier of narcotics to the victim, who was a member of a narcotics distribution network, assaulted and killed the victim for threatening to expose the narcotics network. Jones intended to kill the victim and fashioned this intent beforehand. Further, after Jones killed the victim, he took the victim's wallet to make his death appear to be a concomitant of a robbery." Jones is subsequently brought to trial on a charge of first-degree murder along with other possible charges. During the trial the defense provides compelling evidence that the victim died as a result of an accident, a possibility long since ruled out or eliminated by the investigators.

In reality such an acutely embarrassing situation can only rarely happen to a criminal investigator. If the defense does have strong evidence favoring accidental death, and the prosecutor knows of it, a murder charge will not be filed in the first place. The example simply illustrates a point I made earlier. If we choose to eliminate some possibility from further consideration, we might take special care to ensure that we have ruled out all of the reasons that we can think of for keeping this possibility "alive." The stack labeled *elimination* in Figure 9.5 is designed for this purpose. We might have such a stack for each hypothesis that we have eliminated. The ideas forming the basis for this evidence marshaling operation were drawn from Jonathan Cohen's work on Baconian eliminative and variative induction which I discussed in Chapter 5.

If hypotheses in various areas are refined enough, they begin to resemble possible stories or scenarios. In our example $H_{4.2.2.1}$ and its further refinement, as mentioned above, begins to tell a story of first-degree murder with Harry Jones as the major actor. Our *scenario* stacks shown in Figure 9.5 assist in the process of constructing scenarios from reasonably refined possibilities. As I noted earlier, scenarios or stories are mixtures of what we regard as fact, and some elements that we recognize as pure fancy. We have certain items of evidence marshaled under some possibility. If they can be arranged in a temporal sequence, we have the skeleton of a scenario. Though many parts of the scenario or story will be missing, we have to guess about what they might be. In doing so, we attempt to insert hypothetical events or "gap-fillers." The heuristic merit is apparent; each *plausible* "gap-filler" we identify is a potential evidence item that we might be able to collect. Our scenario stacks help the user make clear what parts of a scenario have a basis in existing evidence and what parts are fanciful.

Not all of our hypothesized "gap-fillers" will be verified by the evidence that they generate; we may have to change our story and revise the hypothesis forming its basis. We may also have to reassess the credibility of other evidence that we already have. In addition, if we have alternative refined hypotheses, we may need to tell different stories; this accounts for the asterisk on the scenario stacks in Figure 9.5. As discovery proceeds, at some point we may begin to have a preference for one scenario, and what it suggests, over others. Suppose that we decide that one hypothesis/scenario should be accepted in preference to others. We now face the task of convincing other persons that the inferential story that we have to tell is one that anyone else should accept as well. As I mentioned, this is where discovery slides, gently in some cases, into justification or proof.

In some contexts, such as in law, history, or auditing, there may be certain elements or points that seem necesary for us to prove in order to convince someone else to accept a chosen scenario or story. Taken together these elements or points might be said to represent a *theory*. For example, if our theory is that Harry Jones committed first-degree murder, there are certain legally prescribed necessary elements of this theory, all of which have to be proved (to a reasonable doubt standard) by the evidence we have. We have to prove that (1) a human person was killed, (2) Harry Jones did the killing, (3) Harry Jones intended to kill this person (it was not an accident), and (4) Harry Jones fashioned this intent sometime prior to the killing (the killing was premeditated). Theories being tested in other contexts may not come with such prescriptions, so investigators are left to their own devices in deciding what needs to be proved in order for someone else to accept one's favored theory.

The *theories* stack in Figure 9.5 allows one to marshal existing evidence under every one of the points or elements thought by an investigator to be necessary in order to convince other persons to accept a certain scenario and the theory it describes. In some cases we may need to consider more than one theory. But just listing evidence favorable or unfavorable to each of the elements or points of a theory is not convincing on its own. Now we do have a justification or proof task on our hands and face all of the argument structural matters that we discussed in Chapters 3 and 4. These structrual matters concern the relevance, credibility, and force of our marshaled evidence on points necessary to sustain ultimate hypotheses or theories that we have generated, discovered, or "abducted."

Finally, Figure 9.5 shows three additional kinds of stacks which I have labeled *compilations*. In discovery efforts in different contexts many things must be kept readily at hand, if not in our minds, especially as the inference task becomes more complex. The three compilation stacks shown are simply examples of the kinds of information, other than that we might use as evidence, that we may have to keep in mind as discovery proceeds. Some of this information may be heuristically valuable. As I mentioned above, in some contexts there are certain rules or established principles that govern what elements or points need to be proved in order to establish some theory. The *rules* stack shown in the figure is simply a compilation of existing rule sets covering different theories. If no such rule prescriptions exist, an investigator may here record elements or points that she believes must be proved. Knowing what we have to prove in order to sustain a theory is certainly an advantage. It also has a certain amount of heuristic value in showing us what kinds of evidence we will need to have in order to sustain some theory.

In some contexts evidence comes from many different sources or actors, and the inference itself may involve the activities of many persons. Keeping track of all of the actors and sources is often a chore on its own. But there is another issue here of considerable interest in many contexts. It may be inferentially valuable to have at hand some record of how our sources of data came into existence. We find out about one source from another source at a certain time. Quite often we may wish to have an audit trail of the means by which new sources are identified by other sources and the time at which such revelations took place. The *actors* stack allows us to establish such trails. The same idea applies to documents. In some contexts just keeping track of the documents that we have searched is a chore on its own. The *documents* stack allows us to do this and also allows us to construct *document trails* showing various, and often interesting, linkages between one documentary source and another.

The network of evidence marshaling operations in Figure 9.5 is a truncated version of the larger network that we have now constructed. I stopped at this point because our present interest concerns the process of discovery. Other evidence marshaling operations on our larger network concern matters of proof or justification and choice. The interested reader may consult another work in which additional evidence marshaling operations are discussed (Schum and Tillers 1991). As far as discovery-related evidence marshaling operations and systems are concerned, Tillers and I make no claim that these devices would turn an imbecile like Inspector Lestrade into an investigative genius like Sherlock Holmes. At the same time we do believe that the manner in which we colligate or marshal existing evidence and thought influences our generation or discovery of evidence, as well as possibilities that we do not yet have but ought to have. Our system can be no smarter than the person who employs it. It will not tell us which questions to ask of existing evidence that are "strategically right." All it will do is allow us to juxtapose our thoughts and our evidence in different ways that may stimulate the asking of such questions.

Chapter 10

End of Discourse

Speaking of the ends or resolutions of discourse, Hobbes said (1651, pt. I, ch. VII, 1988 ed., 30): "Of all *Discourse*, governed by desire of Knowledge, there is at last an *End*, either by attaining, or by giving over. And in the chain of Discourse, wheresoever it be interrupted, there is an End for that time." The time has come for me to review what I believe has been attained in this discourse on evidence. I must also mention points on which I am forced to yield or to give over. The final words on evidence, its properties, and its uses will perhaps never be written. In this discourse we have encountered many issues about which there will be continuing dialogue and debate. As I mentioned in the Preface to this work, the house of evidence has many mansions. The mansions that we have visited include those occupied by scholars in the fields of law, philosophy and logic, probability, semiotics, artificial intelligence, psychology, and history. There may be other mansions that we might have visited.

I will surely yield on the matter of defining the word *evidence;* I have been no more successful than others who have also sought to define this term. In Chapter 2 my approach to this difficulty involved drawing distinctions between the term evidence and other terms that are often used as synonyms for it. Even though the term evidence resists definition, we all have some intuitive sense of what it means. Different disciplines set their own standards for what they will regard as acceptable evidence in various inference tasks. Naturally these standards change in light of experience and increased understanding of phenomena of interest. A psychologist, attempting to assess a person's mental traits and capabilities, would no longer accept as evidence the particular pattern of bumps and indentations on the contours of this person's skull. The diagnostic force of cranial features on hypotheses concerning mental attributes was first proposed by anatomists in the early 1800s and taken seriously to various degrees until 1938 (Boring 1950, 50–60). Lest we sneer at anatomists and psychologists on this point, we might consider how many of the observable signs, data, or indicators now taken as evidence in various disciplines will be regarded as similarly primitive two hundred years from now.

I believe one thing easily attainable on a visit through the many mansions of evidence is *tolerance* for individuals who face difficult evidential problems in many different situations. We do not often envy the juror who must draw a conclusion from a mass of often-dissonant evidence in a case in which a defendant's freedom or life is at hazard. Nor do we envy the cardiologist whose diagnosis based on a mass of evidence in a particular case may suggest the necessity of a risky surgical procedure. There is enormous variance across disciplines in the firmness with which conclusions can be reached about phenomena of interest. To use Mr. Grodman's terms (Chapter 1), the Creator has drawn more red herrings across some tracks than across others. Various disciplines in the physical sciences and in engineering have obviously been able to draw quite firm conclusions from their evidence, or else we would not, for example, have observed so many successful ventures into space. It has been far easier to draw conclusions necessary in order to put people on the moon than it has been to draw conclusions about how a child learns to add and subtract, or to read. Firm conclusions about how best to settle disputes or to distribute resources equitably may be a long time coming.

In evaluating the adequacy of a conclusion drawn from evidence there are many considerations. Two such considerations are: What evidence did a person have to work with? How well did this person use the evidence available? From time to time we do not use evidence wisely, and we experience miscarriages of reasoning of the sort that logicians and probabilists can help us avoid. In other situations, however, even the most skillful logician or probabilist would have difficulty drawing a conclusion from certain kinds of evidence, particularly if there was a large mass of it to be considered. In Chapter 3 I introduced an item of testimonial evidence whose relevance was unchallenged in the celebrated murder trial of the defendants Sacco and Vanzetti. To defend the relevance of this testimony, I found it necessary to construct a chain of reasoning that I believe contains at least seven intermediate links. It contains at least nine such links if attributes of the witness's credibility are to be considered. Each link represents a source of uncertainty that affects the inferential force of evidence. I referred to this testimonial evidence several times during my discourse, in part because it illustrates the following point.

Persons in many disciplines are forced to work with evidence which, on careful examination, is only *weakly circumstantial* on matters at issue. It would help, of course, if the matters at issue were themselves directly observable; in most situations they are not. Events in the past are not directly observable to the historian nor to the advocate, judge, or juror in a legal case. The behavioral and social sciences routinely investigate ongoing processes that are not observable. Suppose, for example, someone entertains the hypothesis that "low self-esteem" (a fuzzy hypothesis) best explains a certain pattern of antisocial behavior on the part of an adolescent. A person's self-esteem, in common with many other mental attributes, is not directly observable *by anyone*. States or levels of these hypothetical attributes have to be inferred from observable behavioral indicators. If detailed chains of reasoning were formed from these indicators to hypothesized mental states, they might have at least as many intermediate links as the chain of reasoning in the trial testimony that I just mentioned.

In many situations we have recourse only to masses of circumstantial evidence, so we must trade off *quality* of evidence for *quantity* of evidence. In doing so, we encounter the assortment of structural and probabilistic difficulties that have formed the subject matter of this discourse. It is common to distinguish between the "hard" and the "soft" sciences or between the physical sciences, on the one hand, and the behavioral/social sciences, on the other. I believe it entirely fair to say that this distinction does not involve the relative intellectual capabilities of persons in these two fuzzy branches of science. What it does seem to involve is the nature of the observable evidence in a problem domain, the precision with which hypotheses can be asserted, and the length of reasoning chains linking evidence to hypotheses of interest. In the "hard" sciences, hypotheses can often be asserted more precisely, and tangible evidence more directly linked to hypotheses of interest is often available. I would not, however, go on record as asserting that lengthy chains of reasoning are encountered only in the "soft" sciences.

Study of structural issues is informative about matters concerning the relevance and the credibility of evidence. But simply identifying links in a reasoning chain is not enough. We must also provide generalizations that serve to license these linkages and then gather whatever ancillary evidence we can find that shows the extent to which these generalizations actually apply in the particular case in which they are being asserted. These generalizations and the ancillary evidence relevant to them form the very basis for any probabilistic assessments that we care to make regarding our belief about the strength or weakness of an inferential linkage.

In some disciplines, such as history, reliance is placed on tangible documents whose authenticity has to be established. The trouble is that the events reported in such evidence may be linked to matters at issue by reasoning chains having many links. In the behavioral and social sciences reliance is often placed on testimonial evidence. As we observed in Chapters 3 and 7, just considering the credibility of such evidence can involve many stages of reasoning, particularly if the evidence comes through a chain of sources or is in the form of an opinion or inference based on other evidence. But the events reported in testimony may themselves be linked to matters at issue by reasoning chains having many links. Each recognized link is a source of uncertainty. A researcher in any discipline is open to the charge that important uncertainties have been overlooked; this raises another issue.

Persons in most areas of research will have had at least some training in statistics. Statisticians are certainly correct in advising us to make a distinction between a statistical hypothesis, concerning the parameter(s) of a probability distribution for some random variable of interest, and a scientific hypothesis, concerning a substantive matter at issue. But they are not to be faulted for being unable to show us how these two hypotheses are to be linked; this linkage requires substantive knowledge about the matters being investigated. As I mentioned at some length in Chapter 4, the jurist Wigmore advised practicing attorneys to carefully establish the linkages beween their evidence and matters at issue, and he provided analytic and synthetic means for doing so. Researchers in many disciplines would be greatly assisted if they took Wigmore's advice and used methods of the sort he developed.

The central topics of this discourse involve structural and probabilistic issues in determining the relevance, credibility, and inferential force of discernible forms and combinations of evidence. But I have also attended to the discovery or generation of evidence and how it might be marshaled or organized. Here is a brief review of specific ideas on such matters that were developed during this discourse.

10.1 EVIDENCE, ARGUMENT STRUCTURES, AND PROBABILITIES

In attempting to understand more about the properties and uses of evidence, we can go part of the distance just by examining structural issues. These issues concern the arguments we construct in an attempt to show the bearing of our evidence items on hypotheses and, possibly, on each other. Study of structural issues is informative regarding establishment of the relevance and credibility "credentials" of evidence. In many instances the arguments that we construct can have an astonishing level of complexity, as I illustrated in Chapter 4. Beginning in the work of the jurist Wigmore in 1913, there is now substantial effort devoted to the study and analysis of *inference networks*. There is no book written on how to construct an inference network appropriate to any specific inference task; nor is one likely to be written any time soon. The reason is that an inference network is always the creation of a person or persons having specific domain knowledge and a particular standpoint relative to the inference task at hand. Some inference problems are recurrent but most others have distinctly unique features whose capture depends upon the skill and knowledge of the person constructing the network. As I discussed in Chapter 4, some computer assistance is now available for persons who construct and analyze inference networks. Unfortunately, there is no computer system currently available that will, on its own, construct an inference network appropriate to an inference problem.

Attention to structural issues provides assistance in the study of evidence. As I illustrated in Chapter 3, by purely structural means we can form a useful and substance-blind categorization of recurrent *forms* of evidence. Answers to two fundamental structural questions provide a basis for categorizing evidence regardless of its content or substance. The questions are: How do I stand in relation to this item of evidence? How does this item stand in relation to matters I am trying to prove? As I noted in Chapter 3, the first question concerns matters to be taken into account in establishing the credibility of evidence. The second concerns how the item of evidence is relevant, directly or indirectly, on matters at issue. The substance-blindness of the classification scheme I presented in Figure 3.11 certainly facilitates probabilistic analyses of the sort I provided in Chapter 7. But, as I acknowledged in Chapter 9, there are equally important studies of the semiotic properties of evidence in which the substance or content of evidence cannot be ignored.

Attention just to structural matters also allows us to identify recurrent *combinations* of evidence. Study of these combinations allows us to adopt more precise terms in our discussions of evidential consonance and dissonance. All *dissonant* evidence is conflicting or at variance, but not all conflicting evidence is contradictory. I chose to label evidence as *contradictory* if it reports events that cannot happen together. Evidence about events that can possibly happen together, but which point us in different inferential directions, I labeled as *conflicting*. One form of consonant evidence is *corroborative* or repetitive in the sense that it reports the same event(s). Another form of consonance involves *convergent* or *confiming* evidence. Here we have evidence involving different events that point us in the same inferential direction. As I noted, convergent evidence can be synergistic in the sense that two or more items of evidence, taken together, can mean more than they do if considered separately. Considering consonance and dissonance both structurally and probabilistically, we observed two "inferential coins." Contradiction and corroboration are the two sides of one coin; conflict and convergence are two sides of the other.

By purely structural means, we are also able to discern two species of evidential redundancy. Corroborative evidence is to some degree naturally redundant, since it involves reports of the same event. Cumulative redundance, on the other hand, involves reports of different events having the following characteristic: If we knew for sure that one event occurred, this knowledge would act to reduce the force of knowledge of some other event. Structurally and probabilistically, it is plain that redundance is a property of the events reported in evidence and not necessarily of the evidence itself; we may have nonredundant evidence about redundant events.

But structural considerations allow us to do more than sharpen our terminology regarding recurrent combinations of evidence; they also facilitate probabilistic analyses such as those I presented in Chapter 8. This leads me to mention the major limitation of purely structural analyses of evidence. Such analyses, by themselves, do not allow us to draw any conclusions. The reason is that the classification and definitional issues just mentioned do not consider the *inferential force* of evidence. By definition, the force, strength, or weight of evidence is an *intensive* dimension, so we expect that it can be graded in numerical terms. At the beginning of this discourse I stipulated that the evidence of concern to us, regardless of its form or substance, is *inconclusive;* it provides some but not complete grounds for a belief about matters at issue. Stated in other words, inconclusive evidence has only a probabilistic bearing on matters at issue. It is natural to suppose, then, that the inferential force of evidence must be graded in probabilistic terms. The question is: What terms shall we employ?

In Chapter 5 four quite different ways of grading the inferential force of evidence were examined. The Bayesian, Shafer-Dempster, Baconian, and fuzzy systems each have unique and important things to tell us about the force of evidence. As I noted, each system "resonates" to particular attributes of evidence and its inferential uses. My belief is that probabilistic reasoning is far too rich an intellectual activity for us to suppose that we can capture all of this richness within the confines of any single formal system of probabilities. In other words, I believe that there is no single probabilistic key that will allow us access to all of the mansions of evidence. I know that my pluralism in this matter is not shared by everyone. But I have many respected colleagues who, although committed to a particular view of probabilistic reasoning, have also been very tolerant of my own obstinate pluralism.

It is only by integrating structural and probabilistic concepts that we begin to gain a true appreciation for the astonishing array of subtleties that lie just below the surface of even "simple" probabilistic inferences. An examination of many of these evidential subtleties is the subject matter of Chapters 7 and 8. One way of describing these analyses is to say that we have examined various forms and combinations of evidence under a microscope. As I noted several times, virtually every inference can be decomposed to reveal additional sources of uncertainty. So we increase the discriminatory power of this microscope by making finer decompositions of a chain of reasoning based on evidence. The different views of evidential force simply supply us with different lens filters that allow us to discern different attributes of evidence and its inferential use.

Here I must yield on an important point. I have been able to use my "Bayesian lens" on more frequent occasions than I have used other lenses in examining various evidential subtleties. One reason is that I have used this lens for such a long time and have become accustomed to it. The Bayesian lens does have a particularly useful feature for capturing certain evidential subtleties; it is the concept of *conditional nonindependence*. Many of the evidential subtleties examined in Chapters 7 and 8, such as state-dependent credibility, transitivity failures, and evidential redundance and synergism, can be captured in terms of patterns of conditional nonindependence. The non-Bayesian lenses that I have also employed in capturing other evidential subtleties have not been with us for very long. Surely someone will eventually be able to give a Shaferian, Baconian, or fuzzy account of the evidential subtleties that I examined only through my Bayesian lens.

In Chapter 7, I focused on evidential properties and subtleties best examined by isolating individual items of evidence and the chains of reasoning linking them to hypotheses of interest. Some subtleties lurk in the individual links themselves and in the number of links in a chain of reasoning. Bayesian accounts of the inferential force of evidence are informative about whether it matters where in a chain of reasoning a weak link or a rare event is located. Both Bayesian and Baconian accounts are informative about the effects of reasoning chain length on the inferential force of evidence and about whether inferential transitivity is conferred in certain chains of reasoning.

I am just vain enough to believe that the credibility-related matters that I examined in Chapters 3 and 7 provide answers to the some of the *credibility-testimony* problems that have been of interest to probabilists since the 1600s. There are more attributes of a witness's credibility than have been commonly recognized. In addition my analyses in Chapter 7 show why credibility and its attributes require more than a single probability in order to capture them in conventional or Bayesian terms. On a Bayesian construal of a credibility-testimony problem it becomes very easy to observe how the behavior of a source of evidence can have inferential force quite apart from that supplied by the event(s) this source reports. But I also provided Baconian and Shaferian accounts of credibility assessment. The Baconian account shows why it is so necessary to consider the *completeness* with which we have covered evidence bearing upon the credibility-related attributes: veracity, objectivity, and observational sensitivity. The Shaferian account is valuable in showing why we must often resort to simpler credibility-related arguments because of the nature and amount of credibility-relevant evidence we have. Elements of the *theory of signal detection* are valuable in the study of credibility-related matters regarding tangible as well as testimonial evidence.

Assessing the force of secondhand, equivocal, missing, and negative evidence requires careful attention to structural and probabilistic concepts. Part of the difficulty is that there is more than one species of testimonial equivocation and more than one species of missing evidence. In addition the structural distinction between missing and negative evidence needs to be carefully noted in any attempt to assess the inferential force of these two interesting and common forms of evidence. One of the most common forms of evidence is that which we obtain at secondhand through a chain of sources. When we examine carefully just the credibility-related links in chains of reasoning from such evidence, we realize just how many uncertainties are involved. People naturally have to cut corners or suppress uncertainties in assessing the value of secondhand evidence. The structural and probabilistic analyses I presented for secondhand evidence show just how many uncertainties may be commonly suppressed.

In Chapter 8 I gave Bayesian, Baconian, and Shaferian accounts of the inferential force of recurrent combinations of evidence. On a Bayesian view, corroborative and contradictory evidence appear as two sides of one inferential coin; conflicting and convergent evidence appear as two sides of another. Resolving evidential contradictions can proceed entirely on credibility-related grounds. Evidential conflict, however, can be resolved on credibility and on other grounds as well. I gave several examples showing how apparent evidential conflict can be explained away under various patterns of conditional nonindependence among events being reported. Particularly interesting are situations in which we have various patterns of consonant and dissonant evidence revealing contradiction, corroboration, and conflict at the same time. Bayesian expressions for the force of such patterns show precisely why counting heads on either side of some evidential matter at issue is not justified (as once believed).

Combinations of evidence items suspected of being *redundant* are, in my view, the most interesting but also the most difficult to study. There are two distinct species of redundancy to which I applied the labels *corroborative* and *cumulative*. Corroborative redundancy is "natural" because it involves successive reports of the same event. Cumulative redundance involves reports of different events and in some cases can also be "natural." These cases occur when we have evidence about two events, one of which is circumstantial on the other. My analyses show why the property we call redundance is a property of the events reported in evidence and not necessarily of the evidence itself. A measure of redundance, related to one imported from *statistical communications theory,* can be applied to events reported in evidence. In my analyses I demonstrated how it is possible to have nonredundant evidence about events that are redundant, even "naturally" so. The probabilistic examples I provided illustrate the two faces on evidential redundancy. The benign face shows verification; the malign face shows the possibility of double-counting or overvaluing the force of evidence.

In discussing the various properties and subtleties in recurrent forms and combinations of evidence, I presented over one hundred numerical examples of the workings of Bayesian and other representations for the inferential force of evidence. Bayesian expressions for the force of evidence frequently have many probabilistic ingredients or variables. The trick is to make these often complex expressions reveal important and interesting evidential and inferential subtleties. For this purpose I performed a variety of sensitivity analyses on these expressions. Such analysis is patently experimental in nature. Different combinations of probabilistic ingredients, representing different situations, are used in an equation for the force of evidence. Quite often the answer supplied by an equation, appropriate to an evidential structure, is counterintuitive or at least surprising. In most cases careful examination of the equation and the structure to which it applies shows why the result should not be surprising after all. The equations in Chapters 7 and 8 provide reference points against which we might compare our intuitions about the inferential force of evidence, at least in Bayesian terms.

10.2 DISCOVERING AND MARSHALING EVIDENCE

It is not possible, in a single chapter, to capture either the variety or the extent of past and current thinking about the process of discovery. Persons in all of the mansions of evidence that I mentioned above have, to varying degrees, taken an interest in the process of generating new evidence, new hypotheses, and arguments linking them. A discourse on evidence would hardly be complete if it did not consider the means by which evidence comes into existence in the first place and then is subsequently marshaled or organized in pursuit of further discovery and the eventual drawing of conclusions. Chapter 9 represents my attempt to capture as much of the excitement in this area as I could. The study of discovery is inherently exciting because the process of discovery is exciting. Nearly everyone enjoys hearing about the imaginative discovery exploits of Sherlock Holmes and others of his ilk. Unfortunately, it is far easier to describe episodes of imaginative reasoning than it is to demonstrate how we all might acquire a more productive imagination when we need it the most.

Discovery, and the imaginative reasoning it involves, is not well understood, though it has been studied by persons from many disciplines. As I noted, Charles Sanders Peirce believed that generating a new idea, in the form of a hypothesis, involves a form of reasoning that is neither deductive or inductive. He identified a third form of reasoning and gave it the names *abduction, retroduction,* or simply *hypothesis.* As our colleagues in the field of semiotics have noted, Sir Arthur Conan Doyle gave Sherlock Holmes investigative capabilities that strongly resemble the abductive reasoning that Peirce described. Philosophers argue about whether or not there can ever be a *logic of discovery.* At least some persons in the field of artificial intelligence argue that there may be such a logic and, further, that computer systems that discover new ideas can be designed. The term *abduction* is currently used with great frequency in the field of artificial intelligence but it has taken on a meaning not evident in Peirce's use of this term.

The process of generating a new idea can be described in many different ways using different metaphors. As I noted in Chapter 9, it has been described in terms of the *bisociation* of intersecting frames of reference, in terms of *chaotic* processes, and in *semiotic* terms as the process of guessing at the meaning of the signs given us by nature. Semioticians also alert us to the fact that there may be different species of abductive reasoning. Scholars of evidence and semioticians have much in common but give every evidence of being unaware of this fact. One point of contact involves Peirce, Holmes, and abductive reasoning. I argued in Chapter 9 that there should be many other points of contact as well. By means of Figure 9.2 I noted that attention to structural matters has significant heuristic value in generating new evidence. The alternative probabilistic systems that I mentioned each have a degree of heuristic power in suggesting new questions that we might ask *of* and *about* existing evidence. I have described probabilistic reasoning as being a very rich intellectual activity; the process of discovery is certainly no less rich.

Marshaling or organizing the evidence that we discover may seem to be the least interesting task of all. However, Peter Tillers and I have argued that this is not so. It may be true that the manner in which we have marshaled or juxtaposed existing evidence plays a significant role in determining how easily we will generate new evidence and new hypotheses. The trouble is that the processes of discovery and later probabilistic inference have many requirements. Our view is that discovery requires not just efficient *search* strategies but also efficient strategies for *inquiry*. Since discovery is a process that gets played out over time in most instances, we may not yet have at hand information that can allow us to generate hypotheses that we will later appreciate as being important. So we have no choice but to keep asking questions. It is far too much to expect that any single method for marshaling evidence can satisfy all of the requisites of discovery and probabilistic reasoning. In Chapter 9 I described a linked network of evidence-marshaling operations which I believe has heuristic value in stimulating inquiry throughout the process of discovery or investigation.

10.3   FINAL WORDS

As I announced in the Preface, this has been a discourse about evidence and not about the people who use it in drawing conclusions of importance to them. I am certainly willing to listen to arguments that the study of evidence can never be completely divorced from the persons who use it. After all, the relevance, credibility, and inferential force of any collection of evidence are all matters requiring human judgment. The extent to which people make such judgments wisely (assuming that wisdom in this matter can always be determined) involves issues that I could not address in this discourse. There is quite enough to be said about the often subtle properties and the uses of evidence that may be very helpful to people in every discipline who routinely make judgments about the relevance, credibility, and force of evidence. The major trouble has been that a better understanding of evidence comes from examining scholarship and experience in many areas, or in many mansions.

I have visited all of the mansions of evidence I mentioned at the beginning of this final chapter and I have, in this discourse, told you about some observations I have made in each one. In closing, I must also tell you that my visits to some of these mansions were not by invitation. Perhaps some of my observations do not adequately reflect the past or current thinking in all of them. In some cases it might be said that I did not actually go inside a certain mansion but merely peeked in one of its windows. Just to make sure, you might visit these mansions yourself. But you should do so in any case; there are so many interesting things to learn about evidence in each one of them.

References

Achinstein, P. 1983. *The Nature of Explanation.* Oxford University Press, Oxford.

Allen, R. J. 1991. The nature of judicial proof. *Cardozo Law Review* 13 (2–3):373–422.

Anderson, T. J. 1991. Refocusing the new evidence scholarship. *Cardozo Law Review* 13 (2–3):783–791.

Anderson, T. J., and W. Twining. 1991. *Analysis of Evidence: How to Do Things with Facts Based upon Wigmore's Science of Judicial Proof* (with accompanying Teachers Manual). Little, Brown, Boston.

Aristotle. 1984. *The Complete Works of Aristotle: Revised Oxford Translation,* ed. J. Barnes. Princeton University Press, Princeton.

Ayer, A. J. 1984. *Philosophy in the Twentieth Century.* Vantage Books, New York.

Ayer, A. J. 1986. *The Problem of Knowledge.* Penguin Books, Harmondsworth, Middlesex, England.

Bacon, F. [1620] 1939. *Novum Organum.* In E. A. Burtt, *The English Philosophers from Bacon to Mill.* The Modern Library, New York.

Baer, E. 1986. The medical symptom. In *Frontiers in Semiotics,* ed. J. Deely, B. Williams, and F. Kruse. Indiana University Press, Bloomington, pp. 140–152.

Baird, J. C., and E. Noma. 1978. *Fundamentals of Scaling and Psychophysics.* Wiley, New York.

Barclay, S., R. Brown, C. Kelly, C. Peterson, L. Phillips, and J. Selvidge. 1977. *Handbook for Decision Analysis.* Decisions and Designs Inc., McLean, VA

Baring-Gould, W. S. 1967. *The Annotated Sherlock Holmes,* Vols. 1 and 2. Clarkson N. Potter, Inc., New York.

Barnard, G. A. 1958. Thomas Bayes—A biographical note. *Biometrika* 45, pts. 3, 4 (December) 1958:293–295.

Barnsley, M. 1988. *Fractals Everywhere.* Academic Press, San Diego.

Bayes, T. 1763. An essay toward solving a problem in the doctrine of chances. *Philosophical Transactions of the Royal Society* 53:370–418.

Bentham, J. 1839. *The Rationale of Judicial Evidence*. Bowring ed. William Tait, Edinburgh.

Bergman, P., and A. Moore. 1991. Mistrial by likelihood ratio: Bayesian analysis meets the F-word. *Cardozo Law Review* 13 (2–3):589–619.

Binder, D., and P. Bergman. 1984. *Fact Investigation: From Hypothesis to Proof.* West Publishing, St. Paul, MN.

Bloch, M. 1953. *The Historian's Craft*. Vintage Books, New York.

Boden, M. 1991. *The Creative Mind: Myths and Mechanisms*. Basic Books, New York.

Bonfantini, M., and G. Proni. 1983. To guess or not to guess. In *The Sign of Three: Dupin, Holmes, Peirce*, ed. Eco, U., and T. Sebeok. University of Indiana Press, Bloomington, pp. 119–134.

Boring, E. G. 1942. *Sensation and Perception in the History of Experimental Psychology*. Appelton-Century-Crofts, New York.

Boring, E. G. 1950. *A History of Experimental Psychology*. Appelton-Century-Crofts, New York.

Boring, E. G. 1963. *History, Psychology, and Science: Selected Papers*. Wiley, New York.

Boswell, J. 1791. *The Life of Samuel Johnson L.L.D.* Modern Library ed. Random House, New York.

Briggs, J., and F. D. Peat. 1989. *Turbulent Mirror: An Illustrated Guide to Chaos Theory and the Science of Wholeness*. Harper and Row, New York.

Bunge, M. 1979. *Causality and Modern Science*. 3d ed. Dover, New York.

Burks, A. W. 1980. Enumerative induction versus eliminative induction. In *Applications of Inductive Logic*, ed. L. J. Cohen and M. Hesse. Clarendon Press, Oxford, pp. 172–189.

Busacker, R., and T. Saaty. 1965. *Finite Graphs and Networks*. McGraw-Hill, New York.

Campbell, N. R. 1920. *Physics, the Elements*. Cambridge University Press. Republished as *Foundations of Science*. Dover, New York, 1957.

Campbell, N. R. 1928. *An Account of the Principals of Measurement and its Calculation*. Longmans, Green, London.

Carr, J. 1949. *The Life of Sir Arthur Conan Doyle*. Carroll and Graf, New York.

Cherry, C. 1959. *On Human Communication*. Science Editions, New York.

Chisholm, R. 1982. *The Foundations of Knowing*. University of Minnesota Press, Minneapolis.

Cohen, L. J. 1970. *The Implications of Induction*. Methuen, London.

Cohen, L. J. 1977. *The Probable and the Provable*. Clarendon, Oxford.

Cohen, L. J. 1980a. Bayesianism versus Baconianism in the evaluation of medical diagnoses. *British Journal of Philosophy* 31:45–62.

Cohen, L. J. 1980b. Comments and replies: The Cohen-Burks session. In: *Applications of Inductive Logic*, ed. L. J. Cohen and M. Hesse. Clarendon, Oxford, p. 190.

Cohen, L. J. 1981. What is necessary for testimonial corroboration? *British Journal for the Philosophy of Science* 33:161–164.

Cohen, L. J. 1985. Twelve questions about Keynes's concept of weight. *British Journal of Philosophy* 37:263–278.

Cohen, L. J. 1989a. *An Introduction to the Philosophy of Induction and Probability.* Clarendon, Oxford.

Cohen, L. J. 1989b. Belief and acceptance. *Mind* 98:347–389.

Cohen, L. J. 1991. Should a jury say what it believes or what it accepts. *Cardozo Law Review* 13 (2–3):465–483.

Cohen, L. J. 1992. *An Essay on Belief and Acceptance.* Clarendon, Oxford.

Cohen, L. J., and M. Hesse. 1980. *Applications of Inductive Logic.* Clarendon, Oxford.

Cohen, M. R., and E. Nagle. 1934. *An Introduction to Logic and Scientific Method.* Harcourt, Brace, and Company, New York.

Cooper, G. F. 1990. The computational complexity of probabilistic inference using Bayesian belief networks. *Artificial Intelligence* 42:393–405.

Copi, I. M. 1982. *Introduction to Logic.* 6th ed. Macmillan, New York.

Costello, P. 1991. *The Real World of Sherlock Holmes: True Crimes Investigated by Arthur Conan Doyle.* Carroll and Graf, New York.

Danto, A. C. 1985. *Narration and Knowledge.* Columbia University Press, New York.

Daston, L. 1988. *Classical Probability in the Enlightenment.* Princeton University Press, Princeton.

David, F. N. 1962. *Games, Gods, and Gambling.* Griffin, London.

Deely, J. 1986. The coalescence of semiotic consciousness. In *Frontiers in Semiotics,* ed. Deely, J., B. Williams, and F. Kruse. Indiana University Press. Bloomington.

Deely, J. 1990. *Basics of Semiotics.* Indiana University Press, Bloomington.

De Finetti, B.. 1972. *Probability, Induction, and Statistics: The Art of Guessing.* Wiley, New York.

Dempster, A. 1967. Upper and lower probabilities induced by a multivalued mapping. *Annals of Mathematical Statistics* 38:325–339.

Dempster, A. 1968. A generalization of Bayesian inference (with discussion). *Journal of the Royal Statistical Society,* series B, 30:205–247.

Diaconis, P., and S. Zabell. 1982. Updating subjective probability. *Journal of the American Statistical Association* 77:822–830.

Diaconis, P., and S. Zabell. 1986. Some alternatives to Bayes's rule. In *Information Pooling and Group Decision Making: Proceedings of the Second University of California, Irvine, Conference on Political Economy,* ed. B. Grofman and G. Owen. JAI Press, Greenwich, CT.

Dodson, J. D. 1961. Simulation design for a TEAS simulation research facility. Planning Research Corporation, Los Angeles. Report No. PRC R-194, 15 November.

Doyle, A. C. 1930. *The Complete Sherlock Holmes.* Doubleday, Garden City, NJ.

Dubois, D., and H. Prade. 1980. *Fuzzy Sets and Systems: Theory and Applications.* Academic Press, New York.

Durant, W. 1939. *The Story of Civilization II: The Life of Greece.* Simon and Schuster, New York.

Earman, J. 1992. *Bayes or Bust? A Critical Examination of Bayesian Confirmation Theory.* MIT Press, Cambridge, MA.

Eco, U. 1979a. *A Theory of Semiotics.* Indiana University Press, Bloomington.

Eco, U. 1979b. *The Role of the Reader: Explorations in the Semiotics of Texts.* Indiana University Press, Bloomington.

Eco, U. 1983. Horns, hooves, insteps: Some hypotheses on three forms of abduction. In *The Sign of Three: Dupin, Holmes, Peirce,* ed. U. Eco and T. Sebeok. University of Indiana Press, Bloomington, pp. 198–220.

Eco, U. 1986a. *The Name of the Rose.* Warner Books, New York.

Eco, U. 1986b. *Semiotics and the Philosophy of Language.* Indiana Unviersity Press, Bloomington.

Eco, U. 1988. *Foucault's Pendulum.* Harcourt Brace Jovanovich, New York.

Eco, U. 1990. *The Limits of Interpretation.* Indiana University Press, Bloomington.

Eco, U., and T. Sebeok, eds. 1983. *The Sign of Three: Dupin, Holmes, Peirce.* University of Indiana Press, Bloomington.

Edwards, A. W. 1992. *Likelihood: Expanded Edition.* Johns Hopkins University, Press, Baltimore.

Edwards, W. 1962. Dynamic decision theory and probabilistic information processing. *Human Factors* 4:59–73.

Edwards, W. 1965. A tactical note on the relation between scientific and statistical hypothesis. *Psychological Bulletin* 63 (6):400–402.

Edwards, W. 1988. Insensitivity, commitment, belief, and other Bayesian virtues, or, who put the snake in the warlord's bed? In *Probability and Inference in the Law of Evidence: The Uses and Limits of Bayesianism,* ed. P. Tillers and E. Green. Kluwer Academic, Dordrecht, Netherlands, pp. 271–276.

Edwards, W. 1991. Influence diagrams, Bayesian imperialism, and the *Collins* case: An appeal to reason. *Cardozo Law Review* 13 (2–3):1025–1074.

Edwards, W., D. Schum, and R. Winkler. 1990. Murder and (of?) the likelihood principle. *Journal of Behavioral Decision Making* 3:75–89.

Eells, E. 1991. *Probabilistic Causality.* Cambridge University Press, Cambridge.

Egan, J. 1975. *Signal Detection Theory and ROC Analysis.* Academic Press, New York.

Ekelof, P. O. 1983. My thoughts on evidentiary value. In *Evidentiary Value: Philosophical, Judicial, and Psychological Aspects of a Theory,* ed. P. Gardenfors, B. Hansson, and Nils-Eric Sahlin. C.W.K. Gleerups, Lund, Sweden, pp. 9–26.

Ellis, B. 1968. *Basic Concepts of Measurement.* Cambridge University Press, Cambridge.

Ellis, R. L. 1859. General preface to Bacon's philosophical works. In *The Works of Francis Bacon,* ed. J. Spedding, R. Ellis, and D. Neath. Longmans, London.

Engel, S. M. 1986. *With Good Reason: An Introduction to Informal Fallacies,* 3d ed. St. Martin's Press, New York.

Epstein, R. A. 1967. *The Theory of Gambling and Statistical Logic.* Academic Press, New York.

Fine, T. L. 1973. *Theories of Probability.* Academic Press, New York.

Fisher, R. A. 1959. *Statistical Methods and Scientific Inference.* 2d ed. Oliver and Boyd, Edinburgh.

Fisher, R. A. 1960. *The Design of Experiments,* 7th ed. Hafner, New York.

Fogelin, R. J. 1987. *Understanding Arguments: An Introduction to Informal Logic.* Harcourt, Brace, Jovanovich, San Diego.

Friedman, R. 1987. Route analysis of credibility and hearsay. *Yale Law Journal* 96 (4):667–742.

Gardenfors, P., B. Hansson, and N. Sahlin. 1983. *Evidentiary Value: Philosophical, Judicial, and Psychological Aspects of a Theory.* C.W.K. Gleerups, Lund, Sweden.

Gary, M. R., and D. S. Johnson. 1979. *Computers and Intractability: A Guide to the Theory of NP-Completeness.* Freeman, New York.

Gastwirth, J., Comment on Nesson. *Cardozo Law Review* 13 (2–3):817–829.

Geach, P. 1976. *Reason and Argument.* University of California Press, Berkeley.

Gettys, C., and T. Willke. 1969. The application of Bayes' theorem when the true data state is unknown. *Organizational Behavior and Human Performance* 4 (2):125–141.

Gifis, S. 1984. *Law Dictionary.* 2d ed. Barron's Educational Series, New York.

Gigerenzer, G., Z. Swijtink, T. Porter, L. Daston, J. Beatty, and L. Kruger. 1991. *The Empire of Chance.* Cambridge University Press, Cambridge.

Gjertsen, D. 1989. *Science and Philosophy: Past and Present.* Penguin, London.

Gleick, J. 1987. *Chaos: Making a New Science.* Penguin, New York.

Good, I. J. 1983. *Good Thinking: The Foundations of Probability and Its Applications.* University of Minnesota Press, Minneapolis.

Graham, M. L. 1989. *Evidence: Text, Rules, Illustrations, and Problems.* National Institute for Trial Advocacy, University of Notre Dame, Notre Dame, IN.

Graunt, J. 1956. Foundations of vital statistics (1662). In *The World of Mathematics,* ed. James R. Newman, vol. 3. Simon and Schuster, New York, 1421–1435.

Green, D., and J. Swets. 1966. *Signal Detection Theory and Psychophysics.* Wiley, New York.

Hacking, I. 1975. *The Emergence of Probability: A Philosophical Study of Early Ideas about Probability, Induction, and Statistical Inference.* Cambridge University Press, Cambridge.

Haft, A., J. White, and R. White. 1987. *The Key to the Name of the Rose.* Ampersand Associates, Harrington Park, NJ.

Hale, M. 1971. *The History of the Common Law of England* (1739). C. M. Gray ed. University of Chicago Press, Chicago.

Hall, T. 1977. *Sherlock Holmes and His Creator.* St. Martin's Press, New York.

Hanson, N. R. 1958. *Patterns of Discovery: An Inquiry into the Conceptual Foundations of Science.* Cambridge University Press, Cambridge.

Hanson, N. R. 1965. Notes toward a logic of discovery. In *Perspectives on Peirce: Critical Essays on Charles Sanders Peirce,* ed. R. Bernstein. Yale University Press, New Haven, pp. 42–65.

Hart, H. L. A., and T. Honore. 1985. *Causation in the Law.* 2d ed. Clarendon, Oxford.

Hastie, R., S. Penrod, and N. Pennington. 1983. *Inside the Jury.* Harvard University Press, Cambridge, MA.

Hayes, W. 1988. *Statistics*. 4th ed. Holt, Rinehart, and Winston, New York.

Hecht, S., S. Schlaer, and M. Pirenne. 1942. Energy, quanta, and vision. *Journal of General Physiology* 25:819–840.

Hempel, C. 1965. *Aspects of Scientific Explanation and Other Essays in the Philosophy of Science*. The Free Press, New York.

Hempel, C. 1966. *Philosophy of Natural Science*. Prentice Hall, Englewood Cliffs, NJ.

Hintikka, J. 1983. Sherlock Holmes formalized. In *The Sign of Three: Dupin, Holmes, Peirce*, ed. U. Eco and T. Sebeok. Indiana University Press, Bloomington, pp. 170–178.

Hintikka, J. 1992. The Concept of Induction in the Light of the Interrogative Approach to Inquiry. In *Inference, Explanation, and Other Frustrations: Essays in the Philosophy of Science*, ed. J. Earman. University of California Press, Berkeley.

Hintikka, J., and J. Bachman. 1991. *What If . . .?: Toward Excellence in Reasoning*. Mayfield, Mountain View, CA.

Hintikka, J., and M. Hintikka, 1983. Sherlock Holmes confronts Modern Logic: Toward a Theory of Information-Seeking through Questioning. In *The Sign of Three: Dupin, Holmes, Peirce*, ed. U. Eco and T. Sebeok. Indiana University Press, Bloomington, pp. 154–169.

Hobbes, T. [1651] 1988. *The Leviathan*. Prometheus, Buffalo, NY.

Holdsworth, W. S. 1903. *A History of English Law*, vol. 1. Methuen, London.

Holland, H. J., K. J. Holyoak, R. E. Nisbett, and P. R. Thagard. 1989. *Induction: Processes of Inference, Learning, and Discovery*, MIT Press, Cambridge, MA.

Hoopes, J., ed. 1991. *Peirce on Signs: Writings on Semiotic by Charles Sanders Peirce*. University of North Carolina Press, Chapel Hill.

Horwich, P. 1982. *Probability and Evidence*. Cambridge University Press, Cambridge.

Horwich, P. 1987. *Asymmetries in Time: Problems in the Philosophy of Science*. MIT Press, Cambridge, MA.

Houser, N., and C. Kloesel. 1992. *The Essential Peirce: Selected Philosophical Writings (1867–1893)*, vol. 1. Indiana University Press, Bloomington.

Howard, R. 1989. Knowledge maps. *Management Science* 35 (8):903–922.

Howard, R., and J. Matheson. 1984. Influence diagrams. *Readings on the Principles and Applications of Decision Analysis*, vol. 2. Strategic Decisions Group, Menlo Park, CA.

Hume, D. 1975. *A Treatise of Human Nature* (1739). ed. L. A. Selby-Bigge. Clarendon, Oxford.

Hume, D. 1989. *Enquiries Concerning Human Understanding* (1777), ed. P. H. Nidditch. 3d ed. Clarendon Press, Oxford.

Jeffrey, R. 1983. *The Logic of Decision*. University of Chicago Press, Chicago.

Jeffrey, R. 1991. *Probability and the Art of Judgment*. Cambridge University Press, Cambridge.

Johnson, S. 1969. Rambler No. 43. *The Yale Edition of the Works of Samuel Johnson*, ed. W. J. Bate, and A. B. Strauss, vol. 3. Yale University Press, New Haven.

Johnson, S. 1969. Rambler No. 137. *The Yale Edition of the Works of Samuel Johnson*, ed. W. J. Bate and A. B. Strauss, vol. 4. Yale University Press, New Haven.

Johnson, S. 1773. *A Dictionary of the English Language.* 4th ed. Librairie Du Leban, Beirut, Lebanon, facsimile ed.

Johnson, W. 1946. *People in Quandries.* Harper, New York.

Kadane, J., and D. A. Schum. 1991. Opinions in dispute: The Sacco-Vanzetti case. *In Bayesian Statistics 4*, ed. J. M. Bernardo, J. O. Berger, A. P. Dawid, and A. F. M. Smith. Oxford University Press, New York, pp. 267–287.

Kaplan, J., J. Waltz, and R. Park. 1992. *Evidence: Cases and Materials*, 7th ed. Foundation Press, Westbury, NY.

Kaufman, L. 1974. *Sight and Mind: An Introduction to Visual Perception.* Oxford University Press, New York.

Kellert, S. 1993. *In the Wake of Chaos: Unpredictable Order in Dynamical Systems.* University of Chicago Press, Chicago.

Kelly, C., and S. Barclay. 1973. A general Bayesian model for hierarchical inference. *Organizational Behavior and Human Performance* 10:388–403.

Keynes, J. M. 1957. *A Treatise on Probability* (1921). Reprint of 1st ed. Macmillan, London.

Kim, J. H., and J. Pearl. 1983. A computational model for combined causal and diagnostic reasoning in inference systems. *Proceedings of the 8th International Joint Conference on AI (IJCAI-85)*, Los Angeles, pp. 190–193.

Klir, G., and T. Folger. 1988. *Fuzzy Sets, Uncertainty, and Information.* Prentice Hall, Englewood Cliffs, NJ.

Kneale, W. 1952. *Probability and Induction.* Clarendon, Oxford.

Kneale, W., and M. Kneale. 1984. *The Development of Logic.* Clarendon, Oxford.

Koestler, A. 1964. *The Act of Creation.* Arkana, Penguin Group, London, 1989 reprint.

Kolmogorov, A. N. 1956. *Foundations of the Theory of Probability* (1933). 2d English ed. Chelsea Publishing, New York.

Kolmogorov, A. N. 1969. The theory of probability. In *Mathematics: Its Content Methods, and Meaning*, vol. 2, ed. A. D. Aleksandrov, A. N. Kolmogorov, and M. A. Lavrent'ev. MIT Press, Cambridge, MA, pp. 229–264.

Kyburg, H. E., and H. E. Smokler. 1964. *Studies in Subjective Probability.* Wiley, New York.

Lakatos, I. [1970] (1980). Falsification and the methodology of scientific research programs. In *The Methodology of Scientific Research Programs*, vol. 1, ed. J. Worrall and G. Currie. Cambridge University Press, Cambridge, pp. 8–101.

Lakatos, I. 1980a. *The Methodology of Scientific Research Programs*, ed. J. Worrall and G. Currie. Cambridge University Press, Cambridge.

Lakatos, I. 1980b. *Mathematics, Science and Epistemology*, ed. J. Worrall and G. Currie. Cambridge University Press, Cambridge.

Langley, P., H. Simon, G. Bradshaw, and J. Zytkow. 1987. *Scientific Discovery: Computational Explorations of the Creative Process.* MIT Press, Cambridge, MA.

Lauritzen, S. L., and D. J. Spiegelhalter. 1988. Local computations with probabilities on graphical structures and their application to expert systems. *Journal of the Royal Statistical Society*, series B, 50 (2):157–224.

Le Grand, Y. 1975. History of research on seeing. In *Handbook of Perception: Seeing*, vol. 5, ed. E. C. Carterette and M. P. Friedman. Academic Press, New York, pp 1–23.

Lellenberg, J. 1987. *The Quest for Sir Arthur Conan Doyle: Thirteen Biographers in Search of a Life.* Southern Illinois University Press, Carbondale.

Lempert, R. 1977. Modeling relevance. *Michigan Law Review* 75 (5–6):1021–1057.

Lempert, R. 1986. The new evidence scholarship: Analyzing the process of proof. *Boston University Law Review* 66 (3–4):439–477.

Lempert, R., and S. Saltzburg. 1977. *A Modern Approach to Evidence.* West Publishing, St. Paul, MN.

Lenat, D. 1981. *The Nature of Heuristics.* Xerox Palo Alto Research Center Cognitive and Instructional Sciences Series CIS-12 (SSL-81-1). April.

Lenat, D. 1983. EURISKO: A program that learns new heuristics and domain concepts. *Artificial Intelligence* 21:61–98.

Leon-Garcia, A. 1989. *Probability and Random Processes for Electrical Engineering.* Addison-Wesley, Reading, MA.

Levy, I. 1980. Potential surprise: Its role in inference and decision-making. In *Applications of Inductive Logic*, ed. L. J. Cohen and M. Hesse. Clarendon, Oxford.

Levi, I. 1983. *The Enterprise of Knowledge: An Essay on Knowledge, Credal Probability, and Chance.* MIT Press, Cambridge, MA.

Levi, I. 1984. *Decisions and Revisions: Philosophical Essays on Knowledge and Value.* Cambridge University Press, Cambridge.

Levi, I. 1991. *The Fixation of Belief and its Undoing: Changing Beliefs through Inquiry.* Cambridge University Press, Cambridge.

Lewis, D. 1973. Causation. *Journal of Philosophy* 70:556–567.

Lewis, D. 1986. *Counterfactuals.* Basil Blackwell, Oxford.

Lichtman, A., and V. French. 1978. *Historians and the Living Past.* Harlan Davidson, New York.

Liebow, E. 1982. *Dr. Joe Bell; Model for Sherlock Holmes.* Bowling Green University Popular Press, Bowling Green, OH.

Lindley, D. 1985. *Making Decisions.* 2d ed. Wiley, New York.

Lindley, D. 1990. Thomas Bayes. In *The New Palgrave Utility and Probability*, ed. J. Eatwell, M. Milgate, and P. Newman. Norton, New York.

Locke, J. [1689] 1991. *An Essay Concerning Human Understanding*, ed. P. Nidditch. Clarendon, Oxford.

Losee, J. 1990. *A Historical Introduction to the Philosophy of Science.* Oxford University Press, Oxford.

Luce, R. D. 1980. Comments on chapters by MacCrimmon, Stanbury, and Wehrung; and Schum. In *Cognitive Processes in Choice and Decision Behavior*, ed. T. Wallsten. Lawrence Erlbaum Associates, Hillsdale, NJ., pp. 211–213.

Mackie, J. L. 1974. *The Cement of the Universe: A Study of Causation.* Clarendon, Oxford.

Maguire, J., J. B. Weinstein, J. H. Chadbourn, and J. H. Mansfield. 1973. *Evidence: Cases and Materials.* 6th ed. Foundation Press, Mineola, NY.

Mandelbrot, B. 1983. *The Fractal Geometry of Nature.* Freeman, New York.

Marks, L. E. 1974. *Sensory Processes: The New Psychophysics*. Academic Press, New York.

Martin, A. 1980. A general algorithm for determining likelihood ratios in cascaded inference. Rice University Psychology Department Report #80-03. November.

Martin, D. C. 1980. *Wilderness of Mirrors*. Ballantine, New York.

Mellor, D. H. 1985. *Real Time*. Cambridge University Press, Cambridge.

Mellor, D. H. 1988. *The Warrant of Induction*. Cambridge University Press, Cambridge.

Mellor, D. H. 1990. *F. P. Ramsey: Philosphical Papers*. Cambridge University Press, Cambridge.

Michalski, R. 1991. Toward a unified theory of learning: Basic ideas and a classification of learning processes. In *Proceedings of the First World Conference on the Fundamentals of Artificial Intelligence*, Paris, July 1–5.

Mill, J. S. [1843] 1952. *System of Logic*. Longmans, Green, London.

Mill, J. S. 1865. *A System of Logic: Ratiocinative and Inductive*. 6th ed. Longmans, Green, London.

Miller, R. W. 1987. *Fact and Method: Explanation, Confirmation and Reality in the Natural and the Social Sciences*. Princeton University Press, Princeton.

Moser, P. 1991. *Knowledge and Evidence*. Cambridge University Press, Cambridge.

Mueller, C., and L. Kirkpatrick. 1988. *Federal Rules of Evidence*. Little, Brown, Boston.

Nance, D. 1991a. Missing evidence. *Cardozo Law Review* 13 (2–3):831–882.

Nance, D. 1991b. Hear no evil, see no evil: A comment on Professor Nesson's claims about evidence suppression. *Cardozo Law Review* 13 (2–3):809–815.

Neapolitan, R. E. 1990. *Probabilistic Reasoning in Expert Systems: Theory and Algorithms*. Wiley, New York.

Nesson, C. 1986. Agent Orange meets the Blue Bus: Factfinding at the frontiers of knowledge. *Boston University Law Review* 66 (3–4):521–539.

Nesson, C. 1991. Incentives to spoliate evidence in civil litigation: The need for vigorous judicial action. *Cardozo Law Review* 13 (2–3):793–807.

Nozick, R. 1981. *Philosophical Explanations*. Harvard University Press, Cambridge, MA.

Nunnally, J. 1967. *Psychometric Theory*. 2d ed. McGraw-Hill, New York.

O'Connor, D., and B. Carr. 1982. *Introduction to the Theory of Knowledge*. University of Minnesota Press, Minneapolis.

O'Neill, L. J. 1982. Corroborating testimonies. *British Journal for the Philosophy of Science* 33:60–63.

Park, R. 1992. Hearsay Reform Conference, University of Minnesota Law School, September, 1991. *Minnesota Law Review* 76 (3) entire issue.

Parker, R., and R. Rardin. 1988. *Discrete Optimization*. Academic Press, San Diego.

Parzen, E. 1960. *Modern Probability Theory and Its Applications*. Wiley, New York.

Pearl, J. 1982. Reverend Bayes on inference engines: A distributed hierarchical approach. *Proceedings of the National Conference on AI*, Pittsburgh, pp. 133–135.

Pearl, J. 1988. *Probabilistic Reasoning in Intelligent Systems: Networks of Plausible Inference*. Morgan Kaufmann, San Mateo, CA.

Pearl, J. 1990. Bayesian and belief-functions formalisms for evidential reasoning: A conceptual analysis. In *Readings in Uncertain Reasoning,* ed. G. Shafer, and J. Pearl. Morgan Kaufmann, San Mateo, CA, pp. 540–574.

Pearl, J., and T. Verma. 1987. The logic of representing dependencies by directed graphs. *Proceedings of the 6th National Conference on AI (AAAI-87),* Seattle, pp. 374–379.

Pearson, E., and M. Kendall. 1970. *Studies in the History of Statistics and Probability.* Charles Griffin, London.

Peirce, C.S. 1878. The probability of induction. *Popular Science Monthly* 12 (April):705–718. (Reprinted in *The Essential Peirce: Selected Philosophical Writings* [1867–1893], vol. 1, eds. N. Houser and C. Kloesel. Indiana University Press, Bloomington, pp. 142–154.

Peirce, C. S. [1898] 1992. *Reasoning and the Logic of Things, Cambridge Conferences 1898,* ed. K. Ketner. Harvard University Press, Cambridge, MA.

Peirce, C. S. [1901] 1955. Abduction and induction. In *Philosophical Writings of Peirce,* ed. J. Buchler. Dover, New York, pp. 150–156.

Peirce, C. S. [1903] 1955. Perceptual judgments. In *Philosophical Writings of Peirce,* ed. J. Buchler. Dover, New York, pp. 302–309.

Peng, Y., and J. A. Reggia. 1987. A probabilistic causal model for diagnostic problem solving, parts I and II. *IEEE Transactions on Systems, Man, and Cybernetics,* vol. SMC-17.

Pennington, N. 1981. *Causal Reasoning and Decision Making.* Ph.D. dissertation. Harvard University Press, Cambridge, MA.

Pennington, N., and R. Hastie. 1991. A cognitive theory of juror decision making: The story model. *Cardozo Law Review* 13 (2–3):519–557.

Pennington, N., and R. Hastie. 1992. Explaining the evidence: Tests of the story model for juror decision making. *Journal of Personality and Social Psychology* 62 (2):189–206.

Penrose, R. 1991. *The Emperor's New Mind: Concerning Computers, Minds, and the Laws of Physics.* Penguin, New York.

Pfeiffer, P. 1990. *Probability for Applications.* Springer-Verlag, New York.

Pfeiffer, P. E., and D. A. Schum. 1973. *Introduction to Applied Probability.* Academic Press, New York.

Pierce, J. R. 1961. *Symbols, Signals and Noise: The Nature and Process of Communication.* Harper and Row, New York.

Plucknett, T. F. T. 1956. *A Concise History of the Common Law.* 5th ed. Little, Brown, Boston.

Pollock, F., and F. Maitland. 1968. *The History of English Law before the Time of Edward I.* 2d ed. Cambridge University Press, Cambridge.

Pólya, G. 1954a. *Mathematics and Plausible Reasoning: Induction and Analogy in Mathematics.* vol. 1. Princeton University Press, Princeton.

Pólya, G. 1954b. *Mathematics and Plausible Reasoning: Patterns of Plausible Inference,* vol. 2. Princeton University Press, Princeton.

Pólya, G. 1957. *How to Solve It: A New Aspect of Mathematical Method.* 2d ed. Princeton University Press, Princeton.

Pollock, J. 1986. *Contemporary Theories of Knowledge*. Rowman and Littlefield, Totowa, NJ.

Poole, A. L. 1955. *From Domesday Book to Magna Carta: 1087–1216*. Clarendon, Oxford.

Popper, K. 1968. *The Logic of Scientific Discovery*. Harper Torchbooks, New York.

Popper, K. 1981. *Objective Knowledge: An Evolutionary Approach*. Rev. ed. Clarendon, Oxford.

Poundstone, W. 1990. *Labyrinths of Reason*. Anchor Books, Doubleday, New York.

Ramsey, F. P. [1926] 1990. Truth and probability. In *F. P. Ramsey: Philosophical Papers*, ed. D. H. Mellor. Cambridge University Press, Cambridge, pp. 53–94.

Ramsey, F. P. [1929] 1990. Probability and partial belief. In *F. P. Ramsey: Philosophical Papers*, ed. D. H. Mellor. Cambridge University Press, Cambridge, pp. 95–96.

Reichenbach, H. 1968. *The Rise of Scientific Philosophy*. University of California Press, Berkeley.

Reiter, R. 1980. A logic for default reasoning. *Artificial Intelligence* 13:81–132.

Rescher, N. 1978. *Peirce's Philosophy of Science: Critical Studies in His Theory of Induction and the Scientific Method*. University of Notre Dame Press, Notre Dame, IN.

Rescher, N. 1988. *Rationality: A Philosophical Inquiry into the Nature and the Rationale of Reason*. Clarendon, Oxford.

Roth, M., and L. Galis, 1984. *Knowing: Essays in the Analysis of Knowledge*. University Press of America, Lanham, MD.

Russell, B. [1912] 1959. *The Problems of Philosophy*. 7th ed. (reprint). Oxford University Press, Oxford.

Russell, B. 1960. *A History of Western Philosophy*. Simon and Schuster, New York.

Salmon, W. 1970. Bayes's theorem and the history of science. In *Minnesota Studies in the Philosophy of Science: Historical and Philosophical Perspectives of Science*, vol. 5, ed. R. Stuewer. University of Minnesota Press, Minneapolis, pp. 68–86.

Salmon, W. 1979. *The Foundations of Scientific Inference*. University of Pittsburgh Press, Pittsburgh.

Salmon, W. 1984. *Logic*. 3d ed. Prentice Hall, Englewood Cliffs, NJ.

Savage, C. W. 1970. *The Measurement of Sensation: A Critique of Perceptual Psychophysics*. University of California Press, Berkeley.

Savage, L. J. 1962. *Statistical Inference*. Methuen, London.

Savage, L. J. 1961. The foundations of statistics reconsidered. *Proceedings of the Fourth Berkeley Symposium on Mathematics and Probability*, vol. 1. University of California Press, Berkeley.

Schaefer, R., and K. Borcherding. 1973. A note on the consistency between two approaches to incorporate data from unreliable sources in Bayesian analyses. *Organizational Behavior and Human Performance* 9 (3):504–508.

Schum, D. 1966. Inferences on the basis of conditionally nonindependent data. *Journal of Experimental Psychology* 72 (3):401–409.

Schum, D. 1969. Concerning the simulation of diagnostic systems which process complex probabilistic evidence sets. Aerospace Medical Research Laboratories Technical Report AMRL-TR-69-10. April.

Schum, D. 1977. Contrast effects in inference: On the conditioning of current evidence by prior evidence. *Organizational Behavior and Human Performance* 18:217–253.

Schum, D. 1979. A review of a case against Blaise Pascal and his heirs. *Michigan Law Review* 77 (3):446–483.

Schum, D. 1980. Current developments in research on cascaded inference processes. In *Cognitive Processes in Choice and Decision Behavior*, ed. T. S. Wallsten. Lawrence Erlbaum Associates, Hillsdale, NJ, pp. 179–210.

Schum, D. 1981a. Sorting out the effects of witness sensitivity and response-criterion placement upon the inferential value of testimonial evidence. *Organizational Behavior and Human Performance* 27:153–196.

Schum, D. 1981b. Formalizing the process of assessing the probative value of alibi testimony. Rice University Psychology Department Research Report No. 81-05. May.

Schum, D. 1986. Probability and the processes of discovery, proof, and choice. *Boston University Law Review* 66 (3–4):825–876.

Schum, D. 1987. *Evidence and Inference for the Intelligence Analyst*. vols. 1 and 2. University Press of America, Lanham, MD.

Schum, D. 1989. Knowledge, probability and credibility. *Journal of Behavioral Decision Making* 2:39–62.

Schum, D. 1990. Inference networks and their many subtle properties. *Information and Decision Technologies* 16:69–98.

Schum, D. 1991. Jonathan Cohen and Thomas Bayes on the analysis of chains of reasoning. In *Probability and Rationality: Studies on L. Jonathan Cohen's Philosophy of Science*, ed. E. Eells and T. Maruszewski. Poznan Studies in the Philosophy of the Sciences and the Humanities, vol. 21. Rodopi Press, Amsterdam, pp. 99–145.

Schum, D. 1992. Hearsay from a layperson. *Cardozo Law Review* 14 (1):1–77.

Schum, D., and P. Tillers. 1989. Marshalling evidence throughout the process of fact investigation: A simulation. Reports 89-01 to 89-04, George Mason University, Fairfax. Virginia.

Schum, D., and P. Tillers. 1990. A technical note on computer-assisted Wigmorean argument structuring. Report 90-01, George Mason University, Fairfax, Virginia. 15 January.

Schum, D., and P. Tillers. 1991. Marshalling evidence for adversary litigation. *Cardozo Law Review* 13 (2–3):657–704.

Sebeok, T. 1986. The doctrine of signs. In *Frontiers in Semiotics*, ed. J. Deely, B. Williams, and F. Kruse. Indiana University Press, Bloomington, pp. 35–42.

Sebeok, T. 1986. Semiotics and its congeners. In *Frontiers in Semiotics*, ed. J. Deely, B. Williams, and F. Kruse. Indiana University Press, Bloomington, pp. 255–263.

Sebeok, T. 1991. *A Sign Is Just a Sign*. Indiana University Press, Bloomington.

Sebeok, T., and J. Umiker-Sebeok. 1983. You know my method. A justaposition of Charles S. Peirce and Sherlock Holmes. In *The Sign of Three: Dupin, Holmes, Peirce*, ed. U. Eco and T. Sebeok. University of Indiana Press, Bloomington, pp. 11–54.

Shachter, R. 1986. Evaluating influence diagrams. *Operations Research* 34 (6):871–882.

Shachter, R., and D. Heckerman. 1987. Thinking backward for knowledge acquisition. *Al Magazine* (Fall):55–61.

Shackle, G. L. S. 1968. *Decision, Order, and Time in Human Affairs.* Cambridge University Press, Cambridge.

Shafer, G. 1976. *A Mathematical Theory of Evidence,* Princeton University Press, Princeton.

Shafer, G. 1981. Jeffrey's rule of conditioning. *Philosophy of Science* 48:337–362.

Shafer, G. 1986a. The construction of probability arguments. *Boston University Law Review* 66 (3–4):799–816.

Shafer, G. 1986b. The combination of evidence. *International Journal of Intelligent Systems* 1:155–179.

Shafer, G. 1988. Combining AI and OR. University of Kansas School of Business, Working Paper No. 195. April.

Shafer, G. 1990. Belief functions. In *Readings in Uncertain Reasoning,* ed. G. Shafer and J. Pearl, Morgan Kaufmann, San Mateo, CA, pp. 473–481.

Shafer, G., and J. Pearl. 1990. *Readings in Uncertain Reasoning.* Morgan Kaufmann Publishers, San Mateo, CA.

Shafer, G., and R. Srivastava. 1990. The Bayesian and belief-function formalisms: A general perspective for auditing. *Auditing: A Journal of Practice and Theory.* (Reprinted in Shafer. G., and J. Pearl. 1990. *Readings in Uncertain Reasoning.* Morgan Kaufmann, San Mateo, CA, pp. 482–521.)

Shafer, G., and A. Tversky. 1985. Languages and designs for probability judgment. *Cognitive Science* 9. (Reprinted in Shafer, G., and J. Pearl. 1990. *Readings in Uncertain Reasoning.* Morgan Kaufmann, San Mateo, CA, pp. 40–54.)

Shannon, C., and W. Weaver. 1963. *The Mathematical Theory of Communication.* University of Illinois Press, Urbana.

Shapiro, B. 1982. *Probability and Certainty in Seventeenth-Century England.* Princeton University Press, Princeton.

Shenoy, P., and G. Shafer. 1986. Propagating belief functions using local computations. *IEEE Expert* 1 (3):43–52.

Shenoy, P., G. Shafer, and K. Mellouli. Propagation of belief functions: A distributed approach. In *Uncertainty in Artificial Intelligence 2,* ed. J. Lemmer and L. Kanal. North Holland, Amsterdam, pp. 325–336.

Singh, J. 1966. *Great Ideas in Information Theory, Language, and Cybernetics.* Dover, New York.

Skyrms, B. 1986. *Choice and Chance: An Introduction to Inductive Logic.* 3d ed. Wadsworth, Belmont, CA.

Sominskii, I. 1961. *The Method of Mathematical Induction.* Blaisdell, New York.

Sperber, D., and D. Wilson, 1986. *Relevance: Communication and Cognition.* Harvard University Press, Cambridge, MA.

Staniland, A. C. 1961. *Patterns of Redundancy.* Cambridge University Press, Cambridge.

Starrs, J. E. 1986a. Once more unto the breech: The firearms evidence in the Sacco and Vanzetti case revisited: Part I. *Journal of Forensic Sciences* 31 (2):630–654.

Starrs, J. E. 1986b. Once more unto the breech: The firearms evidence in the Sacco and Vanzetti case revisited: Part II. *Journal of Forensic Sciences.* 31 (3):1050–1078.

Stenton, F. M. 1962. *Anglo-Saxon England.* Clarendon, Oxford.

Sternberg, R. J., ed. 1988. *The Nature of Creativity: Contemporary Psychological Perspectives.* Cambridge University Press, Cambridge.

Stevens, S. S. 1946. On the theory of scales of measurement. *Science* 103:677–680.

Stevens, S. S. 1951. Mathematics, measurement, and psychophysics. In *Handbook of Experimental Psychology,* ed. S. S. Stevens. Wiley, New York, pp. 1–49.

Stevens, S. S. On the Psychophysical Law. *Psychological Review* 64:153–181.

Stevens, S. S. 1959. Measurement, psychophysics, and utility. In *Measurement: Definition and Theories,* ed. G. Churchman and P. Ratoosh. Wiley, New York, pp. 18–61.

Stevens, S. S. 1962. The surprising simplicity of sensory metrics. *American Psychologist* 17 (1):29–39.

Stevens, S. S. 1975. *Psychophysics: Introduction to Its Perceptual, Neural, and Social Prospects.* Wiley, New York.

Stewart, I. 1989. *Does God Play Dice? The Mathematics of Chaos.* Blackwell, Cambridge, MA.

Stigler, S. 1983. John Craig and the probability of history: From the death of Christ to the birth of Laplace. *Journal of the American Statistical Association* 81:879–887.

Stigler, S. 1986. *The History of Statistics: The Measurement of Uncertainty before 1900.* Harvard University Press, Cambridge, MA.

Stone, M. 1984. *Proof of Fact in Criminal Cases.* Green, Edinburgh.

Swinburne, R. 1974. *The Justification of Induction.* Oxford University Press, Oxford.

Swets, J. 1964. *Signal Detection and Recognition by Human Observers.* Wiley, New York.

The Sacco-Vanzetti Case: Transcript of the Record of the Trial of Nicola Sacco and Bartolomeo Vanzetti in the Courts of Massachusetts and Subsequent Proceedings 1920–27, vols. 1–6. 1969. Paul P. Appel, Publisher, Mamaroneck, NY.

Thompson, R. S. 1991. Decision, disciplined inferences, and the adversary process. *Cardozo Law Review* 13 (2–3):725–781.

Tillers, P. 1991. Decision and inference in litigation. *Cardozo Law Review* 13 (2–3), entire issue.

Tillers, P., and E. Green. 1986. Symposium: Probability and inference in the law of evidence. *Boston University Law Review* 66 (3–4), entire issue.

Tillers, P., and E. Green. 1988. *Probability and Inference in the Law of Evidence: The Uses and Limits of Bayesianism.* Kluwer Academic, Dordrecht, Netherlands.

Tillers, P., and D. Schum. 1988. Charting new territory in judicial proof: Beyond Wigmore. *Cardozo Law Review* 9 (3):907–966.

Tillers, P., and D. Schum, 1991. A theory of preliminary fact investigation. *U.C. Davis Law Review* 24 (4):931–1012.

Tillers, P., and D. Schum. 1992. Hearsay logic. *Minnesota Law Review* 76 (3):813–858.

Todhunter, I. [1865] 1965. *A History of the Mathematical Theory of Probability: From the Time of Pascal to that of Laplace.* Chelsea Publishing, New York.

Toulmin, S. 1964. *The Uses of Argument*. Cambridge University Press, Cambridge.

Toulmin, S., R. Reike, and A. Janik. 1984. *An Introduction to Reasoning*, 2d ed. Macmillan, New York.

Truzzi, M. 1983. Sherlock Holmes: Applied social psychologist. In *The Sign of Three: Dupin, Holmes, Peirce*, ed. U. Eco and T. Sebeok. University of Indiana Press, Bloomington, pp. 55–80.

Tursman, R. 1987. *Peirce's Theory of Scientific Discovery: A System of Logic Conceived as Semiotic*. Indiana University Press, Bloomington.

Twining, W. 1984. Taking Facts Seriously. *Journal of Legal Education* 34:22–42.

Twining, W. 1985. *Theories of Evidence: Bentham and Wigmore*. Stanford University Press, Stanford.

Twining, W. 1990. *Rethinking Evidence: Exploratory Essays*. Basil Blackwell, Oxford.

Twining, W., and D. Miers. 1982. *How to Do Things with Rules*. Weidenfeld and Nicolson, London.

Van Caenegem, R. 1988. *The Birth of the English Common Law*. Cambridge University Press, Cambridge.

van Fraassen, B. 1980. *The Scientific Image*. Clarendon, Oxford.

Venn, J. 1907. *The Principles of Inductive Logic*. 2d ed. (reprint). Chelsea Publishing, New York.

von Winterfeldt, D., and W. Edwards. 1988. *Decision Analysis and Behavioral Research*. Cambridge University Press, Cambridge.

Wagner, C. 1979. Book review: The probable and the provable. *Duke Law Journal* 1979 (4):1071–1081.

Walton, D. N. 1989. *Informal Logic: A Handbook for Critical Argumentation*. Cambridge University Press, Cambridge.

Warren, R. M., and R. P. Warren. 1963. A critique of S. S. Stevens' "New Psychophysics." *Perceptual and Motor Skills* 16:797–810.

Warren, R. M., and R. P. Warren. 1968. *Helmholtz on Perception: Its Physiology and Development*. Wiley, New York.

Weatherford, R. 1982. *Philosophical Foundations of Probability Theory*. Routledge, Kegan Paul, London.

Weinstein, J. 1961. Probative force of hearsay. *Iowa Law Review* 46:331–355.

Weinstein, J., J. Mansfield, N. Abrams, and M. Berger. 1983. *Cases and Materials on Evidence*, 7th ed. Foundation Press, Mineola, NY.

Wells, C. 1911. The origin of the petty jury. *Law Quarterly Review* 107:347–361.

Wells, C. 1914. Early opposition to the petty jury in criminal cases. *Law Quarterly Review* 117:97–110.

Whewell, W. 1847. *The Philosophy of the Inductive Sciences*. vols. 1 and 2. 2d ed. Parker, London.

Wigmore, J. H. 1913. The problem of proof. *Illinois Law Review*, 8 (2):77–103.

Wigmore, J. H. 1937. *The Science of Judicial Proof: As Given by Logic, Psychology, and General Experience and Illustrated in Judicial Trials*. 3d ed. Little, Brown, Boston.

Wigmore, J. H. 1983. *Wigmore on Evidence*, vol. 1. Tillers rev. Little, Brown, Boston.

Wigmore, J. H. 1983. *Wigmore on Evidence*, vol. 1A, Tillers rev. Little, Brown, Boston.

Wigmore, J. H. 1940. *Wigmore on Evidence*, vol. 2, 3d ed. Little, Brown, Boston.

Wigmore, J. H. 1970. *Wigmore on Evidence*, vol. 3A. Chadbourn rev. Little, Brown, Boston.

Wigmore, J. H. 1974. *Wigmore on Evidence*, vol. 5. Chadbourn, rev. Little, Brown, Boston.

Wigmore, J. H. 1940. *Wigmore on Evidence*, vol. 7. 3d ed. Little, Brown, Boston.

Wigmore, J. H. 1961. *Wigmore on Evidence*, vol. 8. McNaughton rev. Little, Brown, Boston.

Williams, B. 1986. History in relation to semiotic. In *Frontiers in Semiotics*, ed. J. Deely, B. Williams, and F. Kruse. Indiana University Press, Bloomington, pp. 217–223.

Winkler, R. 1972. *Introduction to Bayesian Inference and Decision*. Holt, Rinehart, and Winston, New York.

Winks, R. W. 1968. *The Historian as Detective: Essays on Evidence*. Harper Torchbooks, New York.

Wulff, H. 1981. *Rational Diagnosis and Treatment: An Introduction to Clinical Decision-Making*. Blackwell Scientific, Oxford.

Yager, R., S. Ovchinnikov, R. M. Tong, and H. T. Nguyen. 1987. *Fuzzy Sets and Applications: Selected Papers by L. A. Zadeh*. Wiley, New York.

Young, W., and D. E. Kaiser. 1985. *Postmortem: New Evidence in the Case of Sacco and Vanzetti*. University of Massachusetts Press, Amherst.

Zabell, S. 1988. The probabilistic analysis of testimony. *Journal of Statistical Planning and Inference* 20:327–354.

Zadeh, L. 1965. Fuzzy sets. *Information and Control* 8:338–353.

Zadeh, L. 1979. A theory of approximate reasoning. In *Machine Intelligence*, ed. D. D. Hayes, D. Michie, and L. Mikulich. Vol. 9. Halstead Press, New York, pp. 149–194.

Zadeh, L. 1983. The role of fuzzy logic in the management of uncertainty in expert systems. *Fuzzy Sets and Systems*, 11:199–227.

Zadeh, L. 1984. A theory of commonsense knowledge. In *Aspects of Vagueness*, ed. H. Skala, S. Termini, and E. Trillas. Reidel, Dordrecht, Netherlands, pp. 257–296.

Zadeh, L. 1985. Syllogistic reasoning in fuzzy logic and its application to usuality and reasoning with dispositions. *IEEE Transactions on Systems, Man, and Cybernetics*, 15 (6):754–763.

Zadeh, L. 1988. Fuzzy logic. *Computer* (April):83–93.

Zuckerman, A. 1986. Law, fact, or justice. *Boston University Law Review* 66 (3–4):487–508.

Zuckerman, A. 1989. *The Principles of Criminal Evidence*. Clarendon, Oxford.

Name Index

Price, R., 48–49, 206, 213
Proni, G., 483, 516

Ramsey, F. P., 31, 51, 223–224, 525
Rardin, R., 182, 523
Reggia, J., 468, 524
Reichenbach, H., 23, 27, 453–454, 525
Reike, R., 60, 81, 529
Reiter, R., 261, 525
Rescher, N., 52, 462, 464, 469–471, 478–479, 525
Roth, M., 105, 525
Russell, B., 22–24, 26, 525

Saaty, T., 169, 516
Sahlin, N. E., 269, 518–519
Salmon, W., 14, 31, 450, 453–456, 459, 473–474, 525
Saltzburg, S., 99, 346, 358, 521
Saunderson, N., 52
Savage, C. W., 212, 525
Savage, L. J., 51, 223–224, 525
Schaefer, R., 353, 525
Schlaer, S., 69, 520
Schum, D., 2, 43, 52, 60, 73, 81, 105, 115, 136, 163, 166, 168, 179, 196–197, 205, 208–209, 257, 261, 293, 305, 308, 312, 314, 324, 327, 335, 339, 342, 346, 350, 356, 411, 446, 457, 490–504, 513–514, 518, 521, 525–526, 528
Sebeok, T., 477–479, 481–482, 486, 516, 518, 526
Shachter, R., 183, 526–527
Shackle, G., 269, 527
Shafer, G., 5, 41, 52, 54, 61, 63–65, 124, 191–194, 209, 223–243, 248, 268–269, 271, 287, 314, 380, 385–386, 390, 459, 464–465, 472–473, 491, 527
Shakespeare, W., 56
Shannon, C., 126, 418–419, 527
Shapiro, B., 35, 37, 527
Shenoy, P., 192, 527
Simon, H., 469, 521
Singh, J., 126, 527
Skyrms, B., 29, 53–54, 144–145, 147–148, 150, 353, 527
Smokler, H., 51, 521
Sominskii, I., 26, 527
Sperber, D., 68, 527
Spiegelhalter, D., 178–179, 181, 183, 521
Srivastava, R., 234, 527
Staniland, A., 127, 527

Starrs, J., 99, 527–528
Stenton, F., 55, 528
Sternberg, R., 459, 528
Stevens, S. S., 16, 198, 206, 211–214, 219, 528
Stewart, I., 474, 528
Stigler, S., 35, 46, 50–52, 528
Stone, M., 98, 356, 528
Swets, J., 100, 108, 318, 334, 519, 528
Swijtink, Z., 35, 203, 519
Swinburne, R., 31, 528

Thagard, P., 33, 469, 520
Thompson, R., 62, 528
Tillers, P., xvii, 60, 91, 140, 163, 166, 196–197, 201, 205, 261, 293, 346, 490–504, 513–514, 526, 528
Todhunter, I., 35, 528
Tong, R., 41, 265, 530
Toulmin, S., 55, 60, 80–81, 160, 529
Truzzi, M., 478, 529
Turing, A. M., 219, 225
Tursman, R., 462, 488, 529
Tversky, A., 232–234, 527
Twining, W., xvii, 6–7, 17, 21–22, 59, 72–75, 81, 135, 139–140, 163, 165–167, 183, 193, 195, 204, 264, 493, 515, 529

Umiker-Sebeok, J., 477–479, 482, 526

Van Caenegem, R., 55, 529
Van Fraassen, B., 149, 529
Venn, J., 34, 529
Verma, T., 180, 524

Wagner, C., 257, 529
Walton, D., 68, 529
Waltz, J., 345, 521
Warren, R. M., 16, 206, 480–481, 529
Warren, R. P., 16, 206, 480–481, 529
Weatherford, R., 34, 40, 529
Weaver, W., 126, 418–419, 527
Weber, E. H., 213–214
Wehrle, W., xvii, 460
Weinstein, J., 332, 356, 522, 529
Wells, C., 55, 57, 529
Whewell, W., 452, 529
White, J., 482, 529
White, R., 482, 519

Subject Index